Warmaking and American Democracy

MODERN WAR STUDIES

Theodore A. Wilson
General Editor

Raymond A. Callahan
J. Garry Clifford
Jacob W. Kipp
Jay Luvaas
Allan R. Millett
Dennis Showalter
Series Editors

Warmaking and American Democracy

The Struggle over Military Strategy, 1700 to the Present

Michael D. Pearlman

 University Press of Kansas

Published by the University Press of Kansas (Lawrence, Kansas 66049), which was organized by the Kansas Board of Regents and is operated and funded by Emporia State University, Fort Hays State University, Kansas State University, Pittsburg State University, the
University of Kansas, and Wichita State University.

Library of Congress Cataloging-in-Publication Data

Pearlman, Michael, 1944–
    Warmaking and American democracy : the struggle over military
strategy, 1700 to the present / Michael D. Pearlman.
        p.   cm. — (Modern war studies)
    Includes index.
    ISBN 0-7006-0938-5 (cloth : alk. paper)
    1. United States—Military policy. 2. Strategy. 3. United
States—Armed Forces. 4. National security—United States.
5. United States—History, Military. 6. United States—Politics and
government. I. Title. II. Series.
UA23.P384   1999
355'.033073—dc21   98-43993

British Library Cataloguing in Publication Data is available.

Printed in the United States of America

10 9 8 7 6 5 4 3 2 1

The paper used in this publication meets the minimum requirements of the American
National Standard for Permanence of Paper for Printed Library Materials Z39.48-1984.

To Lois Bronson Pearlman
(27 November 1941 to 18 September 1996)

Contents

Maps

Acknowledgments

Many people have read many drafts of this manuscript—all of them working, like the author himself, at night or on the weekends, when they could have been enjoying themselves. Randy Briggs produced the maps. Don Vought, Jim Schneider, Jake Kipp, Don Gilmore, Ted Wilson, and Garry Clifford constructively criticized the entire text, as did Susan Ecklund, my extraordinarily competent freelance copy editor at the University Press of Kansas. Others read the chapters about which they have unique expertise: Jim Sack (Anglo-American wars); Don Hickey (1812); John Simon and Mike Perman (Civil War); Mac Coffman, Bill Widenor, and Scott Stevenson (World War I); Martin Blumenson, Chris Gabel, and Rick Swain (World War II); Rick Fried (Korea); and William Conrad Gibbons, Dave Palmer, Horace Hunter, and James Wirtz (Vietnam). Readers will decide for themselves the value of this book. Good or bad, it has been much improved by the efforts of these generous people. My son, Charley, and my late wife, Lois, did not read one page. They put up with a self-absorbed writer who owes them much more than he has ever given in return.

UNITY OF COMMAND: For every objective, insure unity of effort under one responsible commander.

The sixth principle of war

In the U.S. government nobody is in charge. No issues get settled. They are continuously debated.

Former JCS policy and plans officer, speaking off the record in 1994

In politics nobody gets everything, nobody gets nothing, everybody gets something.

President John F. Kennedy

Making a war in a democracy is not a bed of roses.
General George C. Marshall to General Dwight D. Eisenhower, 6 March 1945

Introduction: Terms, Concepts, Theory, Practice

This book is not political, diplomatic, or military history per se. It is about the area where these subjects overlap: what passes for strategy in America's wars against other nation-states, not police actions against various tribes or sects from native Indians to Bosnia. The latter topic is discussed but only in the context of conventional war. The way the colonial militia fought Indians affected the way it fought the British in the American Revolution; the way the army conducted operations against Apaches in 1886 influenced its plan for war with Spain in 1898.

The very term "strategy" is frequently as vague as American strategy itself. In 1929 Basil H. Liddell-Hart, one of the greatest military theorists of the twentieth century, began an article on strategy with the following sentence: "No military term, perhaps no technical term of any kind, has undergone more changes in meaning, suffered more attempts to reach a standard definition, or been more diversely interpreted." After listening to discussions about the war in the Persian Gulf, I conclude that discourse on the subject has not grown more precise since Liddell-Hart's essay sixty-five years ago. I therefore begin this book, where most should begin, with a definition of basic terms.

Theoretically, nation-states employ their resources in ways that accomplish their goals, policy, and purpose. The coordination and direction of all assets (economic, political, moral, and military) is *grand* or *national strategy*. In war or military conflict (violent competition between political units), these goals are called objectives, the means are the armed forces, and the ways are usually called military strategy. Whatever goals a nation has—survival or expansion, material or moral, economic or political, or some mix of these—its policy should be commensurate with its resources. In limited wars for limited objectives, leaders tailor their ambition by adjusting their ends to their means on hand. In so-called total wars for the eradication of the enemy, leaders are not constrained by their stockpile or force structure at the onset of the conflict. They can substantially

1

change and enhance the size and capabilities of their armed forces to fulfill their ultimate goals; that is, they adjust their means to their ends. In either event, military strategy should reflect national policy. In the words of Carl von Clausewitz, the most profound of all military theorists: "The political object is the goal, war is the means of reaching it, and means can never be considered in isolation from their purpose."

Abstract theories aside, the linkage between policy, strategy, ways, and means has always been fragile and frequently frayed. Clausewitz attributed this to "primordial violence"—the emotions that derail rational policy—and to "friction": nothing is easy when someone is "frozen or faint or depressed from privation and fatigue," let alone when someone else is trying to kill them. These insights have great merit but fail to mention other factors highly relevant to U.S. military history, namely, policy itself. Clausewitz acknowledged that policy can "subserve the ambitions, private interests, and vanity of those in power." Then he dismissed what he had just said by stating that that is "neither here nor there." To him, "the aim of policy is to unify all aspects" of a country engaged in conflict with other nations. In short, war "is a clash between major interests," but the concerns of governments conducting war were supposed to be singular, united, and "representative of all interests of the community."

When Clausewitz wrote that war was a "political instrument" and "nothing but the continuation of policy with other means," he was referring to early nineteenth-century Prussia, where the word "politik" meant both policy and politics. "Political" is very imprecise, at least in the American language, which needs a richer vocabulary reflective of diverse interests. Does it mean national or partisan or personal policy—that is, "high" or "low" politics, for want of better terms? It may mean any one or some combination of these. When Abraham Lincoln commissioned certain civilians who could help him win reelection in 1864, he was pursuing a partisan political agenda at risk to his national political policy of winning the war decisively at minimum military cost. Did America's greatest wartime leader use military means to achieve political goals? Yes and no. Since the wars of the United States have been about "low" as well as "high" politics, this book will spend many pages on their partisan cause and effect.

U.S. national strategy has always been the product of disputes between a host of different participants, including political parties, presidents and Congress, elected representatives and bureaucrats, soldiers and civilians, and the various armed services, both active and reserve. Because autocratic leadership has always been abhorrent to America's culture and Constitution, its military strategy has often resembled a French stew: many different elements thrown into the pot. The items were likely to retain their disparate (if not contradictory) characteristics. The final outcome of this process has never been a smooth broth.

Students of twentieth-century political science may see this paradigm as organizational and interest-group politics. It is a bit more complicated than that. In war the whole policy-making process is particularly volatile, far from bureaucratic politics conducted behind closed doors. Success and failure have a public clarity dramatically changing a player's power vis-à-vis competitors. Events may enable an individual or group to dominate the process, at least temporarily. However, supremacy is not likely to last very long. In war, the most capricious activity known to man, triumph is often followed by defeat. After General Douglas MacArthur's masterful landing at Inchon in the Korean War, the Truman administration could not control him. Then he suffered a defeat near the Yalu River as great as his prior victory. To use another metaphor, MacArthur's stack of chips dramatically grew and shrank in two and a half months of warfare.

Although elucidated by modern models of so-called political science, the process examined extends back to the earliest periods of American history, when citizens called each colony "my country" and sought to minimize central control. A European visitor to mid-eighteenth-century New York said about American military policy: "Not only the opinion of one province is sometimes directly opposite to that of another, but frequently the views of the governor and those of the assembly of the same province are quite different. . . . While the people are quarrelling about the best and cheapest manner of carrying on the war, an enemy has it in his power to take one place after another."[1]

The military conflict over land, trade, and security in the Ohio River Valley in the 1750s was a microcosm of the formulation of U.S. military strategy for the next 250 years. French Canada fought Pennsylvania and Virginia; Pennsylvania and Virginia opposed New France as well as each other. Governors, interested in fighting to win promotions in the British Empire, fought legislatures concerned with minimizing the expense of conducting a war. In colonial Virginia, much like America after Vietnam, the chief executive had a far more assertive military policy than most legislators or the public as a whole. The provincial assembly gave Royal Governor Robert Dinwiddie merely £10,000 to dismantle French installations west of the Blue Ridge Mountains. A serious defeat of a small task force led by someone named George Washington altered the distribution of power to make military strategy. It discredited the legislature's claim that it could dictate to the governor the time and place of military operations, à la the War Powers Act passed in 1973. In 1990, to "kick, for once and for all, this Vietnam syndrome," President George Bush sent 527,000 troops, 1,800 warplanes, and 100 warships to the Persian Gulf. In 1757 Governor Dinwiddie deployed two new Virginia militia regiments to help conquer the Ohio River Valley.

Sometimes, such as during World War II, the debates about appropriate strategy were explicitly resolved by bargaining within specific institutions. If not done between the president and Congress, it might be done within the Joint Chiefs of Staff (JCS). The navy wanted a major commitment made to the Pacific; the army and the air force wanted Europe first. The president resolved the issue by supporting both positions, launching simultaneous offenses in both military theaters. In other cases, compromise occurred without formal bargaining—a kind of thesis, antithesis, and synthesis. During the War of 1812, the Republican party planned to capture Canada; the Federalists refused to support the war at all. The result was that the U.S. government was too weak to conquer foreign territory but strong enough to repel most British incursions, America's minimal objective.

Further complicating U.S. strategy was the irregular flow of influence in the decision-making process. In theory, political policy formulated by the national command authority set the parameters for campaign planning and military tactics in the field. In practice, enlisted men might lead and the high command follow. During the Civil War, soldiers in small units, from squad to regiment, began to wage an unlimited war against civilian property and morale a year before Lincoln or William Tecumseh Sherman incorporated these targets into official military strategy.

My brief introduction now over, I only ask a patient reader to withhold final judgment as I spend the subsequent pages trying to prove my case. The argument often assumes that readers have a basic factual knowledge of political, diplomatic, and military history. Those who do not may want to pick up a good textbook on these subjects for a narrative chronology of events.

1

Perennial Issues
in American Military Strategy

Conducting war for political objectives in a democratic setting has been difficult throughout American history, as summarized here. Suffice it to say that the nation's political culture and institutions are incompatible with unity of command, the sixth principle of war. Numerous presidents have tried to subvert the spirit, if not the letter, of the Constitution when formulating military policy, strategy, force structure, and plans. All these attempts eventually failed. There are simply too many ways to affect the decision-making process: through Congress, the media, and elections held in the midst of war, not to mention the armed forces—a sacrosanct lobby because it is considered more noble than politicians. This diffusion of authority, inherent in a pluralist democracy, engendered a goal peculiar to American wars: that of fighting to banish doubts that a democracy can win its wars.

SOLDIERS AND POLITICS, WAR AND POLICY:
RATHER LOOSE CONNECTIONS

Testifying to Congress six weeks before war began in the Persian Gulf, Colin Powell, chairman of the JCS, said: "The fact that military planning must flow from clear political direction is not a new theory. Although we may have had to rediscover it in recent years, I think history will show that it drove [Generals] Eisenhower and Marshall and Pershing and Grant and Washington. You can discover that theory in the works of Clausewitz." Writing in the midst of World War II, John Patton Davies, the State Department's adviser to General Joseph Stilwell, said: "Most American military men think of war as a soldier's job . . . [to be] accomplished as soon as possible, with a minimum of fuss over international political and economic issues," things that drove his client, "Vinegar Joe," to profess his "preference for driving a garbage truck."

Congress seemed to think Davies more accurate than Powell. In 1986 it acknowledged that a coherent master plan from national goals down to military objectives, force structure, planning, and tactics has not occurred very often in American history. It passed the Goldwater-Nichols Defense Reorganization Act, requiring the president to submit an annual report on "national security strategy." Then, from the legislative floor, it subverted what it mandated by changing almost 40 percent of the line items in the defense budget, usually to provide contracts and jobs for its districts. As Tip O'Neill, then the Speaker of the House, said about his colleagues: "The name of the game is power and the boys don't want to give it up."

The contemporary American predicament of national security policy is more than a contemporary problem. Strategy—coordinating political goals with military capabilities—is inherently difficult because war is inherently difficult. Political pluralism (defined as different institutions persistently competing for power) makes it even harder. In 1914 a naval captain wrote that the president controlled policy, the armed services conceived strategy, and Congress provided the military means. "Some governmental organization [is still needed] to bring policy, plans, and means into harmonious cooperation toward the common objective—the purpose of policy." By the 1990s, if not much earlier, diplomats were said to say that thinking strategically about national security was a waste of time. The best America could do was muddle through.

Even when policy has dictated tactics, the causal relationship between means and goals was often unclear, if only because armed conflict is the most chaotic and unpredictable experience known to man. If a warrior makes correct tactical decisions, the indeterminate will and morale of the enemy may still determine the length, intensity, and cost of the conflict. According to Clausewitz, Powell's source of wisdom: "The facts are seldom fully known and the underlying motives even less so. . . . To assess these things in all their ramifications and diversity is plainly a colossal task."

Plans may go astray even if the national command authority somehow penetrates what Clausewitz called the inherent "fog of uncertainty" about the enemy. Ostensibly, the less ambitious the wartime goal, the more likely its accomplishment, or so it would appear if one were not dealing with emotions, spirit, and morale. Human beings, being the creatures that they are, are not likely to risk or sacrifice their lives in action for some mundane object of tangible self-interest. Most soldiers, even more than heads of state, need transcendent goals, especially in America, which could never be a Prussia. Civilian elites with limited military experience periodically hoped in vain that military service could solve the strategic dilemma: could convince soldiers to risk their lives, disregarding personal for national interests. Once subjected to "work and discipline backed by an authority no one can defy," Americans would supposedly embody "self-control, sacrifice, punctuality, and precision." However, despite these recurrent hopes for moral reformation through military training, the armed forces never could transform

America into what Sam Adams called a "Christian Sparta." Nor could they adopt the system of external discipline described by Frederick the Great: "When an officer comes on parade, every man in the barrack square should tremble in his shoes." This being true, the rank and file of the armed forces ("the means") have applied pressure on the goals. General William Westmoreland complained about being caught between two forces in Vietnam: a president with limited objectives, who merely wanted to discourage the enemy, and "the morale of the fighting man, who must be convinced that he is risking death for a worthy cause."

Because a goal must justify the means (as a product must be worth its price), Americans tend to demand utopian war aims like universal democracy and permanent peace. Unfortunately, this prospectus is incompatible with reality. War is really a preventive act to maintain national security, no small achievement itself. Americans, however, raised in an isolationist setting that takes security for granted, expect much more than preservation of the status quo. Note the words of Ronald Reagan, a man who made his fame and fortune echoing public homilies: "Like most of the soldiers I hoped and believed that the blood and death and confusion of World War II would result in a regeneration of mankind. . . . I discovered that the world was almost the same and perhaps a little worse."

In December 1990, on the eve of America's least costly war, the one fought in the Persian Gulf, the president's national security adviser posed the question: "Can the U.S. use force—even go to war—for carefully defined national interests, or do we have to have a moral crusade or a galvanizing event like Pearl Harbor?" He had good reason to worry. If the stated political goals had no value transcending self-interest, one of two things was likely to happen:

1. Combat forces would lose the will to fight, as they did in the latter stages of Vietnam and Korea. ("Why die for a tie?") In 1970 a sympathetic war correspondent found career sergeants, who had joined the armed services in World War II, hopelessly at odds with the unruly rank and file: "Their love affair with the army has turned sour and their remarks about the military are more violently anti[soldier] than those of any SDS [antiwar] protester."
2. Soldiers would fight for cultural reasons, not for political goals. They fought to prove their courage, character, and manliness to themselves, to their community, and to the other soldiers in their unit.

When the latter motive prevailed for the nation at large, as during the Spanish-American War, the military conflict could lack much strategic meaning. The country could fight, at least in part, to attain domestic unity or to experience excitement. This was revealed in analogies citizen-soldiers made to the circus. Twentieth-century GIs called combat "the greatest show on earth"; nineteenth-century soldiers had called it "seeing the elephant" ("I have seen him," wrote one volunteer in the Mexican War, "& am perfectly willing not to see him again"). Anyone who thinks this emotion was confined to a few adolescents or Teddy

Roosevelt's Rough Riders should consider commentary after the war against Iraq in 1991. Psychologists and common citizens spoke of a postwar depression that occurred as public attention returned to more hometown, humdrum affairs devoid of heroics.

True, a few American civilians and soldiers have shrewdly calibrated national objectives with the ways and means of military power. John Quincy Adams, as secretary of state, coaxed Spain to relinquish Florida in 1819 by encouraging General Andrew Jackson to pursue hostile Indians from Georgia into Florida, even into Spanish forts. When the Spanish could not seal Jackson from their colony's border while he was conducting a mere reprisal raid, they realized they could never withstand an American invasion. Dwight Eisenhower, when supreme Allied commander in Europe in World War II, waged a military campaign across a broad front stretching 400 miles from the North Sea to Switzerland. This dispersal of combat power precluded deep penetrations for a great decisive battle that might have surrounded most Germans, west of the Seine or the Rhine. Senior British and American commanders protested what they called "the pernicious strategy of attacking all along the line." "If everyone attacks, nobody can exploit"—a clear violation of "the principle of concentration of force." Eisenhower's own campaign plan—"shoulder to shoulder with honors and sacrifices equally shared"—kept Britain, Canada, America, France, and Russia (along with Polish, Dutch, and Belgian units) in a coalition that might have ruptured over which nation won a race to Berlin. Hitler could not fragment the alliance at the Battle of the Bulge with armor columns aimed at the military boundaries between the British, American, and French forces, all done on the basis of an incorrect prediction that a great offensive would "bring down this artificial coalition with a crash."

Ironically, as America became more immersed in onrushing international events after 1939, Americans had less opportunity to develop strategic breadth and vision based on the principle that war is senseless when not explicitly tied to political goals. Quincy Adams studied Caesar in Latin at the U.S. embassy in Russia in the early 1800s. Eisenhower read Clausewitz three times at the Panama Canal Zone in the early 1920s. Stationed either place today, not those backwater posts of yesterday, they would be swamped in crisis management and message traffic to and from their department headquarters.

An occasional Eisenhower or Quincy Adams notwithstanding, most Americans have not appreciated the acute need to calibrate military means with national ends. Such synchronization has conflicted with the national tendency to separate politics from diplomacy and peace from war. In place of close coordination, by mutual agreement the State Department has usually been the lead agency during peace. In war, the armed forces took control because the "needs of military strategy must dominate the situation," in the words of World War II's army chief of staff. State, said its own secretary, took "care of routine foreign relations" or merely served as minor advisers on the staffs of major military commanders like

George Patton, who had bought a copy of *On War* during his honeymoon but must have had other things on his mind. In late 1944 he complained about a meeting where "Ike was very pontifical and quoted Clausewitz to us [Americans], who have commanded larger forces than Clausewitz ever heard of."[1]

NATIONAL DEFENSE, POLITICAL PLURALISM, AND THE U.S. CONSTITUTION

Civil-military relations are always difficult because war carries operational pressures and demands of its own. Authoritarian states—Germany and Russia—have also encountered problems coordinating military forces with political policy. Bismark, Stalin, and Hitler overruled or replaced the senior officers of their armies when Generals Moltke and Tukhachevskii and the German General Staff tried to operate without government interference. Winston Churchill, a more democratic leader, had his own trouble linking war fighting and political objectives. Britain emerged from World War II too poor and exhausted to contain the Soviet Union or keep the overseas empire Churchill vowed to retain. "As you know," he wrote his foreign secretary in October 1942, "I am very doubtful about the utility of attempts to plan the peace before we have won the war." If this man once said that "political considerations need not be taken into account" (nothing "compares with military glory"), could one expect mere Americans to have a greater grasp of strategy? Churchill has been the inspiration of cold war presidents from John Kennedy to George Bush, none of whom seemed to care that their role model never mentioned Clausewitz, although his prolific writings on military matters did confess (in 1930) that "those who can win a war well can rarely make a good peace, and those who could make a good peace would never have won the war."

While troublesome in all kinds of political environments, coherent strategy and civil-military relations seem particularly difficult in America, where multiple centers of authority are constantly competing for power. Numerous Americans with responsibility for national defense have long believed that their governmental institutions are uniquely ill suited for this task. The need to establish a working consensus between many political players habitually prevented clearly defined ends, ways, and means. Said Louis Halle, a former State Department policy planner: "The larger the group from which a consensus is to be obtained, the harder it is to obtain one. . . . The leadership's attention must be given to this objective . . . as distinct from the objective of making sound policy." By no means was this an isolated opinion in the 1950s of an academic refugee from government employment: other well-placed men said the same thing in 1985. According to one military defense analyst, "In the United States policy and strategy must proceed by innuendo, persuasion, compromise, and almost infinite negotiation and transaction." According to the secretary of state, "democracies have long had difficulty maintaining consistency, coherence, discipline and a sense of strategy."

Military officers, who valued flexibility at the tactical level of war, had to endure it in the realm of strategy. They habitually wanted clarity and consistency from men who had risen to political authority by avoiding commitments that would freeze presidential options. This inherent conflict between military strategists and their civilian superiors led to outbursts of frustration such as those of Admiral Bradley Fiske when he retired in 1916: "From the standpoint of national longevity, politics is a disease."

Franklin Delano Roosevelt was a case in point. As assistant secretary of the navy during World War I, he complained that the chief executive did not seek advice from "a single officer of the Army and the Navy on the question of what we could do to carry out our declared policy." Typical of presidents, Woodrow Wilson had maintained that an armed service simply "stands and waits to do the thing which the nation desires." The services, Roosevelt complained, did not even "know what policies [they] may be called upon to uphold by force." Not surprising, the same thing happened in World War II, when Roosevelt's shoe was on the other institutional foot. He rarely provided the fixed guidance he had requested when he represented the navy to the White House. When the JCS finally got "clear and definite" direction in late 1943, they were "astonished and delighted," said the secretary of war. "You can't treat military factors in the way you do political factors," the army chief of staff would lament. "You have to be very exact, very clearly informed, and very precise in what you say in regard to military things."

Unintelligibility was an occupational technique, not just a personal trait of some presidents. General Eisenhower could write crystal-clear directives to subordinates when deemed necessary: "We must regain the initiative, and speed and energy are essential." He wanted "rocklike decisions" but got ambiguity from FDR in World War II. However, when a politician himself, Ike gave what he called "sphinx-like" speeches to the electorate: "I will go to Korea"—and do what? (The JCS chairman called this "pure show biz.") On other occasions he wrote confidants: "I've kept my mouth closed in every language known to man."

The guidance that the national command authorities gave to the armed forces could be as unstable as the distribution of political power within the United States. Strategists who fruitlessly searched for clear and consistent policies lamented the constitutional separations and fragmentations created to prevent undisputed authority. Dean Acheson, secretary of state during the Korean War, condemned congressional "interference" in security affairs: "In the conduct of their foreign relations democracies appear to me decidedly inferior to other governments." Ronald Reagan's secretary of defense wrote about "having two governments in Washington—one executive, the other legislative."

This diffusion of sovereignty gave Congress more opportunity to affect war than is recognized by those who focus only on the opening round. Granted, when America used its armed forces abroad 165 times from 1798 to 1970, Capitol Hill declared war on only five occasions, usually after the army or navy was already engaged. Although it did push hesitant presidents into wars they tried to avoid in

1812 and 1898, its primary influence was on the conduct and consequences of armed conflict, not its initial cause. In the Civil War, Korea, and Vietnam before 1968, Congress moved Lincoln to wage war on slavery, Harry Truman to include Formosa in America's defensive perimeter, and Lyndon Johnson to bomb North Vietnam more extensively. When Woodrow Wilson withstood similar pressure to demand an unconditional surrender, Congress made him pay by withholding its consent for what Wilson really wanted, the leading role in the League of Nations after World War I. Less belligerent in 1847 and 1973, it forced chief executives to sign peace settlements for less territory than they wanted. James Polk did not get all of Mexico north of the Sierra Madres; Richard Nixon did not force the North Vietnamese army back to North Vietnam. Both men knew the alternative was legislative termination of military appropriations, which would cause them to lose what they occupied, San Francisco or Saigon.

Compare this to legislative bodies in parliamentary systems, superficially the sovereign branch of government. Ministers selected from a national assembly by the majority party elected on a common platform automatically receive support from a centralized organization. Unlike the U.S. Congress, where individual candidates cut policy positions for particular districts, parliaments do not hold hearings to support critics of executive policy in the armed forces. British officials could not understand why Franklin Roosevelt would ever ask his closest aide: "Do you think the people would demand to have me impeached?" if he attacked a German battleship. Nor did they grasp why Eisenhower had to search for a domestic consensus to end the Korean War. In 1941 cabinet ministers told Harry Hopkins that "your President understands the [military] situation. He is the leader of Congress. Surely, they will loyally follow him if he says that the time has come for the United States to enter the war." In 1953 a former prime minister asked, "Who is the more powerful, the President or Senator [Joe] McCarthy? . . . One of the disadvantages of the American system of democracy is that it is sometimes hard to find where effective power lies."

Congress and the president were only two wings of the political triad. Over time, neither could control public opinion, a constant concern of alleged leaders no matter what Congress did. Both the Mexican War and the Vietnam War received strong initial support in Congress, which would barely uphold the president's threat to use military power in the Persian Gulf: 52 to 47 in the Senate; 250 to 183 in the House. In the long run, in each of these three wars, public opinion did not care about the congressional roll call one way or the other. The Mexican War was a military triumph and the Vietnam War a failure; they both cost the Democratic party control of the White House, in the 1848 and 1968 elections, respectively. The war against Iraq, although weakly supported in Congress, had 89 percent public approval at the time of its cease-fire. In this case George Bush was not reelected in 1992 despite (not because) of the war.

Because no political institution can commit public opinion very long, presidents had to shape military operations to sustain political popularity, more so than prime ministers in parliamentary systems that form coalition governments and postpone elections. Roosevelt induced Henry Stimson, an icon in the opposition party, to become his secretary of war. Yet fearing a military defeat right before the 1942 election, he put off the invasion of Europe, to Stimson's deep regret. Other presidents had a different schedule than other military men, if only because they had to say the war was nearly over when they faced reelection. In 1861, 1898, and 1990, respectively, Generals Winfield Scott, Nelson Miles, and Colin Powell said blockades could beat the South, Spanish Cuba, or Iraq. Because none would say this victory would be rapid (according to Scott, it could take three years), their policy of minimal physical risk was unacceptable to Lincoln, William McKinley, and Bush.

The great exception to this generalization about civil-military conflicts over grand strategy happened in the Confederate States of America. Its chief executive, Jefferson Davis, wanted to exhaust and outlast the enemy; his general officers in the eastern theater (Robert E. Lee and Stonewall Jackson) wanted to gamble on winning quick battlefield victories. Their conflicting plans were probably related to the Confederacy's constitution and absence of partisan political institutions, both unique in American history. This one-term (six-year) president, without party affiliation, had no worries about facing the electorate or about carrying Congress in off-year elections. His adversary had to face the more typical political situation. Abraham Lincoln, after 1862, waged the Civil War in a relentless manner, knowing the electorate would hold him responsible for stalemate on the battlefield "whether I deserve it or not." Four score and two years later, Franklin Roosevelt directed U.S. armed forces to capture Rome, Paris, and Manila. These high-visibility landmarks of progress had minimal military importance. Nonetheless, their occupation by American soldiers reinforced Roosevelt's claim, made a week before his reelection in 1944, that his administration was "winning the war and bringing our men and women home as quickly as possible."

Other presidents, who could not sustain a similar claim, chose not to be a candidate and go down in defeat. In 1952 and 1968, Truman and Johnson tried but failed to do what Nixon did in 1972: credibly claim that there was light at the end of the proverbial tunnel. Johnson's secretary of state later explained that "we knew we had lost the war when we couldn't tell the people of Cherokee County [where he was born] when it would finish and how much it would cost."

How did someone like Lyndon Johnson, a man of immense political skill, make such a terrible political mistake? Presidents, like generals, tend to fight the last war, always easier to understand than the present. Unfortunately, like any analogy, the past is often a poor guideline. Lincoln spent the first year of the Civil War as if it were the Mexican War: to be won by a quick march on the enemy capital and dictating a suitable peace. (This mistake cost his party the 1862 congressional election.) McKinley, a veteran of four bloody years in the eastern theater, feared he would have to win the Spanish-American War the way the Civil War was finally won, in a prolonged campaign of attrition, now to be conducted outside Havana. Wilson, raised in conquered southern territory, settled World War I short of unconditional surrender, lest Germany experience what happened to Georgia. Roosevelt insisted on unconditional surrender, lest he repeat Wilson's mistake and let Germany recover to fight another world war. Because Truman took his war to North Korea, brought in China, sank into stalemate, and ruined his presidency, Johnson held ground forces inside South Vietnam: a decision that created the stalemate he feared the moment he committed combat soldiers. Bush, fighting in the Persian Gulf to "kick, for once and for all, the so-called Vietnam syndrome," lifted restrictions and won the war in record time. He lost the subsequent election, held when the conflict seemed like ancient history.

The American public has wanted only one thing from its commanders in chief: quick wars for substantial victories with minimal costs. Because significant battles tend to shed significant blood, this contradictory demand spawned a recurrent debate: whether to execute a frontal campaign to end the war fast by marching on a Richmond or Berlin or to operate in a peripheral theater to reduce the casualties. America adopted the second option when it was too weak or wary to strike directly at the enemy's strength. It invaded Canada, rather than attack the British navy in 1812; it assaulted Santiago and Manila Bay, not the fortress of Havana, in 1898. In 1950 and 1965 it fought the North Korean "puppet" army and the Viet Cong, neither one allegedly able to "act without prior instruction from Moscow" or Mao Tse-tung. It did not attack "the base of the world Communist movement" in the Soviet Union or Red China.

The decision to adopt a flank or frontal strategy has frequently had a partisan political component, as when the Democratic-Republicans (not the Federalists) advocated the invasion of Canada or when the Republicans proposed the overland route to Richmond. Domestic politics also had a direct impact on initial decisions for or against war. In 1812 and 1898, presidents committed unprepared ground forces lest the opposition party profit from their inability to resolve important issues with methods short of war. On the other hand, presidents slowed the preparation for combat in World Wars I and II when they ran for reelection on peace slogans like "He kept us out of war." Finally, during Korea and Vietnam, Harry Truman and John Kennedy, Democratic presidents elected by slim margins, enhanced commitments to those countries of marginal strategic value lest Republicans accuse them of being soft on communism.

More than any other governmental institution, the presidency has had to cope with the problems that multiple centers of power present for national defense. In so doing, it might have been too critical of the American political system. To be sure, pluralism has created inconsistency and ambiguity. It has also ensured a hearing for most sides of an issue and fostered compromise, things that could have prevented authoritarians from making errors of their own and alienating allies unwilling to accept subservience. Because American policy makers knew their own institutional shortcomings better than they did those of Germany, the Soviet Union, or Imperial Japan, they criticized pluralism rather than discuss the demerits of more hierarchical systems. More important, they often tried to counteract the lack of legal sovereignty by skirting the spirit, if not the letter, of the Constitution, which was "suited to the needs of a remote agrarian republic in the 18th century," according to J. William Fulbright, chairman of the Senate's Foreign Affairs Committee in the 1960s. Before his Gulf of Tonkin Resolution gave the president carte blanche to escalate military action in Vietnam, Fulbright worried that Congress was simply too "sensitive to private pressures," public opinion, "parochialism and self-indulgence" to "cope with world-wide revolutionary forces." In 1961 he was simply catching up with the Supreme Court in the Civil War, when the ultimate protector of the Constitution declared that the executive branch "must determine what degree of force the crisis demands."

In 1864 Abraham Lincoln claimed that "measures otherwise unconstitutional might become lawful by becoming indispensable to the preservation of the Constitution through the preservation of the nation." Opinions like this grew more common as America came to play an ever-greater role in military affairs. Compare conflicts at the end of the nineteenth and twentieth centuries: the Spanish-American War with Desert Storm. In both cases, presidents tried to pressure a country to leave occupied territory—Spain from Cuba in 1898, Iraq from Kuwait in 1991. Diplomacy did not work in either case. McKinley went to Congress for a declaration of war. Bush, ignoring threats of impeachment from a legislature still angry over Vietnam, only sought "support." He began bombing Baghdad irrespective of "authorization," which he said he never needed.

Aside from excluding Congress as best they could, presidents have often tried to prevent the military services from participating in fundamental policy decisions about national defense. The services often resorted to friendly congressional committees to voice their mutual grievance at this state of affairs. Their frustration might have reached its apogee late in the Vietnam War, when the JCS had a navy yeoman, stationed with the National Security Council, pilfer documents to discover what operations they might have to execute. Henry Kissinger, the NSC adviser, called this tantamount to "spying on the Chief Executive," an accusation echoing old Anglo-American fears of military conspiracies subverting republican government. Historically, vocal segments of the public have been less concerned with the close coordination of political ends and military means than that a politically involved army would commit the country to slaughter, bankruptcy, and a military state. As Sam Adams said in 1776: "Soldiers are apt to consider themselves as a Body, distinct from the rest of the citizens. . . . They soon become attached to their officers and disposed to yield implicit obedience to their commands. Such a power should be watched with a jealous hand."

Even when the United States supported a permanent military establishment at the height of the cold war, civilians tried to clamp on tighter controls, called "active management at the top." The National Security Act of 1947 made the chairman of the Joint Chiefs of Staff a permanent member of the National Security Council, created to coordinate defense policy at the highest levels of government.

The council, not the Pentagon, became the focal point of military policy; the Joint Chiefs usually reflected civilian leadership. During the Korean War, the JCS issued statements emphasizing that "the worldwide prestige of the United States" was at stake in northeast Asia, a stance the State Department held in opposition to the military's position that Korea was a "strategically unimportant area." During Vietnam, the chairman of the JCS echoed the words of the administration when telling dispirited presidential advisers, after the Tet offensive, that America's goal was only to avoid a communist victory. This was orthodox containment policy as of 1946, when Clark Clifford, a White House assistant, concluded that America will obtain "a fair and equitable settlement [of its conflict with communism] when they realize that we are too strong to be beaten and too determined to be frightened." In 1968, when Clifford was secretary of defense, he and Dean Acheson attacked the mirror (not the author) of military policy: "General, if the deployment is not an effort to gain a military solution, then words have lost all meaning."

From 1947 to 1966, the civilian command structure of the Pentagon grew much greater than the rate of military spending. Its appropriations increased by more than 400 percent; the Office of the Secretary of Defense (OSD) grew from three assistants ($10,000 each) to a deputy secretary, two undersecretaries, a comptroller, an inspector general, a general counsel, eleven assistant and twenty-seven deputy assistant secretaries of defense, along with 2,500 other employees, about 10 percent of Pentagon personnel. Subject to this bureaucratic obstacle course, the army chief of staff met privately with the president just twice during Vietnam. The chairman of the Joint Chiefs had to wait two years to attend the Tuesday morning meetings where civilians helped Lyndon Johnson select targets to be bombed in North Vietnam. "I can take on the Chiefs," Secretary of Defense Robert McNamara told him. "We decide what we want and impose it on them"— a state of presidential supremacy that would not last very long.

Vietnam, which began as the apogee of power for the executive branch, ended in the nadir of White House control of the conduct of war. Critics of Lyndon Johnson—hawks and doves in Congress—initially agreed on one thing: the legislature would not utilize the power the Constitution gave it and thereby be blamed for defeat. Because the White House ran the war, it suffered a substantial reduction of institutional power when policy failed after Tet. Then, for the first time since the colonial era, the legislative branch made military policy at the operational level in an active theater of war. Before 1968, President Johnson prevented escalation by forbidding ground operations in Laos and Cambodia. After 1970, during the Nixon administration, this action was outlawed by congressional statute because the president wanted to do it.

Along with goals and ways, the executive branch lost much of its control over the procurement of military means. In the early 1960s Robert McNamara and his fellow efficiency experts at OSD took contract decisions out of the hands of the serving military and the legislative committees. The armed forces, while disgruntled, changed their senior educational institutions to produce more per-suasive advocates within the Pentagon. At the Army War College, where military strategy was supposed to be studied and crafted, the new curriculum emphasized the planning, programming, budgeting system "to help the Army compete for resources with the other services." Now that expertise meant acquistion, the senior American officer in Europe would ask his colleagues: "How do we develop enough officers with enough of the attributes to influence the formula-tion of military strategy?"

Congress, angry that OSD had taken purchasing decisions out of its hands, looked for an opportunity "to run McNamara out of town." Vietnam filled the bill, especially given McNamara's attempt to manage the conflict and criticize military tactics. To the armed services, this seemed a "serious civilian intrusion into the business of the professional soldier." To much of the Senate, it seemed as if McNamara was trying to run the war "with his only support and approval coming from the computers." His failure as a military strategist in Southeast Asia discredited McNamara's principles of management and procurement, the fields in which his talent really lay. By the time he left the Pentagon, Congress was adding specific line items through the entire military budget. His successors had little time to challenge the new reign of logrolling because the average senior Defense Department official was spending 3,000 hours per year preparing for and testifying to committees. If he did protest the Capitol Hill–military complex, he was likely to be tagged with a fatal political description: "Secretary so-and-so is another Robert McNamara."[2]

FEAR OF POLITICAL INFLUENCE IN WAR
AND MILITARY INFLUENCE IN POLITICS

Robert McNamara committed a fatal error when he violated a cardinal injunction in American political culture. He practiced civilian supremacy in a way that came to symbolize civilian interference with military operations. Strategy is a triad in which government sets policy, policy states war aims, and combat is the means that achieves the goals. However, government means politics, and the American public abhors the politicization of war. When President Polk did this in the Mexican War, he made General Zachary Taylor a martyred "victim" of political machinations— and, hence, the next president of the United States. When Lincoln seemed to do this in the Civil War, even friendly newspapers "advised the President to keep his fingers out of the military pie." With the possible exception of Harry Truman, a great admirer of Polk, few presidents would openly countermand a commander in the field, something condemned in every public opinion poll. When Truman finally did this in 1951, substantial majorities said that "General MacArthur was right," despite the fact that polls also indicated they opposed his plan to attack China. In essence, the body politic supported MacArthur's prerogative and Truman's policy.

To prevent what would be a fatal partisan political charge, other presidents took convoluted steps to avoid military advice. Then their opponents could not say they had heard, but dismissed, senior officers. Franklin Roosevelt talked so much that his service chiefs rarely had time to voice their opinions. Lyndon Johnson rarely met with them at all. John Kennedy and Richard Nixon appointed special advisers outside the normal chain of command. Max Taylor and Al Haig kept other officers at arm's length but, they hoped, in line with White House demands.

The lack of a free and frank exchange of opinions in civil-military relations has not been very auspicious. Sometimes the results have been crude or clumsy, as in 1942, when George Marshall, the army chief of staff, received copies of the correspondence between the president and England's prime minister from a friend in the British mission. In the Civil War, World War I, Korea, and Vietnam, noncommunication was far more costly. General Grant, never discussing with Lincoln his reservations about subordinates commissioned by the White House, had to rely on military incompetents, who caused him to sustain 55,000 casualties in two months' time. Pershing, fearing Wilson would amalgamate the American Expeditionary Army into French and British ranks, refused to learn tactical lessons from his allies about trench warfare, lest his soldiers become so compatible with foreign doctrine he would lose their command. Truman did not forbid MacArthur to risk escalation, although the president traveled almost 5,000 miles to Wake Island in 1950 for a vacuous meeting 96 minutes long. Lyndon Johnson never told the JCS that he would never mobilize the reserves or allow ground forces to attack enemy sanctuaries outside South Vietnam. They never told him they could not win the war; they did not fully comprehend the restrictions under which they would always have to perform.

Glad to shift responsibility for failure, almost no politician openly contested the taboo against interfering in military operations. In practice, almost all violated this prohibition. Republicans, having lambasted the constraints Democrats placed on the armed forces in Vietnam, excluded military commanders from many important policy decisions; for example, the crisis in the Persian Gulf. The JCS relied on their chairman, Colin Powell, to let them "know what's going on" inside the White House. No soldier could be better connected than this self-identified "political general," who would tell even field-grade officers, "You are being given the president's political problems, not military problems, to solve." Nonetheless, he learned about the administration's decision to escalate the troop commitment to allow offensive action when watching the TV morning news. Three months later, on the eve of that operation, Powell pleaded: "Mr. President, you'll be very tempted to try to fix problems yourself. . . . the more you can leave us alone to work our way through it as military professionals, the better it will be."

Senior officers have endured intrusion in military business, which the public loathed, without the revolt that the public feared. Although officers have come no closer to subversion than leaking memos to Congress and the press, fear of a coup existed as early as 1775, when the Continental Congress chose a Virginian to lead soldiers largely from New England. At that time George Washington did not appear to be the best-qualified military commander. No matter. The legislature took heart that officers and enlisted men from different sections of the country would check, balance, and contain the military's natural inclination for glory, plunder, and oppression.

The fact that most American wars have produced postwar presidents does not disprove public fear of military influence on politics. It only shows that feelings on this subject have been ambivalent. The electorate tends to blame politicians for the chronic problems war could not eliminate. They often turned to a self-described "simple soldier" like Eisenhower, who had cut through enemy obstacles on the way to the victory that officeholders squandered. ("We won the war but lost the peace.") As one man wrote on the eve of William Henry Harrison's election in 1840, "The people know [the politicians] are self-seeking, & naturally mistrust the sincerity of their professions. . . . Old generals stand for the country and not for a party." Washington, Jackson, Harrison, Taylor, Grant, and Eisenhower were all boomed for president on the grounds that the divisive state of public affairs necessitated a nonpartisan commander in the White House. Their candidacy would "cement the bonds of our Union," as Taylor claimed in 1848; it would put "America [on the] straight road down the middle," according to Eisenhower in 1952. Likewise, newspaper editors in 1867 wrote that Grant had led the public "to final victory over the rebellion; they look to him to lead them in the equally essential work . . . [of putting] an end to the war of parties and of factions, by which peace has been repelled and the restoration of the Union discouraged and delayed."

Well aware of the political popularity of military men, presidents from Lincoln to Lyndon Johnson have been reluctant to anger field commanders with unequivocal directions, as noted earlier. Politicians might have taken heart at the fact that the public has promoted to commander in chief only officers who projected a nonmartial image: "Old Hickory" (Jackson), "Old Tip" (Harrison), "Old Rough and Ready" (Taylor), "Sam" Grant, and "Ike." All appeared or acted like citizen-soldiers on temporary duty when they led troops in the War of 1812, the Mexican War, the Civil War, or World War II. A young lieutenant, newly arrived to the Mexican theater, offered Taylor, a nondescript old man, fifty cents to polish his cavalry sword. Grant, "the foremost soldier of his time," according to reviews of his memoirs, lacked "the military spirit"; he "never looked at things for a moment merely from the soldier's point of view." Other officers who tried for the presidency but were not elected to the White House looked like popular personifications of the so-called military mind: spit-and-polish martinets surrounded by a glittering group of sycophantic staff officers. Winfield Scott was the "Old Fuss and Feathers" (cocked hat, saber, and spurs) of the Mexican War; George McClellan was the "Young Napoleon" of the Civil War; Douglas MacArthur was the "Douglas MacArthur" of World War II, his very name becoming a generic term for so-called military aristocrats. Unlike "Ike," no one publicly called him "Mac."

Civilian fears about military encroachments did more than crush MacArthur's aspirations to be president and fan a market for political science fiction about coups in the United States. They frequently isolated the armed forces from input to diplomacy, thereby obstructing smooth connections between national goals and military capabilities. In mid-1941, when staff officers conducted strategic planning for World War II without much outside guidance, they assumed that the political objective would be "to eliminate totalitarianism from Europe" but only hold a defensive perimeter on the Pacific Ocean. In December 1942 President Roosevelt briefly floated the idea of "unconditional surrender" at a White House meeting with the JCS. One month later, without further discussion, he announced to the world that U.S. policy was global total victory. With such incidents in mind, the assistant secretary of war wrote the army chief of staff in mid-1944: "Our foreign policy has had far too little relation to our military capacities," despite the fact that no conflict "in history has more clearly shown the truth of Clausewitz's old dictum [about] the politico-military aspects of war."[3]

OFFICERS, POLITICS, OPERATIONS, AND OBJECTIVES

Officers had their own case, for their own reasons, against political pluralism, which was more abhorrent to them than to the commander in chief. A president's expertise lies in the deals and coalitions that got him to the White House; soldiers were accustomed to unity of command within their own institutions. Even when bargaining as everyone must, they had trouble thinking along the diverse and disorderly lines of horse-trading, standard operating procedure in American political circles. If able to do what they fantasized, flag officers would have excluded politicians from essential decisions in the conduct of war.

Even those officers (active duty and retired) who tried to close this gap between political policy and military operations often could not practice what they preached. Just as politicians did not trust most officers, most officers retained the belief that politics by politicians was a sordid business, in George Marshall's words "a swarm." For them, as for Clausewitz, policy was legitimate if it was "representative of *all* the interests of the community" (italics mine). Pluralism and "private interests" were barely acknowledged, except as a deleterious factor in national defense. Soldiers, rarely accepting the proposal that the army could also be an interest group, felt that war for national security in the international arena was honorable political activity. Personal, regional, or group concerns were a blight to overcome.

George Marshall tried to "make decisions without considering the political consequences." He repeatedly said during World War II, "that was for the politicians." Nonetheless, the army chief of staff had to spend enormous amounts of time and energy trying to keep "political considerations from interfering with strategy." He belatedly learned "the great lesson" that public pressures can upset all military plans. "The politicians have to do *something* important every year," he said in retrospect; "the leader in a democracy has to keep the people entertained." A more worldly man by the 1950s, Marshall lectured senior officers at the National War College that they, too, would have to take such factors into their considerations, something he had not done when he declared that "the destruction of the German armed forces is more important than any political or psychological advantages."

Unless elected head of state himself, no military man had much greater access to the White House than did Marshall, particularly in the Truman administration. Most others, kept at a distance, were not even privy to the presidential point of view. In the late 1940s, military planners made calculations about Korea based on strategic priorities and their knowledge of the means on hand. The JCS unanimously recommended that the United States could not and should not defend the peninsula. The president, attuned to post–World War II domestic pressures not to appease aggressors again, committed American forces when the North invaded the South.

Commitments like Korea (made partly for electoral, not strategic, reasons) helped alienate soldiers from civilians and widen the gap between those deciding what to do and those deciding how to do it. Douglas MacArthur enunciated the army's case against multiple centers of authority in 1952: "When politics fails and the military takes over you must trust the military. . . . There should be no non-professional interference in the handling of troops." No matter how extreme the speaker, the theme was familiar to graduates of U.S. military institutions, who prefer war fighting to strategy, policy, and politics. At best, said the commandant of the National War College in 1990, the armed forces "presume there is something unsoldierly about an officer who grows to intellectual stature in the business of military strategy." As for policy, it was tainted by politics, a fatal agent. William T. Sherman explained that the Union army did much better in the western theater of the Civil War "because there was no political capital near enough to poison our minds and kindle into light that craving for fame which has killed more good men than bullets."

A recently retired plans director at the Pentagon told staff college students in 1992 that "strategy is what you do when you have nothing to do. Operations is what you do when you have something to do." This state of mind was even more pronounced in the 1800s, when military publications defined "strategy" as the "art of concerting a plan of campaign," what is now called the operational level of war. They completely ignored policy and goals, that is, aside from winning. In 1897 the senior instructor at the U.S. army staff college said that strategy was "the art of moving an army in the theater of operations . . . to increase the probability of victory."

Antoine-Henri Jomini, a Napoleonic officer concerned with "the purely military part of the art of war," had a substantial impact on the American army. Clausewitz has been far more important to civilian academics, partly because he subordinated military operations to governmental objectives. Perhaps this was the main reason most generals found him impractical and obscure. Even those who would cite him, such as Helmut von Moltke, chief of the Imperial German general staff, maintained that "political considerations can be taken into account only as long as they do not make demands that are militarily improper." Stated more starkly in America, this sentiment permeated the writings of General Emory Upton (1839–81), the greatest exponent of the separation of the armed forces from "mere politicians" after the Civil War. In 1875, the desire to escape "folly and criminality" drove his mentor, William Sherman, to move the office of the commanding general out of Washington—"the political capital of the country and the focus of intrigue, gossip, and slander." Their proposed alternative to civilian supervision—professional autonomy and peer review—was much preferred by the national defense establishment, which praised Upton (in 1916) as "the greatest military philosopher who has ever written in this country" and paraphrased his ideas down to World War II.

On occasion a military man read Clausewitz. His dictum—that war "is merely a special violent phase of human politics"—shocked John McAuley Palmer in 1893. "Here was a fundamental military concept which I had never heard about in my four years at West Point," where the curriculum was filled with mathematics at the expense of tactics, let alone strategy and policy. "None of my professors or textbooks," this brigadier general recalled in the 1940s, "ever told me what war really is." True, staff college publications at Fort Leavenworth, where Palmer met his lifelong friend George Marshall, went beyond drill regulations (the manuals of the 1890s) to elucidate grand tactics. They also mentioned politics—but much like temperance union pamphlets discussed demon rum. According to *The Principles of Strategy* (1921 and 1936), "Any attempt on the part of statesmen to interfere in the conduct of military operations is likely to lead to disastrous results." Further, "Politics and strategy are radically and fundamentally things apart. . . . All that soldiers ask is that once the policy is settled, strategy and command shall be regarded as being in a sphere apart from politics."

After World War II, staff college ideas echoed in the throat of MacArthur. He paraphrased Clausewitz before Congress: "War was the ultimate process of politics, when all other political means failed." However, in words remarkably reminiscent of those once used by George McClellan, he maintained that war should be removed from political hands. During the Civil War, his predecessor wrote that "a statesman may, perhaps, be more competent than a soldier to determine political objectives," an equivocal concession because they were prone to "partisan" distortions of the public good. Once that function was performed, McClellan maintained, "everything should be left to the responsible military head." During the Korean War, MacArthur said the same thing in response to President Truman's attempt to exercise civilian supremacy in an active theater of war: it "introduces into the military a political control such as I have never known in my life or have studied." Did two men who graduated from West Point at or next to the top of their class never study (let alone hear of) the commander-in-chief-clause of the U.S. Constitution?[4]

MILITARY MEN AND THE POLITICAL PROCESS:
CAREERS, MISSIONS, INTEREST GROUPS

Nineteenth-century officers bemoaned "the melancholy fact that the soldier, who has devoted himself to the science of war from his childhood, can never rise above an inferior grade, whilst the command of the Army is entrusted to a *politician*, who has gained distinction by courting the mob." Such sentiments widened the divisions between war and politics, means and goals. They also were ironic, when not disingenuous. From Winfield Scott, McClellan, and Sherman to MacArthur, the most vocal critics of political influence were the most active politicians in the service. Scott would curse partisan influence on the army during the Mexican War but sought a congressional act in 1828 declaring him the "highest officer in rank of the line." Sherman, so distrustful of politicians that he privately favored a military dictatorship, had one of the strongest lobbies in all Washington. When he desperately needed help early in the Civil War against charges of insanity, he mobilized his brother and his in-laws: present and past U.S. senators from Ohio and a leader of the Republican party in Kansas. Sherman was distraught with worry, but his problem had been solved. Commanding General Henry Halleck—another chronic complainer about "Party Politics! Party Politics! I sometimes fear they will utterly ruin the country"—returned him to the field, partly because of the influence of the Sherman clan. Sherman himself may have cursed "unadulterated democracy," but he did not forget the favor. At Lincoln's direct request, he furloughed several thousand soldiers so the president could carry Indiana in 1864. He was not glad to do it but said with sarcasm, "It is useless to complain because the election is more important than the war."

Unlike officers in Third World countries or Caesars in imperial Rome, Americans did not challenge the principle of civilian government. However, as General Phil Sheridan maintained, when professing that he "drank that [precept] in my milk from the time I was born," on a "professional question I have a right to complain and report." Sheridan's statement and the methods of a Scott and MacArthur are instructive about wiggle room within civil-military relations. Those who actively opposed their commander in chief tried to organize Congress, not stage a coup. This political method could produce an effective campaign plan. Compared with policy makers in the executive branch, the senior congressman and senators who chair committees appeared to be eternal. Officers learned to work with them or on them, whatever it took. Hence, when Generals Grant and Eisenhower did become president, they were less combative with the legislature than were their predecessors, Andrew Johnson and Harry Truman. As for MacArthur, when at odds with Roosevelt in World War II, he appealed directly to Congress, writing members and briefing their inspection tours to enhance the profile and priorities of his Pacific command. (He gave Lyndon Johnson, serving simultaneously in the navy and the House, a Silver Star for briefly coming under fire.) "I will be glad," MacArthur hinted to one legislator, "when more substantial forces are placed at my disposition," hopefully in 1944. During the Korean War, the general was less subtle. When Truman proposed a compromise peace, MacArthur protested to Congress: "We must win. There is no substitute for victory."

Within a decade after MacArthur appealed to Congress to change presidential priorities in World War II and Korea, successive generals did the same thing with a twist, asking Congress to upset the budgetary priorities of a Republican president and former army chief of staff. Until the Eisenhower administration (1953–61), military appropriations were evenly divided between the army, navy, and air force. Then, to reduce taxes and balance the budget for the sake of economic growth, Eisenhower gave highest priority to the Strategic Air Command, whose nuclear weapons could deliver what was called "more bang for the buck." The army's new chief of staff, Maxwell Taylor, fought this threat to make his service the Marine Corps for the air force, relegated to protecting runways for bombers the same way the corps captured ports for the fleet. His natural ally was a Democratic-dominated Congress eager to tax, borrow, and spend. To cement this alliance, staff officers leaked classified studies maintaining "the United States is grossly unprepared to meet the communist threat"—support for Taylor's statements that the country needed the "capability to react across the entire spectrum from general atomic war to infiltrations and aggressions." This doctrine of flexible response enabled Taylor and two of his former Senate supporters, John Kennedy and Lyndon Johnson, to wage limited war in Vietnam.

Predictably, Eisenhower was less impressed than Capitol Hill, telling the superintendent of West Point, William Westmoreland, that officers must not "kowtow to the Congress"—a futile demand, he must have known. In the midst of World War II, Eisenhower said, "I can scarely imagine anyone in the United States less qualified than I for any type of political work." In 1962 he confessed to a reporter, "I have been in the most active sort of politics most of my adult life. There's no more active political organization in the world than the armed services of the U.S." Because war fighting is not a competitive industry, the government had to rely on the officer corps for expertise and implementation. Like other participants in the negotiating process that produces American policy, they reflected the vested interests of the bodies that trained them, employed them, and promised them a future, as two colonels confessed in 1960: "We of the military devote too much of the talent of our best minds to interservice debate and to the battle of the budget."

When the different military services sought appropriations, they lobbied at the expense of their sister services. This was not a major issue as long as the United States fought its wars in North America. By definition, continental expansion made the army primary. In the twentieth century—when America's major military efforts took place in Europe and Asia—land, sea, and air components vied for supremacy by proposing different military strategies. Plans were formulated to get funding as much as funding was sought for plans.

The most celebrated military theorist to ever wear a U.S. uniform was Alfred Thayer Mahan, tasked by the Naval War College to do what "Jomini has done for the [army]": establish "the science of naval warfare under steam." In function, he became the greatest propagandist for the favorite weapon of his service, the battleship fleets. From 1890 to 1914, he wrote an enormously influential series of books and articles expounding the theme that world power meant naval power won in decisive battles on the high seas by heavily armed and armored vessels. Advocates of a big navy cited passages as conclusive proof; skeptics were dismissed as heretics. "In one particular," a Naval Academy graduate wrote in 1900, Ivan Bloch's *The Future of War* "is open to criticism. It disagrees radically with Mahan in estimating the value of sea power in history."

The oracle justified an explosion of expenditure. In 1890, the year Mahan's *Influence of Sea Power upon History* was published, the United States spent 7 percent of its federal budget on the navy. By 1907 it was spending 21 percent, primarily in building two 20,000-ton battleships a year with steel armor, turbine engines, electrification, and long-range heavy guns using state-of-the-art optics and mechanical computers. The production time and costs of these capital ships virtually assured that they would be used against each other in fleet-on-fleet engagements. Both admirals and taxpayers were horrified that a multimillion-dollar investment might be destroyed by a much cheaper asset, such as an offshore mine, torpedo boat, or coastal battery. In the Spanish-American War, Mahan and his colleagues insisted that the army (not the navy) storm Santiago Bay. Said the command of the Atlantic fleet: "Of men there were plenty; of the all-important material—ships—there was but little."

Navies—adhering to the tenets and weapon systems of Mahan—gave much less credence to rival theorists, particularly Julian Corbett (1854–1922), a man more circumspect about the influence of sea power on history. Whereas Mahan wrote about decisive line-to-line battles for control of the high seas, Corbett described the more common responsibilities of navies in armed conflict, particularly American warfare: troop and logistics transport, commerce raiding and protection, and fire support for amphibious operations. Whereas Mahan loathed the idea that "the navy [might] become simply a branch of the army," Corbett maintained that "great issues between nations at war have always been decided—except in the rarest cases—either by what your army can do against your enemy's territory or else by the fear of what the fleet makes it possible for your army to do." Corbett's message—building sealift, destroyers, and platforms for invasions—did not favor the construction of capital ships. He remained a relatively unknown naval strategist, although in emphasizing an attack on land-based logistics depots he was more of a Jominian, when it came to tactical planning, than was the Jomini of sea power, Alfred Mahan.

In the final analysis, Mahan overlooked essential elements of his theory for appropriations' sake. His bedrock principle of war was "mass": concentrate one's force against a fragment of the enemy; do not divide the fleet. He therefore opposed the plan to attack Manila Bay in the Spanish-American War, lest this operation divert ships from a decisive battle in the Caribbean. Nonetheless, Mahan soon relinquished his "dread" of retaining the Philippines for much the same reason that the anti-imperialist bloc in Congress opposed the policy. They both believed, in the words of one senator opposed to increased taxation, that "it will make necessary a navy equal to the largest of powers." Both Mahan and Senator George Gray were wrong. "Passing time" dulled what Mahan called "the sharp impression and lively emotions that followed the war with Spain." Because America acquired the Philippines but did not spend the money to protect it, the country created what army officers would call "a military liability" whose defense would be "an act of madness." (As Mahan wrote in 1899, "The issue lies with the voters.") When Japan attacked and quickly conquered the Philippines in World War II, fact disproved the naval theory that "their possession would be an indispensable condition of success."

Interest groups compete for things aside from material resources. They fight over values, ideas, and ideals, which become important interests in themselves. For the armed services, the relevant beliefs were their respective doctrines for campaign planning, war fighting, and command and control, no matter how incomprehensible they seemed to other interest groups, their sister services in particular. Henry Stimson, a World War I army colonel, ruefully recalled "the peculiar psychology of the Navy Department, which seemed to retire from the realm of logic into a dim religious world in which Neptune was God, Mahan his prophet, and the United States Navy the only true Church." Worst of all was its impact on Franklin Roosevelt, its former assistant secretary. According to Stimson, secretary of war, the president "never dares buck the Navy when the Navy is obstinate."[5]

SERVICE COMPETITION, THE U.S. CONGRESS, ACTIVE-DUTY FORCES, AND RESERVES

In 1947 President Truman proposed service unification under a single civilian secretary advised by a supreme military commander with an armed forces general staff—exactly what Roosevelt had rejected during World War II. Truman's effort at eliminating turf disputes and duplication of effort caused a reaction that exacerbated the problem he hoped to solve. Service separation had contained interservice rivalry. With the creation of the Department of Defense, responsible to a single Armed Services Committee in Congress responsible for one vast appropriations bill, there was direct, continuous competition for missions and appropriations, and hence more redundancy. By the 1950s the army—with its Jupiter missiles—shared strategic nuclear weapons with the air force. By the 1960s the navy—with its "SEAL" teams—shared special forces with the army.

Had Congress, the bane of reformers from the 1820s to the 1980s, not amended Truman's bill, the effort might not have failed. Immediately after World War I, the secretary of war noted that a "high degree of centralization, which an effective General Staff employs, inspired many Members of Congress with the fear that it would grow to be a tyrannical and arbitrary power." After World War II, in response to Truman's proposal, senators and congressmen refurbished the old charge of "military autocracy." Hyperbole aside, they worried that consensus testimony from a unified armed forces would reduce their opportunities to influence policy and purchases. When the rhetoric cleared and legislation finally passed, the secretary of defense had no military staff or principal military adviser. The JCS was chaired by a self-described "presiding officer," one of whom would say about service "unification" that cooperation was based on a loose "federation," that is, when it existed at all.

Because the military's joint staff was weak, the secretary of defense gained relative strength, although not enough to prevent complaints about "end runs to Congress by the services." Capitol Hill defended the navy against the air force and the Marine Corps against the army, the strongest proponent of unity of command. Without air- and sealift, the army cannot deploy overseas. Once there, each branch capability has a specific counter: infantry kills tanks with missiles, artillery kills infantry, tanks overrun artillery, helicopters kill tanks. To fight combined-arms warfare, the army (unlike the navy) tends to centralize authority. This, in turn, tends to make it less popular with Congress.

The navy has a special commitment to decentralization at all levels of organization, across the entire service to a ship on the high seas. When its traditions were created in the late eighteenth century, there was no way to send or receive most orders, security notwithstanding. In a fleet action, admirals could rarely communicate with captains once naval guns engaged the enemy and smoke masked signals on the masts of the flagships. As late as 1915, the U.S. Naval Institute gave first prize to an essay declaring that "it is normally imperative for the subordinate commander himself to decide and to act, even before his superior can be acquainted with the special situation which has been met." Even today, navy discourse speaks of "recommendation"; the army tends to use "order" and "command." In a lecture at the Naval War College in 1983, the instructor told the next generation of admirals that each officer "is trusted to carry out missions with the minimum possible instruction; i.e., the less communication from above, the better."

Two blockades of Cuba—fifty-four years apart—demonstrate the different management styles of the navy and the modern presidency, post–World War II variety. During the Spanish-American War, the senior naval officer in the Atlantic virtually ignored the "deep concern" of the White House to deploy forces to protect the eastern seaboard. He raided Puerto Rico on his own initiative, forcing the Department of the Navy to dispatch mothballed Civil War monitors to seaport cities. Nonetheless, the secretary of the navy still wired Admiral William T.

Sampson: "In everything the department has utmost confidence in your discretion. [It] does not wish to hamper you." Things were somewhat different during the Cuban missile crisis in 1962. President Kennedy and Robert McNamara sought to control every detail of the operation from the "Situation Room" in the basement of the White House. "Crisis management" being an affront to service traditions, the chief of naval operations responded as he thought he should: "Mr. Secretary, if you and your deputy will go back to your offices, the Navy will run the blockade." Eight months later, because McNamara was still in charge of the Pentagon, the senior officer of the navy wound up as ambassador to Portugal.

According to the chairman of the JCS in 1950, the navy insists on "more autonomy of decision and action than [is] demanded by the army or the air force. "The Congress, to which he testified, was even more averse than the navy to strong command "from above"—be it the president, a secretary of defense, or a senior military officer. Before World War I, an articulate group of reformers tried to create a general staff on grounds that the "political influences that sap the strength of the nation" had no role in the military dedicated to "national" concerns. True or false, it was hardly an attractive argument to make to the politicians who had to approve this "plan to Prussianize the American Navy," a phrase the secretary of the navy resurrected when fighting reorganization in 1984. When Congress passed the statute creating the chief of naval operations (CNO) in 1915, it denied this office the authority for "general direction." The senior officer in the navy held responsibility for long-range planning, "preparation, readiness, and logistic support," not for operational control of the fleets on the high seas. In 1962 the CNO may have thought the secretary of defense had no more command authority over a captain on his deck than did the CNO himself.

Ironically, because the navy did not have a general staff in name, it had a strong one in fact. Congress felt no need to do to it what it did to the army in 1903—limit its number of general staff officers and mandate constant rotation to the field. Hence, the Department of the Navy frequently displayed more planning expertise than did the War Department. Between 1942 and mid-1945, 296 army officers left the Division of Plans and Operations to go overseas at the expense of experience and continuity. The naval staff, according to the chief of army plans, "knew all the canned language and techniques. It was new to us; we were just country boys"; rotation "raised hell with this division."

Aside from their mutual aversion to central control, Capitol Hill had other reasons to protect the navy from service unification that would have reduced America's tendency to devise strategy by bargaining. Some representatives were simply loyal to the service where they had fought in World War II. In the House, former lieutenant commander Gerald Ford spoke up for the navy. In the Senate, out of gratitude for "the most satisfying experience of my life," former lieutenant colonel Paul Douglas defended "the little army that talks Navy"—so described by Harry Truman, former colonel in the army reserve, who said the Marine Corps had "a propaganda machine almost equal to Stalin's."

Douglas, onetime Quaker pacifist, appealed directly to an acquaintance, the secretary of the navy, to enlist in the marines when he was fifty. When accepted, he was "far prouder" of making private first class in basic training than full professor at the University of Chicago. He subsequently won a Bronze Star for gallantry at Peleliu and a Purple Heart at Okinawa, where he was badly wounded in one of the worst engagements in World War II. No matter that he was hospitalized for fourteen months and never recovered full use of his left arm, Douglas felt "a deep wave of exaltation . . . that at my age I had shed blood in defense of my country." (A younger marine put it differently: "What's that crazy old grey-headed guy doing up here?") In 1950, after becoming a U.S. senator, he introduced legislation mandating four divisions and four air wings for his "beloved corps." His bill, "spelling out in detail what [Congress] wants the executive departments to do," did not please Truman, who had said the marines would remain "the Navy's police force as long as I am President." The Douglas Act of 1951 more than doubled Truman's allotment, from 175,500 to 400,000 marines. Nonetheless, the president "did not dare to veto the bill," the senator later wrote. "The Corps was granted a reprieve." The next year it became a separate service with its own seat on the JCS.

Congressman Carl Vinson, coming from a town in Georgia burned down by Sherman's army, had reasons to favor the navy, other than historical memory. Prior to so-called unification in 1947, when there were separate committees for each military service, representatives identified with their institutional constituents. Vinson, who pushed the Marine Corps Bill through the House by 254 to 30, "got interested in helping the Navy" during his twenty-five years as chairman of the Naval Affairs Committee he ran with total control. The navy, grateful for support for its aviation arm, named a World War II escort carrier the USS *Milledgeville* for Vinson's hometown (population: 9,543). After his retirement in 1962, after fifty years in Congress, the navy, beholden for opposition to merger, named its fourth nuclear-powered carrier the *Carl Vinson*.

The bargaining that created America's force structure took place not only between the armed services and Congress, but also between Congress, the active forces, and the reserves, particularly the National Guard, which provides a tangible constituency in many legislative districts. The federal government pays most of the expenditures of the guard, which the president commands in national emergencies, particularly war. The governor of each state inducts its soldiers, commissions its officers, and runs it on a daily basis. This dual responsibility violates a sacred principle of war. Unity of command drove spokesmen for the active components to try to merge the guard with the federal reserve. Otherwise, said General Omar Bradley, any hope that it can be the basis "for developing an efficient, mobile national army is quite absurd." The guard repeatedly defeated most attempts to centralize command. After World War II, fighting back the criticism that it was an "expensive boondoggle" good for nothing but "riot control," guardsmen became particularly close to legislators from the South. Carl Vinson lectured the secretary of defense: "You leave our National Guard alone. . . . it is a state organization." Seventy-eight years after the Civil War supposedly decided the matter, the guard had no qualms claiming that, under the Constitution, "the states are sovereign."

When the active forces, having learned their lesson, wanted to garner more political support, they courted, if not merged with, the National Guard. In the 1950s the air force generously financed their squadrons, knowing this would win favor from many congressional delegations. In 1973, after the trauma of the Vietnam War, the army desperately sought ways to assure support in future conflicts. Creighton Abrams, the army chief of staff, supported a "Total Force" structure tying active components far closer to the reserves. He built three undermanned divisions, each needing a "roundout brigade" manned by citizen-soldiers that was supposed to ensure that another president could not do what Johnson did in 1965—commit the army without declaring a national emergency to mobilize the reserves. No congressman or senator could then attack a war waged by the regular army without attacking the activity of the National Guard.[6]

LEADERSHIP, STRATEGY, AND THE UNPREDICTABILITY OF WAR

Ambiguity and inconsistency are part and parcel of pluralism. Unfortunately for those searching for national behavior patterns, America's inconsistencies have not been consistent. Its political leadership has vacillated; it has also been firm. Through the military depths and heights of World War II in the European theater—the defeat at the Kasserine Pass (1942) and the victorious landing at Normandy Beach (1944)—Roosevelt demanded the annihilation of the Nazi Reich, despite requests from his military commanders to soften the call for "unconditional surrender." During the depths of the War of 1812—impending federal bankruptcy, threats of secession from New England, and the burning of the national Capitol—James Madison refused to surrender America's proclaimed right to sail, travel, and trade without hindrance on the high seas. His resolution shocked the British but made perfect sense in Washington. Any concession, one cabinet official told another, "would not only ruin the present adm[inistration], but the Republican Party, and even the [republican] cause."

While clear and consistent goals help focus operations, political guidance could never secure military objectives by itself. Even the best generals operating under the clearest directives have had to adjust their military strategy to respond to the unexpected. Paraphrasing Helmut von Moltke's dictum that "no plan can look with any certainty beyond the first meeting with major enemy forces," Eisenhower said, "There is only one thing I can tell you. . . . No war ever shows the characteristics that were expected."

Success or failure on the battlefield could alter political goals. To the astonishment of President James K. Polk, the war against Mexico that began at the Rio Grande ended in the occupation of Mexico City. He thereby fluctuated between his original objective, the annexation of California, and the incorporation of all Mexico, something more commensurate with his military triumph. The final decision was made by the chief clerk of the State Department. Against Polk's instructions—but with support from Congress—he negotiated for the minimal objectives.

Polk's vacillations resembled Harry Truman's behavior during the Korean War, although, unlike Polk, he rode a military roller coaster from the heights of the Inchon landing to the depths of the retreat from the Yalu River. From early June to late December 1950, American policy went through four stages: (1) no defensive of South Korea, (2) preservation of its government, (3) liberation of the whole peninsula, and (4) return to the prewar status quo. (Between goals 3 and 4, the administration debated fleeing to Japan to protect the army or dropping nuclear bombs on China.) Since these goals rapidly replaced each other, decades of debate have not settled who won or lost the war, something dependent on which objective is selected.

Failure at the Yalu River scaled down America's goals in the Korean War. Failure may also lead to a more ambitious policy, as in the case of Abraham Lincoln. The North fought the first year of the Civil War for a single objective summarized in his statement that "I have no purpose, directly or indirectly, to interfere with slavery in the States where it exists." Appropriately, he selected George McClellan as his senior military commander, a conservative who vowed not "to wage war upon . . . the domestic institutions of the land," an acceptable position until he failed to take Richmond in 1862. Then Congress and newspapers charged that "pro-slavery cliques controlling the army" lacked the will "to strike heavy blows." Lincoln, concurring, felt impelled to fulfill his vow that "all indispensable means must be employed" to win the war. He furloughed McClellan and escalated the conflict from a conventional war focused on defeating enemy soldiers to what he called "a violent and remorseless revolutionary struggle" against the wealth, resources, and slave culture of the South. "I never had a wish to touch the foundations of their society, or any right of theirs. . . . They forced a necessity upon me to send armies among them, and it is their fault not mine."

Lincoln's well-known comment that he did not control the war ("Plainly events have controlled me") points to a pervasive phenomenon in modern military conflicts. Mass participation and destruction often wrest control of costs and policy from the national command authorities. Even when political leaders limited their aims to contain what Lincoln called "the butchering business," the price of combat could be immense. In Korea, both sides (combined) suffered over 4 million casualties in a war that maintained the status quo. More often than not, cost eroded moderation, whatever the initial objectives of belligerents. When that happened, the tail wagged the dog—that is, the means determined the ends. During the Civil War, blood, sweat, and tears—along with shortages, taxes, inflation, and frustration—motivated Americans to continue to fight, if only to give meaning to the pain they had endured. ("We have suffered too much to give up now," said a

Virginian in 1863.) In other wars—against Mexico and North Vietnam—the cost of the conflict polarized the public into hawks (for escalation) and doves (for extrication). When Mexico refused to sell California until the U.S. Army fought its way into its capital, hawks insisted on annexing the whole nation. When North Vietnam maintained its objectives after America deployed to South Vietnam, hawks wanted to bomb it to oblivion, not merely protect the government in Saigon. Meanwhile, in both instances, doves captured a major political party: the Whigs in the 1840s, the Democrats in 1972. Polk and Lyndon Johnson, having fought for limited objectives, could not keep the public on a solid middle ground.

World War I is the classic example of escalating goals to make war commensurate with the price of battle. During neutrality, President Woodrow Wilson's objective had been "peace without victory," that is, no "victor's terms imposed on the vanquished," a policy not substantially changed just because America declared war on Germany in June 1917. In August the head of intelligence services at the British embassy wrote the Foreign Office that "sub-consciously [Americans] feel themselves to be arbitrators rather than allies." Then, in seven months of ground combat from Catigny to the Meuse-Argonne, 112,000 U.S. servicemen died in the war. Wilson concurrently escalated his rhetoric and his objectives: "Force to the utmost without stint or limit, the righteous and triumphant Force which shall make Right the law of the world." In part, he demanded the deposal of the rulers of Imperial Germany in order to make a "peace worth the infinite sacrifices of these years of tragical suffering." In part, stronger terms were proposed for fear that the public, demanding commensurate objectives of their own, would turn to Wilson's opponents in the 1918 congressional election. Theodore Roosevelt and Henry Cabot Lodge opposed any terms at all. They insisted on rejecting an armistice, invading Germany, and forcing an acceptance of unconditional surrender.[7]

FIGHTING TO PROVE THAT AMERICA CAN FIGHT

Authoritarian governments have had a unity of command and clear echelons of authority, as if they were war-fighting organizations themselves. Largely for this reason, Americans long thought others had a distinct military advantage. Before the twentieth century, this idea motivated men to fight to prove the capability of democracy to defend itself. From World War I to the Persian Gulf, presidents still felt the need to establish credibility. Allegedly, dictators would pounce at the first sign of the weakness many Americans thought inherent in their institutions. Truman, Kennedy, and Johnson thought of Korea and Vietnam as limited conflicts by which they could avoid World War III by proving themselves to Russia and China, both of which had more respect for U.S. power than these presidents imagined.

In 1929 defense agencies conceded inferiority in superficially confident statements that "our government is democratic and the world war showed that a strong President can assume autocratic powers with the consent of the people." In the seventeenth and early eighteenth centuries, officials responsible for colonial American security against French Canada bewailed that their "Commonwealths" had to face "an Enemy under the Direction of one Despotick Governour," a "great Advantage in time of Warr." This sentiment created a presumption that the executive branch of government must have more latitude in military than in domestic affairs. The executive kept its supremacy provided it was successful, no easy matter in military operations. Once it failed, the legislature would reassert constitutional prerogatives it held in reserve. After military defeats in 1756 and 1862, Parliament (legislating for the colonies) and the U.S. Congress demanded greater effort and more drastic methods from the chief executive and the armed forces. After the Tet offensive in 1968, Congress began to legislate a withdrawal from Vietnam despite cries from some critics of the war, such as Walter Lippmann. He and Dean Acheson still maintained that the legislature is inherently unable to defend national security, largely because it is the branch of government most responsive to public opinion.

Ironically, the common belief that a pluralist democracy is ill suited to defend itself has been an incentive to fight. Whereas other countries waged wars to gain competitive advantage in the international arena, the United States sometimes fought to substantiate the capability of representative government, by no means a foregone conclusion. Aristocrats historically claimed office on the basis of martial prowess. They alleged that the leaders of democracies could not defend their nation. In the words of Alexis de Tocqueville, a French aristocrat: "Men living in democracies have not naturally the military spirit. [They do not readily] rise in a body and voluntarily expose themselves to the horrors of war."

Strategy itself, as a topic to be studied, reflected this indictment of representative government. It emerged as an academic subject of inquiry because of the gap between civil and military leadership arising in the age of democratic revolutions (1775 to 1848). Clausewitz wrote to educate statesmen about military issues and military officers about political affairs—something not deemed necessary when aristocrats (the "statesman and the soldier combined in one person") governed the nation and led the combat forces. On one particular issue, relevant to this discussion, Clausewitz was in a distinct minority. He believed that wars by governments responsive to "the people" were more apt to display "primordial violence, hatred, and enmity" than those waged by governments controlled by hereditary elites. Spokesmen for democracy felt the system they favored was ill-suited for violence because of its passivity. From the eighteenth through the twentieth century, political liberals in the Western world—from Rousseau to Woodrow Wilson—said that "the spirit of monarchies is war and aggression, the spirit of republics is peace and moderation."

The belief in the inherent pacifism of democracy could be reassuring or upsetting. On the one hand, it suggested America could escape armed conflict because, as Tom Paine wrote when encouraging independence in 1776, it would not have monarchs "drag us after them in[to] all the plundering wars." On the other hand, it implied that a democracy might have to rely on a large standing army of professional soldiers, "always dangerous to the Liberties of the People." The solemn duty to repudiate the accusation that democratic governments could not defend their nation was a constant theme in Fourth of July jeremiads between Yorktown and Appomattox from 1781 to 1865. According to this genre, Americans once were "hardy, brave, and patriotic," always "ready to sacrifice their personal interests for the security of their country and their posterity." Unfortunately, since the death of "our revolutionary fathers," especially Washington, "our people are no longer the brave men which they were wont to be—the inordinate pursuit of commerce had rendered us effeminate and cowardly."

A major goal of several American wars, particularly in the early nineteenth century, was to validate the "means," that is, to prove that elected leaders and citizen-soldiers could successfully wage war. To the Republican party of Jefferson and Madison, the War of 1812 was both the antitoxin and the test for "the American experiment" with republican government. "All the public virtues will be refined and hallowed"; the country will "demonstrate to an unbelieving world that a free government is no less resistless in energy and power than it is free in principle." To James Polk, leader of the Democratic party during the Mexican War, victory signified that a "popular representative government," using "citizen soldiers," could prosecute war "with all the vigor [of] more arbitrary forms of government." Friendly newspapers chimed that the capture of Mexico City would "teach foreign powers to dread the free people of this republic." Said one ditty: "A pure Democracy may own / A power as great as that which guards a throne."

The issue of viability resurfaced in the Civil War. One Southerner professed to give his "whole heart to the cause of the Confederacy because I believe that the perpetuity of republican principles on this Continent depends upon our success." Lincoln, for his part, said on 4 July 1861 that the conflict "forces us to ask 'Is there, in all republics, this inherent and fatal weakness?' 'Must a government, of necessity, be too strong for the liberties of its people, or too weak to maintain its own existence?'" Both sides believed that the war was the definitive test of American political institutions and a response to the issue Tocqueville posed: "It is difficult to say what degree of effort a democratic government may be capable of making on the occurrence of a national crisis." As Lincoln explained at Gettysburg, in the most important speech in American history: "We are testing whether [this] nation—or any nation, so conceived and so dedicated—can long endure."

The day Lee surrendered, one Union soldier wrote home that this "struggle has decided for all time to come that republics are not a failure." He spoke too soon. Doubts about the martial capabilities of American democracy persisted, as in the case of Woodrow Wilson, a devotee of Tocqueville: "Quite the best philosophy since Aristotle." In April 1917 he asked Congress to declare war on Germany, an autocratic power, because "the world must be made safe for democracy," seemingly a fragile flower. Two months later his secretary of war was relieved and elated at the public's cooperation with conscription. The "remarkable" registration of 10 million young men for the military draft testified "against the doubt in the minds of some [people] as to whether a democracy could summon its strength." Those individuals "who argue for dictatorship and strong governments are answered by the events of today." America "is in the business of showing democracy is safe for the world."

In the next major conflict, World War II, another president displayed the same faith and fear. During the Battle of Britain (October 1940), Roosevelt took pains to tell the American people that England was providing "proof that democracy, when put to the test, can show the stuff of which it is made." However, on the night before Pearl Harbor, when his closest confidant suggested a preemptive strike against Japan, the president answered: "No, we can't do that. We are a democracy and a peaceful people." He might have added immaturity to his list of national traits. After the conclusion of the contest, the army chief of staff complained about public impatience with meticulous preparation for long campaigns: "We couldn't wait to be completely ready."

Despite presidential proclamations, like that from Harry Truman that "we conclusively proved that free government is the most efficient government in every emergency by our victories over Germany and Italy and Japan," doubts about democracy persisted through the crisis in the Persian Gulf. John Foster Dulles, secretary of state after the Korean War, negotiated alliances throughout the world on the grounds that all democracies need mutual assistance: none, including America, could "adequately match the strength of a powerful totalitarian state." By extending an alliance to Southeast Asia, America sunk into Vietnam, which resurrected old concerns among defense and foreign policy elites. Henry Kissinger rued that the United States lacked the "stamina to stay the course against the Russians who are 'Sparta to our Athens.'" When senior military officers protested arms concessions to the Soviets, he replied, "That's easy for you to say, you don't have to run for reelection." Two years later, when they protested the fatally flawed peace treaty made with North Vietnam, President Nixon retorted: "You don't have any options in a democracy."

Nixon, Kissinger, and Ellsworth Bunker (their ambassador to South Vietnam) were not the only officials to say that Vietnam posed "the question whether a democracy can fight a war when there is no censorship," that is, when there is liberty. Nor was the deputy director of the Central Intelligence Agency (CIA) the only one to maintain "we are so democratic and diverse in our opinions" that Russia and China simply think "we don't have our act together." Maxwell Taylor—former chairman of the JCS and another ambassador to South Vietnam—agreed that unless "a democracy such as ours can learn to exercise some degree of self-discipline, we will be unable to meet the hard competition awaiting us in the decade of the 1970s." Unlike such elites, the general public did not wage war to prove democracy could wage it. Having more faith in the Republic, common citizens were more likely to fight to export their domestic institutions. When Wilson desperately appealed to the electorate in 1919 to assume responsibility for ensuring world peace through the League of Nations, he appealed to the public by saying that "America had the infinite privilege of fulfilling her destiny and saving the world."

When elites espoused a similar missionary outlook on war, it tended to merge with their belief that so-called military character was a public necessity. Before the creation of the Constitution, the willingness to sacrifice comfort had religious overtones. Defeats at the hands of French Canada drove Protestant clergy to tell the colonialists that they must first "sanctify yourselves." Twenty-two years later, during the Revolutionary War, Congress and General Washington banned profanity and ordered religious attendance for the Continental Army: "To the distinguished Character of Patriot, it should be our highest Glory to add the more distinguished Character of Christian" to the American cause.

By the 1770s the moral rearmament message was moving toward secularization. "We shall succeed," said Samuel Adams, "if we are virtuous." Moral merit was not only a military necessity; it was supposed to be a military bonus insofar as leaders of the young Republic felt that war could foster "warlike virtues" of self-control and sacrifice. John Adams predicted that the Revolutionary War would be a "furnace of affliction" producing "refinement in states, as well as individuals." Andrew Jackson, in 1814, urged the citizens of New Orleans—"an opulent and commercial town"—to "shake off the habits which are created by wealth and show that you are resolved to deserve the blessings of fortune by bravely defending them." Douglas MacArthur, returning to piety in 1951, warned that "our need for patriotic fervor and religious devotion was never more impelling. There can be no compromise with atheistic Communism."

Between the Korean War and the War of 1812, other prominent Americans continued the refrain about political purification through armed conflict. Abraham Lincoln, who had complained that America had "grown fat," greedy, and corrupt in the 1850s, said that the Civil War was a "punishment inflicted . . . for our presumptuous sins [so] that our whole people might be redeemed." In World War I, when Woodrow Wilson talked about making "the world safe for democracy," Theodore Roosevelt and other militants talked about making "democracy safe for the world." According to interventionist literature, "the nation is to be saved by the very blood and tears that it must shed." According to Roosevelt's oldest son, writing his father from the first military division America deployed to France: "A cancerous growth had formed in all departments of the republic. The war looks as if it could be three months or three years. For our country's sake I hope the latter."

Lincoln and Theodore Roosevelt notwithstanding, philosophers have rarely occupied the White House. Most administrations have consisted of inconsistent politicians whose conclusions about whether American democracy was triumphant or on trial depended on the occasion and recent events. In 1961 John

Kennedy's inaugural speech informed "every nation . . . we shall pay any price, . . . support any friend, oppose any foe, to ensure the survival and success of liberty." It inspired what a Saigon-based diplomat called "very gung ho fellows," from Robert McNamara down to Philip Caputo, a Marine Corps volunteer. Five and a half years after Kennedy's speech, Caputo left Vietnam as a self-identified "moral casualty," that is, court-martialed for murder because he could not tell the enemy from local civilians. In 1966 he vowed he would never again "fall under the charms and spells of political witch doctors like John Kennedy."

In fact, as Kennedy privately confessed, he made speeches to "scare people" by making us "appear tough and powerful," a philosophy of speaking loudly when your government is a small stick. Just ten days after the inaugural speech that stirred the New Frontiersman, Kennedy returned to the theme of his senior college thesis, published in 1940 as *Why England Slept:* democracy "is divided and disorganized"; "the essence of a totalitarian state is that the national purpose will not permit group interests to interfere with its fulfillment." On 30 January 1961 the president addressed Congress in words reminiscent of Lincoln at Gettysburg: "Before my term has ended we shall have to test anew whether a nation organized and governed as ours can endure. The outcome is by no means certain. The answers are by no means clear." Neither simple hubris nor the arrogance of power caused the Vietnam War. The perceived need to dispel doubt and establish credibility drove Kennedy to commit the likes of Lieutenant Caputo.[8]

2

The Colonial and Revolutionary Wars for North America

Depending on which group was fighting for what cause, the wars for North America were limited or total, secular or sacred, international or internal. The losers lost when they had to divert forces to protect their European interests; the winners won because they had gained local numerical supremacy. Conventional army officers—fighting a limited, secular, and international war—still needed irregular auxiliaries: Indians, rangers, or militia. Jeffrey Amherst and George Washington always hoped to replace these "lazy rum drinking Scoundrels" with light infantry under their command and control, even when deployed in dispersed formation. Neither got the force structure that he wanted. The British needed irregulars and militia for scouting, security, and logistics against the French in the wilderness, where "there has not been ground to form a battalion since we left the settlements." Americans needed them to win the total, sacred, and internal aspects of the Revolutionary War. "We do require their services," Amherst said in 1761, "ill performed though they be, and must endure their indolence and insolence until this cursed war is over. Then good riddance to them all."[1]

AMERICAN OR EUROPEAN THEATERS, 1690 TO 1755

In a sense, the British Empire's series of wars against France for control of North America was a coalition war of semisovereign states. In theory, the king, with the support of the House of Lords and Commons ("the king-in-Parliament"), ruled the empire without concurrence from the colonies. In practice, the colonies had a substantial amount of de facto independence as a result of slow communications with London preoccupied with other concerns. The Crown led Massachusetts and Virginia against French Canada much the way it induced Portugal and Prussia to oppose Spain and France: it disbursed financial subsidies to raise and support their respective armies. This could mitigate but not eliminate basic conflicts about national security and military strategy. America and England, despite a common king, held different priorities and different concepts of war, at least until 1756, when William Pitt became secretary of state for the Southern Department, bearing responsibility for colonial affairs. Prior to his ascendancy, England emphasized the balance of power in Europe—a logical preference for British monarchs who held dynastic title to the German territory of Hannover.

The elector of Hannover (later known as George I) took the Crown of Great Britain largely to tap its resources to protect his ancestral homeland from its powerful neighbors: France, Austria, and Prussia. Situated between Continental powers, Hannover was a tempting target for England's enemies, who lacked the naval power to cross the Channel. In this precarious position, the German principality took priority over the New World and its "long-injured, long-neglected, long-forgotten people," as described by William Pitt, whose parliamentary faction felt the tail wagged the dog. The king committed Englishmen and money to the Continent or allowed Hannover to declare neutrality and sign a separate peace with France. In either case, this "despicable Electorate" conducted business at the expense of the British Empire.

Largely ignored in London, New England raised 4,000 and in 1745 captured Louisbourg, the French fort protecting the mouth of the St. Lawrence River, Canada's transportation network, since all major settlements were built on its banks. This feat of arms—"scarce paralel'd in [all] History," according to Massachusetts public opinion—was the only successful large-scale operation conducted exclusively by American soldiers in the colonial period. (The English navy was involved, not its army.) After one-fourth of the force died of starvation, disease, and exposure, London traded the "Gibraltar of the New World" for what the ministry called "the balance of power in Europe" when France gave up a golden opportunity to overrun Holland and an army commanded by George II's favorite son.

The American colonists were bitter at this betrayal of their military heroes, who captured what the king's ministers disdained as a weak fortification dominated by high ground. (How else could ill-disciplined and drunken volunteers ever take the objective in the first place?) New England responded that their capture of the "stronghold of Satan" was obviously blessed by God. Once it was returned and "the security of the brave and virtuous given up to purchase some precarious advantages for lazy f[oo]ls and idle All[ie]s," Massachusetts wondered if "our beloved Country may share the same Fate with its Conquest," that is, be traded for a peace treaty in Europe. Just as ominous for the future of the British Empire, a group of young Bostonians, among them Samuel Adams, based their protests of war policy on an ideology that would come to fruition in 1776: that the government in London had no legitimacy if it failed to protect local "lives, liberties, and estates."

Obviously embittered, New England was never again so united on behalf of an imperial military campaign. It did not realize that its effort would pay dividends in London. When Louisbourg was captured, Britain had won no battles in the War of Austrian Succession. As the only bright spot on the horizon, the fortress captivated many Englishmen once inattentive to America. It also became an occasion for criticism of the Crown's military policy by an aroused public and parliamentary opposition that thought colonial (versus Continental) warfare would provide trade, riches, and wealth—far more appealing than battles waged to contain France south and west of the Rhine for Holland and Hannover.

These economic calculations and national aspirations made a particular impression on an aspiring politician who lacked the hereditary fortune and family connections by which others acquired high office in eighteenth-century England. Heretofore, Hannover had been the major issue by which the opposition aroused the nation against the ministry. Four months after Louisbourg fell to the Anglo-American expedition, William Pitt added a new element to the standard call that Britain should fight only for "British objectives." Possession of the fort was an opportunity to destroy the weakest component of enemy naval capability, seamen trained in "the great trade carried on by the French to North America." When Great Britain next fought France in the Seven Years' War, Pitt utilized his identification with commerce, colonies, and American concerns to fulfill his personal and patriotic ambition to become what a contemporary called "the most illustrious man of the first country in Europe."[2]

LIMITED OR TOTAL COLONIAL WAR?

Pitt reasoned that France was impregnable on the Continent but vulnerable in Canada to "vigorous and offensive measures," such as mobilizing colonial auxiliaries, interdicting supply lines with the navy, and conducting a campaign, as James Wolfe put it, to "cut up New France by its roots." Neither Pitt (the "Great Commoner") nor General Wolfe was an aristocrat by birth or breeding; they felt such people lacked "ambition to stir [decisive] action." Most senior English officers and officials were titled gentlemen for whom the war for North America remained a gentlemanly conflict to be conducted "on a European footing," what historian Julian Corbett called "limited war" when he coined the term in 1907 in a book describing English strategy before Pitt came to power. Typically, British government ministers only planned to protect disputed territory like the Ohio River Valley, sparsely populated and claimed by both empires. Military action was equally fastidious, that is, unless Americans, Canadians, or Indians (the "savages," "barbarians," and "vermin" on both sides) got out of hand. "To carry on the War in this Country with the same humanity and generosity it is [done] in Europe," French and English officers exchanged prisoners, wine, cheese, beer, and partridge: "a necessary and good example to set in this barbarous country, not only on account of humanity but because of politeness." Marquis de Montcalm, commander of French forces in North America, was one of several foreign errants to the theater who vowed to fight "like a Gentleman."

The same could be said of George Washington, a young militia officer from Virginia who hoped to secure a king's commission to a royal regiment, usually reserved for English gentlemen. Like England before 1756, his particular colony fought a limited conflict in terms of population committed and effort expended. In the 1740s it enlisted only 136 men, the smallest force raised in North America for what was called King George's War. After 1755, feeling a threat from France for the first time, it raised approximately 3,000 soldiers, about 12 percent of its military-eligible population between eighteen and thirty-five years old. Most volunteered for strictly economic reasons, like the rank and file of the British army. Some were truly destitute. More were recent immigrants or artisans unable to compete with slave labor in the Tidewater. Whatever their background, Washington complained that they were "obstinate, self-willed, perverse, of little or no service, and very burthensome to the country. . . . The united vigilance of their officers can not prevent them" from abandoning the frontier posts they were ordered to protect, Virginia's sole objective, despite Washington's own preference for "an offensive scheme of action." In 1755 its governor explained, "The Plan of Operation is no more than to take Possession of the Lands in his Majesty's Name." Except for suggesting a feint to prevent Quebec from sending forces to Ohio, he proposed no action much beyond the contested river valley.

Other colonial Americans felt very differently, especially those from New York and New England, the provinces on the proverbial front line. Their idea of reciprocity with their adversary was dispatching scalping parties, "a barbarous Method of conducting Warr [but of course] introc'd by the French." For Massachusetts, in particular, the conflict met the criteria for total war: noncombatant casualties, use of citizen-soldiers, ideological motivation, and the attempt to eradicate the enemy government. French Canada, by controlling Louisbourg and the Montreal-Albany corridor, held the front and back doors to New England and the northern border of New York. Its 75,000 white settlers (1754) could scarcely match the 1,200,000 British subjects to the south if it were not for certain constitutional and cultural factors.

First, as Benjamin Franklin complained, America had "extreme difficulty bringing so many different governments and assemblies to agree in any speedy and effectual measures for our common defense and security, while our enemies have the very great advantage of being under one direction, with one council and one purse." ("Should this great body once get a head," asked Montcalm's aide-de-camp, "what will become of Canada?")

Second, Canada commissioned an unusual body of officers by eighteenth-century standards. They began in the ranks and won promotion by aggressive action, not by birth, politics, or seniority, as was the norm in Europe. They used Indian allies and methods against Anglo-Americans who spoke of French Canadians as they often spoke about Indians, partly in contempt for those who did not fight without surprise, partly in awe of the best skirmishers in the world. "Our men are nothing but a set of farmers and planters," said one English observer in 1757. "Theirs are not only well trained and disciplined, but . . . march without baggage and support themselves without stores and magazines."

Truth be known, the French lived in fear of their own allies. In the early eighteenth century, Anglo-American forts planted on the frontier began to undermine French influence with Native Americans by changing the objectives of Indian warfare, once waged for intangibles like prestige, honor, and revenge. The British helped make war a commercial activity, to their ultimate advantage. Indians may have attacked English settlements, if only to ransom Anglo-American captives back for market value. They certainly preferred French brandy to British rum. However, these short-term factors could not offset the long-term trend. England sold blankets, jewelry, tools, knives, steel, gunpowder, and muskets to the fierce Mohawks of the Iroquois Confederation at less than half the price the French charged the Hurons and Algonquins in pelt and fur. (The English also paid substantially more for the scalps of their opponents.) The Royal Navy blockaded Canada during war, thereby preventing the importation that maintained its Indian trade. Hence France was obsessed that the British would eventually bribe all the natives to throw the French "entirely out of the continent of North America," as the Iroquois nearly did in the mid-1600s.

Using their sole competitive advantage while they still had Indian allies, Canadian forces raided families along the American frontier. As in all wars, the means helped determine the methods, and the methods the objectives. The French and the English both used Indians or rangers to "do some good." Neither native-born whites nor reds were effective at siege craft or standard battles in open fields, both of which put a premium on corporate discipline. Their natural talents were as guerrillas, a lucrative opportunity for plunder for which there were many volunteers. This meant that useful auxiliaries would do things "their own way," a euphemism for torturing, scalping, and terrifying other Christians or the Indians their enemy employed. (No self-respecting European gentleman would ever do such things himself.) Admittedly, neither side was particularly gallant, but both had an excuse: "What would be a violation [of propriety] in Europe cannot be regarded as such in America," a barbarous place to begin with. The French, in particular, reasoned that "savages" were the only way to chastise its greedy rival, who has "violated the most sacred laws of civilized nations" by crossing any barrier to conquer any land it could.

The Canadian "plan of containment"—an admitted policy of "consternation and terror"—was "calculated to disgust the people of those Colonies and to make them desire the return of peace." It was also supposed to "distress" Anglo-America with self-protection and survival so its money and manpower would not be used to assault Quebec, the heart and spinal column of New France. This plan did not panic London, which wanted its colonies to provide their own defense. However, within British North America, these raiding parties seemed part of a "detestable and wicked Conspiracy" by which Quebec and its Jesuits would mobilize their "frenchified Indians" and one day "drive [all] the English Settlements into the Sea."

For years, Canada's strategy intimidated and confused Americans who huddled together, every settlement (let alone colony) defending itself. While such isolationism never completely vanished, raiding party warfare gradually caused the reaction it was supposed to prevent—a unifying strategy to march on Quebec. As early as 1690, and gathering strength each decade thereafter, the most powerful citizens of Massachusetts proposed decisive action against what they called "the chief Source of New England's Miseries." By the mid–eighteenth century, Governor William Shirley was telling London of "undoubted intelligence that the French design to make further encroachments on his Majestie's Territories," the only viable counter being his plan "to march an army in a few days to the gates of Montreal and pour our troops into the very heart of their country."

As is often true in war, it is difficult to tell where fear ends and propaganda begins. Important segments of New England's body politic had a vested interest in conflict with Canada. Governors and well-placed merchants sought patronage, contracts, or promotions in the British Empire. The 30,000 volunteers who eventually came from Massachusetts also had material motives. Most of them, around eighteen years old, needed a cash bonus to buy new land or start a trade, since their older brothers would inherit the family farm. Others wanted scalps to sell and goods to plunder, as promised by numerous recruiting agencies. Whatever their reward, they were more combative than other merchants illegally trading with Canada or the average citizen still inclined toward isolation and self-defense. (In 1760 the British high commander, Jeffrey Amherst, noted indifference in New England once the French retreated back to the St. Lawrence.) To offset this peace faction's call "to keep the people at home," the militants spoke of an unrelenting enemy made up of "Negro Slaves, Catholicks, Jacobites, and transported Convicts." They also utilized a religious ideology that gave the war in New England its special intensity.

In the 1750s, when Massachusetts supplied 75 percent of all colonists participating in the campaign that terminated French rule in North America, the colony had a sacred mission, at least in its own eyes. In the 1740s and 1750s, religious revivalists inundated New England with rhetoric about soldiers fighting with "true manliness and grandeur" for the kingdom of God on earth. Thereafter citizens vented their religious emotions against "the whole rabble of [the] Antichrist" ensconced in Quebec, and soldiers set forth under exhortations from a man with a vested interest in war. In 1745 George Whitefield was looking for a way to revive the Great Awakening, the religious revival he led in the 1730s. He found it in a Protestant military crusade. New England's citizen-soldiers, like the Indians they hated, may have drunk themselves into a stupor, especially after English officers prevented them from looting Louisbourg in 1745. No matter. When word of victory came back to Boston, Whitefield and company would attest to a religious transformation on the home front: "the people of all ranks arose from their beds to joy and thanksgiving"; "the niggard became generous, the poor forgot their poverty."

How did Massachusetts reconcile its religious convictions with many things it did as far back as 1710, such as merchants refusing to cut profit margins on supplies, thereby preventing a prospective expedition to Quebec? Two wars later, in the 1750s, Massachusetts suffered approximately 2,000 military deaths: three times the per capita fatality rate the United States sustained in World War II. At the same time, they and other colonists contracted to sell the English army steeds and prime beef; they delivered nags and spoiled food. When in military service themselves, Americans primarily provided logistic support to frontline English regiments by laying roads, building forts, manning boats, and driving wagons—"the Works that in inhabited Countrys are performed by Peasants." If these axmen and masons "were left to themselves," Jeffery Amherst complained, "they would eat fryed Pork and lay in their tents all day." New Englanders complained about heavy labor, rioted over beer, and left the service the day their one-year contracts expired. They did not, and probably could not, resolve the contradiction between a buccaneer out to plunder Canada, labor commissary, and Christian soldier who believed that "Warr is an Ordinance appoynted by God for subduing and destroying the Churche's Enemies here upon Earth." This conflict was not unique in U.S. history. Contradictions have been prevalent, if not predominant, in many aspects of many American wars.

When New England's "godly Soldiers," contract workers, or marauders (take your pick) deployed to Canada, many must have been convinced that they were the instrument's of "God's holy will." According to Puritan theology, unpredictable events like disease and death signified divine purpose. According to keen observers of war, such as Clausewitz, "no other human activity is so continuously or universally bound up with chance." Its inherent uncertainty must have reinforced the belief of at least one New England company clerk that military "victory undoubtedly comes from the Lord."[3]

NEW WORLD IDEOLOGY, OLD WORLD POLITICS, AND THE WAR IN NORTH AMERICA

On the one hand, Massachusetts maintained that "Cruel Papists [were about to] fill the British Colonies, seize our Estates, abuse our Wives and Daughters, and barbarously murder us." On the other hand, Americans maintained that they could not (and should not) have to protect themselves, security essentially being the empire's constitutional responsibility. Needless to say, this was not the prevalent opinion in Great Britain. Prior to the French and Indian War of 1755–63 (called the Seven Years' War in Europe), major military conflicts between America and Canada were triggered by war on the other side of the ocean, and London gave this theater little support. The final act in the long conflict for empire dating back to 1690 was far different in major respects. It began in mid-1754, when young George Washington, conducting what might be called a police action, led 159 Virginia militiamen into the Ohio River Valley. It concluded with British commitments of 44,000 men and a £1.4 million reimbursement to America for fighting the war. Like Virginia, a military moderate, England originally had limited objectives to go along with its limited commitment of 790 British regulars in North America in 1754. Its policy was to roll back French encroachments and then "come to a reasonable Agreement upon the Whole" New World, so said Thomas Pelham-Holles, the Duke of Newcastle and (for thirty years) secretary of state for the Southern Department, charged with American affairs. He believed that this plan of action would create a stable peace at the borders of the empire: the Mississippi in the west; the Great Lakes in the north, Nova Scotia in the east.

In 1754 and 1755 the king's ministers were determined to defend existing territory in a manner "as cheap and as inoffensive as we can." Through the last three wars with France, the Crown incurred a public debt of £84 million. Hence Newcastle's ministry firmly maintained that with a population ten times that of Canada, "the Business in *America* must be done by *Americans,*" especially now that he had become first lord of the Treasury and deficit reduction was "our principal object." What is more, to send over English regulars would create a world war. France would strike back in Europe, where Britain was in a precarious geostrategic position. Neither Austria nor Holland, its historic allies, would help contain France if England precipitated war in America. Nor would an offensive be countenanced by Spain, then a neutral courted by all sides. Madrid, worried about the security of its own possessions, said it would join England's enemies when "the danger to the balance of maritime [overseas] power is exposed by the ambitious projects of the British court," a worry to Newcastle since 1738. A threat to eliminate French Canada might create a grand coalition against Britain, such as England traditionally mobilized against French expansion on the Continent. Once that happened, France could easily repeat what it had done in other wars: offset British advantage in America by holding Hannover hostage. On the other hand, Newcastle would not sacrifice the New World lest England lose its base for gaining territory to trade at a peace conference. "If We lose our American Possessions," he wrote in 1750, "France will, with great Ease, make War with us" in Europe "whenever They please."

On the eve of the Seven Year's War, England and France saw little result likely from another global war except status quo antebellum plus a larger public debt. Under commensurate restriction, the local colonial governments of both nations resorted to the same ruse, that of getting their respective Indian allies to attack the enemy's outposts while professing peace: "Our hands are tied." Then the English ministry was discredited by military misfortune in India, the Mediterranean, and the Ohio River Valley, where 72 French regulars, 146 Canadians, and 637 Indians caught a 1,500-man task force under General James

Braddock in a withering cross fire on closed terrain. "We would fight if we could see anybody to fight with," one soldier was heard to mutter.

Nine hundred fifty British soldiers and American militia were killed or wounded outside present-day Pittsburgh. In the next two years, the war got worse. The French captured major trading posts at Oswego on Lake Ontario and at Fort William Henry on the corridor between Albany and Montreal, thereby threatening to turn all the Indians of New York against the settlements of the Crown. Americans were terrified; London was already mad. Newcastle's carriage had been pelted, and he was threatened with bodily harm. The House of Commons abandoned its tradition of deference to the executive "in time of war and public danger." It began a parliamentary inquiry and threatened to reinforce the colonies whether the Crown approved or not. Newcastle, while still hoping to avoid a major military conflict, knew his options were closing: "If we don't make peace, for God's sake let us make war in a different manner from what we have done." No longer able to manage the polity by banquets, patronage, and other techniques common to the aristocracy, he had to rob his critics of the agitator who "has rode in the whirlwind and directed the storms with abilities beyond the common reach of the genie of a tempest." To win 150 more votes in the Commons, the government asked William Pitt to "invigorate the war" and resurrect morale by forming a coalition billed as "the strongest administration that has been formed for many years."

In force structure, the English army now adopted light infantry regiments and tactics, as one American suggested to Pitt after the Braddock ambush. "It is an unpardonable neglect of Duty to be surprized by the French when a few brisk men scattered for two hundred yards on each Side will prevent it. Keep them from surprizing you and they are an Easy conquest." As for Pitt himself, for the duration of the war, he handled parliamentary debates and public opinion, from the mob to the merchants. He also provided the leadership heretofore lacking, as Newcastle admitted in retrospect. ("I know nobody who can plan or push the execution of any plan agreed upon in the manner Mr. Pitt did.") However, in so doing, the new secretary of state for the Southern Department derailed London's inclination to raise funds and long-term soldiers without the concurrence of local America legislatures. Pitt was interested in decisive military victory, not constitutional reform. Other officials complained "that the People in these Colonies are quite unused to War and Martial Discipline." He was willing to look past this problem and do whatever was needed to "quicken and effectuate the speedy Levying of the greatest Number of Men." This meant promising to reimburse the colonies for the supplies and volunteers they mobilized, even if their methods were grossly inefficient for lack of coercive and central government authority.

Because Americans agreed to serve only one campaign at a time, there was a constant turnover of new recruits learning what to do and how to do it, to the aggravation of English officers who thought colonists were "frightened out of their senses at the name of a Frenchmen." They also felt that colonial democracy was tantamount to anarchy when local legislatures insisted on authority to allocate their military men and resources where they preferred, rarely far away from their provincial borders. Pitt did not fight the process on behalf of British military efficiency. As the "minister of measures" standing "above thinking of accounts," he spent his way through institutional difficulties. Newcastle, reduced to "minister of numbers" at the Treasury, was left the hopeless task of keeping interest rates at 4 percent.

In the next five years, Pitt sent so much manpower that half those serving in the American theater were British regulars. As the most vitriolic critic of the Hannover connection in 1755, he had said that continental commitments were the monarchy's excuse "to exhaust our wealth, consume the profits of our trade, and load our posterity with intolerable burdens" (i.e., debt). Now, as a king's minister, Pitt would claim that "America had been conquered in Germany," as if to justify the policy he conducted but had once condemned. Specifically, the government maintained that "by diverting the expense of France" to the Continent, it "maintained our superiority at sea," thereby able to conduct decisive operations in North America. However, Pitt, like most other would-be strategists, had more coherence in hindsight than he did when conducting war. As a minister of the Crown, he could not ignore the king's dynastic concerns nor the many political factions interested in the Continent. Nor could George II, who had opposed sending English soldiers to America rather than Hannover, maintain his old stance in the face of Pitt's substantial opposition. Hence the monarch and the minister he could barely abide sent forces in both directions and later claimed that it was their global plan.

Unfortunately, to divert France, Britain had to divert substantial resources of its own, despite Pitt's vows to the contrary. Making a "concession [to] fatal necessity," he sent 22,000 English soldiers and spent £340,000 a month to wage war in Germany. He and George II also strengthened Newcastle's recent treaty with Prussia, the rising power in Europe. The duke, always partial to Austria, had merely hoped to buy the neutrality of Frederick the Great with mutual guarantees of respective principalities. Pitt got a full alliance at £670,000 per year. The military crisis that brought him to power in London included defeats of Prussia, squeezed in a giant pincer between Russia, France, Austria, and Sweden. Frederick, threatening a capitulation that would expose Hannover, demanded more assistance than Newcastle had the power to provide. Pitt, who could not be accused of pro-German sentimentality, had far more influence over the House of Commons. He increased parliamentary subsidies for the Anglo-Hannoverian and Prussian armies 700 percent in 1758. He thereby maintained the balance of power on the Continent in England's favor with no help from former allies like Holland, which worried about British expansion toward a monopoly in the New World.

Pitt opposed all notions that conquests in America should remain chips to be traded for Hannoverian concerns, George II's plan of action as late as 1759. When the minister acted like a strategist, not a politician, he thought that control

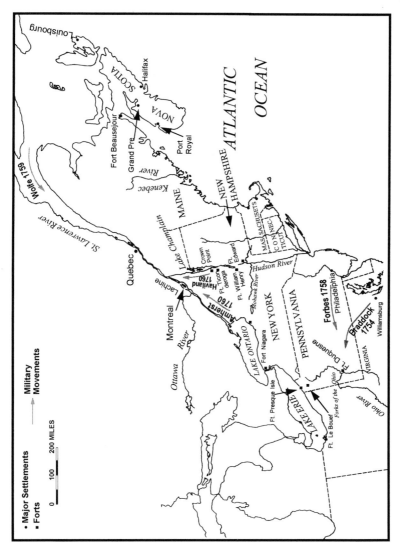

British North American conquest of French Canada, 1758–60

of colonial resources would be the key to world supremacy. Such expectations were prominent in London publications so enthralled by the reconquest of Louisbourg in 1758 that Englishmen overlooked, at least for the time being, the less popular components of Pitt's grand strategy, namely, "smuggling away more British troops to Hanover." Although upset that other nations might now join the fray, he need not have worried about newspaper revelations of grandiose national ambitions. Britain's enemies had already come to a grim conclusion, as the French foreign minister told Spain when convincing it to join the war: if Britain conquers Canada, it "alone will remain rich. . . . France and Spain would become second-rate powers."

Now that America had become a high priority, France might have done what it never did before: trade German territory for land in the New World, provided it won anything to trade. Because Prussia protected England's Continental interests, Pitt won in both theaters. Up to 1760, his strategy and tactics were still emerging and evolving: "all the *data* [for North America] on which we are to ground any Plan are loose and precarious." Furthermore, the old concept of limited and defensive war persisted in government circles. Britain and France still fought for clear and defensible borders that would end all disputed claims on the periphery. Pitt and King George sent men and money to lay siege to French strongholds and establish their own in the Ohio River Valley, the Great Lakes, and Lake Champlain, where three major forts were built within thirty-five miles (£3 million for Crown Point alone) to "secure His Majesty's Interior Dominions from any Encroachments the Enemy may attempt."

These costly commitments to areas of secondary importance were a waste of scarce resources. This remote territory, where thick forests gave the defense a decided advantage, would drop into England's lap whenever Upper Canada's source of supplies fell at Montreal. Moreover, the British dispersal suited the French global strategy by maximizing Gallic tactical advantage in personnel and position: backwoods irregulars versus Anglo-American settlers on terrain where "a thousand men could stop three thousand." When these Canadian "hell-hounds" in control of the internal waterways ravaged the countryside, American communities demanded protection that diverted England from Europe, India, and the Caribbean, to say nothing of Quebec. The French plan was brilliant and successfully executed, up to a point. France sent barely 6,000 men to North America while the English committed 23,000 soldiers and one-fourth of its fleet. Unfortunately, when London finally decided to move toward a new military concept of total victory, France lost all Canada and won nothing in return.

In 1759 Newcastle still believed that the idea of "extirpating a nation such as France from North America . . . is the idelest of all imaginings." Pitt, with ideas of his own, was finally ready to pull resources from local security and have the navy bring an army to the gates of the enemy government. For command, he promoted James Wolfe, who offered his services "particularly in the river St. Lawrence." At last, there was an English general with New England ideas about

"an offensive daring kind of war [that] will awe the Indians and ruin the French."
Wolfe promised friend and foe alike that if "the Canadian vermin" resisted, they
would be "sacked and pillaged," especially by his light infantry, Wolfe's way of
causing mass desertions from forces protecting Quebec. His subsequent destruction of farms, villages, and much of the city was "war of the worst Shape," said
a subordinate. Morality aside, the British Empire had never been greater than it
now was because of Pitt and the men he selected to command. However, the conquest of North America came at a large price. With a truly coherent plan concentrating combat power down the Louisbourg, Quebec, and Montreal axis,
England might have won the war in one or two campaigns, not the six start-stop-
start expeditions that drained its treasury so badly that Pitt's triumph would soon
prove to be a Pyrrhic victory.[4]

TRIUMPH AND FAILURE IN THE BRITISH EMPIRE

In 1759 James Wolfe and 4,500 British regulars conquered the capital of Canada
with support from six American rangers companies and auxiliaries. ("Happy,
happy day! My joy [is] inexpressable," wrote his superior, William Pitt.) To
Jonathan Mayhew, a prominent Massachusetts preacher, the campaign nailed
shut "that Pandora's box, from whence unnumber'd plagues have issued for more
than an hundred years." Another cleric, the chaplain of the Royal American Regiment, the only colonial soldiers Wolfe did not despise, said the conquest of
Canada will make "a lasting impression upon the minds of all the subjects of the
British Government. . . . Gratitude & Joy" was pervasive; "no more complaining
in our streets." Of course, there were some minority opinions. George William
Frederick, soon to become George III, was embittered at greater glory accruing
to Pitt: the "most popular man is a true snake in the grass." Moreover, a few
Frenchmen already suspected that Britain had conquered more than it could govern. The Crown would have to occupy Canada with 15,000 soldiers more prof-
itably employed preserving its dominion south of the St. Lawrence, which was
about to be called into question because Americans and Englishmen had incompatible notions about the causes, key events, and consequences of the recent war.

John Adams, a little-known lawyer who "longed ardently to be a Soldier,"
did no more than carry one military dispatch from Massachusetts to Rhode
Island. He nonetheless felt victory proved America had a destiny to "emancipate
the slavish part of mankind all over the earth." General Wolfe, despite his colonial rangers and 1,000 volunteers, had a different opinion. The greatest contribution of the colonies to the combined war effort were scouts who found safe
terrain and labor that delivered supplies. Habitually, neither activity is much
appreciated by soldiers in close contact with the opposition. They overlook the
eyes and tail of their army, even in North America, where the wilderness could
be as formidable as enemy guns. Wolfe, like most European officers, had few

qualms about treating the colonials with contempt. The campaign against Canada simply demonstrated that "Americans are in general the dirtiest most contemptible cowardly dogs that you can conceive. There is no depending on them in action. They desert by battalions, officers and all."

A famous American painting by Benjamin West, entitled *Death of General Wolfe,* portrayed this remorseless man as a Christlike figure crucified in combat at Quebec. The theme was consistent with the eighteenth-century American conviction that its soldiers would "rise above the Ruins of this World, and become Inhabitants of the Regions of Immortality and Glory." However, faith in the "remarkable smiles of divine Providence upon our national Interest" could not pay the financial interest on the English national debt, which virtually doubled during the Seven Years' War—from £74.6 to £132.6 million. Pitt had not worried, although he had been warned that every American province would try "to throw every Expense of this War [back] on the Crown." He cared only to "elevate Britain to the highest point of glory" and to "lay [France] on her back." However, by 1761, the war had become a substantial burden to Parliament, the public, the London money markets, and the new English monarch, George III—the first of his line to be born, bred, and "glory in the Name of Britain."

Americans were joyful that they finally had "a prince who is native to our country," meaning one who thought the empire more important than Europe. They and Pitt would have cause to recall an old Chinese proverb: Be careful for what you wish; you may actually get it. The latest Hannoverian, with little interest in Hannover, learned how to oppose the ministry when heir to the throne, a rallying point for the opposition in eighteenth-century English politics. He now used Pitt's old arguments to turn the public against the man who claimed that he "was called to the administration of affairs by the voice of the people," not the king. According to the Crown, both Pitt and Newcastle were too generous to Continental allies at the expense of England and too willing to continue what the king called a "bloody and expensive" war. Undaunted by this adoption of old opposition rhetoric, they defended Hannover as a link to Prussia and Prussia as a necessity for diverting France. A separate peace, according to Pitt, would be "no better than an armed truce" as long as France retained any New World holdings giving it the means of "recovering her prodigious losses and becoming once more formidable to us at sea." Granted, "this war has cut deep into our pecuniary [interests, but it] has augmented military faculties" that made Britain "the terror of the world."

However stirring Pitt's rhetoric once was, it did not impress George III, who dismissed him from the ministry in 1761, then Newcastle in 1762. The Crown, facing the specter of government bankruptcy, needed peace with France and Spain to buy time to service its interest payments—£4 million per annum in 1754, £19.5 million in 1761. Closely related to this fiscal problem was the constitution of the British Empire. The government also wanted time for what it called "that greatest and most necessary of all schemes, the settlement [of disputes with]

America." This led to a renewal of the paradoxical debate between England and its colonies over governmental and military self-sufficiency. Britain held that the colonists had no political autonomy but should protect themselves, no easy task for "Obstinate and Ungovernable People, Utterly Unacquainted with the Nature of Subordination." America, which held that London was liable for its military security, simultaneously said that any attempt to infringe on its self-government was "subversive of just rights and privileges."

This king of England, not caring to rule Hannover, wanted to become a real king of North America, not remain the symbolic figurehead of semi-independent states. Military inefficiency provided all the rationale he required. Without unity of effort, colonial money and manpower lay in thirteen diverse provinces, each with different strategies and interest groups. Even William Pitt could employ these resources only in an emergency—and then strictly on a cooperative basis. Therefore, in the 1760s Britain began to redesign and reform these "disunited little Governments." When the foreign threat was at its peak in the 1750s, Americans still tended to think that any reduction of provincial legislative prerogatives was a nefarious "Design for gaining power over the Colonies." They were not likely to change their opinion after French Canada ceased to exist.

Newcastle and Pitt had avoided this controversy, each man for reasons of his own. Newcastle, rather indifferent to imperial efficiency, used appointments to American government positions as patronage to purchase parliamentary support. Pitt, an empire builder, postponed centralized taxation and conscription because "peace, unanimity and good understanding between Your Majesty's Government and the People are absolutely necessary" when waging war in America itself. He had convinced the Crown to dole out his subsidies on grounds that North America was "the fountain of our wealth, the nerve of our strength, the nursery and basis of our naval power." His justification for making it the major theater made other Englishmen adamant to stop the "indulgence to [the] Colonies" and restore "the Constitution [of the Empire] to its true principles." After 1763 this became a mandate to enhance the fragile rule of the king-in-Parliament in the New World. For the last 100 years, one of England's great strengths vis-à-vis France was its uniform tax code, with no exemptions for social rank or regions, excluding the American colonies. Now, correcting that great shortcoming in the British fiscal system, the government declared that Massachusetts had no more right to autonomy than London or the Duke of Kent. Thus began the political controversy over taxation and power that led directly to the American Revolutionary War.

With the extirpation of French Canada, Britain no longer felt it needed to appease its American colonists. The colonists, after the fall of Montreal, felt more self-sufficient, less dependent on London, and less willing than ever to consent to policy "contrary to the fundamental principles of their natural and constitutional rights and liberties." This resistance to imperialism—"worse than Egyptian bondage"—was led by New England, which had recently led the American effort but was disappointed by the outcome of the French and Indian War. The capture of Quebec (the "seat of Satan and Indian idolatry") renewed its old utopian expectations about "shaking off the dust of Babylon," present since the Puritans fled to America from Church of England persecution in 1630.

In actuality, Massachusetts experienced renewed economic depression: per capita income falling to 25 percent of that for white males in the South. Financial dislocation is common after a prolonged military conflict. But in any event the colony blamed London, not the business cycle, for failing to fulfill Pitt's pledge of "proper Compensation for Expenses [as] the active Vigor and strenuous Efforts of the respective Provinces shall justly appear to merit." The problem was that merit lay in the eyes of the beholder. The month Pitt had assumed the post of secretary of state (December 1756), the Massachusetts legislature appealed for assistance: "This Province is so exhausted of its men and money that the necessary defense of its frontiers at this time of the war will be too heavy for them." By 1763, although it received 40 percent of the reimbursements made to all America, this colony was bitter that its special "services and sufferings" were not recognized. Parliament repaid 43 (not 100) percent of its military expenditures. Then, after "we exerted ourselves much beyond our natural strength" and had an internal debt of £387,000 sterling, London imposed a new monetary burden. From 1759 to 1764, Massachusetts's imports were seven times more costly than exports, meaning gold was flowing from the colony. Nonetheless, from 1765 to 1772, the Crown imposed taxes of £835,350,000, despite warnings from the governor when the tax on sugar first appeared in 1764: "The publication of the order for the strict execution of the Molasses Act has caused greater alarm in this country than the taking of Fort William Henry did in 1757."

If Massachusetts had been unique, rather than the most pronounced example of a common phenomenon, there may have been riots but not a serious military conflict throughout America. Virginia was also disappointed by the results of its "overzealous Loyalty in the course of the late war." London blocked new settlements in the Ohio Valley lest it have to fight more Indians. It reimbursed 25 percent of Virginia's military expenditures, a pittance (the colony felt) compared with that for New England. Henceforth Americans, both North and South, complained of having been "lavish [with] their blood and treasure only to bind the shackles of slavery on themselves and their children." In the process, they redirected the rhetoric of the French and Indian War toward Britain, then champing on ingratitude itself, namely from those it felt it saved from Gallic brutality. No matter, according to America, the tyrannical, anti-Christian threat to liberty and property no longer came from popery, Canada, Indians, and France.

Ironically, colonial resistance to England was encouraged by speeches from an old man who resumed his old position as the leading member of the parliamentary opposition. Pitt warned that a squabble over taxes threatened the existence of his greatest achievement, the gains made in the recent war. He specifically predicted that the North American empire hung in the balance once the colonists inevitably sought an alliance with the hated king of France, no

longer diverted to a European theater after George III severed his German connections. The conflicts within the Anglo-American coalition formed by Pitt had
already created the climate for the next American war.[5]

INTERNATIONAL SETTING, INTERNAL ISSUES,
FORCE STRUCTURE, AND STRATEGY

The American Revolution was a world war, a colonial rebellion, and a civil war.
Despite the common political objective of independence from Great Britain, it
had three different sets of military ways and means: coalition operations to offset English sea power, a national army to defeat the king's regiments, and com-
munity-based militia forces to suppress local Tories loyal to the Crown.

By late 1777 the coalition of America and France—with help from Spain
and Holland—waged land or global naval warfare from the North Sea to the West
Indies. Britain, spread too thin with too many places to protect, moved 10,000
men from America just as the Continental army was making substantial improve-
ments. England thus faced the same situation William Pitt had created for France:
diversions around the periphery that enabled its opponent to gain superiority in
the American theater. This was not accidental. France began anticipating fissures
in the British Empire as early as 1710. Immediately after defeat at Quebec in
1759, its lead minister insisted on abandoning all Canada in return for retaining
St. Lucia, Martinique, and Guadeloupe. By maintaining forward naval bases in
the West Indies, Paris could provide significant assistance to abolish British rule
in America, which "would not fail to shake off their dependence the moment
Canada would be ceded" from the French Empire.

To exploit this opportunity, France restrained its tendency for territorial
expansion in Europe, which had diverted its focus from Britain, its traditional
rival. Its first attempt to challenge English colonial supremacy in the 1750s, when
France built fifty-four capital ships, was undercut when France made its main military effort one of ground forces east of the Rhine. Without this diversion after the
Seven Years' War, it increased naval expenditures 600 percent. It was still too
weak to invade Britain: "the wildest folly" which would simply mobilize another
anti-Bourbon coalition in the name of protecting the balance of power. However,
by 1778 it had eighty ships of the line able to activate several military theaters and
revenge recent losses from India to Nova Scotia. Because America could then conduct its colonial rebellion and fight its civil war without British army saturation,
England lost to France for the first and last time in 125 years of armed conflict.

In the civil or internal phase of the Revolutionary War, militia fought loyalists, who constituted some 20 percent of the population. Their war would decide
who and what would govern American localities. In the war as a colonial rebellion, the Continental army fought the king's soldiers for national independence.
While its military objective was always British withdrawal, the strategy changed

with circumstances. Its commander, George Washington, was by nature a fighter, not a Fabian. He preferred decisive battle to the protraction that turned out to be particularly effective. National finance and public will were the weakest pillars of the British war effort, no matter what Washington planned as he took command. In 1775 the Continental Congress still wanted home rule within the British Empire. It merely told him to "harass" and "distress" the English army, depriving them of fresh provisions by driving milk cows away. Washington, an advocate of strategic surprise, was planning offensive expeditions to Bermuda, Florida, Nova Scotia, and Quebec when the British were still besieging Boston. "Enterprises which appear Chimerical," he maintained at this time, "often prove successful from that very Circumstance." Therefore, without congressional authorization, he ordered the invasion of Canada a year before the Declaration of Independence. He lost 5,000 men to battle, disease, and desertion.

By September 1776, one month after British regulars drove Washington out of Long Island, he decided that his army should "avoid a general Action unless compelled by a necessity, into which we ought never to be drawn." While buying time to build a competent army and gain French military assistance, he instituted a new (but temporary) plan to avoid contact with the British "on their own Terms," a set-piece battle on open terrain. Unless certain "of succeeding confine yourself, in the main, to a defensive operation," at the operational level of war. Win a few engagements, primarily for the sake of American morale. "Skirmish and harass the Enemy as much as possible, gain their flanks and rear." Do the best you can "without hazarding the bad Consequences of a defeat and rout."

The best tactician of this plan of operation was Nathanael Greene, the American commander in the southern theater from 1780 to 1783. "The more he is defeated," wrote one frustrated British officer, "the further he advances in the end. He has been indefatigable in collecting troops, and leading them to be defeated." Greene himself described the strategy of protraction that he executed better than anyone else: "Few generals [have] run oftener or more lustily than I have done. But I have taken care not to run too far." Both he and Washington believed that the best means to wage their war of national independence was a conventional force because it excluded "the great unwieldy mass of people without order or connection" from direct military action. Other leaders in other colonial rebellions—as well as other rebels in this particular conflict—would have relied on raiders, irregulars, and guerrillas to conduct hit-and-run warfare. Greene and Washington wanted uniformed soldiers in standing regiments serving for the duration of the conflict in any or all the American states. Because Greene, who felt one regular was worth four militiamen, never got the "permanent Army" he wanted, dire necessity forced him to conduct a "kind of partisan war" that seemed a diversion from "more important concerns." Misfortune made him a genius: "I have been obliged to practice by finesse that which I dared not attempt by force."

Whether or not a conventional force structure was the best means to beat the British, it was not well suited to wage a civil war for local political control.

Rebels conducted operations to prove their contention that the king-in-Parliament and the royal governors-in-council could not govern the countryside. Their strategy was mobilization of the population, begun by loyalty oaths to the rebellion. The means were the local militia units that abetted the insurrection while obstructing anything helpful to the Crown. By late 1777 an English general concluded: "We have not only armies to combat, but a whole country."

Planned or not, America deftly combined the militia and the Continental army to use different strategies in different types of conflict for the common goal of independence. They even seemed to complement each other in the wars against British regulars and Tory loyalists. Because "the damned scouting Parties" forced "market men [to] sneak through at the risk of their lives," Royal regiments controlled only territory that they occupied. Isolated, the British had to draw supplies 3,000 miles across the Atlantic, an unprecedented logistics effort not again attempted until World War II. This meant their army could not move much beyond navigable water. It also meant that the Admiralty could not solve its chronic shortage of able-bodied seamen by moving them from cargo vessels committed to deliver 120,000 tons per annum. By 1778, twelve men-of-war remained at Spithead for lack of 1,400 sailors. This gave a nautical advantage to Franco-American joint operations at Yorktown, the battle that won the war. Shortly before it took place, Washington admitted that "no land force can act decisively unless accompanied by a maritime superiority." On that "fundamental principle . . . hope of success must ultimately depend."

For its part, the Continental army made a major contribution to the militia's war against the loyalists. According to the Crown's plan for pacification, British regulars were to hunt down guerrillas, build loyalist militias, and establish local governments. Greene's raids with conventionally organized soldiers provoked English battalions to remain in large formations and chase him in fruitless sweeps that left loyalists exposed to guerrilla terror. In retrospect and theory, the militia and the Continental army worked hand in glove. In fact, they were terribly at odds. They did not fight over funds, flag officers, and equipment, per the twentieth-century rivalry between active forces and reserves. The conflict between the militia and the Continental army concerned fundamental issues of political philosophy and military strategy.[6]

AN IRREGULAR OR A CONVENTIONAL WAR?

When George Washington took command of the Continental army, it was little more than the Massachusetts militia renamed to rally support from the South when New Englanders were facing execution for their capital crime: shooting over 1,000 British soldiers at Lexington, Concord, and Bunker Hill. Washington's appointment was part and parcel of this sectional transaction. He was not the best-qualified military candidate, at least in 1775. Horatio Gates and Charles

Lee, British officers who retired in America after serving in the French and Indian War, had more command experience and far better records, but neither was a member of the Virginia elite. Where Washington led, the South would follow—or so John Adams reasoned at the time.

Washington would prove the right leader, even if selected for the wrong reason: politics, not experience. He was exceedingly versatile, able to switch between protraction, partisan raids, and set-piece battles. He was also a military diplomat able to join the French without the residual hostility always near the surface among Massachusetts men with bitter memories of the colonial war. However, Washington had one particular shortcoming Gates and Lee did not share. These former lieutenant colonels of the king's Forty-fourth and Forty-fifth Royal Regiments welcomed militiamen, whom they considered natural soldiers trained in firearms and construction tools from their infancy near the frontier. Lee maintained "that all the essentials necessary to form infantry for real [combat] service may be acquired in a few months." Gates said he never saw "better soldiers than New England men." Washington, a former militia colonel, was far less accommodating to what he called "raw and undisciplined" Americans "totally unacquainted with every kind of Military skill." He insisted on enlistments for three years or the duration of the conflict in order "to bring Men to a proper degree of Subordination . . . alone equal to the exigencies of modern war." Militia was "useful as light parties to skirmish the Woods," but not for "making or sustaining a serious attack."

During the French and Indian War, Washington's ambition was a royal commission and a subsequent career in the British army. When his sponsor, Edward Braddock, ran into a hostile tomahawk in the Ohio River Valley, Washington lost the recommendation needed to "distinguish [him] from the common run of provincial officers." He had to retire to Mount Vernon, where he ordered for his parlor busts of his heroes, none noted for militia-like qualities: Marlborough, Caesar, and Frederick the Great. Unable to join a regular army, Washington would try to re-create one in the Revolutionary War. Various European officers fighting with or against America had contrary opinions. Lafayette and Steuben favored a light force-raiding party strategy, not just as a "dire necessity" during a transition to conventional war: Washington's position on the issue. More radical, Lee and Gates talked about conducting a "people's war," as did the opposition in England's Parliament who predicted "every thicket will be an ambuscade of partisans." Finally came Hessian officers, British rangers, and the English commanding general, Henry Clinton, who respectively described the militia as "warlike, inveterate and numerous," skillful scouts, and "excellent marksmen," especially in "small ambush" operations. Everyone seemed to have the highest praise for a force structure he did not know firsthand. Washington thought the world of regulars; Europeans praised irregular formations.

As frequently happens, the debate about military effectivenes was also about domestic politics. Continental army officers and militiamen came from different social backgrounds. The latter were common citizens; the former were elites. In the realm of religion, militiamen were likely to be from evangelical denominations hostile to the Church of England. In economics, they believed in a communitarian policy wherein prices were regulated and "subordinate[d] to the public good," instead of "Making Self the Predominant" concern. As for political philosophy, they were unadorned democrats (or populists) who held that government should be directly and immediately accountable to the numerical majority: not to the hereditary rulers of Great Britain nor to a natural aristocracy professing to be "the authoritative guardians of virtue" in America. In short, they embodied the most revolutionary aspects of the American Revolution: the ideas that "all men are created equal" and that the people are the sovereign rulers of the country. Under these principles, there were to be no ranks and distinctions between citizens. Leisured gentlemen with formal education had no special claim to political or military leadership. No one being much better than anyone else (every man a "mister"), the majority of ordinary people knew best.

The militias always had the potential to be the most democratic institutions in America. Whereas civil government was usually restricted to property owners, in the militia, where all men were supposed to serve, soldiers could elect their junior officers. However, once the Indians vacated the Atlantic coastline, the institution became an elitist organization under a high command that craved the prestige accruing to colonels and felt it had a special social function: a "well regulated militia composed of their leadership, freeholders and other freemen" (note the gradations of citizenship) was to "promote good Order and a just Sense of the Subordination." In 1775, many of these senior officers, still loyal to the royal governors who bestowed the highest ranks, left the body or were politically purged. Other prosperous citizens avoided service by paying a moderate fine. This left a social vacuum filled by a new class of officers publicly beholden to their subordinates and frequently lacking landed property at all. John Adams, "always for a free republic, not a democracy," called them "awkward, illiterate, illbred" men. Other gentlemen said that they were the "damn'd riff raff—dirty, mutinous, and disaffected." As one old colonel complained about the new militia in 1776: "The people have been induced to believe they ought not to submit to any appointments, but those made by themselves."

For many "Men of Low Rank" the militia remained a political institution, even in the midst of a war. It provided a base for aspiring politicians, often radical democrats. In June 1776 the (Philadelphia) Committee of Privates wrote the following about the upcoming Pennsylvania constitutional convention: "Let no Men represent you disposed to form any Rank above that of Freeman. . . . select men uneducated, with unsophisticated understanding." The leaders of the Continental Congress and the officers of its army hardly agreed. They were rationalists, cosmopolitans, and moderate Whigs who favored a natural aristocracy wherein individuals held responsibility by social rank "superior to local prejudices." They favored academic training for a learned ministry and episcopal or unitarian theology. They believed in world markets for economics: "let trade be as free as the air." As for government or military office, they preached deference to "respectable Citizens of Fortune and Character," the wise and worthy "gentlemen of independent means." "A simple democracy," said the surgeon general of the Continental army, "is one of the greatest of evils." To yield authority to the rank and file, Washington said in 1775, "was to surrender command of the army to those whose duty it is . . . to obey."

The militia forces distrusted the Continental army on a political principle rather alien to Washington and Greene, both of whom believed "the Evils of a standing Army are remote" on the American scene. Militiamen embodied the radical Whig tradition of Anglo-American thought wherein standing armies were composed of idle rich officers and idle poor soldiers—aristocrats and paupers. At the very least, a professional military force provided economic sinecures for parasites living off taxpayers: witness America after the French and Indian War. Rebels had believed that Britain imposed its "oppressive" stamp and tea taxes as part of a conspiracy to "enslave" Americans to support England's bloated army. Only Tories believed the taxes repaid the debt the Crown acquired defending its subjects from French Canada.

Nonetheless, padded military payrolls were a relatively minor issue to people with long memories of English atrocities. Editorials and sermons from denominations associated with Scotch and Irish dissenters said a standing army was "the means, in the hands of a wicked and oppressive sovereign, [for] establishing the most intolerable despotism." Because oppression was tempting to all officeholders, full-time soldiers ("the instruments of tyranny") were a dangerous expedient for a republican state. America would be safer if it "preserved its peace, as well as its freedom," by relying on local militiamen mobilized for emergencies near their homes. Granted, they could not provide expeditionary armies serving long tours or far away. No problem. That was a tool of imperialism—the policy of monarchs, not the common man. By contrast, the militia claimed that "every Man that wishes to secure his own Freedom and thinks it his Duty to defend that of his Country should, as he prides himself in being a Free Citizen, think it his truest Honour to be a Soldier Citizen."

Ideology aside, militiamen believed they could perform the necessary military tasks, even against British regulars in the colonial rebellion component of the Revolutionary War. They cited their victories at Lexington-Concord, Saratoga, and King's Mountain, where they mobilized their numerical advantage in the countryside, most Tories coming from commercial centers. Militia chose the time and place of attack to ambush advanced or rearguard units, second nature to rural people hunting British soldiers like they shot wild game. The human targets thought fire "from an unseen Enemy" was murder. Washington, while no friend of the militia, was eager to exploit this fear. He encouraged common soldiers to clothe themselves in hunting shirts "justly supposed to carry no small terror." The British reaction was not surprising. Few Englishmen were gentlemen when it came to operations against the Irish, Highland Scots, and other "savages," such as the militia. "Very few parts of America," they complained to London, "know, as yet, what the horrors of War are. If their houses, farms, and other property was destroyed, their resentment would turn upon Congress."

When the British won the engagements, such as Germantown and Camden, the citizen-soldiers claimed that they were not to blame. Continental army officers, trained in linear tactics, deployed them in open fields, where the militia received a bayonet charge preceded by musket volley fire. Charles Lee, the foremost proponent of the militia and "desultory war," condemned all such confrontations, where the British army was invincible: "Decisive Action on fair Ground is talking Nonsense."

George Washington could deny slow-moving, overloaded British regulars accessible targets by moving outside their killing range. But no force could be more elusive than bands of common citizens on their home terrain against English officers used to performing what Lee called "the tricks of the parade" for the "amusement of royal Masters and Misses in Hyde Park." He might have had Braddock in mind, since Lee and Horatio Gates were part of the task force ambushed by an enemy they could not see. Washington, himself in the expedition "to attain knowledge in the Military Art" from Braddock, a "Gentlemen of great good Character," was shamed at defeat "by a trifling body of men." He never forgot Braddock's rigid refusal to let the Virginia detachment "engage the enemy in their own way." Nonetheless, he drew few lasting lessons about what others called "Wood Country War." One tribal auxiliary of the expedition had said that Washington "was a good natured man, but with no experience, and would by no means take advice from the Indians." His opinion about these "Savages" lay far from that of Lee, who had taken a squaw and joined an Iroquois tribe, "hospitable, friendly and civil to an immense degree."

The same irregular tactics that defeated Braddock in a forest were effective at Bunker Hill, where Americans inflicted three times as many casualties as they sustained. One British officer wrote that "the defense which the rebels made is exactly like that of the Indians"; they occupied "heights which command the passes, proper trees to fire from and very rough and marshy ground." This placed England in a strategic dilemma. If it were to avoid another financial crisis, it had to win before French intervention could make the colonial rebellion a global war. On the one hand, as one English general explained, "a few more such victories [like Bunker Hill] would have shortly put an end to British dominion in America," enforced by fewer than 50,000 soldiers from Hudson Bay to Grenada.

Washington was less impressed than were many Britons. He was "fully convinced that our Liberties must of necessity be greatly hazarded, if not entirely lost, if their defense is left to any but a permanent standing Army." His arguments were mainly tactical, although that may not have been his foremost concern. The military strongpoints of the militia—concealment and evasion—could easily become a political liability to a new nation desperately seeking foreign aid and domestic legitimacy. Militiamen might be as invisible to Frenchmen and to fence-sitting segments of America as they were to British military intelligence. If so, they might exhaust the enemy but "discredit our cause" and lose the war for lack of public and diplomatic presence, as Washington would tell the Continental Congress. The French criticized the Continental army for a "spirit of liberty, independence, and equality" incompatible with conventional military operations, the only strategy they could comprehend. If Washington's own soldiers were too unconventional for the comfort of their allies, one wonders how Frenchmen could ever coordinate with militiamen whom they described as "a lot of curious people" and "armed peasants who have sometimes fought." Those whom Washington called "the first Troops in Europe" would view partisan warfare, à la Charles Lee, as criminal behavior from a desperate insurgency, not a functioning government or an army worthy of combined operations.

The Continental army had a political function the militia could not fulfill. It was the functional substitute for a capital city, a rallying point in time of war. As Nathanael Greene told a fellow officer in 1781: "While there is an army left in the field the hopes of the people are kept alive but disperse that [army] and their spirits will sink at once." For Washington and Greene, the militia had some legitimate functions: to acquire information, procure supplies, and augment, in emergencies, the Continental Line, as they did at Saratoga, the victory that enticed France to join the war. However, special circumstances surrounded this battle in the Hudson River Valley. Indian scouts and some notorious Canadian mercenaries (well-known demons to the people of New England) headed the invasion down the familiar Montreal-Albany corridor, where the English now played the old role of the despicable French enemy. After General John Burgoyne warned rebels to expect "devastation, famine, and every concomitant horror," settlers on their own accord mobilized in droves, to the dismay of a British sergeant. ("Numerous parties of American militia swarmed around like birds of prey.") The commander of British forces in Canada was of the opinion that "it is not the number of [Continental] troops that is to be apprehended, it is the multitude of militia and men in arms ready to turn out at an hour's notice." Washington and Greene might have replied: Oh, if Saratoga were only the rule, not an exception to it.

The high command chronically complained that the militia forgot exactly who was supposed to support whom, whose mission had priority, and whose plans were foiled when so-called auxiliaries took resources from its command. Washington objected that local security and "small excursions" against "a secondary objective" diverted "our attention from more material objects," namely, major enemy bases or formations. The militia and irregular raiding parties did know their place: "They come in, you cannot tell how; go, you cannot tell when; and act, you cannot tell where; consume your provisions, exhaust your stores and leave you at a critical moment." In short, "they are an exceeding[ly] dirty and nasty people [unfit] for the business of real fighting."

The Continental Congress called partisan strategy "the most ruinous,

THE COLONIAL AND REVOLUTIONARY WARS   61

destructive, [and] expensive way of supporting a war." Neither it, Washington, nor Greene could understand militiamen, whose fundamental loyalty was not to "the cause of our Country" or even to the states where they were born. To cosmopolitans in "labor to discourage all kinds of local attachments," the militia appeared unable to abide "the Restraint indispensably necessary to the good order and Government of an Army." Actually, they were simply faithful to the local communities to which they returned, no matter how disruptive their so-called desertion was to the national effort. In America, especially New England, generations of the same families lived and died in the same place. Over one-quarter of the Lexington militiamen who shot the first rounds of the war were related to the captain of their company. This provincialism was incompatible with the Continental army, as conceived by Greene: "All the force in America should be under one Commander raised and appointed by the same Authority, subjected to the same Regulations and ready to be detacht where ever Occasion may require." The biggest obstacle to effectiveness was "the folly of short enlistments," the quintessence of the militia. With a long-term force Washington believed that he could fight and win a decisive battle, rather than prolonging the conflict until one side or the other fell from exhaustion.[7]

THE HIGH COMMAND OF THE CONTINENTAL ARMY

Because George Washington maintained that "discipline is the soul of the army," he employed drillmasters such as Friedrich von Steuben, "an officer educated in the Prussian school." This former aide-de-camp of Frederick the Great turned men accustomed to lax militia laws into dependable soldiers of the Continental Line. About the time Steuben became inspector general (1778), Charles Lee "lamented that America has servilely copied the Defects" of Europe. He did not speak for Congress, which raised the military limit on lashes 300 percent in response to complaints like those from the adjutant general that "the principles of democracy universally prevail."

When Washington took control of the Continental army, it seemed "a mixed multitude under very little discipline, order, or Government." To him, "there was an unaccountable kind of stupidity in the lower class of these people," as well as "among the officers of the Massachusetts part of the army who are nearly of the same kidney with the privates." Believing in continuity between social and military rank—that men with "Fortune and reputable Families generally make the most useful Officers"—he was appalled to see one captain (no doubt a barber) shaving an enlisted man. Thereafter Washington tried, with limited success, to make his army a mirror image of the British, where officers were gentlemen by birth and breeding, not just by act of Congress.

In 1776 at least one British aristocrat said that the colonies could never win because they lacked "a proper division of different ranks of men." Washington never could recruit enough first-rank gentry to fill the officer corps, especially at the top. He did the next best thing by finding young men reminiscent of himself in the 1750s, when this ambitious young man, born into modest circumstances, used his heroic action at the Braddock expedition to become a celebrated militia colonel and join the first families of Virginia. He recruited a new generation of young men (some good, some bad) wanting to join the service and win social rank.

Benedict Arnold, a great battlefield brigade commander, had been a druggist, heavily indebted to English merchants, when this former private in the French and Indian War helped found a militia company for "gentlemen of influence and high respectability." (In his case, ambition completely overwhelmed ideology; he turned traitor after failure to make major general.) Nathanael Greene, a more reliable appointment, was an ironmonger deemed unworthy of a commission by "the Gentlemen" of East Greenwich, Rhode Island, who thought him "a blemish" to their militia company. War was his "Opportunity [for] traveling the shortest Road to the greatest heights of Ambition"—indeed, a way to enter "the golden pages of History." To Colonel Alexander Hamilton, Washington's aide-de-camp, it was an alternative to a "groveling" career as a clerk in a merchant countinghouse. In 1769 this "bastard son of a Scotch peddler" (to quote John Adams) wrote a friend that "I wish there was a War."

Washington and his ambitious coterie built the officer corps of the Continental army in their own image, or the image they wished themselves to be. "They ought to have such allowances," he petitioned Congress, "as will enable them to live like and support the Character of Gentlemen." By 1777 officers wore insignia, received far greater pay, and collected pensions four times greater than those of the privates whom they led. The democratic wing in Congress and militiamen protested that large land grants given to general officers would subvert the Republic by creating a new Tory class. They could do little about social barriers in the Continental army, observed as soon as Washington assumed command. "Everyone," said one visitor in 1775, "is made to know his place and keep it, or be tied up and receive thirty or forty lashes, according to his crime." French aristocrats were shocked that senior Americans would not let subordinates inside their tents. Europeans, more secure about their status and prestige, were less concerned about small proprieties.

In 1776 Washington wrote Congress that "till the bulk of your Officers are composed of such people as are actuated by Principles of honour"—the classic motivation of aristocrats in war—"you will have little to expect of them." To his distress he discovered that, in the minds of his subordinates, honor meant personal promotion, often detrimental to the cause of independence. "Not an hour passes," he noted, "without complaints about rank. . . . we can scarcely parade a detachment without a warm discussion on the subject of Precedence." Resignations to protest "our honor as Soldiers" (from the high command to first lieutenants) would chronically afflict his efforts to build a seasoned army for the duration of the war. One-fourth of his general officers vacated the Continental army. In the midst of the siege of Yorktown, Washington would have to create a military board to settle disputes among captains about who outranked whom in the Massachusetts Line.[8]

DECISIVE BATTLE OR PROTRACTION?

General Washington and the advocates of a militia-intensive defense not only differed about what type of force was needed but also disputed the correct way to employ it. Ambush and protraction was the single strategy of the militia. For Washington, it was only one of several methods Once France sent over a division and thirty-six men-of-war, he reverted to taking the strategic offensive, partly for fear that America was losing its political will. "We are at the end of our tether," he wrote in 1780, after his army had shrunk from 26,000 to fewer than 15,000 men. "Now or never our deliverance must come."

Protraction had become a double-edged sword, dangerous to both sides. Henry Clinton, the senior British army commander in North America, thought it had become the strong suit of the Crown: "I have all to hope, and Washington all to fear. . . . Time alone would soon bring about every success we could wish." To Washington's consternation, too many Americans seemed to have much the same plan insofar as they hoped to win the war in London, primarily through dissension and financial collapse. The war had doubled England's national debt (now almost £243 million) and increased its level of governmental spending: 22 percent of economic output. This situation appalled opposition politicians in Parliament, where seats were held by large landholders. With land-tax revenues increasing almost tenfold from 1775 to 1780, they complained that the result of the conflict was that Englishmen "ourselves were to be taxed and stamped." Those more concerned with national defense worried over England's credit rating, a critical advantage in recent wars against France, Spain, and other financial risks. Nonetheless, in 1781 George III and his inner circle were relatively indifferent to these fiscal concerns. The Crown complained that calculations about "the load of debt we labour under" were "only weighing events in the scale of a tradesman behind his counter" (shades of William Pitt). If utilitarian interests determined policy, the English would end up like the Dutch: "rich perhaps as individuals, but weak as a state."

If disinterest to budgets had been policy in 1775, the Crown might have heeded its commanding general a week after Bunker Hill: "You must proceed in earnest or give the business up. . . . In all their wars against the French, [these Americans] never showed so much conduct, attention and perseverance as they do now." However, at the time, the king and his ministers, led by the lord of the Treasury, believed that once "these rebels have felt a smart blow they will submit." As the preeminent power after the Seven Years' War, Britain could "finish the rebellion in one campaign," no need for mobilization irrespective of cost— what Pitt had done, to Newcastle's despair, in the late 1750s.

Once the Crown finally realized the depth of the conflict in 1777, France had made it a world war fought in India, Gilbraltar, and Guadeloupe, as well as Carolina. Lord Jeffrey Amherst, military commander in the French and Indian War, told the ministry it would need 40,000 more soldiers if it were to conduct "an Offensive Land War with any effect" in North America. Britain, in turn, dispatched 5,000 men from Philadelphia to protect the Caribbean. It now had little choice but protraction: hold seaport strongpoints from Charleston to New York City, establish loyal governments in areas outside New England, and hope to conquer the French West Indies. If successful, this would isolate and bankrupt the rebels, forcing substantial territorial concessions between the Hudson River and South Carolina. Failure would entail what could be called the domino theory of the Crown: a "train of consequences" throughout the empire until "poor" little England stood alone. "A small state," said King George in 1780, "may certainly subsist but a great one cannot get into an inferior situation [without] be[ing] annihilated."

Confronting an opponent as stubborn as George III, Washington had to conduct "a glorious offensive campaign" and score "a decisive stroke," if only to arouse the parliamentary critics of the king. After Saratoga and French intervention, when his own prime minister lamented that the "enormous expense" of the war could not "be repaid by the most brilliant victories," George III was ready to let the hated Pitt return to government to ensure support from the House of Commons. His old adversary would not join in a minor capacity. Once the military situation stabilized in 1778, he was no longer needed. According to the ministry, winning every vote of confidence with decisive majorities: "The opposition is at present if not dead at least asleep." Indeed, the impact of a vocal but ineffective minority "deluding" Americans "that a little further resistance must make the Mother Country yield" was to stiffen the perseverance of the king: "I am resolved to shew the world that neither Zeal, Activity nor Resolutions are wanting in me."

Within America, disputes were more divisive and debilitating. Years of hardship were breaking down the collective morale of the public, the Continental Congress, and the Continental army. Newspapers complained that the country was fighting as if it desired "to protract this destructive war. We should change our means—bring out thousands, . . . storm the [enemy] in their strongholds, and never pause until we force them from our shores." Congress, in lieu of sending Washington the men and money he needed, sent him military advice: "We have had a noble army melted down by ill judged marches." Its senior commanders were "timid, speculative [men], without enterprise." They engendered "languor in all the branches of the army" and desired "a long and moderate War."

Washington, who had always wanted to be a great warrior, was now convinced that "in modern wars, the longest purse must chiefly determine events." He told Congress he could do better if his troops could "live upon Air, or like the Bear, suck their paws for sustenance." More ominously, he saw in every large formation "the most serious features of mutiny and sedition." Near desperation, he called for "one great vigorous effort at all hazards," while he still had an army at all. Then, in 1781, Charles Cornwallis, the British commander in the southern theater, fell onto the Yorktown (Virginia) Peninsula, "quite tired of marching about the Country in Quest of Adventure" and Nathanael Greene, whom he had chased all the way from Georgia, burning and looting the countryside when he could not catch up with Greene.

This fortuitous event probably saved America from a terrible mistake that could have lost the war. Washington, who had precipitated the Seven Years' War by marching a meager force straight toward Fort Duquesne in 1754, had been planning to attack the bulk of the British army exactly where his opponent expected: their fortified bastion and major depot, New York City, the scene of his most humiliating defeats, when the British drove him from Brooklyn Heights and Manhattan in 1776. If Washington's prospective attack were successfully conducted, it would certainly be the decisive victory (and sweet revenge) he sought. If not, it would have been terribly costly to both the Continental army and the French navy, Washington's hope to win the war for the last three years.

When France signed a treaty of alliance in 1778, all of America's military elements hoped to enhance their special capabilities. Militia units in Maine obtained Catholic priests from the French fleet to arouse Indians to attack the British, exactly what Massachusetts protested during the French and Indian War. Washington, for his part, may have been inspired by a different old colonial fear, that of France catching Anglo-America between military jaws by marching south from Canada and sailing north from the West Indies. When he heard of the pending alliance in April, he grabbed the first opportunity to switch from protraction to decisive battle, specifically hoping to close a Franco-American pincer on New York City. All his subordinates called to a council of war said that the Continental army could not survive the pending attack on British fortifications: it would expend their supplies, plunge public morale, discredit their performance in the face of the militia, and discourage any French expedition. Washington, as if oblivious, foreclosed the plan only when the French naval commander refused to run the risk of grounding his ships in New York harbor's shallow waters. Washington needed the fleet to prevent the British army from escaping his attack, an extraordinary presumption considering the condition of the army under his command.

By 1781, grim conditions had gotten much worse because of inflation and financial collapse. Unable to delay while on the verge of losing his army to wholesale desertion, Washington was more determined than ever to storm New York. He was not dissuaded by his calculation that he would need to augment the Continental army with at least 17,000 militiamen, a force he maintained could not stand up to the British in conventional battle. Nor was he cowed by what he witnessed in 1780: 2,000 Continentals beaten back from a blockhouse held by 160 Tories on the outskirts of Manhattan. Washington was saved from his aspiration to wage a decisive battle he was actually likely to lose, by forces (fortunately) beyond his control. The local militia would not mobilize. The French navy refused to navigate the narrows between British guns on Brooklyn Heights and Staten Island. Washington cursed, "I wish to the Lord the French would not raise our expectations of a co-operation or fulfill them." However, Admiral de Grasse was still willing to run a decided risk. Without approval from Paris, he brought his entire West Indies fleet to the coast of Virginia to separate Cornwallis and his 7,000 soldiers from rescue by the British navy. In the process, he stripped commercial convoys and the whole French Caribbean of naval defense.

When Washington heard what Grasse planned, he was "overcome with great joy," marched 5,800 men from New York to Virginia, and pounced on Cornwallis just as fast as he could. Encircled, the enemy was forced to capitulate to the French navy carrying 100 pieces of siege artillery, the Continental army, 7,000 French soldiers, and 3,000 American militiamen turning out like they did at Saratoga, to revenge British atrocities. (Washington's plea to mobilize was of no consequence.) By massing on a significant fragment of the British army caught in an exposed position, Washington won a climactic battle that came none too soon. The commanding general of the French army said that "these [American] people are at the end of their resources." Much the same could be said about France, whose finance minister was informally discussing terms with his English counterpart behind America's back. After the Seven Years' War, 60 percent of his government's revenue was already committed to servicing its debt. Now, after building a major navy and subsidizing the Continental army, Britain's historic enemy was more financially depleted than Britain.[9]

THE AMERICAN REVOLUTION AS A CIVIL WAR

At Yorktown, Washington was able to switch from protraction to decisive battle. But aside from military versatility, other issues separated him from militia leaders. The latter targeted Tories and espoused utopian goals, such as "tyranny and oppression utterly extirpated from the face of the earth." Their idealism sanctioned transgressions of the established rules of "civilized" warfare, far different from what one Whig called a "civil war with mildness and a revolution with order." Washington, always conducting a conventional conflict for national independence, abided by eighteenth-century proprieties and the code of the Anglo-American elite. He never changed his methods much, even after some English officers, in frustration, gave "free liberty to [their] soldiers to ravage at will." When Americans captured a British ship flying a truce, Washington ordered its release lest the incident "Imput an Infringement on the sacred dignity of a Flag." When paroled officers sneaked back to fight, he ordered them home because "we have pledged ourselves to the enemy."

Vengeance and the redistribution of local power and property were issues that concerned local militias; they had no place in Washington's concept of a just or proper war. For specific political, economic, and military reasons, other leading figures in the nation were also rather tolerant of the Tories in their midst. Colonel Alexander Hamilton wanted them to keep investing in the economy of the former colonies; other Americans feared bad feelings might cost the country "our most lucrative trade" with the British West Indies. Aside from commerce there was a fear of institutionalizing mob rule. Greene wanted to end "a state of civil war" and win loyalists to the Whig side by "reason and moderation." He threatened to hang the "rabble" that plundered and killed Tories they considered their sworn enemies.

Washington had initially hoped that the militia would be a police force (not a strike force) in their local communities: protecting residents from attack, even those still loyal to the king. However, he was never confident that "even Veteran troops, under the most rigid and exact discipline," would not begin to plunder, alienate the public, and destroy their own military perseverance. If such a fate could befall Washington's command, he was forever fearful about the militia beyond his effective control. For the duration of the war, he denounced "scouting parties" that ransacked citizens under the "specious pretense" that their victims were Tories whose property and products were about to be "taken within the Enemy's Lines." Even if they were, they still deserved "every indulgence [which] good judgment will permit."

No wonder the militia worked reluctantly with central authority, in particular Washington's headquarters. Largely for this reason, he curtailed their auxiliary responsibilities: intelligence acquisition, logistics procurement, and raids on enemy detachments. As a reliable replacement, he did what the Duke of Cumberland, captain general of the British army, proposed in the French and Indian War when he warned that "till Regular Officers with men that they can trust, learn to beat the woods & to act as Irregulars, you will never gain any certain Intelligence." Washington, like French and English aristocrats who felt that real irregulars are "not at all to be depended upon," organized the best militiamen into light infantry regiments "under proper regulations." Under his command and control, they would capture the key English redoubt at Yorktown with a bayonet charge in the middle of the night. No one would have given this mission to mere citizen-soldiers. However, the militia, whom Washington called an "independent Corps," did not exist simply to support conventional operations. It specialized in fighting the civil war within the American Revolution.

If 20,000 British soldiers and 30,000 "Hessians" were to pacify America, they would have to mobilize economic, political, and military support from some 400,000 colonists still loyal to the Crown. About one-tenth of these Tories fought for King George; London needed a lot more. In 1779 the secretary of state for the colonies wrote General Clinton in New York: "Our utmost efforts will fail of their effects if we cannot find the means to engage the people of America in support of a cause which is equally their own and ours. . . . Induce them to employ their own force to protect themselves in the enjoyment of the blessing of the [British] constitution to which they shall have been restored."

When nonetheless left without support and protection from the British army, loyalists were no match for rebel militiamen "Impudent of Restraint." Tories were loyal to the Crown for two essential reasons, depending on the region where they lived. South of the Potomac, loyalists were likely to be economic, religious, or racial minorities (including blacks and Indians) who needed London for protection against majorities. To the north, they were conservatives believing that republican government is "destitute of stability, borders upon confusion and anarchy, and is distinguished by perpetual struggles between different leaders fired with ambition or glowing with revenge." They often thought their duty was "to be quiet and sit still." They simply could not thrive in conditions of upheaval, which rebels celebrated as "a State of Nature." Nor could they match their opponents in morale, if only because they were committed to the status quo, with all the imperfections of existing institutions. Few, if any, European observers would say of the Tories what they said of the rebels: "What soldiers in the world could do what was done by these men, who go about nearly naked and in the greatest privation."

The rebels, being rebels, were simply more aggressive than were loyalists, one of the few things about which Cornwallis and Thomas Jefferson would agree. The ruthless English general complained that "our friends will not stir" to protect themselves. ("I must say that when I see a whole settlement running away from twenty or thirty [rebel] robbers, I think they deserve to be robbed.") Jefferson concurred insofar as saying that the civil war pitted different types of political personalities: a "timid man[who] fears the people is a Tory by nature. The strong and bold [who] cherishes them, is formed a Whig." If true of Whigs, then it was particularly true of democrats who made up much of the militia. They were perfectly willing to inflict violence on their own initiative without authorization from a standing army or central government because local approval provided all the legitimacy they needed.

Loyalists maintained that "perfection in anything human is not to be expected," even if they won the war. Rebel militia believed they were fighting against "an infernal gang" for "the benefit of the whole world." Their millennial rhetoric was a bit excessive for most Whig-deist elites who generally separated secular from religious concerns. Like others who subsequently struggled to ensure America's national security, Washington referred to "the republican model of government" as a political "experiment intrusted to the hands of the American people." The closest he and Greene came to setting a utopian goal was their attempt to confirm the viability of republican political institutions, at least when guided by those from a superior social class. Washington told the president of the Continental Congress that the few officers "who act upon Principles of disinterestedness are, comparatively speaking, no more than a drop in the Ocean." Greene, although a former blacksmith, talked like the lord of the manor surveying the great unwashed: "The great body of the People . . . are exceedingly avaricious. . . . The sentiment of Honour, the true characteristic of a soldier has not gotten the better of [selfish] interest."

When the war began, many prominent men not only believed personal virtue was crucial if corruption were not to destroy republican political institutions. They felt the war might help avoid the danger by instilling self-denial. John Adams, the day before independence was declared, looked forward to a "furnace of affliction" that would produce "many virtues, which we have not, and correct many errors, follies, and vices. . . . The people will have unbounded power [but] are extremely addicted to venality." In 1777 he received a letter from a surgeon general of the Continental army: "a peace," said Dr. Benjamin Rush, "would be the greatest curse that could befall us. . . . Liberty without virtue would be no blessing." By 1779 the elite had lost substantial hope, after abject scrounging for supplies to carry on the conflict. Patrick Henry asked Jefferson: "Do you remember any instance, where Tyranny was destroyed and Freedom established . . . among a people possessing so small a share of virtue and public spirit?"

In part, these disappointed men had reduced problems of primitive infrastructure to immoral greed. The Continental army primarily starved due to insufficient roads, draft animals, and wagons to get goods to military depots—not just because there was "a herd of monopolizing, extortionate and peculating traders" hoarding essential supplies. No matter, many Founding Fathers had given up the dream of a republic of virtue halfway through the Revolutionary War. By 1787 Hamilton and James Madison, both lately active at Washington's military headquarters, wrote a federal constitution based on a different political model: one where private avarice and self-interest checked and balanced one another.

Militiamen would be anti-Federalist opponents of the Constitution created by the cosmopolitan, Whig, Episcopal-Congregational-Unitarian leadership of the Continental Congress and its army. Committed to local government, members of the local defense force wished to abolish the office of the governor of Massachusetts, to say nothing of central government in London or Philadelphia. They were even more serious about theology, as recognized by Britons who said that "at the Bottom [this is] very much a religious War." Some observed that these rebels were not against government provided it was based on "fatal Republican Notions and Principles." That did not mean militia fought for a secular ideology. Protestant dissenters preached, as imperial officials complained, that able-bodied men who did not stain their weapons "with the Blood of the King's Soldiers and their Abettors, would be renounced by the Lord Jesus Xt [Christ] at the Day of Judgement." When they did their duty and won the war, according to the *New-Hampshire Gazette,* "Liberty will triumph, wealth flow in through ten thousand channels, and America [will] become the glory of all lands."

Religion notwithstanding, there was a lot of questionable action in the civil war, as leaders of the Continental army would attest: the self-professed patriots of Georgia "exceed the Goths and Vandals in their schemes of plunder, murder, and iniquity." Some rebels took vows not to become a "lawless set of banditti." However, most participants in this partisan conflict were not reluctant to transgress the code of limited, conventional warfare. The rebels won partly because they had the motivation of those fighting a holy war for holy stakes, as revealed by one militiaman in 1779: "It is a shame and disgrace to the virtuous sons of Liberty, while the ALMIGHTY is fighting our battles without, to suffer those Devils of all colors within." Reasonably well-mannered irregulars put "halters about the Necks to terefy and Deter" Tories. More violent rebels inflicted more extreme measures, besides the standard tar and feathers by which community standards were enforced in the late eighteenth century. Israel Putnam instructed his patrols "to kill all tory Villains found in arms against their Country or carrying any Cattle or Goods to the Enemy." Charles Lynch, who gave the phrase "lynch law" to the American language, sentenced Tories to thirty-nine lashes. If the victims did not shout "Liberty Forever!" he "hung [them] up by the thumbs until [they] did."

Rebel militia like New York's Committee for Detecting Conspiracies constituted the de facto judicial system anyplace the British army could not occupy. The "dirty little war of terrorism and murder" (to quote a British commander) had strategic significance. It determined which side would control the population and resources for reinforcement and supply. "By such skirmishes," a London publication predicted, "the fate of America must be decided. They are therefore as important as battles in which a hundred thousand [men] are drawn up on each side." Oblivious commanders like Cornwallis still looked for what the Crown originally expected in 1775: one decisive action restoring British rule. Absent Washington's flexibility, they could not switch to pacification and protection, no matter what the ministry said in 1781 about conducting a "settled plan, always securing and preserving what has been recovered, not taking possession of places at one time, abandoning them at another." Tories, left behind in pursuit of Nathanael Greene, could not handle the militia, as Cornwallis already admitted to London: "Loyalist numbers are not so great as had been represented and their friendship is only passive."

By 1783 the Continental army had achieved its goal—independence from Great Britain. George III would have continued the war, but Commons refused to support it any longer. Even the ministry recoiled from the consequence of keeping what they occupied: New York City. Just as France gave up all Canada to wean America from Great Britain, Britain abandoned the lower Hudson, to the wonder of George Washington. After Yorktown, he brought out his old plan to storm its ramparts in battle. Because the French navy and state militias refused to join him once again, he never fought the decisive battle at the strategic center of the war, an action he was likely to lose, with consequences fatal to his cause.

Decisive battle aborted at New York ultimately proved irrelevant. Parliament gave up that city in hopes of breaking what might become a permanent American alliance with France. American diplomats made independent motions toward accepting Britain's generosity, although that would violate the Franco-American treaty forbidding a separate peace. Forced to defer by America's threat to act unilaterally, the French foreign minister predicted that "we shall be badly paid for what we have done for the United States." Much the same sentiment came from

George III: "Knavery seems to be so much the striking feature of [America's] inhabitants that it may not in the end be an evil that they become Aliens." Still faithful, 100,000 Tories were forced by militia to abandon £150 million in land and property. Half of them settled in Canada, thereby giving the former French territory a population loyal to the Crown. In 1777, according to John Burgoyne, Canadians showed "no promise of use in arms" in defense of the British Empire. In 1812 mobilized émigrés would help discredit the plans America's warhawks had to win the next military conflict with England. Whatever U.S. politicians said, Old Tories were certainly not inclined to rise en masse against British "tyranny and oppression" by supporting an American invasion of their new Canadian homeland.[10]

3

1812 and Mexico: Partisan Political Wars in the Early Nineteenth Century

In 1812 and 1846 the party in power went to war expecting military success would solidify its hold on the federal government. In 1815 it ended its conflict with Britain desperately defending upstate New York, New Orleans, and the Atlantic coastline. This was a far cry from the triumphant series of battles leading to the occupation of Mexico City in 1847. Ironically, the public repudiated the political opposition to the War of 1812 but rejected the incumbent party in 1848. Apparently, the opponents of a war may be more successful when opposing a successful war. No one can blame failure on them.

DOMESTIC ROOTS OF THE WAR OF 1812

From 1796 to 1812, the long war between Napoleonic France and Great Britain resembled a fight between a tiger and a shark—one supreme on land, the other in water. Neither able to strike a decisive blow against the other, both countries struck at expanding U.S. trade and transportation between Europe and the Western Hemisphere. Because England had more warships and merchantmen than any other nation in the world, it had less need for America's commerce and more power to do it harm. In June 1812 the U.S. Congress declared war on Britain for preventing trade and travel, inciting hostile Indians on the frontier, and dragging 6,000 Americans into the Royal Navy—one way of reducing Britain's shortage of sailors.

Members of the Democratic-Republican party (hereafter called Republicans) "appealed to the God of Battles" because they stood convinced that the British offenses, specified previously, were part of a "deliberate and systematic" plot to reduce America back to "colonial vassalage." In fact, with Napoleon threatening to destroy the balance of power on the Continent and then invade

England, Britain had no time to conspire. Nonetheless, many Americans always seemed ready to believe that the ad hoc policies of the mother country wre much more coherent than ever was the case. In 1776 the colonies felt the Crown was trying to make them de facto slaves by taxation without representation. By 1812, when England wished to minimize its responsibilities in the New World, American proponents of war stood convinced that the objective of a "rapacious and tyrannical Power" was to destroy "our freedom."

The War of 1812 was "the second war of independence," according to President James Madison and Congressman John C. Calhoun. Their home regions, central Virginia and up-country Carolina, had been particularly nasty battlefields for Tories and British raiding parties committing "rapes, murders, and the whole catalogue of cruelties," so Madison cursed in 1781. However, 1812 was more than a historical flashback. It was the first of several highly partisan political wars. In part, a political party's decision to fight, where to fight, and how was a response to a mounting domestic challenge. An important (but not announced) war aim of each administration was preservation of its predominance. Not just a matter of keeping one's job, each believed that their tenure was a national necessity, as the secretary of the Treasury noted in 1811: a transfer of power to the opposition would "lead to a disgraceful peace, to absolute subserviency to Great Britain, and even to substantial alterations in our [American] institutions."

While not the sole partisan war, the War of 1812 was certainly the most partisan political war in U.S. history. (The Civil War split the nation along sectional, not party, lines.) In Congress, 81 percent of the Republicans voted to declare war; 100 percent of the Federalists opposed the resolution. Republican newspaper editors wrote about "the truth and justice of the great cause in which this country is engaged"; Federalists said it was an "overwhelming calamity." Their geographic stronghold was New England, the bastion of anti-French sentiment ever since Massachusetts led the American attack on Canada in the colonial wars. Whereas Republicans, whose base was the Southeast and the West, said that the British Empire conspired to put the United States under a new imperial yoke, Federalists replied that "*Mr. Madison*'s war" was "undertaken for *French* interest and in conformity with repeated *French* orders." In short, they asked, why trade a momentary English inconvenience to become a "submissive satellite" to a Continental autocrat?

Republicans, the "war hawks" of 1812, won control of the government in 1800 by running on peace and neutrality, while the Federalists were fighting France in an undeclared naval war and threatening to invade Spanish colonies. The challengers portrayed their opponents as political pickpockets devoted to large armies, navies, budgets, debts, and taxes—hardly popular in any election. In control of Congress and the White House over the next ten years, Republicans reduced the debt 43 percent by cutting defense, accounting for 50 percent of the federal budget in 1799. The army shrank from 14,000 to 3,287 soldiers; the navy's budget was reduced 67 percent. In 1800 it had thirteen frigates on line and six new seventy-four-gun vessels under construction. In 1806 dozens of militia-manned small gunboats provided coastal defense bereft of any capacity to take the battle to the enemy on the high seas. This did not disturb most Republicans one bit. "If the United States shall determine to augment their navy, so to rival those of Europe," one congressman expounded, "the public debt will become permanent; direct taxes will be perpetual; the paupers of the country will be increased."

When England and France each renewed their attacks on U.S. commerce in 1805, the Republicans did not have many military options. If they now tried to build a fleet to fight the British, they feared they would just provoke a preemptive attack as when the Royal Navy had destroyed the Danish fleet at anchor in its home port. Did America want to build frigates just "to have our towns Copenhagened"? Economic sanctions, which Madison had called the "commercial weapon," once seemed a viable alternative to fighting outnumbered and losing. Sequentially, Republicans tried (1) total nonimportation, (2) total nonexportation, (3) no commerce with Britain and France, (4) prohibition of imports from the enemy of whichever nation respected America's rights, and (5) nonimportation against only Britain.

If any particular policy had worked, the others would not have been tried. Republicans passed restrictions; smugglers shipped goods. President Madison and commercial coercion were discredited, even within his own party. By 1812, a national election year, one party newspaper was printing, "Every American cheek is flushed with shame, our constitution is ridiculed for its weakness." One Republican congressman confessed that a "government not able to defend itself against all aggressions ought to be changed." The electorate began to agree. The defense policy fiasco was resurrecting Federalist fortunes. Between 1804 and 1810 its representation grew from 28 to 43 percent in the electoral college, 25 to 37 percent in the Senate, and 18 to 22 percent in the House. Concurrently, many leaders of the Republican party came to the conclusion that, economic sanctions having failed, they could declare war or submit to Britain, which would destroy all party unity. As a leader in the House told his father-in-law, Thomas Jefferson: "Only a change in our foreign relations would enable Mr. Madison to ride triumphant, put down his opponents in Congress, and silence the growlings of those who ought to possess his entire confidence."

Important to all political parties at all times, retention was especially important to the Republicans in the early 1800s. The concept of a loyal opposition, one that disagrees with the administration but supports the nation at large, would not become common until the 1840s. Intellectually, as of 1812, America had not accepted the principle of pluralism, by which it actually conducted public life— that is, competing parties can protect political liberty by pusuing their own institutional interests. The relative absence of this argument had an ironic impact on American politics. Instead of creating a nonpartisan environment, it placed a great premium on party unity. Jefferson, the first Republican president, warned one of Madison's Republican critics about what the country needed in 1811, "the union of all its friends to resist its enemies within and without. If we schismatize on men and measures, if we do not act in phalanx, I will not say our *party*, the term is false and degrading, but our *nation* will be undone. For the Republicans are the nation."

Representative government was supposed to rely on self-sacrifice, not self-interest. Now that the Republican party controlled the federal government, it believed that "the rage of party spirit" was based on crude "pound, shilling, and pence patriotism." Its leadership perceived the conflict with Britain as a national opportunity to "immolate all selfish passions on the altar of a common country." Said James Monroe, secretary of state, it could "exterminate all party divisions in our country, and [thereby] give new strength and stability to our government." He and fellow Republicans believed that the Federalists were "a malevolent and traitorous conspiracy" of cryptoaristocrats out to replace the Republic with "a Hanoverian monarchy," à la George III. "If we do not kill them," warned Elbridge Gerry, about to be vice president, "they will kill us," politically. If that happened, "we shall disappoint not only America but the whole world" because, as Jefferson wrote a party newspaper, "the last hope of human liberty in this world rests on us." A vigorous national defense, Madison told Congress in mid-1813, "would demonstrate to the world the public energy of our political institutions."

By 1812 almost all Republicans had reversed their prior opinion about how war would affect their political fortunes. When they had been the opposition party in the 1790s, they espoused the radical Whig belief that wars destroyed republics by transferring prerogatives and property from the citizenry to the chief executive and his military minions feasting off expenditures. As late as 1809, Jefferson told Madison, "I know no government which would be so embarrassing in war as ours." A few ideologists remained committed to the old ideal. The majority (including Jefferson) now concluded that power need not be incompatible with liberty and that conducting war was less dangerous than making more concessions. Across the nation, party newspapers and leaders reiterated a common theme: capitulation to Great Britain (as the Federalists allegedly advocated) would discredit the American political "experiment" by showing that elected governments could not perform the essential responsibility of national defense. "Republics would be the most disgraceful of all forms of government, for they would be the most feeble." Citizens would take "refuge against such wrongs in a military despotism." Worst of all, Americans would discredit the American Revolution. "We must now oppose the encroachments of Great Britain by war or formally annul the Declaration of our Independence and acknowledge ourselves her devoted colonies." Those final words, from Madison, were echoed by Andrew Jackson, about to be called a despot by Federalists themselves. He extolled the Tennessee militia he would take into battle: "We are the free born . . . citizens of the only republick now existing in the world. . . . The advocates of Kingly power shall not enjoy the triumph of seeing a free people crouch before the slaves of a foreign tyrant."[1]

POLITICAL PARTIES AND ALTERNATIVE STRATEGIES

The Federalists wanted to make the armed conflict a limited war fought in a limited way with limited means—perhaps because they realized that large wars can create large dangers for minority political parties. In 1798, when they held power and engaged French forces on the high seas, they did not take the foreign threat as seriously as Republicans did in 1812. Federalists said France attacked America's commerce, not its sovereignty per se, but they still passed the Alien and Sedition Acts, which threatened to imprison their Republican opponents: war gave "a glorious opportunity to destroy faction" and "crush the [pro-]French party in this country."

In 1812, when the political shoe was on the other foot, Federalists would have agreed with what Madison wrote Jefferson in 1798: "Perhaps it is a universal truth that the loss of liberty at home is to be charged to provisions against danger, real or pretended, from abroad." Jefferson (the so-called civil libertarian) now suggested to President Madison a healthy dose of tar and feathers, if not rope and confiscation, for all Federalists south of the Potomac. ("In the North [where they are more numerous], they would give more trouble.") Warned that in the event of war they would be treated like the "Tory opposition" in the revolution, Federalists refurbished the old Republican gunboat strategy. Rather than build a navy, they would arm merchantmen for self-defense: "the systematic protection of our maritime rights by maritime means." This attempt to distinguish "resistance" from "reprisal" failed in the Senate by 16 to 16, each "no" coming from Republicans with a more assertive plan of their own.

The Republicans proposed a wholesale invasion of Canada by a citizens' militia, the fruit of American manhood. In opposition, Federalists restated the medieval theory of the "just war"—that the damage one inflicts must not exceed the damage one received. An expedition would be immoral because it was "not immediately connected with the defense of our sea coast and [our] soil." Republicans responded by saying that this war was "pure self-defense against the designs of the British to reduce us to subjection"; the ways and means were incidental. Moral or not, the Republican plan made perfect sense according to competitive military strategy, whereby one nation tries to be strong in areas where its enemy is weak. No sane person could think that America's advantage vis-à-vis Britain might be sea power. In 1812 the Royal Navy had over 200,000 sailors and 1,000 ships. The United States had 4,000 men and 180 vessels, all but 15 being gunboats mounting one or two small weapons. America's obvious strength was ground combat in Canada, whose population was 7 percent the size of the United States, and much of that French, still resenting the English conquest of 1763. Left to prevent the greatest loss of Crown territory since the American Revolution were a mixed bag of (1) provincial militia ("a mere posse, ill arm'd, and without discipline," according to the English), (2) Indian auxiliaries, and (3) 6,000 low-grade regulars deemed "the rubbish [only] good enough for the Canadian market."

The conquest of Canada, said James Monroe, was "not an object of the war but a means to bring it to a satisfactory conclusion." The operation could achieve a host of objectives—sometimes complementary, sometimes contradictory. Hostile Indians would lose their armaments, since British agents based in Canada allegedly instigated the renewal of "savage warfare" on the northwest frontier. The British navy would lose its base at Halifax by which America's coastline was blockaded. Perhaps most important, the invaluable West Indies would lose cheap Canadian food and fuel. Thus, by military means, America would finally enforce effective economic sanctions against the British Empire. London investors would lose their plantation profits, and the average Englishman would lack sugar for his tea.

Presumably, once the army occupied Canada, a foregone conclusion, the government would decide what to do with it. Not just an end or a means, the British colony was a different objective for a number of different interest groups. Those from the West wanted new territory for settlers. Those in the East wanted a bargaining chip to trade for good behavior by the Royal Navy. It was probably no accident that the administration did not state its own policy. Since 1787, when a young James Madison wrote the seminal essay on political pluralism ("Federalist Number 10"), he had been profoundly aware of the "great variety of parties and interests" in America. As president since 1809, he used ambiguity to manage disputes in ways to alienate the smallest number of citizens he could.

The Republican party was hopelessly split into those who wanted war, those who wanted minimal expenditures, and those who wanted both at the same time. Lacking strong presidential leadership, all sides prevailed. In 1812 Congress declared war without increasing the size of the army, still two-thirds of its peace-time authorization. Federalists soon would say that the administration was the first government ever to go "to war in order to raise an army," getting military funding no other way. Many Republicans did not care. They papered over the disparity between means and objectives by maintaining Canada was a cheap way to beat Britain. Henry Clay, the speaker of the House, already told Congress "that the militia of Kentucky [his home state] are alone competent to place Montreal and Upper Canada [modern Ontario] at your feet." According to Jefferson, the invasion would be a training exercise for the United States, a country "where even the elements of tactics are unknown." The "weakness of the enemy on land will make our first errors innocent"; the campaign "will give us experience for . . . the final expulsion of England from the American continent"—surely one of the worst predictions ever made.

In 1812 America's problem was not national goals or military ways, two components of the strategic triad. The difficulty lay in the means: militiamen used as an expeditionary army. They had been a headache to George Washington; they would be more like a brain tumor at the beginning of James Madison's war, where the militia constituted a greater part of the force structure than it did in the American Revolution. For both legal and military reasons, Madison and Jefferson, of all people, should have foreseen the problem of conducting a strategic offensive with a self-defense force. The federal Constitution, which Madison largely drafted in 1787, speaks of "calling forth the Militia to execute the Laws of the Union, suppress Insurrections and repel Invasions." It said nothing about it being an expeditionary army, nor did Congress (divided on the issue) make a statement of its own. Because of lagging enlistments in the federal forces, Madison had to draw upon state militia, "who, it may be presumed, will cross the [border] line without raising Constitutional or legal questions"—bad prediction number two.

As for capabilities, legalities aside, the militia had a spotty record, even in self-defense. When Jefferson had been the governor of Virginia and faced British troops in 1780, his "here today and gone tomorrow" militia units would not defend Richmond, let alone march to the Ohio River. Neither he, Madison, nor James Monroe, formerly a colonel on Washington's staff, forgot Washington's dictum that militiamen might harass but never conduct a decisive attack. Unfortunately, when Republican presidents tried to reform the militia, they ran up against republican principles formed to oppose and harass kings. Congress rejected Jefferson's and Madison's proposal to make its best soldiers a ready reserve because that gainsaid the ideal of "the whole Province under arms." The militia was to be a local institution and not to be deployed outside the state. Otherwise, Republicans traditionally feared, all military power would gravitate to the executive branch.

Republican ideologists still believed that "patriotic ardor" and numerical superiority could carry Canada in 1812. The Federalist governors of Connecticut, Massachusetts, and Rhode Island used the same ideology to deny Madison use of their militia. In 1775, when these states led the resistance to British imperialism, they desperately recruited a Virginian to command their soldiers in hopes of making New England's conflict a national cause. Now its Federalists talked as if Virginia, the bastion of the Republican party, had assumed the mantle of King George. Since their own regions had been reduced to "the feeble expression of colonial complaints" to the national capital, some Federalists looked forward to a British military victory that "will turn out the Administration," so they told the British Foreign Office. If not defeated, the Republicans would raise a 60,000-man army to yoke the North as slaves "to the carriage of some southern despot."

New England Federalists maintained that if the president could mobilize the militia to "carry on an offensive war," he could "produce a military consolidation of the states." Lest Madison destroy the American "confederacy," the governors insisted that the government could only petition the militia to repel invasions or enforce the law. Governors, not presidents, held the sole "right of determining when [those] exigencies exist." Governors, not presidents, held sole authority to assign militia command. Federalists uncomfortable in the role of an organized opposition resorted to hyperbole to disagree with the administration. They claimed they were saving the country from tyranny, rather than proposing a different policy. Their resistance was more than mere annoyance to the government of the United States. It had an enormous impact on its power to prosecute the war.

Jefferson and Monroe, charter members of the Virginia political dynasty of the Republican party, would look at New England, the Federalist bastion, and ask its leading citizens how and why it threw out the British in 1776 but would not loan a dime for others to fight the War of 1812. "Oh, Massachusetts!" Jefferson wrote General Henry Dearborn. "How have I lamented the degradation of your apostasy. . . . [Its] parricide party would have basely sold what their fathers so bravely won from the same enemy."[2]

LOSING ON THE BORDER, WINNING ON THE WAVES

New York and New England were the indispensable base from which to control Lake Ontario and the St. Lawrence, key terrain for both sides in the War of 1812. Neither America nor Canada had sufficient roads, draft animals, or wagons to transport a substantial military force, except by water. The river and the Great Lakes provided the line of communication, as well as the main zone of battle. New York would be a cauldron of military operations. New England became the center of antiwar activity. From 1710 through 1775, it had provided men, resources, and enthusiasm for the campaigns against Canada. Unless the enemy was under attack, the region then reasoned, France or Britain would use Montreal as a base to arm the Indians, slip down Lake Champlain, and "lay all the back parts of New England open" to destruction. In 1812 the section retained the best-trained and best-equipped citizen-soldiers on the continent. Massachusetts had 40 percent of all artillery possessed by U.S. militias. Only it and Connecticut required every town to store camp equipment, gunpowder, and ammunition. (Virginia stocked weapons for barely 20 percent of its men.) A large number of individuals from the Republican/frontier sections of New England volunteered for federal military service. However, on the Canadian border, America's expeditionary army would sorely miss that organized militia in the grip of state control.

If President Madison could have executed the war the way he wished, he would have massed his force against Montreal, a bottleneck for all transport passing from east to west. America's most militant states, Kentucky and Ohio, still demanded immediate action in the Lake Erie theater to provide relief from Indian attack. Meanwhile, in New York State, many citizen-soldiers ("the most violent democrats") said they must get "orders to act" along the Niagara or they were going home. Consequently, the armed forces approached Canada on two secondary fronts characterized as "the tail of the lion"—between Lakes Huron and Erie toward Upper Canada, and between Lakes Erie and Ontario in western New York. They also moved up the Lake Champlain Valley toward Montreal, the decisive objective to be seized "at one stroke," before Britain could come to its rescue and an impatient Congress reconvene that fall.

American military resources had been sucked into peripheral areas. By 1813 some 800 Britons and 4,000 Indians would tie down 20,000 Americans in the

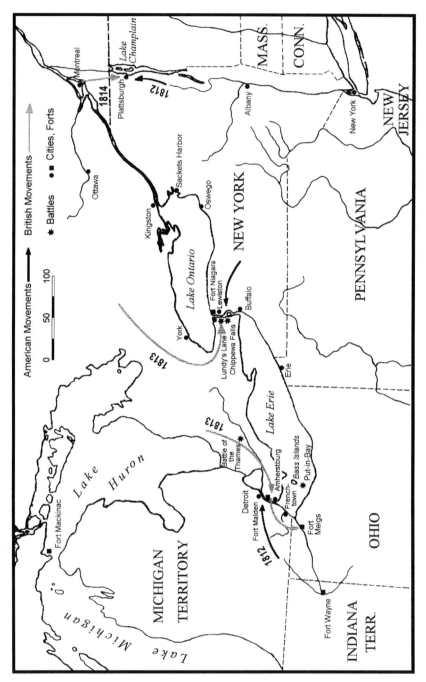

War of 1812, northern theater

Michigan Territory. By 1814 almost 1,000 U.S. regulars (including Major Zachary Taylor) would be deployed to contest enemy control of the Mississippi River. Back in 1812 the administration had hoped to turn a political necessity (the attack on Upper Canada) into a military advantage. Simultaneous operations would prevent lateral mobility on the Great Lakes; the enemy would be unable to block at least one penetration deep into its territory. In fact, the British military commander, Sir George Prevost, had not planned to counter each attack. That spring, he largely stripped Canada of manpower west of the mouth to Lake Ontario on grounds that "an effectual defense of the open Country would be in vain." Better to protect what was defensible and truly irreplaceable: Halifax and Quebec, bastions from which to rescue the rest of Canada after the conclusion of the European war. After making this difficult decision, Prevost was pleasantly surprised. No American penetration got much beyond the border from Detroit to Montreal.

A three-pronged offensive is never easy to coordinate; in 1812 it was virtually impossible. Most of America's senior military commanders were superannuated survivors of the Revolutionary War. At least one of them (Henry Dearborn) was not sure if he belonged near Lake Champlain, on the Niagara border, or protecting Boston Harbor. Communications with Washington were obviously inadequate. The secretary of war could not tell one general when another "might deem it expedient to commence offensive operations," all of which lacked transportation and supplies. Common citizens near the border could have filled these shortfalls. Many spent the war selling horses and cattle to the enemy, partly to prevent invasion and plunder if British forces were deprived of the goods they wanted. As for America's own disadvantaged soldiers, they were largely militiamen, the preferred force of the U.S. Congress. However expedient for a balanced federal budget, they were hardly the ideal military body for a synchronized offensive along multiple avenues of advance.

American units crossed into Upper Canada on 12 July. Four and five months later the other commands executed their invasions, hardly textbook coordination. In place, on time, or not, many militiamen believed that they were on the border to prevent an invasion, not conduct one themselves. Since the war was being fought over maritime rights, some of them had made the logical (but incorrect) assumption that their government planned to conduct its offensive operations on the high seas. At two fronts (Niagara and the Montreal corridor), almost two-thirds of the militiamen claimed that they could not legally cross out of American territory. The others were ill prepared to advance, no matter what they believed. Worst of all, American military commanders did not know which units would claim which constitutional clause. Who would remain on American soil, and who would cross into Canada, either for looting or to end the war quickly—both being old citizen-soldier objectives? All Kentucky and most Ohio militia units crossed the Detroit River. Pennsylvania, Vermont, and some New York units would not cross the border at all. Others from New York threatened mutiny if they did not invade, were then beaten back, and cited the Constitution in refusing to return. Apparently legal stricture, like beauty, was in the eyes of the beholder—in this case the colonel, the sergeant major, and the rank and file. "My apprehensions for the safety of the province are considerably diminished," Lieutenant General Prevost concluded by the end of the year, "such an enemy cannot be considered as formidable."

Disgusted at this performance, southern militia officers, like Andrew Jackson, assured the president that their own men ("the choicest of our citizens") had no "Constitutional scruples [about] any boundaries," Spanish Florida in particular. However, the law of the land was not the only reason for military failure in Canadian territory. Northern militiamen who did cross the border did not do very well when they faced the enemy. Their slow-loading flintlock muskets required a massed volley fire from linear formations. This required strict military discipline to be effective on an open battlefield without prepared positions. Militia units in a democracy were notoriously weak in command and control, as one of their so-called commanders later confessed: "With militia a retreat becomes a flight, and the battle once ended the army is dissipated." An Ohio newspaper, observing the virtual disintegration of militia units by early 1813, asked its readers: "Where is the spirit of '76? Where is the patriotism of 1812?" By 1814 the most pro-war state in the Union, excepting Kentucky, was conscripting soldiers, buying substitutes, and conceding every male would not do his military duty.

The secretary of the Treasury came to much the same conclusion in 1812, after observing the military engagements on the U.S.–Canadian border. Albert Gallatin lamented that this "series of misfortunes exceeds all anticipations made even by those who had the least confidence in our inexperienced officers and undisciplined men." They were simply "not the species of force," an American newspaper said, "on which to rely for carrying on war, however competent they may be to repel an invasion." Whether the militia could do even that much was about to be tested, although Britain did not want to initiate offensive operations. The Crown lacked military resources for secondary theaters until the French army was defeated. It also understood that as far as America was concerned, Napoleon was just an unsavory associate against a common adversary, namely, them. Unfortunately for the United States (certainly not the Crown), Napoleon invaded Russia two weeks after Congress declared war on Great Britain. He would never recover from this mistake, although not clearly apparent before 1813. In 1812 the British government feared that if it pushed the United States too hard, a Franco-American parallel course could become a formal alliance, as had occurred in the American Revolution. This deleterious development could give Napoleon a new foothold in the New World.

England, against its own inclinations to stay on the defensive in North America, was lured to counterattack by circumstances and situations it could not control. Like French Canada against Anglo-America before 1760, British

Canada believed it had only a few options to offset the numerical advantage of its southern neighbor. It might attack enemy territory because the Crown lacked manpower to cover all the area it had to defend. It could make overtures to disaffected minorities, that is, slaves and Indian tribes. These options were closely related and became policy. To find allies among Indians abandoned by the British after the American Revolution, offensive operations were needed to show "that we are earnestly engaged in the War." Native Americans would fight to loot settlers who invaded their tribal lands, not to protect European colonial territorial integrity.

Largely out of necessity, English officers found themselves arming and leading Indian forays across Canadian and Spanish borders. As often happened, these engagements were marked by mutual atrocities: mutilation, wanton destruction, the killing of women and children. Englishmen tried to impose restraint, without much success. Indians deferred to Canadian fur traders (their primary source of weapons, tools, and utensils) far more than they did to gentlemen with a commission from the Crown. The English maintained that if they did not support and accompany their allies, the consequences would have been much worse than they were. Probably true, the English still used threats of "a war of extermination" to force Americans to surrender before the Indians got "beyond [their] control." Americans, for their part, demanded revenge for the incitement of brutalities the British could not stop. Senior American officers declared that no quarter would be given to white men "fighting by the side of an Indian" and offered a forty-dollar bounty for each dead Indian a soldier produced. By late 1813 the policy was amended by the secretary of war to make use of Indians. Subordinates were to turn Native Americans loose until there was not a single "British settler west of Kingston," at the mouth of Lake Ontario. James Madison, a Virginia gentleman, thought this order "more severe than may be proper" and softened the directive, although not much. Thereafter, American soldiers were supposed to take prisoner all male Canadian settlers who "may be disposed to do us harm."

On all sides of all borders, numerous villages were burned to the ground: Buffalo, York, Prophetstown, and others, not to mention Washington in August 1814. English and American army regulars professed to each other that they had no intention to pursue a system of warfare "so little congenial to the[ir] character," but both had problems controlling the so-called barbarian elements: Indians and citizen-soldiers on each side. Everyone soon had ample evidence (if any was needed) that they were facing what Americans called a "a new race of Goths, outraging the ordinances of God and the laws of humanity." Not to be outdone, the British Empire said it faced a "conspiracy threatening greater barbarism and misery than followed the downfall of Rome." By 1814, when U.S. officers were writing that the "whole [Canadian] population is against us; [every] foraging party is fired on," the American invasion had turned out to become the greatest single contribution to the creation of Canadian loyalty to the Crown.

Britain certainly humbled America's expeditionary army. However, England was quickly humbled by U.S. naval forces, once described by the *Times* of London as a "few fir built frigates with strips of bunting, manned by outlaws." The Madison administration had merely hoped to save its homebound packets and defend its own coast. Instead, in a series of single-warship battles on the high seas in the first six months of the war, the United States sunk or captured three British frigates, two sloops, one brig, and one military transport. By December 1812, as Federalists praised themselves for having created a navy so strong it could survive twelve years "of democratick misrule," English military periodicals were exclaiming that the entire conflict "has been marked by events on land and at sea . . . diametrically opposite to public expectation." The next two years would not lessen the shock. When Britain substantially increased its warships at Halifax station and grouped them to fight single vessels, America switched strategies. Its navy and privateer schooners (the volunteer militia of the ocean) raided commerce from India to Dover. That merchantmen would not sail up and down the English Channel without convoy protection caused further "mortification" to the nation "whose flag till of late waved over every sea and triumphed over every rival." By the end of the entire conflict, to the dismay of Britain, the United States had won the battle of the maritime body count: some 2,000 vessels captured, 1,500 lost. Public "feelings of favor to the Navy," wrote an official of the Crown, "rendered the military triumph [in Canada] no compensation for the disaster."

In the interior of America, where the U.S. Army was supposed to win the war, the navy triumphed on Lakes Erie and Champlain. There, commerce raiding was unimportant. Admittedly, America would have to fight British vessels "man to man and gun to gun." However, the Royal Navy could not sail its heavy vessels on the St. Lawrence west of Quebec. Washington, loath to challenge enemy men-of-war on the ocean, stripped men and guns from half its vessels bound for the Atlantic, which became a secondary theater after 1813. America sent these resources west, along with the former superintendent of the New York Navy Yard to lead what had become "a ship-builder's war." He hastily constructed bases along the rivers and the lakes to create and support a "brown water" capability. By the time the British army was ready to mount its own offensive, these facilities were producing warships carrying 110 guns. America, although now on the defensive, controlled the avenue for mobility and supply in the Northwest, as well as the Lake Champlain route for invasion between New York and Montreal. In 1814 Plattsburg Bay would be the site of the decisive battle of the war. Without superiority on these crucial waters, the Duke of Wellington informed his government, any army would be wasted and Britain have no "right from the state of war to demand any concession of territory from America." This sober message from their premier general to accept the status quo would disappoint Englishmen eager to revenge the naval losses that cast a pall of "gloom" over what they called their "high and honorable minds."[3]

THE BRITISH INVADE, THE FEDERALISTS GLOAT, THE MILITIA FIGHTS

Once Napoleon appeared defeated in late 1813, Britain moved beyond "plundering and ruining the [American] peasantry," that is, conducting raids to divert the enemy from the Canadian border. By 1814 England held the objectives America thought it had in 1812: to strike down the "detestable American government" in a preemptive war. In concrete terms, this meant the British Empire wanted to do what French Canada aspired to do in 1754: take sole possession or control of Maine, the Mississippi River, New Orleans, and all military installations on the northern waters, as well as securing extensive territory for its Indian allies south of the Great Lakes. If a firm barrier were not erected now, time and population would inevitably favor America, which was (according to London) the real cause of this war. "Strike! Chastise the savages, for such they are," wrote the *Times,* the voice of the America haters. This group talked about "blustering democrats" the way William T. Sherman would later talk of the Confederacy and Franklin Roosevelt about Nazi Germany: "It was our business to have given [America] a fearful memento [so] that the babe unborn should have remembered" the pain inflicted. We must "give them a complete drubbing before peace is made."

English newspapers found America "destitute even of the brutish quality of being beaten into a sense of their unworthiness and incapacity," at least by the forces the Crown deployed in 1813. They and Madison's worst political enemies took heart when Britain transferred 13,000 seasoned veterans to the Western Hemisphere, twice as many soldiers as Wolfe had at Quebec in 1759. By all reason, this formidable force would finally make Madison "fall victim to the just vengeance of the Federalists" and sue for a humiliating peace. The president looked "shattered" but persevered as the enemy attacked from New England to the Mississippi Valley. Just as the American invasion of Canada had destroyed pro-America sentiment, the English invasion virtually destroyed Britain's friends in America. The Federalists would have been better off if the Republicans had conquered Canada in 1812. They could have continued to justify their acts of obstruction on grounds the conflict was not "connected with the defense of our sea-coast and soil." The British military offensive put them on the political defensive, no longer able to say that the war "was absolutely unjust," that is, an act of aggression "against the nation from which we are descended." Republicans could now label the British "water[borne] Winnebagoes," a simile that tied an Indian albatross around the Federalist neck.

Partisan charges that Federalists were Tory traitors mounting a "steady, systematical, and energetical opposition" to national defense were not without substance, especially concerning the fringe wing of the party. It made overtures toward negotiating a separate peace and alliance with a foreign power wherein Massachusetts would never make war on Canada; Britain would give it material aid for defense from federal agents and the federal army. Other Federalists, while less extreme, were also obsessed with "domestic tyranny," their professed motive for preventing Madison from raising all the means he needed to accomplish anything more than staving off defeat. When Canadian farmers would not sell provisions to the English on credit, New England eased the cash flow crisis by illegal trade, a regional tradition dating back to the colonial wars. It purchased English Treasury notes with gold obtained from smuggling supplies to the enemy's army and its navy blockading seaports south of Connecticut. American regiments in western New York lost half their men for lack of pay. Meanwhile, the governors of New England refused to mobilize state militias.

Essential to conduct any war, central authority was especially weak in the first decade of the nineteenth century because the national government was small, fragmented, and based on a Republican philosophy that mistrusted power. In the winter of 1814, Federalists at the Hartford Convention would have made this state of affairs a permanent condition through a series of constitutional amendments, such as a provision that war must be declared by a two-thirds vote of Congress. Federalists debated what to do with a "dying" government about to "dissolve into the original elements" of sovereign states. Parliament debated the "ruffian system of warfare," particularly the destruction of the White House and the national Capitol. These actions were defended by arguments the English had used since their wars against the savage Irish and the barbarian Scots: they "came to treat with a regular government but have [had] to deal with a mob and mob leaders" instead.

No doubt the British reference included the militia, said to be an American mob in military garb, especially when assigned to be an expeditionary army. However, in 1814, militiamen conducted their customary function of local self-defense in standing organizations with unit cohesion, not in formations quickly constituted on the Canadian border. In the defense of Washington, they were maneuvered into meeting English regulars in the worst position, on open terrain. Elsewhere, they were on both the tactical and strategic defense, fighting behind earthworks, parapets, and canals. When pushed from one field fortification in front of Plattsburg, Baltimore, and New Orleans, they fell back to the next position prepared in depth. British officers at those engagements would not talk about American militia, as they did while raiding Washington: "They seemed country people, who would have been much more appropriately employed in attending to their agricultural occupations than in standing with muskets in their hands on the brow of a bare green hill." The French ambassador to America summarized the new state affairs in early 1815: Three large attacks saw "Wellington's best corps flee before the militia."

Apparently cowed by nightmares of another Saratoga, the British commander withdrew from the Lake Champlain corridor with visions of "the Enemy's Militia raising En Masse around me." Because the navy, not the army, was the decisive factor in this campaign, militia glory would have to lodge at

New Orleans. Andrew Jackson, the senior American officer in the southern theater, had left almost all his regular army components at Mobile to guard the Gulf Coast. Tennessee, Georgia, and Kentucky militiamen under his command would have to bar the way up the Mississippi River. When they helped inflict some 2,000 casualties on the cream of the British forces led by Wellington's brother-in-law, they redeemed what Jackson had lamented was "the reputation of the once brave and patriotic Volunteers."

Myths about democracy and citizen-soldiers aside, Jackson actually won the battle with engineers, artillery, and naval gunfire, not Kentucky rifles. He also practiced a draconian discipline that must have been the envy of regular army officers such as Winfield Scott. Scott executed federal soldiers four at a time for desertion yet lost control of the militia in 1812. "These vermin who infest all republics" left him a prisoner of war: fleeing battle across the border and failing to return. In Jackson's case, however, when these men were "taken [with] the home mania," he threatened them with grapeshot and charged with desertion the first militiamen executed since the Revolution. In New Orleans he jailed one critic of martial law and the judge who would free him on a writ of habeas corpus—both on the grounds that "personal liberty cannot exist at a time when every man is required to become a soldier."

Federalists would declare Jackson a military dictator—but they had a vested interest in losing the Battle of New Orleans. They not only were counting on a "few right blows struck in the right place" to humiliate the administration; they were counting on regaining control of Capitol Hill. Loss of the mouth of the Mississippi River would sever contact with the states west of the Blue Ridge Mountains. That region gave the balance of national political power to Republicans at the expense of Federalists, who had opposed the Louisiana Purchase and were glad to see territory they never wanted lost in a war they did not support. Military victory meant their political defeat, rubbed in by one national newspaper headline: "Glory to Jackson. Glory to the Militia. . . . Glory Be to God That the Barbarians Have Been Defeated."[4]

INTERNATIONAL IMPASSE, DOMESTIC TRIUMPH

Because treaties reflect military situation maps, America's militia and navy created the conditions for a status quo antebellum settlement. "If we had either burnt Baltimore or held Plattsburg," a British negotiator said, "we could have had peace on our own terms." Those particular setbacks were not the only factors. Repatriated English officers testified about facing much tougher opponents in regular American army units. Winfield Scott laboriously trained his brigade to professional standards, took the tactical offensive, and won engagements *in* Canada on open terrain, unheard of when the war began back in 1812. To at least one other officer, Scott's battle at Lundy's Lane (July 1814) was "the finest subject for the pen and pencil of the poet and artist that has occurred since the coming of Christ."

Along with enemy military competency, there was the recurrent cause of war termination in Hannoverian England—the growth of the national debt: £400 million in 1800, £625 million in 1812, £840 million in 1815, the year of the Treaty of Ghent. Even before the government predicted that "the continuance of the American war will entail upon us a prodigious expense," taxation took 35 percent of production and per capita income—far more than the public was willing to sustain, especially now that the government bore the onus of aggression. Aside from English taxpayers in general, there were specific economic interests agitating for peace, primarily the parliamentary lobbies for overseas commerce now afflicted with American privateers and the cotton textile industry, which processed American raw materials and sold them back as cloth.

America "escaped a sound flogging"—"a lamentable event to the civilized world," according to the *Times* of London. Federalists were less willing to admit that the English had retired "with the recent defeats at Plattsburg and Lake Champlain unavenged." They said that the Treaty of Ghent was proof of Republican defeat and "Mr. Madison's submission," since it "obtained [not] one single avowed objective for which [he] involved the country in this bloody and expensive war." Because Britain did not renounce its conduct on the high seas, the document was more a cessation of hostilities than a firm foundation for a lasting peace. Nonetheless, because the United States established its military credibility, England now was careful to observe what Americans called "the utmost courtesy towards the crews of our ships," even when Napoleon went on his last warpath before Waterloo in 1815.

The Republican party could stake a claim to other favorable results of the war. Now bereft of European allies, Indians would cease to be a substantial obstacle to national expansion, however much they troubled small settlements on the frontier. Even more important to many political activists in 1815 was the feeling that there "never was a more glorious opportunity for the Republican party to place themselves permanently in power." When Madison submitted the peace treaty to the Senate, he said that "the Government has demonstrated the efficiency of its powers of defense." The republic survived; the Federalists would not, as Jefferson and others predicted: "The triumph over the Aristocrats and Monarchists is equally glorious with that over the enemy." The war left the nation in debt, but it proved "that our government is solid [and] can stand the shock of war. . . . Its best effect has been the complete suppression of the party deeply involved in the parricide crimes and treasons of the war."

With that charge wrung around its neck, the Federalist party disintegrated by 1820. Without an organized opposition, the Republicans broke into competing factions led by regional and personal political chieftains. Andrew Jackson, the symbol and personification of citizen-soldier combat power, emerged from the pack on the base of appeals to militia units better organized than parties in the 1820s.

By 1830 he and his followers formed the Democratic party. Their opponents, who called themselves Whigs, were led by Henry Clay, the man who once claimed the Kentucky militia would win the War of 1812. They failed to conquer Canada but to Clay's eternal regret helped Jackson become an icon at the Battle of New Orleans. In the mid-1840s the Jacksonians would lead the country into its next major military conflict, during which a former Federalist warned fellow Whigs, including Abraham Lincoln, that "by God, I opposed one war, and it ruined me. Henceforth I am for *War, Pestilence,* and *Famine.*"

During the Mexican War, regular army officers would have to put up with "contemptible appointments" made to "citizen political soldiers" eager to boost their postwar careers. According to professional soldiers, their competition thought themselves "all great Jackson men [who] must have his soldierly qualities." Good or bad, they would have to become federal volunteers. When the United States invaded Mexico, it left its state militia at home. No matter, there were still enough disputes between regulars and amateurs to keep the new expeditionary army fully occupied. Regulars, remembering the defeats of 1812 and victories of 1814 on Canadian territory, felt they had to win the war by themselves because "the ordinary operation of civil affairs, in our beloved country, is deadly hostile to every principle of military discipline." Citizen-soldiers, remembering Jackson, went down to Mexico to rescue "kid glove dandies" like Winfield Scott, who had said in 1814 that "our handsome little army" would "be disgraced if we admit a militia force into our order of battle."[5]

DOMESTIC POLITICAL ORIGINS: THE MEXICAN WAR, 1846–48

All in all, the Mexican War was somewhat less partisan than the War of 1812, if only because the Democrats, the dominant political party of the period, were internally split along sectional lines. Furthermore, the Whig opposition in the Senate supported the declaration of hostilities in May 1846. However, President James Polk, Democrat from Tennessee and protégé of Andrew Jackson, made war a partisan activity in ways not done by his predecessors or successors, James Madison and Abraham Lincoln. Although the vote for war in 1812 had been split along party lines, Madison initially tried to conduct it on a nonpartisan basis, to the consternation of Republican congressmen. They complained that the president, to win over the opposition, was "appointing too many Federalists to office." Few could ever accuse Polk of doing the same thing.

Soon after the presidential election of 1844, Polk listed his objectives in foreign affairs: resolving the border between Oregon and Canada, annexing Texas at the Rio Grande, and acquiring New Mexico and California. Ever since Marco Polo visited Kublai Khan in Cathay in the thirteenth century and returned to Venice to write sensational stories about the riches of the Orient, trade with China has periodically beguiled the Western imagination. In 1843, after Britain used the Opium War to force China to open five new coastal ports to foreign trade, visions of cornucopia resurfaced in America, then undergoing a series of economic downswings—1837, 1839, and 1841. In 1844, the year of Polk's election, the price of hogs and corn reached a twenty-year low; cotton sank to its all-time depth. In 1846 the president addressed Congress, asserting that "the home market is inadequate to enable [Americans] to dispose of the immense surplus of food and other articles they are capable of producing, even at reduced prices."

To get to the "inexhaustible markets" of China, ending economic busts, America had to get to California, an underpopulated province of Mexico. In Mexican hands it was "doomed to dissolution and barren waste." Under U.S. rule, "one of the most beautiful regions on the face of the earth" would "immediately blossom like a rose." San Francisco Bay, "one of the great natural anchorages of the world," would control "the trade of the northern Pacific" and increase "the resources and wealth of the nation to an incalculable degree," according to both political parties. The Democrats lost the presidency to the Whigs because of the economic panics of 1837 and 1839. The Whigs lost the presidency to Polk when the depression of 1841 occurred while they ruled Washington.

The political consensus for obtaining California as a staging base to China broke down over proper ways to get it. The Whigs, who represented most members of the large companies active in the China trade, were "not averse to extending the limits of the republic, provided it can be done by fair and just means," that is, "an honest purchase." Party leadership came primarily from settled communities, established professions, and prestigious institutions, like Philadelphia law firms and the Presbyterian Church. Order, deference, and dispassion laced their politics and rhetoric. Their social code did not sanction armed conflict unless clearly fought for self-defense. War "of an aggressive character" or "inordinate territorial aggrandizement" did not pass their test, nor would the Mexican War. Henry Clay, the party's elder statesman and last nominee for president, condemned it in 1847, although his favorite son and namesake had recently died in battle at Buena Vista: "War unhinges society, disturbs its peaceful and regular industry, and scatters poisonous seeds of disease and immorality."

Democrats, since conception under Andrew Jackson in the late 1820s, were far more prone to resort to armed conflict. Individualism, rights, and expansion often appeared in their discourse, along with denials of basic Whig beliefs about natural harmony between labor, capital, and agriculture. If America were to preserve equality and democracy by avoiding the class conflict associated with industry and urbanization in places such as England, its "increasing population [could not] be cramped and confined" within its present boundaries. "The preservation of the union" from the forces of disruption depended on provision of cheap land and territorial growth to the Pacific Ocean, at least according to the Jackson Democrats. By the 1840s the party was split along geographic and ideological lines. Spokesmen for the southeastern seaboard lined up against the Southwest: sectional loyalists opposed so-called party hacks. South Carolina, a bastion of congressional war hawks in 1812, was led by its senior United States senator, John C. Calhoun. No longer saying, as he did in the last war, that battle would produce "the real spirit of union," he now was trying to cut new ground along the path blazed by Thomas Jefferson after the heated debate between the North and the South over slavery in Missouri in 1819.

In 1815 Jefferson thought the Federalist party was doomed. By 1820 he believed that the old Tories had infiltrated the Republican ranks to accomplish their historic agenda of oppressing the agrarian South. According to Jefferson (and later Calhoun), the enemy sought to construct a "venal and oppressive" central government that would consolidate all power in its hands. Then, aside from subsidizing corporations that "plundered [the] ploughman," they would give slaves "freedom and a dagger" to force all whites to evacuate the states south of the Ohio River, where "the true political faith" of the American Revolution still survived. Having lost faith in the electoral process, Jefferson proposed constitutional restrictions similar to those Federalists tried to pass in the War of 1812, political pluralism taken to its extreme. Calhoun would do the same thing in the 1840s under what he called the doctrine of "concurrent majorities." If it was enacted, his state and region would gain the legal right to veto federal policy within their jurisdictions. If not stopped now, the government was supposed to become so oppressive that secession was foredoomed.

As of yet, Calhoun lamented, the South had not embraced nullification because of division along Whig/Democratic lines. The only way it could form what he called a "union among ourselves" was to dissolve the party organization based on a Southwest-Northeast alliance formed by his old rivals, Jackson and Martin Van Buren, one a war chieftain, the other a political boss. In the mid- to late 1840s, Calhoun reiterated fears about a White House–war–partisan connection first expressed in 1835, when he accused Jackson of "uniting in the President the power of the sword and the purse" in order to create "a war party" interested in conflict and government contracts at the expense of true republican principles. Calhoun's policy toward Mexico was reminiscent of his policy toward Indians, contrasted with that of the Jacksonians. The Jacksonians used force to acquire land to sell and tribes to govern, with patronage agents doing the president's bidding. Calhoun merely supported "masterly activity," by which pioneers settled and Indians "dwindled." The same method should be used with Mexico. Because "our population is rolling toward the shores of the Pacific with an impetus greater than what we realize," expansion had no need for military action whose real purpose was to reap credit from the public's unfortunate "inclination for conquest and empire."

For foreign and domestic reasons, the Calhoun policy was unacceptable to the dominant Democratic faction once led by Jackson ("Old Hickory"), now led by "Young Hickory," James K. Polk. They felt that if Mexico lost control of California, it would sell the province to England, which would fortify and keep it from the United States. Just as important as their chronic suspicions of Britain, mainline Democrats expected political benefits from an assertive policy. As opposed to Calhoun, they believed that the alliance between the "planters of the South and the plain Republicans of the North" was the best "antidote for sectional prejudices" and the only way to ensure "fidelity to the compromises of the Constitution," that is, states' rights. War, far from lamentable under Democratic leadership, could "cement lasting friendships . . . [among] men from all parts of the Union." That would ensure the rights of the South to avoid interference from "fanatics and knaves," code names for New England Whigs.

Polk, in particular, was not loath to take political advantage from national expansion, especially when his home state was so closely divided that party workers named it "the hard fought battlefield." If handled skillfully, expansionism could be decisive, as shown in the 1844 election. Polk's cohorts claimed to possess "conclusive" evidence of a plot "between the abolitionists of England and America" to turn an independent Texas into a forward base to destroy states' rights and slave property principles. "The Southwest is in a *blaze of enthusiasm*," wrote Polk's campaign manager, Gideon Pillow. "We now entertain *no doubt* of carrying Tennessee by a large majority."[6]

FROM COERCIVE DIPLOMACY TO LIMITED WAR

Whigs once claimed that Andrew Jackson was a "wanton [warmonger noted for] cruelty and useless bloodshed." Partisan hyperbole aside, Jackson had certainly been ready to use force in pursuit of national objectives, as in 1818, when he coerced Spain to sell Florida to the United States. In late 1845 Polk sent a personal envoy to Mexico City with a pledge of $40 million for California, New Mexico, and acquiescence in the annexation of Texas to the Rio Grande. Like Jackson, he held a physical threat in reserve, warning of "a corps of properly organized volunteers [to] invade, overrun and occupy Mexico." All the time, the administration believed "there will be no war," even if Mexico "kept up appearances of a fight for a while." Its government was so weak that even after war began, Washington believed it would take the "first chance" to make an "amicable arrangement of all differences." By bowing to limited demands, Mexico would gain money, not lose more blood and territory to its neighbor to the north.

The Mexican government proved too weak at home to make concessions abroad. From 1829 to 1846, it was rent with coups, rebellions, twenty different heads of state, and several constitutions: empire, republic, dictatorship, and finally something Santa Anna called a "prudent democracy." Americans, who had taken Texas out of Mexico and brought it into the Union, were hated figures and widely blamed for the last twelve years of government mismanagement. The quickest way for one Mexican president to be overthrown was to be accused of trying to avoid a "glorious and necessary war" to preserve the territorial "integrity of the republic." The quickest way for a replacement to solidify his position was to proclaim, as Santa Anna would, that "my duty is to sacrifice myself and I will know how to fulfil it! I am decided to die fighting" the United States.

Polk hoped to buy California but could not even get Mexico to relinquish its claim to Texas, lost in battle since 1836. It thought about the Rio Grande the same way Harry Truman would think about Korea and Lyndon Johnson about Vietnam. The river valley was merely the first domino in an aggressor's "grand design" to take everything it could get: next California, then Chihuahua, Tamaulipas, and so on. Better not "open a vast field for the insatiable voracity of our neighbors." Once the process began and Americans flooded into the outlying provinces, no one could know where or if it would stop short of the nation "annexed en masse by the United States."

California, like Texas before it, lay far beyond the grasp of Mexico City. Nonetheless, in the face of public outrage, no regime could sell territories it could barely govern unless it could prove the alternative was national extinction. Unfortunately, this was not indisputable as long as Mexicans reprinted and quoted English newspapers still embittered over the War of 1812. The London *Times* and others assured their Latin American readers that the United States was just a "boasting" bully with "imperial pretentions"; it did not have the government, army, and officer corps to invade anything more substantial than an Indian tribe. Such contempt, foreclosing painful concessions, led to a war that threatened the extinction Mexico ultimately feared.

All this was not clear to President Polk. He sent an American army on a mission of coercive diplomacy, brandishing force when money, diplomacy, and verbal warnings did not acquire his objectives. However, military demonstrations around the northern periphery and the Gulf of Mexico elicited little except public declarations that "defeat and death on the Sabine would be glorious and beautiful" compared with an "infamous and execrable" peace signed in Mexico City. Nonetheless, as Polk once predicted, neither Mexico's president nor its congress was "mad enough to declare war." Maintenance of the Mexican army (21 million pesos per annum) was twice the net revenue of the government, which was already deeply in debt. Consequently, Polk had to take the initiative by provoking a minor and measured clash of arms, as described by his adviser, Thomas Hart Benton, chairman of the Senate's Committee on Military Affairs: Polk "wanted a small war, just large enough to require a treaty of peace and not large enough to make military reputations dangerous for [his] Presidency. Never were men at the head of a government less imbued with military spirit, or more addicted to intrigue."

Addicted or not, the administration was not very good at the intrigue, certainly no match for Santa Anna, soon to resume leadership of Mexico's government. Polk's plans to the contrary, he got a protracted campaign terminated only by the occupation of Mexico City, a far cry from the brief border skirmish at the Nueces River that was supposed to start and stop the conflict in 1846. The

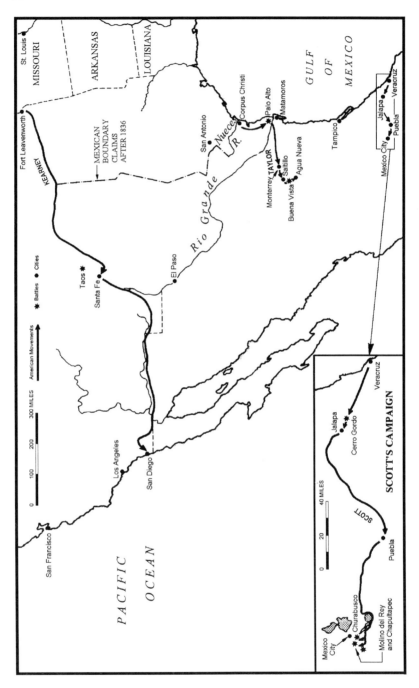

The Mexican War

president positioned troops in south Texas and waited for Mexico to negotiate. When it did not respond, he ordered General Zachary Taylor to occupy the disputed area between the Nueces and the Rio Grande. Shortly thereafter, American and Mexican forces clashed on 24 April. Polk quickly attached the congressional resolution on the war to appropriations for Taylor, thereby tying presidential policy to support for troops in the field. While clever in the short run, this made the vote a misleading indicator of long-term support, particularly because the Democratic majority in the House of Representatives prevented all debate on policy. This was fine with most Whigs, who realized that dissent during war "requires much prudence in its management." Five hours after Polk submitted his claim that Mexico "invaded our territory and shed American blood upon American soil," the House voted 172 to 14 for war. The next day, 13 May, the Senate voted 40 to 2. Calhoun complained privately that if Congress had been granted one day to examine the evidence, less than 10 percent of its members would have supported President Polk.

Within months Calhoun was saying that "the administration and the country are already tired of the Mexican War"; Polk was saying that "peace must be conquered in the shortest space of time." Consequently, the White House reassessed its original plan of action to wage a peripheral, low-casualty campaign. Under that concept of operation, the navy was to blockade Mexican ports, raising the enemy's level of discomfort. Some regular army units were to grab California and New Mexico, the ultimate objectives, while others were to hold defensive positions south of the Rio Grande until the dispirited enemy, after charging into the military wall, made peace by accepting this fait accompli. Mexico, still uncooperative, would not charge or negotiate. It threatened to conduct a guerrilla resistance of indefinite duration. Meanwhile, the U.S. public—and individual citizens of various political persuasions (including antiwar Whigs)—vacillated between stopping the war as "folly" and a "vigorous" prosecution taking "the most direct and shortest road to [Mexico] City."

Calhoun, no favorite of the administration, advised the president to continue the cordon defense at the Rio Grande because expansion into arid territory inhospitable to slavery would reduce the congressional strength of the South. Senator Benton, Calhoun's enemy since 1819, had already warned Polk that this would only "prolong the war and ruin the Democratic party." A third (but highly informal) presidential adviser seconded Benton at the expense of Calhoun, although Santa Anna did it through intermediaries lest "his countrymen form an unfavorable opinion of his patriotism." Mexico's past president told Polk's secret emissaries that America would have to subject his country to more military pressure (at least take Tampico) if its rulers were to have a credible excuse for selling territory. Hardly a disinterested observer, this man who rose to the top of the political pile by fighting invaders in the 1830s was playing a duplicitous game with Washington and Mexico City. He wanted America to humiliate the government that had exiled him to Cuba in 1844. Then he could return on a wave of public approval as the savior of the homeland from the Yankee horde. If he then got caught between anti-American sentiment and the American army, that was a small price for the presidential palace.

The day Polk signed the bill expanding the U.S. Army he ordered the navy to let Santa Anna sail right through the American blockade. Then he tried to create the military conditions Santa Anna said he needed, as explained in Polk's party newspaper: "Bring pressure home to the people of Mexico . . . [to] feel the evils of the war . . . so they may appeal to their Government for peace." Meanwhile Santa Anna, back in Mexico City, would tell his constituents that he was luring the Yankees, "blinded by pride," to their destruction.[7]

WARS BETWEEN GENERALS AND POLITICIANS

Polk's new policy to prosecute the war "with increased energy and power in the vital parts of the enemy's country" created civil-military conflict on the American side. The "inactive" strategy now abandoned, the army grew fivefold from 8,500 to 47,000 men, along with 70,000 volunteers in state regiments. Officers were not ready for this sudden augmentation, having believed that "Mexico may bluster" but is not "insane"; "she will soon be driven to terms." Unprepared, they were quite reluctant to take recent recruits into offensive operations before they were trained, disciplined, and indoctrinated. Polk, as a devotee of Jackson, had far more faith in the inherent abilities of citizen-soldiers, "the best troops in the world." He had far less faith in his senior officers. Their professional prudence was certainly not the way to win the trust of a president who believed they "are all Whigs and violent partisans. Not having the success of my administration at heart, [they] seem disposed to throw every obstacle in the way of my prosecuting the Mexican War successfully." Caution meant protraction, and protraction was part of a plot "to see the Government embarrassed" and "turn this war to party & political account."

Winfield Scott, the commanding general of the U.S. Army and the most partisan of the lot, had received votes at the Whig presidential nominating conventions in 1840 and 1844. In his military capacity, he planned campaigns with methodical care: "head-work, the slow, scientific process." Unfortunately, Scott's profound knowledge of history, theory, and operations did not impress the president, who would complain that "if I had a proper commander of the army, who would lay aside the technical rules found in books, . . . Santa Anna & his whole army could be destroyed or captured in a short time." Polk wanted a no-frills soldier, not "a visionary" nicknamed "Old Fuss and Feathers." Scott survived because Polk surmised he could not find someone more politically correct. In fact, Zachary Taylor, in command near the Mexican border, was lukewarm on politics; he had never voted for president in his life. Polk still gave credence to the poison-pen letters of his confidant, Gideon Pillow, a Tennessee militia colonel whom Taylor did not trust leading troops in combat because he was "a lawyer with much to learn as regards his new profession."

Taylor did not like amateurs, even if he looked like a sloppy militiaman himself (hence his nickname, "Old Rough and Ready"). Nonetheless, Pillow was convinced that Taylor's personnel decisions were "intended to drive the President's friends [namely, himself] in disgrace from the service." After he "paid him back in full" through reports direct to Polk, the president described Taylor as a "bigoted partisan" who was "hostile to the administration." That notion was not only wrong but also self-defeating. It did not help the president select an army commander. By statute, some professional officer had to fill that role. "Nothing but stern necessity"—and the opportunity to escape personal "responsibility of any failure of the campaign"—forced Polk to conclude that Scott was "the best we could do," faint praise for the man about to conduct the most skillful expedition in U.S. history, aside from Desert Storm in 1991.

Scott, the symbol of professionalism, held equally strong feelings about the Polk administration, accusing it of plotting to sabotage the efforts of "every general who would not place [the] Democracy above God's country." This close association between senior officers and the antiwar party is an object lesson in the ironies of political-civil-military relations. Like most coalitions, the Whig-army alliance was produced by a common enemy, the western Democrats. Polk and other war hawks of 1846 never favored a professional military force, "contrary to the genius of our free institutions." Nor did they support the breeding place of "snobbish officers," the U.S. Military Academy, where according to a graduate named William T. Sherman, cadets "are easily convinced of the vast superiority of themselves over everybody else." Jackson, Polk, and other western Democrats sent their offspring to West Point to get a free education at the foremost school of civil engineering. However, knowing a sore point among the electorate, they proposed its abolition on grounds that military commissions should be available to "all citizens, like every other department of government." The Academy, allegedly "aristocratic and anti-republican," made the officer corps an "exclusive privilege." In 1846 nearly 75 percent of it came from West Point (in 1990, only 13 percent did so).

Rather than the standing army, Democrats favored the state militias and federal volunteers, where elected politicians or the men in the ranks chose the officer corps. In a war not supported by most Whigs, Democrats virtually monopolized the newly commissioned commanders. However, the administration and the standing army that it loathed still had a common interest in a short, quick war. Polk wanted the conflict to end before antiwar sentiment could swell against him. Regulars desired to "settle the business" quickly for reasons of their own. Rather mum about the cause and wisdom of the war, the officer corps was outspoken about the impact of the conflict on their careers. Professional soldiers had been smarting over claims that they were "kid glove dandies" in need of help by citizen-soldiers since at least 1815. Frontier politicians were especially inclined to say that "a corps of women would be as serviceable against Indians as a corps of West Point graduates." The regulars, in turn, sick of patrolling Indian territory, were loath to share the "glorious chance" to fight a conventional battle, something that might not reappear for another thirty years. They wanted to win the Mexican War "before the volunteers arrive," claim to have "rescued [the army] from annihilation," and subject it to relentless attack "in and out of Congress."

"This Mexican affair is a glorious thing for West Point," gushed Captain Robert E. Lee, class of 1829; "every one must see the difference between the commencement of the present war & the last." Lieutenant Edmund Kirby Smith, class of 1845, "hoped now that Congress will give us the credit of being ready & willing to do our duty. . . . [It will] let the Military Academy alone for the present." But however much "the sons of West Point covered themselves with glory," especially in the first engagements, where "there were no volunteers with us," newly minted officers frequently outranked them in the field. They turned to Whigs for institutional protection from "Mustangs," "Mohawks," "mushroom generals," and "vile Volunteers"—not endearing terms for citizen-soldiers. The Whigs, in turn, needed senior officers to win national elections, especially because of their antiwar position.

Polk grasped one component of antimilitary ideology by invidiously comparing the standing army to "citizen soldiers . . . ever ready . . . to rush with alacrity, at the call of their country, to her defense." Whigs grabbed the other pole with charges of "Executive usurpation," that is, ramming through Congress this "horrible war" without open debate. At the same time, they paraded their participation in it to dodge the Democratic charge that they were "traitorous, aristocratic, tory federalists" whose "aid and comfort" to Santa Anna did "more to prevent a peace than all the armies of the enemy." Military service would likely pay political dividends to future standard-bearers or the sons of the pillars of the party, Daniel Webster and Henry Clay—that is, before they died in military service under Scott and Taylor, respectively. Their commanders survived to receive Whig presidential nominations, thanks to party loyalists also critical of the war. Abraham Lincoln, who said the conflict was "unnecessary and unconstitutional," was a charter member of the club to nominate Taylor for president in 1848. With him at the top of the ticket, Lincoln thought Illinois Whigs could pick up another congressional district, although he actually would lose Illinois. Taylor was far more popular in Massachusetts, which he carried almost two to one, even though (or because) its legislature led the nation in condemnations of this "war against humanity."

Polk understood the Whig temptation to nominate a "military chieftain," such as it condemned. He had two ways for dealing with senior officers supposedly "opposed to the administration." First, Polk became commander in chief in fact as well as title. Eventually, he lamented, constant pressures on the presidency made it "impossible to give much attention to the details in conducting the war." One wonders what level of minutiae Polk aspired to control. He delved as deep as buying steam transports and trying to plan America's first major amphibious invasion, that at Vera Cruz in 1847.

When Polk could not be his own military commander, he tried other ways to lift credit for winning the war from Whigs in the upper echelons of the army. He took special pains to praise enlisted men, who "would gain victories over superior forces if there were not an officer among them." Because officers had to be among them, Polk commissioned eleven new generals of volunteers directly from civilian society, all loyal Democrats. To command above the brigade level, where most of these appointments took place, the president adopted Benton's suggestion for legislation making this militia colonel, who had never seen a real battle, America's first lieutenant general since George Washington.

The bill making Benton supreme commander of the entire theater was dead on arrival at Capitol Hill. Whoever filled Washington's military slot seemed sure to fill it in postwar politics. In 1813 generals, the secretary of war, and the secretary of state fought among themselves for the three-star billet that never was created due to jealousy among Federalists and civilians with no hope to be the commander "destined for the President's chair." In 1846, when Whigs and eastern Democrats rejected the Benton proposal, Polk turned to Gideon Pillow, "one of the shrewdest men you ever knew." Jacksonians made little distinction between military and political operations. When Pillow engineered Polk's nomination at the 1844 Democratic convention, one member of their state delegation told him that he was "a great General and in the first war we have I shall command the Malitia [sic] of Tennessee." Apparently, this also seemed sensible to Polk, who made this thirty-five-year-old attorney, who had saved his brother from a murder charge, a major general in the army marching toward Mexico City in 1847, second in command to Winfield Scott.

Hardly surprising, descriptions of Pillow were divided along partisan lines. Polk called him "a gallant and highly meritorious officer"; Whigs called him a "third-rate Country lawyer." Professional soldiers who saw Pillow firsthand agreed with both depictions: brave but "as consummate an ass as any army, modern or ancient, has ever" had. At the Battle of Cerro Gordo, where his brigade suffered eighty casualties in a few minutes, he attacked two hours late and from the wrong direction, after ignoring advice from the elites of the army, engineers such as Lee, Joe Johnston, and P. G. T. Beauregard. ("Human stupidity," said Lieutenant Daniel Harvey Hill, "can go no farther than this.") But whatever Pillow's worth in battle, he occupied an excellent position for spying on Scott and performing an all-purpose mission as "the confidential officer of the Government, upon whom the President relied to guard and protect the honor of the country."

When Polk let Scott command in the field, the latter gushed that he would take any volunteer general Polk wished to send. At least initially, Scott and Pillow leaned over backward to accommodate each other. The commanding general not only asked "the President's other self" for approval about negotiations with the Mexican government. He listened to advice about military tactics from this citizen-soldier known for bonehead frontal assaults. Pillow, in turn, flattered Scott's vanity, as advised by Polk's secretary: "The good fame of an officer in any manner subordinate depends on the name [he gets] in official reports and the opportunity given him by the command." Kept out of combat by Taylor, Pillow could not afford to tangle with Scott, lest the hope of the Tennessee Democrats for a new General Andy Jackson go up in smoke.

This artificial interlude of mutual forbearance was only temporary. There were simply too many personal and political conflicts between Scott and the Pillow junta dating back nearly to before Pillow was born. Scott always hated amateurs and political generals, *"utterly unfit for any military purpose."* In the War of 1812, when drilling his brigade near the Canadian border, he feared infiltration by citizen-soldiers looking for another chance to loot. By 1818 Scott stood convinced that "Gen'l Jackson and the Western militia seem likely to throw all other generals & the regular troops into the background." Jackson, reciprocating, labeled Scott one of the "intermeddling spies and pimps of the War Department." In 1835, when President Jackson controlled that agency, Scott dared disregard his advice to force the Seminole Indians to stand and fight by chasing down their women and children. Never Jackson's equal at irregular warfare, Scott took three heavy columns on a conventional sweep of the Florida swamps and blamed his failure, at a court of inquiry, on the militia the president urged him to use: I could have won with "good troops, not volunteers." Now in the Mexican War, run by Old Hickory's disciples, Scott felt subject to a "continuation of the Jackson persecution," never forgetting Pillow was a member of Tennessee's first political family.

Never one to believe that the regulars needed much assistance, Scott felt that volunteer units were an excuse "to give commissions or *pay* to western Democrats. Not an eastern man, not a graduate of the Military Academy and certainly not a Whig would obtain a place." Never one to doubt that a cabal of "conspirators coalesced" against him, Scott was as paranoid as Polk, especially after Pillow told the press that he himself "was in command of all forces engaged." By inference, Scott stood around and watched. No cause for alarm, this was a national blessing because Tennessee's leading citizen-soldier possessed a "masterly military genius and a profound knowledge of war, which has astonished the mere martinets of the profession." Scott, more outraged than astonished, thereupon arrested Pillow. That action only confirmed Polk's suspicion of his "extreme jealousy lest any other Gen'l Officer should acquire more fame in the army than himself." The president released his friend and convened a court of inquiry to investigate Scott for bribing Mexicans to accept the treaty Polk had offered them. The president, finding a new commander in William O. Butler, former Democratic candidate for governor of Kentucky, may have done a service to his party but not to Robert E. Lee: "General Scott having crushed the enemy and conquered a peace, can now be turned out as an old horse to die."

Although Scott and Pillow were world-class prima donnas, their friction and respective reliefs transcended their egos, making each man a martyr for their respective positions about the role of the expert in a democracy. Pillow, who thought removal by the villainous Scott would make him a national hero of the first order, symbolized the cause of the common citizen-soldier. Scott, "the great cause of our success," according to Lee, symbolized the standing army that credited itself with winning the war. "He is really a very great man," said Lieutenant George McClellan, who attributed his hero's persecution to the national "folly" of military appointees recruited from urban saloons and the county courthouses. Scott, while unwilling to give credit to citizen-soldiers, shared it with McClellan's alma mater, where (Scott claimed) cadets were uniformed in the gray cloth his brigade wore when they beat the British in 1814. "This army, multiplied by four, could not have entered the capital of Mexico" if not for the "science of the Military Academy," Scott's grave site in 1866.[8]

WINFIELD SCOTT AND LIMITED WAR: MILITARY ART, MEXICANS, AND VOLUNTEERS

Scott and James K. Polk obviously had different opinions about the contributions made by professional soldiers and volunteers. Otherwise, they had a great deal in common, although both denied it to the day they died. They both were waging a limited war for the acquisition of outlying provinces, particularly California. True, Polk was tempted toward greater acquisitions, but he never accepted the total annexation position of various newspapers that wrote "like the Sabine virgins, [Mexico] will soon learn to love her ravishers." Polk needed a conflict to get a treaty; Mexico would not cede territory any other way. Scott, whom Polk hated, was the ideal tactician, as the general put it, "to conquer a peace." He sought to win the war without leaving Mexico or America too embittered to negotiate, as might have happened if he had measured his accomplishments in blood. As it was: "Vera Cruz must be taken with a loss not to exceed one hundred men; for every one over that number I shall regard myself as his murderer . . . although I know our countrymen will hardly acknowledge a victory unaccompanied by a long butcher's bill."

Granted, aside from enemy lancers and cavalry, Scott did not face first-class competition. Most Mexicans would not forgo personal, factional, and sectional rivalries, if only for the duration of the American invasion. This perpetuated serious personnel problems, from the rank and file through the senior leadership. Since the provincial governments ignored the capital's call for better recruits, Mexican lines were manned by undernourished campesinos unfamiliar with the machinery of field artillery. The whole Mexican effort seemed paradoxical to Americans. "A stubborn and foolhardy people, who do not know when they are conquered," resisted at the political level, refusing to concede defeat. At the same time, in any particular battle, according to Lieutenant Ulysses S. Grant, they "simply quit, without being particularly whipped, but because they had fought enough."

Whatever Mexican soldiers did, Scott still faced operational problems that dismayed the American public as well as his peers. Taylor said he himself would need at least 25,000 men to capture Monterrey, let alone Mexico City, whose conquest took 30,000 French army regulars and an Austrian archduke eighteen months in 1861. Half of Scott's original contingent were volunteers who returned home months before the end of the war. He still won the war in six months with 10,000 men, many suffering malaria and chronic dysentery. One need not say, as did Grant, that Scott's strategy and tactics were "faultless." One still may wonder who else could have maneuvered and preserved what soldiers called "our little sickly and enfeebled army" from Vera Cruz to Mexico City—260 miles into enemy territory, without supply lines for food, water, ammunition, and reserves. The Duke of Wellington was once of the opinion of the condescending London press: Scott "cannot capture [Mexico] city and he cannot fall back upon his base." In 1848 Europe's greatest general said that Scott's "campaign was unsurpassed. . . . He is the greatest living soldier."

To be sure, the U.S. Army had what generals call moral or psychological ascendancy over its opponent before they ever met on the battlefield. Mexico had long described itself as Poland and America as the "Russian threat" of the Western Hemisphere: a barbarian horde with great "tenacity, endurance and energy" eager to eradicate a more refined but weaker nation. However, a failure in battle would have shredded the reputation of American invincibility. Scott's military operations sustained, if not enhanced, the myth. His opponents selected the time and place of contact: close terrain and high ground naturally suited to the defense. Scott still managed to place men and mobile artillery on the enemy's flanks and rear, rendering their lines "panic struck." His tactical deployment of this decisive weapon offset the numerical disadvantage he faced throughout the conflict, frequently two or three to one. To quote Lee, one of the West Point engineers who found ways around the enemy's strongpoints, Scott "sees everything and calculates the cost of every measure." To quote a Mexican field commander: "If we were to plant our batteries in Hell, the damned Yankees would take them from us."

Scott, a military intellectual with a self-described "predilection for France," had studied Napoleon's campaigns intensely, as interpreted by Henri Jomini, the military theorist whose books occupied a prominent place in Scott's baggage train since the War of 1812. No doubt, Scott recalled Napoleon's foredoomed strategy in Spain, where he lost 75,000 soldiers to what Jomini called a popular uprising by "a fanatical people . . . under the appeal of its priests." Fear of a repetition of this event was common in America when Scott set out for Mexico City in 1847. Analogies were also drawn to other protracted guerrilla wars: Napoleon in Russia and the U.S. Army's inability to defeat the Seminoles for less than $40 million dollars.

Professional soldiers, such as Scott and Taylor, thought military conflicts should be waged between armies—ideally between men like themselves, common citizens and the public not invited. In Mexico, they warned their subordinates:

"We have not come to make war upon the people or peasantry of the country," a self-defeating enterprise. "We may ruin and exasperate the inhabitants and starve ourselves. Not a ration for man or horse would be brought in, except by the bayonet." Reminiscent of English quartermasters gouged by colonial Americans in the French and Indian War, U.S. officers purchased substandard supplies at "the highest prices," paying gold for worn-down nags and work cattle said to be mustangs and prime beef. All ranks supplemented their diet with eggs and potatoes, three cents each from the local vendors.

The Polk administration wanted to "pressure" the citizenry "to use their best efforts to bring about a state of peace." It had reason to complain that "mild treatment" encouraged Mexicans "to wish the continuance of hostilities"; even Santa Anna, through his local agent, sold mules and cattle to Scott's contractor at Vera Cruz. While tough talk was easy in Washington, in Mexico the mass of population seemed "sufficient [to one soldier] to have crushed our whole force into utter annihilation without the aid of any other arms than clubs and rocks." Officers took care to advance without breeding more hatred for Americans, as noted by a Spanish diplomat who said that common people "received them more like travelers than enemies." Said a thankful lieutenant: "The dark eyed Senoritas chat, sing, ride or promenade with us, as if we were not heretic invaders and conquerors of their native land."

Scott, in particular, was soft on enemy citizens but hard on his own soldiers: "A rigid discipline is the first and great want of this army." Fifty lashes was standard punishment for illegal entry and petty theft; hangings for rape and murder, even after soldiers were found mutilated, presumably by criminals, since Scott's policies forestalled systematic guerrilla resistance. U.S. military volunteers were less appreciative than the natives, feeling Scott and company were aliens of some sort. They wondered how "in the nineteenth century an American citizen is subjected to the dishonor of being publicly . . . tied up and whipped like dogs in a market yard in a foreign land."

The American army went deep into Mexico on the false assumption, encouraged by Santa Anna, that the next Yankee victory would force negotiations that would end the war. The expedition was on the outskirts of Mexico City when he asked Scott to breach the outer defenses of the ancient fortress and await concessions, standard operating procedure in limited wars. Scott, having planned to threaten the city, not capture it, declared a two-week armistice and wrote his opponent that too much blood had "already been shed." To misinformed Mexicans, he looked weak and on the verge of defeat. Others, more aware of the facts, wanted Scott to proceed, defeat, and discredit the incumbent government, exactly what Santa Anna wanted when he was out of power. Either way, Mexican mobs screamed, "Let the Yankees die!"; their congress forbade talks until Americans went home and indemnified their country for the entire cost of the war. Santa Anna, under these circumstances and in light of his claims about victory, could not make the concessions he secretly promised, especially after American newspapers reprinted in Mexico City revealed his prior collusion with the Polk administration. He consequently used the two-week armistice to rebuild his defenses. That was the last time any American fell for his swan song about needing one more excuse before he could surrender. A loyal intermediary, defending Santa Anna, maintained America was to blame. His client could not capitulate with honor to the ragged force of less than 10,000 men Scott was given to command.

The whole affair seemed "strange" to one officer: "a conquering army on a hill overlooking an enemy's capital, which is perfectly at our mercy, yet not permitted to enter it, and compelled to submit to all manner of insults from its corrupt inhabitants." Scott subsequently explained to an angry secretary of war that if America "wantonly" drove the government out of Mexico City, "we might scatter the elements of peace, excite a spirit of national desperation, and thus indefinitely postpone the hope of accommodation." Accurate as far as it went, Scott's statement made no mention of his trepidation at letting citizen-soldiers loose in a city laden with gold, at least according to legend. Some young Americans were satisfied to fight "one hard battle, come out safe, [and] then return home with some honor." Others, away from their families for the first time in their lives, foresaw "a grand jubilee in the halls of the Montezumas," that is, a unique opportunity to frolic in ways their strict Anglo-Protestant culture did not allow. Such behavior was tacitly accepted back home if it was restricted to a den of sin and iniquity, one reason a substantial number of veterans joined private (filibuster) expeditions to Latin America after the Mexican War. During the war itself, highly questionable conduct could be justified on grounds of necessity: "the yoke of papal oppression [would be placed] upon every state of this Republic" if Mexico won the war. In fact, many citizen-soldiers went on a spree even before they left the United States. "The sooner they are removed the better," said a newspaper in Cincinnati. When what the regulars called the "lawless, drunken rabble" got to Mexico, they could be particularly tumultuous, especially when they anticipated "gaining glory and honor" but found boredom behind the front lines.

Appalled by the indiscipline of their own subordinates, some officers of volunteer units concluded that militiamen should be confined to their home locales. The farther they got away from "their own firesides," the more they acted according to "a new morality." Professional soldiers were less shocked by what they witnessed and probably less impressed by the statements that citizen-soldiers were "honorable men at home." Most of the volunteers came from Texas, Tennessee, Kentucky, and Mississippi, whose governors offered to fill all the military manpower quotas left by Massachusetts, Connecticut, and Rhode Island. According to President Polk, "Experience has proven that no portion of our population are more patriotic than the hardy and brave men of the frontier." According to the army, which had policed conflicts with Indians since the 1780s, pioneers were hardly paragons. They had a long history of trading guns, selling liquor, and stealing tribal land, all the while "sneering at the authority of the United States." In Mexico, where common Americans came into contact with another "miserable, ignorant, filthy race," their conduct seemed no better to the regulars who sympathized with Mexicans as they often did with "poor harmless" Indians whom "we had to fight."

"The people are very polite to the regulars," wrote George McClellan, "but they hate the volunteers . . . [who] think nothing of robbing and killing Mexicans." Scott wrote the secretary of war that "our militia and volunteers have committed atrocities . . . sufficient to make Heaven weep, & every American, of Christian morals, blush for his country." Zachary Taylor told his soldiers that "such deeds cast indelible disgrace upon our arms and reputation." He was probably preaching to the West Point choir.

Scott and his army received plaudits from Congress for their "good" behavior and his "judicious conduct." Had the president not despised professional soldiers, he might have concluded that they should not be burdened with political generals and volunteers. Polk needed strictly disciplined soldiers to win the war without creating lasting bitterness. The standing force of 1846, which Grant called the most "efficient army for its number and armament [that] ever fought a battle," was uniquely suited for the mission of coercive diplomacy. Nonetheless, the president also sent down to Mexico what a West Pointer called an "undisciplined compound of material." They might have confirmed propaganda about destruction at the hands of Protestant America if it were not for officers who "hate volunteers as they do the devil. There is no love lost," said a citizen-soldier, "for the volunteers hate them."[9]

PARTISAN IMPACT AND PEACE TREATY

If Scott had not threatened his raucous volunteers with capital punishment, he might not have maintained the discipline required to capture and control Mexico City. His mastery turned out to be a mixed blessing; Scott was too successful for the political goals he sought. While engaged in a limited war, American had captured a major prize, the enemy capital. Polk escalated his objectives, originally set when the army was encamped in South Texas. His new set of annexations included territory as far south as Tampico and a United States canal zone across Mexico's narrow waist. After all, nations rarely trade the enemy's seat of government for the chance to buy an outlying province, even one described (like California) as "the garden of the world." If America did that, it would relinquish most of what it conquered, hardly sensible to the president and the secretary of state, who now wanted territory commensurate with "the blood which has been shed and the money which has been expended."

For domestic political reasons, Polk selected Nicholas Trist, the chief clerk of the State Department, to negotiate a peace. The president had learned an important lesson from congressional refusal to make Thomas Hart Benton lieutenant general. He did not want senators to reject a treaty to deny credit to a fellow politician who might be their rival for the White House. At the same time, the president needed a civilian commissioner, if only to take credit for peace from Winfield Scott. Because Trist was an obscure civil servant, he could be trusted to perform as instructed, as well as be ready to join Scott's expedition the day it landed at Vera Cruz. Then a loyal protégé (a Gide Pillow in diplomatic garb) would be present whenever Santa Anna decided to negotiate, hopefully long before the army ever got to Mexico City.

The administration, trusting Scott even less than Congress, told Trist to consult Pillow and gave him the power to suspend combat, as well as relocation of the army. Scott, enraged, thought this "an attempt to place me under the military command" of a mere "functionary of my government." This exacerbation of civil-military relations, bad to begin with, paid no dividends. All hopes to the contrary, Mexico would not concede.

By August 1847 Washington virtually gave up on limited war and talked of taking over "all Mexico," not just San Francisco, Santa Fe, and San Diego. Nonetheless, Trist still did not use his military leverage for maximum territorial gain lest this destroy the Mexican government, the legitimate adversary and America's best hope for eventual peace. If that happened, the military expedition would turn into a conflict "against the [Mexican] People," a nightmare for him and Scott, who suddenly discovered common ground with Trist, a West Point graduate himself. They desperately wanted to avoid a long-term occupation responsible for dealing with anarchy, crime, and popular "resistance." For domestic reasons, they also opposed what Trist called a new "war of conquest." Scott, a Whig ashamed of "territorial aggrandizement at the expense of Mexico," hoped a peace between moderates on both sides of the border would refute the "parties" of war, that of Polk and Santa Anna. Trist, a Democrat worried that the conflict was splitting the United States, feared secession movements among anti-war elements, especially in the North.

By mid-1847 Scott and Trist, who had become fast friends, were more committed to Polk's original policy than was Polk himself. Their impatience to arbitrate compromised both parties—Washington and Santa Anna—especially when they raised a slush fund on "condition that he would conclude a peace." After stories about "foreign gold" surfaced in Mexican politics, they tried to soothe the pride of the beaten enemy with pleas to end "this unnatural war between the two great republics of this continent." This just encouraged further Mexican resistance and inflamed the pride of the Polk administration: Why would Americans bribe or beg, if winning; the loser, not the winner, is supposed to say the war was a mistake? Serious negotiations began only after U.S. forces occupied the capital and threatened to destroy the remains of the government, although that was always the last thing Scott had in mind.

Even some U.S. Army regulars, by 1848, lost all patience with politics and procrastination. As the North would propose after failure to defeat the South in 1862, the quartermaster of the Fifteenth Regiment wished to "impose crushing contributions, burn every town that offers resistance, blow up their churches and take no prisoners"; then the enemy "will humbly sue for terms." Trist, although under pressure from below and above, never hid the fact that he still was "resolved and committed to carry home a treaty" consistent with the terms the administration gave him back in 1846. In late 1847 the secretary of state wrote "not to make another offer. . . . The Mexican government must now first sue for peace." No matter. Trist still supported Scott's policy of armistice and restrained force. He pointedly condemned Gide Pillow for wanting "to capture the capital and *then* make peace." To say the least, Polk was taken aback by "an impudent and unqualified scoundrel" who would not do "the simple duty with which he was charged." He had become, Polk reasoned, "the perfect tool of Scott."

Whatever one thought of Scott, he did what he pledged to do in September 1846: "satisfy the expectations of the American people" but minimize damage to Mexico. At an affordable cost, he combined military victories, generous terms, promises to leave Mexico, and new threats along the line of President Polk. (Scott had become the good cop, Polk the bad.) The army had abolished taxes in occupied territory. As of December 1847 it would seize and keep its own revenues—a hint it would finally ravage the countryside, although under proper military supervision. This fulfilled the strategy Scott embraced in April, that of wielding simultaneously "the olive branch & the sword." Together, they enabled Trist to secure Polk's minimal terms: the purchase of California, Arizona, and New Mexico for $15 million—63 percent less than America's original offer. Of course, this bargain price did not count the operational costs of the conquest—$170 million dollars and 13,700 American dead.

Polk fired Trist for "insubordination" but confessed to his diary that the treaty "should not be rejected on account of his bad conduct." More to the point, Polk could not get anything more than Trist delivered. The Whigs controlled the House of Representatives after gaining thirty-eight seats in the 1846 elections. Before the armistice, a thin majority passed a resolution that the war was morally wrong; a vote to withdraw troops in the face of the enemy lost, 41 to 137. Now that a cease-fire removed soldiers from immediate danger, it would be far easier to challenge the president of the United States. Even Whigs who had counseled "prudence, moderation, and discretion" to their colleagues would not pass appropriations for any treaty getting more territory than Trist had stipulated. At worst, Polk worried that the new Congress would withhold men and money to renew prosecution of the war. Then he would have to withdraw his remnant army, as some Whig senators expressly demanded, or risk its physical safety. Either way, for lack of a treaty, Polk might lose California to boot.

The war had long since failed to be "brief, cheap, and bloodless," in the words of Senator Benton. Now that it was "long, costly, and sanguinary," it became a liability for Polk. He was particularly vulnerable among the volunteers he used to dilute Whig control of the regular army. They had not been prepared for military discipline, where soldiers "are but machines and obey without [a] murmur." The military, focused on winning a quick war, was not prepared for them. Food, equipment, shelter, and sanitary facilities were lacking. By August, 60 percent of the First Tennessee had suffered death or discharge largely from disease. When they and other volunteers mustered out of the service, usually as soon as they could, they returned home "complaining most bitterly of the discomforts and risks to which they have been subjected." Their anger brought joy to opponents of a president not above blame, having stocked the ranks with threadbare tents and uniforms lest he run up the national debt. When the Whigs carried Polk's home state in 1847, accusations also fell on Gideon Pillow, who was blamed for the "terrible carnage among the Tennessee troops." The only person to gain major office in this state on the basis of the war was the sole Whig officer in its volunteers, who ran for governor on the slogan he used under General Taylor at the Battle of Monterrey—"Boys, follow me."

John Sherman (Whig from Ohio) was a rising politician whose sense of public opinion would shape policy in the next two military conflicts. In mid-1847 he said that "nothing but a series of victories has sustained the administration in prosecuting the war. There is no doubt but that a large majority of the people consider it an unjust aggression upon a weak republic." Because Polk apparently agreed, he wanted to end the conflict, if only to rob the hated Whigs of the antiwar issue in the 1848 presidential election. Nonetheless, having given up on negotiations, Polk ordered Trist to return to Washington just as the "Peace party" seized power in Mexico City and set up a "provisional government" to negotiate. Trist stayed and created what one observer called a treaty "negotiated by an unauthorized agent, with an unacknowledged government, submitted by an accidental president to a dissatisfied Senate." Some political circles thought the method was ample cause for rejection. Most apparently agreed with newspaper opinion: whatever the faults of the treaty, a now "aimless and endless foreign war is far worse." "We are glad to get out of the scrape even upon these terms."

Despite political disunity and horrendous civil-military relations, America rarely calibrated national goals and military means better than it did in the Mexican War. At least one modern West Point strategist wrote that "it provides an excellent example of the concurrent pursuit of political intercourse and military operations which Clausewitz considered as normal." Considering the accomplishment, it was a shame that the president and the commanding general of his army scarcely talked to one another.[10]

POLITICAL CONSEQUENCES OF MILITARY SUCCESS

Congress had split between those who opposed all territorial conquests and those who wanted all Mexico. When Polk submitted terms substantially short of maximum expansion, the Whigs had no important issues to use against the Democratic party in 1848. They did not draft a platform and nominated Zachary Taylor, who ran on personality, not partisan identification. Henry Clay lamented the selection of a "mere Military Chieftain" in the tradition of Andrew Jackson: such people will succeed each other "until, at last, one will reach the Presidency who, more unscrupulous than his predecessors, will put an end to our Liberties." All such qualms to the contrary, Clay and Webster "acquiesced" in Taylor's nomination because a political "fever" for the general was "spreading far and wide," especially where the war was popular and the Whigs were not—the West and the South. Taylor's presence on the ticket allowed the party to "turn the war thunder against" their rivals. "The noblest Roman of them all" subsequently won the 1848 election because of his heroic military record and because the country "considered him a victim" of political machinations. As Taylor wrote his family soon after his great battlefield victory: so what if "Scott, [Secretary of War] Marcy, Polk and Co. . . . [left] me exposed to the enemy" by taking 9,000 soldiers away. "Through the blessings of divine providence I have disappointed their expectations. . . . The battle of Buena Vista is the best reply I can make to them or their slanderous attacks."

The White House mixed partisanship with war fighting when they stripped Taylor of much of his army because they thought him a Whig. Henceforth, while Scott took the bulk of the regulars with him toward Mexico City, Taylor retained some two cavalry squadrons, three artillery batteries, and 4,000 citizen-soldiers whom he believed "were never intended to invade or carry on war out of the limits of their own country." Largely for this reason, he once wanted to hold a line in Northern Mexico, à la John C. Calhoun. Nonetheless, when now ordered to take up a "strict defensive," an outraged Taylor moved forward to engage Santa Anna and 20,000 soldiers confident of defeating a mélange of amateurs while the U.S. regulars were at sea off Vera Cruz. On George Washington's birthday, while the fife and drums played "Yankee Doodle," Taylor led militiamen at Buena Vista to their greatest triumph since New Orleans in 1815. Most professionals, yet to land, were none too happy; a bit like Taylor himself. They all worried, in his words, that the praise the riflemen received from their hometowns "must prove injurious to keeping up a respectable regular army." No matter that "Old Rough and Ready" felt artillery carried the day, much as it did at the Battle of New Orleans; the man who had bellowed "Double-shot your guns and give 'em hell!" assumed the mantle of Andrew Jackson, although not as the mortal enemy of the Whig/Federalists. Taylor (not Scott or Pillow) would soon be commander in chief because he had led what newspapers called "indomitable volunteers," "not unworthy [of] the old guard of Napoleon."

President Taylor died sixteen months after being sworn into office. Former president Polk, white-haired and careworn by the war, had already passed away in Tennessee. Despite his plans, the Mexican War had not anointed a new Jackson to lead his party in 1848. Gideon Pillow hoped but failed to fit the bill as the heroic citizen-soldier with exploits (according to Pillow) "unequalled in the history of American arms." Nonetheless, the Tennessee Democrats got their revenge when the Whigs nominated Winfield Scott in 1852. "I would be willing to be a *slave* & work in the *mines* of Mexico, the balance of my life," said Pillow, "for the pleasure of *beating him.*"

Pillow's aspirations notwithstanding, the Democrats chose another candidate to use the Mexican War as a stepping-stone. In late 1846 Polk offered Senator Franklin Pierce the post of attorney general. When Pierce refused the position but volunteered for the army, Polk made him a brigadier in Pillow's own division. Wounded in front of Mexico City, Pierce pleaded with Scott and got permission to take his troops into the capital. ("For God's sake, General, this is the last great battle, and I must lead my brigade.") His wish granted, Pierce became a hero, to Scott's regret. In 1852 Pillow organized a political circle of Mexican War volunteers who got the nomination for "the Young Hickory from New Hampshire." Then, chanting "We Polked you in 1844, we shall Pierce you in 1852," they reaped their revenge: attaching Scott for being "fed by the Treasury" (collecting $350,000 in cumulative salary for forty years of service) and for having made "a pack-mule" of volunteers who toted "sixty pounds all day, under a forced march" to Mexico City. In short, their former commander was a haughty aristocrat who hated the common people.

The mind and command style that made Scott a great general made him a terrible candidate. Desperate Whigs tried to out-Jackson the Jacksonians with claims that he was raised on the frontier, slaughtered Indians, and loved militiamen—all to no avail. Even stalwart Whigs called Scott a "bundle of wind & vanity"—and a "conceited, aristocratic ass." The only commanding general to win a war, then lose an election got forty-two votes in the electoral college. In a different field of endeavor, the battlefield, Santa Anna had done better in 1847.[11]

"WHEN THE FOREIGN WAR ENDS, THE *DOMESTIC WAR* WILL BEGIN" *(NEW YORK GAZETTE)*

The Polk wing of the Democratic party believed that territorial expansion had always "cemented" the nation across class and sectional lines: "As you augment the number of states, the bond of union is stronger" because of the necessity for "mutual support." Needless to say, not everyone was nearly this confident nor half so proud at adding nearly 600,000 square miles to the national domain via war with Mexico. At least one Calhoun Democrat predicted that the conquered territory would lead to the "fearful alternatives of a dissolution of our Union, or a degrading submission to dangerous usurpation, insult and outrage" for the South.

This prediction proved wrong: territorial expansion led to both civil war *and* constitutional reconstruction, not to one or the other, although most of the South thought no such thing in 1848. Calhoun warned against expansion but was apt to be considered a "poor old man [who] has truly outlived his greatness." Thus his claim to be the spokesman for his section diminished on the eve of fulfillment of his great desire, that regional unity would replace partisan political identity. This came about as a result of what he wanted to avoid, growing unity in the North against the expansion of slavery. By 1847 Calhoun agreed with an old antagonist, Senator Daniel Webster, Whig from Massachusetts, who warned that "the future is full of difficulties and full of dangers." President Polk, who thought that statements from the Websters and Calhouns were contrived to disparage his achievement, could never fathom their fears. "What connection slavery had with making peace with Mexico is difficult to conceive. I put my face alike against Southern agitators and Northern fanatics."

The president's political party proudly proclaimed that it "waged, to a successful termination, a glorious War." The officer corps of the regular army was more ambivalent, although convinced its exploits were "not surpassed by any military achievement in *all* previous history." Extremely proud of its alumni's conduct of operations, West Point celebrated the Mexican War for years to come. On the other hand, when it came to political objectives, many professional officers leaned toward the opinions of Webster and Calhoun. Barely three months after proceeding to the Rio Grande, Taylor called the conflict one of "conquest and aggrandizement at the expense of a weak power." Scott confided to England's ambassador that, as an American citizen, he was ashamed of the war. This opinion was not restricted to the high command. Take the quartermaster of the Fourth Infantry Regiment. In 1885 this former first lieutenant wrote that the conflict with Mexico "was the most unjust war ever waged by a stronger against a weaker nation. It was an instance of a republic following the bad example of European monarchies." He concluded that "nations, like individuals, are punished for their transgressions. We got our punishment in the most sanguinary and expensive war of modern times."

The author of these words, Ulysses Simpson Grant, was not an armchair observer. In America's next conflict, when many other officers were still applying the limited ways and means of Winfield Scott, he would help devise the more drastic methods required to defeat the South, beginning with Missouri, Tennessee, and Mississippi, whose political leaders and volunteer soldiers played crucial roles in the Mexican War. In 1862 Grant won national fame by demanding his opponent's "unconditional surrender," a phrase that would reverberate through government policy in the next three wars. When he first uttered those fateful words at Fort Donaldson, he had no doubt he could demolish the enemy commander. Grant's memoirs would record, "I had known General Pillow in Mexico, and judged that with any force, no matter how small, I could march up to within gunshot of any intrenchments he was given to hold."[12]

4

The Civil War: Policy
Out of Political Control

One war may provide an abysmal model for another. In 1861 the North planned to wage its contemporary conflict as the nation had conducted the Mexican War: march a disciplined army on the enemy capital and replace an obdurate regime. The president of the Confederacy, perhaps recalling public impatience with the Mexican War, pronounced in the Northeast, planned to exhaust the Union's will by stopping its army short of Richmond. Both sides drastically underestimated their opponent's resolve. From unforeseen necessity, not political plan, the war "degenerate[d] into" what Abraham Lincoln called "a violent and remorseless revolutionary struggle." Because the South ostensibly fought for political independence, not preservation of slavery, the North would resort to arming former slaves to destroy the secessionist challenge to the American polity.

THE WAR AIMS OF THE SOUTH: INDEPENDENCE OR SLAVERY?

The simple fact that the Civil War began when the South seceded from the Union after the Republican victory in the 1860 election encapsulates the paradox of Southern strategy. Secessionists declared their political independence to protect their "domestic institutions" from what Jefferson Davis, president of the Confederate States of America, called the "steady progress towards a transfer of the government into the hands of the abolitionists." He was certainly not unique. The governor of Arkansas said that Abraham Lincoln's administration would simply mean "the Union without slavery, or slavery without the Union." This being the case, the South might have used its military capabilities to reverse the plurality of 1860 in subsequent elections, 1862 and 1864. It could have promised to stop fighting if voters restored Democrats to power. This would have solved the South's stated fear that it "will become another Africa or St. Domingo" governed by radical Republicans akin to John Brown, the instigator of an abortive slave rebellion in 1859.

Reversing an election was feasible given the power the South possessed. However, it insisted on complete, nonnegotiable independence: an objective beyond the means it could deploy against the determined opponent it faced. The North was only committed to fight Southern independence, certainly not chattel slavery, an institution not likely to survive anything approaching total war. In 1755 the governor of Virginia complained that blacks, thinking "the French will give them their Freedom," had become "very audacious" after hearing of the Anglo-American defeat at Fort Duquesne. During the War of 1812, thousands of slaves eagerly joined British colonial marines with the expectation (their officers noted) to "meet [up with] their former masters" in the Chesapeake Bay. Hence, in 1861 there was ample precedent for what Southern unionists and conservative Yankees were already saying: that an unremitting military struggle for Southern independence would destroy slavery. As General William Tecumseh Sherman would write his brother in 1864, the institution was killed "as the natural, logical, and legal consequence of its self-constituted admirers. . . . They are the [real] abolitionists."

For lack of sufficient means, secession was impractical. However, the South did have enough military strength to change the balance of power among competing political parties. In the 1860 election, Democrats had said that "to vote the Democratic ticket is to vote for Peace and the Union; to vote the Republican ticket is to vote for Civil War." Republicans replied that this was just "the old game of scaring and bullying the North into submission to Southern demands and Southern tyranny." If the Battle of Bull Run proved nothing else, it showed that Stephen Douglas was a better prophet than Abraham Lincoln. The subsequent list of casualties might have given his Northern Democrats a winning issue in subsequent elections when they claimed, as in September 1862, that the citizenry "could readily settle the present difficulties of our country by electing men who would put affairs in such a state as would bring the Southern Confederacy back into the Union without any fighting." They were hardly helped by statements from their erstwhile party brethren that "we are not fighting for slavery. We are fighting for INDEPENDENCE and that, or extermination, we shall have." Jefferson Davis, a loyal member of the Democratic party right up to secession, undermined the political campaign strategy of the Northern Democrats.

In 1860 Davis tried to return Franklin Pierce of New Hampshire to the White House to ensure the existence of slavery. Why did he and other Southern politicians now adopt the John C. Calhoun position against partisanship and demand total independence, something even Northerners like Pierce opposed? Ironically, the South could not win a war for independence but could not fight one for slavery. As George Randolph, future Confederate secretary of war, told the Virginia Secession Convention in 1861: the argument of Southern ideologists that the institution was something to be proud of "is recent—it is not backed by sympathy abroad—it has hardly yet had time to be understood and appreciated by our own people."

Explicitly fighting for slavery seemed "the height of folly" to Southerners who felt "there is no instance in history of a people as numerous as we are, inhabiting a country so extensive as ours, being subjected if true to themselves." Only 3 percent of the white population held twenty slaves or more; only 25 percent owned any at all. Furthermore, even newspapers speaking for the planter elite, in the words of the Richmond *Examiner,* admitted there was "lurking in the Southern community a deep-seated feeling of aversion to slavery." Robert E. Lee had called it "a moral and political evil." Davis, as paternalistic on his plantation as a slave owner could possibly be, privately call it "an evil for which there is no cure."

Writing home during the Civil War, slave-owning officers were likely to say that they were fighting for independence and liberty. Indeed, according to one recent study, they were more likely to espouse this ideology than was any other group of soldiers, from the North or South. If slave owners did not want to think they were simply fighting for slavery, one need not doubt that yeomen farmers (some 80 percent of the South) would not wage war, as they put it, "for no rich man's slaves." It was common knowledge that those who would have to be the rank and file of the army had opposed secession in 1861, when Jefferson Davis was condemned as "a renegade and traitor" by a crowd outside his hotel in Chattanooga. Barely 37 percent of the electorate from counties with the lowest ratio of slaves voted for secession, no matter that it might not mean a long and bloody war. In 1861 many Southerners thought it was a temporary ploy to renegotiate the Constitution of the Union. Others said the North would not resist: "A lady's thimble will hold all the blood that shall be shed." Still, as long as secession was perceived to be a defense of slavery, it lacked a strong public mandate. Lincoln exaggerated only somewhat when he suggested on 4 July 1861 that outside of South Carolina the political majority was not "in favor of disunion." Everywhere but there, Mississippi, and Florida, the vote was very close. In Virginia and North Carolina, it initially failed by large margins. In Georgia it passed because proponents rigged the count.

Slavery could never provide the legitimacy independence could by evoking memories "planted down in the depths of the American heart." North and South, the country viewed the American Revolution as "the great political consummation" of human history and the moral standard for all events, war and peace. In 1812 and 1848, proponents and opponents of expeditions to Canada and Mexico argued their positions with claims that contemporary soldiers did or did not emulate their "patriot ancestors." In 1861 both sides once again appealed to the example of the Founding Fathers by arguing about which one really followed in the footsteps of George Washington—"the god of America," Europeans observed. If secessionists could solidify their claim that the "Confederate States of 1861 are acting over again the history of 1776," their authority would not only be secure in the South, where unionists would be labeled "Tories" and the Union army called "the Northern Hessian horde." They could sanction secession among segments of the North, which might then oppose Lincoln the way the parliamentary opposition confronted King George. During the Civil War, the peace wing of the Democratic party would accuse the administration of acts like "those perpetuated by the Mother Country against the colonies," that is, re-creating a military despotism to "deprive us of the cherished principles for which our fathers died."

In 1888 a Confederate veteran recalled that the South "had never been able to understand how any reasonable mind could . . . fail to see the unlawfulness and iniquity of coercion, and they were in a chronic state of surprised incredulity, as the war began, that the North could indeed be about to wage a war that was manifestly forbidden by unimpeachable logic." Abraham Lincoln was able to push the "Copperhead" Democrats to the political margins because he captured Washington's mantle in the North. Jefferson Davis did the same thing in the South—"and the war came." They understood the symbolism of the American Revolution as well as anyone could. When debating Stephen Douglas in 1858 or at Gettysburg in 1863, Lincoln claimed his opponents proposed ideas equivalent to "the divine right of kings." On the way to his inauguration, he said that from the moment he read Parson Weems's *Life of Washington* as a child, he believed the soldiers of the Revolutionary War fought for the principles to which he was committed in 1861. In 1862 he ordered all Union armies, from Arkansas to Virginia, to advance south on George Washington's birthday, 22 February. That same day Davis, standing next to Washington's statue and Washington's portrait on the Great Seal of the Confederate States, was inaugurated president of its government, moved from Montgomery to Richmond, in part to give it legitimacy by proximity to Mount Vernon.

If Davis, "a second Washington" to his following, convinced constituents that "Southern valor still shines as brightly as in the days of '76," tradition would uphold secession, no small factor in a region respectful of the past. In mid-1861 Richmond's foremost newspaper stated, "There is no doubt that the South is more rife with treason than any community that ever engaged before in a struggle with an adversary." By the spring of 1862, that problem was temporarily solved because citizen-soldiers of the South had accepted the historical analogy, as testified by men who wrote that they fought for "rights guaranteed to us by the blood of our forefathers on the battlefields of the Revolution."

Secession also resonated in the day-to-day life of the common people of the South, who scorned work "not compatible with thorough and perfect independence." Since the 1820s they had worried that outside forces threatened the autonomy and self-sufficiency that made them free men, not slaves, a status to be reserved for blacks. Political leaders (especially Southern Democrats) had focused this fear on taxation and commercial corporations, particularly railroads and banks. When the sectional conflict became an independence movement, secession subsumed these other concerns. As one Georgia preacher wrote his son in 1862: "We are fighting for our liberty and independence, not for our [material] interests."

The phrase "fighting for independence" foreclosed the option of using armed conflict to enhance one's bargaining position. The very idea was unacceptable to hard-core Confederates because it had been unacceptable to the revered Founding Fathers in 1778, when the British Empire offered to resolve the issues that grieved them in 1774, such as the repeal of all internal taxes passed since 1763. However, the Continental Congress then had French allies. It could sensibly reply that it would negotiate nothing but a schedule for British withdrawal. The Confederacy, for want of foreign support, was hardly in the same position. Nonetheless, according to one of its officials, "the temper of the people" made reunion on any terms "as impossible as the annexation of the Confederate States to Great Britain in their old colonial condition."

Jefferson Davis followed the same fight/don't bargain formula, this time to defeat. His strategy was to affect political elections in the North, but mainly by prolonging the conflict until its committment collapsed. He ignored sage advice from Generals Lee and Beauregard, somewhat inconsistent themselves. Although more willing to run military risks to win decisive battles, they were also ready to string along enemy public opinion: "We should bear in mind that the friends of peace in the North must make concessions to the earnest desire that exists in the minds of their countrymen for a restoration of the Union, and that to hold out such a result as an inducement is essential to the success of their party." No matter what Lee told Davis, Davis told his public not to "hope to elect any candidate in the North" by appearing "to listen to reunion. . . . Victory in the field is the surest element of strength to a peace party." Soon thereafter Lincoln won reelection, morale crumbled, and 72,000 Confederates deserted in the next four months rather than face what one soldier called "four more long years of war."

Davis—a West Point graduate, Buena Vista hero, and former U.S. secretary of war—had hoped to serve at the front. Confederates, longing for a Caesar or Napoleon, made him president to get a commander in chief who would command, not preside. They got what they did not need: a de facto general staff and war department rolled into one chief executive. The South had some of the greatest battlefield tacticians in American military history. They did not have a grand strategist who could focus on correlating ends with capabilities. Consequently, when their political goal seemed virtually hopeless, their top leaders would not or could not modify it. Davis's response to fundamental strategic problems was to tour the battlefield (a tonic for the ailments that afflicted him in Richmond) and fantasize about a field command: "If I could take one wing and Lee the other, I think we could between us wrest a victory," defined as nothing short of Southern independence.

Until the last year of the war, independence was an objective that produced "unity and harmony" in a society divided into slave-owning and non-slave-owning groups. Whether secession was the goal or a means, it also guaranteed slave property and white supremacy. However, the blood, sweat, and tears of the conflict created fissures between the primary and ancillary war aims of the South. By late 1864, desperation forced Southerners to choose. Some planters talked of trading independence for slavery, as did Alexander Stephens, vice president of the

Confederacy, "halfhearted" secessionist, and advocate of talks with Northern Democrats. Contrary to his position that slavery was the "cornerstone" of the south and the "immediate cause" of the Civil War, Davis and Lee maintained that if they had to set priorities, then "slavery must go," even if this necessitated the enlistment of black soldiers, as favored by one Georgian who had "lost two noble sons" in battle. In early 1865 this man entreated Davis to "take hold of all the means that God has placed within our reach to help us through this bloody war for the right of self-government. . . . I had rather live with any people [presumably free blacks] than the Yankees, and so every one talks whom I hear speak on this subject."

This gentleman should have spoken to a broader body of the Confederacy. As a whole, the South remained hopelessly ambivalent, as did many individuals. Those who maintained that the South must "prosecute the war of independence with all the weapons and resources at our command" also said that by emancipating the few slaves who would enter the ranks "the institution itself will be preserved." Those who opposed the innovation said that if the South adopted emancipation it would fail the standard of George Washington because we would "gain our independence by the valor of our slaves." The legislation that finally passed by one vote in March 1865 was a monument to equivocation. Davis and Lee had asked for emancipation and conscription. They got a bill by which slave owners would decide whether to enlist their chattel and could refuse to manumit "as a reward for faithful service in the war against the common enemy."

The slavery-first wing of the Confederacy blocked the last-ditch efforts of the Davis faction. The "political independence at any price" faction had already stymied the efforts of the Stephens bloc to help Democrats with pledges to negotiate if they were returned to power in Washington. Three days before the 1864 election, the vice president complained that hard-core secessionists feared Northerners with "liberal terms of compromise" more than they did Abraham Lincoln. "With a view to our ultimate and permanent separation from the Yankee people, McClellan might be more perilous," according to the Davis band. If he "were President, there might be some appearance again of 'Union men' amongst us." By contrast, Lincoln's "fanaticism" and Grant's "fury" had redeeming virtues. They would "revive our courage and reanimate our efforts" for complete independence. By this time, less belligerent Southern citizens and soldiers had their own agenda. They were holding on "to hear some terms of peace before they run clear over us."

The stubborn commitment to fight on against overwhelming odds defined heroism. At least one junior officer told his Yankee captors, "There are about one hundred thousand high-toned chivalric southern gentlemen whom ye may extirpate, but can never subdue." True or false, this state of mind could be counterproductive for either objective, the retention of slavery or the preservation of independence. Davis told the Confederate Congress in 1863 that the Emancipation Proclamation will "calm the fears of those who have constantly evinced the apprehension that this war might end by some reconstruction of the Old Union." By late 1864 he had nothing to fear aside from 900,000 Union soldiers. The

North had too many bitter memories to negotiate about reunion on the basis of slavery. As early as September 1862, two ministers petitioned Lincoln for emancipation on the grounds that "the struggle has gone too far and cost too much treasure and blood, to allow for a partial settlement." By mid-1863 even Union soldiers who professed to "hate the negroes and believe them better off" as slaves were making war on the South's "peculiar institution." Those people who howl that we are "fighting for the nigger" simply could not "see the difference between the means employed, and the end in view." "We are in war and [will do] anything to beat the south." Furthermore, "as long as slavery exists . . . there will be no permanent peace."

The reign of Union soldiers in the South meant freedom for blacks. Military occupation—search, seizure, arrests, and curfews—meant "slavery" for whites. Plantation owners wrote to their families about "the most desolate, destitute, & degrading condition" beyond all imagination. "If it would close this war, I would be willing to give [the slaves] all up."[1]

THE WAR AIMS OF THE NORTH: DEMOCRACY OR LAW AND ORDER?

When the South left the Union in 1861, many assumed the North had no compelling reason to wage a prolonged struggle against its independence. "The enemy, in yielding the contest, may retire into their own country, and possess everything they enjoyed before the war began." This plausible conclusion was the South's strategic miscalculation. The North never felt about the Civil War the way its descendants did about Vietnam in 1972—that it could go home, forget the recent unpleasantness, and cultivate its own interests. The Confederacy never grasped that the North believed its own fundamental institutions were at stake in the War between the States. Hence Union as well as Confederate soldiers wrote, "I am engaged in the holy cause of defending & preserving [my] home" to be made "secure only in the continuance of the government of [my] country."

Because Northerners believed that secession would destroy the foundations of representative government, many had their own trouble recognizing the depth of the South's commitment to it. Abraham Lincoln, in particular, had a vested interest in denying the intensity of the crisis, having run for president saying calls for secession were a Southern political bluff. When secession occurred, his belief that it was an attack on democracy caused him to feel its support was limited to a small, slaveholding elite. By mid-1862 a similar conviction that the conflict was *the* test to determine if "popular government" could maintain itself "against a formidable internal attempt to overthrow it" motivated Lincoln to fight with an intensity that neither he nor the South could have predicted in 1861.

Mid-nineteenth-century America was a paradox, the most radical and most reactionary nation in the Western world—one of the last to practice chattel slavery, one of the first to allow any male citizen to hold any office irrespective of paternity or wealth. Most Americans believed that they had a duty to protect and propagate their political institutions. Secessionists not only claimed that they were purifying representative government by abolishing contaminants like political parties "trampling the minority under their feet." They said that submission to Northern coercion meant they would "give up the principle of the right of a people to make their own government." (Then "Washington would have labored and lived in vain.") Union volunteers believed the same tenant dictated a different course of action. Commanding officers and privates said the North was "fighting to tell the world that republican government can be sustained." If it fails, "the aristocrats of Europe" will repeat their "old cry that such is the common lot of all republics."

William McKinley, at that time an eighteen-year-old private and later the U.S. president in America's next war, felt he was "doing nothing but [that which] my revolutionary fathers before me have done." Those in agreement had trouble comprehending that secessionists had wrapped their own cause in Washington's robe. A radical Republican like Zach Chandler, senator from Michigan, might lament the "Little Bo-Peep policy" of not tearing right into Dixie. Lincoln simply thought the common "people of the South have too much sense to attempt [to] ruin" the only political system where one of them (he himself) could become head of state. In March 1861 he told an agitated officer named William Tecumseh Sherman to not worry about war: "We'll manage to keep house."

Lincoln's initial policy was to restrain his military force while he appealed to what he poetically called "the mystic chords of memory, stretching from every battle-field and patriot grave." Residual Union sentiment in the South was not just a figment of his imagination, as Confederate conscription teams and tax collectors learned from the resistance in the hills of Carolina, Georgia, Tennessee, and Alabama. Jefferson Davis did not need to read about it; it was always on his mind. This was why he had to appeal, from the beginning of the war, to the South's bedrock sense of honor: that of protecting family, home, and community against outside threats. A month before the first Bull Run, he said that "in this war, rapine is the rule: private residences . . . are bombarded and burnt." Always worried that the South might settle short of complete independence, Davis had a vested interest in total war. Lincoln, at least at first, refused to accommodate him.

Union army officers, for their own reasons, were also reluctant to acknowledge the necessity to take the kind of measures Jefferson Davis was anxious to condemn. "We cannot make good soldiers out of thieves and robbers," was common opinion. "Self-preservation to say nothing of humanity requires that discipline be maintained." Virtually nothing was more important than order to officers who never ceased to complain that violence inflicted on civilians weakened their own army. Their daily responsibility was imposing rules and regulations on common soldiers who always had the potential to become (and sometimes became) a mob beyond their control.

When military men had larger political objectives in the Civil War, they usually differed from men like Lincoln, at least in emphasis. The president would condemn secession as the "essence of anarchy" but primarily wanted to make democracy credible for the world. Officers stressed the other major political objective of the North, that of preserving the fragile "foundations of civil society." Secession was rebellion and rebellion was criminal disorder, a sensitive subject since the 1830s, when rioting took place in numerous American cities. The topic resurfaced as secession, according to the *New York Times,* a week before the bombardment of Fort Sumter: "The issue is between anarchy and order— between Government and lawlessness—between the authority of the Constitution and the reckless will of those who seek its destruction."

Southerners might have been incredulous about the motivation of what they would call "a nation of thieves and robbers." Their skepticism notwithstanding, law and order was the common motif of the Union's most important generals: McClellan, Grant, and Sherman. In 1861 McClellan and Grant used almost the same phrase—McClellan: "The Govt is in danger, our flag insulted & we must stand by it"; Grant: "We have a Government, and laws, and a flag and they must all be sustained." Sherman, more loquacious, felt that the real cause of the secession was "unadulterated democracy," that is, millions of Southerners "thinking themselves sovereign and qualified to govern." This was "but the beginning of the end": first "disunion, civil war, [and then] anarchy universal on this continent." Any man with these chronic fears of disruption would let his troops loose only if he felt there was no other way to win the war.[2]

GEORGE MCCLELLAN AND CITIZEN-SOLDIERS: A GENERAL VERSUS HIS MILITARY MEANS

Indiscipline and disorder are apt to be particularly pronounced in a civil war, where the enemy and the rules of engagement are not clear to most participants. For senior officers, to release the destructive potential of their soldiers in this situation was to risk relinquishing command and control. McClellan never could unleash this power. Grant did it after a year of war. Sherman, who began the war as a devotee of McClellan, ended it as the most thorough practitioner of total war in the high command.

A Philadelphia gentleman, McClellan never liked the rank and file of the regular army. However, "these wretched Dutch and Irish immigrants" seemed a bargain compared with citizen-soldiers who thought regular army officers were "unsympathetic, overbearing and tyrannical" martinets. As a twenty-one-year-old lieutenant, McClellan wrote that "the idea of being killed by or among a parcel of volunteers [under Gideon Pillow] was anything but pleasant." In fact, throughout the Civil War, he maintained a Mexican War mind-set resembling that of his mentor, Winfield Scott, whom he replaced as Union general in chief in November 1861. McClellan set out "to thoroughly organize, discipline & drill" raw recruits until they were "a real Army," such as that which captured, occupied, and pacified Mexico City in 1847. Although McClellan was a gifted administrator and instructor, it was virtually impossible to elevate the Union army—16,000 men in 1860, 637,000 in 1862—to the standards of Scott's expedition: 10,000 men, almost half regulars, the most professional force the United States would ever field to fight a major conflict, aside from Desert Storm in 1991.

McClellan praised his own performance in transforming volunteers into a force that was "magnificent in material, admirable in discipline and instruction, excellently equipped and armed." Privately, he placed little faith in these men, no matter how much they cheered and broke ranks to touch his horse, as if he were the source of their salvation. Since the 1820s, War Department policy was to use professional soldiers as a cadre for each large group of ertswhile civilians making up the rank and file in each major conflict. Winfield Scott, never partial to citizen-soldiers, kept the regulars largely intact. His adherent, George McClellan, would have done more than that. Reminiscent of the stripping of Zachary Taylor of his cadre in 1847, McClellan pleaded that each and every regular be immediately "united in one body," namely, under him. Ironically, his least-trained subordinate was the man most trusted, Alan Pinkerton, military intelligence. This former railroad detective was good at surveillance, a responsibility closely related to his civilian line of work. However, McClellan accepted his inflated estimate that the enemy had a two-to-one numerical advantage. This grossly overstated figure expressed McClellan's own fears about poor Union troop quality in quantitative measurements comfortable to a West Point–educated engineer. More accurate were statements other officers made in 1894 and 1863: "McClellan never realized the mettle that was in the grand Army of the Potomac." "They have the English bull-dog in them. You can whip them time and again but [they are] as full of pluck as ever. . . . Some day or other we shall have our turn."

When successful, in limited engagements, McClellan did not mention the resolve and courage of his men. "I accomplished everything . . . by pure military skill." He was hardly the only general officer in American military history with a large ego. One thinks immediately of Patton and MacArthur. However, neither of these World War II commanders ever spared their troops hard fighting because he thought the mission too difficult for them. At Buna or the Bulge, they demanded that exhausted troops attack enemy positions under horrendous conditions, a malaria-invested jungle or subzero temperatures. McClellan would attack only with well-rested soldiers, "overwhelming fire," and favorable force ratios—all being "necessary to enable this Army to advance with a reasonable certainty of success." Because he conducted such "long and tedious labors" turning volunteers into decent soldiers, he was simply reluctant to expend his assets, à la European generals before the French Revolution. He too thought it took five years to produce infantry that could lay down a volley fire, then make a bayonet charge in formation; more time was needed for cavalry, engineers, and artillery. Because men like these were so hard to replace, generals like them were reluctant to fight.

McClellan lamented "the dreadful responsibility for the lives of my men." The same obligation depressed Grant, who was not the heartless butcher many people thought he was. The real difference between McClellan and his eventual successor was not that McClellan was "tired of the sickening sight of the battle-field." It was their respective opinions about the capacity of citizen-soldiers. Grant had an abiding faith in the rank and file, even if they denied this plain-look-ing man the adulation they bestowed on the charismatic McClellan. Sustaining 55,000 casualties in six weeks during the Wilderness campaign, he had to replace half of the Army of the Potomac, usually with conscripts and recent immigrants. Volunteers, class of 1861, felt the substitutes were mercenaries thinking only of how "to keep out of danger." Grant believed they would be "ready for duty from the moment they report." He would tell the White House that "no other troops in the world" could have withstood the pounding "our men did," even though he wanted anyone the government "can rake and scrape." As for the wounded, evac-uated to the North, they could "think of nothing but staying away from the army until this fighting is over."

Unlike Grant, McClellan believed the government could send him only raw recruits to train—and train, and train. He did not trust them to fight and did not trust them not to loot—activities that "should be treated as high crimes." On the way to Richmond, they did their fair share of foraging and plundering the coun-tryside, despite McClellan's prohibitions. Ten miles outside the enemy's capital, when the Union commander should have concentrated all his attention on over-coming the opponent's defensive positions, he worried that he might not "control fully this army of volunteers. . . . I will do my best to prevent outrage and pillage but . . . I hope that I shall not be forced to witness the sack of Richmond."

McClellan always worried that his soldiers would be "demoralized by suc-cess [or] disaster" and that he could not keep this "contest free from the usual horrible features of civil war." Confederates booby-trapped the countryside with land mines, "the most murderous and barbarous thing [McClellan] ever heard of." He still held to his fundamental conviction that the conflict should be waged exclusively "against armed forces and political organizations," the classic sign-post of limited war. "The confiscation of property . . . or [the] forcible abolition of slavery" was simply not "the means by which we may gain our ends." That end—McClellan's goal—was the rapid restoration of "peace and good order": what conservative Democrats called "the Constitution as it is, the Union as it was, and the Negroes in their place."[3]

THE FAILURE OF DECISIVE BATTLE

Just as Scott entered Mexico City and dictated an acceptable peace, McClellan always hoped to "bring this war to a speedy close" by crushing the rebellion "in one blow" outside Richmond and arresting the agitators who had led the Southern people astray. His fixation on fighting "a decisive battle" was not unique, as judged by people on both sides of the wire. At West Point McClellan, a cautious tactician, and Robert E. Lee, a daring risk taker, had been active members of the Napoleon Club, students and faculty meeting to discuss the climactic battles the emperor waged in 1805–6, not the long campaigns of attrition he fought after 1808. During the first years of the Civil War, leading newspapers looked for the appearance of an American military genius who would execute the emperor's art of war. The *New York Herald* (1861) foresaw another Waterloo; the *Richmond Enquirer* (1862) said that the South "must have an Austerlitz before we can have a peace."

Decisive battle was both cause and effect of the standard definition of heroic action. In turn, heroic action was another cause of war, at least for many men who fought at the front. American soldiers have often been a rather nonpolitical lot more concerned with displaying their courage to themselves, their comrades, and their communities than with the balance of power and national security. "Private soldiers," former private Sam Watkins recalled, "fought as much for glory as the general did." This meant closing the distance between armies by moving forward without flinching, breaking the enemy's lines, pursuing remnants of its army, and forcing its capitulation.

Unfortunately for the nineteenth-century image of manliness, this concept of military courage was not very functional once swords and bayonets ceased to be the ultimate weapon. Equally unfortunate for a nation subjected to attrition warfare, a decisive battle was no longer likely when rifled muskets and cannon had a killing range of 700 and 2,000 yards. Closing with the enemy (called "shock action") could be suicidal, as common soldiers learned in the Civil War. By 1862 men like Watkins who once looked forward to losing an arm to prove themselves heroes were simply thankful to be alive. On both offense and defense, soldiers began "to fight a great deal lying flat on our breasts" behind "rocks, fallen stumps, or anything we can get." This dismayed senior officers on both sides. Between battles (not just in basic training) they drilled soldiers, whose ranks rarely broke when on the tactical defense, testimony to combat discipline. Attack at full tilt was a different matter: Missionary Ridge and Gettysburg becoming anomalies. "The men," said a Confederate colonel in 1864, "seemed possessed of some great horror of charging breastworks which no power, persuasion, or example could dispel." "A fresh furrow in a plowed field," Sherman wrote Grant, "will stop the whole column and all [immediately] begin to intrench."

All this was perfectly reasonable to the rank and file. "In our youth," explained one Michigan volunteer, "we acted upon impulse regardless of consequences, now we think before we act." "The veteran American soldier," said Major General John Schofield, "fights very much as he has been accustomed to work his farm or run his sawmill: he wants to see a fair prospect that it is 'going to pay.'" But however judicious for those on the front lines, such tactics increased the cost of war for the nation as a whole. Without punching a hole and a vigorous pursuit, the final stages of decisive battle, quick victory was impossible, according to Napoleonic tenets of warfare.

Neither side had a distinct qualitative advantage in the American Civil War. General officers were educated in the same military academy and trained in the same antebellum army. Most enlisted men came from the same backgrounds (rural Protestant America), with the same cultural traits and tendencies, despite slavery in the South. Theoretically, Northern industry might have readily mobilized overwhelming resources. However, the Confederate government packed away its states' rights ideology and sponsored a crash program of industrialization. The North failed to arm its infantry with the very latest rifle, the most important weapon in this war. The old guard that controlled the ordnance department until late 1863 disliked magazine-fed weapons. They distrusted the initiative, which threatened to spring from semiautomatic weapons unloaded whenever a target appeared. To get a substantial volume of fire from the standard one-shot rifle ordnance fielded, Union soldiers had to use volley fire. This meant they had to mass and thereby present dense targets for Confederates to kill. As Schofield said in his postwar memoirs: "The greater the mass, the greater the loss—that is all."

Quantity (not quality) was also relatively equal. The North had nearly twice as many men in uniform but had to deploy 33 percent to guard logistics and communications, a problem confronting all invading armies. Because the South was usually on the strategic defensive, it could choose the time and place of attack. Grant, no whiner, said in his memoirs that "there were no large engagements where the National numbers compensated for the advantage of position and entrenchment occupied by the enemy." In summary, a short war, let alone a decisive battle, was probably impossible against an enemy that would try to mobilize all its resources to wage a military conflict. It eluded Europe's greatest tacticians—Wellington and Napoleon. At Waterloo, Wellington beat a French army already exhausted and attrited in Russia. At Austerlitz the emperor only won what proved to be an armistice against Austria and Russia. McClellan's shortcoming was not his failure to win a decisive battle. It was his adamant refusal to admit that new methods were required.[4]

THE PUBLIC, THE POLITICIANS, AND THE TRANSITION TOWARD TOTAL WAR

Lincoln's dispute with George McClellan was about means, not ends. The general professed that he would "do nothing to render ultimate reconciliation and harmony impossible, unless such a course were imperative to secure military success." Lincoln said much the same thing but really meant it, particularly that "it was our duty to avail ourselves of every necessary measure." The eradication of the Confederacy was the fundamental issue. Compared with that, the means that obsessed McClellan was a minor concern. As long as McClellan held out hope for success, Lincoln withstood critics of the general's caution and "declared emphatically that he will not back down on Mac." He did not issue guidance, aside from keeping a substantial force between Lee and Washington, D.C. After the president's hopes for resurrecting Southern unionism finally waned in mid-1862, he gave McClellan direct instructions to "strike a blow." Because the general's methods proved insufficient, the North (not just the president) decided to escalate. Lincoln later told Grant that public and congressional opinion "forced" him to act, that is, assume more control of the conduct of the war than he was inclined to do.

By late 1861 political parties had flip-flopped their traditional positions on military professionalism. The Democrats, the champions of citizen-soldiers since the rise of Andrew Jackson, now defended the prerogatives of professionals like McClellan to conduct operations without political interference: "Let the Army do its own business and we [in Congress] do ours." Former Whigs now used Jacksonian rhetoric about "common sense" and "the real heroes" springing "from the ranks of the people" to attack the devotees of "military science" hesitant to wage relentless war. In January 1862 Republican Congressman Thaddeus Stevens used a metaphor heretofore restricted to the radical press: it was time to treat "this rebellion with iron gloves." That theme would dominate political debate in the North for the rest of the year, especially after high hopes were dashed that summer.

In April, Union forces surrounded Memphis and captured New Orleans. In May, McClellan slowly moved toward Richmond while his protégé, Don Carlos Buell, crawled toward Chattanooga without confiscating supplies lest "acts of plunder" lead to "the demoralization of the troops and the destruction of their efficiency." Common soldiers of the Army of the Ohio were quite critical of this "dancing-master policy." Important constituents were already writing their representatives that "caution is educated [into professional soldiers] until it is hardly distinguishable from cowardice." Nonetheless, the North still indulged their style of warfare as long as "the end of the struggle" seemed near. Then McClellan was thrown back toward Washington, and sensational stories about Confederates killing wounded prisoners filled the press. Buell, meanwhile, fell back to Kentucky. By July, patience had run dry, as shown by Senator William P. Fessenden—a moderate Republican leader heretofore known for his judicious temperament. With three sons in military service and some blunt letters from voters about "wanting our army to kill somebody," he announced from the Senate floor: "White kid-glove warfare" was over.

Since November 1861, military volunteers had been saying that "we have been playing with Traitors long enough"; "the time has come to march through this nest of vipers with fire and sword, to liberate every slave." Still too radical for most professional soldiers, their opinions were echoed in what officers called "the savage appeals of our journals back home." The call of the *Chicago Tribune* and the *New York Times* "to wage war in deadly earnest" was now matched by politicians reflecting the opinion of their constituents. "We are growing more radical every day," one voter wrote Senator Lyman Trumbull (Rep.-Ill.). In July 1862 John Sherman, the junior senator from Ohio (another former moderate, like Fessenden and Trumbull) was far more aggressive than his older brother, William Tecumseh, yet to become a demonic figure in the mind of the South. The officer opposed emancipation and loved West Point as an island of social order in an ocean of democratic anarchy. The politican, having criticized the Military Academy for not infusing "the right spirit to carry on this war," favored a policy "ordinarily . . . shocking to our sense of humanity": we must utilize "the whole physical force of this country—whites and blacks, free and slaves—[to] desolate, if necessary, every State that stands in the way." Congress, bowing to pressure, passed two acts authorizing Lincoln to "employ as many persons of African descent" as deemed necessary to "suppress this rebellion." It was still trailing the public's opinion that total abolition would "secure a speedy peace" because it struck a heavy blow.

Ulysses S. Grant, then in northern Mississippi, wrote his own political mentor, Congressman Elihu Washburne, in June that the Southern "masses" were just intimidated, not really disloyal, an opinion he held for another year at least. In August 1863 he would tell Sherman to impress their soldiers with "the importance of . . . abstaining from taking anything not absolutely necessary for their subsistence. They should try to create as favorable an impression as possible upon the people" of Mississippi. Sherman (that's right, Sherman) agreed wholeheartedly: "The Policy you point out meets every wish of my heart." Washburne was less impressed, having heard very different ideas from Galena, their hometown, as early as January 1862. One journalist then wrote him that local people "were becoming [so] *desperate*" that they could have "rebelled" for not beating down the South. Six months later, he got a similar message from Edward Kittoe, a Galena civic leader. This sixty-year-old physician, who would direct medical care on Sherman's march through Georgia, told Washburne that "the iron gauntlet must be used more than the silken glove." The next month, July, Washburne informed Grant: "A different policy is about to prevail. The administration has come up to what the people have long demanded—a vigorous prosecution of the war."

The privates, the public, and the Congress—in chronological order—felt that the Lincolns, Grants, and Shermans grossly overstated the residual strength of Union sentiment in the South. One speaker told a rally that the region "is as unanimous [about secession] as the Colonies were in the Revolution." This must have warmed the heart of Jefferson Davis, since it conceded that he had won his local ideological contest for political legitimacy. He should have known it was also a mandate for the remorseless war that the North was about to bring to the depths of the Confederacy.

In retrospect, the path from limited to total war may seem smooth after mid-1862. Henry Halleck, who had replaced McClellan as the Union army's general in chief in July, ordered his field commanders to handle "all active [Confederate] sympathizers . . . without gloves," a far cry from his position barely six months earlier, when he wrote about Scott and Taylor's wisdom not to make the civil population "feel the weight of war." However, in practice, the transition to what Sherman would call "a hard species of warfare" was still inconsistent and uneven. He, for one, was not quite ready to "bring the sad realities home to those who have been directly or indirectly instrumental in involving us in its attendant calamities."

Lincoln had been leaning away from what he called the "rosewater" policy of reconciliation since McClellan's failure at Richmond. Soon thereafter, he asked Northern Democrats, "Would you give up the contest leaving any available means unapplied?" He irrevocably crossed the Rubicon toward the iron glove and total war in November 1862, the last month in a series of state and congressional elections. In response to direct demands from close political allies that "the time has come for the adoption of more decisive measures," Lincoln retired Don Carlos Buell on 24 October, five days after asking him "why we cannot march as the enemy marches, live as he lives, and fight as he fights." He still was not quite ready to pull the plug on George McClellan, whom he tried to provoke into last-minute action before the election with bitter commentary: "I have just read your dispatch about fatigued horses. Will you pardon me for asking what the horses of your army have done since the battle of Antietam [17 September] that fatigues anything?"

After the Peninsula campaign, Lincoln kept McClellan and his coterie of conservative Democrats in command of the Army of the Potomac while temporarily transferring the bulk of its regiments to the Army of Virginia, a new formation led by officers with a Republican persuasion. The day after the last ballots were cast in November, Lincoln, no longer having to keep up pretenses, retired McClellan altogether. The secretary of war wanted McClellan court-martialed after Antietam to ensure he could never resume active duty. That would be an admission of failure right before an election, something no politician ever wants to do. Hardly surprising, the nation knew the military situation, judging by the fact that the Democrats gained another 20 percent of the seats in the House of Representatives and legislative control of several northwestern states.

The peace faction of the Democratic party said the election was a mandate for opposition to forcible reunion and the iron-glove policy the administration had just begun to implement. This was self-serving and not really valid, since the winners really ran against what they called "the interminable nature of this war." In late October one Republican told Lincoln that "if we are beaten" in the Illinois election, "it will be because McClellan and Buell won't fight." Lincoln, in turn, told another party leader the lesson he had learned by mid-November: "If the war fails, the administration fails, and that I *will* be blamed for it, whether I deserve it or not." To do better at the polls in the next canvass, when Lincoln himself faced reelection, the president would have to do far better on the battlefield, even if this meant no more vacillation about a tougher, meaner war.

In 1864 Lincoln again discouraged the removal of generals before a national election, overlooking the lesson he should have learned in 1862: the only important political issue was success against the enemy. Yet unlike many other members of his own party, who would flinch at the massive butcher's bill about to be presented, he never wavered once he finally determined that "decisive and extreme measures must be adopted" even if "it is impossible to foresee . . . all the ruin which may follow."[5]

THREE MILITARY STRATEGIES FOR THE NORTH

When George McClellan, the advocate of traditional ways and means, failed to end the rebellion with "one blow" as promised, Lincoln, Grant, and Sherman assumed the task of devising alternatives to decisive battle, no matter how unpleasant their methods proved to be. Each of them had what a Confederate official called "revolutionary vigor." As Lincoln said in words appropriate for all three: "I shall do all I can to save the government."

The new iron-glove policy had three major components. At different times and different places, one element might be paramount. None ever became the Union's sole strategy. By and large, but never exclusively, Lincoln tended toward attrition: placing Union military strength on Confederate strength and beating it into submission. Grant and Sherman preferred other styles of warfare more difficult to label for lack of a simple term. They both tried to place Union strength on an enemy weakness, military or civilian.

Lincoln, caught in a maelstrom no one could fully grasp, would disarm critics by saying "my policy is to have no policy." Not completely true, he adopted attrition in late 1862, after McClellan failed to crush Lee at Antietam in September. Whereas Henry Halleck concluded that McClellan "does not understand strategy and should never plan a campaign," politicians disenchanted with formal military education equated strategy with "stratagem," cunning tricks played by those who lacked the will to press home the attack. "Any commander who relies wholly upon STRATEGY must fail," said Congressman John McClernand, a newly minted major general of volunteers. "Neither Caesar nor Cromwell were graduates of West Point." The president, who once thought secession was political posturing, now had no doubt he was in the midst of "one of the greatest wars the world has ever seen." Shortly after Antietam, which he visited with McClernand, he said in a mood of great depression that "McClellan is responsible for the delusion that is untoning the whole army—that the South is to be conquered by strategy. . . . The War is to be carried on and put through by hard, tough fighting; and no headway is going to be made while this delusion lasts."

The next major battle in the eastern theater was at Fredericksburg (December 1862), where the North suffered 12,653 casualties out of 114,000 men; the South took 5,300 casualties from 72,000. Lee was not elated nor Lincoln in despair. The former, knowing his opponent was still standing, said such victories "inflict no loss upon the enemy beyond the actual loss in battle." Lincoln, meanwhile, told his staff that "if the same battle were to be fought over again, every day, through a week of days, with the same relative results, the army under Lee would be wiped out. . . . No general yet found can face the arithmetic. The end of the war will be at hand when he shall be discovered."

Grant became the grim mathematician—but not by choice. In 1864 he sought to execute what today is called the operational art—weaving sequential battles by separate formations into a campaign to accomplish one's strategic objectives. Ideally, he would pin and strike the enemy with one force while another maneuvered in search of a weakly held route to some vital target. The war never unfolded as neatly as he planned, for reasons explained later. Nonetheless, Grant, who did not win a major battle after breaking the Confederate lines at Chattanooga in late 1863, won the war with a campaign that forced Lee to surrender in 1865.

"We always understood each other so well," Lee said about McClellan shortly after Lincoln relieved Lee's old assistant in the corps of engineers during the Mexican War. "I fear they may continue to make these changes till they find some one whom I don't understand." As for Grant, Lee understood him, at least at the tactical level of war. In the spring of 1864 he anticipated his new opponent's march route and beat him to terrain objectives: Wilderness Tavern, Spotsylvania, North Anna, and Cold Harbor. Lee did not anticipate what James Longstreet predicted: Grant "will fight us every day and every hour till the end of the war." To Lee's surprise, once (or repeatedly) beaten, Grant would advance, rather than retreat. "The art of war is simple enough," the Union commander told one young officer. "Find out where your enemy is. Get at him as soon as you can. Strike at him as hard as you can and as often as you can, and keep moving on." This new concept of operation—striking often and moving on—replaced decisive battle as the military formula to win the war.

Sherman, searching for an alternative to attrition, called Grant's original concept of converging separate commands on a common center "enlightened war." The failure of the plan in mid-1864 helped force him to become the most innovative strategist in a conflict where the staggering costs of strength-on-strength engagements made them a last resort. Except for those who knew Sherman very well, few Confederates could believe that their scourge had great sympathy and admiration for their soldiers of the South. Before the war, he had spent the happiest years of his life in service with them at outposts from Charleston to Louisiana. Now, when he bypassed Confederate strongpoints, he reduced the number of "dead and mangled bodies" among fighting men on both sides. "Whenever a result can be accomplished without the carnage of battle I prefer it." With a touch of sarcasm, Sherman wrote Grant in 1865, "I had to content myself with the material fruits of victory without the cost of life which would have attended a general assault."

At the same time that Sherman let enemy armies escape his grasp, he struck economic infrastructure: part strategy, part retribution. He blamed civilian non-combatants for starting a terrible war poor Southern soldiers had to fight: a "brave but deluded enemy," he wrote Grant. To spare fighting men on both sides, Sherman conducted what he called "statesmanship" (what the twentieth century termed "psychological operations" or "terrorism," depending on whether one approved of its use). "If the North can march an army right through the South, it is proof that the North can prevail. . . . Even without a battle, the result, operating upon the minds of sensible men, would produce fruits more than compensating for the expense." Once Sherman made the inhabitants "fear and dread us" and believe "that war & individual ruin are synonymous terms," the South would become "so sick of war that generations would pass away before they would again appeal to it."[6]

GRANT'S OPERATIONAL AND LINCOLN'S POLITICAL ART OF WAR

Grant, despite his postwar reputation as a butcher, was not an attrition warrior by choice. Like McClellan, he preferred more subtle military methods. Unlike McClellan, after his own plan for quick victory failed, Grant did not overestimate the opposition, blame his problems on the president, and demand twice as many troops. He was prepared to wage war relentlessly until cumulative battles "inflicted upon the enemy severe losses, which tended in the end to the complete overthrow of the rebellion." Although it was not Grant's original design, "this kind of war," said one Southern veteran, "would wear [us] out eventually."

Grant preferred not to use the Union's numerical superiority in force-on-force battles against the South's hardest target, the Army of Northern Virginia under Robert E. Lee. He planned to use the Army of the Potomac, the largest single formation he had, as a pinning force while smaller armies hit the softer targets Lee was supposed to be screening—Richmond, railroad lines, farms, and factories. In fact, the assault on Lee was Grant's concession to the administration. Washington was uncomfortable with his initial proposal to place all the Union's major forces south of the Confederate capital, a scheme dreaded by officials in the rebel war department who felt that, if this ever happened, "Richmond cannot subsist a week." Henry Halleck, with worries of his own, feared that Lee might grab this opportunity, strike north, and capture Washington. Having "very little faith" in winning by "destroying lines of supply," he added a substantial component of attrition to Grant's target list. "We have given too much attention to cutting the toe nails of our enemy instead of grasping his throat. . . . Every man we can collect should be hurled against Lee."

When Lincoln promoted Grant in 1864, the idea of coordinating attacks around the circumference of the Confederacy seemed new to America's first lieutenant general since George Washington. In fact, it already occurred to privates

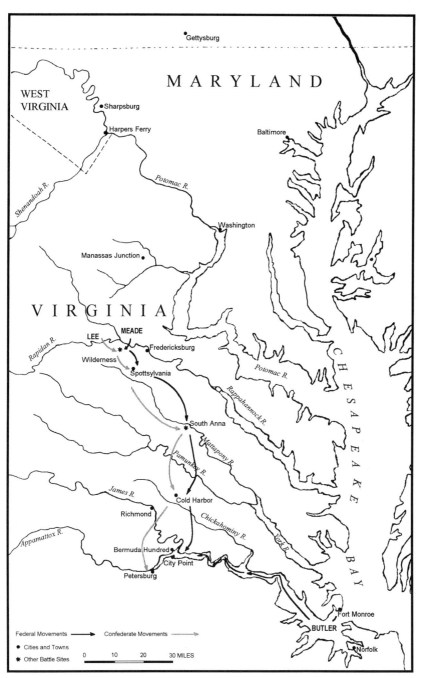

Civil War, eastern theater, 1864

and the president. That March, a Vermont volunteer wrote his hometown paper: "I would have all the armies clear around Secessia hammering away at them at once, so that the rebel armies in each quarter . . . would stop their reinforcing from one point to another." In January 1862 Lincoln told Buell and Halleck: we must menace the enemy "with superior forces at *different* points at the *same* time. . . . If he *weakens* one to *strengthen* the other, seize and hold the weakened one." Unfortunately for the Union cause at this time, Buell and McClellan were too slow to perform as required, partly because Confederate raiders collapsed their supply lines. Being unwilling to respond by taking food and fuel from civilians, Lincoln adopted a crude scheme of attrition in December.

In May 1864 Grant would try to implement the strategy Lincoln had talked about in early 1862. However, as the first true military commander of all Union forces, he would try to do it on a far larger scale, some 320,000 men in five field forces: (1) Nathaniel Banks with 40,000 soldiers and sailors in New Orleans aimed at Mobile; (2) William Tecumseh Sherman with 100,000 men at Chattanooga aimed at what Grant called "the heart of Georgia"; (3) Benjamin Butler with 35,000 men at Norfolk to be sent up the James River, a high-speed avenue of approach to Richmond; (4) Franz Sigel with 26,000 men in West Virginia to cut the railroads "connecting Richmond with all the south and the southwest"; and (5) George Gordon Meade's Army of the Potomac, 120,000 men abundantly supplied from 4,300 wagons. "Wherever Lee goes there you will go"—a pinning, not a maneuver, mission.

Only Meade and Sherman would perform as required. Grant, like Lincoln in 1862, had to execute a complicated plan with incompetent subordinates who drove him toward attrition as the only way to win the war, hardly a surprise. Win, lose, or draw—from Grant's first engagement, at Belmont in 1861, he had rarely been able to synchronize pinning movements and flank attacks on a battlefield, let alone in an area of operations stretching from New Orleans to northern Virginia. In 1865 Grant acknowledged that "it but rarely happens that a number of expeditions, starting from various points to act upon a common centre, materially aid each other. They never do, except when each acts with vigor, and either makes rapid marches, or keeps confronting an enemy"—exactly what Sigel, Banks, and Butler failed to do.

Grant's military campaign was saddled with Lincoln's political interpretation of the Civil War. To the president, the primary issue was always the preservation of constitutional democracy against the embittered losers of the 1860 election. Subsequent political referenda could not be delayed until an armistice because "if the rebellion could force us to forgo or postpone a national election, it might fairly claim to have already conquered and ruined us." In 1864 Lincoln believed the Confederacy had to lose simultaneously by battle and by ballot. Sigel, Butler, and Banks—three influential politicians—had military commands largely to help the president's political prospects. They would do so much military damage they nearly cost him reelection.

Lincoln appointed Sigel a brigadier general of volunteers as of 17 May 1861—the same date and rank as Grant, a day after Butler and Banks. An immigrant who left Germany after liberal reform seemed hopeless, Sigel settled in St. Louis, where he became director of public schools and a leader of his nationality. "The enthusiasm in his favor among our German population is unanimous," one newspaper editor wrote Lincoln during the war. This was true in New York, where Sigel's speeches declaring that "you as Germans have the duty to sustain the government" brought out voters in 1863. It was crucial in the Midwest from the late 1850s, where Germans were a swing vote in swing states. Lincoln, then an aspiring politician, condemned nativism (a rare practice for Whigs) and purchased part of a German-language newspaper—a wise political investment. In the 1860 presidential election, German-American voters helped provide the Republican margin of victory in Pennsylvania, Indiana, and Illinois. In 1864 Lincoln confessed to Gustave Koerner, former lieutenant governor of his home state, that the German vote would probably cost him Wisconsin, Illinois, and Missouri, especially with their beloved John C. Fremont, lately of St. Louis, dismissed from military command.

Fremont, an embittered egotist, blamed battlefield defeat on insufficient supplies from Washington. He was ready to run for president as a third-party candidate, if only to wreak revenge on the administration. No small threat, it drove one U.S. senator, allegedly speaking for Lincoln, to promise Fremont a new military command if he would drop out of the race. Since 1844, third-party candidates had decided three of the last five presidential elections by taking support from an established party, usually the Whigs, more independent voters than what Lincoln called the "double-drilled army" of Democrats. In 1848 and 1856 Lincoln attacked splinter groups for splitting the anti-Democrat vote. In 1860, with a 39 percent plurality, he won the presidency as a Republican—a party too young to rely on historical loyalty, especially from voters willing to have joined what had recently been a third party itself. Germans were so angry at the ouster of Fremont that Missouri would nominate Grant at the Republican National Convention. Sigel's selection to succeed Fremont in command of the Department of West Virginia was "a very judicious measure," so said Carl Schurz, Lincoln's political adviser on the German-American community. Two hundred thousand German-American soldiers made up 10 percent of the Union army; 300,000 would cast almost 10 percent of the forthcoming vote.

Ben Butler and Nathaniel Banks were important politicians and frequently mentioned candidates for president. Banks could sway swing people like himself, former members of the American party, getting 875,000 votes in 1856 when he was the "Know-Nothing" Speaker of the House. Butler, a self-described "Andrew Jackson Democrat," could influence voters tempted to return to that party if it nominated pro-war candidates. Ever since Jackson's election in 1828, the Democrats were the political majority in America—one reason Lincoln had won no more than one term in the U.S. House. There, in the Mexican War, his

Whigs hindered a president's powers to command. When president himself, Lincoln tried to make the Civil War a nonpartisan cause lest he stumble worse than James Polk, who made his own war a partisan issue by commissioning men for loyalty to the Democratic party. Lincoln, having condemned that particular "rascality," claimed his own appointments proved that "in considering military merit . . . I discard politics." In fact, it proved that he played politics differently than Polk. To Republicans who wanted their brethren to hold all important positions, he said "it was mere nonsense that a minority could put down a majority in rebellion." Lincoln's secretaries of war and the navy were both Democrats, as was George McClellan, whom he retained through the election of 1862, partly to keep this a bipartisan war. After him came General Ben Butler, who had nominated his old friend Jefferson Davis for president at the Democratic National Convention in Charleston, South Carolina, in 1860.

Now in demand at political rallies for hanging Southerners who desecrated the flag, Butler was a volatile factor in the presidential politics of 1864. The White House thought him "the smartest damned rascal that ever lived" and feared he might "make common cause" with John C. Fremont's anti-Lincoln alliance. Lincoln, worried about the election until election day, asked Butler to be his running mate in March. Because the vice presidency was a dead-end job, Butler chose to stay at Fort Monroe in command of the Union's Army of the James, where he had a chance to do what he long wanted: strike "a lightning-like blow on Richmond." This former militia commander of the "Jackson Musketeers" knew the surest way to win the White House. His father had served under his role model and the namesake of his older brother, Andrew Jackson Butler, at the Battle of New Orleans. In 1864 the entire Butler entourage was convinced that the man who captured "the nest of the rebellion" would be elected president in 1868, especially if he were a citizen-soldier, if only because the Academy had rejected Butler's application to the school in the 1830s.

Out of apparent jealousy, Butler hated West Pointers. They responded in kind. Halleck, class of 1839, called it "little better than murder to give important commands to such men as Banks, Butler, [John] McClernand, [and] Sigel, but yet it seems impossible to prevent it." Grant was a bit less resigned. By 1864 he had developed a standing operating procedure for handling well-connected men supposedly lacking in military talent. In late 1862 he was saddled with McClernand, former congressman from central Illinois. The Northwest was rife with talk about an armistice when this leader of the War Democrats outlined to Lincoln, his old friend and neighbor, a plan to win their region back in favor of the war. He would use his political network in Illinois, Iowa, and Indiana to raise the regiments he expected to command in operations against Vicksburg, the Confederate Gibraltar on the Mississippi River blocking Midwest access to the markets of the world.

In McClernand's original concept of the Vicksburg operation, Grant was to stay in his Memphis headquarters, from where he would support McClernand's campaign in the field. He hardly wanted McClernand in any capacity but could not remove him without cause. To Sherman's astonishment, Grant made McClernand the point of attack across the Mississippi River, then waited for a mistake such as he made in unauthorized releases to the press, the same prima facie cause Winfield Scott used to remove Gideon Pillow in the Mexican War. Grant contacted Washington, which transferred McClernand but kept him in the army, a typical political compromise. The congressman held nothing against Lincoln, subtly on Grant's side but not forced to alienate an ally who blamed a "clique of West Pointers who have been persecuting me for months." (Like other good Jacksonian haters of the Academy, McClernand would send his son to West Point: Brigadier General Edward J., class of 1870.) In 1863, still friendly with the president, McClernand was available to lead midwestern rallies against Peace Democrats, a service for which he got command of a new army corps under Nathaniel Banks in 1864. Grant, as of then, explained his standing operating procedure to the War Department: "The earnest desire on my part to do the most I could with the means at my command without interference with the assignments to command which the President alone was authorized to make, made me tolerate General McClernand long after I thought the good of the service demanded his removal."

In 1864 Grant would do the same thing with Sigel, Banks, and Butler that he had done with McClernand: wait for a mistake before he sought to replace them. Whether McClernand was as bad a general as Grant believed—or as good as McClernand thought he was—did not matter much in 1863. Vicksburg was relatively easy, at least compared with the Wilderness campaign. In the former operation, Grant had marched 200 miles in eighteen days, fought five engagements, and conducted a six-week siege at a total cost of 7,373 casualties. The cost of biding one's time with inept subordinates was not too great to bear. In early 1864 Grant could not imagine that the campaign in Virginia could claim 55,000 casualties in forty-two days. "The world has never seen," he wrote his wife, "so bloody or so protracted a battle as the one being fought."

Not knowing what was about to happen, Grant wished to be what he called a rare commodity: "a gentleman who has no axe to grind" with the president of the United States. Halleck told him that to get Lincoln to replace the likes of Banks and Sigel he would have to make "a definitive" demand for "removal as a military necessity." That was simple to advise but difficult to do. Halleck hated all political generals but certainly had not done it, nor suggest that he and Grant go to Lincoln together, although Halleck had been a successful attorney used to making oral arguments and had worked with Lincoln for the last eighteen months. The task would be far more difficult for Grant, a reticent man barely three years removed from clerking at his father's dry goods store. Even after "disasters" due to the "incompetency" of Sigel, Banks, and Butler, Grant would be reluctant to pressure Washington. He thought McClellan's "main blunder" had been to cross the political barrier and "become the critic of the President." The last thing he wanted was to be "McClellanized" himself, that is, an object of partisan dispute. As "a 'good soldier,'" he told Halleck, "I do not believe I have the right to criticize the policy or orders of those above me" who "at least intend for the best."

Rather typical of civil-military relations in America, neither Grant nor Lincoln sought a private conference where they could raise and discuss all their concerns. Most professional soldiers, especially before the Civil War, were wont to erect barriers between war, politics, and politicians, whom they described as a "rotten collection of demagogues" winning office by "flattering the people" so badly they refused to obey authority. Grant's own views of the matter were not nearly this heated, but both he and Lincoln wanted to avoid another McClellan situation, actually irrelevant in their case. The problem with McClellan was not too much contact with the president. It was that he complained to the opposition party—instead of talking to a commander in chief who really had no wish to interfere lest he assume "all the responsibility in the case of failure." Nonetheless, McClellan kept Lincoln in the dark as much as he could, then complained that the president sabotaged his plans, as when Lincoln removed a corps from McClellan's march on Richmond to protect the capital from Confederate raids.

Lincoln came to a tacit understanding with Grant. "The quietest little fellow [the president] ever saw" scarcely murmured about patronage appointments to military command. As for the White House, already criticized for putting political "fingers [into] the military pie," it gave Grant private possession of the military plan. Only Lincoln, Grant once said, had a right to know what Grant planned; only Lincoln, of all the men Grant met, never asked what Grant's were.

Both the soldier and the politician were remembering the precedent of Zachary Taylor, although remembering different aspects of this particular soldier-president. Grant would recall that his military role model did "the best he could with the means given him" in the Mexican War. Lincoln recalled what a potent challenger an irate war hero (his candidate for president in 1848) could be. In 1864, when Lincoln's own critics were touting Grant for president, he sent two envoys to sound out his political ambitions. To Lincoln's relief, Grant replied, "I hope to remain a soldier as long as I live."

Grant was at the pinnacle of his prestige, yet to be tarnished in effusive bloodletting on the way to Richmond in mid-1864. He was in a position, newspapers noted, "to compel the administration to obey him rather than he them." Nonetheless, he would not use his enormous political leverage to purge the Union army of political appointees, perhaps a tragic product of Grant's great strength, his "absolute confidence" in ultimate success. Grant, observed George Meade, was "almost too confident and sanguine," attributes that put him "under the influence of those who should not influence him," in this case the president of the United States. When Lincoln, to Grant's relief, did not ask him for his plan, Grant missed a golden opportunity to explain the importance of proven commanders for each field army. Not confronted, the president could maintain that the Sigels, Banks, and Butlers were no worse than the Buells and McClellans, professional soldiers whose "sinking courage [he had] to sustain in critical times." Politically, at least the former would "give great relief while, at worst, I think, they could not injure the military service much."

Lincoln did tell Grant that "celerity was absolutely necessary," lest the country exhaust its moral and economic resources. Unfortunately, many of his military commissions would create the situation he feared: one where even a leading Republican despaired about "our bleeding, bankrupt, almost dying country." The president seemed to ignore a fact obvious to Northern and Southern newspapers, let alone the Confederate high command: "The grand struggle of the war upon which we are about to enter . . . will shape and determine the Presidential contest." In short, patronage would not hold a political candle to the cost and rate of progress on the battlefield.

Sigel and Banks proved so bad that Grant asked that they be "relieved from all duty." (Phil Sheridan and E. R. S. Canby, replacements who should have taken command that spring, would conquer the Valley and Mobile for the Union in late fall.) Butler would be the biggest disappointment because he had the best chance to end the war. Grant had considered replacing him, if only because this lawyer–politician–military governor of New Orleans had never led a large column against the enemy. His doubts were allayed by meeting Butler and finding they both planned to launch a deep envelopment on Richmond. Grant may have overrated the military importance of mental capacity. As a man of average intellect but monumental fortitude, he may not have grasped that Butler, "always clear in his conception of orders," simply lacked the willpower Grant had in abundance. Still, as a final precaution, Grant provided Butler with a "sufficient number of able Generals to render him all the necessary aid to execute the details." This was a subtle way of notifying Major General William "Baldy" Smith that Grant expected this top West Point graduate, "one of the most efficient officers in service," to take command of the battlefield.

Smith was one of a handful of men Grant brought with him from the west, where Smith planned and organized the daring night attack up the Tennessee River that broke the Confederate siege of Chattanooga. Unfortunately, his doubts about Butler brought out the worst in Smith, a brilliant but erratic prima donna. Moreover, unlike Grant, he was under no illusion that General Butler would relegate himself to administration, such as John McClernand, another political general, failed to relegate Grant in 1863. No West Pointer, such as Grant, would accept a military support role for a Jacksonian politician such as McClernand; no Jacksonian hero-to-be, such as Benjamin Butler, would accept this role for a West Pointer, such as Baldy Smith. Smith's conviction that Butler would be "helpless as a child on the field of battle" was hardly conducive to a command climate necessary to conduct a mad dash for Richmond through unknown territory.

When Butler disembarked eighteen miles south of Richmond, the Confederacy could call fewer than 10,000 soldiers to stand between his 39,000-man army and the capital of the South. On the first day of operations—5 May—750 of these rebels blocked Butler's path, caught his advance guard in a small ambush, and drove them back behind their lines. This took the spirit right out of his army, which began to ask the embarrassing question: "How long will it take to get to Richmond if you advance two miles every day and come back to your starting point every night?" In the meantime, Butler entrenched and forgot his mission: to cut Lee's supply lines at Richmond and force him to retreat while the Army of the Potomac followed in hot pursuit. On 9 May Butler wired the War Department that "we can hold out [here] against the whole of Lee's army." This was hardly vital when Lee was busy seeking "a crowning victory" against Meade on the Rappahannock: something to force Lincoln to recall Butler, Sigel, and even troops from Sherman to defend Washington. Grant soon concluded that the Army of the James was "as completely shut off from further operations directly against Richmond as if it had been in a bottle strongly corked."

After Butler dug in, Confederates south of the James sent 7,000 reinforcements to Robert E. Lee. The war north of the river became the frightful campaign of attrition Lincoln predicted back in December 1862. He was far better prepared than was the nation at large, which, in the words of the *New York Herald,* anticipated "quick work and great results" from Grant, whose victories at Vicksburg and Chattanooga had not cost lots of Union blood. Now, in the midst of recruiting new volunteers, the War Department withheld Grant's casualty reports "for fear the country could not stand the disclosure." A week into the Wilderness campaign headlines in the *New York Times* read "VICTORY! / A Decisive Battle / LEE'S ARMY ROUTED." The sort of operation McClellan once promised seemed to be occurring; Lee fell back and Grant moved forward, apparent proof of military triumph. When the facts about Union carnage leaked out, the disappointment was even worse. Antiwar Democrats suddenly switched the brunt of their attacks on the administration heretofore accused of a policy of racial "amalgamation in social and domestic life." They now focused on the state of the war: "Who shall revive the withered hopes that bloomed on the opening of Grant's campaign?"

As Lincoln's political stock descended, Butler appeared a more viable presidential candidate to a band of Republican leaders, pro-war Democrats, and newspaper barons. Henceforth, he became someone the White House wanted ever more strongly kept inside the army, even if they thought him "perfectly useless & incapable for [military] campaigning." Grant, the good soldier, accepted Washington's decision, even appeared to be "cowed" by Butler. Butler himself reacted with more vigor than he expended south of Richmond: "Hurrah for Lincoln and [Andrew] Johnson! That's the ticket."

Since the Army of the James could or would not fight its way up to Richmond, the Army of the Potomac had to fight its way down to the James. To do so, Grant ordered Baldy Smith's XVIII Corps north to join Meade. He reported just in time to take the point of attack at Cold Harbor, the bloodiest ten minutes in American military history, 7,000 Union casualties. "It was not war; it was murder," said one Confederate general. Another witness to events was the chairman of Senate Military Affairs: "If that scene could have been presented to me before the war, anxious as I was for the preservation of the Union, I should have said: 'The cost is too great; erring sisters, go in peace.' "

Nearly twenty-five years later a Union general wrote that Cold Harbor "was the dreary, dismal, bloody ineffective close of the Lieutenant-General's first campaign with the Army of the Potomac"—hardly a hurrah for the operational art. However, one more great opportunity still existed. The Army of the Potomac, having tried to turn Lee's right flank since it entered the Wilderness, slipped down to link up with Butler. Grant now hoped to launch Baldy Smith on Petersburg, a railroad junction south of Richmond such as both planned to attack when pondering ways to defeat Lee back in January. Grant had finally beaten him to a soft target with strategic significance; Petersburg barely held 2,000 men. By now, however, the Army of the Potomac was "utterly unnerved" by "nothing but fighting, starving, marching and cussing for 50 days with no cessation," as officers wrote their families. Their regiments took one look at even hastily built earthworks and refused to budge: "No amount of urging, no heroic examples, no threats, or anything else, could get the line to stir one peg." This opportunity squandered, the defense at Petersburg hardened as Lee caught up with Grant, now reduced to conducting a laborious siege south of Richmond.

Unbeknownst to much of the Army of the Potomac—still rife with "McClellanism," said congressional critics—Grant had grimly done what was necessary. Lee long acknowledged that once Richmond is besieged the war, then one of exhaustion, "will be a mere question of time." However, to citizens on both sides, the Virginia campaign then seemed to be an endless string of inconclusive bloodshed, intolerable in an election year. Confederates predicted that "we will get our independence by Christmas, won't we be a happy and free people." Both they and Northern Democrats were wrong. The Republican party retained control of Congress and the presidency for two reasons.

First, Grant adjusted his strategy to win political dividends. Sherman was supposed to have kept Joe Johnston "so busy he cannot . . . send any part of his command against" Meade, Sigel, or Butler. Now, when "everything hinges on the election," so said Grant's military aide, he pinned Lee while Sherman conquered Atlanta—in "the very nick of time [to] save the party of Lincoln," the Richmond *Examiner* lamented. As late as 30 August, a caucus of dispirited Republicans agreed that "Lincoln cannot be re-elected, unless great victories can be attained soon, which is next to impossible on account of the worn-out state of the armies of the Potomac." Seven days later, one traveler reported clanging bells, bonfires, and "the shouts of rejoicing multitudes" all the way from New York to Chicago. Sherman had flashed the proverbial light at the end of tunnel. For the North, it meant "The Dark Days Are Over. . . . we can see our way out." For the South, it meant "the end has come. . . . We are going to be wiped off the face of the earth."

Second, neither side reacted to battle as it would to commercial markets: when the price goes up, demand goes down. In war, where the price is blood as well as money, cost can increase demand that may help eliminate doubt about the worth of political objectives. Eighteen sixty-two was the year of the "iron glove"; 1863—for both the North and the South—was the year of "not in vain." In February the *Richmond Enquirer* editorialized: "Two years, and an abyss of horror and hatred, and the blood of our slaughtered brothers crying aloud from the ground, all prohibit impious union" with the enemy. At Gettysburg in November, Lincoln delivered the most important speech in American history: "We here highly resolve that these dead shall not have died in vain."

The elections held during the last half of the war were the best evidence that Lincoln spoke for the North and the *Enquirer* for the South, in particular for soldiers "not as near whipped as the citizens at home." In 1863, even after major military defeats at Gettysburg and Vicksburg, veterans shouted down unionists and voted down moderates in elections that upheld the Confederate government. The next year, Lincoln received 53 percent of the popular vote but 78 percent of the ballots cast by the Union army. "I can not vote for one thing and fight for another," one soldier told his family. In truth, Lincoln's reelection was a mandate about means, not about ends, insofar as his opponent, George McClellan, also vowed to fight "until our land was saved." Soldiers rejected his candidacy for the same reason they rejected the "silk-glove" or "rosewater" strategy. "You and a large portion of the Democratic party," one private wrote his father, "are retarding instead of hastening the end of this horrible war." The rank and file concurred with Republican pamphlets against Democratic calls for negotiations: "You should [not] lay down your arms, abandon your conquests, and leave to a set of designing and knavish politicians the settlement of terms of peace."

For Union soldiers, Lincoln had become synonymous with victory and "unconditional surrender," a term Lincoln never used. This was also the case in the South, as one rebel deserter told his captors that October: "The whole dependence is upon the election . . . it being openly avowed that if Lincoln is re-elected, they will of necessity have to yield." Richmond newspapers put the best face on the bad news: Lincoln's "brutalities render our success more certain by rendering failure more dreadful and intolerable." By then the editorial writers were far more fierce than the average soldier. "The Yankee election," said a Confederate War Department official, has "depressed the army a good deal." A Virginia private wrote his sister that "many are anxious for the war to stop and they don't care how." In June, Southerners expected victory by Christmas. By 25 December nearly 200,000 rebel soldiers had deserted their virtually hopeless cause. They left behind 160,000 malnourished men to face 600,000 Yankees, 300,000 more in reserve. By April 1865, at Robert E. Lee's last battle, it was "a handful to a houseful," said one Confederate. "We could do nothing but shoot and run . . . like a flock of wild turkeys."[7]

SHERMAN, CITIZEN-SOLDIERS, AND THE WAR
ON THE SOUTH'S WILL TO MAKE WAR

Civilians joined the ranks and learned to fight like soldiers during the Civil War. Professional soldiers learned to think like civilians insofar as they slowly drew conclusions many common citizens already had made regarding how to win this war. William Tecumseh Sherman exemplifies this process. Quite conventional in 1861, he became the ruthless warrior of legend by 1864. To save time and trouble, he and fellow officers might have consulted a September 1861 edition of *Harper's Weekly* magazine. "To molest their homes," it said about the rebels, "and jeopard[ize] their 'personal property' is to attack them where they are weak."

In World War II, marines said that "the Japanese fight for their emperor, the British for glory, and the Americans for souvenirs." Sherman called them "trophies" in 1865. The local inhabitants, who reluctantly provided the prizes, called the activity looting and plunder. Whatever the terms, American soldiers have searched for spoils since the first war with French Canada. During the Revolution, George Washington's threat to execute looters could not prevent "the Ravages of our own Troops who are becom[ing] infinitely more formidable to the poor Farmers and Inhabitants than [is] the common Enemy." In the Civil War such behavior was committed by the South against itself. The *Richmond Enquirer* reported in mid-1862 that "the Yankees cannot do us any more harm than our own soldiers have done." Could reasonable people expect more forbearance from the North? Sherman certainly did in 1861, according to his "old West Point notion that pillage was a capital crime." Gradually changing, he just sanctioned the way the rank and file acted on their own. Thirty years after the war, one volunteer revealed exactly who led whom: "The idea of the soldiers upon the subject of 'confiscation' were, during the first months of the war, a long way in advance of those held by the double-starred generals, and the statesmen at Washington who were steering the ship. It was about two years before the latter caught up with the procession."

True to Academy conventions, Sherman was a "poor innocent" who believed wars were government monopolies run by professional officers; they were not fought by, between, or against civilian populations. He wrote home from the first Bull Run: "No Goths or Vandals ever had less respect for the lives and property of friends and foes" than the Union's volunteers. They "never will be fit for an invasion and when tried will be defeated and dropt by Lincoln like a hot potato." George McClellan never rid himself of such notions, nor his private oath "not [to] permit this army to degenerate into a mob of thieves." Sherman, his admirer, once thought "a better officer [than McClellan] could not be found." As late as 1863, he said McClellan was a victim of politicians and unforeseen forces. He never would "join the hue and cry against him," knowing he himself barely escaped the same fate "of the early heroes" now "swept as chaff before the wind." "In revolutions,"

Sherman wrote his wife in 1864, "men rise and fall. Long before this war is over
. . . you may hear me cursed and insulted."

Like McClellan, Sherman loathed citizen-soldiers: "no cohesion, no real discipline, no respect for authority." Like McClellan, he had externalized his dread
of these "anarchical elements" by overestimating the opposition. McClellan
counted two and a half Confederates for every one real soldier in Virginia; Sherman thought he was outnumbered five to one in Kentucky, his area of operations
after Bull Run. The significant difference between Sherman and McClellan was
not where they started but how dramatically Sherman changed. This admittedly
nervous man—prone to doubt, depression, insomnia, and hyperactivity—fell
under the spell of a calm and self-possessed superior officer. Grant, under horrendous pressure, sat quietly, whittled, and claimed he did "not feel"—certainly
did not show—"the slightest doubt." This struck Sherman as a "faith in success"
reminiscent of "the faith a Christian has in a Savior." It "made us [meaning Sher-
man] act with confidence."

How Grant, a miserable failure in civilian society, could have so much confidence in war, the most unforgiving yet capricious activity known to man, is inex-
plicable. Sherman would call him a mystery, even a "mystery to himself." What
matters is that Grant favorably compared volunteers to "veteran troops in point of
Soldierly bearing, general good Order, and cheerful execution of commands"—
all quite important when reaping food and forage from the Southern countryside.
Inevitably, soldiers transgressed his rule against taking household property "without an enquiry as to their [the owner's] status in this Rebellion." When that happened, he fined specific units, imprisoned individuals, and mustered certain
officers from the service—all without resorting to a blanket condemnation of his
men as a mob. Command style tends to be contagious in the military; subordinates
emulate their superiors. Sherman wrote his wife in 1861 that his recruits were
"the most destructive men that I have ever known." By November 1862 he was
writing Grant: "I have full confidence in the spirit of my men."

Sherman's conversion was never total. He never stopped cursing democracy,
anarchy, and "the amount of plundering and stealing done by our army"—inter-
related issues in volunteer regiments where firm discipline could ruin a political
career by alienating subordinates, one's future constituents. This "defective system of organization"—wherein "each colonel comes into the field expecting to
run for Congress"; every corporal for justice of the peace—dismayed the *New
York Times*. One can imagine the reaction of West Pointers. In mid-1863 Sherman told Grant's chief of staff that he was so ashamed he "would quit the service
if I could." Nonetheless, these outbursts of frustration aside, interior disorder no
longer obsessed him like it did McClellan. Sherman sometimes claimed to "have
checked it" for the most important reason: "On the discipline of our armies must
be built the future Government of this country." Often he admitted to confidants,
"I suppose I'll have to bear it"; "these men are of no common sort, for they think
for themselves."

Citizen-soldiers not only did what official iron-glove policy allowed: taking food, fuel, wagons, and farm animals to supply the Union armies. They scoffed at general orders against plundering private homes, knowing full well no soldier would be hung "for the benefit of traitors." Joe Wheeler's Confederate cavalry, nabbing looters here and there, was the most effective discipline Sherman had. "Serves 'em right," he would say, "hope they shoot 'em." As late as mid-1862 he issued orders to "prevent petty thieving and pillaging, it does us infinite harm"; and to restrict all activity "to acts of war controlled by educated and responsible officers." Sherman winced when "old friends look on me as a brutal wretch," but he was coming to conclude, as he later put it, that the time had come to "cease to quarrel with our own men and [go on] to subdue the enemy."

Sherman would explain that "no large army, carrying with it the necessary stores and baggage, can overtake and capture an inferior force of the enemy in his own country," especially when raiders strike its supply lines and then "depart as soon as the mischief is done." However frustrating, this type of military predicament was not new to the United States. In mid-1862 British writers recorded Northerners saying, "'We must annihilate [the South],' with as little remorse as [Americans] have before displayed in destroying the Indians." Sherman had a direct pipeline to public opinion through his younger brother, a U.S. senator from Ohio. Hence his grasp of what the country was demanding was far better than that of McClellan, who was misled by close contacts with Democrats condemning "confiscation, subjugation and extermination." John Sherman showed his sibling newspaper complaints that he was too "lenien[t] to the rebels" and warned of the demand that they be "conquered by the employment of their slaves, by terror, energy [and] audacity rather than by conciliation."

General Sherman, while complaining that "it would be folly to send parties of infantry to chase these wanton guerrillas," remembered some practical lessons he had learned in the early 1840s. The Second Seminole War had demonstrated the truism that Indian warriors, too elusive to be cornered, could be beaten only by the starvation and destruction of their tribes. Most officers had been happy to forget this deployment to Florida, where, as one forgotten general put it at the time, "the best concerted plans may result in absolute failure and the best established reputation be lost." Lieutenant Sherman, for his own part, felt "this is the kind of warfare which every young officer should be thoroughly acquainted." As if he were back in the Everglades, not Tennessee in 1862, Sherman told Grant, "We are not going to chase through the canebreaks and swamps [but] visit punishment upon the adherents of that cause which employs such agents," that is, the populace, not just the raiders.

Other Union officers felt that guerrilla warfare was a desperate act by an enemy "fast giving up the ghost." Sherman felt "guerrilla bands [were] a thing more to be feared than open organized warfare." He thanked fate that Jefferson Davis, a gentleman West Pointer like himself, would not "adopt the Indian policy of ambuscade . . . derogatory to the high pretences of his cause [and] courage." Sherman would forcibly banish ten families each time a guerrilla fired on a riverboat. But due to Richmond's choice of official strategy, the situation behind Union army lines never quite justified Sherman's pet proposal: transport all the "malcontents" to Madagascar, then "repopulate" the South with "the whole population of Iowa and Wisconsin."

Unable to execute mass deportations, Sherman hit soft civilian targets by destroying resources, demoralizing the inhabitants, discrediting the government, and causing mass desertions. Once a conventional soldier well suited to fight dynastic warfare, he developed a rationale reminiscent of eighteenth-century French and English officers sent to fight in colonial North America. "In Europe . . . wars are between kings or rulers through hired armies, and not between people." This particular conflict, "no common war," had to be waged against the resistance of "the people of the South" who were "more formidable and arrogant" after beating the likes of McClellan and Buell. "We are forced to invade [and] keep the war South until they are not only ruined [and] exhausted but humbled in pride and spirit." Then, a thoroughly pacified population will never dare "raise their hands against our consecrated Government."

Sherman characterized his strategy as "statesmanship," a euphemism for terrorism. Once having worried that pervasive looting would cause the "country to rise and justly shoot us down like dogs," he now came to use his men the way French and English officers used their Indian allies between 1700 and 1815—to threaten their opponents with a savagery they would not commit with their own clean hands. "The soldiers and people of the South," Sherman later wrote, "entertained an undue fear of our Western men. . . . This was a power and I intended to use it." The cost of this power was a rank and file not controlled by army rules for a discriminate and proportional punishment of the South. "Farms disappear, houses are burned and plundered, and every living animal killed and eaten," he wrote his brother in 1863. "General officers make feeble efforts to stay the disorder, but it is idle."

Sherman's lament to the contrary, the rank and file were better behaved than they seemed to officers with West Point standards or appeared in the legends of the South. Rape, assault, and murder were rare, if only because most men wanted "a good deal of fun" on "a gay old campaign." They had already had enough bloodshed to last a lifetime. The homes most badly damaged were those already abandoned by leaders of the Confederacy. Major General Oliver Howard wrote that Georgians "are terrified and believe us a thousand times worse than we are." One wonders what would have happened if he and Sherman had been able to rein in all their men as they tried to do. Could Sherman have sent a credible threat to the commander at Savannah warning that he would let his volunteers loose if Confederates did not surrender this vital seaport city? He warned: "I shall make little effort to restrain my army—burning to avenge a great national wrong they attach to large cities which have been so prominent in dragging our country into civil war." If Sherman's men had obeyed the standards he had set, would he have been able to instill the dread and terror he set out to imprint in the mind of the South? Could he have made a vice like looting into a military asset that played a substantial role in winning the war?[8]

UNION SOLDIERS, SOUTHERN WOMEN, CONFEDERATE DESERTERS, AND GENERAL SHERMAN

One hundred thousand armed men will damage any locale to which they deploy. Even without malice or forethought, fields will be trampled, woods cut, animals butchered, crops destroyed. One feels the South overstated the malevolence of the North, even after the "iron glove" became the official policy in the latter half of 1862. In July, Grant issued orders to forage "in an orderly manner" and confiscate personal property only in response to guerrilla raids. Southerners from Mississippi to Richmond accused him of violating "all rules of civilized warfare." Hyperbole was nothing new in the crisis of the Union. South Carolina began the chain reaction of secessions by saying Abraham Lincoln was a closet John Brown who would use patronage appointments to place insurrectionists in post and custom offices throughout the South. (Lincoln "has openly proclaimed a war of extermination against the leading institutions of the Southern States. He says that there can be no peace so long as slavery has a foothold in America.") When Union soldiers subsequently arrived, they were called "thugs." Treated as if the "army was a horde of Cossacks and vandals whose mission was to burn, pillage, and destroy," soldiers gave the South some of the treatment it expected and yet was outraged to receive.

Historically, friendly women have softened the rule of American military occupation. Despite orders against fraternization from those concerned with policy objectives, soldiers mitigated the hardships for pretty companions on lonely nights, be it Mexico in 1848 or Germany in 1945. In the Civil War, contacts between Southern females and Northern soldiers only made things worse. At a minimum, the former took pride "to look as ugly as possible." More often, they mounted a more active defense. One soldier wrote his parents from Alabama in July 1862: "The *ladies* of the place allow no opportunity to pass, to insult our soldiers & our flag." ("The men are just as mean as the women," said another soldier, "but a little bit more discreet.") The inevitable reaction became a point of demarcation between limited and total war. When insulted for hurting noncombatants, a provost marshal under Sherman replied that "the women of the South kept the war alive—and it is only by making them suffer that we can subdue the men."

Initially, Union occupation was a propaganda windfall for hard-core secessionists always worried that loyalism "was a latent sentiment in the bosom of the Southern community." Physical defense of one's home was the essence of Southern honor, and honor remained a substantial motivation to the bitter end. It certainly became the major theme of the political oratory, as Jefferson Davis told the

Mississippi legislature in December 1862: "The question is will you be free, or will you be the slaves of the most depraved and intolerant and tyrannical and hated people upon earth." In mid-1863 a European observer wrote that "nothing could exceed the intense hatred and fury with which excited citizens speak of the outrages they have undergone." At the front, Confederate soldiers displayed the same spirit in letters to their families: "I certainly love to live to hate the base usurping vandals, if it is a Sin to hate them, then I am guilty of the unpardonable one." But as they were speaking, morale was breaking. After Gettsyburg and Vicksburg in July, Confederate soldiers lost faith in inevitable victory. Desertion rates began to rise, not to be stopped until the end of the war.

The "thieving hordes of Lincoln" did not help the Confederacy sustain support for a prolonged war. By mid-1863 its former assets had become major liabilities. Ladies who had shamed men to go to war and wrote letters sustaining their morale now begged them to desert, if only to stop Yankee "ruffians stalking into my house [and] making all sorts of demands." One lieutenant from Mississippi reprimanded his wife: "Be a woman." Others had trouble remaining a soldier. The most frequent neuropsychiatric illness in the Civil War was an emotional depression termed "nostalgia," thought to be caused by preoccupation with one's home. Stonewall Jackson, no therapist, denied furloughs on grounds that men should place their country first. He was an eccentric (if not a fanatic) who talked directly to God. A more reasonable man was Sherman's opponent from Chattanooga to Atlanta, Joseph E. Johnston, who sympathized with the poor deserters whom he shot in a desperate attempt at deterrence: "Those soldiers of the laboring class who had families were compelled to choose between their military service and the strongest obligations men know—their duties to their wives and children."

In 1861 Lincoln believed that the plain people of the South would never fight to overthrow a republican government for the sake of rich slave owners. He grossly underestimated the willingness of many common Southerners to do what they claimed: fight "down to the point where the women and children begin to suffer for food and clothing . . . rather than be equalized with an inferior race." When destitution occurred, Confederate desertion developed a class component that could not be contained by claims that slavery "gives the [white] poor an elevated position in society that they would not otherwise have."

Richmond ignited a time bomb of internal conflict in 1862. Against the wishes of Jefferson Davis, the legislature exempted owners and overseers of at least twenty slaves from military conscription, ostensibly to keep blacks under male subjugation. The "twenty-nigger law," which helped only "the aristocracy," according to its critics, reflected the South's chronic inability to set unequivocal priorities: political independence or chattel slavery. By December, soldiers were openly complaining "that they are torn from their homes, and their families consigned to starvation, solely in order that they may protect the property of slaveholders."

Davis to the contrary, Southern nationalism was simply not strong enough to withstand class conflict exacerbated by the invasion of the Union armies. Elsewhere, such as the Balkans, successful secessionists have been able to exploit their region's cultural incompatibility with the mother state. However, Americans—North and South—shared a common language, religion, and history, as revealed when common soldiers made an impromptu armistice to celebrate American independence on the Fourth of July. Soldiers could rarely see their opponents in battle, since most were fought in thick woods, but their commonality was clear whenever they traded coffee, tobacco, newspapers, and gossip during a lull in the fighting. One Tennessee volunteer, who loathed "Yankee hate and Puritan barbarity," went to a Northern outpost, ate a good breakfast, and found the enemy "mighty clever and pleasant fellows."

When a sense of nationality had to be pitted against the welfare of one's family, political commitment was apt to be outgunned, particularly in the South. In the North, most families were nuclear: parents, children, and perhaps a grandparent or two living in a community of nonrelatives. In the South, families were more often extended networks: groups of brothers and cousins married groups of sisters, and married couples lived near their kin. This extended family network could be a very vulnerable target for the Union army behind the battle lines. Young men from the same locality joined the same Confederate company, since they were cousins, in-laws, and next-door neighbors, all in one. When a letter written by or for one's wife arrived in camp, it might tell of her economic deprivation, as well as that of nephews, nieces, and cousins who farmed the neighboring fields. The soldier had to consider the plight not only of his immediate family but also of his extended family, his dead buddy's children, and his neighbor's wife and kids—all the same people. These circumstances caused a volunteer's "soul to sink in anguish," as Sherman knew and planned: "If they claim to be men they should defend their women and children and prevent us reaching their homes." Confederates from enlisted men to Robert E. Lee said that "half of the desertions from the southern army [are] caused by the letters they receive."

By mid-1863, with some 30 percent of Confederate soldiers absent from their units, "deserter" was not necessarily a term of reproach. (They included, one officer wrote his father, "some of the bravest men of our army.") By mid-1864, with some 40 percent gone, desertion had become a duty when one's home was at risk. That year the Confederate Congress passed a law punishing anyone abetting the act. It could hardly prosecute the newspapers habitually read by soldiers with time to kill. Like Davis, zealous publishers proclaimed "the hell of horrors which the people of Georgia will have to endure when Sherman becomes their lord and master." The claim that he "leaves the country perfectly impoverished wherever he has been" was hyperbolic. (One scholar believes he severely damaged about 12 percent of Georgia.) More important, it may have done as much inadvertent damage as pleas from starving relatives to come home. What soldiers called "blood-and-thunder editorials" begged them to hold the line with Johnston and Lee. One can imagine the response among the rank and file who read that "no man, woman, or child will escape [Sherman]. Universal ruin awaits us all."

Like all effective terrorists, even ones with his scruples, Sherman thrived on newspaper publicity and aimed at mass psychology: specifically at producing in "the people of Georgia a thorough conviction of personal misery which attends war." Once that was accomplished, he hoped to convince the state to make a separate peace with the U.S. government. If done, he promised to prevent "the ravages of a hostile march" to the sea, a contingency that scared him, like it scared them, since he never escaped the fear that his army might degenerate into a lawless mob.

Sherman, who relaxed by reading the knight-errantry novels of Sir Walter Scott while he trampled through the South, left "the chivalry [of the Confederacy] perfectly confounded and horror stricken," according to a war correspondent of the *Chicago Tribune*. Nonetheless, he was unable to force separate Southern states to surrender on their own. In Georgia and South Carolina he therefore had to conduct the type of campaign many civilians and privates had advocated since late 1861. In a chain of diffusion of ideas about how to fight the war, the professional soldier had come to agree with his brother, who came to agree with the public in mid-1862. The last step in this process occurred when reluctant staff officers came to agree with General Sherman. His judge advocate, a religious man born in Alabama and responsible for enforcing the rules of war, admitted that "it is terrible to consume and destroy the sustenance of thousands of people and most sad and distressing in itself to see and hear the terror and grief of these women and children." Nonetheless, he concluded, "it is mercy in the end" because the operation will "paralyze their husbands and fathers fighting us" in the field.[9]

FROM SOUTHERN SLAVES TO YANKEE SOLDIERS

Along with Southern families, the softest target the Union army could hit was the slave labor system. In 1862 the North began to keep runaways, recruit Northern freedmen (only 45,000 available), and arm 1,400 Louisiana mulattoes—"about the complexion of the late Mr. [Daniel] Webster." This politically tepid policy would soon be discarded, along with George McClellan and other moderate ways that failed to win the war. Making former slaves into combat soldiers would facilitate each of the North's three strategies. It would strengthen Lincoln's strategy of attrition by increasing manpower. Furthermore, as radical Republicans argued two months before Bull Run, the recruitment of blacks would increase Confederate desertions as more Southern soldiers worried about the safety and subsistence of their families back home. But whether or not black soldiers pillaged and looted as whites did, they would also give Grant more men to practice the operational art, using Meade to pin Lee while trying to maneuver with Butler, who had a whole military corps of colored regiments in the Army of the James.

Born of necessity, this new recruitment policy was begrudgingly accepted within the Union army. "I wouldant lift my finger to free them," wrote one private, "but if we cant whip the rebils without taking the nigers I say take them and make them fite for us any way to bring this war to a close." In the process of ending the war in this manner, the conflict between states over constitutional rights became a race war between Southern blacks and whites. Lincoln, a Whig who had spent most of his life in pursuit of respectability, inherited the role and language of John Brown, as revealed in his second presidential inaugural: "Every drop of blood drawn with the lash shall be paid by another drawn with the sword." Despite his personal hopes to the contrary, the conflict "degenerate[d] into a violent and remorseless revolutionary struggle." Lincoln, a self-described "fatalist," said this was "Divine Will"—certainly not the only explanation. Black soldiers as military means changed the nature and objectives of the war.

The month after Fort Sumter, Lincoln began receiving letters suggesting the enlistment of slaves. A year later he still lagged behind public and congressional opinion, especially that of radicals who complained about his being "born of 'poor white trash' and educated in a slave State." Even moderate Republicans reported that those "who are determined to preserve the unity of the government at all hazards, agree that we must seek the aid and make it the interests of the negroes to help us." However, while Lincoln was moving toward emancipation, he told a leading proponent of black soldiers "the time" was not right to change recruitment policy.

Lincoln well knew that he was riding a process he could not control. As Federal troops moved into an area, slaves fled into their ranks. Lincoln had to decide if he would try to stem this tide or do decisive damage to Southern productivity. If he chose the latter and emancipation became an objective of the war, enlistments would probably decrease. (There were even reports of a military coup to prevent the proclamation.) Lincoln then would need blacks to offset the loss of white manpower. By mid-1863 the president was elated about events he had stoically accepted in mid-1862. "Raising colored troops," he wrote Grant and the military governor of Tennessee, "will soon end the contest . . . [by] weakening the enemy and strengthening us." They are "the great *available* and yet *unavailed* force for restoring the Union."

With great expectations, Lincoln planned to organize "a negro army," break into "the interior of rebeldom," and recruit 62,000 more soldiers from its slave population. Then, "the bare sight of fifty thousand armed and drilled black soldiers on the banks of the Mississippi would end the rebellion at once." Such predictions were not uncommon in the North. So many Yankees put so much faith in black warriors that Democratic newspapers and Confederate officers made a concerted effort to discredit them as soldiers. One Union general told the commander of the First (Colored) South Carolina "to risk as little as possible in [their] first enterprise because of the fatal effect on public sentiment of even an honorable defeat."

Pollyannaish or not, the president's new recruitment policy tapped a reservoir of commitment to the Union most white men could not duplicate. This was not just because former slaves, at least according to some whites, had "long habits of obedience and subordination" suitable to military institutions. Nor was a slave simply "used to suffering and seeing his own blood flow." As stated earlier, many common soldiers were primarily concerned with proving their capacity and courage, as was the Pennsylvania recruit who declared how "I longed to be a man, now the opportunity has offered." If whites had this motivation, one can begin to appreciate what combat service must have meant for blacks, heretofore treated as if they were subhuman. "When God made me I wasn't much," one new recruit told a former slaveholder, "but I's a man now."

African-Americans—from Frederick Douglass to riflemen in the field—described the military experience as a transition "from passive submission, shame, [and] disgrace" to "the glory and brilliant aggressiveness of a free soldier." They even took "a grim satisfaction" that most Southerners would not take their surrender: "With us there was to be no play-soldier." No wonder newspapers, recruiters, and white officers "never saw such enthusiasm" and "fiery energy" as was displayed by volunteers in the colored units who "realize that they have the rights of men." "They never feel sure of it until they get the muskets, because they have been told so many times that they were enlisting for soldiers, and found themselves laborers" instead.

Once the slaveholder, as Douglass put it, fell "by the hand of his slave," the Civil War crossed a Rubicon far wider than emancipation, a policy that already drove Southern legislators to raise "the *black flag,* asking and giving no quarter," and pushed Lee to write of "no alternative but success or degradation worse than death." Hereafter, the political ground was cut out from under moderate Northern Democrats and Southern Whigs, as Halleck told Grant in 1863: "There can be no peace but what is forced by the sword." Southern rhetoric became ever more laced with "grand holocaust," "war of extermination," and Davis's depiction of Yankee policy: "They debauch the inferior race, hitherto docile and contented, by promising indulgence of the vilest passions as the price of treachery." One officer commanding weary Confederates at Petersburg gave thanks: "I have aways wished the enemy to bring some negroes against this army. . . . it has had a splended effect on our men."

Throughout American military history, race has been a major cause of the escalation of the violence of war. In 1756 and 1814 enemy solicitation of Indian allies (and occasionally slaves) drove conflicts with France and Britain in the direction of no-holds-barred. In 1863 the Southern rank and file, "enflamed at seeing a negro in arms," did not need the official guidance that "slaves in flagrant rebellion . . . cannot be recognized in any way as soldiers subject to the rules of war." African-Americans, who knew from the beginning that "dere's no flags of truce for us," retaliated in kind. There was also "a general gritting of teeth" in Sherman's army, irrespective of race.

Unlike his brother John, Sherman would have kept "this a white man's war," if he possibly could. Then he would escape accusations from West Point classmates on the other side "that we had to call on *their* slaves to help us to subdue them." At the most, he would have used runaways as construction workers, servants, and cooks—functions they performed for nearly every Union unit operating in the South. However, in this capacity, African-Americans were as badly abused by Northern soldiers as they had been by former owners. True, by mid-1862 there was certainly a growing "desire among the soldiery to take the negro from the secesh master," according to one army colonel. But this only occurred from a "desire to destroy everything that gives the rebels strength."

Once African-Americans were committed to combat, their status improved, at least within the army. They often proved braver than most officers, a joy to enlisted men of any race who thought their captains "worse than a niger driver." That made blacks Union soldiers, not runaway slaves, even in the eyes of some who believed that "God never intended a nigger to put white people Down." A private from Illinois wrote home, "When you hear eney one say that negro soldiers wont fight just tell them that they ly for me." Privates from Wisconsin, less concerned with proprieties than General Sherman, had a more direct response. They asked twenty-three rebels if they knew of Fort Pillow, where Nathan Bedford Forrest, the Confederacy's fiercest fighter, slaughtered 200 black prisoners to "demonstrate to the Northern people that negro soldiers cannot cope with the Southerners." Whatever the reply, they killed them all. "Where there is no officer with us, we take no prisoners. . . . We want revenge for our brother soldiers." Farewell to fraternization.

Black soldiers were not only a cause of mutual atrocities and an issue to suppress Union sentiment in the South; they also became a pledge Lincoln's conscience would not let him disavow. In other words, he could not treat them as if they were but a means for his end of suppression of secession. During the 1864 presidential election, the Democratic party said that only abolition kept the South from rejoining the Union. Even friendly critics reminded Lincoln of his statement on the eve of the Emancipation Proclamation: "If you could save the Union without freeing any slave, you would do it." They, several Republican politicians, and newspaper publishers, who once attacked Lincoln for excessive caution and called for the iron-glove policy, now suggested that he revoke the decree to rob McClellan of his strongest issue. Lincoln, however, remained adamant on what he called a debt of honor to those who "have helped mankind on to this great consummation" of preserving "the great republic": people have "proposed to me to return to slave the black warrior of Port Hudson & Olustee. I should be damned in time & eternity for so doing. The world shall know that I will keep my faith to friends and enemies, come what will." By mid-1865 there were 186,000 African-Americans in the Union army, 72 percent recruited from slaveholding states. After nearly 200,000 desertions, there were 160,000 white men in the army of the Confederacy.[10]

FROM A LONG STRUGGLE OF ATTRITION
TO A "SPLENDID LITTLE WAR"

The Civil War would be a monumental event in the hearts and minds of those who fought it and those who heard about it for the next thirty years. Some veterans from the North, such as William McKinley, would spend the postwar decades trying to prevent a repetition of similar military events. Others—from the South, like Bedford Forrest, Fitzhugh Lee, and Joe Wheeler—would use prospective wars to show their old enemies that old rebels could be loyal to the government. In the 1890s, memorials to Civil War heroism pervaded popular culture, after a twenty-year moratorium on the subject while veterans dealt with postwar traumatic stress. Those too young to have served felt about the Lincolns, Lees, and Grants the way those men felt about Washington in 1860: that their predecessors shamed a third-rate generation coming to maturity after great deeds were done. During a colonial rebellion in Cuba, Teddy Roosevelt, Leonard Wood, and others would leap to grab their own opportunity for military heroism. McKinley, meanwhile, had nightmare flashbacks of events he hoped he would never have to witness again.

5

The Spanish-American War:
Stumbling into the Way
to Fight a Limited War

Reminiscent of the War of 1812, the Republican party fought Spain to retain power in Washington. That objective required military victory before the congressional elections of 1898. President William McKinley's dilemma was that this goal seemed to require an assault on Havana reminiscent of the Union army's march on Richmond, the worst experience of his life. Fortuitously, he fell into the peripheral strategy of the Naval War College and the army chief of staff: that of capturing the Philippines and Puerto Rico. Both campaigns were executed brilliantly. Neither would have won the war by November if the Spanish had not sent their fleet into Cuban waters, where it was destroyed. This exposed Spain to a potential bombardment that could have incited a revolution, the specter that impelled the government to sue for peace. The hold of the monarchy on the Spanish people was less than that of McKinley on the American electorate, precarious indeed.

CAUSES OF THE CONFLICT: CUBA VERSUS SPAIN,
CONGRESS VERSUS PRESIDENT

The Spanish-American War of 1898 can be traced to the "Ten Years' War" within Cuba (1868–78) and to political competition inside the United States. Natives staged a colonial rebellion for independence from the Spanish Empire. Democrats contested Republicans, and Congress contested the president in the most volatile and competitive period in American political history. Between Ulysses S. Grant's election in 1872 and McKinley's in 1896, no presidential candidate received a majority of the popular vote. (Third- and fourth-party candidates ran in each contest.) From the Forty-third through the Fifty-fourth Congress (1873 through 1897), Democrats controlled both the House of Representatives and the Senate twice; Republicans did so four times; and six times Congress split. When the electorate changed their political preference, the turnover was greater than at any other time, except the Great Depression of the early 1930s. The Forty-third Congress (1873 to 1875) had 194 Republicans in the House and 92 Democrats; the Forty-Fourth Congress had 169 Democratic congressmen and 109 Republicans. From 1889 to 1897 the Democratic delegation numbered 159, 235, 218, and finally 105.

Aside from this close and combustible contest for partisan control, institutional competition between Congress and the president marked the political environment. The national Democratic party was a coalition of minority groups— Southerners, Catholics, recent immigrants, opponents of the tariffs, and so forth. As such, they favored power in the hands of Congress, the institution that represented state and district pluralities, not the national majority from coast to coast. Republicans also tended to favor authority in the legislature, their antebellum roots laying in the Whigs, a party named after the parliamentary opposition to the kings of England. In the early 1830s, Whigs organized to contest "executive usurpation" by "King Andrew" Jackson, one of the most assertive presidents in U.S. history. After the Civil War, although Republican candidates were likely to win the White House, congressional Republicans still wanted to rule. "The executive department of a republic," wrote John Sherman, four-term congressman and six-term senator, "should be subordinate to the legislative department. . . . The limitation of the power of the President . . . is an essential requisite of a republican government." "The most eminent Senators," said George Frisbie Hoar, three-term congressman and five-term senator, "would have received as a personal affront a private message from the White House expressing a desire that they should adopt any course . . . they did not approve. If they visited the White House, it was to give, not to receive advice."

In this contentious setting, foreign affairs were highly politicized, beginning with America's reaction to Cuba's first insurrection—from 1868 to 1878. The political dispute within the United States pitted senators and some congressmen—mostly Republicans—against the Grant administration, especially its secretary of state, Hamilton Fish, a descendant from a long line of wealthy New York City bankers. Fish—to whom the president deferred—did not want to risk war for impoverished, largely nonwhite insurrectionists unlikely to provide stability, law, and order as conservative bankers defined those terms. The most vocal congressional critics of the secretary's refusal to grant the insurgents belligerent rights all came from the Midwest—John Logan, Matthew Carpenter, Oliver Morton, and John Sherman. This was probably not fortuitous. The Northeast was secure for Republicans and the South for Democrats. The Midwest was closely contested political territory, and said Sherman (Ohio) on the Senate floor: "In the region of the country where I live . . . [public] sympathies are strongly excited in favor of the insurgents."

In the 1870s Senator Morton (Indiana) condemned Spain for "atrocious and satanic barbarism." In 1896 the Chicago *Tribune,* the leading Republican newspaper in the Midwest, wrote that if "Spain wants to go to war, the war will be a welcome one and she will get all the fighting she wants." For some twenty years language like this may have provided the margin for victory in the region's closely contested elections. When America finally did go to war in 1898, one-third of the House of Representatives opposed intervention; only one-fifth of the Midwest delegation voted no.

Newspaper and congressional calls for an assertive foreign policy usually followed party lines. Democrats berated Republican presidents for timidity. The GOP did the same thing by attacking Grover Cleveland, the era's only Democratic president, for two alleged failures in the late 1880s. First, he did not secure fishing rights and border claims from the British Empire in Canada—a patent Republican attempt to court the Irish vote in New York, a state Cleveland carried by 1,150 votes and thereby won the 1884 election. Second, he did not exclude Chinese immigrants from California—a swing state Cleveland would lose by 7,000 votes when he lost the White House in 1888.

Because the party out of power attacked the administration for a weak or tepid foreign policy, the party in power encouraged assertion lest its rival replace it. In 1891 Republican politicians such as Senator William Chandler from New Hampshire told President Benjamin Harrison that the annexation of Hawaii would "divert attention from stagnant political discussions." In 1895 a congressman from Texas told Cleveland's secretary of state that "one cannon shot across the bow of a British boat in defense" of the Monroe Doctrine would nullify critics of the administration's domestic policy.

Whether presidents adopted or rejected the advice to assert a more aggressive foreign policy, the political debate had a profound impact on the Cuban rebellion, which, after 1878, had slumbered for lack of international support. Many insurrectionists took exile in America, where they surely were encouraged by the militant mood of newspapers, Congress, and the opposition party, whoever that might be. In mid-May 1895 Republicans attacked "the supineness, dilatoriness and lack of National and patriotic spirit which has characterized the [Cleveland] Administration" and said, that June, they themselves would make foreign affairs the major issue in upcoming state elections. Perhaps agreeing with its own Democratic supporters that the Venezuelan border issue was "a winner" from every political angle, the administration soon challenged English claims in Latin America. "Today, the United States is practically sovereign on this continent," the secretary of state notified London during a dispute about the boundary of British Guiana, "and its fiat is law upon the subjects to which it confines its interposition." The same year that these and other bellicose statements pledged the United States would use "every means in its power," Cubans renewed their armed revolt against Spain.

Opposition to "Spain and her feudal lords," support for independence from a Catholic monarchy, and the removal of "medievalism from our front doors" was a popular stance for Congress to assume. Consequently, in April 1896 it passed by overwhelming numbers a joint resolution granting the insurgents "all the rights of belligerents [to purchase supplies] in the ports and territories of the United States"—247 yeas, 27 nays, and 80 not voting in the House; 57 yeas, 12 nays, and 20 not voting in the Senate. Those few who voted no were insulated from political challenge, 17 of the 21 Republicans and 12 of the 18 Democrats coming from the eastern seaboard states, both north and south.

Cleveland paid little heed to this strong vote in Congress. A chief executive on the Andrew Jackson model, he did not shape legislation; he annulled it, issuing twice as many vetoes as all preceding presidents combined. As for Cuba, Cleveland never wavered from his conviction that the Constitution gave the president the exclusive authority to recognize foreign governments and grant belligerent rights. Moreover, like policy makers in the Grant administration, he felt that the Cubans did not merit American support. If "the most inhuman and barbarous cutthroats in the world" won their war for independence, anarchy would prevail. If they just prolonged the costly conflict, Spain might sell the colony to a first-rate power. Then the United States would have the German navy as a next-door neighbor stationed in the Caribbean and blocking up the coastal trade.

The public's disapproval of this position did not phase Cleveland much. By 1895 his political stature was already damaged beyond repair by the worst depression of the nineteenth century—30 percent unemployment, 800 bank failures, a 600 percent increase in interest rates, and a 20 percent decrease in prices for farm products. Through it all, foreign issues and domestic, Cleveland would not modify his personal motto, "inflexible duty." Consequently, he was not renominated by his party, let alone reelected by the public. He was replaced in 1897 by a more flexible man, William McKinley from Ohio, a good Republican with a very different political background.

Cleveland's entire political career had been spent in the executive branch—as mayor of Buffalo, governor of New York, and president of the United States. McKinley was a creature of the legislature—a six-term congressman and chairman of the House Ways and Means Committee from 1889 to 1891. Cleveland vetoed city council street-cleaning contracts, state legislature mass transit regulations, and U.S. Congress private pension bills. McKinley had to bargain, negotiate, and compromise, as would anyone responsible for tax and tariff bills. In response to strong public and congressional sentiment, he would modify the contours of a legislative package. He could not banish pressure groups and felt he should not try. When he did take an unpopular stand on his favorite issue at an inappropriate time (the protective tariff during a "high price scare"), he lost his bid for reelection to his seventh term in the House in 1890.

A Republican presidency freed congressional Democrats to concentrate on Cuba at a time they were desperately searching for an issue. In the 1896 election the party had suffered its worst defeat in thirty-two years, Lincoln's second term. It emphasized domestic issues—especially inflation to provide relief to debtors by backing paper money with silver, not just gold. McKinley's inauguration

(1897) coincided with an upswing of the business cycle, making the economy a Republican issue. Hence the liberation of Cuba, barely mentioned in the 1896 party platform, became the Democratic theme for 1898.

As mentioned earlier, the Democrats were a loose, diverse, and disparate coalition of import-export merchants in favor of low tariffs, urban working-class Catholics, cotton planters, and wheat farmers. ("I'm not a member of any organized political party," went one vaudeville joke. "I'm a Democrat.") On most domestic issues—social or economic—they were woefully divided. Merchants wanted deflation (a strong dollar) to purchase imports from abroad. Farmers, being debtors, wanted inflation and high prices for cotton and wheat. As evangelical Protestants, they wanted to prohibit saloons and parochial schools, exactly what urban Catholics wanted, along with cheap cloth and food. Cuba could unite the party as no other issue could. "The Democrats," wrote a Washington reporter in late 1897, "present a more solid front than I have ever seen."

Symbolically, support for Cuba and opposition to Spain struck a responsive chord with a host of Democrats. German and Irish Americans were anti-imperialists, since Britain had the greatest empire in the world. They favored independence for nearly everyone from nearly every empire—Cubans, Boers, and Filipinos. The fact that Spain was a Catholic country was an added incentive. Wartime patriotism would discredit the charge—widespread during this period of rampant nativism—that "foreign elements [were] ready tools of demagogues" and that Catholics were loyal only to their pope. In 1898, when debate on the Spanish-American War kept Republican-sponsored bills for immigration restriction off the floor of the House of Representatives, Congressman John F. Fitzgerald (John Kennedy's grandfather) declared in the Capitol rotunda: "If war does come, no more valiant, brave and heroic defenders of the national honor and the preservation of the Government will be found than the members of the Catholic Church. (Loud and enthusiastic applause.)"

Like the Irish Catholics of the urban East, the wheat farmers of the Great Plains had a symbolic stake in the liberation of Cuba. At least as early as Hamilton Fish, East Coast financial interests were indifferent, if not hostile, to aiding the insurgents in a brutal civil war along race and class lines. This gave interventionists a populist tinge, even if Republicans. In 1896 John Sherman made a point of noting that "'the better class of inhabitants'" supported the colonial administration, where "the rights of the poor and feeble and ignorant are totally disregarded." Theodore Roosevelt and Henry Cabot Lodge, sons of bankers or investors, denounced "the craven fear" of the "selfish money interests" inferior to "the popular instinct," at least in policy toward Cuba. If Republicans could talk this way, one can imagine what Democrats were thinking in the political aftermath of 1896. Prominent bankers had financed the Republican campaign against paper money—one way to reduce interest payments to banks. To wheat farmers and other debtors from the West, a war against Spain—like the election they recently lost to Wall Street—would be a "fight between the money power and the people." This time, on this issue, they felt they could beat the "organized band of conspirators who put dollars above the higher interests of the nation."

Finally, within the Democratic party, there was the congressional mainstay from what was called "the solid South." Like wheat producers, cotton planters hated the finance capitalists of the Northeast. Like the Irish, they loathed an empire based on military conquest and wished to show their loyalty at the same time. In their case the evil empire meant the Republican party, a strong federal government, and the American Civil War—until the 1960s called the "War of Northern Aggression." In 1873 the Spanish hung a former Confederate naval officer sailing a former Confederate blockade-runner full of guns and ammunition to a rebel stronghold near Santiago de Cuba. In 1897, a year before America landed an expedition at the same location, John Sherman, now McKinley's secretary of state, protested the counterinsurgency tactics Spain used in Cuba—"the cruel employment of fire and famine [against civilians] to accomplish by uncertain indirection what the military arm seems powerless to directly accomplish." Spain replied, no doubt with a smirk, that "to crush rebellions . . . all civilized countries . . . have proceeded in the same manner"—for example, "the expedition of General Sherman, that illustrious and respected general, through Georgia and South Carolina." Rubbing more salt into America's political wound, Spain also pointed out that "a military and dictatorial system, in the States opposed to the Union, lasted many years after the termination of the bloody contest."

The Spanish military commander in Cuba, Valeriano Weyler, had been military attaché in Washington in the 1860s. New York newspapers, calling him "the devastator of haciendas, the destroyer of families, and the outrager of women," paid no attention to Spain's analogy between its "Reconcentration" policy and Civil War and Reconstruction in America. The South certainly did. Its congressional representatives called the empire "carpet-bag government." Unlike the McKinley administration, well aware of the racial composition of the conflict in Cuba, it ignored the warnings of Winston Churchill, a young English military observer sympathetic to Spain: "Two-fifths of the insurgents in the field are negros . . . [whose triumph will create] another black republic" in the Western Hemisphere.

Democrats would sponsor resolutions to recognize the rebellion as the sovereign Republic of Cuba, bills invariably defeated by Republican opposition. Senator Samuel Pasco of Florida, former Confederate prisoner of war, said the white population of the island overwhelmingly supported the revolt, patently false. Senator John Tyler Morgan of Alabama called the guerrilla insurgency an "open, public civil war." Congressman Joe Wheeler called the insurrectionists "our brethren struggling for liberty." This was something of a political flashback for these men and their whole region. Thirty-five years before debating intervention on Capitol Hill, Major General Wheeler had led Brigadier General Morgan and a whole corps of Confederate cavalry against the secretary of state's big brother and General Weyler's role model, the "illustrious and respected" William Tecumseh Sherman.[1]

Feeling that the conduct of foreign affairs was emblematic of a "really great nation," Theodore Roosevelt, assistant secretary of the navy, and Henry Cabot Lodge, senator from Massachusetts, lamented America's "hap-hazard" performance. Actually, it was transacted more consistently than they believed, although in a partisan context natural to politicians who tended to take military security for granted. Congressional Democrats attacked the Republican president for weakness before the Spanish Empire, just as Republicans had attacked his Democratic predecessor. Most Republican legislators did not rally to McKinley, just as many Democrats had left Cleveland on his own. In 1896 the Republican party platform on this issue had been longer and stronger than that of the Democrats: "We watch with deep and abiding interest the heroic battle of the Cuban patriots against cruelty and oppression. . . . The United States should actively use its influence and good offices to . . . give independence to the Island." To reverse that stance was to risk in the upcoming congressional election what one Democrat had feared Republicans would do back in 1891: to grab all the political "capital there is to be made in an attempt to assert national self-respect."

Office retention, pure and simple, was not the sole motivation of Republicans in 1898. In 1896, the Democrats repudiated Cleveland, a conservative from the East, and nominated William Jennings Bryan on a populist platform pledged to "protect the people from robbery and oppression" by big business, high finance, and marketplace monopolies. Publicly and privately, Republicans had described the campaign against the Bryan Democrats as a battle to halt "the triumph of sectionalism and communism," a national "disaster which would be second only to 1861." In the election they broke the political stalemate that had existed since 1875. Republicans now had a 13-seat majority in the Senate, 139 in the House, and the first president elected with a majority of the popular vote since Grant in 1872.

Cuba threatened to upset the whole Republican applecart, as indicated by losses in New York and Kentucky in 1897 and a very narrow victory in Ohio, McKinley's home state. Cabot Lodge, who could sound like a radical populist when it came to Cuba, told one important Massachusetts constituent who opposed intervention that "the course you are advising leads straight to free silver and Bryanism" via repudiation of the Republican party. Conversely, Knute Nelson, senator from Minnesota, wrote one of America's leading railroad investors that "a popular war might do more than anything else to relieve the country from the nightmare of the free silver question. The success of Bryanism [and] Populism would inflict infinitely more damage on this country than a short, sharp war with Spain."

Lodge and Nelson were two of many Republicans who feared repudiation in an off-year election even greater than that which they had suffered in 1890, when they lost seventy-eight members in the House of Representatives. If the Democrats monopolized the "free Cuba" issue, GOP legislators predicted that 1898 would be "the greatest defeat ever known." They informed senior members of the administration that "Congress will exercise the [constitutional] power and declare war in spite of [the president]!" One angry senator told the secretary of state: "He'll get run over and the party with him!" One sad citizen entreated the Speaker of the House to contain jingoism. The so-called czar, Thomas B. Reed, on McKinley's side, replied: "Might as well ask me to stand out in the middle of a Kansas waste and dissuade a cyclone." After the political dust settled, when the war and election were over, Lodge told one forum that "this public sentiment drove Congress forward to meet the popular will, which members and Senators very well knew could be fulfilled by war and in no other way."

McKinley, although said to be supported by the "quiet but influential class" of people, could not defy Congress and would not sacrifice his party under any circumstance. Nonetheless, he delayed congressional action for a few months while he desperately sought some alternative to armed conflict with Spain. He had only a brief window of opportunity until the onset of the rainy (disease) season, June through October, would prevent military operations in Cuba. By April, one way or the other, the president needed to settle the Cuban problem if he were to nullify its impact on the November election. War was certainly the option he favored least of all.

"War" is an imprecise term meaning anything from a futile search for Seminoles in the 1830s to the Battle of the Bulge in 1944. To most people the word usually evokes the type of military conflict they remember from their youth. For McKinley that meant the Civil War in which he—"a handsome, bright, gallant boy"—served in some of the worst fighting in U.S. history. In 1898 he may have been thinking of Antietam—where "the colors of [his] regiment were riddled and the blue field almost completely carried away by shells and bullets"—when he told a young interventionist, "I have been through one war; I have seen the dead piled up; and I do not want to see another" or when he told the senior senator from Indiana, "It isn't the money that will be spent nor the property that will be destroyed but the thought of human suffering that must come into thousands of homes [that] is almost overwhelming."

This sentiment was not peculiar to McKinley. In the North, some of the most vocal doves were the most highly decorated veterans of the Civil War. One week before Congress authorized "forcible intervention" in Cuba, General (retired) John Schofield—recipient of the Medal of Honor and former commander of the Army of the Ohio—was quoted as saying that he found it "hard to conceive how people can look upon war as in some manner tending to enhance the glory and dignity of a nation." One of the few congressmen to speak against an emergency appropriation to begin mobilization was Henry H. Bingham (Rep.-Pa.), once a brigadier general of volunteers (brevet rank) and a recipient of the Medal of Honor for actions at the Battle of the Wilderness, May 1864. He told his House colleagues on 8 March 1898: "This generation has had one war, sufficient for it and for all time to come. . . . We want no war with Spain."

Bingham may have spoken for many members of his generation from his section of the United States. He certainly did not speak for all generations nor for all regions of America. The South, to repeat, was far more militant. After Congress passed the appropriation for mobilization, "Fighting Joe" Wheeler from Alabama let out a rebel yell. Apparently, former "traitors" felt the need to prove their patriotism, especially since Republicans were loath to let the loyalty issue die. As late as the 1890s, the GOP still proposed federal control of southern elections, as was done in Reconstruction, to "end the right of a set of rebels to command the Union army from the floor of Congress when they could not defeat them upon the field." Now, from 1896 to 1898, the South took great pride in pointing out that America's counsel in Havana was the nephew of Robert E. Lee and a former Confederate general himself. As the representative of America, Fitzhugh Lee risked lynching by angry Spanish mobs but, according to a congressman from Kentucky, himself a former rebel, Lee would "give up his lifeblood for that flag which once he fought against but which now he loves as devotedly as any man on American soil." In the same debate, Joseph W. Bailey, the House minority leader from Texas, said: "This war, if it be a war, will have at least one compensation. It will forever efface from the memory of our countrymen those dreadful times of civil strife, and the men whose courage made the first Manassas [referring to a Confederate victory] will join with those who immortalized Gettysburg, and together they will consecrate a new battlefield combining the glories of both."

Within the North, sentiments like these had more appeal to the post–Civil War generation than did Bingham's angry retort that Spanish atrocities in Cuba were similar "to the dead line at Libby"—the Confederate prison camp at Richmond. Vis-à-vis veterans of the Grand Army of the Republic, younger men had the same inferiority feelings their elders once felt toward those who had waged the Revolutionary War. Carl Sandburg, a famous biographer of Abraham Lincoln, was twenty years old when he saw limited action in the Puerto Rican campaign of the Spanish-American War. He would recall that "over all of us in 1898 was the shadow of the Civil War and the men who fought it to the end." Theodore Roosevelt was thirty-nine when he disregarded the anger of the administration by quitting the Department of the Navy in order to see "active service anywhere." He would say that those who fought "in the iron years from '61 to '65 . . . bore the heaviest burden that any generation of Americans ever had to bear; and because they did this they have won such proud joy as it has fallen to the lot of no other men to win." Roosevelt later admitted that the Cuban expedition "wasn't much of a war, but it was the best war we had." It gave him some of what he wanted: "chances of death, and hardship, of honor and renown."

A resurrection of the combat of the Civil War was Roosevelt's dream. (After the war, he would say that he commanded the Rough Riders "with honor. We lost a quarter of our men" and over one-third of the officers, "and all this within sixty days.") This same scenario was McKinley's nightmare, literally. The president could not sleep without sedatives, he paced back and forth, his face "haggard" and eyes "sunken" as he anxiously awaited "any news which has in it a token of peace." Nonetheless, as McKinley acknowledged, he was in diplomatic quicksand: the more he struggled, the more he sank. He raised a $50 million military appropriation to frighten Spain to make concessions that would stop its most abusive counterinsurgency operations and grant Cuba domestic autonomy within the Spanish Empire. However, as Spain made concessions "as fast and as far as they can," leaders of the rebellion threatened to shoot anyone advocating home rule. After all, complete independence, via U.S. assistance, seemed to be in the offing.

McKinley hoped Spain would sell or sever ties with Cuba, since the insurrection could be squelched only by a reign of "destruction and devastation" that would make the island utterly "worthless." Although 400 million pesos in debt, Spain was not pragmatic from a utilitarian point of view. Reminiscent of Mexico in the 1840s, its government was too weak to relinquish nominal control of territory it could scarcely govern. The more subjected it was to coercive diplomacy, the less it could defer to threats. It was precariously perched on an unstable political environment, much like the McKinley administration. Madrid officials, especially in the Department of the Marine, bewailed "the ignorant masses." They knew they had "to reckon with the excitable nature of our nation and the evil of a press which it is impossible to control," words one could have heard in Washington. In both countries, elements outside government ridiculed the prospective military opponent (American crews will desert their ships "as soon as fire is opened") and insisted there be no compromise on Cuba lest the nation "live with a stigma of humiliation and shame."

Spain, a parliamentary government, was a constitutional monarchy presiding over a country divided between royalists and republicans ready "to spring at each other like savage dogs," according to America's naval attaché. When the country had a real empire in the New World, Cuba had strategic significance, the fortress of Havana protecting treasure ships sailing from Central America. In 1898 it still was important but largely for sentimental reasons: what remained of God's so-called gift for eliminating the last Muslim enclaves from western Europe in 1492. Cuba gave the crown what fragile prestige it still retained in the hands of an unpopular Austria-born queen regent living to pass the throne on to her son. Its independence, according to one member of the Madrid government, "strips us of the very last memory of a glorious past," now the moral glue of modern Spain. To declare an armistice, said the U.S. ambassador, "would cause [a] revolution"—from the left, from the right, or from the army that intimidated the government with threats of a coup. The ambassador's reports from Spain read a lot like letters from Republicans in Congress, except he was talking about Madrid, they of Washington. He reported to McKinley that the regency had to "seriously consider the contingency of war in order to save themselves, and possibly the Dynasty, from [being] overthrown."

By 1898 Spain no longer controlled the countryside of Cuba, where its army, by its own account, was "without the power to fight or hardly even to lift their arms," a reference to 100,000 casualties, primarily from dysentery and malaria. "They know that Cuba is lost," the American ambassador cabled, but Spain had to lose it honorably. It was "no more than a romantic ideal," lamented Admiral Pascual Cervera, whose squadron would engage an American fleet nearly twice its size in what he called an act of military "suicide" that would strip Spain of self-defense. Others chirped about "the proud deeds of our ancestors." Cervera, a self-described "man without mad passions," said that to fight "a decisive naval battle" to keep America out of Cuba was to act "like Don Quixote, go out to fight windmills and come back with broken heads."

Domestic politics prevented Spain from granting independence and U.S. officials—although angry at the rebels—from accepting anything less than the rebels approved. Ipso facto, this committed America to Cuban independence. McKinley's "great ambition," Lodge wrote Roosevelt, "is to restore business and bring back good times." To do that, the administration felt it needed the cessation of combat inside Cuba; it "inflamed the American mind . . . [and] disturbed the peace and tranquility of our people." Two weeks after the secretary of state wrote these words to the ambassador to Spain, the president expressed similar sentiments also growing inside the business community now reconciled to war. When asking Congress for authority to enforce a peace settlement, McKinley stated that the conflict "beget[s] a perilous unrest among our own citizens. . . . Issues wholly external to our own body politic engross attention and stand in the way of that close devotion to domestic advancement that becomes a self-contained commonwealth."[2]

WAR PLANS AND CAMPAIGN PLANNING: FRONTAL ASSAULTS OR PERIPHERY PECKING?

As late as 7 April 1898, Theodore Roosevelt wrote a friend: "The President doesn't know what message he will send [to Congress] or what he will do if we have a war." McKinley had spent almost all his energy trying to establish peace in Cuba. He had raised $50 million dollars to coerce a settlement, not mobilize an expedition. Almost all bluff, the president forbade spending the money on anything but coastal defense, which would not fire a single round in the entire war.

Once again, the public was far more assertive than its so-called leaders. By the time Congress passed its resolution for armed force on 20 April, the strongest cry in the country was "On to Havana," hardly a judicious proposal. This Spanish bastion contained 60,000 soldiers, 105 stationary guns (4 from Krupp with twelve-inch barrels), and 150 pieces of field artillery, along with three lines of mines, torpedoes, and steel cable blocking a forced entrance to its harbor. This prospect chilled McKinley, who had spent four bloody years hearing "On to Richmond." But having failed to avoid armed conflict, he had no clear notions how to wage it while somehow avoiding a repetition of the American Civil War.

The United States did have a few contingency plans floating around Washington. The joint army-navy board proposed landing thirty miles west of Havana, marching quickly on the capital, and thereby producing a "certain and probably speedy" victory of prime importance to the president. There was also an idea from Fitzhugh Lee. Despite Cleveland's advice against retaining this unreliable war hawk, McKinley kept Lee as counsel in Havana to give his policy bipartisan and southern support. In March the old commander of the Army of Northern Virginia cavalry sent Washington an alternative to "On to Havana," one to strangle the city on all sides: (1) blockade Havana harbor, (2) land supplies for insurgents at an inlet sixty-six miles east of the city, and (3) help Cubans cut communication lines to the capital at a railroad node to the hinterland.

When Lee joined the diplomatic service in 1894, he had just completed a biography of his Uncle Robert and was lecturing about the Civil War, probably the source of inspiration for his concept of operation. As a general officer, his experience had been different from that of McKinley, who had fought exclusively at a tactical level where every offensive action seems like a frontal assault. Lee's plan bore remarkable resemblance to Ben Butler's amphibious landing up the James River, a back door to Richmond. Old Yankees may not have been as impressed as old Confederates. Butler never made the rapid progress Grant intended in 1864, thereby forcing the Union to conduct a laborious siege that prolonged the conflict until 1865. Lee's plan went to the War Department, where it languished, perhaps because it would take more time than the public gave McKinley, who wanted to end the conflict before the fall elections. Hence it did not provide the president with much practical hope of avoiding a bloody frontal assault.

The president rued and young men relished some sort of resurrection of the Civil War, the patriotic fare of histories and Memorial Day addresses throughout the Gilded Age. Bright young navy officers had a different model of armed conflict, that of "a purely naval campaign," influenced by their favorite conflict—or at least the one they wished to duplicate. In 1812 the navy had saved the nation while the army hung on for dear life. After 1883 the navy underwent extensive modernization, changing the force structure it had had since its creation in 1775: moving from sail to steam, from wood to steel, from smoothbore to rifled naval guns, from single-ship action to fleet engagements, and from coastal defense to command of the high seas. On the eve of the Spanish-American War, the U.S. Navy had six first-class battleships, two armored and ten light cruisers, but also a cabinet secretary bored by "the necessity of having some scheme to attack arranged for instant execution in case of an emergency." This Massachusetts politician notwithstanding, a generation of officers stood ready to "act offensively" from the onset of war.

The naval construction program was designed according to the "go-get-'em" school of blue-water strategy: "The way to keep the enemy from your door is to go for him so actively that he cannot afford to do anything but defend himself."

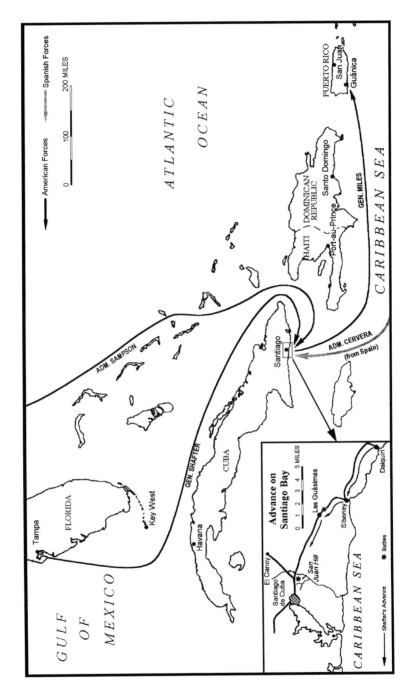

Spanish-American War, Caribbean theater

Its priorities had shortchanged the barges, tugs, and troop transports the country would need to support a substantial projection of ground forces onto Cuba. Nor did the navy seem to mind that disembarking troops and supplies was an army mission for which the army was not trained, cause for the future "muddle" near Santiago Bay. In all fairness, the navy might have replied that it made no sense to support a sister service not prepared to conduct a foreign expedition.

The U.S. Army seemed to have remained, in the words of Congressman George McClellan Jr., "little better than a clumsily organized National police force" geared to watch Indians and stop domestic riots. Even John Schofield, its recently retired commanding general, called the navy "the *aggressive* arm of the national military power. . . . In special cases," he concluded in 1897, land "forces may be needed to act in support of naval operations . . . but such service must be only auxiliary, not a primary object." For credible reasons, such as the army's concurrence, the navy expected that they would have to win the next international conflict largely on their own, especially after America declared war near the eve of Cuba's rainy season. That April, the secretary of the navy told the Atlantic fleet commander that the army would not be available before October.

Since 1895, when hostilities between Spain and the United States became a distinct possibility, personnel at the Naval War College and Office of Naval Intelligence had been perfecting a plan by which their service could get maximum credit for the liberation of Cuba. One area of operation they selected was Manila Bay in the Philippines. If the navy sank the antiquated squadron and sealed off the weakly defended capital of that Spanish colony, it reasoned that America could trade Manila for Cuba at a peace conference, especially after a "purely naval war" softened up Havana and San Juan (Puerto Rico) with blockades and bombardments.

In September 1897 McKinley heard of naval plans during a carriage ride with Roosevelt, who was not very happy that "the Army may not be employed." He personally wanted "a serious land war" so he could get a chance to fight, knowing that he would "be useless on a ship." Whether Roosevelt disclosed everything or withheld some information, the president seemed barely informed about the campaign the U.S. Far East Fleet was supposed to execute when the war began. He brought General Schofield to the White House for unofficial advice, much the way John Kennedy would bring Maxwell Taylor and Richard Nixon sought Al Haig. Schofield suggested a peripheral approach, initial attacks on Puerto Rico and the Philippines. It barely registered with McKinley and his cabinet, preoccupied with Cuba and domestic politics. They only dispatched Commodore George Dewey after he telegraphed Washington that the fleet had to vacate its Hong Kong base leased from Britain exclusively for peacetime purposes. Dewey then went to Manila and destroyed the Spanish fleet without suffering a single fatality. By this fortuitous event, McKinley began to stumble into a military strategy: avoid Havana; attack the periphery; concentrate strength against weakness, not against strength.

After the navy's action at Manila—but before the army disembarked for Cuba—the State Department and McKinley floated a proposal for restoring the Philippines to Spain in return for evacuation of the Caribbean. Neither the Naval War College nor the U.S. government took the pride of the Spanish army into account. It and the jingoist press in Madrid said it still could rout America's "untrained militia." Under threat of a military coup and more riots in the streets, where Civil Guard cavalry was charging pro-war demonstrators, the Spanish government could not make any reasonable trade that would deny its army the chance to bloody the invader.

Whenever possible, the senior officers of the U.S. Army would deny the Spanish the battle they wanted by executing the peripheral strategy McKinley was unwittingly adopting. In fact, if they had full authority, they would have conducted it much better than the president, since they felt no compulsion to liberate Cuba before the November elections. Unlike the commander in chief, they had gotten Civil War assaults out of their mind. For the last thirty years, the army served in low-casualty conflicts, primarily rounding up Indians running off the reservation. McKinley, as a specialist on tariff legislation, paid little attention to these low-profile operations. The service could do other things than reenact Grant against Lee. As Major General William R. Shafter, the commander of the V Corps, told a group of officers while en route to Cuba: "We were a long way from the Civil War. . . . The country was no longer accustomed to hear of heavy losses in battle and would judge us accordingly."

The army's commanding general, Nelson A. Miles, was a crockery store clerk when the Civil War began. He, the inspector general, and the secretary of war— all Civil War volunteers—trusted little but professional soldiers "fully armed, equipped, drilled, and disciplined." Even more than McKinley, they wanted to avoid large bodies of "hastily organized" citizen-soldiers, such as Miles had led in the Wilderness campaign, "a spectacle of horror without a parallel." Volunteers, by their very nature, were "neither equipped nor instructed, or even supplied with ammunition to fight a battle." A standing army was "the best conditioned military body in the world," not the operations Miles recently conducted.

Miles had been one of the army's most successful Indian fighters. In those campaigns he had placed a premium on small units and maneuver, not the ponderous frontal attacks he futilely led at Fredericksburg in 1863. As an institution, the army emerged from the Civil War vowing not to use assault waves again. For strategy in Cuba, Miles proposed the same ideas that worked in the West. There, effective officers respected the rights and responsibilities of Indian scouts, absolutely essential for conflicts won by destroying the food supply of hostile tribes. Now, in April 1898, Miles proposed using "a small force of regular soldiers" to harass the enemy and give "succor to the insurgents," that is, making filibustering official military policy. While natives conducted the bulk of the land campaign in Cuba, the U.S. Army was to take San Juan (Puerto Rico), "the first objective." The occupation of this choke point and coaling base would prevent hostile warships from entering the Caribbean. Then a U.S. naval blockade and guerrilla destruction of cattle and crops (their primary tactic) would starve out the Spanish. This would complete the plan to "compel the surrender of their army on the island of Cuba with very little loss of life."

Miles's military strategy combined appropriate ways and means for limited objectives. It ignored racial prejudice, institutional rivalry, partisan pressures, and public demands. Washington, which had had far less faith in Indian auxiliaries than did army officers on the frontier, had just as little faith in the Cuban insurgents. In 1886 the War Department instructed Miles about "the necessity of making active and prominent use of the Regular troops" in the campaign to capture Geronimo. In 1896 it cautioned Shafter "against putting too much confidence in any persons outside of your troops." At the same time, the army's plan deferred to the navy far more than the navy wished. A blockade may have been effective in theory but had several problems in practice. It was long and laborious, wore down machinery, and exposed the fleet to Caribbean hurricanes. Thus, in late April and early May, Washington witnessed a series of military conferences strange to those who believe the services always fight for the major wartime mission. The navy, worried that "the burden is likely to fall upon the[m]," demanded that the army, whatever its condition, conduct an assault on Havana "at once." The army, specifically Miles, pleaded unpreparedness, decried "thoughtless" sloganeering reminiscent of "On to Richmond," and implored the president to adopt "more judicious measures."

The secretary of the navy, John Davis Long, had the president's ear, and not simply because he was a personal friend to whom McKinley confessed his deep anxiety about the war. General Miles's plan to slowly strangle Spanish ground forces resembled the Anaconda strategy that Winfield Scott gave Abraham Lincoln back in 1861. Scott had barely considered the time factor; Miles never mentioned time at all. McKinley, reminiscent of Lincoln, responded, "I deplore the war but it must be short and quick to the finish." As the White House personal secretary wrote that spring, the president "is solicitous to the last degree for the welfare of our troops and sailors, but he is determined not to delay prosecution . . . a day longer than necessary."[3]

INTERNAL CONFLICT AND FOREIGN WAR:
WHITES, BLACKS, SOUTH, EAST, AND WEST

Aside from the time factor, general public demand overruled Miles's plan to confine the war to small elements of the regular army. National interest in enlistment had been high since the *Maine* sank in Havana harbor (15 February). After Dewey's dramatic victory at Manila Bay, up to a million citizens volunteered for military service, which suddenly lost the lurking horror associated with the 1860s. (A "Mild-Mannered War," read the *Austin* (Texas) *Daily Statesman;*

"Nothing of the Grim Visage about It.") High spirits stretched from Theodore Roosevelt, now with the Rough Riders, down to obscure members of the First Texas Volunteers. "This is going to be a short war," said Roosevelt, "I am going into it and get all there is out of it." Texans worried that "the marine boys won't leave us any work to do. . . . I hope Blanco [Cuba's governor-general] won't surrender, we will all chip in and make him a present of a gold walking stick if he will give us a fight."

The secretary of war wrote a friend: "There is going to be more trouble to satisfy those who are not going [overseas] than to find those who are willing to go." For the emergency, the administration planned to expand temporarily the regular army by 50,000 men. Then Congress wrote its own mobilization legislation according to the age-old Anglo-American principle that citizen-soldiers are better than "mercenaries" because they fight for "liberty and the rights of man." Within weeks there were five applicants for each of 200,000 new military billets: ten times more volunteers than were inducted in the first six weeks of the Civil War. This meant that the U.S. Army, totally unprepared to expand tenfold in three months' time, would spend months simply trying to provide supplies, facilities, and training camps for volunteers inundating the institution. Only 35,000 of these men ever got overseas. The others inadvertently served the nation by causing confusion and delay at ports like Tampa, originally selected when large forces were not contemplated. This logjam meant that peripheral operations were the only feasible strategy if McKinley was to win the war before November.

Volunteers might not have helped America conduct military operations. However, if McKinley and Congress excluded their participation, incumbents would have paid the stiff price at the polls they had avoided when they declared war ostensibly to save Cuba. That particular objective was the occasion, not the cause of the Spanish-American War, as one senator indicated when he wrote in April that "those who have been most eager for [armed conflict] are casting around for reasons to give for it." The question, heretofore ignored, is why the American public had such great concern for Cuba in 1898. Like the citizens of every other country, they have rarely insisted that their government intervene to prevent atrocities beyond its borders. In 1849, 1894, 1978, and 1994, there was no mass outcry or compelling political demand to prevent the slaughter of Hungarians, Armenians, Cambodians, or Bosnians, although each story was widely carried in the American press.

Cuba, unlike Armenia, was only ninety miles from America. Geographic proximity did not increase human suffering but, by implication, measured and reflected the strength of the United States. Cuba, said the *New York Daily Tribune,* was "within sight of our own shores." A former ambassador to Spain wrote in a magazine article widely discussed in the press that if the United States did not prevent atrocities in the Caribbean, it would be a declaration that America "is incapable of protecting its own interests and of guarding the peace of the new world. In its final form the question is for us one of moral dignity."

If Americans had confidence in their own strength and cohesion, they probably would not have been preoccupied with Cuba, where disorder on their doorstep seemed proof of U.S. incapabilities. The class and sectional conflicts disclosed in the depression and the elections of the 1890s drove many people to believe, in the words of Theodore Roosevelt, that they were living through "the greatest crisis in our national fate, save only the Civil War." America wanted to prove to itself that it was not disintegrating by driving Spain out of the New World. And it wanted to do this not just with professional soldiers but with a diverse mixture of citizen-volunteers. Their cohesion in combat would help dispel nagging doubts about disunity, as revealed in the newspaper commentary of Finley Peter Dunne, America's most quoted satirist. "We're a gr-reat people," Hennsey told Dooley shortly after the Spanish-American War. "We ar-re that," Dooley replied. "An' the' best iv it is, we know we ar-re."

McKinley also sensed that the war was an act of national healing. In the face of enormous pressure from 30,000 applicants for commissions, the president was more careful than was Lincoln that soldiers be led by competent commanders, not well-connected politicians. To grateful applause from the journal of professional military men, nineteen of the twenty-six major generals selected were officers in the standing army. Two notable exceptions were old southern gentlemen reappointed to the U.S. Army thirty-seven years after they left it to join the Confederate cavalry.

Wise or foolish, Joe Wheeler and Fitzhugh Lee were pushed forward by the public, especially the South. Their commissions were the last of several endeavors to use military conflict to prevent—or bury—the Civil War. Two weeks before Fort Sumter, the secretary of state proposed unifying the nation by provoking war with Spain over Cuba, long an objective of Southern expansionism. To facilitate reunion in 1865, Grant and Francis Blair wanted Yankee and Confederate veterans, serving in the same units, to drive the French from Mexico. In 1875 Ben Butler had a similar idea: that a military campaign against lawless elements across the Mexican border "would put an end to all the questions arising out of Reconstruction." Two years before Grant's worst subordinate general made that statement to the secretary of state, Grant's most intimidating old adversary had notions of his own. In 1873, during a war scare with Spain over hanging American gunrunners, Nathan Bedford Forrest volunteered to lead 5,000 former rebel raiders "in [a] war with a foreign power." William Tecumseh Sherman had once written the War Department that he did not care if it "costs 10,000 lives and breaks the Treasury. There never will be no peace in Tennessee till Forrest is dead." In 1873, as commanding general of the U.S. Army, he recommended "that devil" to the secretary of war: "He would fight against our national enemies as vehemently as he did against us, and that is saying enough."

By 1898 Forrest was dead, along with Grant and Sherman. Wheeler and Fitzhugh Lee were in their sixties. The latter took command of the VII Corps, with Grant's grandson on his staff. He never left Florida because the assault on

Havana (which Lee thought a bad plan) never took place. Wheeler got overseas, as the cavalry commander of the American expedition to Santiago. Subordinates would call him "just a weak, old man" of "no more use here than a child." No matter, McKinley needed "Fighting Joe" to bury bitter remnants of the Civil War. His appointment was "a symbol that the old days are gone," as the president explained to this erstwhile rebel. Wheeler, in the excitement of first battle, forgot what he was told and yelled to his troopers: "Come on men, we've got the Yankees on the run."

The former Confederacy was anxious to furnish "proof that now more than ever [it] is the home of the best American patriotism." If nothing else, this would encourage the Republican party to overlook the way whites disenfranchised blacks, the GOP unionists in the South. Blacks, for their part, had associated military service with freedom, equality, and proof that "we are true American citizens" ever since taking up arms in the Civil War. Some 9,000 members of their race entered the new voluntary army presumably to show that "the coolness and bravery that characterized our fathers in the [18]60's have been handed down to their sons of the 90's." For Booker T. Washington, "there was no more significant feature in the Spanish-American War than General Joseph Wheeler leading black regulars against the Spaniards." According to one white soldier writing to the *Washington Post,* this was especially important at San Juan Hill. "If it had not been for the Negro [Tenth] cavalry," Roosevelt's Rough Riders, never known for tactical dexterity, "would have been exterminated." One can only wonder how that contingency would have affected the domestic impact of the war. The Rough Riders proved to be the single most reassuring and important symbol of national unity.

However useful to the nation's sense of well-being and the Republican party's political fortunes, the existence of the First U.S. Volunteer Cavalry (commonly called the Rough Riders) was largely fortuitous, as far as the White House was concerned. Administration officials warned Roosevelt, who organized the unit from scratch, that he would "end his political career" if he deserted his post as assistant secretary of the navy, where his "unbounded energy" was needed to help the department carry out its decisive wartime responsibilities. The secretary of the navy called "him a crank and ridiculed him to the best of my ability," but Roosevelt still felt it was his "sacred duty" to "run off to ride a horse and probably brush mosquitoes from his neck on the Florida sands." Three and one-half years later, after McKinley's assassination, Roosevelt was president of the United States, largely because at San Juan Hill he led what he described as "a regiment of crackerjacks—American from start to finish, in the best and fullest sense of the term."

No matter what the Civil War generation still believed, North against South was no longer the foremost conflict within America. By the 1890s it was superseded by debtor versus creditor, poor versus rich, West versus East—all of which were mixed together in the Rough Riders, which one contemporary writer called "the most unique aggregation of fighting men ever gathered together in any army." Newspapers from all regions depicted this regiment as a microcosm of America: ranch hands from the Southwest, farmers from the Plains, New York bankers, and Ivy League athletes, including Sergeant Hamilton Fish III, grandson of Grant's secretary of state. The Rough Riders were "the most representative body of men on American soil," for in it were "cowboys and millionaires, side by side, all men equal." It was "democracy, the highest and the lowest, the rich and the poor, the young and the old, ready to fight side by side" and "mingle their blood on a Cuban trail."

Roosevelt sensed what was good for the country's self-confidence and for his own political career. In his memoirs of the war, he said about the regiment that made him a national celebrity and the Republican candidate for vice president in the 1900 election: "There could be no more honorable burial than that of these men in a common grave—Indian and cowboy, miner and packer, and college athlete—the man of the unknown ancestry from the lonely Western plains and the man who carried on his watch the crests of the Stuyvesants and the Fishes, one in the way they had met death, just as during life they had been one in their daring and their loyalty."

As the incarnation of more national cohesion than the nation really had, the Rough Riders basked in publicity that eclipsed the standing army, making up 85 percent of the expedition. Shafter, like Winfield Scott in the Mexican War, requested and got virtually all the regular army regiments placed in his command. No matter, they were all equally ignored by the press. When asked by a correspondent, "Are you a hero?" one brigadier general sardonically replied: "No, I am only a regular." But however picturesque, Roosevelt's boys had to do something heroic, if they were to be heroes. If not for the charge up San Juan Hill as one of only three volunteer regiments in the V Corps, they might not have received much more attention than other volunteers less gratifying to America and barely recorded by the local news. At base camps in America, citizen-soldiers from the Southeast brawled with those from the Midwest who sang "Marching through Georgia." The boys from Kansas and Iowa tore down the tents of New Yorkers, "a peculiar lot of fellows . . . [profoundly] impressed with themselves." However, these particular units did not get to Cuba, where America's attention was focused; the Rough Riders certainly did.[4]

CONDUCTING WAR IN CUBA: THE ARMY
VERSUS THE NAVY VERSUS THE ENEMY

Roosevelt, at his base camp in South Texas on 10 May, was hoping to "get [his] troops down with the first expedition, drill or no drill," ready for war or not. Two weeks later, the navy confirmed that Admiral Cervera's Spanish fleet had crossed the Atlantic and was hiding at Santiago Bay in southeast Cuba, a region of operations previously reserved for the insurgents because it had been a base of rebel strength since the 1870s. The new target gave the Rough Riders their opportunity to take part in a war that, according to Roosevelt, demonstrated that "the country was indeed one when serious danger confronted it." More important to military strategy, it gave McKinley an unforeseen opportunity to avoid the march on Havana he authorized on 2 May, after the president was advised that "the country will demand that our soldiers make a landing and do something." Now, he could invade Cuba in an area of operations the Spanish army could not reinforce, Santiago lacking railroad lines to the Havana bastion 700 miles away.

The U.S. Army had barely 15,000 men prepared to take the field in late May when McKinley, through the War Department, ordered General Shafter "to sail at once with what forces you have ready" to help capture or destroy Santiago Bay. Washington identified "the enemy's fleet in the port," not its soldiers, "as the primary objective." It was silent about which service had ultimate responsibility for executing the operation. McKinley stood on the sidelines directing Shafter and Rear Admiral William T. Sampson, commander of the North Atlantic Station, to confer and "determine a course of cooperation best calculated to secure desirable results." Perhaps a suitable way to write tariff legislation, McKinley's field of expertise, this was hardly the way to settle an argument about service roles, missions, and costs in blood and equipment.

Truth be known, the debate could not be resolved because, as of yet, there was still no grand strategy on how to win the war. Washington instructed Shafter to act with "the utmost energy" and "the least possible delay" because after the army accomplished its mission at Santiago Bay (whatever that exactly was), Shafter was to redeploy to a deepwater harbor on the northern coast of Cuba, where he would join a "formidable" force of 70,000 soldiers still scheduled to march on Havana in mid-June. The administration continued to raise raw recruits, calling out 75,000 more men in May. In the meantime, for the Santiago operation on the other side of the island, it assembled a relatively small body of professional soldiers and some elite volunteers to wage what McKinley did not know would be the decisive land campaign in a remote area far away from the colony's capital. The president combined the peripheral strategy of the small, professional military with a mass force of citizen-soldiers mobilized to assault major fortifications. However, for officers fighting in Cuba, the Santiago operation seemed to proceed "without any definite plan of action." To begin with, the administration never appointed a unified (interservice) commander, the first essential step for joint operations. Reminiscent of debates in early May, when the navy proposed and the army protested a ground force assault on Havana, there were interminable arguments in July, never conclusively settled, over which service should attack and which hold its position. At White House planning sessions, Captain Alfred Thayer Mahan, the great maritime theorist, spoke on behalf of the proposition that the army had been sent to Cuba to help destroy the enemy fleet or be destroyed itself: "If we lost ten thousand [soldiers], the country could replace them; if we lost a battleship, it could not be replaced."

The army was so sensitive about its honor that Shafter would not invite Sampson to the ceremonial capitulation on grounds that "the surrender of Santiago was made to *me*" (italics mine). Furthermore, at the direct instruction of the secretary of war, the army took "immediate possession" of all Spanish shipping left in the bay, to the ire of the navy. Perhaps it needed tokens of respect to compensate for begging Sampson to force his way "into the harbor and save lives of our brave men that will be sacrificed if we assault the enemy in his entrenchments without aid." The army need not have been so touchy about being cast in the shadow of the navy. Mahan and company had not carried every argument because McKinley never fully grasped the periphery strategy he practiced. Naval supremacy was its sine qua non, something even the War Department felt in its gut when given false reports that the Spanish navy had escaped from Santiago Bay: the "darkest day of the war," said its cabinet secretary. The Department of the Navy was correct when it held that "armored vessels must not be risked" against coastal artillery on high bluffs and naval mines in a narrow inlet 350 feet wide.

Ground forces at the tactical level were not much better organized than the joint war plan and campaign. Enemy positions were not reconnoitered, infantry lacked artillery support, and primitive lines of communication prevented sufficient delivery of essential items from Florida to the front. Forty pieces of artillery, 3,000 mules, and 200 ambulances lined the docks at Tampa; 16, 500, and 12 of them, respectively, ever made it on board ship. Soldiers had to be sustained on rifles, hardtack, castor oil, and bacon. For the Santiago campaign, the navy would demand that the army be the hammer and attack. Because of a lack of troop transports and barges that naval construction priorities ignored, the ground forces had too little combat power to do much more than its sister service envisioned in 1896: "garrison and hold places captured by the Navy." The army now concurred with this premise of grand strategy: that it was not the means to conduct decisive military action in a foreign war. Shafter said he was "in position to do my part" while the navy navigated into Santiago Bay, "the sure and speedy way" to win "without further sacrifice of life." That position, at this time, just confirmed to the navy that "our sister branch of the service is a spoiled child [that] takes every exertion on our part as a matter of course."[5]

UNCONDITIONAL SURRENDER AND LIMITED WAR

The U.S. Army was not equipped or prepared to win the Spanish-American War, at least not without a lot of military help and a little compromise of armistice objectives. Theodore Roosevelt held out for "unconditional surrender" and a climactic battle worthy of Lee and Grant. But after the army scaled the heights overlooking Santiago on 1 July, even he had to admit that "the lack of transportation, food, and artillery has brought us to the very verge of disaster." Two hundred five Americans died in that charge up San Juan Hill; 1,180 were wounded. Those less obsessed than Roosevelt with military honor for his generation felt they had had enough. George Kennan, a magazine writer doubling as a Red Cross worker, said of the suffering: "If there was anything more terrible in our Civil War, I am glad that I was not there to see it."

Joe Wheeler could not remember facing more lethal rifle fire in 1864. Bullets still proved less deadly than the weather. The expedition overlapped the rainy season wherein soldiers said "the roads were in fearful condition and the cement-like mud clung to our shoes with the tenacity of glue." Everything was drenched: uniforms, sugar, salt, and flour, not to mention the trenches in which men fought and slept. Yellow fever, typhoid, and malaria would cause 2,500 fatalities. If the enemy had not surrendered in mid-July, only 10 percent of the American force could have continued to fight.

These conditions upset the high command's hopes to fight a war of limited liability by withdrawing to more hygienic ground and waiting for Santiago to starve. Supply depletion was supposed to force the Spanish fleet out of its base into the guns of the American blockade. Then, after the U.S. Navy won its campaign for uncontested supremacy, the American military could roam at will, taking any soft target in the Caribbean. Unfortunately, this plan seemed too time-consuming to some very interested parties. It did not appeal to McKinley, who just wanted "to do it quick," nor did it appeal to some enlisted men living on half rations and "drenched to the skin" while terms were discussed, a "flag-of-truce gag." Said one sergeant just beyond enemy lines: "Damn Strategy! I've never read about it. . . . I am in favor of going up there and beating the faces off them dagoes, and then let the war correspondents make up the strategy, as they seem to be the only ones who are worrying about it."

Whether this enlisted man knew or cared, he had more in common with the commander in chief than with the flag officers trying to conduct a limited war. The Naval War College at Newport had long rejected the notion "that war means the total ruin or complete wiping out of the enemy." (That "would be the negation of all progress, naval and social.") Shafter and Miles thought much the same way, their habits shaped by having policed the West for the last thirty years, where the army was always more ready to negotiate than settlers and presidents wanting to hang renegades. Now Miles, who had virtually ignored White House directives to get an "unconditional surrender" from Geronimo, would have treated the Spanish like a tribe wandering off the reservation, that is, apply just enough force to relocate them to areas of no real importance.

In fact, the U.S. military often dealt with the Spanish better than with the native insurrectionists they were supposed to help. Nelson Miles's original plan to make the insurgents the major land component of the war mirrored army-Indian relations at their best, where officers said friendly tribes had "a full sense of their duty and a determination to fulfill it at any cost to themselves." At their worst, racial animosity made army-Indian conflicts terribly brutal and alliances arrangements of convenience. The indispensable confederate in one conflict

(Cherokees against the Creeks) could readily become "a degraded race" of savages who got in the way "of our peace, happiness, and prosperity." In Arizona, when Miles was department commander, the army deported its Apache scouts to Florida, along with Geronimo and the other renegades they helped run down. In Cuba and Manila, the same racial discrimination was directed at dark-skinned rebels who were becoming the army's excuse for delay in winning the war. They might be useful for scouting and small-unit ambush, as were Indian auxiliaries. However, the erstwhile guerrilla conflict had now become a conventional war. "All the Cubans we have met here are dirty nasty niggers who eat our rations, will not work, and will not fight," Shafter wrote his mother on 2 August. "Not a man of them was killed during all the fighting, [from Las Guasimas to Santiago Bay] they were skulking back in the hills."

Granted some Americans, particularly Civil War veterans, welcomed the prospect of joint operations with insurgents. George Dewey, who fought his way into New Orleans in 1862, expected help from Filipinos similar to that received from Negroes, "the only friends we had in the South." He never quite got it, nor did he need it, at least compared with the Civil War. Number one, the Spanish were far less recalcitrant than was the Confederacy. Number two, the rebels did not engage in pitched battles such as those by which former slaves won some respect. Undergunned natives had survived as long as they did by evading Spanish strongpoints, that is, conducting on a tactical level the U.S. military strategy on an operational level. They avoided enemy pillboxes and trenches, fighting (instead) from a prepared ambush according to their maxim: "The advantage always goes to the one who waits, not to the one who advances." Americans, despite claims of moral superiority, took this idea to its ultimate conclusion by avoiding Havana altogether. Miles, rather alone, would give the guerrillas "a good share of the credit" for gathering intelligence and holding 7,000 Spanish soldiers (away from Shafter's flanks) at Guantánamo. Shafter, more typical, wrote the secretary of war that "if we intend to reduce Santiago, we will have to depend alone upon our own troops and will require twice the number we have."

When army officers could conduct a military operation without political interference, they might come to understandings with the Spanish reminiscent of eighteenth-century dynastic warfare between Christian aristocrats. Pitched battles were avoided and fortress walls damaged just enough to give a worthy opponent justification to haul down his flag, that is, if the Manila command could fulfill its desire "to surrender to white people." To be sure, blows were exchanged, sometimes ignobly. On the trail to Santiago Bay, Spanish snipers using dumdum bullets picked off litter bearers and medical personnel. However, those preliminary engagements notwithstanding, both sides were happy to face "an enemy that will come out and fight," at least when the campaign reached its climax. The U.S. Army, tired of "bush-wacking" conflicts with Indians, developed great respect for Spanish soldiers delivering volley after volley "full in our faces, standing as they did." The Spanish contrasted Americans who charged up

San Juan Hill with former slaves or native savages of "doubtful origin" who "shot their noble victims from ambush and then immediately fled."

In this situation American military authority protected the Spanish from those they had abused. The U.S. commander in the Philippines ordered "pillage, rapine, or violence by the native inhabitants or disorderly insurgents must be prevented at any cost," the same rationale for Shafter's order to bar armed rebels from Santiago. McKinley, having no experience with limited conflict or police actions on the frontier, vetoed Shafter's suggestion to withdraw and allow the Spanish to leave their base, no matter that Shafter would call them "the most orderly, tractable and generally best-behaved men that I have ever known." The corps commander told Washington, "We [would only] lose some prisoners we do not want and the arms they carry." McKinley responded in words reminiscent of Lincoln's to McClellan: "What you went to Santiago for was the Spanish army. If you allow it to evacuate . . . you must meet it somewhere else. [What you propose] is not war."

McKinley worried that an American withdrawal from San Juan Heights would have a deleterious "effect upon the country," that is, on public opinion, which was never far from his mind. The election aside, the president did not understand the ad hoc peripheral strategy he employed, judging by his instructions to come to grips with the enemy. Neither was it grasped by Theodore Roosevelt, although he had explained the navy's plans to McKinley before the war. They both assumed the conflict would end with what Roosevelt called "the great Havana campaign," postponed because the V Corps had become, in Shafter's words, "an army of convalescents." McKinley resembled George Washington redeploying to attack New York City after Yorktown in 1781. He did not realize America had already fought the decisive battle of the war, in his case a fleet engagement outside Santiago Bay.

Ramon Blanco, Cuba's governor-general, had not allowed his sister service to scuttle its ships (and thereby save its sailors) on grounds that "if we lose the squadron without fighting, the moral effect would be terrible, both in Spain and abroad." The navy grumbled about a "sacrifice to vanity" that merely signaled the fact that "Spain was becoming a nation of the fourth class." Nonetheless, after the U.S. Army took San Juan Hill and cut off all food and supply trails to Santiago Bay, Cervera's fleet sailed forth with bugles blowing and flags on every mast, looking to Americans as if it were dressed "for a regal parade or a festal day." Inside four hours, every ship was sunk or blazing, all done so quickly it surprised the survivors, although they were long convinced their "small and poorly equipped squadron" was on a suicide mission. "They came at us like mad bulls," said one American captain. "It succumbed gloriously," and "Spain will never forget it," said envious army officers such as General Blanco, now shamed and more determined to "vanquish or die" in Havana, what he had promised Madrid to get it to send Cervera to Cuba.

Neither Blanco nor Theodore Roosevelt would get to fight at Havana. The destruction of Cervera's squadron created the contingency the admiral predicted in April: the exposure of Spain to U.S. bombardment sailing off its coast with "impunity." This was certainly not Washington's initial plan. The navy planted such stories to get Madrid to keep all its warships home, ceding control of the Caribbean and the Philippine Sea. (Washington pressured Britain to bar Spanish access to the Suez Canal, although passage of its reserve squadron to Manila would have left its coast totally exposed.) America's bluff worked better than any American dreamed after Spain still sent Cervera to Cuba. Once he got there, Madrid got nervous and gave him the option to sail home. By then, Cervera was too low on fuel to flee destruction. The monarchy, witnessing American ships shelling Manila, Santiago, and San Juan, feared that an attack on Valencia or Barcelona could set off an internal uprising. This contingency had driven the government to war with America. Now, three days after Santiago capitulated, it implored France to broker an armistice "with extreme dispatch."

If Madrid were "to save our unfortunate country from new disasters," it needed a peace settlement even quicker than McKinley, who needed to liberate Cuba before the November election. Fortuitously, the ad hoc U.S. strategy attacked the weak spots of the Spanish Empire—first Manila, then Santiago, and Puerto Rico (described later). Paradoxically, the threat to attack Spain was the crowning act of the periphery strategy, Havana being the strongpoint to be avoided at all costs. Planned or not, this course of action proved quite effective. Without ever storming Havana, the United States could drive the enemy army out of the Caribbean, partly because many important Spaniards were not too sad to lose Cuba (a drain on government resources) provided their army could return home with what it called "the honors of war."

The U.S. Army was more than happy to grant its adversary what General Miles called "generous terms." Washington still instructed Shafter to "accept nothing but an unconditional surrender": words that made Joe Wheeler, the erstwhile Confederate, ache for the Spanish commander who only wanted "to maintain his honor and prestige as a soldier." McKinley had problems of his own. Like Grant at Fort Donaldson in 1862, he was only asking "unconditional surrender" from an army. He did not demand it from a nation, nor had Lincoln, whose party platform simply called for "terms of peace . . . based upon an unconditional surrender of hostility" to the government. McKinley actually offered the Spanish fairly comfortable conditions, giving its soldiers parolee (not prisoner) status and sailing them to Spain at U.S. expense. However, the very phraseology, "unconditional surrender," was becoming America's criteria for military success irrespective of specific content, as when Washington wired Shafter on 15 July: "Have you received the absolute surrender of the enemy? We are awaiting the conditions." In World War I Woodrow Wilson would pay a stiff political price for rejecting the wordage. In 1945, bowing to public demand, Harry Truman would accept the slogan but, like McKinley, try to add specific content that might avoid a bloody fight to the finish. In 1898, before the formula hardened and distinctions completely blurred, McKinley had more political space for diplomatic maneuver than did his successors in the next two wars.

Spain was willing to concede what one congressman called "the unconditional surrender of Cuba," provided it lost its empire to a strong nation-state, not a ragtag insurrection. Consequently, the administration could call any fudge of the phrase "a gracious act on the part of a victorious nation." McKinley agreed to Spanish demands to replace "surrender" with "capitulation," a word implying contractual rights for the defeated party in Spanish military terminology. Repatriated senior officers wound up in prison but escaped the hangman's noose. Defeat was so complete individuals were not blamed and Madrid escaped revolution. In 1902 it could stage a coronation of the queen regent's son as King Alfonso XIII. His regime survived another twenty years, but bygones were not bygone. The future leader of the extreme right wing, Francisco Franco, five years old in 1898, would recall that when his generation began its "life we saw our childhood dominated by the contemptible incompetence of those men who abandoned half of the fatherland's territory to foreigners." Parliamentary democracy: may it rest in peace.

Thanks to the "capitulation," America's armed forces avoided the last act in the campaign for Santiago, let alone start a new one for Havana. The army never had to storm the trenches on the high ground above the bay where, according to a captain in the Tenth Cavalry, "our attack would at least have been checked— and possibly repulsed." Nor did the navy run the mines in the harbor, as it was about to do in mid-July, even if no one had yet determined which service was to execute the main effort and which was there to assist.

Military action then shifted to the periphery: back to the Philippines, where antagonists wisely negotiated an armistice without consulting Washington, and to Puerto Rico, the softest target in the Spanish Empire. Nelson Miles, the man with the best grasp of the periphery strategy, had wanted to make the island America's first and foremost military objective. By the time he landed on 27 July, Puerto Rico had lost its strategic value as a choke point preventing the Spanish fleet from ever getting to Cuba. Its early conquest would have been a misfortune for America. If Cervera had had his wish and stayed in Spain with a fleet in being, its coast would not have been potentially vulnerable to American bombardment, the final circumstance driving Spain to sue for peace. At the same time, although no one knew it in 1898, the preservation of the fleet would have been beneficial for American national security in the postwar world. Spain would not have lost what the captain of Cervera's flagship called "the only power which could have weight in a treaty of peace." America, with uncontested control of Manila Bay, would retain the Philippines, the worst result of the entire war.

As for Puerto Rico, the U.S. Army and Navy clashed once again, this time because that island was weakly defended. Each wanted to attack with minimal assistance from its sister service. A fleet voyage toward Spanish home waters was the quickest way to force Madrid to concede. The navy still advised its delay to deploy warships to San Juan: it "can be destroyed from the water and may yield without much resistance [after] a proper show of naval strength." Miles, for his part, maintained that the control of "all military affairs on the land of this island can be safely left to the army," a position that got some congressional support. Senators pressured Washington to commit their state volunteers: "They want to get into or near a fight." Tactically, this is not what Miles had in mind. He completely outflanked the Spanish from the moment he landed on an unprotected beach: "Gin'ral Miles' gran picnic an' moonlight excursion in Porther Ricky." Mr. Dooley characterized the three-week campaign. Suffering only seven total fatalities, he cut off San Juan in a manner similar to Fitzhugh Lee's original plan for Havana. However, the man whom Theodore Roosevelt called a "brave peacock" could not crow all that loudly that he had been right all along. McKinley, having finally learned there was no need to fight this conflict as if it were the Civil War, suspended all hostilities a week before Miles would have occupied the whole island.

The entire war—Manila to San Juan—cost America $250 million and 5,462 lives, only 379 killed in combat. The public decried the disease rates, particularly deadly among the volunteers, but McKinley weathered the storm, unlike James K. Polk, president during the Mexican War. Political wrath now focused on the secretary of war even for those, such as a writer for the *Boston Herald,* who asserted, "That the situation was not worse is due more to Spanish incompetency than to our own effectiveness." But whatever people thought of the government, the country gained renewed faith in its strength and its future. It also reduced conflict between its economic classes and geographic sections, although not between the army and the navy nor between the races despite the belief of a white officer in the Tenth Cavalry. John J. Pershing hoped in vain that "our black heroes [have] fought their way into the hearts of the American people." Nonetheless, having won at San Juan Hill the respect of Theodore Roosevelt, who would promote Captain Pershing to general, he was on the route to command in 1918 an army a hundred times the size of the V Corps. In the meantime, Republicans retained control of Congress in November 1898, an ideal time for them to face election. The fighting had stopped, but no peace treaty was yet signed. Roosevelt, Lodge, and other speakers for the GOP could hold before the public the specter of a president who won a war but was repudiated before he could "secure the fruits of peace." That appeal helped the White House accomplish its essential objective of the war. In the final analysis, it fought Spain to control Washington, not Cuba.[6]

THE AFTERMATH OF A VICTORY

Although considered "a splendid little war" shortly after its conclusion, the conflict with Spain had political and military liabilities unforeseen by McKinley, the army, or the Naval War College in 1898. On the political front, the Republicans' war hero, Theodore Roosevelt, would be the latest (and greatest) reincarnation of Andrew Jackson, a citizen-soldier leading volunteers to exploits that overshadowed professional soldiers, at least in the hearts and minds of the electorate. Unfortunately for his party, his personal following was so great that Roosevelt could run as an independent in 1912, get more votes than the Republican candidate, and enable a Democrat to win the White House, for the second time since Lincoln. This man, Woodrow Wilson, would struggle to avoid World War I, wind up taking the country into combat, and face the threat of repudiation in an off-year election with less success than McKinley in 1898.

As for military (not political) strategy, America had occupied the Philippines when an armistice terminated the Spanish-American War. In the fall of 1898 the Democrats ran against its acquisition and the Madrid government stalled for time. Because Republicans, thanks to McKinley's military victory, retained control of Congress, Washington would not agree to a final peace treaty without acquiring the archipelago, suddenly seen to be a base from which America could dominate commercial enterprise in the Far East. The nation might have been better off if the opposition party had won. America would be in no position to defend the Philippines from Imperial Japan. In 1942, on the rim of the entrance to Manila Bay, some 75,000 soldiers conducted the largest surrender in American military history. When McKinley spoke about the acquisition of the islands back in 1899, he asked one audience: "What nation was ever able to write an accurate program of the war upon which it was entering, much less decree in advance the scope of its results?" Dewey's easy victory in 1898 led to the death march from Bataan.

6

World War I: Fighting a War, Saving the World, Losing the Electorate

Woodrow Wilson needed to convince America, let alone himself, that World War I was worth the pain and suffering it caused. He felt it could introduce a new era of world peace, prosperity, and democracy, that is, if won under his leadership, on his political terms. To do this, he deceived his allies and his military commander, hiding his resolve not to merge the American Expeditionary Force with the French and British armies. This increased the difficulty of training recruits to survive on a very lethal battlefield. The ensuing casualties strengthened the president's political opponents who sought unconditional surrender, not a League of Nations that embodied Wilson's hopes and aspirations.

NATIONAL AMBITION, DOMESTIC POLITICS, AND A NEW WORLD ORDER

The national election of 1900 revealed a role reversal from 1897 on the issue of military action. Leading Republicans, some reluctant to fight over Cuba, defended the conquest, occupation, and retention of the Philippine Islands. The Democratic party, so quick against Spain, opposed counterinsurgency in the Philippines as "an act of criminal aggression and a wicked exercise of despotic power." The southern wing of the party, still smarting over its military occupation after the Civil War, was particularly opposed to this "unnecessary war," with exceptions like Thomas Woodrow Wilson, a southern-born professor of government whose ambition lay in taking "a leading part in public life and . . . a *statesman's* career." Wilson maintained that the United States must look "into the tasks of the great world at large, seeking its special part and place of power," words quite similar to those of Henry Cabot Lodge, the Republican who would cross his path at the end of World War I. Wilson said America was a major player in the world arena "whether we will [it] or not"; Lodge said likewise, "weal or woe." But whereas Lodge perceived international relations in terms of rank and national hierarchy, Wilson was more comfortable with concepts of redemption. "No man is a true American in whom the desire to do mankind service does not take precedence over the desire to serve himself."

Wilson would flit between liberal and conservative positions on domestic issues but always mixed necessity and idealism in foreign policy. At his second presidential inaugural in 1917, he would declare that Americans are "citizens of the world. . . . Our own fortunes are involved, whether we would have it so or not." Four weeks later, when asking Congress to declare war against Germany, he transcended stoic acceptance of a grim situation to proclaim America had no "selfish ends to serve." Its sole objective "is to vindicate the principles of peace and justice in the life of the world."

The main international event of the Wilson presidency—and of the first third of the twentieth century—was the war pitting Germany, Austria, Turkey, and Bulgaria (the Central Powers) against Britain, Belgium, France, Serbia, Italy, Romania, and Russia (the Allies or Entente). Begun with rapid maneuver, it stagnated into trench warfare from Switzerland to the English Channel on the western front. Rapid-fire artillery and pontoon machine guns spitting out 600 bullets a minute ensured neither side could decisively penetrate the other's military lines, where three rows of trenches were followed by dugouts, sometimes forty feet deep. Warfare became an attrition campaign of gross national product in which each side hoped to exhaust the other's economic vulnerabilities. Britain had been the largest and Germany the second-largest food importer in the world. Now Germany, the greatest land power, acquired economic reinforcements in the form of raw materials extracted from its military conquests, primarily on the eastern front. The English, who had the largest navy and the greatest economic investment in the Western Hemisphere, imported their own economic reinforcements, primarily from the United States, a fact that inexorably drew America into the war.

To prevent the Central Powers from harvesting resources from Romania to the Baltic, the Entente tried to run a supply line through the Turkish Straits to keep Russia in the war and Germany contained. This perfectly sensible objective produced the disastrous Gallipoli campaign, where Britain suffered 250,000 casualties. It was far more successful against a less important economic objective, that "of strangling Germany at sea." By controlling the surface of the Atlantic Ocean and the bulk of Europe's gold supply, the Admiralty reduced Germany's trade with the United States from $345 million per annum before the war to $2 million by 1916.

Less successfully than England, Germany tried to interdict overseas trade, which provided 66 percent of Britain's normal food supply. After the Royal Navy bottled up the Imperial surface fleet, the Central Powers had to employ submarines, heretofore a "tedious experiment" primarily useful for harbor defense.

Because Germany had only nine submarines able to reach England's western coast in 1914, the Entente's trade with America mushroomed from less than $3.5 billion (1911 through 1913) to $9.8 billion (1915 through 1917). Meanwhile, German casualty rates grew far faster than its fleet of submarines, each modern U-boat taking one year to move from contract to launch. In 1915 the country lost over 600,000 soldiers on the western front. Although prewar studies indicated that 222 submarines were needed to starve Britain, the pressure to employ the 39 the Germans now had increased as the land war sank into a ghastly stalemate.

President Wilson would not concede that Germany's military predicament warranted "the abridgment of the rights of American citizens in any respect," that is, their claim to loan money or export products that were not immediate implements of war. Nor would he sacrifice the prerogatives of neutrals to travel safely on any passenger ship, even one bearing the flag of a belligerent. His reasoning, in inverse order of importance to him, involved national security, economic prosperity, domestic politics, and international prestige. "The honor and self-respect of the nation is involved," as well as the opportunity to create what Wilson would call "a new international order."

If submarine warfare were to force America to withdraw its commerce, English naval power could not counterbalance German superiority on land. If Germany won, U.S. security would be at risk, according to conversations Wilson had in late 1914 and mid-1915. An Allied defeat would force the United States "to take measures of defense . . . fatal to our form of government and American ideals"; "it would change the course of our civilization and make the United States a military nation," when its true forte was international trade. "We are making more manufactured goods than we can consume," he said on the eve of his 1912 presidential campaign. "If we are not going to stifle economically, we have got to find our way out into the great exchanges of the world."

Intimately related to the state of the economy was domestic politics—a high priority for all politicians. Wilson was especially sensitive, having been elected president with less than 42 percent of the popular vote after Theodore Roosevelt split the Republican electorate as a third-party candidate in 1912. Wilson would have to do much better in 1916, which did not seem likely in 1913, when America fell into economic recession. Then the European war created an enormous demand for American exports, particularly cotton, copper, steel, petroleum, and wheat, whose price per bushel grew from $.95 in 1914 to $2.40 in 1917. None of this was lost on the Wilson administration, whose secretary of the Treasury (Wilson's son-in-law) wrote the president in August 1915: "Great Britain is and always has been our best customer. . . . The high prices for food products have brought great prosperity to the farmers, while the purchasers of war munitions have set factories going to full capacity." On the other hand, Robert Lansing, the new secretary of state, warned that curtailment of exports would produce "industrial depression, idle capital, idle labor, numerous failures, financial demoralization, general unrest and suffering among the laboring classes." In short, it would resurrect the depression of 1893 that had relegated the Democrats to a minority party for the next twenty years.

Wilson agreed with his cabinet. One month after receiving Lansing's memo, he lifted his ban on private loans to belligerents in order to maintain Allied purchases in American markets. He liked to describe his policy in lofty language: "America is not selfish in claiming her rights; she is merely standing for the rights of mankind." America at large also wanted to retain the right of neutral trade along with neutrality itself. "The opinion of the country," the president said in mid-1915, "seems to demand two inconsistent things, to maintain a firm front in respect of what we demand of Germany [strict adherence to these rights] and yet do nothing that might by any possibility involve us in the war." As a public servant and desperate politician, Wilson "wished with all my heart I saw a way to carry out the double wish of our people." He would be disappointed, but not shocked, that he eventually failed.

Wilson's political judgment was sharper than that of his critics on the left or right. The populist wing of the Democratic party—led by William Jennings Bryan in the State Department and Claude Kitchin, the majority leader of the House—firmly held that military preparedness in defense of trade served the "predatory interests" of big business. The interventionist wing of the Republican party—led by Theodore Roosevelt and Massachusetts senator Henry Cabot Lodge—firmly felt that the future "peace and safety and national character of [the] country depend upon our going to war." The political extremes had something in common, both wanting a significant sacrifice from the American people. The interventionists would spill its blood for "absolute insistence upon our rights"; the isolationists would give up treasure in the form of trade. Neither group had Wilson's political appeal in the 1916 election: peace *and* prosperity.

Successful electoral campaign strategies rarely solve security dilemmas. Wilson could not convince Germany to relinquish submarine warfare unless he held it to "strict accountability." Those words ran a big risk, said Edward M. House, Wilson's unofficial counselor and "second personality"—"his thoughts and mine are one." Now that Wilson so warned the kaiser, more than prosperity and reelection was at stake. "Our action in this crisis," House told Wilson, "will determine the part we will play when peace is made, and how far we may influence a settlement for the lasting good of humanity. We are being weighed in the balance, and our position amongst nations is being assessed by mankind."

After Wilson issued his ultimatum to Germany on 18 April 1916, the Imperial government agreed to terminate underwater attack without warning lest it "necessarily force the United States into war." While Germany went out to improve the situation against the military opponents it already had, it gave itself a loophole by stipulating that the British must also "observe the rules of international law." That November, Wilson would gain almost 3 million more votes than he received in 1912, reelected on a platform of "peace with honor, he kept us out of war," prosperity, and progressivism—a domestic reform movement Wilson defined as follows: "No body or group of men, no matter what their private interest is, may come into competition with the authority of society" against the public interest. In the meantime, Germany was building 108 new long-range submarines, and the president privately rued that "something might occur on the high seas which would make our neutrality impossible."

To avoid a future choice between war and humiliation, Wilson could (1) convince England not to wage economic warfare, (2) enhance American military power to intimidate Germany, or (3) broker a peace between the warring powers so that no one would interdict international trade. He would try—and fail—to do all three. In 1916 Britain suffered over 1,400,000 casualties: the bloodiest year to date in its military history. It was in no mood to relinquish its competitive advantage against Germany: sea power and economic warfare, that is, the capacity, in the words of the Admiralty, to "starve the whole population—men, women and children, old and young, wounded and sound—into submission." Wilson to the contrary, England escalated its strategy of strangulation by blacklisting those Americans who traded with the Central Powers and by seizing noncontraband goods such as cotton, always upsetting to any southern politician. Wilson never would forget or forgive it for "infringing upon our rights as a neutral." In March 1917 he denounced with equal fervor "German militarism on land and English militarism on sea." If Germany had not declared unlimited submarine warfare in January, "I was ready then and there," Wilson later said, "to have it out with Great Britain."

England would not relent. America would not prepare, at least not enough to intimidate a German high command that confessed to the kaiser in September 1916 it had "no faith in being able to force a favorable decision by means of war on land alone." Wilson, on occasion, was frank with the American public, as when he told one audience, before his reelection campaign swung into high gear, that "you may count upon my heart and resolution to keep you out of the war, but you must be ready if it is necessary that I should maintain your honor." These somber words to the contrary, there was no political consensus for a preparedness program that would elevate the United States much beyond its status as the seventeenth-largest army in the world. Wilson proposed constructing capital ships (to "build a navy bigger than Britain's and do what we please"), federalizing the national guard, and instituting voluntary training to acquire a mass reserve. This was too strong for Kitchin and Bryan but too weak for Roosevelt and Lodge. At a minimum, the militant wing of the Republican party demanded universal and compulsory military training for all reasonably healthy males between eighteen and thirty-five. This provided a golden opportunity that few Democratic politicians could pass up, least of all Wilson, elected by a fluke. He weakened his own calls for "reasonable preparedness" by repeatedly accusing his opponents of a foreign policy that "can only be a reversal from peace to war." Consequently, when America went to combat in 1917, it had enough ammunition in its arsenals to fight a major European battle for a day and a half.

Aside from political expediency, Wilson had other reasons for ambivalence about military preparedness. He worried it would undermine the appearance of American neutrality and his credibility as an honest broker. More than any other course of action—certainly more than backing down Germany or Britain—Wilson wanted to mediate a compromise settlement that would prevent wars and ensure neutral rights. "It would be a calamity to the world at large if we should be drawn actively into the conflict and so deprived of all disinterested influence over the settlement." The Wilson presidency, at least according to Wilson, coincided with a pivotal point in human affairs. "This war will vitally change the relationships of nations," and Wilson had the chance to be what House called "the prophet of a new day."

The president believed the war in Europe, having changed the way Europe thought about war, presented "an unparalleled opportunity" to create "an enduring peace." On the eve of the conflict, there were three major schools of opinion on the root cause of war, a subject widely debated since the 1890s: (1) one articulate but relatively small group of liberal intellectuals believed that international commerce was about to abolish warfare as an irrational activity adding nothing to "wealth, prosperity, and well-being"; (2) another relatively small group of elites believed that armed conflict was "drastic medicine" but beneficial for the body politic because it "elevates the human heart beyond the earthy and the common" pursuit of material gratification; (3) a third group, occupying the political center and probably representing majority opinion, accepted wars and the governments that made them as inevitable facts of life, equivalent to illness and bad weather. However, by early 1915 the average European was shocked to find that war was none of the preceding. It had not been abolished no matter how wasteful. Neither was it a glorious or natural occurrence. As one French veteran later recalled: "I did not know [in 1914] that for four years I would be condemned to live the life of a mole."

As for Woodrow Wilson, his own mind had moved from the second position toward the first. Like most southerners raised in the backwash of the "lost cause" of the Civil War, he had at least a muffled belief that war "as an economic proposition [was] ruinous," but as he told House in 1913, "there was no more glorious way to die than in battle." By November 1916 the horrendous casualties and futile tactics at the Somme and Verdun drained the martial romanticism from Wilson, as from much of Europe. He now described war as a "mechanical game of slaughter" stripping combat of "all its charm." Nonetheless, Wilson took heart that this "unprecedented human waste and suffering" had one redeeming aspect. "Both sides have grown weary of the apparently hopeless task of bringing the conflict to an end by force of arms."

Wilson did not realize that this "vast, gruesome contest of systematized destruction" would actually prevent him from making the type of peace he wanted; partly because of new internal challenges to European governments, and partly because of the diplomatic problems of coalition warfare. To mediate, he would have to know the war aims of the belligerents, kept secret because public opinion blanched at spending blood to expand an ally's dominion at the expense of their foe. This was especially true once fringe elements in European politics began to acquire new adherents to their alternative explanation of the cause and effects of war. Similar to the populists in the United States, radical socialists and other self-identified "representatives of the revolutionary class" did not maintain that war was an eternal fact of life, nor was it morally enhancing or disruptive to trade. It was a ploy of the ruling strata, be they capitalists or kings. Through conquests and contracts, these elites enhanced their wealth by spilling the blood of the poor. As for the liberal opinion that war was not productive and therefore would be stopped, the "soldiers of the revolution" dismissed that as "petty bourgeois" pacifism.

Military failure, by discrediting old regimes, had sparked revolutions in 1793 and 1870. Now legendary, the Paris Communes continued to inspire (or horrify) the left and right of Europe. By 1915 the call for "the working class in all lands to overthrow the rule of capital and seize political power" had affected war aims by reducing receptivity to Wilson's quest for "a peace without a victor's terms imposed upon the vanquished." Political leaders in both coalitions were hearing and warning that a failure to fulfill their objectives of expansion could cause "the worst kind of dissatisfaction among the lower and middle classes. . . . The disillusioned nation would believe that it had sacrificed the bloom of its youth and the strength of its manhood in vain."

Wilson pinned his hopes for mediation on the military fact that "never before in the world's history have two great armies been in effect so equally matched." In fact, the parity hindered negotiation. Both sides feared losing any ally, no matter how weak. Junior partners joined their coalitions for territorial objectives. If they were aggrieved and left before the consummation of a settlement, the enemy might resume fighting in hope of victory. This fear kept Germany from buying peace with Russia at the expense of Austria or Turkey. It kept England and France from making peace with Austria at the expense of Serbia and Italy. Rather than expose this dilemma and fuel the radical fire that "the capitalist war" was waged for annexations, not for self-defense, governments kept their aims secret, even from Wilson, who would need to know them if he were to mediate a peace.

The more subtle European diplomats—especially Britain's foreign minister, Edward Grey—dodged Wilson's inquiries by putting the onus back on the United States. He maintained that if the Allies were to renounce territorial ambitions that would enhance their national security, America would have "to join in repressing by force whoever broke the [hypothetical] Treaty." Wilson could not make this commitment without congressional approval (he could not get it in 1919), but Grey nurtured notions having a decisive impact on military strategy when America went to war. In 1917 Wilson presumed that a nonvindictive settlement required proof that America would rescue France and England in a crisis. It also depended on gaining much more influence than it ever could have as an ally merely plugging holes in their sectors on the western front.

Wilson's "peace without victory" speech (22 January 1917) was the greatest statement of his objectives during the neutrality period. He predicted the creation of an "international concert . . . of power which will make it virtually impossible that any such catastrophe should ever overwhelm us again." One paragraph later, in the most revealing words of the presentation, Wilson told the Senate that "it is inconceivable that the people of the United States should play no part in that great enterprise." Nine days later, he lost his race to mediate a peace before facing the choice he rued for the last two years, war or a humiliation that would prohibit America from playing an important role in building a new order for the postwar world. The German army having lost another million men in 1916, the kaiser was ready to accept his navy's claim that "the U-boat war will lead to victory." Although Berlin had only 100 submarines to deploy, it announced it would sink all ships on the Atlantic, no matter what flag they flew.

Wilson's reelection had convinced him that the United States did not want "to go to war no matter how many Americans were lost at sea." After Germany's decision to challenge his ultimatum, he went through three months of emotional tension and depression similar to the anguish President McKinley endured on the eve of the Spanish-America War. McKinley's physical symptoms had been insomnia; Wilson's were severe headaches and extreme irritability. In late February he snapped at his cabinet—especially his son-in-law at the Treasury—for "pushing the country into war." In mid-March he confessed his fear to a newspaper publisher that "to fight you must be brutal and ruthless, and the spirit of ruthless brutality will enter into the very fiber of our national life."

By April the president regained his self-control, the character trait he particularly prized, and calculated that if he could not secure his political objectives as a noncombatant, he would do it as a belligerent. Wilson incorrectly assumed that the war was in its final stages. He correctly believed that there would be a peace conference at its conclusion. "If America stayed neutral," he told a delegation of pacifists, "the best she could hope for was to 'call through a crack in the door.' " Wilson hoped the price for a place at the conference would be small in money and manpower, but that was not the decisive factor, as foretold in a conversation he had in 1916 about not forgetting what he once taught in college history classes: "A hundred years from now it will not be the bloody details that the world will think of in this war; it will be the causes behind it, the readjustments which it will force." However, before Wilson could state the cause and shape the final outcome, he would first have to commit America to his crusade. That meant convincing populists and isolationists to fight while simultaneously restraining the militant Republicans who wanted to crush the enemy with an "overwhelming victory." Then, after beating the Germans without arousing a vindictive lust for their destruction, Wilson would have to have the power to impose his vision on the victors (his allies), as well as the vanquished.

It is hard to know if Wilson's rationale was cause or effect; whether he declared war to construct his new world order or whether, forced into the conflict, he conceived a goal to make it worthwhile. One way, the other way, or a bit of both, his task would not be easy. In his haste to redeem what disillusioned Europeans called "the damnable waste and unfairness of this war," Wilson ignored the fact that armed conflict is usually a preventive (not a constructive) policy. It can stop situations from getting worse; it rarely makes them much better. Near the end of World War II, a former Wilsonian named Walter Lippmann advised America to set "the minimum terms which are certainly necessary rather than maximum terms which may be desirable." He should not have been surprised that his mentor would fail, no matter how badly Wilson believed that his goals were "the principles of mankind and must prevail."[1]

MILITARY UNPREPAREDNESS AND PROGRESSIVE WAR AIMS

Three months after telling Edward House that "this country does not intend to become involved in this war," a visibly worn and distraught Woodrow Wilson went to his cloakroom on Capitol Hill, regained his physical composure in front of a mirror, and then went out to ask Congress to declare war on Germany. Shortly after Congress complied on 6 April, the president grabbed the hand of a White House assistant and declared with tears and great emotion: "I hate war."

One congressman recalled that Wilson made "a magnificent presentation," convincing many people by sheer eloquence. However, the speech abounded in ambivalence. It was part summons to a crusade against "the existence of autocratic governments backed by organized force," part admission of being caught in a terrible trap. The concluding paragraph began with "distressing and oppressive duty," moved on to talk about America's "privilege to spend her blood and her might for the principles that gave her birth," and ended with the words "she can do no other," as if to say that America had no option but war. A week before the speech, Wilson had asked House: "Is there anything else I can do?"

Aside from the militant wing of the Republican party, Congress was as distressed as the president. One representative from Vermont said there was no public enthusiasm, in striking contrast to the Spanish-American War. A senator from Utah recorded in his diary that "a majority of the people are opposed to this war. I am receiving many protests from all parts of the country." Many of his colleagues had little idea what the conflict would entail. A representative from New York recalled that "at least sixty to sixty-five per cent of the members who voted for war did so in the belief and firm conviction that we would never have to send a single soldier to Europe." The afternoon the House voted to declare a state of hostilities, an aide to the secretary of war testified that the country "may have to have an army in France." The chairman of the Senate Finance Committee responded, "Good Lord! You're not going to send soldiers over there, are you?"

At least initially, Wilson was ambivalent about America's ambivalence toward war. He laced his war message with appeals for "moderation" and "temperateness." No doubt his call for a war "without rancor" had roots in the places he was raised in the 1860s: Augusta (Georgia) nearly hit and Columbia (South Carolina) flattened by a force named William Tecumseh Sherman. Just living in those communities, let alone having a Confederate veteran as one's only teacher in the primary grades, must have bred enormous anxiety about the need for strict control of military power. One of Wilson's earliest memories was of the commotion caused by the fear that Sherman's army would enter Augusta. Years later, Wilson would say that "a boy never gets over his boyhood, and never can change those subtle influences which have become a part of him."

On the other hand, it soon became apparent that America was too indifferent to mobilize for war, let alone for one against Germany, the best army in the world. In the first three months, there were barely 300,000 volunteers, far short of "at least three million men," needed according to a War Department assessment. Industrial mobilization was not much better. Worried that the Allies were wearing down in May and wanting "to bring the war to the earliest possible conclusion," Secretary of War Newton Baker thought that airpower would be "America's most speedy and effective contribution to the Allied cause from a military point of view." Congress appropriated $840 million for 22,000 army airplanes. By July 1918, 37 were ready. As for ground combat, where machine guns were decisive, the United States had only 8,000 by the end of 1917. Training camps lacked rifles, medical supplies, winter uniforms, sanitary facilities, and fully built barracks. The shortages were so acute that the War Department delayed induction of one-fourth of the first military draft.

These deficiencies, prominently featured in the nation's newspapers, gave the Republican party an excellent opportunity for "going after the man in the White House" and his so-called pacifistic secretary of war. The administration wanted to rectify these mobilization shortfalls without inflaming public passions. Thus Walter Lippmann, a prominent young intellectual and a consultant to Edward House, advised Wilson to rely on conscription, "the only orderly and quiet way," not on volunteers who would need stimulation from "a newspaper campaign of manufactured hatred." However, even mandatory military service on an unprecedented scale would not prime America for the effort necessary to win its first foreign war against first-class competition. "It is not an army that we must shape and train for war," Wilson said in June, "it is a nation." Yet, he would admit, "if they cannot go in with a whoop, there is no use of their going in at all." This was no easy task, as William Wiseman, intelligence chief at the British embassy, explained to the Foreign Office: "The American people do not consider themselves in any danger from the Central Powers."

Unlike Europe, where heads of state could readily appeal to historic fears, America's historical hatred was against Britain, its ally in this war. As a country of "variegated elements" and "conflicting cross-currents," it had no consensus on international issues; not so for domestic policy. In the 1910s almost every politician was calling himself a "progressive," including former conservative, Grover

Cleveland Democrats such as Woodrow Wilson. In 1917, when the president looked for a war policy the public would support, he based his appeal on what House called "progressive principles" consistent with Wilson's maxim that "men are not led by being told what they don't know."

Wilson, House, and assistants like Lippmann internationalized themes common in American political culture. They articulated war aims based on their 1916 election campaign on peace, prosperity, and progressivism. To motivate America to play a major role in this awful war, the administration said that victory meant international peace ("a war to end all wars") and prosperity: "equal opportunities of trade with the rest of the world." It would also make "the world safe for democracy." the final item in the trinity. Progressivism promised to take government away from "special interests"—monopolies and bosses at home; militarists and monarchists abroad. Armies fighting for Wilsonian war aims would empower the common people for "the common purpose of enlightened mankind." If the aims of France and Britain belied this objective, they would make the "fatal mistake [of] cooling the ardor of America," Wilson told House. The United States "will not fight for any selfish aim on the part of any belligerent."

To clarify the application of those principles to international relations and to articulate war aims to the public, the administration turned to progressive publicists. One radical wrote that the president was "obviously bidding for liberal support," a comment more cynical than Wilson deserved. The president not only needed help to convince Americans to believe, as Wiseman reported to London, that "they are fighting for the cause of Democracy and not to save themselves." This reluctant commander in chief needed suitable war aims nobly stated to convince himself that he made the right decision when he led America to war. During the neutrality period, he borrowed the phrase "Peace without Victory" from the *New Republic,* which he thanked for editorials that "served to clarify and strengthen my thought." Now he turned back to this magazine and to kindred writers for ways to reconcile peace with military power.

Walter Lippmann, editor at the *New Republic* in 1916, wrote speeches helping Wilson win progressives who supported Roosevelt in 1912. In October 1917 he wrote for the think tank working on the president's war aims that "men will not die and starve and freeze for the things which orthodox diplomacy holds most precious," such as national self-interest and realpolitik. There was a nearly "universal feeling on the part of the common people of the world that the old diplomacy is bankrupt and that the system of the armed peace must not be restored." Because Wilson believed much the same thing about military preparedness and the balance of power, Lippmann's memorandum became the basis for Wilson's major statement of war aims, the Fourteen Points address (January 1918): "The day of conquest and aggrandizement" is to be replaced by "a general association of nations . . . affording mutual guarantees of political independence and territorial integrity to great and small nations alike."

The Fourteen Points address was the first great act of psychological warfare in the twentieth century: launched to motivate Americans, "foment trouble between the Liberals and the Imperialists in Germany," and appeal to Allied public opinion over the head of their governments. The Social Democratic party called it a "beautiful and alluring world peace program." The *New York Tribune,* a Republican newspaper heretofore critical of the president, compared Wilson to Abraham Lincoln, except for the proviso that Europeans living under German military rule suffered from "a slavery worse a thousand times than that of the negro" in the antebellum South. This comparison must have encouraged Wilson, who had written in his *History of the American People* that "it was necessary to put the South at a moral disadvantage by transforming the contest against States fighting for their independence into a war against States fighting for the maintenance and extension of slavery."

Armed forces doctrine holds that psychological operations are effective only when combined with combat lethality. Reluctantly, the Wilson administration came to agree insofar as House talked of "aiding the military situation by diplomacy of a sane and helpful sort." In April 1918, the German Social Democrats failed to prevent the Imperial Army High Command from carving satellite states out of Russia. Wilson, who once talked of peace without victory, returned to a rhetorical pattern he had used over forty years earlier in an essay about the war between "Christ's Army" and "the Prince of Darkness"—"there is no middle course." The president told the nation there was "but one response possible from us: Force to the utmost, Force without stint or limit" directed against the "military leaders, who are Germany's real rulers."

Meanwhile Lippmann, whose grandfather fled Berlin after the Prussian repression of liberalism in 1848, became an intelligence officer interviewing prisoners of war. Before he got near the front in September 1918, he wrote Newton Baker: we "should aim to create the impression that [Wilsonianism has] something new and infinitely hopeful in the affairs of mankind." He soon found out that the German soldier was "not a political animal" and that the cruder themes of standard army propaganda were more effective than those of the president. Military commanders, who thought that political messages were "tainted with radicalism and revolution," offered the enemy a simple choice: hold your position and get shelled or desert and get "succulent rations," now quite scarce thanks to English economic warfare. "Even the most sensitive among them," Lippmann reported back to House, "refuse flatly to believe that America has any ideal purpose. They simply do not believe such things exist among nations."[2]

AMALGAMATED FORCES OR AN INDEPENDENT ARMY?

Because German soldiers and civilians carried out the war despite Wilson's appeals and reduced rations, the president needed an expeditionary army to (1) defeat and discredit the German militarists, (2) prove to allies that collective security was more efficacious than territorial expansion, (3) give America authority at the peace conference vis-à-vis Germans and allies alike.

The first issue would dominate the debate in October 1918, when Wilson and the Allies considered Germany's request for an armistice. The others were at the heart of the most important decision America made during the world war, whether to fulfill or refuse the request of Britain and France to place American units—from divisions to companies—into sectors of their lines. Pure military logic has rarely been so unequivocal, as it was in the case for amalgamation. Because the president's 1916 preparedness program was not much more than an attempt to preempt a Republican political issue, the country was woefully unprepared to fight in 1917. Its army was far too meager to be more than the skeleton for an expedition to be mobilized in 1917, trained in 1918, and committed in 1919, when it was to have 3,500,000 men. The Germans, refusing to cooperate with American plans, devised a schedule of their own. After Allied convoys and other antisubmarine operations neutralized the U-boat as the winning weapon, the German army knocked Russia out of the conflict and massed on the western front with the intention of winning the war in early 1918. That prospective victory would save Germany from having to struggle through another "turnip [for dinner] winter" and would deprive America of the chance to win the war when it would be ready. Therefore, although the United States did not know it in 1917, the American Expeditionary Force (AEF) would have to mobilize, train, deploy, and fight, while Germany was spending its waning assets assaulting Allied lines in 1918.

If America came to the rescue, it might substantiate Wilson's claim that a League of Nations, with U.S. participation, was a viable substitute for security via armaments and conquest. If America were to participate in any meaningful fashion before mid-1918, amalgamation was the only way. English officers who instructed U.S. divisions—and wanted their battalions in their lines—said that "American Commanders and Staffs are almost wholly untrained and without military experience." True, the British had extensive experience taking horrendous casualties. Their comments were still valid, as Americans admitted long after the war. Robert Lee Bullard, commander of the Second Army, would say that "we lacked not only the training, but the organization; and the kind of arms with which we were later to face the enemy."

Most division commanders had been in charge of nothing larger than a regiment (sometimes a company) before the war. Staff officers trained for intelligence, operations, and logistics (G-2s, G-3s, and G-4s) were invaluable but scarce. Out of 5,700 officers in the U.S. Army in 1917, some 250 were graduates of its staff college at Fort Leavenworth, barely enough for corps and army headquarters, echelons actually above Leavenworth's curriculum. In smaller units, where direct contact with the enemy occurs, trained staff was particularly rare. America had to improvise by making its divisions twice as large (28,000) as those of other armies. This made them the functional equivalent of a European corps. It also made it far more difficult for division staff to supply, train, deploy, and maneuver American formations. In March 1918 John J. Pershing, the AEF commander, thought he had only 61 qualified general staff officers in the entire force. In November 1917 he had opened his own three-month staff college, eventually graduating 537 officers on an emergency basis, as Pershing had to admit. ("Our staff officers generally have little conception of [the] problems involved in directing armies.") Another answer was amalgamation, at least according to the Allies. "They lacked the men," Pershing's chief of staff would write, "but had the officers to command them. We had the men and from their standpoint lacked the officers," except for small units, battalion and below.

The U.S. Army also lacked heavy weapons and the specialists to use them. Artillery, tanks, and airplanes were necessary to counter machine-gun fire, but none of these products had been priorities for the prewar army, mostly infantry regiments with a sprinkling of horse cavalry. Total personnel with over one year's experience in field artillery could fill a single U.S. division as configured to fight in Europe. When the United States did mount its first operation as an "independent" army (St.-Mihiel in September 1918), all 3,010 guns and one-third of the gunners came from the Allies, as did all the shells they shot. America would produce 12 percent of its own field artillery, 34 percent of its trench mortars, 19 percent of its aircraft, and 12 percent of its tanks. As General Pershing told Franklin Roosevelt on the eve of World War II: "We were literally beggars as to every important weapon, except the rifle."

Pure logic supported British policy as of December 1917, comparable to American lend-lease policy early in World War II. England's main contribution to the Allied effort would be tanks, planes, shipping, and skilled labor—industrial or military. America would contribute raw materials: cotton, wheat, and riflemen. However, wars are fought to achieve political objectives, foreign or domestic, not to practice military logic. Amalgamation, which meant fighting under a foreign flag, not only would confirm the Republican accusation that Wilson could not lead the nation in war, but also would deprive the president of the international influence for which he waged war in the first place. He would tell confidants that "England and France have not the same views with regard to peace that we have by any means. When the war is over we can force them to our way of thinking," provided he could "carry as many weapons to the peace table as I can conceal on my person."

For starters, Wilson's prospective arsenal included gold, the navy, and his eloquence: the Allies would be his financial debtors, he would have a navy "second to none," and he would speak directly to the common people of Europe, none of whom "could doubt or question my position with regard to the war and its objects." Finally, he counted on an independent and triumphant army with major battles to its credit, that is, unless it disappeared in amalgamation. General Tasker Bliss, Wilson's personal adviser on military matters and a "real thinking man" in the president's eyes, warned of the lack of diplomatic leverage if "the American flag [has] not appeared anywhere on the line because our organizations will simply be parts of battalions and regiments of the Entente Allies." The "deliberate desire" of the Allies is for the United States to send to Europe "a million men [with] no American army and no American commander."

The British government rued what Wilson anticipated: attending "a Peace Conference with our country weakened while America was still overwhelmingly strong." The president of the United States would have turned the tables on England's own plan to mobilize a large army to dominate negotiations after France, Russia, and Germany depleted their armed forces in combat with each other. Its allies and the enemy had both been threats to the British Empire in Africa, India, or the Middle East. England hardly welcomed the notion that Wilson would be "the great arbiter of the war," certainly preventing the establishment of Britain as "the first Power in the World." In the words of its ambassador to Washington: "Let the Americans—a rotten lot of psalm-singing, profit-mongering humbugs—mind their own business."

French officials were also worried. During the Spanish-American War, Jules Gambon, ambassador to Washington, was the most vocal but not the only Frenchman talking about an "American peril." He mediated the peace settlement that ended that war in 1899 so he could take special care that the United States acquired the Philippines, not the Canary Islands in the eastern Atlantic that would have been a way station for the latest barbarian invasion of Europe. In February 1917, when he was secretary-general of the foreign ministry, his nephew warned his brother, the ambassador to Britain, that if America intervened on the Continent, in twenty or thirty years it would be treating Europe like a troublesome Caribbean island. In 1918, after the armistice, the Gambons urged the creation of a united Anglo-Franco front against America.

Allied officials such as these wanted U.S. materials, loans, ships, and labor: all at the cheapest possible price. House and other informed Americans, after consultations with the Allies in April 1917, told Wilson that "no one looks with favor upon our raising a large army at the present." Then, in May, the French spring offensive failed at the cost of 120,000 casualties and mutiny among the rank and file. From that moment until the end of the war (if not through World War II), the French army abandoned what an officer recently called "the Napoleonic maxims of energy, activity, and speed." That same month, Bliss told Newton Baker that "as the foreign gentlemen spoke more and more freely [in Washington] it became evident that what they want and need is men, whether trained or not."

American isolationists would later say that scheming Europeans pretended not to want U.S. troops until America declared war, then convinced poor Wilson to send an army against his own inclinations. This is a myth. The Allies may have wanted all the help they could get, but they did not beg America for "men, men, and still more men" until early 1918, when the Germans launched their final make-or-break offensive. (Once it failed, the British rapidly reduced the number of American soldiers they transported to Europe: 300,000 in July, 180,000 in October.) Pershing wrote Secretary Baker, after the French failure in 1917, that they still "would rather have us work for them than fight for them." The senior military leader in the British delegation sent to Washington that April told the War Department that the United States could never "raise, train, and transport an army of sufficient size to have any effect in the European theater."

To be sure, once Allied officials realized the magnitude of the failure in 1917, many (not all) began to ask for American combatants, but not an American army. In May, General Joseph Joffre asked for U.S. soldiers to "join ours on the French front." In September, George Clemenceau, soon to be prime minister of France, urged Pershing to put soldiers into the line without delay. By 1918 he was telling the Supreme War Council of the Allies that his plan was "to hold out . . . till the American assistance came in full force; after that America would win the war." Amalgamation was an ideal solution for France and Britain, growing dependent on a nation they did not trust. By putting American infantrymen into European sectors under European flags, their armies would get what one officer called "a wonderful transfusion of blood." Meanwhile, according to Pershing, America would never "find out her own strength."

No fool, Wilson was way ahead of the game. Two months before the 1917 French offensive began, he authorized the War Department to plan for raising an army for deployment to the Continent. The congressmen who later said they voted for war on the assumption that "we would never send a single soldier to Europe" should have paid more attention to the president's war message: the conflict "will involve the immediate addition to the armed services of . . . at least 500,000 men." Granted, Wilson had not said where he would deploy them, nor that he already foresaw at least 1,500,000 soldiers in the American army. However, the nation hardly needed this much coastal artillery. Before Congress declared war, Wilson was already planning to dispatch an independent army while the Allies held the line against the enemy. Then, America would "give the final, shattering blow" to Germany, as well as to "selfish" Allied ambitions that would undermine a just and lasting peace.[3]

WILSON AND AN AEF: HIDING AGENDAS
FROM HIS ALLIES AND HIS ARMY COMMANDER

The great problem with Woodrow Wilson's strategy was that if he waited to deploy American soldiers, he would not demonstrate to France and Britain that American military support was a viable substitute for national security through conquest, occupation, and territorial expansion. Even worse, Germany might win the war. Therefore, Wilson had to build his own army and support the Allies at the same time. Hence the contradictory directives he had Bliss and Baker send General Pershing on 26 May 1917, with copies to France, England, and Italy:

"The forces of the United States are a separate and distinct component . . . [whose] identity must be preserved. . . . But until the forces are in your judgment sufficiently strong to warrant operations as an independent command [that is, 1919] . . . you will cooperate as a component of whatever army you may be assigned to by the French Government"—an organization that defined cooperation as amalgamation within its lines.

Wilson met Pershing for the first and last time (until after the armistice) two days before this message. Pershing recalled: "I had naturally thought that he would say something about the part our Army should play in cooperation with the Allied armies, but he said nothing." Newton Baker, Pershing's primary source of information on administration policy, was no less confusing. He wanted America to be "a great power conducting *pro tanto* a war of our own, rather than having our force merged with that of one of the other combatants and losing its identity." He also "sympathized" with Allied opinion that amalgamation was the only way "to bring the war to the earliest possible conclusion" and thereby prevent "the German machine" from knocking France and Russia out of the war. This did not bode well for Pershing's own priority, to withhold men for two years while he created his independent army, especially after he himself told Baker in December that the critical moment was at hand. "The Allies are very weak. . . . It is very doubtful they can hold on until 1919 unless we give them a lot of support this [upcoming] year." Five months later, when the Germans launched their main offensive, Baker wrote Pershing that "exigencies" require the "useful cooperation at the earliest possible moment [of] the largest possible number of American personnel in the military arm most needed by our Allies," that is, infantry. Pershing wrote on the margin of the message: "If this is not amalgamation, what is it?"

Not knowing administration policy, Pershing did not ask for more directives, probably afraid he might receive orders for amalgamation, something no self-respecting military commander would ever want to hear. Orders from Wilson had already caused the greatest humiliation in his life. In 1916, in pursuit of Pancho Villa, Pershing "dashed into Mexico with the intention of eating the Mexicans raw." Ambushed but told to "get his troops promptly in hand," Pershing sneaked "home," as he put it, "under cover like a whipped cur with his tail between his legs." Seething with rage and weeping in frustration, he still felt "soldiers are but to obey no matter what they think." Largely because Wilson figured "Pershing will just do what he is told," he made him commander of the AEF. While always obedient to direct orders, Pershing tried to avoid being told what to do. "It was not my policy," he wrote in his memoirs, "at any time to put anything up to Washington that I could possibly decide myself."

For his part, Wilson did not trust military men, even Tasker Bliss, who would discuss administration policy "as far as I know" or "as I understand it." Most senior officers had ties to Theodore Roosevelt and the Republican party, whom Pershing once said would control Washington as long as "the red-blooded American is still in the large majority." However, partisan identification explains only part of the president's reticence. Playing a double game, Wilson could not be per-fectly clear with Pershing and credible with professions to cooperate with Allies. When they would plead for amalgamation, the president played the good guy inclined to say yes—or at least that he had no "settled" policy. Meanwhile, he cast Pershing as the bad guy with the prerogative to say no.

This scenario, by which Wilson convinced Europeans that he "agreed in principle" with amalgamation but "had to consult his military advisers and be guided by them as to details," deceived some very sophisticated men every bit as deceptive as Wilson himself could be. David Lloyd George, Britain's prime min-ister, told Pershing that while an independent army was correct in principle, it could ensure military defeat. He lamented that "the decision of the President" to collaborate "proved of insufficient value in face of [Pershing's] stubborn intran-sigence." Actually, his complaint about "the shortsightedness of one General and the failure of his Government to order him to carry out their undertakings" described the situation between Lloyd George and Douglas Haig, his own field commander whose strategy of attrition threatened to leave Britain "so beaten and shattered that at the end of the War the American army would be the only one left." The indictment was not accurate, at least for the United States. The "Welsh Wizard" incorrectly concluded that poor Wilson was not to blame, as did the French prime minister who wired Lloyd George that "Wilson is entirely on our side" but "felt bound to adhere" to Pershing's decisions. Reduced to a "state of nervous exasperation" from arguing with the military man about amalgamation, Clemenceau told Marshal Foch, the supreme Allied commander, that it was "high time to tell President Wilson the truth and the whole truth." The western front "had already drunk the best blood of France." Pershing's obstinacy would doom "my country's fate."

William Wiseman, British intelligence officer and confidant of Wilson's con-fidant, Edward House, wrote the foreign office that the president "told Pershing that he may put American troops by battalions in the British line, or use them in any way which in his, Pershing's, judgment may be taken by the necessities of the military situation." Wilson knew exactly which way Pershing would decide, which is why he gave him "authority to act with entire freedom in making the best disposition and use of your forces." That got the monkey off Washington's back. Even retired American generals, equally deceived, wrote Pershing about "what a wonderful thing it is to see a war run by military men instead of politicians."

Unlike his domestic enemies, Roosevelt and Lodge, Wilson no longer felt that war had any intrinsic merit or majesty due to heroism. In all but name, he had become a Clausewitzian, someone who believed (as he once wrote) that a good general "deem[s] himself always an instrument, never a master" of policy. In 1919, when forbidding Foch to occupy the Rhine, Wilson said "it is indis-pensable that we understand one another perfectly." In 1918, at the height of Ger-many's spring offensive, he merely asked Pershing to treat "as sympathetically as possible" Allied requests for reinforcements. Part of his scheme to avoid responsibility, he gave Pershing "entire freedom . . . unique in history," as the general said in his memoirs. Lloyd George wanted House to come to Europe and represent the United States on the Supreme War Council, where Wilson's alter ego might take control of the amalgamation issue. Wilson, no fool, kept House at home. This left Allied governments, in the words of British officials, "dependent upon General Pershing's good will." Unfortunately, "the man on the spot with whom we have to work" was the last person they wanted to see.

If all this implies that Woodrow Wilson could be devious, it is because he could. Clemenceau, no friend, said he "talked like Jesus Christ but acted like Lloyd George." Wiseman, a friend, said Wilson "is by turns a great idealist and a shrewd politician." More to the point, the president was trying to build an army to enhance America's power, save the Allies from their own expansionist policies, and prevent Germany from winning the war. "Justice and mercy and peace" hung in the balance, as well as Wilson's peace of mind. He confessed to House that God would hold him accountable for every dead American soldier. Could this terrible war, under this stipulation, be worth "the lives of our fittest men"? Wilson could not conduct in perfect candor his plan to produce an affirmative answer with a suitable peace. Neither could anybody else.[4]

PREPARING FOR THE GERMANS, ENTREATING WITH THE PRESIDENT

Wilson's pretense to sympathize with amalgamation but defer to Pershing's professional judgment had some drawbacks, especially because Pershing never grasped the president's scheme. Consequently, the AEF commander did not always play his fall-guy role. Take one heated exchange on amalgamation in late May 1918. Lloyd George: "We will refer this to your president'; Pershing: "Refer it and be damned. . . . He will simply refer it back to me for recommendation."

On this occasion Pershing acted in anger or else was simply bluffing. This proud and ambitious man (who else gets the rank he had?) usually lived in fear that the army he was creating would be yanked out from under him. If Wilson ever transferred American troops into Allied armies, even temporarily, "very few would ever come out." If that happened, the AEF would become, in fact if not in name, a forward-based supply bureau filling requisitions for Henri Petain, Douglas Haig, and other Allied field commanders. Pershing would be a rubber-stamp administrator, the role he expected the army chief of staff to perform for him as a real commander of a real army conducting combat operations on the battlefield.

Pershing sent to Washington numerous arguments against amalgamation. The mere fact he did this at a time when he had to organize, supply, train, and deploy the largest single army in American history testifies to his anxiety. Sometimes Pershing would argue that "our forces should not be dissipated," since "when the war ends our position will be stronger if our army . . . [has] played a distinct and definite part." When a soldier searches for political arguments to persuade a politician, it is likely that the soldier is not privy to the politician's political objectives. Based on his sole face-to-face meeting with the president and a subsequent message from Newton Baker, Pershing did know Wilson felt that European trench warfare was just a "delaying action" and that he was to keep the War Department "fully advised of all that concerns your command." This gave him an opening to bring up reasons of tactics, his area of expertise. To the administration and within the AEF, Pershing repeatedly emphasized "differences in national characteristics and [the] military training of troops" to oppose amalgamation. "The methods to be employed must remain or become distinctly our own." Allied "tactics and techniques are not suited to American characteristics or the American mission in this war."

The commanding general was recycling an argument present in U.S. military circles since the Civil War, if not the eighteenth century, when Americans claimed that they knew more about conducting the French-Indian conflict than their English drillmasters did. A decade before Pershing was commissioned, General Sherman wrote that "our Army should be organized and maintained upon a model of our own." Twenty years later, Lieutenant Pershing could read in military journals demands for "an American system of infantry drill"; "almost anything is better than European tactics."

In 1917, to underscore the incompatibility of methods, Pershing emphasized the doctrine the English and French had relinquished in the war: riflery and bayonet attack on open terrain. The Allies had entered the conflict with the conviction that "the offense doubles the energy of the troops" and that "the moral attributes [are] the primary causes of all great success." However, there was something hollow at the base of this belief after forty terrible years of taking the tactical offensive, from the Confederates at Gettysburg (1863) to the Japanese at Mukden (1905). The European officer corps that went into World War I were probably bombastic to overcome their admitted reluctance "to advance under fire. . . . We have to train ourselves and train others, cultivating with passion everything that bears the stamp of the offensive spirit. We must take it to excess; perhaps even that will not go far enough."

After the first year of the European war, most small-unit leaders were dead or disabled. Having lost the personnel able to "exploit the resources of the moment," the Allies went to closed linear formations—a "perfect target," said the Germans, about "this solid wall of khaki men." By the time the first American units landed in Europe, the French and English had changed their doctrine once again. The English relied on tanks, planes, and blockade. The French emphasized meticulous planning, entrenched positions, limited objectives, and a role reversal for combat arms. American military manuals stated that only infantry, by "shock and contact," can overcome the enemy; "the ability to do this is possessed . . . not at all by artillery." According to French doctrine, reproduced to tutor Americans, "the conquest of the ground is made by the artillery. . . . The infantry follows up to occupy and hold." More bluntly, one French combat soldier told a U.S. reporter that America had "the best raw material" of any nation then fighting the war. However, "they need a deal of training. The hardest thing to teach them is not to be too brave. They must learn first to hide. That's the first essential in this war."

Pershing, who condemned this transformation of "the principles of warfare," probably welcomed what he heard and witnessed on the western front. Heretofore, Newton Baker noted, neither Pershing nor the army had been strong proponents of "the importance of good rifle shooting." Now the fact that "the average Allied soldier . . . had all but given up the use of the rifle" became the cornerstone for Pershing's case to Washington. America must teach "superior marksmanship" and practice "open warfare" was his constant refrain. "The methods of training and instruction in [the French and English] armies are very different from our own." Combat operations must be "conducted in all essential elements according to the principles found in [U.S.] standard manuals," no matter that they had been written for campaigns against Indian raiders, Mexican bandits, or Moro tribesmen in the Philippines. Pershing, whose combat experience had been in these missions against undergunned opponents won by maneuver and riflery, adopted the same doctrine for use against Germans armed with the latest technology: "All instruction must contemplate the assumption of a vigorous offensive. This purpose will be emphasized in every phase of training until it becomes a settled habit of thought"—shades of old (not new) Allied strategy.

Pershing would never relinquish what he called "the correct doctrine." In 1918 he terminated all instruction from French officers within the AEF. His opinion was not unanimous within the U.S. Army, especially not in the agency primarily responsible for organizing, training, and equipping divisions. The War Department, which had six times more soldiers under its command than the AEF in late 1917, paid a lot more attention to learning European techniques. Its stateside officers felt that "the opinion of the British, after 3 years of war, should be given great weight. [Unlike them] we have had *no* experience." Pershing to the contrary, the army chief of staff sent out instructions reflecting the opinion of Allied advisers sent to Washington, not the opinion of the AEF commander who wanted those advisers sent home. "In all the military training of a division, under existing conditions, training for trench warfare is of paramount importance."

American conscripts prepared for open warfare through "the hardest, most uncompromising and intensive system of drill" many veterans ever saw. Confused to be in the army to begin with, they did not need an army confused within itself, especially about what was called "the cult of the rifle." Charles Summerall and John Lejeune, commanders of the First and Second Divisions, thought Pershing drastically underestimated the need for more artillery: "The reckless courage of the good soldier with his rifle and bayonet could not overcome machine guns well-protected in rocky nests." Hugh Drum, chief of staff of the First Army, thought that mass was far more important than mobility: "In some cases the enemy's deployment may be so dense that the old time shoulder to shoulder function will be required."

Truth be known, Pershing questioned the wisdom of his own doctrine, although warning doubters in September 1917 that pessimism would be grounds for summary relief. On the one hand, he ordered that the "specialities of trench warfare should not be allowed to interfere with rifle practice." On the other, he toured a British training camp and found its use of mortars "more realistic than anything we had so far seen in our own service." In August 1918 he admitted to his chief of staff that "perhaps we are losing too many men by enemy machine guns. I think this might be met by tanks or possibly by artillery." A study made for Pershing on this issue said that there was nothing wrong with open warfare per se. It was simply beyond the level of military skill most American soldiers possessed: "All formations are habitually lacking in elasticity; there is almost never any attempt to maneuver, that is, throw supports and reserves to the flanks for envelopment."

The Germans would do exactly this in their March 1918 offensive: bypassing strongpoints and enemy firepower. At the Somme in 1916, the Allies took 500,000 casualties to capture ninety-eight square miles in 140 days. On 21 March, to Pershing's secret satisfaction, the Germans captured 140 square miles and 21,000 British prisoners for one-tenth the price paid on the Somme. German accomplishments seemed to vindicate his doctrine that Petain ridiculed: "Americans dream of operating in open country, after having broken through the front." But whatever Pershing may have thought, it was not just the tactics (or ways) that enabled the Germans to stage a momentary breakthrough on the western front: it was primarily the means. On the eve of World War I, the German army contained more veteran noncommissioned officers than the total manpower of the U.S. Army (115,000 German NCOs; 98,500 American soldiers). America conscripted recruits, described in Pershing's memoirs, as "ignorant of practically everything pertaining to the business of the soldier in war." They were just beginning to learn preliminary infantry skills, such as caring for weapons and marching in formation, when the Germans were retraining the best soldiers in the world's best army to overcome its sole shortcoming, its tendency for tactical density to maintain cohesion and concentration in battles of annihilation. Now, firing tons of gas (not high-explosive) shells to incapacitate the first line of defense, they attacked in depth with fire teams armed with light mortars and machine guns, flamethrowers, smoke, and grenades.

Pershing, still proclaiming that the "rifle and the bayonet remain the supreme weapons of the infantry soldier and that the ultimate success of the army depends upon their proper use," was making a virtue out of a necessity. Rifles were about the only up-to-date weapons the United States had en masse. Many mortar and machine-gun platoons, so designated in America, never saw mortars or machine guns until they arrived in France, sometimes not until they reached the front. When they finally got them, they were often poorly deployed by battalion commanders who understood little about these weapons. In short, Pershing was trying to elicit high-grade labor from a semiskilled workforce led by the 6,400 new junior officers his training program graduated each month.

Not something to be proud of, the AEF's emergency school system was prima facie proof of unpreparedness, confirmed by the commander of the First Division. ("I have much difficulty in getting officers who know anything.") One thing they knew was the burden that they bore, as one of his artillery officers wrote home in 1918: "We have changed from the stereotyped trench warfare to a warfare of maneuver which requires a great deal more military knowledge and ability to carry on properly than it does to 'sit tight.'" Other than conveying that distressing fact, official doctrine and methods did not help much. Pershing issued general pronouncements; details were left to his assistant chiefs of staff. This was standard operating procedure considering his rank and other responsibilities. However, in this instance, there was too much confusion about what "open warfare" meant against the Germans, since it essentially described what small mounted units did against Indians on the Great Plains. Until the War Department distributed a revised training circular in October 1918, it was barely defined and rarely specified in meaningful detail. Hunter Liggett, the commander of the U.S. I Corps, had to devise "some practical line for open warfare," as he told headquarters. "I can find nothing in the mass of literature I have received which teaches this essential question."

Practicality, in general, was not the strong suit of the AEF. Those Germans who faced Americans said they were "absolutely tenacious," "reckless," and "endowed with great energy." They were also awkward, mechanical, and unable "to exploit changing conditions by quick decisions." The absence of this ability, according to the enemy, "would have been even more conspicuous in the course of mobile warfare which is the true test of both leaders and rank and file." Pershing, who wanted to do exactly that, certainly recognized the need for thorough training. It was his justification for keeping American units out of combat for a year and a half. Yet he did not fight their premature commitment with the same utter tenacity he used to fight amalgamation. In mid-1918, 300,000 Americans a month arrived in France, often to be rushed right to the front, where many men who had never fired a rifle were hardly ready to practice open warfare. George Catlett Marshall, the G-3 of the First Army, would admit that it was very "difficult to carry out any operation exactly according to Hoyle [or Pershing?] because of the limited amount of training and complete lack of experience on the part of the men and the young officers." Other AEF leaders would have agreed, according to the evaluations they filed on their units during the war. Even Pershing might have concurred, judging by the cables he sent the War Department: "Officers from colonel down, including some generals, are ignorant of the handling of units in open warfare including principles of reconnaissance and formation of attack."

Granted, conscription acquired a few Alvin Yorks—backwoods marksmen naturally able to conduct open warfare Pershing-style. However, they were a rare commodity in modern American society, as George Marshall later explained: most military recruits "hadn't seen a weapon except in a shooting gallery and had never been in the woods, other than a park." York, a mountain man who single-handedly would ambush a German battalion, could sneak up on deer or hit wild turkeys in the head from fifty yards away. He was amazed that other recruits in his division "missed everything [on the rifle range] but the sky."

German intelligence reported that "neither officers nor men [in the AEF] knew how to make use of the terrain." But even if America had an Alvin York on every corner, one doubts whether Pershing could have conducted the type of warfare he told Washington he planned. To be fair, since at least the 1870s, every modern army had been struggling to learn how to conduct the tactical offensive in the face of modern firepower. They would also grapple with the predicament through World War II, where for every instance of "blitzkrieg" in an age of mechanized warfare there were several examples of attrition warfare, such as Stalingrad, Okinawa, and the Siegfried line. Even after 1919, the War Department stated that the tank was a useful infantry "auxiliary" that could never replace the bayonet. Pershing, in the midst of war, was tussling with an extraordinarily difficult problem. Nonetheless, the question persists: Why did he insist that typical American doughboys, the least prepared soldiers on the western front, conduct open warfare that required tactical expertise "by all troops engaged in the action"? Furthermore, draftees were supposed to do it according to "the standards of West Point" and Germanic military proficiency, which neither the French nor the English could claim to emulate. It seems likely that Pershing's insistent demands for "American methods" and "a doctrine of our own" were directly related to his fear that his creation, the AEF, might otherwise be snatched away from him and amalgamated into Allied formations.

Tactical incompatibility need not be a military objective, especially for a coalition. Since 1973 the U.S. Army has accepted the fact that an effective alliance needs "interoperability," that is, mutual doctrine and equipment within the NATO forces. It has worked nearly as hard to make itself compatible with West Germans as Pershing once opposed the process when it came to the French and the British. Never sure what President Wilson really wanted, the commander of the AEF was doing all he could to protect his institutional independence, including keeping experienced French commanders away from his training centers and exploding with anger when four infantry companies fought exceptionally well under an Australian corps commander. Consequently, American soldiers would be even less prepared for the savage warfare they would face at the Meuse-Argonne.[5]

FIGHTING AND FINISHING THE WAR: PERSHING, WILSON, AND UNCONDITIONAL SURRENDER

The U.S. Army might have fought more proficiently had it been able to fight when and where it planned—in 1919 on the Lorraine front in the Saar River basin, where the terrain was relatively open. However, war is mankind's most unpredictable activity. One rarely does what one wants; one usually reacts to an enemy who purposely upsets carefully made plans. The Germans tried to win the war in March 1918, before Pershing was ready in 1919. Despite the brilliant tactics of small units, they could not get to Paris. When German infantry penetrated enemy lines, the Allies used railroad lines for lateral mobility and plugged the gaps before they hemorrhaged. By the time the western front stabilized in July, the Germans had suffered another 960,0000 casualties and depleted most of their waning energy, supplies, and morale. On 8 August Douglas Haig, the British Expeditionary Force commander, launched a limited counteroffensive to pinch off an exposed German salient east of Amies. Near there, in 1916, on the first day of the Battle of the Somme, he suffered 60,000 casualties. Now, armed with 530 tanks and 800 planes, he collected 16,000 surrenders in what General Erich Ludendorff called "the black day of the German army. . . . It put the decline of our fighting power beyond doubt." The British, heretofore expecting the war to last as late as 1920, decided to stretch the engagement into a campaign. In the next three weeks they captured 50,000 prisoners and 700 heavy guns by employing over 1,000 tanks. On 27 August Haig wrote his wife: "The German Army is thoroughly war weary and our attack will still go on!" That same day he implored the commitment of all American soldiers to battle "to enable an advance to be made without delay."

These events upset almost every plan and schedule Pershing had. The AEF had sent many of its best regimental officers and NCOs back to the States to prepare new divisions for 1919, when combat was supposed to culminate. Others had spent much of their tours in the AEF school system. They were barely familiar with the units to which they were assigned when combat became decisive in the fall of 1918. Sixty-seven more officers attended the staff college that October, leaving assault divisions fighting on the American line. Timing aside, the sector for the offense was also changed—to occupy decisive territory, according to Haig. His target was the railroad track running from Strasbourg to Flanders: the means for German lateral mobility and retreat to new defensive lines. Pershing's choice had been an area south of Germany's fallback routes to Cologne and Coblenz. As France, Britain, and Belgium simultaneously converged toward the center and the northern sector of the line, America would have diverged due west.

Haig's proposal faithfully adhered to the military principle of combining combat power on a mutual objective, even if that meant a 300-mile envelopment from the Meuse to the Channel. Nonetheless, military orthodoxy might not have been what carried his case. Foch and Pershing may have concurred for reasons barely hinted at in Pershing's terse depiction: "It was agreed that the American Army should operate as a unit under its own commander on the Meuse-Argonne front." The Allies got what they wanted: an American attack on the southern shoulder of the giant German salient. Pershing got what he wanted: a definitive commitment to renounce requests for amalgamation. As a bonus, Pershing also got a chance to show up the French, whose condescension he

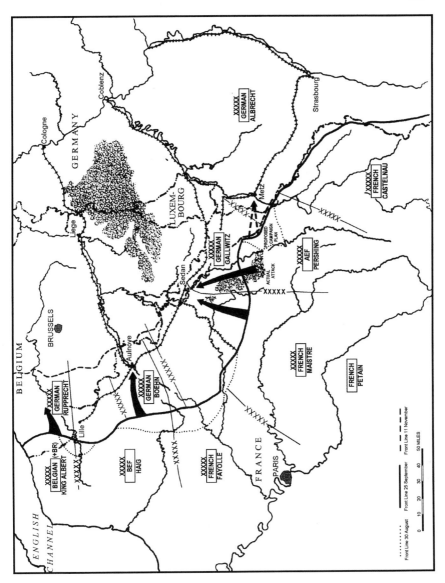

World War I, western offensive, 1918

loathed. "In my opinion, with which some of the French fully agreed, none of the allied troops had the morale or the aggressive spirit to overcome the difficulties to be met."

"The French," George Marshall later recalled, were "very, very tired and the Americans very, very cocky." Pershing gave his allies what they had lacked since their 1917 offensive turned out a miserable failure. Petain and Foch had said: "We must wait for the Americans." The absence of amalgamation meant that fresh recruits noted for "bravery and audacity and relish for danger" would not fill their ranks. However, by placing them on a near flank, a large-scale French offensive might be feasible for the first time in a year, as suggested by a battle fought that July. The Americans and the French had launched a combined operation to pinch off a twenty-five-square-mile salient on the Marne, some thirty-five miles northwest of Paris. The U.S. Twenty-sixth Infantry Division suffered 4,000 casualties, 66 percent more than the cautious French divisions on both its flanks. "Without Americans," elated French officers told their U.S. counterparts, "this [offensive] would have been impossible. We owe it all to you."

In October those fresh, young Americans, "fighting with intense *individual* passion," would draw "the best German divisions to our own front and consume them," so said Pershing. In the process, the AEF would clear a path for the French army to march to Sedan, a location of enormous military and political significance. Aside from being the major junction on the southern half of the great railroad line, it was where the French had surrendered 83,000 soldiers and lost the Franco-Prussian War in 1870. Now in 1918—after Foch and Pershing reached their understanding—the only thing left was for the inexperienced AEF to punch fifty miles through four defensive belts placed on what Pershing soon called "the most difficult [terrain] on the Western Front."

The Meuse-Argonne turned out to be the most ferocious military campaign in U.S. history, engaging 1,030,000 soldiers and claiming 122,000 casualties—twelve times as many men and twice the cost Ulysses S. Grant sustained in the Wilderness campaign. Pershing (like Grant) began the campaign hoping to avoid frontal attacks, although he had even less room for maneuver. The sector was narrow and congested; in one area 600,000 men advanced on three main roads along a twelve-mile front of woods, barbed wire, booby traps, and what one soldier called "mud, mud, mud, mud." The defense had observation posts; the offense was virtually blind. If Pershing had successfully trained an army of marksmen, it would not have mattered very much. Commanders from infantry companies to army corps reported, "I couldn't point out any targets"; "no one was visible," despite horrendous noise. When Americans did break into the open, nests and pillboxes caught them in cross fire until it seemed to a typical doughboy that "every goddamn German who didn't have a machine gun had a cannon." Open warfare "proved useless," said the secretary of war. Tactics was "just massed infantry stuff," said Captain Mark Wayne Clark. General Billy Mitchell of the army air service, later filing a brief for his particular branch, would write that "the art of war had departed," Pershing's plans kaput. "Attrition, or the gradual killing off of the enemy, was all the ground armies were capable of."

The U.S. attack stalled for lack of skill, firepower, and supplies unable to navigate the craters on the road net to the front. Pershing had hoped that "the youth and enthusiasm of vigorous young Americans [would] more than offset their lack of training." An officer who once served on his staff, George S. Patton, would recall that "untutored courage [proved] useless in the face of educated bullets." After three weeks about 100,000 stragglers clogged the American sector, many dropping back just to search for food. To control these so-called "deadbeats, deserters, evaders of battle and danger," the AEF organized a follow-up force of military police in linear formations. One MP called this tactic "moral support," an inspired euphemism that did not impress the French high command. It believed the logjam proof of incompetence: "The American Army was literally stuck with paralysis because 'the brain' didn't exist, because generals and their staffs lacked experience." Therefore, on 12 October, Foch broke his understanding with Pershing and tried to place a French general in tactical command of the U.S. Army. Pershing refused on grounds of national honor: that such an event "would forever obliterate the part America has taken in the war."

Pershing cursed the French and blamed his problems on "too much attention to trench war methods." (In 1919, while at peace, the AEF would renew training, having witnessed its tactical inability "to reap the full fruits of victory.") In the meantime, Pershing drove the army to "push on regardless of men or guns, night and day." He recorded in his diary that "if we keep on pounding, the Germans will be obliged to give way." (Asked when, he admitted: "I do not know.") In late 1918 the U.S. Army was at the stage of human expenditure its allies left in 1916, after the battles of the Somme and Verdun. One general staff officer would recall that "there was not brought home to us the need for conservation of manpower." Pershing authorized officers to shoot down men who ran from the enemy. If any officer, no matter what his rank, did not attack "with all possible energy," he was "to [be] relieved on the spot." "Give it up, and you're a goner," one general told another thrown back twice with heavy losses; "you'll lose your command in twenty-four hours."

American soldiers on minimal food, sleep, and water—and without any hope of relief—conducted a kill-or-be-killed campaign for nearly a month. ("We are not men any more," said one doughboy, "just savage beasts.") They attacked "in close, deeply arranged formations" that Germans attributed to poor training and incompetent leadership. This created "absolutely colossal casualties," according to the German army group commander. By late October, said George Marshall, Americans "were approaching the point of complete exhaustion." The Germans were already there when AEF tactics began to improve.

Pershing's old training program had a relatively small component of "specialists," that is, those trained in the "special form of warfare" required to break through the first line of trenches before "maneuvering in the open fields." This familiarized some Americans with mortars, machine guns, poison gas, and the light cannon "which smashed machine gun nests at point-blank range." On-the-job-training at the Meuse-Argonne spread this experience through the AEF. By October, as it was confronting continuous belts of enemy entrenchments (not the thin layer open warfare presumed), the army was using a lot fewer marksmen and a lot more area-suppressive fire. Chemical shells and light machine guns pinned the enemy, while the "bombers" did the permanent damage with their mortars and grenades. Years later, one lieutenant said that "we learned small unit tactics from the Germans. They were costly teachers."

As American soldiers were learning their craft, Pershing learned that Germany had finally asked Wilson to do what the president wanted to do in 1915: arbitrate a peace settlement short of military victory. Negotiations with the enemy, especially when it was still on French soil, cut against the grain of senior U.S. officers who had argued against amalgamation on grounds that "Berlin can only be taken by an entirely homogeneous American army." They looked at armed conflict through the perspective of their predecessors, which was living memory for the generation that joined the service after the Civil War. Many of them had attended West Point in the 1880s, where they marched before Sheridan, received diplomas from Sherman, and shook hands with Grant, whom Pershing called "the greatest general our country has produced." When they deployed west after graduation, their companies (let alone regiments) were commanded by old veterans. Bored with garrison duty and an occasional skirmish, these men regaled their young subordinates with recollections of the greatest event in their lives, "our battle lines during the Civil War." It is hardly surprising that officers predicted the western front would come "down to a tug of war like Grant had against Lee." When that happened in late 1918, Pershing aspired to "compel [an] unconditional surrender" by "fight[ing] on until we bring Germany completely to her knees."

One wonders whether unconditional surrender was feasible, considering the military situation at the time. One will never know. The English high command believed the "enemy is fighting a very good rearguard" action just as British combat power reached its culminating point. Responsibility, therefore, would fall on Americans who had just sustained over three times the monthly casualty rates of the Civil War. By the accounts of the rank and file, they were "a fucked-up mess": "all weak, starved, sick, emaciated." Even before the Meuse-Argonne offensive began, said the chief of staff, AEF logistics, "supply and transportation are not improving, on the contrary getting worse." Staff officers struggled to get the army to the line of departure. They would estimate they needed 100,000 more horses to reach limited objectives, let alone go another 300 miles to Berlin.

Be that as it may, armies are not measured against ideal standards of readiness. They fight a specific enemy, in this case the Germans, who had enormous problems of their own. Their own transportation was depleted, according to intelligence filed after the armistice. Their soldiers, according to their officers, wanted "nothing except rest and peace." Unknown to the Allies, the German command had doubts that its army could handle a domestic revolution, let alone an invasion by any organized force.

In late October Pershing warned the Allied Supreme War Council that "victorious armies are prone to overestimate the enemy's strength and too eagerly seek an opportunity for peace." However, when it came to unconditional surrender, he was not talking just to Foch but to a president who thought he was "glory mad" and taking unneeded casualties. As the secretary of the interior noted at the time Pershing was begging to fight on: "Any kind of blood-thirsty talk drives [Wilson] into the cellar of pacifism." "The thing that holds me back," Wilson once told his personal secretary, "is the aftermath of war. . . . I came from the South and I know what war is, for I have seen its wreckage and terrible ruin."

Wilson acknowledged that he might turn out to be the "advocate [for the enemy] against American Prussianism." If a peace were not in place by late November, he confessed the shame he would feel once "our troops destroyed one single German town," along with telling his cabinet six days before the armistice, "I was a boy at Columbia and heard near relatives tell of the outrageous deeds of Sherman's troops." Typical of practitioners of psychological warfare, Sherman's bark was worse than his bite. But the amount of damage done was not as important as his objective to make the South "so sick of war that generations would pass away before they would again appeal to it." When Sherman wrote those words in 1864, he was aiming at the likes of Nathan Bedford Forrest. He hit a seven-year-old named Thomas Woodrow Wilson, who would preside over the government for which Sherman terrorized the South.

Wilson, anxious to stop American troops from invading Germany and "setting up a government ourselves," was dealing with historical memories of what he had called the "dark chapter of history." Aside from Sherman, Reconstruction was a period of "fear, demoralization, disgust, and social revolution." The North was not the danger in 1918, but the "billeting of troops on the civil population will ensure hatred and ultimate disaster," reminiscent to Wilson of what he once called "the blue-coated armies which stormed southward." Now "the Kaiser was needed to keep some order." Unless the Germans had a stable government of their own, "we might witness bolshevikism worse than in Russia."

Wilson worried about Britain and France, along with Sherman and Lenin. "It is certain that too much success or security on the part of the Allies would make a genuine peace settlement [that is, on his terms] difficult if not impossible." Erstwhile friends would feel little need to court his favor once Germany's power disappeared. For all these reasons, Wilson briefly considered recognizing the Imperial German government if it would just withdraw its soldiers back within its borders. Then some of his closest advisers "irritated" the president, "more disturbed" than House ever saw him, by pointing out his promise not to "bargain or compromise with the governments of the Central Powers." If Wilson negotiated and thereby reverted to his old peace without victory position, he would court "a political disaster" in the upcoming congressional election. Wilson's first response was to declare, "I am dealing with human lives, not politics." His second response was to acknowledge that "public opinion . . . was as much a fact as a mountain and must be considered." Hence Wilson's partisan opponents, "harping on the danger of an incomplete peace," forced him to adhere to his own progressive tenet that "a stable and enduring peace" required the enemy's political institutions "must be crushed out, root and branch." No cabinet officer could answer the question the president asked on 8 October: "How could he have correspondence with Germany under autocracy?"

Wilson was caught in a trap. To await or demand a revolution in the German constitution meant prolonging the war, but to whose advantage? Every day the United States got stronger, the reason England wanted peace before America took "our place as the first military, diplomatic, and financial power of the world." Every day Wilson grew weaker vis-à-vis the Republican party's unconditional surrender wing, part of the price he paid for keeping Pershing in the dark. By distorting military training with the doctrine of "open warfare," it spawned heavy casualties, creating a desire for a victor's peace per Wilson's opponents.

Ultimately, the decision whether to continue the war was up to Germany, which had problems of its own. Based on some vague American pronouncements about demanding surrender if the Allies "must deal with the monarchical autocrats," Germany felt it could still negotiate a settlement if it democratized. Wilson worried that Germany would resume war rather than accept humiliation. He did not worry about what could happen if Germany accepted terms that he and the Allies assumed it would reject. The kaiser and his military court, banished from authority, would never have to acknowledge defeat. The onus for that act fell on the fragile successor government, as German diplomats warned Wilson and Lloyd George told his cabinet. Stigmatized for giving up when the army was still on French territory, the Weimar Republic would give way to the Nazis who would drive everyone into a far worse war.

In November 1918, when Germany replaced its monarchy, Wilson finalized arrangements to negotiate an armistice that prevented an armed expedition to Berlin. Neither the French army nor the U.S. Army was pleased, but neither was in a position to prevent it. Clemenceau would not call Wilson's bluff to make a separate peace. Senior officers had no choice outside mutiny against the commander in chief. Pershing would soon say that "they never knew they were beaten in Berlin. It will all have to be done all over again." However, in 1918, soldiers could not budge the president's conviction that "the gentlemen in the Army who talk about going to Berlin and taking it by force are foolish." The AEF commander had to settle for Sedan as a consolation prize.

According to the Foch-Pershing understanding, the AEF was supposed to pave the way and guard the flank, not liberate Sedan, a mere "fetish" to Americans. However, boundary lines were never sacred. In early October Petain declared that if the U.S. Army did not advance more rapidly, he would move into

Pershing's "zone of action . . . in order to overcome resistance." Pershing, stung by the suggestion that he needed Petain's aid, may have been looking for a chance for revenge. On 5 November he found it. While Wilson was completing the negotiations that would prevent the AEF from advancing into Germany, Pershing broke his deal with Foch by distributing to his subordinate commands that "General Pershing desires that the honor of entering Sedan should fall to the First American Army."

With that message, one of the strongest disciplinarians in American military history mandated a madcap race to glorify his army at the expense of the French. His personal colors were carried by the First Infantry Division, which he had trained in 1917. But before what Pershing called "the best damned division in any army" could barge into the French road net, it had to cross through the sector already occupied by America's Forty-second Division. In the process, one of its regiments literally ran across a man dressed strangely in thick muffler, floppy cap, and riding whip, with no brown belt. They arrested Douglas MacArthur as a German spy but did not shoot him on the spot. One wonders what would have happened in World War II and Korea if "Pershing's Pets" had performed their mission with the dispatch Pershing might have expected.

The French army, the Forty-second Division, the I Corps, and the First American Army all screamed to AEF headquarters that the action of the First Division was   "a military atrocity." Pershing reined them back lest anarchy become a standard procedure. Then he singled out the division for its "splendid record" in the war. Meanwhile, the French liberated Sedan, and Wilson concluded terms with the democratic government now representing Germany. A member of Pershing's AEF inner circle later recalled: "The armistice ended two wars for us—the one with our friends, the other with our enemies."[6]

WILSON AND LODGE: THE GHOSTS OF THE CIVIL WAR AND THE LEAGUE OF NATIONS

Pershing to the contrary, Woodrow Wilson rejected unconditional surrender on grounds it "would throw the advantage to the military party in Germany." The president imposed his will upon his army, something he could do whenever he chose to speak clearly to the command. However, Senator Henry Cabot Lodge would soon remind the world that the "Commander in Chief can make or agree to an armistice" but "the President was not the only part of the government necessary to the making of a treaty." The Republican party and the U.S. Congress had a role to play in ending the war. Until Theodore Roosevelt died in 1919, he was the opposition's foremost spokesman and odds-on favorite to be its presidential candidate in 1920. Inside the Senate chamber, where a two-thirds vote was needed to ratify a treaty, Lodge was the Republican leader and its ranking member on the Foreign Relations Committee. He had ample opportunity to

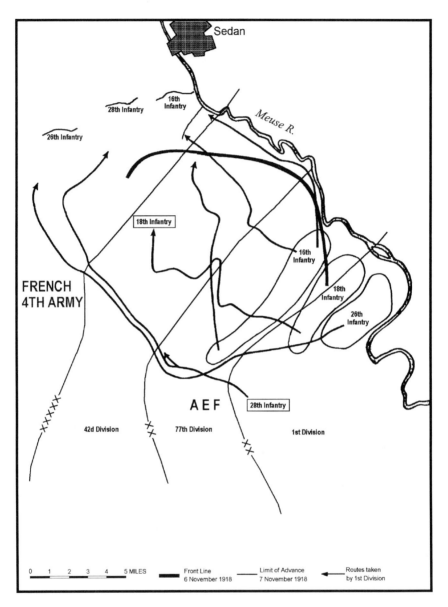

First Division's march toward Sedan, November 1918

obstruct a final settlement, if only because he and Roosevelt had a vision of war termination compatible with that of Pershing, not Woodrow Wilson.

The Civil War was "not mere history" for this generation of Republicans. At age seven Roosevelt had seen Lincoln's funeral procession pass by his home in 1865. Lodge had personally known many Civil War heroes; "the war pervaded everything," he wrote about his childhood. "To have been alive and in a sense a witness to such a mighty conflict . . . left an ineffaceable impression, none the less lasting because it was unconscious." Woodrow Wilson said much the same thing about his own youth, but with significantly different emotions about an event he later described as "destruction . . . hardly matched in the annals of modern warfare." Young Lodge followed "with the deepest interest Sherman's march to the sea." On the eve of World War I, he remembered "the blind rage with which I assailed our Democratic Irish groom when he told me that Sherman would never get through."

Roosevelt and Lodge had spent much of their political lives looking for an event to enable their generation to "leave an indelible mark in history" commensurate with the Civil War. True, they led the government into the Spanish-American War, from which they hoped the country would "emerge gloriously on the great world stage." Within two years, the public had reverted to general apathy, confirming that the episode could not hold a candle to those who "bore the heaviest burden that any generation of Americans ever had to bear, the burden of saving the Union." In 1914 Roosevelt and Lodge thought they had finally come across something of equivalent stature, when once again "the freedom and the civilization of the Western world was at stake." After America finally entered the world's largest war, they had a far different concept than Wilson about the way it should be fought and finished. Roosevelt accused the president of the policy of Democrats in the Civil War: trying to win "with kid gloves," rather than fight "no matter what the cost." (Nothing but total war "would spell ruin for the world, just as in 1864 a premature and inconclusive peace would have spelled ruin to the United States.") Lodge, speaking in the Senate, said "the Republican Party stands for unconditional surrender and complete victory, just as Grant stood." In short, "we must go to Berlin."

By early October Wilson reluctantly concurred with Lodge's statement that "the American people mean to have a dictated and not a negotiated peace." Moderates tried to wrap their own terms in the sacred slogan of the militant position, something they would also try to do in the closing days of World War II. In this case Wilson's secretary of the Treasury told a rally in Chicago that German evacuation of conquered territory "means unconditional surrender." (In fact, it was America's minimal demand.) Three weeks later, despite this attempt by Democrats to blend in with the Civil War, the United States conducted a congressional election filled with sectional enmity reminiscent of Reconstruction. In the 1890s Lodge had been one of the last Republicans to abandon the charge that the Democrats had been the party of treason and rebellion against the Union. In 1918 he got the bloody shirt out of the attic, where it had been gathering dust since the Spanish-American War. The Wilson administration and the leadership in Congress were virtually all from the South. They put price controls on wool and wheat but not on cotton, whose price inflated 400 percent. This made planters happy but embittered farmers who accepted the argument that "the South is running the Government and running it selfishly." Republicans, especially Lodge, played to this regional resentment against Dixie Democrats. By sweeping the western and midwestern states, they gained control of the Senate, where Lodge became majority leader and chairman of the Committee on Foreign Relations.

From his new position in Congress, Lodge would control the Senate's tempo and manner for considering the treaty that would end World War I. He was also busy with Wilson on a personal basis. Lodge had a festering dislike for southern Democrats, whose patriotism was suspect for favoring states' rights or a League of Nations that might substitute "an international state for pure Americanism." ("I never expected to hate any one in politics with the hatred I feel towards Wilson.") Events in 1918 inflamed all these emotions, as well as giving Lodge a new opportunity to exploit what he long felt was the major lesson of the Civil War, that the American people respond to appeals based on nationalism. He could criticize Wilson without subjecting Republicans to the charge "we are not loyal to the war" by taking a more punitive position than the president. Politically successful in November, Lodge believed "this wonderful election" mandated "a victory worth having," that is, invading Germany, loading it down with "heavy indemnities," and dividing it "into its chief component parts."

Although the election was won largely on domestic concerns, key politicians felt the primary issue was Germany's attempt to trap America and "her allies into peace not based on unconditional surrender." That Wilson, ambivalent about the kaiser, was too late to force abdication until after the election seemed the great mistake. By contrast, said one prominent Democrat, "the reactionary Republicans had a clean record of anti-Hun imperialistic politics." Lodge would have added that the public repudiated Wilson's conviction that the presidency had "absolute" responsibility for "conducting the war and safeguarding the nation," something Lodge found suited to a "dictatorship or an autocracy." When Wilson still imposed an armistice on the army, he ended the hope of "winning the war in the only way which could justify our sacrifices." This pushed Lodge toward a commensurate punishment of the president, that is, getting "rid of Wilsonianism and everything connected with it." The obvious target was the League of Nations—to Wilson, the embodiment of "our purpose in this war."

Numerous books discuss in great detail the president's submission and the Senate's rejection of membership in the League of Nations, as contained in the Treaty of Versailles. New light might be shed by placing the issue in the context of the wider debate about ends, ways, and means for World War I. For Wilson, "the essentially American" issues included open (not secret) diplomacy, removal of trade barriers, and freedom of the seas, rejected by London as "directed absolutely against the British Navy." In the final analysis, he felt "the most essential part of the peace settlement" was the establishment of "a general association of nations" to guarantee the independence "and territorial integrity [of] great and small states alike." By comparison, the national borders of European governments were not "worth fighting a war that engulfs the world," especially after Germany shook off "military autocracy" in November 1918. "If properly treated," it could "be a bulwark for peace in Europe."

For Lodge, this philosophy of collective security was too unfocused and too sentimental to accomplish what he considered the "sole purpose" of the war— "to put Germany finally and completely in a position that it will be physically impossible for her to break out again and attempt to conquer and ruin the world." The democratization of the Reich, so important to Wilson, was irrelevant to the most important man in the U.S. Senate. Progressivism to the contrary, Lodge maintained that "the German people" were not misled by their political bosses. They always had "the government they prefer." The right peace settlement would fortify Allied positions on the Rhine River and extend a defense alliance to England and France. Vague global commitments, such as the president put into his League of Nations' covenant, were no substitute for firm "barriers" around Germany. Otherwise "we shall have fought in vain," the phraseology Republicans used in the Civil War.

Lodge planned to block Wilson's peace plan in the Senate and force Democrats to campaign on the issue in the 1920 election against a Republican party unified by its opposition to the administration. Then, after "we have destroyed Wilson's League of Nations and . . . have torn up Wilsonianism by its roots," a Republican president (perhaps Lodge himself) would renegotiate a postwar settlement reflecting the senator's geopolitics. Wilson fell into this trap, although he could have scuttled the scheme by accepting mild amendments to the treaty. Lodge knew the tendencies of his enemy and predicted that the president simply could not compromise, at least with him. In Wilson's mind the upper-class senator from Massachusetts embodied the militarism and privilege he abhorred: warmongering mixed with radical New England abolitionism. Furthermore, Wilson was under enormous self-induced pressure to end the war with a settlement worthy of its cost. "I consented to [young men] being put in the most difficult parts of the battle line, where death was certain," he said in the last public speech he ever made. Their mothers bless me "because they believe that their boys died for something that vastly transcends the immediate and palpable objects of the war," that is, the mundane national interests so important to Senator Lodge.

To solicit public support for the League of Nations, Wilson reiterated the themes of his recent war aims: peace, prosperity, and democracy. Without collective security, America must have high taxes, "a great standing army," and a government such as Imperial Germany, "the only sort that could handle an armed nation." Then, on 2 October the stress of conducting a struggle to make the war worthwhile produced a massive cerebral stroke. The debilitating illness magnified the most dysfunctional tendencies in a man who once said that a "politician must be an opportunist." Wilson's strength became rigidity and his principles became pursuit of perfection. What is more, his belief in his own indubitable wisdom (common among aging professors) led to a fatal underestimation of the volatility of power in American politics. "Let [the president] once win the admiration and confidence of the country," Wilson had written, "and no other force can withstand him," certainly not the U.S. Senate. "Let Lodge hold out the olive branch." In short, the president was asking the Senate to do what he would not ask of Germany: submit an unconditional surrender. "We must hit [congressional critics] hard and not mind if the blood comes."

Wilson thus entrusted the issue to the American public, a foolish decision considering he lost the last election at a far more auspicious time. In 1918 Democrats could claim that a repudiation of the president would "give aid and comfort to the enemy," no longer credible in 1920. Wilson and Lodge both hoped this election would be a solemn referendum on national security policy, for a League of Nations to create a new world order or for the protection of national interest via military preparedness. In fact, it was neither. The 1920 election (like those of 1918 and 1916) was primarily a referendum on the state of the American economy. After every major war there are significant readjustment problems: high unemployment, low demand, and high inflation—the worst of all possible worlds. When the polls opened, there were 4,750,000 workers without work, 450,000 farm families without farms, and 100,000 business bankruptcies, not to mention a cost of living twice as great as in 1914. Warren G. Harding, the Republican candidate for president, won 61 percent of the popular vote and thirty-seven of forty-eight states. The Democrats, bearing the burden of incumbency, carried only the solid South, except for Tennessee, which went Republican for the first time in its history. In the concurrent congressional election, the Republicans won 10 new seats in the Senate and 303 seats in the House, giving them the largest congressional delegation in the history of the party. "It wasn't a landslide," said Wilson's personal secretary. "It was a tidal wave."

The American people had repudiated Woodrow Wilson, who concluded, "We had a chance to gain the leadership of the world. We have lost it." They also repudiated Henry Cabot Lodge, who had bitterly opposed Harding's nomination at the Republican National Convention. Virtually everyone interpreted the election as a mandate for isolation, which was certainly the mood of the country by the time Harding went to the White House in 1921. In retrospect, both Wilson and Lodge had a brief window of opportunity after the war to steer America toward strong leadership in international affairs. Until the Democrats lost the presidency, Lodge could not do much more than obstruct Wilson's initiatives. By the time Wilson left, Lodge's own opportunity was overtaken by domestic events. As the senator privately confessed in 1924, the whole dispute over the League "was not without its elements of tragedy."[7]

THE GHOSTS OF WORLD WAR I

By January 1937, 70 percent of the American respondents to an opinion poll felt U.S. participation in World War I had been a mistake. Military men are said to prepare to fight the last war. Doing much the same thing in foreign policy, the public tried to avoid the next war by cutting the ties to Europe that got it into the last war, thanks to Woodrow Wilson. His primary legacy for the 1930s comprised the ideals that shamed the mundane facts of the Treaty of Versailles. Few people wanted to fight Hitler, when he was relatively weak, to protect a peace settlement perceived to be unjust.

The troublesome task of trying to explain to America that it could not turn back the clock to isolation fell to Franklin Delano Roosevelt, former assistant secretary of the navy in the Wilson administration. FDR would remember the errors made by Wilson, whose portrait hung in his White House office, along with those of Roosevelt's wife, his mother, and that of John Paul Jones. In World War II the president would vow not to repeat his predecessor's errors and consequently made new mistakes of his own. However, FDR was not the only American to be haunted by the memory of Woodrow Wilson, whose reputation was rehabilitated in the next world war. By 1945, 83 percent of the respondents to opinion surveys said it was "very important" for the United States to join an international organization "with police power to maintain world peace."

As for Wilson himself, his life was the topic of the 1940 Pulitzer Prize–winning biography. In 1944 it was the subject of an epic feature film made by the producer of *Gone With the Wind.* Seen by over 10 million Americans by February 1945, the most expensive movie made to date won five Academy Awards. *Life* called this melodrama about the president's martyrdom for the League of Nations "one of the best pictures ever made"; the government's Office of War Information said it was "vital to the psychological warfare of the United Nations," the name for the grand alliance in World War II. When FDR saw *Wilson* while attending a wartime conference at Quebec, his blood pressure rose to 240 over 130, causing his physician to increase his medication for hypertension.

Roosevelt used the moral of the movie to help win reelection in 1944, when Democrats said that a Republican victory would return to power the obstructionists who prevented "the immortal Woodrow Wilson" from ensuring a lasting peace at the end of World War I. He would not mention his own similarities with the late Henry Cabot Lodge: their demand for unconditional surrender, refusal to differentiate the German people from their government, and the attempt to construct a postwar alliance of the victorious powers, as opposed to a world-wide forum for collective security. Lodge, robbed of the ideas that proved him a true prophet, fared much worse than Woodrow Wilson. To play the senator in the movie, Darryl Zanuck (a colonel on leave from the Signal Corps) cast an English character actor whose last performance was that of a Nazi colonel in Norway.

A foreboding presence in *Wilson,* Lodge insisted on "a realistic peace," for which he was blamed for causing World War II. Ironically, the proponent of the Lodge perspective with the most popular appeal was Wilson's erstwhile disciple, Walter Lippmann, who had become America's foremost columnist and critic of "Wilsonian ideology." In 1922, as "a result of experience in psychological warfare and in seeing the war," Lippmann wrote a landmark book on the thesis that public opinion is always "discolored with prejudice." He would not be content with just denouncing the roots of progressivism: faith in rule by the people and direct democracy. In 1943, one year before a highly critical biography of Lodge went through four printings, Lippmann wrote another best-seller, pertinent to Lodge. In *U.S. Foreign Policy* he stated, "If we construct our foreign policy on some abstract theory of rights and duties, we shall build castles in the air. We shall formulate policies which in fact the nation will not support with its blood, its sweat, and its tears."

While a Lippmann or two favored Lodge, Wilson's public stature rose toward the mythological heights of an Abraham Lincoln, the last casualty in his own war, or that of Robert E. Lee, another Southern idealist who fought for a lost cause, although not the one identified in *Wilson:* an "international police force to enforce the peace." Harry Truman, World War I battery commander, thought Wilson was "one of the greatest of the great Presidents." In late June 1950, when the North Koreans invaded the South, he sent American troops to the peninsula to conduct a "police action" despite all military plans to avoid deployment there. The day President Truman made his decision, he explained his action to an assistant: "I believed in the League of Nations. . . . It failed because we weren't in it to back it up. Okay, now we started the United Nations . . . and in this first big test we just couldn't let them down." Judging from these comments, the Korean War was national penance for the failure to fulfill Wilson's vision in World War I.[8]

7

World War II: Public Reluctance, Military Missions, Political Demands

Despite administration efforts to make World War II a crusade inspiring self-sacrifice, it rarely became more than an onerous obligation to be concluded as fast as possible, at minimum feasible cost. At the same time, because Japan and Germany were so frightening and formidable, they had to be defeated so badly they would not wage aggression again. These conflicting goals produced inconsistent objectives that White House rhetoric could not finesse. Contradictions pervaded American combat operations. To "defeat the Axis powers at the earliest possible date" required taking daring risks, such as done by Ernie King at Tarawa and George Patton west of the Seine. On the other hand, if only because the public would be terribly discouraged by a defeat, the armed forces were to exercise judicious caution, à la Omar Bradley at the Falaise pocket, Raymond Spruance in the Marianas, and Chester Nimitz postponing the invasion of Okinawa. Given an impossible wish list, it was amazing that America's military and political leaders did as well as they did, even if they would need the atomic bomb to give the public all it wanted. "God bless democracy!" George Marshall wrote a confidant after the war. "I approve of it highly but suffer from it extremely. This incidentally is not for quotation."[1]

ROOSEVELT AND THE FAILURE TO RESURRECT WILSONIAN WAR AIMS

Unlike the majority of the American public, Franklin Delano Roosevelt was never disillusioned with participation in World War I. Although FDR was a member of the Wilson administration, his military objectives had been more compatible with those of his relative and hero, Theodore Roosevelt. Wilson had been profoundly sad to commit his country to armed conflict. FDR's major regret was that he was not allowed to "follow in the steps of T. R.," that is, resign his post as assistant secretary of the navy "and form [his own] regiment of rough riders." Uncle Ted said of his charge up San Juan Hill: "I commanded my regiment with honor. We lost a quarter of our men." Franklin, inspecting Belleau Wood in 1918, said "our men have undoubtedly done well. . . . One of my Marine regiments has lost 1200 men & another 800." To make himself acceptable to the electorate in 1936 and 1940, Roosevelt proclaimed, "I have seen war and I hate war. . . . As long as it remains in my power to prevent [it], there will be no blackout of peace in the United States." At the time, the U.S. public blamed France and Britain for obstructing Wilson's war aims. Roosevelt told confidants to consider the alternatives to the Treaty of Versailles: "America never knew [what] its 'reward' [would have been] if Germany had won."

Until December 1941, when Japan attacked Pearl Harbor and Germany declared war on the United States, Roosevelt's self-described problem was "to get the American people to think of conceivable consequences without scaring the American people into thinking that they are going to be dragged into this war." He did what he could to aid Britain, Russia, France, and China and waited for events to drive home the "unalterable facts" that the United States was "a vital factor" in the world and that the Axis powers threatened its "simple self-preservation" with a "reign of terror and international lawlessness." Meanwhile, the president surrendered the initiative even in confidential discourse. In January 1941 the army and the navy drafted a document using the words "decide to resort to war." Roosevelt substituted the phrase "should the United States be compelled."

Roosevelt's policy reflected American opinion as revealed in the polls he confidentially received before they were published. He rarely, if ever, took military action contrary to their conclusions. According to his principal speechwriter, the president "knew that we could do what we had to do only if Americans realized that we had to do it." In mid-1941, up to 67 percent of the public said it was more important to see the Axis defeated than remain at peace; 83 percent believed that the United States would become directly involved in the conflict. At the same time, only one-third said that they wanted to declare hostilities. As the chief of naval operations (CNO) said in February, "The difficulty is that the entire country is in a dozen minds about the war."

In 1934 students at the Army War College concluded that "it would require flagrant enemy acts and properly handled propaganda to arouse the nation to the point of prosecuting a war." The administration established several propaganda agencies, but its activities were futile if only because Roosevelt would not articulate a clear plan of action to support. The government awaited public opinion; the public awaited presidential policy. In August 1941 the country got the Atlantic Charter, the last hope to prevent the conflict from becoming what a speechwriter called "the first war in American history in which the general disillusionment preceded the firing of the first shot."

Issued at the first Allied summit conference during World War II, the charter rehashed the tenets of Wilsonian liberalism—political democracy, national self-determination, free trade, and world peace. Roosevelt, who went over every word, believed that "the Joint Declaration [issued with Winston Churchill, prime minister of Britain] will affect the whole movement of United States opinion." It turned out to be "a propaganda bust." After its issuance, 74 percent of the public still opposed belligerency, but nearly twice as many felt it was more important to stay out of the war than to defeat Germany. The charter itself was probably not to blame, since most people barely noticed it at all. In January 1942, 79 percent of those polled could not recall hearing or reading anything about it. By contrast, in late 1943, 85 percent said they knew that General George S. Patton had slapped a private in Sicily.

Sophisticates remarked that the Atlantic Charter was "a dud" largely because Woodrow Wilson "took all the shine out of these platitudes." Criticism like this even reached into the ranks of liberal publicists, the group that once helped Wilson promulgate his Fourteen Points. Some prominent writers said the nation was hungry for "a crusading faith, the kind that inspired the soldiers of 1917," but the old "battle cries" could not inspire a generation worn and weathered by the Great Depression. They proposed making economic security a high priority in World War II, but the balance of power in Washington did not allow such notions to flourish. During World War I Congress and the president argued about unconditional surrender and postwar occupation, not about political reform and Wilson's domestic agenda. In World War II there would be a general consensus, at least among civilians, for unconditional surrender, not for political reform. According to one official from the Office of War Information, the president believed that "if he attempted to give the war a social purpose, he would arouse the hostility of the same groups which had opposed his domestic policies." Hence, while everywhere from England to China politics moved toward the left, FDR told his chief White House assistant: "Cut out this New Deal stuff. It's tough to win a war."

The Atlantic Charter was as meaningless to most soldiers as it was to the nation at large. "Maintaining the morale of the men was a continuous battle," said George C. Marshall, the army's chief of staff. One prominent newspaper editor wrote the government's director of public information that draftees home on leave "don't give a tinker's damn." Pearl Harbor did not change this very much. Most GIs continued to say that they were fighting "because I have to" or to "get the job done" so they could go home and resume their lives where they had left them. Their options at home, while better than a trench, might not inspire much fortitude at the front. Polls and magazine articles would continue to document that draftees were "depression-conscious and worried sick about postwar joblessness." In 1945 this would create a demobilization crisis before Japan surrendered, as soldiers tried to race each other back to America for early opportunities at limited employment.

The lack of wartime fervor, even during the war, had a direct impact on mobilization, strategy, and operations. Like the politicians, the senior officers in the armed forces constantly read opinion polls and reports. (The army even established its own research bureau that conducted 200 surveys about "what the soldier thinks.") Like the politicians, the Pentagon was keenly aware that "the burdens of the war effort" would have to be carefully "adjusted to maintain the morale and the will to fight of the civilian population." Indeed, for the United States, morale took the place of ideology and survival, the factors that motivated Russia, Britain, Germany, and Japan. Because neither soldiers nor civilians had what General Marshall called "that tremendous spirit that comes of defending your own home," they had to continue to receive comfortable allotments of consumer goods. Most important, the "prolongation of the war" was simply not an option for America. The Joint Chiefs of Staff (JCS) and their war planners repeatedly lectured the British that the public would "not countenance a long war of attrition."

Politicians and flag officers were also well aware that "the United States could not stand for another Bataan." If we took "a third of the losses suffered by the Japanese," Marshall said in mid-1942, "we would probably have been subjected to an investigation by Congress, certainly to considerable public clamor in the press." This pressure not to lose a major battle drove the administration to withhold information about the "gruesome" losses, starting with Pearl Harbor. Veterans subsequently complained that "there was very little American blood, very little tension, very little horror" in the stories, photographs, and drawings presented to the public during most of World War II. Half the army's recent recruits in mid-1942 thought that a few bombing raids would defeat Japan; 25 percent believed they would return home inside twelve months of being drafted. In the meantime, soldiers were to be well supplied with far more than beans and bullets—hence movies, cigarettes, crates of Coca-Cola, and a post exchange for every military unit. As for the general public, just 34 percent said in 1945 that they had made "any real sacrifice for the war." No matter, George Marshall once again found himself "under heavy pressure" to reduce requisitions and thereby "permit civilian production to go ahead for civilian goods." Much like Lincoln complaining of McClellan in 1862, Marshall recalled in 1957: "It was a long time before [most Americans] came to recognize there was a terrible, costly hard fighting that would have to come before there was an end of the war."[2]

TO WIN THE WAR WITHOUT AN EXPEDITIONARY ARMY

Having failed to inspire public opinion, Roosevelt's policy was not to have a policy as *Webster's* defines the term: a definite course of action to guide and determine present and future decisions. Without an "answer to the question: 'Where should we fight the war, and for what objective?'" the high command of the armed forces said they could not field and train an appropriate military force. Out of frustration the CNO and the army chief of staff devised their own long-range plan and sent it to the White House to prod guidance from the president in late

1940. "To some of my very pointed questions, which all of us would like to have answered," Admiral Harold Stark got "a smile or a 'please don't ask me that.'" Henry Stimson, the secretary of war, said that tracking Roosevelt's ideas was like "chasing a vagrant beam of sunshine around the room."

Although the army complained about "nebulous national policy," Roosevelt had a general concept of operations. Before Pearl Harbor, he tried to coax America by depicting war fought on the cheap. In the 1920s and 1930s, when Americans said that World War I had been folly, they did not talk of naval or aerial operations. They invariably thought of trench warfare on the western front, as Roosevelt did in his strongest antiwar pronouncement, delivered three months before the 1936 election: "I have seen men coughing out their gassed lungs. I have seen the dead in the mud." Now, beginning in late 1937, Roosevelt described capital-intensive methods of applying military power in "a modern way." Large ships and heavy bombers would wreck the enemies' economies; no need to fight their armies on the ground. As if Hitler and Hirohito shared his own major problem, that of public morale, he said that "the German people would crack under aerial attacks"; "there might be a revolution in Japan."

The last battles of the war make Roosevelt's forecasts seem incredible. When fought in 1945, the Axis cause was hopeless. Nonetheless, although bombing inflicted over 2 million casualties on Japanese civilians and left another 22 million without homes, the Imperial army inflicted 45,000 casualties on U.S. forces at Okinawa. (Admiral Nomura would tell the Strategic Bombing Survey: "The Japanese people obey government orders.") The Germans suffered 600,000 civilian bombing fatalities (ten times that of Britain) but inflicted 300,000 casualties on the Russians during the campaign for Berlin. Roosevelt, not knowing the future, anticipated the imminent collapse of the Nazis as late as November 1943. If the cross-Channel operation by the Anglo-American armies was still necessary in mid-1944, he predicted an "invasion of Germany with little or no fighting." In the words of a major speechwriter for the president, FDR could be one "of the really Olympian optimists of all time."

Essentially, Roosevelt's scenario of bombers, blockade, and support to the Allies was a new version of the old maritime strategy, hardly shocking for a former assistant secretary of the navy. One retired fleet commander wrote the president in mid-1940 that *we should never send an army of millions abroad in any future war. . . . The frontier must be the enemy coast.* If infantry were needed, let the Allies field them, as proposed by Ernest J. King, CNO after Pearl Harbor: "It should be our basic policy to provide the manpower of Russia and China with the necessary equipment to enable them to fight." The navy worried that a large expedition would change priorities from capital ships to troop transports, escort vessels, and landing craft. "The [Naval] Yards and Construction people," George Marshall said after the war, "threw water on everything concerning taking an army to Europe."

Unlike the admirals and the president, most of the American people were skeptical that the conflict could be won from the sea and the sky. Unlike April 1917, when Congress declared war presuming no need to send an army to the western front, 65 percent of the public felt it would have to commit substantial ground forces if America became a belligerent. It was this "tremendous fear of another AEF with its heavy losses," a leading interventionist wrote the White House, that kept public sentiment stuck at the stage where, at best, some 30 percent approved a declaration of war. Because 70 percent of the public believed that military aid reduced the "chance that we will have to fight the Germans later on," Roosevelt's lend-lease policy undercut his plan to coax the country into ever more military responsibility. Almost 75 percent of the public said that the nation should declare war if the Allies were losing. American military assistance was supposed to prevent either one from occurring. As the president told his secretary of war ten weeks before Pearl Harbor, the army's "assumption that we must invade and crush Germany" would elicit "a very bad reaction."

One might think that Roosevelt's military strategy would abruptly change in mid-December 1941, after Japan, Germany, and Italy made the decision the United States would not make for itself: to move its responsibility into direct combat. Roosevelt no longer had to fear that, if he mentioned a new AEF, the American public might be horrified, stop lend-lease, and retreat into true neutrality. Nonetheless, U.S. strategy changed more slowly than international events. Roosevelt's initial response to the status of belligerency was that it gave him a new opportunity to win the war by industrial production. Heretofore, he had appealed for "the same spirit of patriotism and sacrifice as we would show were we at war." However, by making promises that America would not enter combat, he fostered the complacency that prevented it from being "the arsenal of democracy." U.S. industries produced only 60 heavy bombers in 1940 and 313 in 1941. From July 1940 to June 1941, it manufactured eighty-three medium tanks.

The CNO told the president in mid-1941 that "it just isn't in the nature of things to get results in peace." The army would agree with the navy, while adding its own caveat that "air and sea forces will make important contributions, but effective and adequate ground forces must be available to close with and destroy the enemy within his citadel." It is hard to imagine anyone less likely to concur with an anti-AEF strategy than George Marshall, who often wondered why Roosevelt selected him for chief of staff in 1939. He later concluded that he had been the candidate of Harry Hopkins (Roosevelt's closest assistant), that Hopkins "was the champion of the Army," and that Roosevelt was only paying close attention to bombers and the navy. In short, the president accepted Marshall, whom he did not know or trust, as "the best of a bad bargain."

In World War I, Marshall was G-3 (plans and operations) for the First Infantry Division and the First Army, where he helped plan and execute the Meuse-Argonne offensive, the largest ground operation the United States had ever conducted. He also became the protégé of John J. Pershing, the AEF commander, whom he served as aide-de-camp in the 1920s. During World War II, on a biweekly basis, he visited Pershing at Walter Reed Hospital to update him about the progress of the war, which meant progress toward a new AEF, at least to proud old doughboys. Although Marshall was too dutiful to request any position for himself, his personal ambition was to follow the footsteps of Pershing, whose full-length portrait hung on the wall behind Marshall's desk, which was Pershing's old desk in the War Department. Even before Pearl Harbor, Marshall began to build the mass army he hoped to command in the European theater. "The principle of our providing the munitions while other troops do the fighting" seemed to him to be what amalgamation had been to his mentor in World War I: "a fallacious and humiliating proposition." In 1942, when executives on the War Production Board maintained that America's great contribution should be production and shipping, the army chief of staff wrote the president that "the morale of the hostile world must be broken not only by aggressive fighting but as in 1918 by the vision of an overwhelming force of fresh young Americans being *rapidly* developed in this country."[3]

THE ARMY AND PURSUIT OF A MILITARY STRATEGY

At Pearl Harbor Japan decided that America would enter the war, but U.S. military strategy still lacked firm form and direction. Dwight Eisenhower, then director of Army War Plans Division, noted in his journal in January 1942: "The struggle to secure adoption by all concerned of a common concept of strategical objectives is wearing me down." This uncertainty was inevitable as long as the enemy had the initiative. Then, in May and June 1942, the navy stopped Japan's advance at Midway and the Coral Sea. Army strategists seized this opportunity to stop what they called plugging "urgent ratholes" and "giving our stuff in driblets all over the world." "At long last," Eisenhower said that spring, "if we can agree on major purposes and objectives, our efforts will begin to fall in line and we won't just be thrashing around in the dark."

The army would soon propose a cross-Channel operation that would concentrate troops in England to invade northern France in 1942 or 1943. It made this recommendation for several reasons, not the least of which was the fact that it gave the army planning staffs "a target on which to fix [their] sights" and "a definite and consistent long-range strategic concept of operations." Without a "clear course of action" to coordinate military efforts throughout America and across the globe, the army warned that "future planning will be haphazard and at random"—as it had been before 1942. The head of army logistics continued to complain that "those responsible for various phases of supply are forced to make their own uncoordinated assumptions and guesses . . . [about] the placing of orders, production, and delivery."

Pearl Harbor did not immediately discredit Roosevelt's concept of a lend-lease, airpower, sea-power way to win the war. On 3 January 1942 the president wrote Henry Stimson that victory in the final analysis depended on "our overwhelming mastery in munitions"; America's allies being so "extended" they could not arm their armies, "our own fighting forces" would have no special claim on American production. Eleven days later, Roosevelt presented to George Marshall a proposal removing the military chiefs from direct allocation of military resources, to be kept in the hands of Roosevelt, Churchill, and their closest civilian assistants: in his case Harry Hopkins, a strong proponent of lend-lease. Then and there, Marshall threatened to do what he later called "a very reprehensible thing," especially for "a military official," that is, resign on grounds that he "could not continue to assume the responsibilities of Chief of Staff" under these circumstances. It may not be too melodramatic to say that the size, state, and mission of U.S. ground forces hung in the balance.

To Churchill's consternation, the president made "a preliminary agreement [to] try it out [Marshall's] way." One can only surmise what thoughts went through his mind. Marshall was not the preeminent military adviser he would become in 1944, when he wrote many presidential statements on military policy. In 1942 he only saw the message traffic between Roosevelt and Churchill thanks to leaks from a friend inside the British embassy. However, while dispensable to Roosevelt's maritime strategy, Marshall portended serious domestic consequences. FDR's political opponents were already charging that he was his "own strategist." Polls confirmed what every politician knew: that the public, by three to one, wanted military men "to have the final decision on military and naval plans." As a result, Roosevelt would claim, particularly before elections, that "at all times . . . there has been a very substantial agreement" between him and those "trained in the profession of arms."

Aside from potential to cause a partisan political embarrassment, Marshall and his cause, a new AEF, drew support from the U.S. Congress and the Union of Soviet Socialist Republics. (War makes strange bedfellows.) Congress was far more isolationist than Roosevelt. Nothing could be more interventionist than the expeditionary army the War Department was planning in 1942: 192 divisions; nearly 13,600,000 soldiers. Nonetheless, the legislature held Marshall in such high regard that over the heads of the navy and without support from the White House, he convinced it to appropriate money specifically for troop transports.

Aside from Marshall's Job-like willingness to answer every question and complaint Congress had about the service, his influence lay in the difference between him and FDR. The president was charming, would cut deals, and was suspected of everything under the sun. Marshall made no pretense at friendship, gave no favors, and was thoroughly trusted to keep Roosevelt from providing cronies with contracts and jobs grounded in national defense. In May 1940 Roosevelt appealed to Congress to raise the regular army to 255,000 men; Marshall asked for 335,000; Congress authorized 375,000. "Never in U.S. history," wrote *Time* magazine, "has a military man enjoyed such respect on Capitol Hill."

Marshall's influence with Congress helped ensure the U.S. Army had a substantial role in World War II. It also helped ensure he would not play the role he particularly wanted, that of commanding general of the field army he created and preserved in the face of the lend-lease–bomber–naval strategy. In 1943, when word went through Washington that Marshall would leave the Pentagon to become supreme allied commander (Europe), Republican newspapers and legislators charged a "domestic coup d'état" by New Dealers "to turn the War Department into a global political organization." Roosevelt's relations with Capitol Hill were bad enough after the November 1942 election, in which Democrats lost fifty seats in the House and eight in the Senate. Largely to keep them from getting worse, the president chose someone else (Eisenhower) to be what Roosevelt described to Pershing as "the Pershing of the second World War."

The U.S. Congress supported George Marshall; the Soviet Union supported his cause, a large expeditionary ground force for the European theater. As early as January 1942, a symbiotic relationship had developed between the Red and American armies, which understood they might not survive—certainly not prosper—without direct support from one another. To withstand the invasion of 4 million Axis soldiers, 3,500 tanks, and 3,000 planes, the Red Army said it needed the Anglo-Americans to divert thirty to forty German divisions from the eastern front in 1942. The American army believed it would need the Russians to contain the bulk of the Germans in the east if it were to attempt an amphibious invasion, what Marshall called "the most difficult undertaking military forces are called on to face." If the Red Army was subjugated, U.S. ground forces "could undertake little of a positive nature to bring the war to a successful conclusion." In short, the army believed that the fate of the world and the fate of the service were synonymous, and they were both in a precarious state in 1942. Three months after Eisenhower noted in his journal that "we've got to keep Russia in the war," Marshall wrote the president that "the most pressing need is to sustain [it] as an active, effective participant. . . . That issue will probably be decided this summer or fall."

If a cross-Channel invasion were not in the offing, the alternative seemed bleak, at least for the army. Marshall, Eisenhower, and the War Plans Division said that in the European theater America would have to rely on strategic bombing. Ground combat forces would take "up an offensive against Japan," although there was not much need for an AEF in the Pacific. The vast distance between strategic objectives, the primitive infrastructure, and the limited expanse of land east of the Philippines were ideal for a navy–marine–airpower strategy. By contrast, northwestern Europe had the harbors, transport, and terrain to support an enormous ground force, the only way to capture the German capital. Hence Europe was the natural theater for U.S. army operations, as it had been since 1917, when Marshall's mentor wrote the Wilson administration that "the war must be won on the Western front."

The opinion of the army—but not the navy—was much the same in 1942. Both brought their institutional interests to the debates on strategy held with the president and the British. More than any other military service, the army felt that "time is the most vital factor in planning" and that "long-range decisions for the conduct of the war must not be dominated" by reactions to unforeseen events. Its soldiers were mass-trained by drill sergeants and its equipment mass-produced by machine tools difficult to modify. The army had to synchronize and maintain a very long supply line—beginning with factories, railroads, harbors, and shipping in the United States, and ending with harbors, storage facilities, and forward bases in a theater of combat operations. As Marshall tried to tell the president in mid-1943, another shift in war plans would disrupt mobilization "as far back as the Middle West of the United States."

Never quite appreciating the army's point of view, Roosevelt felt its war planners were "always conservative and saw all the difficulties," rather than follow his own example, which was to focus on opportunities and have faith that they would somehow find what they really needed when they really needed to find it. As to the president's "habit of tossing out new operations," Marshall called this his "cigarette lighter gesture"—strategy by wave of hand. In part, FDR was a politician who typically felt "it is a mistake to look too far ahead," did not want to make a categorical decision, and said "it is sufficient to take each step as it comes up." In large part, as Marshall complained, he was also a man who "knows the navy like a book but knows very little about the army." More important, he did not seem very willing to learn: "Ordinary Army methods of presenting things to the President [get] us nowhere. He is quickly bored by papers, by lengthy discussions, and by anything short of a few pungent sentences."

Compared with the army, the navy had far more capacity for flexibility in planning and conducting war. Its own army (the Marine Corps) rarely moved far beyond the beachhead. Its road net—the ocean—could not be cratered and was too vast to clog. Its primary weapons, capital ships, were versatile in mission and few in number. On successive days—or in successive hours—a battleship could bombard bunkers for amphibious invasions, provide air defense artillery for an aircraft carrier, or engage enemy ships at sea. While its hull and deck could take two years to produce, the special equipment that modified a vessel for a short-term contingency was not a major problem. It could be built in advance, kept in storage, and bolted down on short notice.[4]

NORTH AFRICA: MILITARY STRATEGY AND POLITICAL SURVIVAL

In World War II, two "former naval persons," Roosevelt and Churchill, constituted the highest command, often to the consternation of Anglo-American army planners who felt, as Eisenhower put it, that "the doctrine of opportunism so often applicable in tactics, is a dangerous one to pursue in strategy." FDR's favorite phrase was "freedom of action"; he scribbled "no closed minds" across memos sent to the JCS. Churchill, being a man of letters, said much the same thing with a flourish: "In swiftly changing and indefinable situations, we assign a large importance to improvisation, seeking to live and conquer in accordance with the unfolding event."

In 1941 Roosevelt agreed with Churchill's public statement that "this is not a war of vast armies, firing immense masses of shells at one another." However, by late 1943 FDR was ready to send a large expeditionary army to Europe for reasons of his own—the 1944 election and irrevocable commitments to unconditional surrender and a postwar league of nations based on an alliance with the Soviet Union (all discussed later). Churchill, under less pressure to change, did not have a British equivalent of George Marshall, a persuasive proponent of decisive land warfare with his own constituency in the legislature. The English system of cabinet government was "an elective dictatorship," said two military officers. Their war minister was a leading figure of the majority party in Parliament, where soldiers did not testify about strategy, as pointed out by a British general who made several trips to Washington: "In London, the armed forces and their chiefs are to some extent insulated from the seasonal and seismic fluctuations of politics. The United States Chief of Staff stands right up against the elected representatives of the people, and his popular responsibilities are far more direct than those of his British counterpart, if he indeed can be said to have one."

When the British army did exert influence, it was not in the direction the U.S. Army wanted. Although far from saying so, the English looked upon the German blitzkrieg that knocked them off the Continent in 1940 as a blessing in disguise. Unlike World War I, when Britain could not "wrest an army from France and Flanders" because of its commitment to the western front, England could adopt a peripheral strategy, something debated but narrowly rejected from 1915 to 1918. In the 1940s, the British not only remembered the frightful casualties at the Somme and Passchendaele, battles mounted to reduce the pressure on France, now a dead hostage. They also recalled their own surprise in mid- to late 1918, when English tanks and planes spearheaded attacks that captured 65,000 German soldiers and 700 heavy guns. In World War II the English wanted to make the first major battle of the cross-Channel operation a replica of their last battles in World War I. Then, according to a British joint intelligence prediction, "collapse may, as in 1918, ensue with startling rapidity."

With that in mind—but with some technological changes—Churchill conceived a strategy in which infantry and artillery had minor roles. Strategic bombing and naval blockades would produce "great misery" and despair in "the morale of the German people," the "weakest link" in the Nazi juggernaut. Covert agents would "set Europe ablaze" with resistance movements. Then, in 1942, Allied armies should mobilize their best soldiers to engage second-rate German units in a secondary theater "where only comparatively small forces can be brought into action. . . . If we could achieve [this] series of successes even though these might be comparatively small in extent, it seemed fairly certain" to the British that "a point would be reached at which Germany would suddenly crack," even with its physical capabilities intact. Then—and only then—should the Allies conduct a cross-Channel invasion that, if done before "there is a German collapse," would "inflict on us a military disaster greater than that of Dunkirk." Under this plan, "there would not be needed vast armies on the continent such as were required in World War I. Small forces, chiefly armored, with their power of hard hitting, would be able to win a decisive victory."

The American army's senior officers called British strategy "groping for panaceas." "Our troops," said General Brehon Sommervell, chief of service forces, "must meet the Germans and the Japanese on the battlefield and in such numbers as to deliver telling and decisive blows." Churchill sided with the British military, hardly a surprise. So did Franklin Roosevelt in 1942, despite the domestic political problems that could ensue. No politician likes to argue with any constituency, least of all with one that has a strong following in Congress and the press. Roosevelt dodged the political danger by a series of devices. He forbade taking notes at meetings, leaving everyone wondering exactly what he said, nor did he let Marshall bring up unwelcomed issues, often doing all the talking himself. The president also ensured a broad array of military opinions, at least one of which was bound to support him, and found someone else to overrule the American army, the role of Winston Churchill.

To ensure there was no unanimity that critics could say he ignored, Roosevelt sabotaged the attempt to institute what army planners called "an authoritative Joint Staff of the Armed Forces of the United States." Although Congress historically has been the greatest opponent of service unification, seven different bills in March 1942 proposed the enactment of a consolidated department of national defense with a single chief "charged with the duty of directing, under the President, all naval and military operations." In July Roosevelt took the steam out of this legislative proposal, backed by newspapers such as the *New York Times,* by informally creating the JCS. Denied the written charter it requested, let alone statutory protection, its members served at the pleasure of the president. It became a forum where the navy, the army, and the army air force (not fully independent until 1947) discussed their various opinions, came to a unanimous consensus (they never took a vote), or agreed they disagreed. Then they had to appeal to the president for final adjudication, just as the president planned. Admiral William Leahy, its presiding officer, Marshall lamented, was "more the chief of staff of the president and less the chairman of the chiefs of staff." He carried FDR's guidance to the armed forces, not its point of view to FDR. Leahy never had much opportunity to suggest that Roosevelt amend the initial job description that he gave him: "sort of a 'legman.'" The president "did most of the talking," Leahy later wrote, "he always did."

Roosevelt's most subtle procedure for discounting military advice was to stack the deck at coalition meetings and get the British to overrule the army. Even George Marshall, who saw through most of FDR's acts, was always worried "when Churchill got hold of him," as if the prime minister led the poor president astray. Roosevelt was profoundly ambivalent about the army's proposal to invade the Continent in 1942 with "whatever personnel and equipment is actually available at the time." He, too, was anxious to open "a second front to compel the withdrawal of German air forces and ground forces from Russia," although from motives different than those of Marshall and Eisenhower. They needed Soviets to tie down Germans if the army were to assault the beachheads and play a major role in the European theater. Roosevelt needed the Soviets if his lend-lease strategy were to have any feasibility. Somebody had to bell the German cat. Even those Britons who predicted a sudden collapse of Germany said the collapse would occur only after a futile "winter campaign in Russia."

In the long run, Roosevelt needed the Soviet Union. In the short run, he wanted a tactical victory before the 1942 congressional elections, something incompatible with Eisenhower's plan to launch five or six Anglo-American divisions in a "sacrificial" operation designed "to keep 8,000,000 Russians in the war." Eisenhower gave the invasion "about 1 [chance] in 5" to establish a beachhead and hold on by one's fingertips, hardly auspicious for Roosevelt's electoral success. "The silly headlines," according to somber sailors and soldiers, still insulated the public from bad news on the battlefield. "We got a hell of a beating" in Burma, General Joe Stilwell said in May: "INVADING JAP FORCE CRUSHED BY STILWELL," read newspapers in the United States.

Roosevelt probably agreed with Marshall's feeling that "support must not depend upon giving a favorable press report of every action." However, as a practical politician, he had to accommodate public opinion more often than he tried to change it. If the landings on the continent of Europe "lead to disaster," as the War Department admitted they might, Congress could have gone under Republican control in November 1942. Then the legislature, influenced by complaints that the armed forces had no unity of command, might have penalized the president, who had actually followed army advice. After indicting Roosevelt, incorrectly this one time, for being an amateur strategist, Congress would have reintroduced legislation to create a supreme military commander in place of a weak JCS. Roosevelt might have become in name only what he loved to be in fact and title: *the* one and only commander in chief. Because he avoided a tactical defeat by sending the army against beachheads in North Africa held by Vichy Frenchmen armed with obsolete weapons, Roosevelt retained a Democratic majority in Congress—by just ten votes in the House. This ensured that FDR and Churchill "really ran the war." The chairman of the JCS later said that Anglo-American military men "were just artisans building definite patterns of strategy from the rough blueprints handed us by our respective Commanders-in-Chief."

Whatever Roosevelt's reasons for discarding the advice of the army, he did so indirectly by getting Churchill to do it for him. FDR had more in common with his fellow political leader than he did with his own military chiefs. They not only shared slants on strategy: improvisation, naval backgrounds, and faith in strategic bombing. They also wanted to retain firm control of their nations' war effort, and both commands were shaky in 1942. The prime minister's plans had failed in Norway, Singapore, Greece, and Crete, let alone Gallipoli in World War I. Then, on 21 June, the day after Eisenhower told the JCS that ground forces could hold a beachhead on the Continent like "Tobruk has been held," Tobruk (the British strongpoint in Libya) fell to the Germans.

The fall of Tobruk, said American reporters in London, created a "supreme political crisis" for Churchill, already in a state of depression and exhaustion caused by the string of defeats and 35 percent public approval of his conduct of the war. Churchill might not survive another military disaster. He knew it, Roosevelt knew it (and worried about it), and if Churchill ever overlooked it, Roosevelt was there to remind him. Through confidential messengers, FDR referred to the cross-Channel operation as a "sacrifice landing," a remark that deeply disturbed Churchill, an opponent of "sublime heroism utterly wasted" on the western front ever since protesting a proposed offensive to come to the assistance of Russia in World War I. (At the ensuing Battle of Loos in September 1915, British soldiers suffered 80 percent casualties.) In mid-1942 the president sent George Marshall to London to get agreement to launch an Anglo-American invasion (at least three-fifths British) across the English Channel that fall. One doubts whether Roosevelt was shocked when the prime minister vetoed the proposal in favor of action in North Africa. Privately, Churchill had repeatedly told him that "no responsible British military authority" felt the U.S. plan had "any chance of success."

To say the least, the high command of the army was angry with the British for forcing on them the invasion of North Africa. Eisenhower called the decision "the blackest day in history." George Patton, about to lead forces ashore at Morocco, agreed that "the operation is bad and is mostly political," while Henry Stimson called it the "wildest kind of diversionary debauch" from the invasion of the Continent. An English undersecretary for foreign affairs visited the War Department in August and reported back to London that the army was "violently jealous" of Churchill, who allegedly was "dominating and bamboozling the President." American generals were as friendly to the British "as they would be to the German General Staff if they sat round a table with them." Stimson, while not privy to Roosevelt's missive that he was "inclined to support continuing the campaign in the Middle East," knew enough not to put all the blame on the British. Churchill, he recorded in his diary, had adopted the plan to invade North Africa "knowing full well I am sure that it was the President's great secret baby."[5]

CONFLICT WITHIN WAR: THE ARMY, THE NAVY, THE AIR FORCE, AND THE ENGLISH

There were several informal alliances within the grand alliance of the United States, the United Kingdom, and the Union of Soviet Socialist Republics. The

U.S. and Red Armies had an institutional interest in each other's good fortune. Churchill and Roosevelt had personal stakes in each other's political prosperity. If either lost control of the war "to some military figure," as their opponents said they should, a disconcerting precedent would be set. Finally, there was the fragile alliance between the U.S. Navy and the British chiefs of staff based largely on their common enemy, the "strategic concept" of the U.S. Army. "The Pacific fellows," George Marshall said in retrospect, were the only American military men who wanted the invasion of North Africa in 1942.

In November 1940 Admiral Harold Stark, then CNO, was an architect of the "Germany first" strategy that stated the United States "should direct [its] efforts toward a strong offensive in the Atlantic as an ally of the British," but it should "do little more in the Pacific than remain on a strict defensive." Roosevelt passed over several senior candidates when he selected Stark, a personal friend since World War I, because "we think alike." To the irritation of commanders, planners, and staff who thought him too responsive to the president, the admiral tried to mirror Roosevelt's strategy, at least as far as Stark (or anyone else) could understand it. When Stark left Washington for a post in London following the shake-up caused by Pearl Harbor, Ernest J. King took his place. The highest echelon of the navy then resumed its traditional stance (never abandoned by most subordinates) that the navy was *the* military service in, of, and for the Pacific Ocean. As the head of the British military delegation in America wrote Churchill in July 1942, the cross-Channel operation is George Marshall's "first love, but . . . King's war is against Japan."

An early invasion of northwestern Europe would have prevented the Pacific from receiving anything approaching equal recognition. "It is remarkable," Marshall recalled in 1956, "but King accepted [North Africa] without a quibble. . . . Usually he argued over all our plans." The idea of attacking Germany in the Mediterranean was a variant of traditional maritime strategy as articulated by the navy in September 1941: Anglo-American forces might land at "distant regions where German troops can exert only a fraction of their total strength." This not only gave sea power a major responsibility but also gave King an opportunity to challenge the premise of Europe first. If the Allies would not mass their power for a decisive battle against Germany, then he could argue that America should commit its resources to fight Japan.

In 1942, when the War Department was engrossed with the survival of the Soviets, King predicted that "in the last analysis Russia will do nine-tenths of the job of defeating Germany." Certainly hyperbolic, he was still more prescient than the army, although he was right for the wrong reason. If Eisenhower and Marshall overstated the danger to the Soviet Union, they used the threat to argue for their cross-Channel strategy. If King overstated the power of the Red Army, he did so to support the navy's agenda. In March 1942 he had written Roosevelt and the other service chiefs that offensive action in the Pacific was "more urgent" and important than an invasion of the Continent. In July, when Churchill refused to approve a cross-Channel operation, King launched what would be his largest (and last) direct assault upon Germany first, this time with allies in the army. Together, King and Marshall overturned the major tenet of the Stark-Marshall memorandum (November 1940) that "the issues in the Orient will largely be decided in Europe." They proposed that the United States "assume a defensive attitude against Germany, . . . turn to the Pacific and strike decisively against Japan . . . with all available means."

Marshall was not just bluffing to put pressure on the British, as he would maintain after the war. For months the War Department had been trying "to concentrate rather than scatter U.S. forces" around the world. "Germany first" would allow it to make long-range plans and mass combat power in England, the shortest overseas lines of communication at a time when shipping was critically stretched. In July, when Europe meant dispersals through the Mediterranean, it lost much of its appeal to the U.S. Army, which adopted a position military planners expressed as early as March: "If the British are not willing to implement [the cross-Channel] concept this year," America should "concentrate U.S. offensive effort in the Pacific Area."

King momentarily sold George Marshall. He could not sell Franklin Roosevelt, who wrote the service chiefs that their proposal was exactly what Hitler wanted. It would not provide a decisive place to fight, nor would it support Russia or England, both in need of help. Lest anyone forget who was who, Roosevelt signed his response "C in C," for commander in chief. King never made another frontal assault on Europe first. He supported the strategy in principle but created facts and "clarified" phrases to modify it in practice. While he could not make the Pacific the first national priority, he helped make it a close second, contrary to the original plan to hold a static perimeter at the "Pacific Triangle" (Alaska to Hawaii to Panama) until Germany surrendered.

From mid-1942 to mid-1944, a paradox existed in American military strategy. Despite verbiage about European priority, the country made equivalent expenditures to the war with Japan. King helped create this contradiction by instigating what one biographer called "an active fighting constituency in the Pacific with a rightful call on American resources before the Allies undertook major operations against Germany." Rather legalistic, this hardly does justice to the human meat grinder at Guadalcanal, the longest battle in U.S. history, August 1942 to January 1943. To the president and the JCS, King justified the commitment as defending the sea lanes to Australia, consistent with Roosevelt's instructions for "a holding war." To Chester Nimitz, the commander of naval forces in the Pacific, he was confidentially describing it as the first step toward the conquest of the Marianas, the hub of the central Pacific and a forward base to China and Japan. So far no one in high authority had approved anything beyond New Guinea and the Solomons. Outside the confines of the navy, King would not mention the Marianas for another year, May 1943.

Once committed to Guadalcanal, Roosevelt had to reinforce the effort, for personal and political reasons. Aside from the fact that his oldest son was leading raider units behind Japanese lines, there was the prospect of suffering a tactical defeat on the eve of the November elections. Having dodged that danger by rejecting the cross-Channel invasion of Europe, he was not about to allow a failure somewhere else. The price of success proved to be 7,000 men, twenty-nine ships, 400 planes, and Roosevelt's finding himself "far more heavily engaged in the southwest Pacific than I anticipated a few months ago." At the time, no one knew, least of all the navy, that King's campaign had paid dividends in Europe. To Germany's dismay, the battle for the Solomons drew Japanese submarines out of the Indian Ocean, where they could have cut America's supply lines to Russia via the Persian Gulf and to English forces in North Africa via the Red Sea. By November, Roosevelt was writing Joseph Stalin that having "hit the Japanese very hard . . . we are going to press our advantages in the Southwest Pacific." Whether Roosevelt knew it or not, Ernie King was on his way to the Marianas.

The Casablanca Conference (14 to 24 January 1943) soon confirmed how hard it was not to exploit a victory. King went there hoping Roosevelt, Churchill, and the combined chiefs of staff would acknowledge his progress in the Pacific and approve further action with ever more resources. Marshall and Henry "Hap" Arnold, commander of the army air force, had ideas of their own. Unable to forge a common plan, the American military delegation brought to the conference a shaky, three-part program—for the navy, an offense in the Pacific; for the army, the cross-Channel invasion; for the air force, strategic bombing of Germany. No service chief could be sure what was on Roosevelt's mind, unlike Winston Churchill, who was much better informed. In November FDR confidentially put forth "forward movements directed against Sardinia, Sicily, Italy, Greece and other Balkan areas." Two months later, a week before the conference, he met the JCS briefly, gave permission to propose a cross-Channel invasion, then had them travel separately to Casablanca to prevent their reaching a common understanding on the eve of an important military meeting.

Churchill arrived with a ship full of prepared plans and technical experts. Roosevelt allowed two army planners to come and make the case for the invasion of France. "I was shooting off the hip all the time," Marshall recalled after the war. He "had done a magnificent job," according to his sole assistant, "but he had been almost entirely on his own," something that spoke volumes about his colleagues and his boss, the president.

As the army was running into its worst ambush this side of Custer at the Little Bighorn, Roosevelt "joked continually" and appeared convinced that the war would turn out just as he planned. Meanwhile, the navy was pursuing its own interests with the British chiefs of staff, heretofore willing to sanction operations "on a scale sufficient only to contain" Japan. King traded naval escorts "to do Sicily" for a change in Pacific theater strategy from defensive to offensive operations, while denying an abrupt shift at all. "Germany is our prime enemy," but we must still take "a position of readiness from which we can operate against

Japan after Germany has been defeated." The English may not have known it, but King had just redefined the meaning of "Europe first." To them, it still meant beat Hitler and then turn to attack Japan. To America, it now meant beat Japan down to the verge of surrender right after Germany.

While King was securing his immediate objectives and Marshall was losing the cross-Channel invasion, Hap Arnold was working on behalf of the air force, more than a branch but less than a service. While part of the army, it had de facto autonomy and a representative (Arnold) on the JCS. This anomalous compromise satisfied no one, least of all the flyers themselves. If the army air force were to emerge from World War II as the fully independent service that it wished to be, it would do so on the strength of its performance in strategic bombing, its completely independent mission. Accomplishments in joint operations, such as fire support for ground forces or the interdiction of enemy armies, would support the army's case against independence: because airpower was indispensable for success on the ground, the air force should not become a separate service.

Before Casablanca, the army air force had been supporting ground forces in North Africa, searching for submarines in the Atlantic, and bombing sub pens in France. It had not dropped a single payload on the enemy homeland, despite Arnold's words at the conference: "No one is keener to go for targets in Germany than the U.S. Air Commanders in the United Kingdom." If the army invaded France, as George Marshall now proposed, it could not survive, Marshall admitted, without "strong air support." The army air force knew what Leahy would say: "Whether Germany is bombed or not, American forces must be adequately protected. If those troops are neglected, the Joint Chiefs of Staff could not face the people of the United States." Consequently, the ambition of the air force depended on postponing the invasion of the Continent, clear to its war planners who already drafted documents proposing at least a year and one-half of preparatory bombing.

In January 1943 the Allies decided to conduct "the heaviest possible bomber offensive" to destroy "the morale of the German people to a point where their capacity for armed resistance is fatally weakened." Sicily was to be occupied to open the whole Mediterranean for new operations. Then, at the Trident Conference in May, the allies decided to invade Italy. Once again, King supported the policy, as did the air force, which wanted bases to bomb southern and eastern Germany, as well as the Romanian oil refineries. To the army, all this meant more delay in confronting the Wehrmacht head-on and in formulating a strategic concept by which it would fight World War II. It had complained about the lack of solid direction since November 1940, and the army's aggravation did not mellow with age. In July 1943 John Hull, head of the European section, wrote Thomas Handy, the chief of the War Plans Division, that "until a firm decision is made" about long-term Allied strategy, "we are in an indefensible position wherever a question is raised concerning the dispatch of troops to various theaters" around the world.

The consensus of U.S. army strategists for a cross-Channel operation began to crack from the bottom to the top. Reminiscent of George Marshall's former proposal to concentrate combat power in the Pacific, his subordinates began to accept the Mediterranean strategy. In July 1943 two colonels in the War Plans Division advised their boss, Major General Hull, that because Roosevelt and Churchill adopted "a time-consuming strategy of pecking at the periphery of Europe," the army must accept the fact that a cross-Channel invasion would not be "the opening wedge for decisive defeat of the German armies," something to take "place in the air over Europe, on the ground in Russia, and at sea" (FDR's original strategy). Hull wrote his boss, Tom Handy, that because "our commitments to the Mediterranean" have created their own momentum, we must now make "an all-out effort" there (exactly what Churchill had planned). Even Marshall now urged the JCS that if Roosevelt and Churchill endorsed more operations in southern Europe, "the decision be made firm in order that definite plans could be made with reasonable expectation of their being carried out." No doubt, he was reflecting the latest word from Leahy, FDR's "leg man" to the armed forces, that "we may not mount Overlord," code name for the invasion of France.[6]

UNCONDITIONAL SURRENDER AND D DAY: POLITICS AT HOME AND ABROAD

Just as the U.S. Army was beginning to accept, with deep regrets, the Mediterranean and maritime strategy, the president of the United States was finally accepting the need to mount the cross-Channel invasion of France. When FDR met with the senior command on 10 August 1943, the day before the Quadrant Conference with the British at Quebec, he "astonished and delighted" the secretary of war with his definite commitment to Overlord. Exactly what happened must remain hypothetical. Roosevelt rarely explained himself to his wife, let alone the armed forces. "The President never 'thinks,'" she told one journalist, "he *decides.*"

Some factors seem probable, despite Roosevelt's baffling methods. Politics is paramount for politicians. In 1942 Roosevelt tried (but barely failed) to mount an invasion of North Africa right before the congressional election. In 1944 he himself was up for reelection. The people whom he saw almost every day, Leahy and Hopkins, said Mediterranean operations had "little value for ending the war." If this were right, Roosevelt would soon be in serious political trouble. Every opinion poll indicated that on domestic issues, the country preferred the prospective Republican candidates. If there were no definitive evidence that the war was nearly won, Roosevelt would have no advantage as the incumbent commander in chief. It was also clear from the polls that the public perceived the invasion of France to be the light at the end of the tunnel, something shining so brightly that

Hopkins would complain in August 1944 "that everybody thinks the war is over." That November, the *New York Times* would conclude that "Franklin D. Roosevelt had been re-elected in a war year as a war President who could promise the country victory in the war and, on the basis of victory, a lasting peace."

Aside from reelection, three interwoven goals required a cross-Channel invasion: defeating Germany before Japan, forcing its unconditional surrender, and building a long-term alliance with the Soviet Union—the foredoomed hope for a lasting peace. Pearl Harbor had changed the public's geostrategic priorities, but not those of the president. Before December 1941, substantially more Americans were willing to risk war to stop the Germans than the Japanese. After Pearl Harbor, according to the government's surveys, 62 percent of the public (vs. 21) wanted to "put most of our effort into fighting Japan." FDR resisted as best he could, suppressing reports of the death march from Bataan until 1944. In private he maintained that the "defeat of Germany means the defeat of Japan, probably without firing a shot." In public he said in his State of the Union message (January 1942) that "the dreams of empire of the Japanese and Fascist leaders were modest in comparison with the gargantuan aspirations of Hitler and the Nazis."

In 1943, despite Roosevelt's profession of Germany first, America had as much combat power committed against Japan. With forthcoming offenses by King and MacArthur about to draw even more resources, the president would need to create a countervailing condition by launching a major invasion of Europe in 1944. After he did this on 6 June three-fourths of the army's air groups and two-thirds of its divisions were fighting in France and Italy.

Marshall told Roosevelt in mid-1943 that public impatience with a "protracted European war" would "culminate in peace short of complete victory," hardly welcome to someone committed to "no result save victory, final and complete," Roosevelt's words two days after Pearl Harbor. In World War I he had been virtually the only member of the Wilson administration to call the armistice a "patched-up peace" and favor fighting as far as Berlin. At Casablanca he condemned Wilson's constraints on Pershing: "The unwisdom of this policy had long ago become apparent to all." The maritime strategy would enable the nation to bargain from a position of strength, not compel unconditional surrender, an objective opposed by Admirals Leahy, King, and Nimitz. Off the record, the CNO told reporters that "the American people will [grow] weary and pressure at home will force a negotiated peace." Unconditional surrender was "just another phrase" to the navy's high command.

As a policy, unconditional surrender was a fait accompli that Roosevelt gave the American military. He mentioned it seven days before Casablanca, then moved on to other business, implying it was just an item for future consideration. The president thereby covered his tracks so that he could say the JCS was informed and had not disagreed. Caught off guard by Roosevelt's announcement that unconditional surrender was America's objective, Marshall "was too busy [at Casablanca] to react" to that fateful phrase. Senior officials in the government's propaganda agency (Office of War Information) felt that unconditional surrender was something combat soldiers gave or received in the field. As a statement of national war aims, it confused ends with means: "In this war we are never going to have a political policy which governs military action. We are going to take military action which conditions policy." As for the phrase itself, the propaganda experts said that Nazi leaders exploited its lack of specificity. Hitler could claim unconditional surrender "means slavery, castration, [and] the end of Germany."

Joe Stalin agreed with American propagandists and Eisenhower with Stalin, although privately believing "the German is a beast." Given a choice to "mount a scaffold [or] charge twenty bayonets, you may as well charge bayonets" was Eisenhower's opinion. To reduce enemy resistance, the JCS asked Roosevelt to clarify the conditions of "unconditional surrender" by drawing a distinction between the guilty leadership clique of "gangster overlords" and the innocent German "people," reminiscent of Marshall's favorite propaganda for GIs, Frank Capra's "Why We Fight" movies, said to be "the inside story of how the mobsters plotted to grab the world!" In fact, neither FDR's speeches nor Capra's films were clear or consistent about whether the enemy was the Wehrmacht, the Nazi government, or the German people.

When the president finally had to make a choice, he demanded unconditional surrender from all three, a policy without precedent, according to the State Department. Roosevelt put particular emphasis on subduing the population of the vanquished, as when he spoke to Marshall of "feeding the Germans for years from soup kitchens and giving them nothing else." An "inconclusive peace," he often told America, "will run the risk of another World War in ten or twenty or fifty years . . . when the [German] babies of today have grown into fighting age." GIs, with their own surrender policy, would prevent World War III in their own way. Very lenient toward the "average German soldier, just a young man drafted [like us]," they were apt to slaughter the SS, "Hitler's bad boys," on the spot. One frontline practitioner explained this de facto no quarter: "Better to get rid of the fanatics than to have our sons over here in another twenty-five years."

Combat soldiers were not Roosevelt's only audience. His statements about unconditional surrender promised Stalin no separate peace and Germany appropriate punishment. They also were supposed to inspire the home front to work harder than it had. Complacency, if not apathy and profiteering, did not disappear after Pearl Harbor. FDR openly complained about America's pampered past and emphasized the need for unstinting sacrifice. (He privately mentioned what "a good thing" it would be "if a few German bombs could be dropped over here.") Under these circumstances, Roosevelt would not soften the phrase "unconditional surrender" lest new words muffle the impact of his call for greater effort. If nothing else, the slogan was an attention-getting device for a man who "believed his primary obligation was to concentrate the attention of public opinion upon the winning of the war." The maritime strategy may have won at the Casablanca Conference, but the president urged the press to call this the "'Unconditional Surrender' Meeting."

If Roosevelt were to fulfill his goal and "eliminate Germany as a possible and even probable cause of a third World War," he felt he would have to solidify a long-term alliance with the Soviet Union. Firm military ties with Russia had been his objective even before he became an active belligerent. In 1941 Roosevelt refused to accept a Japanese empire in north Asia, lest the Imperial army, with access to American oil and scrap metal, tie down Soviet forces along the Manchurian border when Roosevelt wanted to free them to fight Hitler in Europe. Thirteen months after Pearl Harbor (largely the result of that rejection), Roosevelt used unconditional surrender to assure Stalin that he would not negotiate with Germany. By 1943 he feared Stalin might take that option himself. American intelligence, having broken Japan's diplomatic code, was well aware that in late 1942 Russia had accepted—but Germany rejected—suggestions for a status quo ante bellum settlement, something to enable Germany to concentrate on Japan's primary enemy, the United States. By mid-1943 Stalin's bargaining position was enhanced dramatically, suggesting that Hitler might request the settlement he previously refused. From July through September, from Kursk to Kiev, Axis armies lost approximately 1,400,000 soldiers, 3,000 tanks, 5,000 planes, and 25,000 field guns along a 650-mile front. Shortly thereafter, Western capitals were rife with rumors about a separate peace in Eastern Europe. Harry Hopkins, convinced that Russia could fight one more year before reaching utter exhaustion, mentioned this in print two months before the Tehran Conference: "If we lose her, I do not believe for a moment that we will lose the war, but I would change my prediction about the time of victory."

Hopkins was putting a brave face on the disaster of Stalin ever making a separate peace with Germany, something Roosevelt would not do, despite advice and consent to seek out the pre-Nazi ruling class. Forty percent of the American public approved negotiating with German generals, if they overthrew Hitler. Several officials in the War and State Departments, as well as the Office of Strategic Services, urged FDR to encourage a coup by promising to support Germany against Soviet expansion. Roosevelt refused because he believed that "the whole nation has been engaged in a lawless conspiracy against the decencies of modern civilization." Nonetheless, if Stalin cut his own deal, FDR would have to retract at least one of his military goals: achieving decisive progress in 1944, fighting without a ground force greater than the AEF, winning on the basis of unconditional surrender before public morale dissipated.

Heretofore, Roosevelt believed that the answer to this unpleasant array was the strategic bomber, to be built at the expense of all other items, even his beloved navy. By mid-1943 it had been demoted from *the* winning weapon to one more system in the total Allied arsenal. Four months after the Casablanca Conference announced the bombing campaign against Germany, the Allied political and military high command met in Washington to assess its preliminary results. The bad news indicated that a protracted air supremacy campaign would have to be waged before effective bombing could ever be conducted. The next six months confirmed this pessimistic prediction. In August, when air force doctrine held that 5 percent losses were barely acceptable, 30 percent of the heavy bombers raiding Ploesti were shot down. In October another 214 were destroyed over Schweinfurt and Regensburg, each crash losing a ten-man crew. Worst of all, no end seemed in sight. German fighter command was supposed to expand 56 percent by mid-1944.

This predicament confounded Hap Arnold and the proponents of airpower, who assumed bombing would proceed (not follow) the cross-Channel landing. In fact, 75 percent of the tonnage eventually dropped on Germany fell after D day. Nonetheless, there was a silver lining to attrition before 6 June. The army air force had planned to win air superiority over the battlefield by bombing aircraft factories deep in Germany, the highest-priority target in early 1943. They won it as much by diversion as by destruction. Germany had to switch production from Stuka dive-bombers to short-range fighters dedicated to urban air defense. In early 1944, over its own cities, it lost thousands of planes, not truly decisive, since nearly all equipment was replaced. Of crucial importance, it lost 2,500 pilots attempting to intercept Allied bombers with long-range fighter escort. The latter were the hunters; the former were the "bait," as bomber crews suffering the bulk of air force casualties came to describe their role in the war. Marshall, using far less abrasive language, had predicted this occurrence in mid-1943: "One of our primary objectives [is] to force the Luftwaffe into the air where we can get at it and destroy it." By June 1944 the Allies had killed most of the German aces, had tactical air supremacy over the battlefield, and maintained a virtual monopoly over the beaches. Soldiers are never so vulnerable as when packed in troop transports or landing craft. On D day one British sailor said, "The Luftwaffe is obviously smashed." It conducted only 250 sorties the entire day, 22 against Allied shipping. The Allied air forces conducted almost 15,000 sorties of their own. As Eisenhower told American troops before the invasion: "If you see a plane, don't worry. It's one of ours."

In the air war over Germany, the enemy lost more than the sky above the English Channel. By deploying some 30 percent of its heavy guns, 20 percent of its ammunition, and 2 million men to protect its cities, Germany reduced its force-to-space ratio of men and firepower on the battlefield. This forced it to leave gaps on the front line or strip itself of reserves, creating more maneuver room for the Allies no matter what option the enemy chose. In 1944, the great year of the Soviet and Anglo-American offensives, the Allies would need these clearings and tactical air supremacy to offset the inherent advantage of the defense, especially in places like Normandy, where thick hedgerows favored prepositioned German infantry. The sticking point would then be whether the grand alliance could hold itself together through 1944. When the United States pledged to invade France at Tehran in late 1943, that problem was largely resolved. There, Roosevelt told one son, a bomber pilot himself, "Nobody can see how—with a really concerted drive from all sides—the Nazis can hold out much over nine months after we hit 'em."

The commitment to a second front was not only an inducement to Stalin to stay in the war. It was also a down payment for a role in a postwar league of victor nations. Haunted by memories of Woodrow Wilson, Roosevelt was convinced that America "will be only too glad to retire all their military forces from Europe." Someone would have to provide ground forces to control future generations of Germans. No candidate seemed available aside from the Soviet Union.

The American military, by the nature of the profession of arms, thought far less about a world without war. At Tehran one American strategist remarked that Stalin's policy was "that the Soviet Union would be the only important military and political force on the continent of Europe." Nonetheless, senior American officers were not in a position to ask Roosevelt a crucial question: After Germany's unconditional surrender, who would be available to contain Russia? Logically, this might lead to a Mediterranean strategy to occupy Central and Eastern Europe before Stalin got there or to restrict lend-lease, neither one acceptable to the American army. It always opposed periphery pecking. As to equipping Russia, once supposed to lose to Hitler in six weeks, the army had reversed its opinion and became its foremost proponent, aside from Roosevelt himself.

The army knew that lend-lease abroad meant fewer divisions for a new AEF. This was part of a compromise implicitly struck with the president. American ground forces would play a far greater role than Roosevelt envisioned in 1941 but would be a far smaller force than the 334 divisions discussed in army plans as late as October 1942. The country eventually mobilized 90, while concurrently providing its allies with equipment and supplies for 2,000 infantry or 555 armored divisions. America would mobilize a smaller segment of its population than any other power, 7.8 percent. This sufficed, said Marshall, because of "air superiority [and] Soviet numerical preponderance." He therefore opposed the State Department's proposition to withhold military aid in order to restrain Soviet expansion. He also vetoed the proposal of the chief of his War Plans Division to retain equipment so we will "be strong enough militarily at the peace table to cause our demands to be respected" by the Russians. In World War I Pershing raised similar points to get Wilson to oppose amalgamation with the armies of Britain and France. In 1944 his former aide wrote Roosevelt that "lend-lease is our trump card in dealing with [the] U.S.S.R. and its control is possibly the most effective means we have to *keep the Soviets on the offensive* in connection with" our invasion of France (italics mine).

The U.S. Army had invested an enormous amount of time, effort, and prestige in the cross-Channel operation, which the British persisted in calling "a nebulous 2nd front." Until the army established a secure lodgment in Normandy, its commanders naturally worried far more that the Soviets would not attack and pin down Germans than about the postwar balance of power. In late June, when the West was still pinned down and might be pushed off the Continent if Germany committed its strategic reserves, 1,250,000 Red Army soldiers, 6,000 planes, 30,000 heavy guns, and 5,000 tanks tore a 250-mile gap in German lines. Within twelve days, twenty-five German divisions effectively vanished: "a greater catastrophe than Stalingrad," said Wehrmacht headquarters. After the American breakout in August 1944, new pressures arose on the JCS to minimize any interallied conflicts that could delay the defeat of Germany. The United States still had a war in the Pacific, and "with reference to [the] clean-up of the Asiatic mainland, our objective should be to get the Russians to deal with the Japs in Manchuria (and Korea if necessary)." JCS position papers as late as June 1945 continued to state that "the maintenance of the unity of the Allies in the prosecution of the war must remain the cardinal and overriding objective of our politico-military policy with Russia." When it came to "big military matters," such as killing German soldiers and taking pressure off American ground forces, Marshall and Stimson said "the Soviet government kept their word" and "carried out agreements to the day," as opposed to Marshall's comment on the British: "We just didn't understand them and they certainly didn't understand us."[7]

KING, MACARTHUR, AND ROOSEVELT:
OPPORTUNITIES AND AMBITIONS

For General Marshall, Normandy was the vital terrain from which to launch a decisive campaign. For Admiral King, the Pacific equivalent was the Marianas—Guam, Saipan, and Tinian. From there, the navy could move due west toward the China–Formosa–Luzon triangle, a choke point for Japan's vital imports from the "South Seas Resource Area": oil, rubber, tin, tungsten, and lead. After that, it would move northwest toward the Shantung Peninsula of China to establish a base from which to sever what King called the "inner ring" (the Yangtze River Valley, Manchuria, and Korea) that provided coal, lumber, fish, and wheat. The U.S. Army had long held that any plan that discounted soldiers was "contrary to logic and historical precedent." The navy, faithful to its own "strategic concept of maximum destruction of resources," maintained that a "truly effective blockade" could win the war "before [an] invasion and even before Japan is subjected to an intensive air offensive."

General Douglas MacArthur, supreme Allied commander in the Southwest Pacific Area (SWPA), had plans of his own: an army–army air force advance up the spine of New Guinea to the Philippines, which he called "the Holy Grail." Both plans—the army's and the navy's—required assets from the other service. Before King could proceed to Formosa, he would need 200,000 additional soldiers to garrison supply bases across the central Pacific. MacArthur would need shipping, since even he could not walk across 800 miles of water from western New Guinea to Leyte Gulf.

In this debate, King's great advantage was provided by the fifteen fast aircraft carriers launched in 1943. Before B-29s were armed with atomic bombs in 1945, carriers were the most powerful—but one of the most vulnerable—

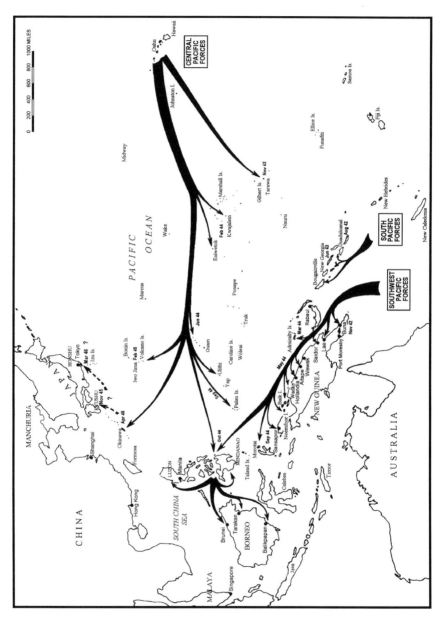

Pacific theater, World War II

weapons in the Pacific theater. America had to find somewhere to use them, and SWPA was not the appropriate place. With aviation fuel and ordnance stacked right below a carrier's teakwood deck, a well-placed bomb or torpedo could cause secondary explosions that might sink a vessel it took three years to build. Carrier warfare meant concealing your ship's position and discovering those of your opponent, as done at the Battle of Midway in June 1942. The U.S. Navy found a Japanese task force, dropped thousands of bombs, landed a few, and in the space of five minutes changed the entire momentum of the war in the Pacific by destroying four carriers, 332 aircraft, and 2,155 highly trained sailors and aviators. In SWPA, the narrow passages between long islands would be a lethal gauntlet to run. Carriers were far better suited to an area where they could approach a small atoll from any point on the compass. The president knew this, army planners knew this, even MacArthur knew this, although he still wanted to use carriers against New Guinea, the second-longest island in the world. King milked this fact to make the central Pacific, where Admiral Chester Nimitz was supreme Allied commander, the main avenue of approach to the Far East.

In theory, military strategy postulates a way and then acquires the means. America often built the means, then looked for how and where to employ it. King exploited this procedure, but he did not create the carriers that made it feasible. That responsibility primarily lay with the only civilian to whom he completely deferred, a congressman from backwoods Georgia who took only three airplane rides in his life.

Exactly why Congressman Carl Vinson, known inside Washington as *the* permanent secretary of what he called "my navy," championed large aircraft carriers remains a mystery. It was irrelevant economically to his landlocked constituents, none of whom worked in a shipyard or base. If Vinson had a geostrategic vision, he confined it to executive sessions of the Naval Affairs Committee, which he joined in 1917, when FDR was assistant secretary, and chaired from 1931, before Roosevelt was president. Vinson published no articles, made few speeches, and communicated by raising his eyebrows. He may have best revealed his motives in a statement made near the end of his fifty-two-year career in Congress: "I wanted to serve on a committee where I could see the results of my labor. When you authorize a big carrier you can see the results." Whatever his motivation, Vinson had more to do with acquiring the means that drove American strategy than did the navy's "gun club" of battleship admirals or the president, who favored a more balanced fleet. FDR was worried about isolationist opinion when he signed without fanfare "the third Vinson bill" to expand the navy in mid-1940. Then Vinson, without encouragement from the White House, promptly added a supplemental appropriation that mandated the construction of twelve new aircraft carriers which, according to him, "must spearhead the attack."

A fellow congressman once said that it felt like "treason" to vote against a Vinson bill. He may have had no idea how the vote in June would affect World

War II. It passed right after Germany panicked America by crushing France. It created the force that crushed Japan. The navy would win the Battle of the Atlantic against German submarines with destroyers, land-based aircraft, and the small ("jeep") carriers Roosevelt preferred. Without the large carriers, battleships, and 15,000 planes funded in 1940, it could not have projected its combat power far beyond the Alaska–Hawaii–Panama perimeter to be held in the "Germany first" strategy as conceived in 1940. Whether many Americans realized they were building a force to fight what was then considered the secondary threat, the Japanese certainly realized that the bill was closing their window of opportunity to expand in the Pacific. Two months after the supplemental appropriation, its prime minister told a military conference that "now is the most advantageous time for Japan to start a war."

Large carriers legitimized an offensive in the Pacific long before Germany surrendered. King used the first half of 1943 to expand the verbal mandate of the Casablanca Conference to "maintain unremitting pressure on Japan." By the Trident Conference in May, he had increased the commitment in the Pacific "to the maximum consistent with the minimum requirements in the Atlantic." That formula, worthy of a Philadelphia lawyer, could blow a chasm in the concept of fighting Germany first, provided King could prove it was better to "hitch off and shoot" carriers across the central Pacific than it was to settle for "inch by inch progress" with land-based aircraft in SWPA.

At Trident, the Anglo-American Combined Chiefs of Staff withheld consent to attack the Marianas. Not expecting King to accept defeat, the British predicted he would spring a trap at the next summit conference in August by ensuring enough "progress before 'Quadrant' regarding operations in [the] Pacific that his position will be impregnable." They were right about his methods but wrong about his timing. The Allied conference at Cairo in late November would set specific objectives and the alternative routes to the Far East. Before it met, King wanted to begin "the offensive phase" of the war, that is, when the United States "attack[ed] the enemy at places of our own choosing." To do this, he needed to create facts and confirm the theory of his joint planning staff that "carrier aircraft, although untested, are equal to the task of supporting amphibious operations against island fortresses in the absence of land-based air." He would do it by projecting combat power from Pearl Harbor 2,000 nautical miles to Tawara, a small atoll in the Gilbert Islands.

In June the JCS planning staff set 1 December as D day for the capture of what Nimitz called "the front door to the Japanese defenses in the central Pacific." Then, right before the Quadrant Conference in mid-August, it moved the date to 15 November, no doubt influenced by King, who never deferred to staffs and plans contrary to his agenda. A major in the New Zealand army, who had shipped coconuts off Tarawa before the war, warned that the tide over the reef 600 yards from the beach would be too low to navigate in mid-November. If correct, all but the first echelon, which would have special landing craft, would have to cross on foot and wade ashore. He advised delaying the operation until mid-December, a position tacitly supported by the ground force commander, who worried that naval gunnery and dive-bombers might not compensate for all the other shortages. "The Marines are crossing the beach with bayonets," said Major General Julian Smith, "and the only armor they'll have is a khaki shirt."

The disconcerting information got to the naval task force commander but not all the way up to King. What came down from the CNO was pressure to conduct the operation by 20 November. High tide or low, the navy would bring to Tarawa an enormous amount of firepower that would supposedly "obliterate" the enemy from all sides of the atoll. Three battleships, four heavy cruisers, and twenty destroyers would fire 3,000 tons of shell; 375 planes from three large and five "jeep" carriers would drop 275 tons of bombs, all on an islet three miles long by a half mile wide. No matter. Over 3,000 Japanese infantry ensconced in concrete pillboxes and bunkers under four feet of absorbent sand survived to meet the marines, some wading in water up to their necks. More than 1,000 Americans were killed and 2,000 wounded in the conquest of the bloodiest battlefield (per square yard) in American military history.

Aside from low tide, marines had to contend with lightly armored landing craft that could not take a shelling, water-damaged radios precluding shore-to-ship communication, and a navy whose mission was "to get the hell in and get the hell out." When it hovered around a landing site, as at Guadalcanal and Bougainville, it was a sitting duck for planes and submarines. Yet despite these problems, the marines took Tawara because of small-unit tactics, human willpower, and the circumstances in which they engaged the Japanese. On small islands in the central Pacific, from which there was no escape or retreat, "the opposing forces were like two scorpions in a bottle. One was annihilated, the other nearly so," according to one private.

The senior command of the corps and the navy had motives of their own. "Had the Marines failed at Tarawa," said Lieutenant General Holland Smith, "no Marine would have commanded another major operation. Command in the Central Pacific would have passed to the Army," a service with a different style and doctrine. It viewed ships as transport and fire support for infantry. The navy viewed ground forces as amphibious support for the fleet. Consequently, riflemen were more safe but ships more exposed during what the navy called the army's "slow, methodical way of fighting." This led to bitter interservice conflicts "beyond mere healthy rivalry," as George Marshall said to King.

In the Marianas, Smith relieved an army general for "laggard action." From Washington, nine months later, the CNO suggested disciplinary action at Okinawa. Newspapers reported the commander of the Tenth Army saying that it was "suicidal" to charge "the toughest [obstacles] yet encountered in the Pacific." King, in a fury, wired Nimitz that "such views show lack of appreciation of the naval problem regarding continuous support for ground operations." Nimitz, conducting the most costly battle in naval history (34 ships sunk, 368 damaged), stood down Lieutenant General Simon Buckner for gaining less than a thousand yards a day against a labyrinth of caves: "I'm losing a ship and a half a day. If this line isn't moving within five days, we'll get someone here to move it so we can all get out from under these kamikaze attacks."

The U.S. Navy and Army drew different lessons regarding tactics. The Japanese drew no strategic lessons at all. They never believed they could win a war of gross national product. By their own staff estimates, America had ten times their total matériel potential in steel, oil, labor, and so forth. However, paying close attention to the prewar debate within the United States, Japanese military men believed that they were strong in what America seemed to lack: unity, discipline, fortitude, and what they called the way of the warrior: "Common sense will not accomplish great things. Simply become desperate and crazy to die." In words attributed to Rear Admiral Keiji Shibasaski, "A million Americans could not take Tarawa in a hundred years."

One marine division took Tarawa in three days without discrediting this type of assessment. Although some newspapers admitted that "in the course of recent battles [Americans] have shown a fighting spirit little expected of them," the consensus opinion in ruling circles was that U.S. victories were a temporary setback; the opponent could stand no "further bloodshed." As late as mid-1945, most Imperial army officers planed to throw back the next amphibious invasion, this time against the home islands, by killing 33 percent of the assault troops at sea, another 20 percent on the beachhead. After that, the "evil and ugly [American] plutocracy" would not "continue an unprofitable war" and would come to accept the Japanese empire, at least in northeast Asia. Shrewd or not, the plan made no provision for the atomic bomb.

The initial response to "terrible Tarawa" supported the prediction that the United States would flinch in front of an entrenched defense. The public was horrified by photographs of the bloated bodies stacked up on the beach after Roosevelt lifted press censorship of casualties shortly before the invasion because he felt the home front had grown too complacent. However, the Japanese were not fighting newspapers and politicians, who demanded a congressional investigation of the operation. They faced a band of American samurai, one of whom said, "If the Marines could stand the dying, you'd think the public could at least stand reading about it." They would also have to stand seeing it in the movies. The corps shot *With the Marines at Tarawa,* a combat training film of what was supposed to be a textbook assault. It was "gruesome but the way the war is out there," a correspondent told FDR. Despite the qualms of the secretary of the navy, the president released the film, which received an Academy Award to go along with four Medals of Honor, forty-six Navy Crosses, and 248 Silver Stars won by the original cast. Unfortunately, the movie subsequently drove down enlistments by 35 percent.

Those still not cowed were apt to believe that "if you weren't a Marine, you weren't much of anything." The corps recruited volunteers at age seventeen;

many were younger but lied about their age. They were far more more eager and impressionable than the average GI, "idiotic adolescence" some old veterans recalled. Granted, a few army divisions were conspicuous for what William Styron, novelist and marine, has called "that mysterious group trance known as esprit de corps." The First Infantry, Eighty-second Airborne, and Fourth Armored stand out because they were exceptions. One could not say about the typical soldier, a twenty-six-year-old draftee, what a former marine said about the corps: it "was a society unto itself, demanding total commitment to its doctrines and values, rather like one of those quasi-religious military orders of ancient times."[8]

Because marines, who "really did assume they were invincible," took Tarawa the day the Cairo Conference began, King had momentum at an ideal time. The JCS was fed up with the fact that the Grand Alliance had still not selected a main avenue to Berlin—the cross-Channel or the Mediterranean strategy. Lest indecision also plague the war against Japan, American planners now clearly stated that "when conflicts" over resources exist, "due weight should be accorded to the fact that operations in the Central Pacific promise a more rapid advance towards Japan and her vital lines of communication." This point was not lost on the navy's informal ally against the army, the army air force, whose state of affairs resembled that of the navy. They both acquired a very expensive weapon system, then looked for where to use it, in one case aircraft carriers, in the other the B-29 long-range bomber, a $3 billion project, as opposed to $2 billion for the atomic bomb. King's argument had a clause that came back to haunt the navy when final credit would be calculated for beating Japan: his route promised "the earlier acquisition of strategic air bases closer to the Japanese homeland." Hence the air force, about to make Tinian the busiest airport in the world, joined the navy in support of going to the Marianas, home for 1,000 B-29s in 1945.

King thought the Cairo Conference ratified his strategy. He overlooked the Clausewitzian aphorism that war is waged against "an animate object that reacts," in this case Douglas MacArthur, who was far from happy with the plan to make SWPA a tar baby keeping Japanese ground forces away from clogging the central Pacific avenue of approach. He already appealed to Marshall to uphold the honor of the army: relegating most soldiers "to garrisoning and supply" would be "completely destructive of morale." Now he began to exploit the public shock at Tawara, a "tragic and unnecessary massacre of American lives," disregarding his own losses on the eastern edge of New Guinea, three times greater than marine fatalities at Guadalcanal. There was no room for ground maneuver once marines landed on a small atoll. MacArthur still told Roosevelt that "frontal assault is only for mediocre commanders. Good commanders do not turn in heavy losses."

To abstract arguments, MacArthur added military facts to impress Washington officials anxious "to show progress in the Pacific War" and less than thrilled that he had advanced just 280 miles in 1943. If MacArthur could land halfway up New Guinea six months before the navy got to the Marianas, scheduled for

1 October 1944, the army would be closer to the Philippines than the navy was to Formosa, King's target for cutting Japanese supply lines to their "South Seas Resource Area." MacArthur first would have to capture bases in the Bismarck Archipelago, which gave the enemy air supremacy along the coast of New Guinea. It was supposed to take several months. He pushed the landing forward one month and accomplished the mission in a matter of weeks, using detailed intelligence to bypass enemy strongpoints and personally lead 1,500 troops onto the Admiralty Islands, where he seemed to a *Newsweek* reporter like Washington crossing the Delaware. Then, after telling subordinates "to hold the airstrip at any cost," he returned to New Guinea to complete a campaign that would inflict nearly twenty times as many fatalities as it would sustain: 26,500 enemy versus 1,600 Americans. SWPA, whose poorly charted coral reefs were so dangerous to the navy's capital ships, proved relatively safe for infantry that could disembark behind enemy lines in flat-bottomed boats. This enabled MacArthur to avoid many attrition battles, advance 1,400 miles in nine months to the eastern tip of New Guinea, and be one step away from the Philippines long ahead of Pentagon predictions.

Back in January 1944, MacArthur said that he had "no political ambitions," only the "ambition to return to the Philippines," a statement playing right "into the hands of the people who would really like to make him a candidate" for president, according to the secretary of war. Five weeks after the Pentagon tentatively approved a Philippine operation in March, MacArthur publicly declared he would not accept any party's nomination. Various journalists surmised a simple quid pro quo in which Roosevelt would send him sufficient resources to reconquer the islands. The truth seems more complicated, especially since the JCS had only sanctioned an invasion of a southern province of the archipelago to get air and naval bases, possibly to go next to Formosa. To go to Luzon, Roosevelt might need MacArthur nearly as much as MacArthur needed him.

Roosevelt's management of the war had always been political dynamite, giving the MacArthur presidential campaign its most effective issue: "The shortest way to victory would be to place an experienced military man in the White House." Its claims on behalf of a nonpolitical war were barely scratched by the fact that MacArthur's military proposals contained thinly veiled warnings about "profound political repercussions," as when he told Roosevelt in July that if he bypassed Luzon, the American people would register their "resentment against you at the polls this fall." In fact, Roosevelt needed no pressure from MacArthur to go to Manila, although he would welcome it for reasons of his own. FDR probably encouraged MacArthur to take the lead and responsibility. Then Roosevelt could claim that he was bowing to military expertise, rather than sending men to die in a military campaign of dubious justification, as MacArthur tacitly admitted in a letter to the army chief of staff. ("A decision to eliminate the campaign for the relief of the Philippines, even under appreciable military considerations, would cause extremely adverse reactions among the citizens of the United

States.") If this hypothesis is correct, then MacArthur in 1944, like Churchill in 1942, only pushed Roosevelt in the direction he distinctly wished to be pushed.

Back in February 1942, when the military situation in the Philippines was so bleak that MacArthur recommended "*immediate* independence and neutralization" of the islands, FDR ordered that "American forces will continue to keep our flag flying so long as there remains any possibility of resistance." At the time, he thought it "mandatory" to "establish . . . in the minds of all peoples complete evidence that the American determination and indomitable will to win carries on down to the last unit." Hence, for the first five months of the war, the president riveted U.S. attention on Luzon, where some 75,000 soldiers eventually conducted the largest surrender in U.S. history. In private, the president thought MacArthur's conduct of command (such as letting his air force be destroyed on the ground) was worthy of court-martial. Publicly, he gave him a Medal of Honor, if only to "offset," as George Marshall put it, "any propaganda by the enemy directed against leaving his command" on Bataan. Since the Philippines was now a symbol of untarnished heroism—the contemporary version of the Alamo—there was no other landmark in the Pacific, short of the Imperial Palace in Tokyo, that had nearly the significance that Manila had for the electorate in 1944.

By contrast, the Marianas were barely known outside the War Plans Bureau of the navy. From there, the armed forces could move due west to Formosa, King's alternative to Luzon. However, the CNO to the contrary, many naval officers doubted whether Saipan had the harbor capacity to mount a massive invasion of what was a stronghold of the Japanese army. In mid-September 1944, when all the military staffs conducted their calculations on tactical and technical grounds, the consensus opinion was that the navy would need up to 200,000 more soldiers to support and supply the occupation of Formosa, certainly impractical before the election. King remained the final holdout. Even Chester Nimitz and Bill Halsey—two of the navy's three four-star admirals in the Pacific—favored Luzon. The third, Raymond Spruance, had an idea of his own.

Roosevelt thought King was "the shrewdest strategist" in Washington. King thought Spruance the only man in the navy smarter than himself. When they conferred in mid-July 1944, the commander of the Fifth Fleet suggested bypassing both Formosa and Luzon, to go straight from the Marianas to Okinawa, temporarily a soft target and the best staging base for a direct attack on Japan. True, there was a political downside, but Spruance was not a member of the Democratic National Committee. Okinawa was no household word before it was hardened and became the scene of the greatest battle Americans would ever fight in Asia. Even in the midst of the battle (May 1945), only 33 percent of the public could locate Okinawa on a map (74 percent could find Manila).

Spruance may have given brilliant military advice, but it barely got a nod from Ernie King. If the CNO had studied the idea and presented it to Marshall and Arnold, they well could have supported the proposal. Then Roosevelt might have consented to bypassing the Philippines, rather than face the heat of overruling a consensus in the JCS. For Arnold, Okinawa would have meant around-the-clock attacks on Japan with medium-range bombers, not just B-29s all the way from the Marianas. For Marshall, it meant land-based air cover for an invasion of Kyushu, the southern island of metropolitan Japan. American soldiers on enemy soil, according to the U.S. Army, were simply indispensable, and, as Marshall told MacArthur, "our great objective is the early conclusion of the war with Japan."

Four years before the United States suffered its first casualty in World War II, officers at the Army War College were convinced that public stamina would be America's greatest weakness. In May 1943, when most strategists were predicting V-J Day in 1947, the army chief of staff told the JCS that they had to win by 1945, an opinion shared by Frank Knox, the secretary of the navy. A Rough Rider with Teddy Roosevelt at San Juan Hill, Knox was not squeamish about blood on the battlefield. Nonetheless, after Tarawa, he wrote friends and naval officers that "we must be prepared for casualties on a scale we have never known since the Civil War—[but] are not at all prepared for them. . . . When [the public] finds out that the war with Japan will take a couple of years more, I wonder whether they will have the guts to stay with it to the finish."

By the spring of 1944, America's self-described "strategy of attrition and economic pressure" had produced mixed results. Submarines sinking Japanese shipping far faster than it could be built helped reduce war production 40 to 50 percent. On the other hand, on Capitol Hill, George Marshall had to spend valuable time lobbying against prospective legislation to begin demobilization. That May, he asked various Pentagon planning committees for ideas to get the war over fast.

The army, as an institution, was inherently less flexible than the navy, for reasons discussed earlier. Nonetheless, before the war, when sailors were planning an island-to-island campaign across the Pacific, the War Plans Division complained that a navy (unlike an army) need not occupy all points along communication lines. During the war the army staff remained a fertile source of new ideas, if only because the navy would have the daunting responsibility of testing innovative thinking under live fire. In late 1943 some of these planners had suggested going from the Aleutians directly to Hokkaido, the northern island of metropolitan Japan. Now Marshall, in 1944, asked them to study the possibility of going from the Marianas straight to Kyushu. If this plan was adopted, America would replace a peripheral strategy in the Pacific the same year it executed the cross-Channel invasion, its antithesis in the European theater. However, the United States would blend this direct approach to Japan with bypass operations more familiar to the British, since it would skirt Imperial army strongpoints in the western Pacific.

General Hideki Tojo, war and prime minister of Japan, would later say that the United States won the war by bypassing strongpoints like Truk and Rabaul, destroying merchant shipping, and keeping its aircraft carriers in constant operation. All these innovations were rather fortuitous. Congressman Vinson, not the navy or the president, created the aircraft carrier fleets. The destruction of 95 percent of Japan's merchant shipping was also inadvertent, although it was the bottleneck of the enemy's economy. Japan, while importing 75 percent of its foodstuffs and raw materials, used its shipbuilding facilities for its war-fighting navy rather than replace its cargo losses. Submarines, accounting for two-thirds of those sinkings with just 2 percent of U.S. naval personnel, were never ordered to do exactly what they did. In 1942 Admiral King told cautious captains to sink more ships or lose their commands. His subordinates came to the conclusion that they could meet their quotas and stay alive if they avoided warships (King's own priority) and attacked merchantmen deemed unworthy of protection by the Imperial navy, whose doctrine (like that of America) emphasized decisive engagements against enemy fleets. As a result, while destroying over 1,000 vessels, only 15 percent of American subs were sunk, as opposed to 67 percent of the Germans during the Battle of the Atlantic—the highest fatality rates of the entire war, aside from those for kamikaze pilots.

Bypass operations, Tojo's first reason for America's success, were also a chance discovery rather than the product of systematic planning. As such, the tactic never was exploited to its full potential by the United States. For every Rabaul bypassed there was at least one or two Attus, Kiskas, Palaus, New Georgias, and Luzons taken for no good military reason. In March 1942 Churchill pointed out that Japan, in a fit of enthusiasm, "is spreading itself over a very large number of vulnerable points. . . . All their islands will become hostages to fortune," specifically commando raids to create "a reign of terror among the enemy's detached garrisons." This proposal appealed to the president, then desperate for a victory to boost domestic morale, even if more symbol than substance. FDR created a Marine Corps raider battalion led by the former commander of his bodyguard detachment (Evans Carlson) and his eldest son, Jimmy Roosevelt. However, by 1943 "Carlson's Raiders" were defunct, partly because the Marine Corps, wanting to execute large invasions, said small-scale raids had "little strategic value." All that remained was a movie, entitled *Gung Ho,* about their attack on Makin Island in August 1942. At the end of the film, a wounded marine asks his platoon leader: "Tell me, when do we go to Tokyo?" The restless American people had a Hollywood spokesman a step or two in front of the high command.

Only gradually did the American military come to appreciate Japan's vulnerability to bypass operations. What is more, they did this largely for fear of public impatience, not from campaign strategy per se. FDR told the JCS that if the United States maintained the pace of progress established at Guadalcanal and western New Guinea, 200 miles a year, it would reach the enemy homeland about the year 2000. (*Life* magazine, more precise than the president, wrote that America "shall be able to make a bloody landing in the summer of 1957. After that we can proceed to the conquest of Japan.") At Casablanca he condemned the "island-to-island advance across the Pacific," the navy's primary war plan since the 1930s. "Some other method of striking Japan must be found."

As late as August 1943, Douglas MacArthur, soon to become the self-proclaimed prophet of bypass brilliance, was demanding a frontal assault on enemy headquarters at Rabaul, if only because a viable operation against this 100,000-man bastion would subordinate the central Pacific to SWPA. Rebuffed, he subsequently admitted that "the paucity of the resources at my command made me adopt this method of campaign as the only hope of accomplishing my task," that is, getting to the Philippines without expending all his power getting there. "Then," as he told one subordinate, "I'm going to meet the enemy head on." All in all, the U.S. military was only a hesitant convert to bypass operations that left behind what King called "a thorn in the side of our communications to the western Pacific." It usually conducted "intermediate jumps," not long leaps. A few strategists on the navy staff talked of "proceed[ing] to the heart of Japan by the most direct route"; there was "no reason for playing along the side of the road." However, the theater commanders were not receptive to Marshall's suggestion to "by-pass selected operations [the Philippines or Formosa] and choose new objectives, including Japan proper."

MacArthur, hardly surprisingly, responded that not going to the Philippines would betray a "great national obligation." Nimitz, for reasons of military caution, supported this objection to a big bypass. Like other nonaviators, this submariner repeated the old naval maxims against engaging installations: "To the maximum extent practicable our amphibious operations should be conducted with the support of shore based aircraft. Tactical situations in which the fast carrier task forces are more or less immobilized in support of protracted fighting on shore should be avoided." Nimitz thereby echoed the "step-by-step mopping up process" traditionally proposed in the Pacific: in his case, Leyte to Luzon to Formosa and then to northern China.

General Marshall was in no position to demand compliance with his more daring plan. First, the JCS usually gave suggestions (not orders) to theater commanders, who had a great deal of autonomy in their areas of operation no matter what their prior association with any service chief. This was true for Eisenhower, once Marshall's war plans director, let alone for MacArthur, who was army chief of staff when Marshall was a lieutenant colonel training captains at Fort Benning. Second, Marshall still had doubts of his own. He predicated his plan on certain conditions that had yet to happen: namely, the decisive defeat of the German army in northwestern Europe and the Japanese fleet in the central Pacific, most likely at the Philippines Sea.

A climactic defeat of the enemy fleet had long been the dream of naval strategists schooled in the doctrine of Alfred Thayer Mahan. Thanks to the bills Carl Vinson passed through Congress, 1944 seemed the year to put theory into practice. According to an archetypal naval aviator, the best pilots flying the best planes were now "backed up by the greatest fighting fleet in the history of the world"—20 carriers, 12 battleships, 13 cruisers, 56 destroyers, and a rotating pack of submarines. It still did not create feelings of invulnerability, at least in the high command. The navy in general (Nimitz in particular) balked at facing the type of "scissor's battle" Nimitz arrayed for the Japanese at Midway: capital ships, land-based aircraft, and anti-air artillery catching the enemy between sharp blades.

This contingency ran too large a risk for carriers whose vulnerability, according to the *Naval Institute Proceedings,* constituted "the Achilles' heel of our present system of waging offensive war." Their destruction, Marshall acknowledged, would immediately reverse "the balance of seapower" in the Pacific. Since 1906 the United States had presumed that Japan would sensibly preserve its fleet for its own climactic battle near its home bases, the area where it would maximize its strength. King and company, still fearing "a Japanese trap and a bloody nose," did not realize how badly they already had crippled the enemy by destroying its most valuable asset from the Coral Sea to the Marianas.

According to American doctrine, the decisive target was the Japanese carrier, not even its planes. Either one seemed more important than the naval aviators selected at age fourteen for ten years of intense training. At the Coral Sea (May 1942), the first naval battle ever waged beyond the range of big guns, the U.S. Navy downed seventy enemy flyers, putting them on the road to what they were in 1944, second-string replacements with half the training of their American counterparts. Nonetheless, even flyers chose to celebrate the latest version of harpooning the great white whale. "Scratch one flattop" entered naval lore next to "don't give up the ship": hence the institutional expectations of the navy on the eve of the invasion of the Marianas, two years after Midway, the last major naval engagement with the Japanese.

Nimitz hoped to "provoke these people into a fleet action." King feared that if the enemy's ships did not stay to defend the hub of the central Pacific, "we'll just have to go into the Inland Sea and dig them out." Then Raymond Spruance, in tactical command at the Battle of the Philippine Sea, pulled back his carriers and battleships to protect troop transports and logistics from Japanese air attack on the grounds "we could not afford to gamble and place [them] in jeopardy." (What, marines more important than capital ships?) By tradition, the navy allots a commander autonomy in battle, then brickbats in retrospect. "The enemy had escaped," said the official report filed by the carrier task force commander. Over 400 of its aircraft were destroyed and its pilots killed, but "his fleet was not sunk." Unofficially, that "is what comes of placing non-aviators [like Spruance] over aviators" with the "skill and imagination" to make the "difference between a reasonably expeditious victory in the Pacific and a long drawn out, exhaustive war."

Aside from a crippling defeat of the Imperial fleet, George Marshall's other stipulation for launching an attack directly toward Japan was the defeat of the German army in France. That would have allowed him to commit men, equipment, and shipping (the scarcest element) to the Pacific theater. Unfortunately, in late August 1944 American ground forces missed their opportunity to surround a German army group in Normandy, which then escaped across the Seine to prolong the war into mid-1945. Ironically, Marshall had trained most of the generals who failed to close the Falaise pocket when he ran the Infantry School at Benning from 1928 to 1933.[9]

SUCCESS AND FAILURE IN NORMANDY

Under Lieutenant Colonel George C. Marshall, the Infantry School was remarkably innovative, according to instructors Omar Bradley and J. Lawton Collins: "If anybody had any new idea," Marshall "was willing to try them instead of saying, 'Why don't you let the thing alone instead of stirring things up.'" One suspects that Marshall's tolerance for any "screwball idea" was tacit admission he had not found the answer to the question all armies asked after World War I: How can one break the stalemate of the trenches and bring decisive battle back to land warfare?

The German solution was to concentrate tanks into special Panzer units for deep penetrations into rear areas. Marshall was far more skeptical about the ability of armor to culminate a high-speed campaign. "In the first phases of a war," large units would maneuver over wide areas; however, battle "is going very soon to end in the mud." Hence Marshall was more partial to vertical envelopments with airborne divisions, later proven to be too lightly armed to be decisive. Otherwise, he had no solution for stalemate aside from warning that "each situation is unique and must be solved on its own merits."

When Marshall left Benning in 1933 to take a position of little influence, adviser to the Illinois National Guard, the army easily reverted to its conventional doctrine that the "primary mission" of all other weapons was "to facilitate the rifleman." Heavy armor, assigned to the infantry branch, would knock down obstacles. Light tanks were assigned to cavalry, the army's equivalent of naval aviation when it came to daring action. However, its mission was just reconnaissance. Few Americans thought tanks could make a breach, take a hit, and exploit the gap—all at the same time. The staff college at Fort Leavenworth said little about mechanized formations; a sure way to flunk tactics was to advocate a deep attack with exposed flanks on a narrow front.

"Armor is more than a branch. It is a state of mind," according to an old army adage. When Marshall became chief of staff in 1939, he did not have the time to change the army's frame of reference. Most of his energy went to mending political fences and expanding the army tenfold: "We were in a struggle for survival against the misunderstanding of our public and the failure of our Congress to resist criticism and the magazines who played up the men to desert." Issues like the pace of warfare became the province of the deputy chief of staff for ground forces, an old artillery officer who believed that blitzkrieg warfare was impossible without total surprise. Otherwise, heavy cannon in antitank units would kill armor when it tried to strike deep. With Lieutenant General Leslie McNair in charge of doctrine, training, and force structure, the army emphasized artillery

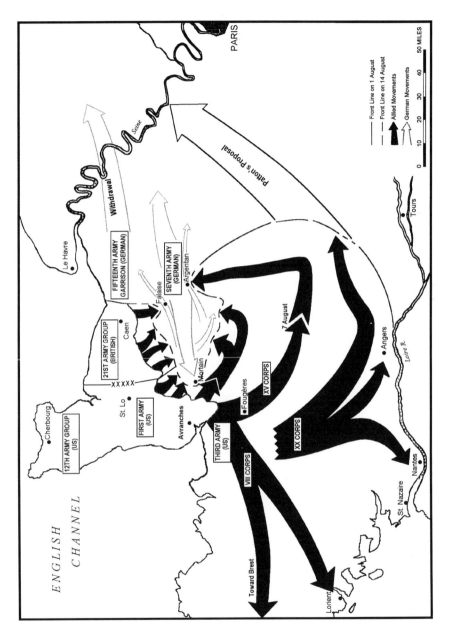

Normandy/the Falaise Gap, August–September 1944

rather than tanks and mobility. It continued to train to the pace and style of conventional infantry: advance five miles in three hours, dig in, and secure the flanks. Unfortunately, for the first six weeks in Normandy, the army moved nowhere near that fast.

An amphibious invasion must first get ashore. The Anglo-American command in the European theater spent so much time and effort on the issue of the landing that they barely considered what to do after securing a lodgment. The United States, which had the most men and firepower, landed in the worst possible place for maneuver, the thick hedgerow (or Bocage) area. The British Commonwealth forces, on the best terrain, lacked the equipment, reserves, and confidence to strike deep. Seven weeks after the invasion of 6 June, the Allies were occupying positions they expected to conquer in fifteen days. By late July the common nightmare was a resurrection of World War I—stalemate and trench warfare—but this time with the Allies just fifteen miles from being pushed back into the sea.

Between the world wars, Dwight Eisenhower, now supreme commander of Allied forces in northwest Europe, was one of the few infantrymen who believed that armor could conduct decisive "envelopments of, or breakthroughs in, whole defensive positions." In North Africa and Sicily, when the Allies simply pushed back the Axis, he seethed at accusations of undue caution. Now in Normandy, Ike told Omar Bradley, commander of the Twelfth Army Group, to "pursue every advantage with an ardor verging on recklessness." Bradley, more conventional and a former commandant at Benning, distinguished firepower from maneuver, far different from the blitzkrieg doctrine of deep attack. On 25 July, per his instructions, 1,500 heavy bombers dropped 4,400 tons of explosives on Germans occupying a key road junction. This sprang the VII Corps under "Lightning Joe" Collins to begin an exploitation that did not stop until the Allies outran their logistics near the German border on 15 September. (At D+100 the Allies were where they had expected to be on D+360.) By then, they were too tired, weak, and poorly supplied to smash through twenty German divisions that had established a new line of defense at the so-called West Wall. Rather than allowing most of them to escape from Normandy in August, far better to have surrounded the Germans after they committed the "greatest tactical blunder" Bradley could imagine.

Military orthodoxy suggested—and the Anglo-Americans predicted—that once they had secured their initial lodgment (ca. D+20), the enemy would withdraw and make the Allies cross a series of rivers under fire. Left alone in Normandy, the Allies would take three months to deploy at least thirty-five divisions, build up a mass logistic base, cross the Seine at D+90 in a set-piece operation, and then conduct a "showdown battle for Germany." Hitler, however, refusing to give up anything he had conquered, insisted that his armies drive deep between the Americans to the south and the Commonwealth forces on their north. The Allied high command, having broken the German military codes, read the orders to "attack recklessly to the sea" and barely believed their good fortune that the enemy was putting its neck in their noose. "This is an opportunity," Bradley said on 9 August, "that comes to a commander not more than once in a century. We're about to destroy an entire hostile army . . . [and] go all the way from here to the German border." Well, not quite.

Bradley seemed affected by the unspoken directive to the army after Bataan and the Kasserine Pass: Don't lose another battle; you (army Europe and army Pacific) already lost one each. Unable to free himself from worry about a counterattack and German forces in Brittany or south of the Loire River, Bradley could not make an unequivocal commitment to the option of George Patton, a critic of Leavenworth tactics for being "much too timid," too concerned with "moving supplies," and for ignoring what was really needed—"some means of making the infantry move under fire." (Without instructor permission, he added tanks to the school's tactical scenarios.) Patton may have been what Bradley later called him: "the strangest duck I have ever known." He might have been what Eisenhower said: "the finest leader in military pursuit the United States Army" ever had. Whether he was either one—or both—the old horse cavalryman was emphatic that the object of the Normandy campaign should not be a methodical buildup, especially when one might "surround and destroy the German army west of the Seine." Now that he had his chance to gain immortality by conducting "the fastest and biggest pursuit in history," Patton proposed crossing the river before 300,000 German soldiers could get to it. His own Third Army would have to make a deep penetration into unknown enemy territory while the First Army was holding off Germans twenty miles from the Atlantic. If they persevered, then the Axis (not the Allies) would have to cross the Seine under fire while other Allied units closed in from their rear. "We may end this in ten days," Patton wrote "but Bradley won't let me."

Patton admitted that "it is a little nerve-wracking to send troops straight into the middle of the enemy with front, flanks, and rear open," but he pumped himself up by recording in his diary, "Do not take counsel of your fears." His high-risk plan failed to provide much help for one of Bradley's major responsibilities, the safety of Americans who needed Patton to double back against two Panzer armies attacking due west. On the other hand, Bradley could not forget the golden opportunity to end German resistance on the western front. Falling between these two stools—or rather two envelopments: one deep, one shallow—he did neither with the requisite purpose, mass, strength, and speed. Patton, surrounded by what he derisively called "good doughboys," complained that "we oblige tanks to deploy in the manner of infantry." The commander of the XII Corps "has been thinking a mile a day good going. I told him to go fifty and he turned pale."

Because the U.S. Army could not move enough combat power to the critical place at the critical time, Bradley feared executing the short envelopment to close the Falaise pocket, let alone the deep one to the Seine. On 16 August he told Patton that nineteen enemy divisions were "beginning to pull out. You'd better button up and get ready for them," not head due north. He would explain: "I much pre-ferred a solid shoulder at Argentan to the possibility of a broken neck at Falaise." At the time, Patton wrote that Bradley's "motto seems to be, 'In case of doubt, halt.'"

According to his own intelligence reports, Bradley grossly overestimated the combat power of the enemy. After fighting two months without relief, the four Panzer divisions trying to escape the trap had 83 tanks and virtually no artillery. The XV Corps of the U.S. Army, digging in at Argentan, had 300 tanks, 416 heavy guns, and fire support from the air force in complete control of the sky. When it finally closed the gap on 19 August and ended the Normandy campaign, 10,000 more Germans were killed and 50,000 captured, along with hundreds of tanks, thousands of trucks, and tens of thousands of horses. Eisenhower said "it was literally possible to walk for hundreds of yards at a time, stepping on noth-ing but dead and decaying flesh." However, by then, some 240,000 Germans had crossed the Seine, largely unopposed. Once reequipped, they reconstituted the defense at the Siegfried line, forty-five miles from the German border, where the Allied advance ground to a halt in mid-September. For the next five months, fighting in terrible weather with limited supplies, the Americans waged a pro-longed infantry–artillery–attrition battle costing some 400,000 casualties. ("It had been our Passchendaele," recalled one division commander.) After the war finally ended in the spring, Patton, America's foremost armor officer, was reputed to have said: "I do not have to tell you who won the war. You know artillery did."

In March 1945 Bradley admitted that his failure to bag the German army was his biggest mistake of the war. The event was on his mind during the Korean War, when he was chairman of the JCS. When some 50,000 disorganized communist soldiers escaped the American envelopment at Inchon, Bradley concurred with a pursuit across the Thirty-eighth parallel, rather than take the risk that North Korea would reconstitute its army, as Germany did in late 1944. This action, ter-minating near the Yalu River, brought Communist China into the conflict. Then the Korean War, almost over in September, lasted another two and a half years. As Churchill said after World War II: we won't repeat our mistakes; we'll make brand-new ones.[10]

BACK IN THE PACIFIC: ANOTHER OPPORTUNITY NOT TAKEN

After Japan lost the Marianas in July 1944, operations officers in its army's gen-eral staff feared that America would head directly for the home islands, not pre-pared for attack at this time. They need not have worried. In Normandy, Omar Bradley won a tactical victory but failed to destroy the German army. At Saipan, Raymond Spruance permanently crippled Japan's naval aviation but failed to sink its surface fleet. George Marshall's two stipulations for bypassing the Philippines not being met, he was hesitant to head northwest despite warnings "that the American public will *not* support a lengthy war with Japan." In 1938 this same premise had driven Army War College students toward a swift victory strategy in their war games. When senior officers played the game for real in 1944, they were more cautious.

The army chief of staff would not fight for a high-risk strategy in the central Pacific, where the CNO was the "executive agent" of the JCS. Marshall was always wary of meddling in the navy's plans, lest interservice conflict invite civilian leadership to take a greater part in military business, something that "scared [him] to death." As for Ernie King and Charles "Savvy" Cooke, his assistant chief of staff for naval war plans, they were as concerned as any soldier that "the American people will weary of [the war] quickly and that pressure at home will force a negotiated peace before the Japs are really licked." Nonetheless, in the final analysis, they were creatures of military habit. As King pointed out repeatedly to gain support for his campaign strategy, the U.S. Navy had wargamed the conflict with Japan hundreds of times since 1906, always fighting across the central Pacific to the China–Formosa–Luzon triangle. King was not about to rethink what was carved into the corporate mind of the navy, least of all in the midst of a war, when naval staffs were primarily tasked with "the execution of current plans" and when King and Cooke had thousands of immediate problems on their minds, from defective torpedoes to Douglas MacArthur. Did it testify to prescience or inflexibility that Chester Nimitz said in 1965 that "nothing that happened in the Pacific [at the operational level] was strange or unexpected" to graduates of the Naval War College?

King's preference for Formosa was not diminished by the fact that Okinawa was a step closer to completing the ironclad blockade and was, in many ways, a less dangerous target. (Formosa had sixty-five Japanese air bases and was far too large for the navy to attack from any angle.) The Philippine alternative had military plausibility, especially for Nimitz, who agreed with the argument MacArthur had made ever since King kept aircraft carriers out of his hands, that landings supported by naval-based (rather than land-based) aviation were excessively hazardous. On 3 October the JCS directed MacArthur to take Luzon and Nimitz Okinawa, but only after the Philippines were secured, beginning with air bases at Leyte in its central island group. These orders, secured by Leahy, Roosevelt's "legman" to the Pentagon, formalized decisions made in July, when MacArthur convinced Nimitz at their conference with the president, King conspicuously absent. At the time, the CNO was inspecting the fleet at Pearl Harbor, a stone's throw from the meeting to which he was not invited, another Roosevelt stacked deck.

On 10 October, largely to mislead the Japanese about the target of the next American invasion, the navy raided Okinawa. With virtual impunity, U.S. carriers dropped 600 tons of explosives on ships, ports, and airfields. (A Japanese Pearl Harbor, seventy planes were destroyed on the ground.) The raid testified to the dispensability of land-based aviation for U.S. power projection, at least if it had the element of surprise. However, by this time it was too late to change the sequence of objectives in the western Pacific. Carriers withdrew from the Ryukyus to support the landings in the Philippines, a worse diversion from a decisive area than North Africa in 1942. Before they could return to Okinawa in April 1945, the enemy had six months to prepare caves, tunnels, and bunkers along every avenue of approach. The navy would have to do what it hated—hover around the battlefield, not shoot and scoot. Almost all the close air and fire support for American infantry came off naval platforms, forty aircraft carriers and eighteen battleships. There was virtually no ground-based aircraft launched from northern Luzon, where terrain was ill suited for airfields, something MacArthur failed to tell Nimitz in July 1944. During the final five months of action—in the Philippines, Iwo Jima, and Okinawa—America's armed forces suffered half the total casualties they would sustain in the entire Pacific war. (One lesson learned: attach a grave registration platoon to each infantry regiment lest the latter spend all its time evacuating its dead.) This statistic seemed to prove what Marine Corps planners said back in 1937: "'Playing safe' by venturing too little may end in greater loss than that resulting from a bold stroke with its chances of strategic surprise and its effect on enemy morale."

King, Cook, Marshall, and Bradley chose to avoid tactical risks associated with a 1,400-mile leap to Okinawa or a 100-mile drive to the Seine. In the process, the protraction of the war confronted them with what Marshall called "a general let-down" and its "effect of public reaction on [military] morale." When push came to shove, even politically astute flag officers prioritized short-term military issues. One would be surprised if they had assumed the president's ultimate responsibility, that of maintaining public support. Unfortunately, because they conformed to their job description as military men, the domestic morale problem came to the fore after Germany surrendered in May 1945.

War-weariness was rapidly growing inside the United States, not to mention in the elite military units. The Marine Corps sustained 26,000 cases of combat fatigue at Okinawa, including 1,000 infantry shell-shocked after assaulting one Japanese strongpoint. "The grinding stress of prolonged heavy combat," one marine later said, was "enough to make us drop in our tracks. How we kept going and continued fighting I'll never know," especially with no light visible at the end of the tunnel. "Even if I live through it, what next, the great battle of the Japanese mainland?"[11]

UNCONDITIONAL SURRENDER, DEMOBILIZATION, AND THE ATOMIC BOMB

Having witnessed the demand for instantaneous demobilization after Germany signed an armistice in World War I, George Marshall had long been expecting a sharp reduction in American morale. This indelible memory of November 1918 shaped his resolve to minimize responsibilities after the Nazi defeat. In Europe this meant no operations in the eastern Mediterranean, where internal instability might require a long-term occupation by an army about to be dramatically reduced. In the Pacific it meant beating down Japan to a position where its surrender would occur shortly after V-E Day. Otherwise, there might not be a capitulation at all, something Marshall predicted in 1943: "The collapse of Germany would impose partial demobilization and a growing impatience . . . throughout the United States." This mood could lead to a compromise settlement along the lines the Japanese army was hoping to obtain: retention of its core empire (Formosa, Manchuria, and Korea) and no change in the political institutions of Imperial Japan.

Considering the enormous perplexities of war, America's military timing was extraordinarily good. By the time Germany surrendered, the United States had made what Marshall called the "preparation for the final kill." Its armed forces surrounded the home islands of Japan from the south and east. The United States had also obtained a pledge from the Soviet Union to attack the Imperial army in Korea and Manchuria, thereby completing the ironclad blockade. However, the denial of imports of strategic items from oil to coal and protein did not mean that a mere mop-up operation was in the works. The U.S. military, especially the army, planned on the premise "that defeat of the enemy's armed forces in the Japanese homeland is a prerequisite to unconditional surrender." Even before Japan strongly reinforced Kyushu, the first home island to be invaded, American officers made an "educated guess" that the cost of conducting what were foreseen as the toughest landings and follow-up battles in World War II would be somewhere between 200,000 and 1 million casualties, one-fourth of them fatalities. As the secretary of war recorded in his diary, "Once started in [an] actual invasion, we shall in my opinion have to go through with an even more bitter fight to the finish than in Germany."

Admiral Leahy would later complain that "the Army did not appear to be able to understand that the Navy, with some Army air assistance, already had defeated Japan." Pity the U.S. Navy could not surrender to the U.S. government on behalf of the Japanese army. The latter did not feel it had already lost, at least by the standard of unconditional surrender, completely foreign to an institution whose code forbade surrender of any kind unless approved by the emperor himself. (The U.S. psychological warfare campaign was using the phrase "cease resistance.") Annapolis alumni seemed to think of war as a venture to liquidate if the costs became too great. The Japanese army thought of style and values perpetuated by military means. It was still relying on what one of its officers called "suicidal bravery, ardent patriotism, and fierce loyalty" to protect "the sacred soil of the homeland."

Admiral King would write that the navy "in the course of time would have starved the Japanese into submission." Time, however, was a waning asset, especially to Marshall, who would later say that American "political and economic institutions melted out from under us" in 1945. The Office of War Mobilization and Reconversion confirmed what the media had been saying since late 1944: that a "national end-of-the-war psychology" insisted on the immediate resumption of production of consumer goods. Tacitly recognizing that war-weariness had reached epidemic proportions, a chorus of newspapers and government officials warned, as did the *St. Louis Post-Dispatch,* that "there is only one road to Japan's total defeat—a long, hard road necessarily marked by death." Far less public, military intelligence briefed the JCS that total victory through a standoff strategy of encirclement, blockade, and bombardment might well take "a great many years."

Reasonably sane people prefer to avoid amphibious invasions against fortified beaches. Before the invasions, Marshall spent days in a cold sweat over "the awfulness of the consequences that could occur should one of these go wrong." Nonetheless, he thought no "temporizing measure" could defeat "the last ditch tactics of the suicidal Japanese." The Imperial armed forces—along with the emperor—would have welcomed his conclusion that only an invasion would suffice. Looking for an opportunity to redeem a string of humiliating defeats back to Midway, they could now "smash the inordinate ambitions of the enemy nations" on a battlefield of their choosing. Japan had lost the air and naval capacity to fight off a blockade, but it had used Okinawa to buy time for its soldiers to carve out an interconnected "mass of caves" on terrain the U.S. Army deemed "unsuited for large-scale mobile warfare." With this scenario of infantry versus infantry, America might have abandoned its demand for unconditional surrender or substantially augmented its military means. It did neither, aside from work on a secret weapon yet to be tested in New Mexico.

Unconditional surrender, more a battle cry than a statement of political objectives, had two competing definitions, when it had any clear definition at all. The first one did "not mean absence of terms," said a Judge Advocate lawyer, "but whatever terms are imposed do not result from a bargain or a barter with the enemy." The victor laid down all conditions. For the vanquished, those conditions were unconditional. According to the second, surrender was "not subject to conditions or limitations." The victor had absolute freedom because the vanquished "is actually signing a 'blank check'" with "no contractual elements whatever."

The armed forces and career diplomats preferred the first definition, as did Republican politicians and newspapers, such as the *Chicago Tribune,* along with certain religion-based publications, such as the *Christian Century* and the *Catholic World.* Other publications, from the *New York Times* to the *Daily Worker,* used the second definition, as did political appointees in the State Department and southern Democrats. As for Franklin Roosevelt, he did what he typically did; he chose both options and selectively used them as he saw fit. For Germany he preferred no specifications, despite requests from Stalin, Churchill, and his JCS that he define concrete terms. As for Japan, Roosevelt wanted no negotiations that could alter the terms he specified, the same policy Wilson took toward Germany in 1918, certainly not considered unconditional surrender at the end of World War I. This distinction was hardly popular for treating Japan more leniently than its European ally. Consequently, the president was opaque, as in his pointless reference to Grant's conversation with Lee at the end of the Civil War: "'Take the animals home and do the spring plowing.' . . . That is what we mean by unconditional surrender."

So-called clarifications like this mystified the Japanese as much as they did most Americans. They consequently thought U.S. policy toward Germany foretold the position toward them (both were called "unconditional surrender"). It did not clearly move in that direction until FDR died in April 1945. At the Cairo Conference (November 1943), the communiqué drafted by Harry Hopkins, at Roosevelt's instruction, made the obligatory demand for unconditional surrender. Then it set specific stipulations consistent with a series of position papers drafted by State Department professionals and Asia specialists. None of the points were draconian compared with those directed at Germany. Japan was to be "stripped of all" its overseas conquests in order to isolate a nation Roosevelt believed was genetically disposed toward lawless violence. The communiqué said nothing about an invasion, which certainly was not inadvertent. Roosevelt wanted China to conduct the postwar occupation of Japan, but its leader, Chiang Kai-shek, about to face a civil war, deferred the duty back to the United States. He and Roosevelt then agreed "that as soon as Japan's military power has been broken, the Japanese in Japan proper would be permitted to work out their own destiny without outside direction." In short, there would be no occupation, let alone transformation of a society such as Roosevelt planned for Germany, where a generation was to be fed from U.S. army trucks so that they would learn how badly they were beaten. Hence, at Tehran in December, Roosevelt and Stalin agreed that the Allies would only control "islands in the vicinity of Japan." That alone, they hoped, would deter a renewed "course of aggression."

For once, America's political objectives were perfectly consistent with the military means available in late 1943. Over objections from Admiral King, who still hoped for a major naval base in continental Asia, Roosevelt quashed new operations in the China–Burma–India (CBI) theater, lest they divert soldiers and landing craft from the invasion of Europe. CBI became a backwater campaign, such as Italy after D day. With most ground forces now committed to France, a reasonable military strategy was to win the war against Japan from the sea and the air. This could force an "ultimate surrender," provided terms were not too harsh. They were hardly sufficient for what Allied planners later called the "absolute military control of Japan" itself. It was no accident that the top brass of the navy—Leahy, King, and Nimitz—all spoke against unconditional surrender. That implied a protracted occupation, which only the army could provide.

After Franklin Roosevelt died on 12 April the new president, Harry S. Truman, spoke to his military advisers about "preventing an Okinawa from one end of Japan to the other"—something that could kill 500,000 Americans, "the flower of our young manhood." His fear is not surprising considering the last time the new commander in chief commanded any combat soldiers. In the fall of 1918, outnumbered Germans were supposed to be on their last legs in the Meuse-Argonne offensive when they killed or wounded almost half the soldiers in Truman's Thirty-fifth Infantry Division. Twenty years later, the former army captain vividly recalled a "pile of [dead] American soldiers in all sorts of ghastly positions" and an old, hard-boiled sergeant who yelled at Truman's battery: "Now you sons of bitches, you'll believe you're in a war."

To mitigate the casualties, the secretary and assistant secretary of war, Henry Stimson and John McCloy, advised Truman to settle for "the equivalent of unconditional surrender," that is, remove the phrase that inflicted a great "loss of face" but still accomplish the "vital war objective of preventing Japan from again becoming a menace to world peace." This meant the transformation and retention of the emperor as "a constitutional monarch." Like most other people in the government who thought there was a viable alternative to ever greater bloodletting, Stimson believed Hirohito was a passive witness in a political system "under the complete dominance of the Japanese Army" since the 1930s.

Unbeknownst to Stimson, a self-described "kindly-minded Christian gentleman," the emperor was actually an active participant in Japan's military-political complex. The War Department, ignorant of his complicity, hoped not to have to govern the island "in any such matter as we are committed in Germany." Its wish to use the emperor to "lessen resistance by those Japanese who would accept Imperial commands" got a new lease on life in Truman's first speech on war aims, when he asked for "unconditional surrender" solely from the Japanese military. The War Department not only felt itself already too involved in European government, reform, and relief but also wondered whether America had the perseverance to carry on the war. Since December 1944, Stimson had bewailed the fact that "our noble people" had even failed their quotas for scrap paper and victory gardens. "They have no more notion that they are in a war [where] sacrifices are needed—just so many children," he told George Marshall. However, what Stimson perceived in the civilian population was nothing compared with what he saw in army units redeploying from Europe to the Pacific: "These men were weary in a way that no one merely reading reports could readily understand."

Marshall's own recommendation about unconditional surrender was a bit more subtle than that of civilians in the War Department. He advised Stimson and Truman to change its "precise terminology" into "something which might be psychologically more conducive to the earliest defeat of Japan." Nonetheless, he wanted to retain "the phraseology" (implicit recognition that it was a war cry), because a new slogan would send the wrong signal to Americans, Russians, and Japanese. U.S. soldiers and the public might abandon "the firm determination" to fight, the Soviets might withhold "cooperation against Japan," and the enemy might get the "impression that we are growing soft." This, in particular, had to be avoided because it was absolutely true.

Japan, the side that was losing the war, seemed to suffer no such problem. Despite "increasing devastation," it appeared prepared to mount a "more desperate and bitter resistance." According to Marshall: "We had to assume that a force of 2.5 million Japanese would fight to the death as they did on all those islands we attacked. . . . Despite what [air force] generals had to say about bombing the Japanese into submission, we killed 100,000 in one raid in one night, but it didn't mean a thing."

Japan's Supreme War Council, like the U.S. Army, "did not believe that Japan could be defeated by air attack alone." To counter the prospective invasion, it prepared 12,725 kamikazes to destroy 30 to 40 percent of the troop and supply transports right off Japan. (The primary freighters, LSTs, were short for landing ship tanks—or "large, slow targets," said those who sailed them.) Cliffs and hills would foil radar and visual warning, precisely what ships need against airplanes. The American army prepared for thousands of caves manned by "determined and fanatical [soldiers] whom we would have to exterminate, almost man by man." To prevent the campaign from becoming another Okinawa, where bayoneted rifles were the ultimate weapon, Marshall was in the process of introducing a host of old and new equipment—body armor, a "super flamethrower," poison gas, and tactical nuclear weapons.

Some JCS elements wanted to use "all-out gas warfare" as a strategic weapon to "bring home with great force to the Japanese the hopelessness of continuing the war." Marshall, while hoping this could convince Japan that it faced "extermination," primarily thought of using gas to sicken soldiers who manned underground fortifications. Planners not privy to the Manhattan Project called gas "the single weapon hitherto unused which assuredly can decrease the cost in American lives." Marshall, better informed, also planned to use the atomic bomb. It was "a wonderful [tactical] weapon [to] protect and prepare for landings" by hitting communications and divisions in reserve. These "straight military objectives" were morally preferable to targeting cities with a weapon of such "primordial considerations" that Marshall lost his legendary self-control. He went into John McCloy's office rubbing his hands in agitation and saying, "Please don't let them ask me whether or not we should drop the atomic bomb on Japan. That's just not a military question."

One more military way to avoid a "fight to the death" was Marshall's idea to proceed directly to the Tokyo plain now that Japan had stripped Honshu of assets to build up Kyushu, where up to 900,000 combatants (ten times as many as fought on Okinawa) would hold prepared defensive positions stocked with food and ammunition. Whereas the Germans were deceived about Normandy, Japanese military intelligence predicted the exact locations, nearly the exact date, and the division strength of the invasion shortly before Douglas MacArthur presented his plan. He heretofore had leaped no farther than the range of the army air force, a tendency now known to the enemy. "There should not be the slightest thought," MacArthur told Marshall, "of changing the [Kyushu] operation. Its fundamental purpose is to obtain air bases under cover of which we can deploy our forces into the industrial heart of Japan."

The Inchon operation in Korea (September 1950) attests to MacArthur's willingness to run risks as great as a long leap to Honshu, provided they furthered his agenda. In Korea that was the rollback of communism. In World War II it was the assumption of supreme command of all military forces in the Pacific theater. The navy had not and would not consent to that appointment, but at least as far as Kyushu was concerned, the JCS had given MacArthur an important concession. In other invasions in the central Pacific theater, the senior army officer assumed direction when troops hit the ground. For Kyushu, MacArthur had "primary responsibility for the conduct of [the] operation including control, in case of exigencies, of the actual amphibious assault." Granted, it was not the supreme command of all elements that Eisenhower had for Normandy, but it did provide a leg up on Nimitz and the navy by giving MacArthur ultimate authority over 1,300 troop transports, cargo vessels, and landing craft. If the invasion of Kyushu were scrubbed in favor of Honshu, the issue of command would be reopened, this time in an area of operations beyond the range of MacArthur's ground-based air force. Carriers would have to provide virtually all close air support and interdiction over the beaches, as they had done on Okinawa. This would give the navy a new chance to gain control of the next amphibious assault, which would be the single most important event in the campaign for Japan. Unless that new guy in the White House was already willing to cross MacArthur, the army was heading straight into the guns of Japan.[12]

Neither tactics nor technology encouraged Henry Stimson to doubt America faced a "score of bloody Iwo Jimas and Okinawas" unless it softened its political stance. Most career diplomats and east Asia experts would agree. Led by Under Secretary of State Joseph Grew, a former ambassador to Japan, they opposed what they called "a strict" or "rigid interpretation" of unconditional surrender and had "no idea of interfering with the form of the government of Japan." They wanted to state specific demands and retain Hirohito as the "de jure sovereign." Then the Japanese people could be induced to obey the emperor's directive for cooperation. For protection from media charges of appeasement, Grew was associating his policy with that of the navy's high command, impressive in some quarters but hardly convincing to the State Department's political appointees.

James F. Byrnes, Archibald MacLeish, and Dean Acheson—secretary of state and the assistant secretaries for public affairs and congressional relations— led the effort to create "a surrender policy for Japan consistent with surrender policy for Germany." Each had his own reason for their common position. Byrnes, known as "the assistant president" when heading war mobilization for Roosevelt, looked upon Truman as a temporary caretaker who could kill a Byrnes presidency with a grossly unpopular decision such as retaining Hirohito. MacLeish, a Pulitzer Prize–winning poet with no political ambition, felt the institution of the emperor was "the basis for much of the beastly behavior of the

Japanese." This zealous New Dealer on domestic issues and Wilsonian in foreign policy had hoped to make World War II a crusade for everything from public health to world disarmament. Sorely disappointed, he bitterly complained about "the tragic outlook of all liberal proposals, the collapse of all liberal leadership, and the inevitable defeat of all liberal aims." The reformation of Japan was his last chance to get the type of peace "which alone will justify this war."

Acheson—no politician, New Dealer, or Wilsonian—had never made policy distinctions between Japan and Germany. In mid-1941, when Roosevelt, Grew, and the armed forces hoped to "reach a *modus vivendi* with Japan" in order to concentrate on the Nazis, Acheson pushed the rest of the administration toward freezing all trade with all Axis nations. The oil embargo he initiated that August, when assistant secretary of state for economic affairs, "caused the Japs to decide to go to war," he said in 1950. In mid-1945, arguing with Grew, the so-called Prince of Appeasers, Acheson said that if the emperor were not important to the militarists, who fought in his name and for his honor, why should "the military element in Japan be so insistent on retaining the Emperor"?

There was far more consensus within the American public than there was within the State Department or the Truman administration. From late February through June, opinion polls sent directly to the White House and printed on the front page of the *Washington Post* repeatedly stated that only 10 to 18 percent approved "working out peace terms" with Japan. Three percent favored governing the island through the present dynasty. Thirty-three percent wanted to execute Hirohito, 11 percent wanted imprisonment, 9 percent wanted banishment, and 17 percent wanted him tried. Presumably, he would then be hung in accordance with a court of law.

Editorials in the *Post* inspired by the navy were almost the only body of opinion in Washington to challenge unconditional surrender in a public forum. Even that was more style than substance. The same day the paper published a front-page story claiming that Japan sought a "conditional surrender" (the liquidation of its empire in return for no postwar occupation), the editorial page attacked the Cairo communiqué. It said that old policy merely pared Japan "down to its volcanic core"; America had to "clearly recognize the necessity of stamping out militarism *in* Japan" (italics mine). But whether the specific terms of a conditional surrender were strong or weak, could Truman's first major act as president, thanks to a cerebral hemorrhage, be the repudiation of the war cry of the man whom he dutifully called "the greatest of our war Presidents"? Unlike the *Post,* the former vice president could hardly say: "What we are suggesting, to be sure, is conditional surrender. What of it?"

Truman hung Roosevelt's picture on his White House office wall, as Roosevelt had hung one of Woodrow Wilson and Marshall one of John J. Pershing. He told one confidant, "I haven't been elected president. . . . I'm going to try to follow Roosevelt's policies as much as possible." Truman should have said that he would follow his predecessor's policies as he best understood them because he privately admitted he never had a conversation "about the war, or about foreign affairs, or what [Roosevelt] had in mind for peace after the war." When Truman entered the White House, a heated confrontation was in the making with Russia about the implementation of agreements concerning Poland. He spent days laboriously going over the record of the Yalta Conference, since every time he read the ambiguous accords he "found new meanings in them." One doubts Truman ever looked at the Cairo communiqué.

No one is more devoted to a dead president's slogans than his former understudy. When Truman met the JCS and military service secretaries in June 1945, he said that "he did not feel that he could take any action at this time to change public opinion" about unconditional surrender. He had already addressed a joint session of Congress three days after he took office, asserting that "the vision of our departed Commander in Chief . . . must and will remain unchanged and unhampered!" ("Unconditional surrender" was the main applause line.) He was advised by Byrnes and Roosevelt's secretary of state, men who presumably knew what Roosevelt had in mind, that anything other than unconditional surrender would seem "too much like appeasement of Japan." That would produce "terrible political repercussions in the United States" and lead to the "crucifixion of the President."

Up until the Potsdam Conference in late July between Truman, Churchill, and Stalin, the administration was still not committed "to any particular definition of unconditional surrender," according to a civilian in the War Department. That the president assigned John McCloy to write a policy statement indicates that he was leaning in the direction of Stimson, Marshall, and the army. However, once Byrnes got hold of the Potsdam Proclamation, its final draft was a compromise: too strong for the soldiers and career diplomats but too weak for the political appointees who controlled State Department policy. Truman rejected the position of MacLeish, who said that the enemy's propaganda ministry would use any terms whatsoever to claim "war-weary" America was about "to call off the Japanese war." The official government statement demanded unconditional surrender solely from "the Japanese armed forces," as had Truman since 8 May. The State Department, which lost the intraagency tug-of-war on this particular issue, would have included "the emperor, the government, and the people." As for the crucial debate about postwar occupation, the proclamation went beyond the Pentagon but fell short of State: only "points in Japanese territory" (not the entire nation) were to be occupied. "The terms of the Cairo Declaration," which limited "Japanese sovereignty" to its home islands, were officially superseded. Potsdam demanded "a new [political] order" ensured by a "stern justice [for] all war criminals." However, those "war criminals" might simply be the military men who broke "the laws of war" in the field of operations.

The Potsdam Proclamation retained substantial ambiguity, to the consternation of the State Department, which warned that vague terms, under international law, are "interpreted favorably to the state which accepts them." It said nothing about the emperor and his dynasty. Paragraph 7 insisted that "the authority and influence of those who have misled the people of Japan . . . must be eliminated for all time." Who they were was not specified—one could read Hirohito in or out. The U.S. government was deliberately vague; it had not made up its own mind. The State Department wanted to "take over the government of Japan." The War Department merely wanted to influence "the political action of the enemy government" to be retained to enable a small force to occupy Japan.

Whatever way it was interpreted, the proclamation failed its function, according to the JCS—that is, "to induce Japan's surrender and thus avoid the heavy casualties implied in a fight to the finish." It did not help the peace faction, primarily in the foreign ministry. Stimson and Grew felt that this "Dr. Jekyll" element represented "a large submerged class of Japan who did not favor the present war." Supposedly, defeat had discredited the militarists, the "Mr. Hyde" Japan; "it is not a nation composed wholly of mad fanatics." In fact, the doves were a small body of wealthy men who lived in fear of American military destruction, a communist revolution produced by prolonged war, and assassination by the Imperial army, never friendly to big business. If they were to end the conflict, they would need to be able to convince others that they could negotiate what the armed forces called "peace with honor." This phrase, later used by America in the Vietnam War, was defined by Japan as "the protection of the fundamental character of our government."

At most, unnamed parties hinted through Sweden that although there would be no discussion of "the Japanese constitution . . . the Imperial power could be *somewhat* democratized" (italics mine). This was hardly satisfactory, in either form or substance. Even Joe Grew, "hoodwinked" by Hirohito, according to widely read newspapermen, took a firm public stance that unconditional surrender meant "termination of the influence of the military leaders," words written for him by MacLeish. Under these circumstances, according to Japanese officers, diplomats, and the minister of foreign affairs, "it was taboo for us to speak about the problem of peace," let alone compose terms "in any concrete form." As long as America "continues to insist on the formality of unconditional surrender . . . our country and His Majesty would unanimously resolve to fight a war of resistance to the bitter end."

America's premier hawks were also disappointed. They perched in the southern bloc of the U.S. Senate, a substantial role reversal from World War I, when Republicans and the U.S. Army were proponents of unconditional surrender while Wilsonians (such as McLeish) and southern Democrats were its leading opponents. Robert Taft, a conservative Republican from Ohio, cited Wilson's Fourteen Points on the Senate floor. The Republican minority leader from Maine and the whip from Nebraska proposed terms similar to the Cairo communiqué, now acceptable to Japan. Meanwhile, Alben Barkley, the majority leader from Kentucky, and Richard Russell from Georgia opposed any terms at all, no matter what the American army wanted. Yankee military units tramping through the

South in 1864 had destroyed the Russell family textile factory. Historical memory apparently convinced him that national security meant overwhelming force. He once told a Republican colleague, "You'd be more military minded too if Sherman had crossed North Dakota."

Like many other southerners, Russell carried a grudge against the army but loved the navy, which he loyally supported on the Naval Affairs Committee. In 1945, when Russell noted that the War Department "has never taken [the] Pacific very seriously," he was not impressed by what was called a "high military authority" who petitioned Truman to retain the emperor and forgo occupation of Japan. Like Sherman, permanently emblazoned on his mind, Russell would have made war unmitigated hell so that the vanquished would never challenge the victor. He told the Senate—and wired Truman at Potsdam—that leniency would only repeat the mistake made in World War I, when "weak and half-hearted methods" cost America a "golden age of permanent peace." The conflict should be carried on "until every Japanese is as firmly convinced as are the people of Germany that they have really lost this war completely." In short, they should be "brought groveling to their knees," begging "us to accept their unconditional surrender."

The American public backed Russell's hard-line policy with their words but not their blood and treasure. It insisted on fighting until we have "completely beaten [the enemy] on the Japanese homeland" (84 percent approval). It also required release from economic rationing as well as at least partial demobilization from the day Germany surrendered (72 percent approval; the rest wanted something greater than "partial"). Truman would recall that "Congress and Mamma and Papa put such pressure on us that the discharges were much faster than they should have been." The under secretary of war warned that "we must prepare ourselves to win our war with Japan the hard way—by killing Japanese soldiers right through the ruins of Tokyo." Oblivious, the citizenry forced the War Department to release 450,000 soldiers from ground combat units at the very time the army was replacing the navy as the primary service in the Pacific theater. Experienced and decorated infantry, whom George Marshall called "the first team," were the first to leave; Medal of Honor winners were discharged upon request. Next came the men who "make a unit dependable in battle"—the seasoned noncommissioned officers who "make the wheels go." Veterans with not quite enough service to be released were now on "short time," the limited tours typical of Korea and Vietnam. Henceforth, GIs lost their major motivation. They had to put in a few more months, not win the war, to go home. They would certainly be reluctant to come to grips with an enemy who did not surrender under any circumstances.

Fearful of a postwar public backlash against the army, the War Department devised its system for demobilization with maximum input from "the soldiers themselves," as deduced by thirty statisticians who had been sampling opinion since 1943. Its priorities certainly reflected civilian values, no small issue to a military that had responded to critics of "militarism" by claiming compatibility with American society. Now, individuals "who have earned the right to leave through long and dangerous service overseas" would have the "first chance at a civilian job," quite important because of the fear peace would reintroduce the Great Depression only ended by mass expenditures for World War II. However, this plan took place at the expense of military capability. The army had begun to treat GIs as a constituency, not a military means, wherein their lives, let alone their convenience, were "nothing more than tools to be used in the accomplishment of the mission." As war planners had long feared, demobilization occurred "regardless of the effect on the prosecution of the Japanese war." It also took place without satisfying Congress, which said its "mail on the subject was growing daily" and the army must "reduce its size immediately by [another] 1,000,000 men."

George Marshall later said that "demobilization could only be done with reasonable justice on the basis of the individual, and not on that of the units." Whole divisions were gutted and "made almost unfit for combat," no matter what responsibilities they had at the time. In the Pacific, rifle companies fighting Japanese infantry in northern Luzon lost their combat-experienced leadership lest the whole theater suffer morale problems. Washington feared a reaction if veterans of Europe received preferential treatment vis-à-vis those who had fought longer, in the most austere conditions, "while feeling that they were still being considered a relatively unimportant part of the world war." In Europe, combat readiness was even worse. The Forty-fifth Infantry Division, scheduled to invade Honshu in 1946, lost all its artillery officer corps, save the commander himself. Eisenhower said it would take at least six months of training for European theater divisions, designated for the Pacific, to be ready to fight Japan.

Compared with morale and motivation, training was a minor issue. Mere "efficiency" dropped in the Pacific. Divisions in the European theater of operations (ETO) approached mutiny, even the elite. General Maxwell Taylor tried "to stir up enthusiasm for new worlds to conquer" in the 101st Airborne, one of two army divisions to have won a Presidential Unit Citation. "We've licked the best that Hitler had in France and Holland and Germany. Now where do we want to go?" The heroes of Normandy, Eindhoven, and Bastogne screamed "home." Commanders of lesser divisions spoke of "a very disturbing situation approaching open sedition," a problem now before the commander in chief. Truman gave all ETO soldiers passing through America thirty-day furloughs to "have the best time [they] know how." To no avail, he still wrote Marshall that protest over redeployment "is cause for disciplinary action."

Congress might have replaced rebellious veterans with eager young men, such as those who made great marines, but it proscribed assigning eighteen-year-olds to army combat units without six more months of training. This virtually stopped new infantry from reconstituting old divisions, as MacArthur complained to Marshall. The former said he might have to delay the invasion of Kyushu until 1946, a nightmare scenario for the army chief of staff who feared military policy would become a partisan issue in an off-year election—repudiating the president and creating a divided government in the midst of a world war, per Wilson and Lodge in 1918. But, unable to fight the flow of events, Marshall admitted he was desperately trying to keep "one step ahead of public opinion," Congress, and the press. He did not have many options. In the American governmental system, a desperate appeal to preserve combat capability could not be kept confidential. It would do what military intelligence feared: confirm the Japanese army's argument that it could still "stave off defeat" because of "war weariness in the United States."

In summary, America's goal was "the early unconditional surrender of Japan" and a "rigid interpretation" of the declaration. Its methods included demobilization of those combat soldiers able to conduct assaults on fortified positions. On more open terrain, mediocre infantry could call on artillery and close air support to clear obstacles in its path. More difficult and demanding methods were now required. Ground reconnaissance would have to precede suppressive fire from naval guns to light mortars, all working to get tanks and flamethrowers into position to shoot down the mouth and close up a cave. Each situation would be different, depending on everything from the enemy position on a slope to the precise gradient of the hill. This was certainly not the time or the place for on-the-job training, but as Marshall told Eisenhower in March, "Making war in a democracy is not a bed of roses."

America, like a Greek drama, needed a deus ex machina to solve its dilemma on open display before Japan, whose intelligence stated that partial demobilization and industrial reconversion aroused so much optimism "for an early termination of the war" that heavy casualties would immediately "decrease fighting morale among the [American] people and the military." With U.S. resolve so brittle, the Japanese army reasoned that a climactic battle on the beaches would force it to make a compromise peace. That was the strategic setting on 6 August, when one specially modified B-29 took off from the Marianas to test the JCS assumption that, the Imperial army notwithstanding, Japan "as a whole is not pre-disposed toward national suicide."

On 10 August, after America dropped the only other atomic bomb in its arsenal but warned of "a rain of ruin from the air, the like of which has never been seen on this earth," the emperor overruled the army, which still had 2.35 million men under arms inside Japan, having not yet suffered the massive devastation inflicted on the air force and the navy. In fact, the Japanese army had recently sneered at its erstwhile Axis ally for surrendering when some 2.5 million Russians fought their way through Berlin. Pleading for the chance to "find life in death," it maintained that "if we are prepared to sacrifice 20,000,000 Japanese lives in a special attack [kamikaze] effort, victory shall be ours!"

Hiroshima turned out to be the military's face-saving device, even more efficacious than an abrogation of "unconditional surrender" by the United States. The emperor could now capitulate without challenging the valor of the army; one member of the peace faction would tell an American interrogator that the atomic bomb "was a good excuse." More typical citizens would still tell American reporters that the United States never "would have dared attempt a seaborne invasion," a statement that made Richard Russell absolutely livid.

Prisoners of war, interrogated by captors in search of any information about atomic bombs, had said that America had 100 stockpiled. Lest the "whole nation be reduced to ashes" by this nonexistent arsenal, the government accepted the Potsdam Proclamation on "the understanding that [it] does not comprise any demand which prejudices the prerogatives of His Majesty as a Sovereign Ruler." Allied terms actually assured "sovereignty" to the Japanese nation, not the dynasty. The rulers of the island were insisting (as one Japanese diplomat confirmed) that there would be no change in the political institutions of Imperial Japan, even if no Japanese empire remained to be ruled. They were accepting, twenty months too late, the sole demand of the Cairo Conference for the liquidation of all overseas possessions. By now this was "conditional surrender," according to NBC radio news.

In reply, Truman issued another carefully drawn compromise between the doves in the War Department, who thought "the Emperor was a minor matter," and the hawks at State, who wanted his head. He did not demand Hirohito's abdication or expressly guarantee the existence of the throne. He only specified that the government would "be subject to the Supreme Commander of the Allied Powers," thereby enabling the army to rule Japan through the Japanese. Truman's conditions were nonnegotiable, no matter how Hirohito saved face by proclaiming a "cessation of hostilities" because "the war situation has developed not necessarily to Japan's advantage." Truman, for his part, could maintain that there "is no qualification" and that "the warlords of Japan and the Japanese armed forces have surrendered unconditionally." He probably crossed his fingers and hoped that the more hawkish elements in America would agree. Until then, the country had not conclusively decided how to define unconditional surrender (whether "no contractual elements" was more important than "not subject to conditions") and whether to execute the emperor.

The president was happy to end the war on the basis of this exchange with Japan. This proud former artillery officer had no qualms about tactical nuclear weapons that enhanced the combat power of his old military branch. "A half dozen batteries with atomic explosives can wipe out an entire front on the other side," but "I never had a happy feeling," he later confessed, "about killing noncombatants by dropping a bomb. . . . That would have been murder." Truman fed himself a fable that "soldiers and sailors are the target, not women and children." In fact, according to Stimson, the bomb was dropped to "administer a tremendous shock which would carry convincing proof of our power to destroy the [entire] Empire." Hirohito, the cardboard warrior on the receiving end, was not the only one to suffer vicarious bomb shock. Truman complained of dreadful headaches and went around mumbling that he could not stand wiping out more cities and killing "all those kids."

Elements of the U.S. government still insisted on hard-core versions of unconditional surrender. The American embassy in Tokyo forwarded Hirohito's name on a list of individuals to face military trial—that is, before the War Department terminated the process and perhaps the career of the unnamed foreign service officer responsible for the action. Senator Russell, trying to take the issue out of the hands of the executive branch, introduced a bill that would force the government to try the emperor as a war criminal. Supported on the Senate floor by the Democratic left and the southern right, the bill died in committee from general neglect, much the way the heartfelt demand for hanging Jefferson Davis rapidly subsided after the Civil War. Most of the American people were simply too tired and too grateful for having avoided an invasion and a hostile occupation. They did not pay sustained attention to the retention of Hirohito and the possibility that they might not have won the war exactly as the president said they did. Truman must have been relieved, for he had risked his political career. The JCS were not surprised. They spent the war worrying that public will would be exhausted short of achieving unconditional surrender. Perhaps it had, although no one would admit it.[13]

THE POLITICS OF THE SURRENDER CEREMONY

The last item of business was the formal ceremony in which the Japanese would read a script written by the U.S. State Department: "We hereby proclaim the unconditional surrender to the Allied Powers." America had fought the entire war without a supreme commander in the Pacific theater. The navy and the army could not agree; the president would not make them. However, if a committee were to govern Japan, the Soviet Union would demand at least as much authority as any single American military service. Hence the president finally nominated MacArthur as supreme commander *for* (not *of*) the United Nations, a distinction that enabled Truman to designate Chester Nimitz to represent America at the surrender MacArthur conducted. To have it "take place on American soil," the president chose the battleship *Missouri,* which he had dedicated by saying, "Missouri is the 'Show me' state," and this "will show all the world the invincible power of the United States Navy."

In spite of orders from the supreme commander to remain anchored at Tokyo Bay, a hasty naval launch beat an airborne division about to be dropped on enemy soil. ("Our first wave," said a marine, "was made up entirely of admirals trying to get ashore before MacArthur.") Naval aviators swooped down on Japanese runways to brag about which air service landed there first. Like the army, the Russians were not happy. "Our role" at the surrender, said Nikita Khrushchev, "was that of a poor relative at the wedding of a rich man." Stalin told America's ambassador that the "control of Japan [was] the first question requiring settlement" with the United States. No matter. Carl Vinson was pleased. The congressman from

Milledgeville had suggested that the surrender take place on the *Missouri* with Admirals Nimitz and Halsey present. Like most in the naval aviation community, he never thought much of Spruance. The final standing for most valuable player in the war against Japan: the U.S. Army and Navy in a photo finish, the Soviet Union a distant third.[14]

DOWN WITH ONE WAR, ON TO ANOTHER

The atomic bomb had some collateral benefits for Harry Truman, aside from enabling America to avoid reducing its political goals or enhancing its ground forces. Clearly angry with Stalin for establishing Soviet satellites through Eastern Europe, he now could do what no American had planned as late as 24 July. According to JCS planners, northeast Asia would fall entirely within the orbit of the Soviet army, as tacitly admitted when George Marshall disappointed the Red Army chief of staff by saying America could not launch an amphibious invasion of Korea to catch the Japanese in a pincer à la Normandy-Bagration. Two weeks later, after Japan surrendered, the army noted that the president was "anxious" to send forces "promptly" to Korea to prevent Russia from setting up "friendly" governments throughout northeast Asia. "This," Henry Stimson wrote back in July, "is the Polish question transplanted to the Far East."

In September, nearly a month after Soviet forces crossed into northern Korea, the XXIV Corps of the U.S. Army, stationed in Okinawa to invade Japan, disembarked at Pusan and Inchon despite protests from the War Department, which realized that its "toehold" on the mainland of Asia existed at the pleasure of Joe Stalin. Dean Rusk, the army staff officer who drew the Allied demarcation line, "was somewhat surprised that the Soviets accepted the 38th parallel since I thought they might insist upon a line further south in view of our respective military positions." In the next five years, the balance of military power between communist and anticommunist forces on the peninsula did not change much. Little was in place to stop the North Korean army when it crossed the boundary in June 1950 to unify the country under a communist regime. Then Truman, Acheson, and Rusk, the secretary of state and assistant secretary for Far East affairs, believed that America had to enter its next war or else see South Korea become another Soviet satellite.[15]

8

Korea: Fighting a War
While Fearing to Fight One,
the Specter of Escalation

To establish credibility with the Soviet Union and the American electorate, Harry Truman sent combat forces to Korea, where all U.S. strategists had felt America should not fight. Once committed to a limited war against so-called pawns of the Kremlin, Truman could not withdraw, even after Douglas MacArthur, pursuing a conclusive victory, precipitated the fight with China the administration tried to avoid. The war sunk into a stalemate, and the president was repudiated for failure to hold out creditable hope of a suitable peace. His successor, Dwight Eisenhower, might have escalated the so-called police action into a nuclear war, precisely what Truman had been fighting to prevent. The dilemma was resolved by Joseph Stalin's death and unforeseen concessions from China, which in 1953 suddenly allowed prisoners of war to repatriate to Taiwan. That had been the major issue of contention since Truman fired MacArthur in 1951.

RED CHINA, DOMESTIC POLITICS, AND
THE END OF BIPARTISAN FOREIGN POLICY

In 1945 Harry Truman sent ground forces to Korea largely because he could not keep the Soviet Union out of Poland. Angry that Eastern Europe was becoming a communist satellite, the president vowed to prevent this from recurring throughout northeast Asia. Joseph Stalin was happy to give America southern Korea in hopes of receiving permission to occupy Hokkaido, which he had been planning to invade when the United States dropped the atomic bomb. Stalin's control of this portion of the Japanese archipelago bottling up Vladivostok, his major naval base, was not incompatible with U.S. Army postwar plans. The War Department had hoped to share "the burden of the occupation" and the "enforcement of the provisions of unconditional surrender" with at least 30,000 Soviet soldiers. Truman, however, was in no mood to trade. When he declared that America would not share control of metropolitan Japan, Stalin indignantly replied: "I and my colleagues did not expect such an answer from you."

Now that the American army occupied Korea south of the thirty-eighth parallel, it had little idea what to do, according to officers who complained of "little or no practical guidance." In July 1947 Lieutenant General John R. Hodge, the military governor, wrote the JCS: "I have always been aware that Korea has been low on the agenda . . . but Washington must become aware that it may soon reach the point of explosion." Among those paying virtually no attention was the commander of military forces in the Far East (CINCFE), Douglas MacArthur. When Hodge pleaded for help and a visit from his boss, MacArthur replied he was "too preoccupied." Privately, the supreme commander told his staff that he "didn't want any part" of that "messy situation." In 1948 the State Department assumed responsibility for Korea, including supervision of military advisers. MacArthur was pleased, his aide recalled. Now "the coffee drinking diplomats" he barely tolerated in Tokyo would "stew in their own juice."

For the next two years, the State and Defense Departments debated what to do with Korea, portending numerous disputes through the Korean War. Dean Acheson, the secretary of state in 1948 and a strong proponent of Korea since 1946, upheld his department's claim that Soviet control of the peninsula would be "a threat to the future security of the Pacific." This contingency seemed particularly ominous after Mao Tse-tung founded the communist People's Republic of China (PRC) in 1949. Now that Nationalist (noncommunist) China under Chiang Kai-shek could not prevent Russia from replacing Imperial Japan as the dominant force in the Far East, post–Imperial Japan would have to fill the void, a prospect that worried Russia since 1945. Not yet an economic powerhouse, Japan required cheap food from South Korea simply to survive, let alone become the new centerpiece of anti-Soviet influence in the North Pacific. A communist South Korea "would have affected the whole economy" of the region. "Were Japan [then] added to the Communist bloc," Acheson told the British, "the Soviets would acquire skilled manpower and industrial potential capable of significantly altering the balance of world power."

The Defense Department worried far more about combat power ratios than it did about what the State Department called "an ideological battleground upon which our entire success in Asia may depend." The "forces in Korea would be a military liability," trapped between Soviet naval bases at Vladivostok and Port Arthur, then overrun by hordes of infantry. To protect Japan, "neutralization [of Korea] by air action would be more feasible and less costly than large scale ground operations." State notwithstanding, military planners maintained that "every effort should be made [in 1947] to liquidate or reduce the U.S. commitment of men and money in Korea as soon as possible."

Truman sided with the Pentagon, despite an emotional commitment to Korea. He had a far stronger interest in capital investment, consumer price stability, and

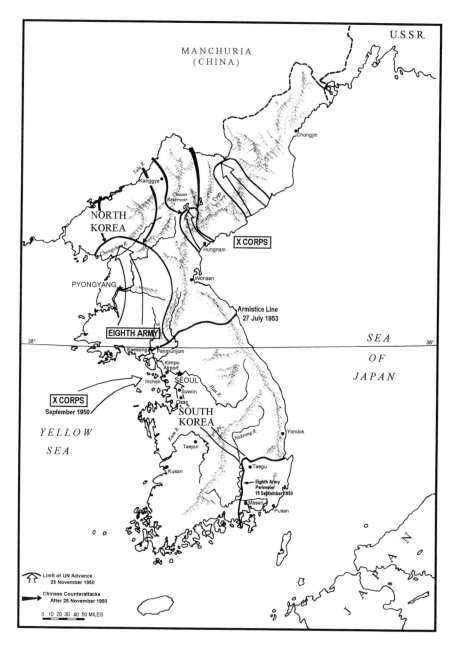

The Korean War

liquidating the $250 billion debt carried over from World War II. His belief that balanced federal budgets were imperative for economic growth meant a $13 billion cap on military spending. Between 1948 and 1950 the president, the military, and the Congress all clearly stated that America would not fight for South Korea. Years later Soviets would still cite these pronouncements as proof that "we just can't trust you Americans."

Well aware that its budget prohibited war on the Asian mainland, the Pentagon formulated a "carefully considered and comprehensive plan" to contain communism by holding a string of offshore air and sea bases from the Aleutians to the Philippines. This would maximize its high-technology weaponry and minimize its scarcest resource, manpower on the ground. Reminiscent of the George Marshall memorandum to mount "a strategic defense in the East" (November 1940), infantry and armor would not be sunk into "unimportant areas" like Asia, where no nation ranked above thirteenth in the Defense Department's priorities for military aid. Ground forces should be preserved for Europe, where aside from a skeleton American ground force in the late 1940s, a few rivers stood between the Red Army and the English Channel. As for the atomic bomb, Truman confided, "It is used to wipe out women and children and unarmed people. You have got to understand that this isn't a military weapon"; we will "never use it for war." The European priority for conventional defense was so widely accepted in the administration that even Acheson withdrew his commitment to Korea when testifying to Congress the month before the North Korean invasion. "We cannot scatter our shots equally all over the world. We just haven't got enough shots to do that."

Having to devise a way to reduce the commitment to Korea "as soon as possible with the minimum bad effects" on national credibility, the Defense and State Departments dumped responsibility on the United Nations. In private, Acheson called the institution "window dressing" for the United States, that is, when it was not a complete "monkey house." Theoretically, if North Korea ever did invade the South, according to a JCS study (1949), U.S. military units could be part of a "police action" conducted by an international force. In reality, Acheson told the Senate in January 1950 that no UN force would ever exist because of Russian vetoes. Yet by making South Korea a UN ward and having it create an independent government, a burden was lifted from the United States. Neither State nor Defense anticipated Harry Truman's emotional attachment to the UN.

In the meantime, different compartments of the U.S. government tried to specify exactly where America would draw its "defensive perimeter" in the Pacific. Since Korea, by consensus, was discounted, Formosa (also known as Taiwan) became the divisive issue regarding where to plant American military assets. The USSR and the PRC openly disputed rival claims to Manchuria in 1949–50. Although Acheson had opposed Japan and Germany with equal fervor in World War II, he made a clear differentiation between major communist countries, at least at this stage of the cold war. If successful in "detaching [China] from subservience to Moscow," its "inevitable" adversary in northeast Asia, he would duplicate his great success of 1948, coaxing Yugoslavia out of Stalin's orbit. To do this in the Far East, the United States had to terminate aid to Chiang's anticommunist faction now governing Formosa. Otherwise America would "substitute for the Soviets as the imperialist menace to China." Geopolitics aside, Acheson was simply skeptical about Formosa's military prospects in the final round of the Chinese civil war. Its conquest "is widely anticipated and the manner in which civil and military conditions have deteriorated under the Nationalists adds weight to this expectation."

Acheson's remark was hardly judicious for anyone on thin ice with Republicans in a Congress dead set against bipartisan harmony. Having lost the last five presidential and nine of the last ten congressional elections, the GOP would not repeat its mistake of running what the public called a "dignified" and "clean" campaign, as it did in 1948. After Truman successfully attacked Republicans for plotting "to go back to the days when big business held the upper hand and forced the working man to take only what they wanted to give him," they searched for populist targets of their own, although ones for cultural, not economic, issues. They did well to look past the president: a midwestern farm boy, bankrupted small businessman, and graduate of the Kansas City Law School's nighttime course. Far better to focus on the type of East Coast Establishment figures whom Truman had lambasted in 1948 for domestic (not foreign) policy—Acheson, Averell Harriman, Robert Lovett, Paul Nitze, and the other "bright young men born with silver spoons in their mouths" who held senior positions at State and Defense. They would be accused of lacking anticommunist credentials when their real sin was to be a "pompous diplomat in striped pants with a phony British accent," as Senator Joe McCarthy described the secretary of state. An alumnus of Groton, Yale, and Harvard, Acheson was "the perfect foil for my attacks," said Richard Nixon, then a congressman from California. The "best-dressed man in America" (1949) barely hid his contempt for people less refined and intelligent than he, meaning the public, the press, and Capitol Hill, whose place in foreign policy was "the function of people who don't know and don't care and are just generally raising hell" for the "thinking cells of government," that is, Acheson himself.

Partisan bitterness and disputes about China made politics barely civil even before Acheson made a statement that, by his admission, "absolutely took the roof off everything." In January 1950 Alger Hiss, a personal friend and former State Department official, was convicted of perjury after denying that he passed documents to a communist agent in the 1930s. Acheson, advised to say "no comment, the matter is before the courts," faced a "yelping pack" of media "fools" with smirks on their faces. When he said "I do not intend to turn my back on Alger Hiss," Nixon declared that "traitors in the high councils of our own government have made sure that the deck is stacked on the Soviet side." In March, Senator Robert Taft, the leader of the Republican conservative wing, announced that in the impending fall election, in which he was running for his third term, the

GOP would make "softness toward Communism" a major issue. Thereafter, until the end of the Korean War, partisan politics was as vituperative as it has ever been in U.S. history. In May, opinion polls showed that 40 (vs. 28) percent of the public believed that Joe McCarthy's accusations about a major "spy ring" in the State Department were "a good thing for the country." Truman, of a different opinion, said they were "just as bad in this cold war as it would be to shoot our soldiers in the back." To say the least, this domestic environment was hardly ideal for the development of a defense policy devoted to nothing but the national interest.[1]

FORMOSA, THE DEFENSE PERIMETER, AND THE FUTURE OF DOUGLAS MACARTHUR

In World War II Franklin Roosevelt encouraged two major myths about America's allies: Joe Stalin was a social democrat; Chiang Kai-shek ran an honest government. Congressional conservatives who ridiculed the former claim as "flagrant Communist propaganda produced as a result of White House pressure" still espoused the latter. Through the 1948 election, they had a begrudging understanding with the Truman administration whereby the president got aid for Turkey, Greece, and South Korea and they got up to $94 million a year for Chiang Kai-shek. This compromise had been an important component of the bipartisan foreign policy that existed until Chiang's defeat in 1949, whereafter Republicans accused Acheson of appeasing Mao Tse-tung, delayed funds for South Korea, and insisted that Truman support fortress Formosa, from which Chiang bombed the mainland and attacked coastal shipping. This may have planted in the mind of Communist China the notion that a U.S. defeat on the Asian mainland would terminate aid to Formosa, one of Mao's objectives when he entered the Korean War.

Before Korea, Douglas MacArthur was not a tool of the Democratic White House or the Republican camp in Congress, although both sides were eager to claim his support. The general had his own agenda now that the military occupation of Japan was nearly over. Other old soldiers who never die might fade away into retirement, not this seventy-year-old man who was always of the opinion, in the words of one subordinate, that "he was a man of destiny with a divine duty to perform in this world." In 1949, when he feared his career was about to close, he displayed physical and psychological symptoms informally diagnosed as Parkinson's disease. These muscle tremors and memory lapses would vanish the moment he found a new mission fighting communism in the Korean War.

MacArthur was obviously searching for a new role and new arena when he began to focus his attention on Formosa. Whereas Republicans wanted to make Chiang Kai-shek a bulwark against Chinese communism and Acheson would have rid America of the entire island, MacArthur would have replaced Chiang, whose "capability and will" he questioned, as part of his own grand plan to turn

Formosa into the major military strongpoint on "the western strategic frontier of the United States." His own military strategy had dramatically changed from the time he opposed invading Formosa in debates with the navy during World War II, just as it had changed from the early 1930s, when he said that infantry was the "decisive arm," particularly compared with "the airplane as a weapon of war." Having used airpower and sea power to his decisive advantage against the Japanese army in 1944, he became convinced America should not try to be a power on the mainland of Asia. By 1945 MacArthur no longer wanted to build bases in China. In 1961 he would tell President John F. Kennedy not to send ground forces to Vietnam. In 1950, when MacArthur said the United States needed "naval and air supremacy and [only] modest ground elements to defend bases," Formosa was the place from which he planned to control "the entire eastern periphery of China."

Like JCS planners in Washington as far back as 1945, MacArthur was inconsistent about the exact mission of U.S. forces on offshore bases. Sometimes he said they were there to prevent any "hostile movement into the Pacific." Other times, they were there to project combat power onto the mainland. The best possible case, at least for MacArthur, was to do both at the same time. If the Red Chinese launched an invasion of Taiwan, generally expected for August 1950, MacArthur planned to conduct "one of the decisive battles of the world—a [defeat] so great it would rock Asia, and perhaps turn back Communism."

MacArthur obviously felt that America had a mission to dominate the Pacific and that he had a destiny to fulfill. This self-proclaimed expert on "Oriental psychology" was convinced that "Asiatics adore a winner and despise a loser." When he provided the "aggressive, resolute, and dynamic leadership" they craved, MacArthur not only would foster "the civilization and Christianization" of the Orient but also would succeed where his longtime rival had failed—a man of whom he said his "fine patrician Virginia nose does not tolerate the daily smells of Asia."

George Marshall and MacArthur emerged from World War I as the shining stars of different factions within the U.S. Army: Marshall representing the so-called Pershing clique surrounding the commander of the AEF, MacArthur the protégé of Peyton March, the army chief of staff. In 1947, as Truman's special envoy to China, Marshall told Chiang that he could not stop the communist revolution with "military force." MacArthur later called this advice tacit "appeasement to the Red Chinese." Now, in 1950, if Mao Tse-tung tried to invade Taiwan, MacArthur—with carrier- and land-based aircraft—would try to do what Marshall had said could not be done. Not complete fantasy, MacArthur's scenario impressed Mao, who was worried that a setback would severely damage the prestige of his regime, still having to "pacify" 3 million "political bandits" and armed "special agents" of Chiang on the mainland. This made the Red Chinese, struggling to add landing craft and marines to its light infantry–intensive army, more cautious than MacArthur wished they would be: "I pray nightly they will try" to attack. The CINCFE was paying so much attention to Formosa that he did not know, or seem to care, what was happening in Korea, other than to say something that would come back to haunt him. In March 1949 he issued a directive that the soldiers of the Republic of South Korea (ROK) not receive heavy weapons able to provide more than a "token resistance" to a communist invasion. Doing otherwise would lend credence to "allegations of being a threat to [the] North."

On 5 January 1950 President Truman publicly restated his position that the United States "will not provide military aid or advice to Chinese forces on Formosa," a position unanimously supported by the Democratic caucus in the Senate. Nonetheless, a different policy was gathering enough advocates in Washington to leak out to the public through the press. Its proponents included the second echelons of the Truman administration, particularly Dean Rusk, a recent volunteer for what Acheson called "the dirtiest job in the entire Department of State," that of assistant secretary for Far Eastern affairs. State's director of public affairs said "the overwhelming majority of Americans" now demanded active opposition to communist expansion. Rusk was more disturbed by international opinion, particularly because "the loss of China to the Communists" had created a perception that there has been "a marked shift in the balance of power in favor of [the] Soviet Union." Lest defeatism produce "further losses" that would enhance Russian strength, he stressed that the United States must "take a dramatic and strong stand that shows our confidence and resolution." Heretofore dubious about Formosa, he said in May 1950 that it was the place to draw the line because it was "not subject to the immediate influence of Soviet land power."

That spring, Acheson and Truman were admitting to prominent Republicans that because of the "considerable deterioration in our position," the country must take "early affirmative action" against the "communist menace particularly in the East," partly to discredit "men like McCarthy" before the American public. However, neither one was willing to defend Formosa, a far cry from the JCS. When its chairman, General Omar Bradley, visited the Far East in mid-June, MacArthur gave him a memorandum about Formosa as an "unsinkable aircraft carrier and submarine tender." In communist hands, it would constitute "an enemy salient in the very center" of America's defensive perimeter between Japan and the Philippines. Because MacArthur's paper presented the argument better "than anything the JCS had produced," Bradley read it to the National Security Council (NSC) the day after he got back to Washington on 24 June. Once he finished, the meeting switched to another issue—how America should respond to the invasion of South Korea—something Bradley suspected was a communist "diversion to distract us from an imminent attack on Formosa," a place of real importance.[2]

THE DECISION TO FIGHT BUT NOT GO TO "WAR"

On 24 June 1950 Kim Il Sung, a former battalion commander in the Soviet Far East forces, sent 90,000 soldiers, sixty bombers, thirty fighters, and 154 T-34s, the best medium-sized tank in the world, across the thirty-eighth parallel to unify

Korea under his communist regime. On 25 June, when President Truman was about to leave Kansas City to attend an emergency meeting on this crisis, one of his aides told a newspaperman: "The boss is going to hit those fellows hard." Meanwhile, the boss warned a member of his cabinet: "You and I both have seen two world wars started [for] less."

Neither Truman nor the rest of the American nation knew exactly what he was going to do. "Everyone was vaguely aware that the U.S. was committed to Korea, but only vaguely committed," wrote *Time* magazine, "part hope, part good intentions, part bluff and part indecision." Before ever meeting his inner circle of thirteen advisers that evening, Truman made the fundamental determination to intervene. Thereafter, the debate concerned how to do it; whether to do it was not discussed. The lesson Truman and company had derived from the 1930s was that world war was the product of appeasement, something that "had encouraged the aggressors to keep on going ahead." Since 1946, Acheson was saying that intervention was less dangerous than isolation, a policy that failed after World War I. Rusk would recall that "the Korean decision was in the process of being made for an entire generation since Manchuria," the Japanese aggression in 1931.

Some forty years after the commitment to Korea and four years after the Soviet Union fell, official documents surfaced, calling into question Truman's rationale. They indicate that Stalin was every bit as frightened of the United States as it was of him. Not wanting to test U.S. resolve, let alone wage war against the West, he approved Kim Il Sung's invasion only because it promised to be a quick victory in a location America discounted and would not defend. However, no one in the U.S. national command authority believed they had anywhere near that much military credibility in late June 1950. Therefore, there was unanimity, Omar Bradley said, that "we must draw the line." At the time it was Bradley's understanding that it would not be drawn by American ground forces, to be excluded from Korea, a terrible place for them to fight. No matter, as Acheson told the army's chief of staff on 26 June, "It was important for us to do something even if the effort were not successful."

Truman thought his options were a small conflict now or a total war later. "If we are tough enough there won't be any next step" from Stalin. The problem was how to be tough enough to stop what Truman called "a Frankenstein dictatorship" but not start a general war ending with atomic weapons, something he called "totally unthinkable for rational men." Initially, his answer seemed easy and the commitment slight: send military supplies on the assumption that the South could hold the North, still thought to be a "wretched little satellite government" of the Soviet Union. When that proved fallacious, limited escalation was in order. "Turn the Air Force loose and we'll stop those tanks," one high-ranking officer said. When they got two or three from a column of eighty tanks, Truman had to take another step. On the sixth day of the crisis, the president finally decided that American ground forces had to be deployed, although one reinforced battalion should suffice.

The responsibility for containing communism now fell on 504 men used to comfortable garrison jobs in Japan, where they had had virtually no training with heavy weapons and large-unit operations. Furthermore, the entire U.S. Eighth Army was at two-thirds strength (from two divisions in each corps to two squads in each platoon), a situation ill suited to a force whose doctrine was to fight in two-up, one-back formations. Task Force Smith, as it would be known in history, still took heart at what was being said in Washington: that it was to conduct a "police action" and "suppress a bandit raid." On 5 July it bought time for the reinforcements that saved South Korea, although not the way Washington foresaw. Its men, who packed their dress uniforms for the postbattle victory parade, expected to find "a motley horde armed with old muskets." Within two hours, they suffered 185 casualties and were destroyed as a functioning unit. Nonetheless, the North Korean People's Army (NKPA) had to pause to start a chain of inquiries regarding why U.S. soldiers were there at all. Moscow and Peking may have been as surprised as Kim Il Sung, who had promised he would unify the country by 15 August, the fifth anniversary of the Korean liberation from Japanese occupation. The Chinese Communist party newspaper, heretofore predicting a procession to the sea, now warned that Washington would not "concede defeat" and began to call Korea "the central problem of international relations."

Surprised or not, the so-called bandits were better trained, better equipped, and in far better condition than their "green and flabby" opponents flown over from Japan. Red Chinese army observers were shocked by the severity of NKPA discipline; American soldiers were shocked by their firepower ("These crooks over here got big guns!"). By the time the JCS understood "just how good these North Koreans were," the administration had to reinforce to protect its credibility. The army's chief of staff, J. Lawton "Joe" Collins, would explain: "We rushed into Korea with no advance planning [or] any fully thought-out ideas concerning our objectives or the means we would be willing to expend to attain them. As each situation arose we extemporized, unsure what the next step would be, until we were far more committed than we had expected to be."

When Truman first used "police action" to describe Korea, it was still plausible to claim "we are not at war." Unfortunately for his credibility, he stuck with these words up to November 1952, the last time he officially used the phrase "police action for the United Nations—and nothing else." By then, "Harry's police force on the call," as American forces sardonically called themselves, had suffered approximately 50,000 dead and 100,000 wounded. Douglas MacArthur would have no problem ridiculing the president when he said that even if Truman was not waging war against Red China, China was certainly waging war against the United States.

As far as Truman was concerned, "state of war" was a politically incorrect description of a conflict waged with a Soviet satellite for the purpose of avoiding a war with the Soviet Union, especially when the phrase might later trigger the defense alliance with the PRC. If Stalin honored his commitment to Mao Tse-tung,

Truman could witness the condition he had described in 1945, when he said, "We can't ever have another war, unless it is total war, and that means the end of our civilization." He definitely knew that he lived in an era in which some prominent politicians, generals, and pundits already suggested a preventive war with Russia while America still had a nuclear advantage. In July, the first month of the Korean "conflict," 50 percent of the public said that they were "actually in World War III." Limited war not yet having entered the American vocabulary, Truman would try to convince the country that it was not at war. His fear that it might otherwise insist on no-holds-barred was no mere theory for the man whose presidency virtually began by dropping the atomic bomb in response to public demand for unconditional surrender in World War II. The public, according to *Time* magazine, never heard from Truman "the ringing phrases of a Churchillian or Rooseveltian [wartime] performance." Soldiers in Korea, according to one officer, "listened for the trumpet, but heard only an uncertain sound." The president was sitting on a political time bomb he could not contain. When he finally fired General MacArthur in 1951, an emotional dam burst and the country took out its stored-up wrath on Harry Truman.

Truman's reluctance to say "war" was also related to his aversion to the governmental body with the sole power to declare it. His hero was James K. Polk, who "had the courage to tell Congress to go to hell on foreign policy matters." Truman not only told the Senate (Republican) minority leader that "I just had to act as Commander-in-Chief"; he felt that to have awaited congressional authorization was to "tie the hands of a successor president." He still needed legal justification to commit troops to Korea, where America had no treaty obligations in June 1950. The UN Charter might replace the U.S. Constitution, but Truman did not use it as a crude subterfuge. He was pleased to make Korea a UN cause even if (or because) it was only authorized to "maintain or restore international peace."

Acheson, who encouraged Truman to commit forces without congressional sanction, also played a major role in involving the UN, although he may not have realized the ramifications. On Saturday night, 24 June, when the first North Korean echelon crossed the border, much of official Washington was out of town or reach. The first people to get to the State Department and manage the crisis situation were Dean Rusk and John Hickerson, the past and present assistant secretaries of state for UN affairs. They convinced Acheson to involve the institution they loved largely to give a transcendent moral purpose to American self-interest. Acheson, no Wilsonian, probably blanched but appreciated Rusk's other point, that America should not be stuck as the sole policeman of the world. A few minutes later, Acheson called Truman and suggested the UN track, to which the president enthusiastically agreed. Three days later, after Acheson briefed congressional leaders about Korea, Truman exclaimed: "But Dean, you didn't even mention the U.N.!"

Truman, like Rusk, worshiped Woodrow Wilson and the lost cause of the League of Nations. As a senator in 1943, he helped sponsor U.S. membership in an international organization with "military force" for the postwar world. As Democratic candidate for vice president in 1944, he attacked Republicans for being "as determined, as bitter, and as dangerous as the band who set themselves against the League of Nations and gave to Wilson's peace in 1920 a stab in the back." As president in 1945, his first decision was to host the conference to draft the charter and to ask "every American . . . to support our efforts to build a strong and lasting United Nations organization." When the Senate ratified the UN treaty, old Wilsonians gloated that their "saint on earth, a martyr," had been vindicated, "the record of the United States of 1920 has been expunged," and "if [Senator Henry Cabot] Lodge doesn't turn over in his grave, I would be willing with you and other competent grave diggers to help him or even hang him up [by] his heels like Mussolini." Harry Truman was hardly ready to witness the deflation of these high hopes. On 25 June 1950, when the president decided to oppose the North Koreans, he turned to John Hickerson and said: "In the final analysis I did this for the United Nations. . . . In this first big test we just couldn't let them down."

Walter Lippmann, an apostate Wilsonian, would later say that Korea "was the test of a theory to which we were committed [that] we would all join together to enforce peace. It didn't work very well," in retrospect. At the time of the North Korean attack, however, one magazine correspondent wrote that "a good many old hands in the U.N. headquarters [were] astonished at the speed and decisiveness with which the organization acted," first to ask members "to furnish assistance" to repel the aggressor, then to ask the United States to designate the leader for a United Nations military command. Russia, by boycotting the proceedings for failing to give Communist China Chiang Kai-shek's UN seat, enabled America to get the institution's support in Korea—valuable, according to the JCS, "for worldwide political reasons" even if "virtually useless from a military point of view."

This propaganda boon came to America at a steep price. Now that Truman's boyhood hope for a "federation of the world" showed a spark of viability, thanks to a Soviet tactical error, he would bear a heavy burden in order to preserve it. By November, several magazines and newspapers were saying that the UN "stands to become [the] powerful instrument for peace its framers overwhelmingly meant it to be." By December, after China entered the war, Truman felt he had to accept substantial military danger by keeping the army in Korea largely "to bring the United Nations through its first great effort on collective security." In 1953 he would end his presidency, like he began the conflict, telling America that "if we let the Republic of Korea go under, the United Nations would go the way of the League of Nations."

Whatever happened in the future, in June 1950 all components of Truman's commitment to Korea seemed mutually supporting. The president did not want to call the Korean "conflict" a war lest it become World War III fought with strategic nuclear weapons. Only Congress could declare war, and he did not want Congress to decide the issue. The UN Charter, Truman's sacred cause, entailed no power to make war, only to "restore international peace and security" through an international police force. However, this seamless web would shred if America ended up suffering protracted casualties from a substantial enemy, no matter what Truman called Korea. That would happen if the Red Army replaced the NKPA, since, in the unanimous opinion of the NSC, all American forces would then be sitting ducks for ninety submarines, 2,000 combat planes, and thirty-five divisions—the total Soviet forces in the area of operations, at least by 1951. Hence the Truman administration waited to commit ground forces until it had assessed the Soviet response to an American request to "use its influence with North Korean authorities to withdraw their invading forces." (Off the record, government officials said that the "influence" of the Kremlin on North Korea was the same as that of "Walt Disney on Donald Duck.") When, on 29 June, the Russians sent a euphemistic note denying all responsibility, Truman and the State Department's experts concluded "that the Soviets are going to let the Chinese and the North Koreans do the fighting for them."

If the conquest of South Korea had been truly vital to the Kremlin, it might have used serious threats to deter an American military response. When it feigned that the regime in the North was completely independent, it encouraged the U.S. troop commitment. The administration had long worried that the Soviet Union would divert America to peripheral areas while it attacked "the centers of power" such as Iran, Truman's initial concern on 24 June. Policy makers were now "of the opinion that the Russians were trying for a quick and easy victory in Korea and that they were not trying to get us off balance in order to start a major all-out war." This meant that America could fight a conflict that would not be a war, at least against its real adversary, the Soviet Union. It also meant that the onus of escalation would be on Harry Truman, something Truman never forgot.

The final reason America intervened in Korea was because America *could* intervene in Korea, northeast Asia being one of the few places where "the U.S. is capable of conducting immediate general offensive operations with its armed forces," according to the NSC. Even if the four divisions in Japan were ill prepared, they were there, along with 639 fighters and bombers. If Soviet grand strategy was to probe for "soft spots" around its perimeter, as Truman thought, then this was a unique opportunity to "meet their challenge without getting embroiled in a world war." Best of all, the direct opponent in Korea was just a proxy. Worst of all, "the capacity of a small Soviet satellite to engage in a military adventure challenging the might and will of the US, can lead to serious questioning of that might and will." When Truman committed the navy and air force, let alone Task Force Smith, European allies exclaimed, "Thank God, this will not be a repetition of the past"—their own reference to appeasement in the 1930s. The North Atlantic Treaty Organization (NATO) would soon curse America's overcommitment to Korea, but not in June 1950, when the State Department knew that Europe waited to see if "America will neither put up or shut up."

There was a paradox in America's plan to fight a proxy, avoid its sponsor, prove its credibility, and maintain "collective security," the recurrent phrase at the

White House in mid-1950. If the Soviet army were not directly involved, it was probably because Korea was a low priority compared with Germany, Iran, and other flash points in the cold war. Initially, U.S. policy makers only sensed their dilemma; they would not fully appreciate it until Douglas MacArthur threatened to use virtually the complete American arsenal to attack another alleged proxy, the Chinese communist armed forces. Then, Omar Bradley would finally say succinctly: "This strategy would involve us in the wrong war, at the wrong place, and with the wrong enemy." First, however, MacArthur would have to bring over 300,000 Red Chinese soldiers into the Korean War.[3]

THE RESURRECTION OF DOUGLAS MACARTHUR

General Douglas MacArthur was as surprised as anyone in Washington at the invasion of South Korea. Military intelligence for the peninsula was the responsibility of the Korean Military Advisory Group, which reported through the State Department, not directly to him, commander of military forces in the Far East (CINCFE). If the general had known of the impending attack, it is doubtful he would have cared. Like Acheson, he had publicly excluded Korea from America's defense perimeter, part of his own long-standing policy not to fight on the mainland, as opposed to throwing back communism when China would invade Formosa.

On 25 June MacArthur believed that the North Koreans were only executing a "reconnaissance in force," similar to other border incidents in the last two years. Two days later, when this assessment was discredited, he told John Foster Dulles that anyone who advised throwing Americans into the breach along the thirty-eighth parallel "ought to have his head examined." Dulles, then visiting Tokyo as a Republican consultant to the State Department, found MacArthur so despondent and deficient that he advised the president to bring him home. In fact, now would have been the best time to get rid of the general, before Truman (like Franklin Roosevelt) would feel compelled to portray him as a hero, especially if Pusan became another Bataan. As of yet, the aging CINCFE had done nothing but overlook the danger of a communist invasion and then lament that "all Korea is lost." However, Truman (the so-called feisty little man) was already intimidated. "The General," he told Dulles, "is involved politically in this country and he could not recall MacArthur without causing a tremendous reaction." Within three weeks, to build up national morale, Truman would be praising MacArthur's military genius on the radio as Roosevelt had done in late 1941.

Ever fearful of the general he felt compelled to preserve, the president warned him against "the slightest implication" America was "planning to go to war against the Soviet Union." MacArthur, at the time, was still in a fog and not even thinking of fighting North Korea. On 25 June, when the JCS authorized the use of air and sea power, the CINCFE used them solely for evacuees. Omar

Bradley had not given directives to attack North Korean tanks streaming toward Seoul on the false assumption that MacArthur would seize the initiative. This state of affairs would not recur. By 28 June, once MacArthur realized America would actually fight for Korea, he shed the physical symptoms of Parkinson's disease he had exhibited when he thought his career was about to end. His hands and voice no longer shook; he no longer lost his train of thought, probably because of hormones secreted in a period of heightened excitement. He seemed "buoyant" to one *Life* magazine reporter. "His eyes possessed that same luminous brilliance which I had sometimes seen in the faces of fever patients." From now on, MacArthur would not wait for authorization to do almost anything he could to destroy the enemy in a decisive battle for decisive political objectives. Korea had become, as he later put it, "Mars' last gift to an old warrior."

On 29 June MacArthur ordered bombing north of the thirty-eighth parallel on his own authority, toured the front, and demanded two American divisions and a regimental combat team as "the only assurance for holding the present line." When the Truman administration concurred, the die was cast and MacArthur proceeded to practice strategy by fait accompli, as he had done in World War II. If Washington complained that a proposed operation was "too big a gamble," he informed his staff to tell them "I said this is throwing a nickel in the pot after it has been opened for a dollar. The big gamble was Washington's decision to put American troops on the Asiatic mainland." Two days after the mauling of Task Force Smith, MacArthur wrote the JCS that he would halt "the enemy advance," then "fully exploit our air and sea control, [to] strike by amphibious maneuver, behind his mass of ground forces." Washington, far less ambitious, was praying to save some credibility by holding off the enemy at the Pusan perimeter. "The United States reverses in Korea," according to the State Department, dismayed NATO and Japan so profoundly that they "will begin to seriously question the validity of their military and political association with the United States."

The JCS was astonished at the scope of MacArthur's ambition, far greater than interdicting the enemy supply route running through Seoul. He planned to use "the hammer" of an amphibious invasion by the X Corps at Inchon "and the anvil" of the Eighth Army at Pusan to "crush and destroy the armies of North Korea" prior to uniting the peninsula under an anticommunist regime. The Pentagon did not emphasize the fallacy of dividing one's forces by 180 miles in the face of a strong enemy. It was simply too astonished at the mention of Inchon, where one narrow channel was easily blocked and the high tides necessary to bring assault waves ashore occurred only a few times a month. MacArthur's proposal had barely one advocate inside the high command, Matthew Bunker Ridgway, army assistant chief of staff for operations, a paratrooper used to fighting behind enemy lines.

On 21 August 1950 the JCS sent their executive agent, J. Lawton Collins, the army's chief of staff, on one last attempt "to try to argue General MacArthur out of" his plan. They should have saved the airfare. In the 1930s Collins had been a captain teaching tactics at the infantry school when MacArthur was chief of staff. In 1943 MacArthur booted him from the Pacific to Europe on grounds he was too young for a major command. The army has a way of preventing embarrassing situations where a nominal superior calls a man "general" and the other man calls him "Joe," as was the case when Collins met MacArthur in Japan. When an officer becomes chief of staff in his early fifties, his former superiors are supposed to catch the hint and retire. In 1949 this seemed especially likely if the older party was not part of the "European theater clique"—Eisenhower, Bradley, Collins, and Ridgway, who took over the army after World War II. Since MacArthur still would not retire—and no one dared force him—the institutional solution did not work.

MacArthur, like Truman and the JCS, read history for lessons learned. The JCS, which never felt that Korea was worth a big risk, feared another Anzio (1944), where an American army corps had been caught behind enemy lines for nearly five months. MacArthur foresaw another Quebec (1759), where General James Wolfe had braved inhospitable currents to meet the enemy where it was not prepared. He told Collins and Admiral Forrest Sherman that "the very arguments you have made as to the impracticabilities [of Inchon] will tend to ensure for me the element of surprise. . . . I seem to have more confidence in the Navy than the Navy has in itself." Said the commander of the First Marine Division, who would take the assault wave ashore: "It was more than confidence which upheld him; it was [a] supreme and almost mystical faith that he could not fail."

The only person left to overrule MacArthur was the president of the United States, who proved more supportive than the JCS. If Truman would not take on MacArthur before he began to fight, he would hardly overrule the CINCFE holding off North Korean tanks at the Pusan perimeter—especially after MacArthur's general plan (sardonically dubbed "Operation Common Knowledge") had been leaked to the press some three months before the 1950 congressional election. That fall the election seemed to be, in the words of the Republican Senate leader, a mandate on whether "the blood of our soldiers in Korea was on the shoulders of the Secretary of State." No one in the Truman administration seemed beyond reproach. In September the president begged George Marshall to leave retirement and become secretary of defense. This congressional icon in World War II was now lambasted for failing to save Chiang Kai-shek from himself. "General Marshall," said Senator William Jenner (Rep.-Ind.), "is not only willing, he is eager to play the role of a front man for traitors."

Harry Truman was an experienced politician used to giving and getting election year brickbats without holding a personal grudge. However, Jenner's charge of treason against Truman's hero was out of bounds: "an all-time low for attacks in the Senate." The president was loath to do anything that might lose the upcoming election to the likes of him, McCarthy, Taft, and Nixon. If, in the vernacular, a Washington weenie overruled a muddy-boot soldier with the guts to end the war, there would be political hell to pay, even if the weenie was president and the soldier was a five-star general living in a palace in Japan. On the other hand, if

MacArthur "rapidly" destroyed the North Korean army, as he promised the administration he would, Democrats would gather in the glory for rolling back communism right before the election. That was certainly more inviting than the alternative scenario predicted in the Pentagon as late as 24 August: "A military stalemate could last several months. It is a bleak prospect for our troops, the American people, and the UN cause."

On 7 August, via presidential emissary Averell Harriman, Truman offered MacArthur a deal: "Tell him two things. One, I'm going to do everything I can to give him what he wants in the way of support; and second . . . I don't want him to get us into a war with the Chinese communists." Thereafter, Washington's military instructions became even more slack. Until MacArthur was finally told he was fired in April 1951, most directions to him were suggestions, guidelines at best, partly because at Inchon, despite a general consensus that MacArthur was wrong, he appeared to have been absolutely right.

Knowing of MacArthur's World War II penchant for landing behind enemy lines, the communists planted thousands of mines in most of the harbors they controlled, with one notable exception. "Our intelligence," said a North Korean general, "told us it was impossible to launch a full-scale amphibious operation at Inchon. . . . All available reinforcements have been sent to the Pusan front," aside from 2,000 second-class soldiers left in the vicinity of the beachhead. They had no response to America's strong suit: naval gunfire and air strikes that suppressed virtually all resistance within twenty-five miles of the landing, where the X Corps suffered only twenty-five fatalities.

Actually, Inchon may only have been the straw that broke the communist camel's back. The NKPA was excellent at the tactical level, in direct contact with their enemy. It lacked the operational art the Soviets had shown in World War II, that of planning and conducting military campaigns, probably because Stalin withdrew his advisers and technical specialists so he could escape Truman's wrath by denying all responsibility. After overrunning Task Force Smith, the North Koreans paused to "liberate" towns in the southwest, rather than move directly toward the absolutely vital port of Pusan. Subsequently, at the Pusan perimeter, they dispersed around the circumference, where they conducted piecemeal local attacks instead of concentrating for a breakthrough. This stalled their offense that could not afford to stall lest snowballing deficits in logistics doom the operation.

After six weeks of warfare, North Korea was critically short of food, fuel, ammunition, spare parts, and manpower, largely due to America's land and naval airpower. It attacked infantry concentrations at the front, now fighting at near 50 percent strength, and napalmed the rubber in the tread of communist tanks. It also blew up roads, bridges, trucks, and supply dumps stretching to the Yalu River. Meanwhile, the United States shipped virtually everything available to the Far East, including tanks on display at military museums. On the eve of Inchon, the UN command had a two to one advantage in manpower and a five to one advantage in deployable armor at the Pusan perimeter. The Inchon operation hit an opponent on its way to the deck. Nonetheless, it seemed testimony, as Ridgway wrote MacArthur, "to the incomparable brilliance of your unsurpassed leadership and judgment." One doubts MacArthur filed a dissent.[4]

TO CROSS OR NOT TO CROSS: THAT WAS THE QUESTION

Inchon was the closest thing to a decisive battle the U.S. Army ever fought, but it failed that Olympian designation. It did not end the war. Approximately 40,000 North Koreans escaped the trap and recrossed the thirty-eighth parallel to carry on the conflict. Few Pentagon flag officers expected this would happen, even those opposing Inchon. On 7 September, the same day the JCS asked MacArthur to reconsider the envelopment, Omar Bradley wrote the secretary of defense that "after the strength of the North Korean forces has been broken south of the 38th," action north of the border "will probably be of a guerrilla character." The South Koreans "should be adequate to cope with this situation. . . . All United States forces should be removed from Korea as early as practicable."

Like most predictions in war, this one failed to come true. The U.S.–UN forces knocked the North Koreans down and back across the border. They did not annihilate them beyond reconstitution so that the ROK army could cross the thirty-eighth parallel on its own. Because the Eighth Army could never get Anzio out of its mind, no matter what MacArthur told the JCS about not needing a "rapid juncture with the X Corps," it raced out of the Pusan perimeter to link up with the envelopment, not catch North Koreans. Russians advised the NKPA to reconstitute their lines around the thirty-eighth parallel. The rank and file had ideas of their own. They dropped their weapons, abandoned their vehicles, put on civilian clothes, mingled with refugees, and found exfiltration routes back across the border—something Stalin finally ordered on 2 October, long after the process began.

If the X Corps were to block the NKPA escape routes, it would have to race eastward across the peninsula right after landing at Inchon. Instead, at MacArthur's insistence, it fought for a week to recapture Seoul, where the Marine Corps suffered 1,000 casualties in brutal block-to-block warfare. Then, after another week of clearing rubble and rebuilding bridges, MacArthur was ready to drive his cavalcade of spotless staff cars shipped from Japan to an elaborate ceremony at the capital conducted by MacArthur himself. He loved pageantry, and this pageant made headlines, but no one should discount the sincerity of his emotional fervor. Colonel "Chesty" Puller, the legendary thick-skinned marine who led the First Regiment ashore at Inchon, attended the dedication of the restoration of the government of Syngman Rhee, although he was almost arrested by MPs for driving a dirty jeep: "General MacArthur prayed and talked for half an hour, so fervently that you couldn't tell one from the other. All the time, tears as big as buckshot came down his cheeks, evenly spaced, like soldiers at drill."

This diversion notwithstanding, there may have been no way to conduct a truly decisive battle once Inchon began. The X Corps (one marine and two under-manned army divisions) was simply too small to constitute an anvil 200 miles long. Neither Bradley nor MacArthur seemed to realize what field-grade officers who have served in Korea point out: America would have had to deploy a complete army (nine to ten divisions) to create an unbreachable barrier from the Yellow Sea to the Sea of Japan. This being the case, the Inchon operation should not have been conducted, no matter how well executed it was. It did not collapse resistance by a surprise attack deep in the enemy rear. The NKPA soldiers whom the Eighth Army captured knew nothing of the landing. With no Inchon, the Eighth Army, with the X Corps attached, would have concentrated all its resources and attention on one responsibility—catching every North Korean it could. Washington took a big gamble at Inchon under the illusion that it was "standing on the threshold of victory." When the maximum goal that was beyond its grasp allegedly slipped through its fingers, America naturally considered reaching out again by chasing the enemy north of the thirty-eighth parallel, rather than restore the status quo antebellum.

Government policy and position papers, even before Inchon, bear witness to the temptation of total victory. Although "containment" was administration policy, that word would not mean coexistence until late in the Korean War. George F. Kennan, the State Department officer who coined the term, wrote that if the United States could impose "moderation and circumspection" on the Soviet Union, it "might be changed overnight from one of the strongest to one of the weakest and most pitiable of national societies." One wonders if Kennan had not held out hope for a reasonably quick victory, his policy would have won approval at all. In March and May 1950, senior White House, State, and Defense Department officials, including Dean Acheson, condemned what they called "a purely defensive reaction," partly because the American people needed to hope "that some day we would win." "We should intensify our efforts to look for ways to wrest the initiative from the Soviets and to roll them back."

It was never very clear how to defeat Russia without risking the limitless conflict that horrified the president. The secretary of the army suggested using "all means short of war." Then, in early July, the government began to think of crossing into North Korea, just as it had suddenly gone back into South Korea late that June. The northeast Asia division in the State Department suggested that "we should continue right up to the Manchurian and Siberian border, and, having done so, call for a UN-supervised election for all of Korea." Dean Rusk, the head of the whole East Asia branch, was the man who originally selected the thirty-eighth parallel as the border back in 1945. Raised in southern Calvinist traditions, he believed that all aggressors must be taught a mortal lesson they would never forget, a stance that "shocked" the urbane Kennan, his personal enemy. One of the first (and last) proponents of the offshore perimeter defense, Kennan counseled Acheson that "we should make sure we did not frighten the Russians into action."

In August, as the military balance changed in Korea, the Soviet Union made overtures to negotiate a restoration of the status quo. This forced the State Department, institutionally divided, to prepare a position paper for the NSC, which stated: "Present public and Congressional opinion in the United States would be dissatisfied with any conclusion falling short of what it would consider a 'final' settlement of the [Korea] problem." On the other hand, "UN military action north of the 38th parallel would result in conflict with the USSR or Communist China," which MacArthur had been instructed to avoid. In conclusion, there was no department conclusion, aside from "maintaining the greatest possible degree of flexibility and freedom of action."

Not every agency was so equivocal. The armed services, especially the army, had never wanted a commitment to South Korea. One month of war had not changed its mind one bit. However, getting in deeper seemed the fastest way of getting out. The Defense Department worried that if the situation were restored to conditions as of 24 June, "the USSR could re-arm a new striking force for a second attempt" that would mean another redeployment for the U.S. Army already burdened with too few resources and too many commitments, especially in Europe. To make its case less self-serving, the Defense Department added an argument that had wide political appeal: Korea "provides the first opportunity to displace part of the Soviet orbit," although this must be done with "great caution and discretion" lest the government alert Russia and China. One week later, on 10 August, the American ambassador to the UN asked the institution "to insure that Korea shall be free, unified and independent." He was trying to prepare international opinion to support new U.S. political objectives. He alerted China to begin its "Resist-America" mobilization and military preparations to contest the move beyond the thirty-eighth parallel.

The Truman administration was divided about uniting all Korea in an anticommunist government. The Pentagon opposed the State Department and the State Department opposed itself—Kennan on one side, Rusk on the other, Acheson and Paul Nitze somewhere in the middle. After negotiations between State and the JCS, their different recommendations went to the NSC. It wrote, and Truman approved, a statement that authorized the occupation of North Korea with several caveats. If Russia or China intervened, the United States was not to cross the thirty-eighth parallel. If they intervened after the crossing, U.S. forces were to protect themselves, not escalate the action. Finally, only the ROKs were to approach the Yalu River. All this was a very complex and nuanced message to send to Douglas MacArthur, a man who now read all ambiguities as leeway to fight the war he wanted. Three days after getting the government's "guidance," described as "a matter of policy" (not an order), he replied: "I regard all of Korea open for our military operations unless and until the enemy capitulates."

By October the flip side of Douglas MacArthur came forth. On his good days, he was brilliant. On his bad days, he was awful. Worst of all, his assets became his liabilities. His confidence in U.S. capabilities, his audacity in the face of obstacles, and his intuition about the enemy created his success at Inchon in mid-September. They would lead him, the army, and the nation astray near the Yalu River in late November. The State Department did not provide much resistance, even though it had reversed its policy position vis-à-vis the army in World War II. Dean Acheson, who once led the fight "against any proposal for retaining the Emperor" of Japan, was an older (and presumably wiser) man in 1950, when he tried to make defeat "as easy as possible for the enemy to swallow." With his tacit approval, Paul Nitze and others tried to do what State opposed and the War Department favored in 1945: give up the form but capture the substance of unconditional surrender. The UN resolution of 4 October 1950 invited "all sections and representative bodies of the population of Korea, South and North," to participate "in the establishment of a unified government." On 1 October, per instructions from the Pentagon, MacArthur issued what UN sources considered a demand for total capitulation: "The early and total defeat and complete destruction of your armed forces and war making potential is now inevitable. . . . Lay down your arms and cease hostilities under such military supervision as I may direct."

No one in Washington, military or civilian, amended MacArthur's campaign plan or his political objectives. The administration would grow increasingly worried that he was taking unwarranted risks. But it was trapped by Truman's reluctance to discuss "victory" in a "police action," lest the word energize the public to confront Russia and thereby "strain to the breaking point the fabric of world peace." Hence the citizenry was free to define victory any way it chose. After Inchon, according to Harriman, expectations were so great that "it was almost impossible not to go ahead and complete the job."

Within the American political spectrum, crossing the border of North Korea was not an extreme position that fall. The secretary of the navy and some general officers were proposing preventive war against the Soviet Union in the name of "civilization." By comparison, President Truman took a moderate position shared by those on his left and right. According to Republican critics, to halt at the thirty-eighth parallel would simply be appeasement: "The North Korean Army should be destroyed. . . . That is the only way to remove the menace." According to the liberal wing of Truman's own party, proceeding north would strengthen the UN, whose prior attempt to unify Korea was rejected three times by the communist regime. The Americans for Democratic Action and the *New Republic* joined prestigious newspapers, from the *Atlanta Constitution* to the *New York Times,* which supported erasing the border, as did the rest of the country by 2.5 to 1.4 in public opinion polls.

In mid-August, when the war still looked problematic to the public, Truman's assistant press secretary noted that Republicans were planning to make Korea "their leading issue in the congressional elections." Now, GOP campaign strategy was a boon to Democrats, who were quite happy to talk about "our ultimate victory in Korea," not the 25 percent inflation in consumer prices for basic commodities from June to September. The president's public approval rating was at its highest point since his so-called honeymoon in 1945, although it was still 30 points below approval for the Korean War. However, the prestige and power of the Truman presidency were latched to an issue and a military commander it could not command. Nor could the White House control a potential enemy who viewed Truman's actions differently than did Truman himself. On 2 October, the day after MacArthur issued his communiqué to North Korea (quoted earlier), Mao Tse-tung wired Stalin that he had decided "to do combat with the forces of America and its running dog Syngman Rhee."[5]

MACARTHUR, TRUMAN, AND A CHINESE SPEED BUMP ON THE ROAD TO VICTORY

On 9 October 1950 U.S. ground forces crossed the thirty-eighth parallel. Since too many North Koreans had escaped for the South to conduct a mere mop-up operation, the JCS repeated its recommendation to lift restrictions so MacArthur could complete the job. One of the first messages to him from George Marshall, secretary of defense as of 20 September, was a handwritten note saying, "We want you to feel unhampered tactically and strategically." MacArthur would not forget these words Marshall came to regret.

In October, Washington's attention moved from Korea, leaving MacArthur largely on his own. The State Department, which had vigorously debated whether to cross the thirty-eighth parallel, switched its focus to negotiations about Germany's place in the NATO alliance. The Defense Department, which had closely monitored the Inchon operation, was now concerned with how to finance the first three months of the Korean War. White House attention returned to where it had been most of the year, the 1950 congressional election.

Truman, defying conventional political wisdom that a president should not campaign when not running himself, had planned to conduct another whistle-stop tour reminiscent of 1948. In May, between Washington State and Washington, D.C., he made fifty-seven speeches attacking "the prejudices of the extreme right" and heaping praise on "progressive measures." Then, in June, with the Korean War in progress, it would not be presidential to stump in Ohio and the other places Truman had planned. However, a trip to see MacArthur would be "good election-year stuff," in the words of a member of the White Staff staff. Truman's pride in the presidency made him reluctant to go on what Acheson called a "pilgrimage." Then his political counsel reminded him of Franklin Roosevelt in 1944. The top of the national ticket (Truman was the bottom) went to see MacArthur in Honolulu to dramatize progress in the Pacific three months before reelection. In 1950 a similar act would be "an inspired move," according to Senator Millard Tydings, Joe McCarthy's foremost critic, campaigning for reelection himself. It not only would put Truman back in the headlines by posing him with the hero of the hour but also would lend credence to the president's lame claim that "General MacArthur and I are in perfect agreement and have been ever since I put him in the job he has now." The worst Republicans could say about the meeting was "It's about time."

On 15 October President Truman—accompanied by thirty-eight White House reporters and photographers—landed at Wake Island, a 4,700-mile trip, for a ninety-six-minute meeting with MacArthur. There was no agenda, little preparation, and few people with the stature to engage the general about policy. (Neither Marshall nor Acheson would come to pay homage.) Hence the Truman administration lost its one opportunity, if it ever had one, to instruct the theater commander about its global strategy of limited war in a secondary theater. In accordance with the president's guidance, the Pentagon was there to offer to supply whatever MacArthur requested. Dean Rusk was about the only person "to lend a note of seriousness to the meeting" by raising the issue that "Russia was continually urging China to get into the war."

Having been Joe Stilwell's G-3 in World War II (assistant chief of staff for plans and operations), the State Department's representative knew how to "war-game" a prospective military campaign. Rusk made pointed inquiries about U.S. contingency plans and State's number one question: What was the advisability of using Indian and Pakistani troops along the fortieth parallel to separate the U.S. Army from the Soviet Union and the PRC? After the meeting MacArthur had a question of his own: "Who was that young whipper-snapper who was asking questions?" During the meeting Truman was primarily worried about the American electorate. He scribbled Rusk a note of warning: "I want to get out of here before we get in trouble!"

Aside from the 1950 election, Truman had another concern since 3 October, when the PRC warned it would "resist" an American invasion of North Korea. The president asked MacArthur on the fifteenth, "What are the chances for Chinese and Soviet interference?" "Very little," he replied. The day before this exchange, the Far East Command's chief of military intelligence gave a far better answer. "The decision" regarding communist policy "is beyond the purview of collection" at the theater level. In short, ask the CIA. If MacArthur had adopted this tact and said, "Mr. President, your sources are better than mine," the ball would have been in the court of agencies that refused to be conclusive. The CIA said that "intelligence is lacking to permit a valid prediction." The JCS said China has the "potential" (who knows the intention) "to openly intervene." The State Department could not speak with much assurance, since it received less information from MacArthur about communist military positions than his headquarters gave the press. If the president, desperate for someone to speak with confidence, had not got the definitive opinion he wanted to hear, he might have restricted the military campaign in North Korea. Then, MacArthur would not have got what he desperately wanted, an opportunity for a decisive victory.

Truman, like nearly everybody that October, stood in "awe" of MacArthur. His "persuasive powers" and genius for dramatic presentation caused "doubters to doubt themselves," said Matt Ridgway. At Wake Island the general gave the president a rosy prediction that no one probed. Omar Bradley seldom saw Truman "in higher spirits. It was a relief to us all that the Korean War would soon be over." Consequently, while the president basked in a "very friendly" conversation with a "most interesting person," the Pentagon studied troop shortages in Europe and Bradley went back to writing his World War II memoir. MacArthur, who came to Wake Island wary of Truman's "quick and violent temper," left with assurance of "complete unity in the aims and conduct of our foreign policy"— what the president announced the day he returned to the States.

On 24 October, back at military headquarters, MacArthur ordered his subordinate commanders "to drive forward toward the North with all speed and with full utilization of all their force." The Joint Chiefs read the message and reminded him of their directive (27 September) that Americans were not to approach the Yalu. He reminded them of their own words—this was a "matter of policy," not a command—and claimed that "this entire subject was covered in my conference at Wake Island," particularly the forty-minute private meeting with Truman for which no transcript was kept. The JCS could not dispute MacArthur's statement and never countermanded his orders. Meanwhile, the UN command pushed north in what seemed a "complete rout," according to a reporter at Eighth Army headquarters. Then, on 25 October, the First South Korean division, which guarded the right flank of UN forces, was smashed by what its commander called "many, many Chinese." In the next ten days the new enemy would inflict over 1,000 casualties on the U.S. Army.

The JCS were uncertain how to react. Bradley had just told the British Chiefs of Staff: "We all agree that if the Chinese Communists come into Korea, we get out." However, the ten-day engagement was "halfway between" covert action and a major military clash. It was not covered by established policy. The Joint Chiefs, apprehensive that "the situation may get out of hand and lead to a general war," asked MacArthur for his own assessment of the Chinese action. He rejected any "hasty conclusions" and urged that a final appraisal "await a more complete accumulation of military facts." Consequently, after Chinese soldiers broke contact and withdrew on 6 November, MacArthur told the JCS that he would order a "reconnaissance in force," the same term he used in his breakneck race to the Philippines in 1944. "Only through such an offensive effort can any accurate measure be taken of enemy strength."

MacArthur was doing what he did in World War II, proceeding so quickly he overthrew constrictions the JCS put on his theater of operations. As for the PRC, their military objectives were as volatile as those of the United States. In December 1950 Mao Tse-tung would resemble MacArthur, a far cry from where Mao started in April, when he tried to discourage Kim Il Sung from undertaking an invasion that might incite America and tie down resources on an objective other than Taiwan. As late as early October, Mao still hoped that a defensive barrier set up between Pyongyang and Wonsan would stop the "imperialist bandits."

He certainly did not want to provoke what one of his field marshals called "a level of retaliation that would escalate the Korean conflict into another world war," least of all one against American army corps with fifty times more artillery than their Chinese counterparts. However, before Mao could construct a solid line, Americans moved north so quickly they ran into Chinese communist forces (CCF), by mutual accident. China was planning to attack ROK units only when it hit the flank of the Eighth Cavalry. Lin Piao, China's foremost general, was so nervous about battle with America he declined command of the northeast Asia field force. Mao had to turn to Peng Dehaui, who knocked U.S. units back but would not pursue. "All we seem to have accomplished," Peng lamented that fall, "is to convince the Americans that Chinese troops have not entered Korea in any strength."[6]

THE DEFEAT IN THE VOTING BOOTH

MacArthur's military intelligence chief, Charles Willoughby, soon came to the opinion that the U.S. army was not in danger. The American people were far less confident on 7 November, when they went to the polls for the congressional election. The Republicans picked up twenty-eight seats in the House and five in the Senate, almost all for the right wing of the party. Statistically, it was not an overwhelming defeat for the party in power in an off-year election. Democrats had lost twice as many seats in 1946. Nonetheless, neither the White House staff nor Truman's wife had ever seen him more overcome with remorse.

If the president were responsible for letting his political enemies win and his friends down, it was because MacArthur ran into a Chinese army speed bump at a most inappropriate time. While convinced that history taught clear lessons about appeasement, Truman apparently forgot what Franklin Roosevelt had done in 1942. By invading French North Africa, FDR prevented a military defeat on the eve of a congressional election. In 1950, when MacArthur charged into an ambush at a time when America thought the war was virtually won, Democrats began to feel "everything sliding out from under the party." Republican statements that "all the piety of the Administration" about its stand in Korea "will not put any life into the bodies of the young men coming back in wooden boxes" resurrected the charge that Dean Acheson was to blame for giving China to the communists back in 1949. Hyperbole or not, at least one-third of the Democratic candidates later said that this issue hurt them significantly in the 1950 election, among them Millard Tydings, whose defeat made other critics of Joe McCarthy very cautious. As for the president, he told a cabinet meeting that aside from the "McCarthy–Jenner–Nixon poison," the vote turned on "hero worship," a cryptic comment suggesting that Truman felt he had lost to MacArthur. This was hardly auspicious for bringing the CINCFE into line.[7]

MACARTHUR'S ADVANCE, WASHINGTON'S RETREAT

After the initial contact with the CCF, Washington resumed its chronic debate: the Pentagon on one side, the State Department on the other, with the White House floating in between. The Eighth Army was wary since running into Chinese soldiers without any warning. However, it had no firm data about how many Chinese were in Korea or what their objectives were. Since intelligence could find only battalions (not Red divisions), the JCS agreed with MacArthur's prediction that digging in "would condemn us to an indefinite retention of our military forces along difficult defense lines in North Korea." In a nutshell, the Defense Department still felt that a decisive military victory was the only way "for getting our divisions out in order to use them elsewhere," according to the army chief of staff on 21 November.

The State Department was as wary as the Eighth Army. Its office of Chinese affairs predicted Red China's intervention. Most of the department's constituents in the international community—NATO governments and the UN—did not want to proceed beyond the narrow neck of North Korea, approximately 50 miles from the Yalu River border in the west and 130 miles in the east. Nonetheless, in the interagency debate, the diplomats were outgunned, partly because common wisdom in Washington held that "the State Department was a loser" in the 1950 election and Acheson was the largest single liability. Some Democrats thought the problem was primarily style: Acheson "ought to sound as though he had cow manure on his feet." Others said "Americans won't stand for any concessions to the Communists." Either way, the White House was not apt to emphasize what Acheson reminded the NSC three days after the election: "Politically we are not committed to the conquest of all of Korea." It approved MacArthur's resumption of his drive north, "pending further clarification [of] the military objectives of the Chinese Communists."

General Willoughby admitted there were some 833,000 Chinese soldiers in Manchuria with the potential to launch a counteroffensive without notice. On the other hand, "on the other hand" was pervasive in his daily intelligence summaries for the Far East Command. While he could draw judicious distinctions between political predictions of intention and theater assets able to assess only capabilities, Willoughby was also prone to emulate MacArthur in claiming to comprehend the "Oriental mind." If this were not so serious, it might be amusing considering he emigrated from Germany at age eighteen and was a leading expert on European languages and history—his responsibility in the 1930s when he wrote and edited articles, books, and dictionaries for the army service schools.

Recruited by MacArthur in 1940 to keep a record of his accomplishments, Willoughby would compare MacArthur at Hollandia (1944) to Hannibal at Cannae. Reporters, hating his ham-handed censorship, portrayed him as a sycophant telling the boss what he wanted to hear. Actually, Willoughby did not tell him much at all. He spent most of his time writing MacArthur's official history of World War II. Young field-grade officers briefed the CINCFE, usually without him present at all. MacArthur was his own intelligence chief, as he had been in World War II, when he disregarded Willoughby's warnings not to race to a new landing in New Guinea or Kyushu, Japan. MacArthur did not exert overt pressure for optimistic reports. There were few facts available about the Chinese army, whose soldiers were marching at night into the mountains of north-central Korea, where they were camouflaged from U.S. Air Force observation, inaccessible to road-bound U.S. reconnaissance, and immune from signal intelligence detection for lack of communications equipment of their own. The absence of hard data gave MacArthur and Willoughby room to delve into the realm of Chinese communist political motivation, areas where neither man belonged.

In mid-1951 MacArthur's successor, Matt Ridgway, recorded in his diary that "U.S. military teaching rejects as a basis for action guesses as to what the enemy will do." In late 1950 MacArthur and Willoughby concluded that the PRC would not intervene in Korea, which was perfectly reasonable provided one believed that America had no malice and China's motivation never was defensive. They believed—and leaked to *Time* magazine—that if the PRC wanted to fight, it would have sent forces to Pusan in July, when a slight enhancement to North Korean combat power "might have pushed U.N. forces into a Dunkirk on their southern beachhead. Now, for a change, not the free world but the enemy had acted too little and too late." As for the Chinese soldiers who surprised America in late October, they were "volunteers" within North Korean divisions making their final stand at the border, the communist equivalent of the 30,000 South Koreans plugging holes and hauling cargo for U.S. divisions.

MacArthur had bought the story spewed by communist propaganda and Chinese soldiers captured in the field. Mao now had a greater ambition than keeping the United States away from the Yalu. It served his purpose (described later) to "purposely show ourselves to be weak [and] increase the arrogance of our enemies." Like most good deception plans, this one reinforced what his opponent already believed. MacArthur told the American ambassador to Korea on 17 November that some 25,000 Chinese had crossed the Yalu, "certainly no more than 30,000," less than half the number cited in Willoughby's last report to Washington: 64,200 Chinese south of the Yalu plus "a continued build-up." In fact, there were some 250,000 Chinese in North Korea by the second week of November.

By then nearly everyone in Washington—soldiers and civilians—was far less confident than MacArthur. George Marshall said that U.S. units were 20 percent understrength, widely dispersed, and vulnerable to attack. Nonetheless, he ignored his self-imposed rule to communicate solely through the president and the JCS in order to send a "personal message" to MacArthur: "Everyone here, Defense, State, and the President, is intensely desirous of supporting you in the most effective manner within our means." Not only anxious to soothe the antagonism between his and the MacArthur wings of the army, Marshall might have remembered his own tribulations under Franklin Roosevelt, who changed military plans nearly as soon as he approved them. Whatever the reason, Marshall told Dean Acheson: "I think it is a great mistake to confuse everybody by changing orders." Correct in most cases, this may not have been appropriate vis-à-vis a theater commander who needed restraint more than encouragement as he pursued total victory but ran a "serious risk of becoming involved in the world war we are trying to avoid," according to an assistant secretary of defense.

Acheson, although the self-described "first minister of the government," deferred to Marshall when it came to instructing MacArthur. Damaged political goods, the secretary of state was concerned with self-protection, the same motive he attributed to Chinese foreign policy. He wanted to stop at the narrow neck of North Korea or at least the high ground overlooking the Yalu, some ten miles from the Chinese border. Nonetheless, he concurred that if the UN proceeded, the PRC would probably not attack. Unlike MacArthur, Acheson believed that Communist China was more Chinese than communist. It had no good reason to rescue North Korea, a Russian satellite.

Acheson rejected suggestions that he threaten China to prevent its intervention, an ultimatum that might stifle rapprochement and be an insult from which China could not back down. This tough-minded exponent of realpolitik had great faith in the believability of vague assurances of good will, bereft of a specific date for American withdrawal or the creation of a buffer zone keeping America away from the Chinese border. The PRC already heard Acheson say that America would not fight in Korea, not cross the thirty-eighth parallel, and not defend Taiwan, reversed on 27 June in an effort to appease MacArthur and his congressional supporters. It now thought all U.S. statements were a trick designed "to fool us. If we did nothing, the aggressive enemy would surely continue its advance up to the Yalu River and would devise a second scheme," this time against the PRC. Since Red China believed that Washington was ruled by "Wall Street warmongers" and friends of Chiang Kai-shek, Acheson would have been more credible if he simply said: "Cross the Yalu and you'll be nuked."

Polite communiqués would not restrain China or Douglas MacArthur, who would have obeyed a firm, specific order but never received one, as State Department officials privately admitted: Washington had "doubts and misgivings," which were not "quarrels or disagreements" because everyone had "refrained from making issues of these matters or taking them up in ways that might have irritated him." MacArthur felt he had enough airpower to guarantee his prediction (20 November) that "the war is very definitely coming to an end." He ordered it to fly, to "exhaustion if necessary," in order to "destroy every means of communication and every installation, factory, city, and village" that communist forces could possibly use. By late November, U.S. air had wrecked barracks and warehouses anywhere near the southern bank of the Yalu. When he met Truman in mid-October, MacArthur reassured the worried president much like he once told Roosevelt that only minor resistance had to be "mopped up" in New Guinea.

"Now that we have bases for our Air Forces in Korea, if the Chinese tried to get down to Pyongyang there would be the greatest slaughter." Unfortunately, because Pyongyang was now in UN hands, Chinese forces had far less ground to travel before contacting U.S. units heading north. Nonetheless, on 24 November, the day MacArthur began his final offensive, he assured the UN that his "air forces, in full strength, completely interdicted the rear areas . . . [and] there is little sign of hostile military activity."

MacArthur had become what Mao Tse-tung was counting on: a "stubborn, old warrior" who rejected any notion that he had reached what Clausewitz called a "culminating point," the place where "the superior strength of the attack diminishes day by day." North Korea, at its narrow neck, is relatively flat and barely 100 miles wide. Moving north toward the border with Russia and China, MacArthur entered a wide, mountainous range far beyond the reach of naval gunfire that terrified North Korean soldiers because it struck without warning. At the same time, the army pulled away from ports under UN command, making it dependent on trucks with limited load capacity, since the air force had destroyed railroads throughout North Korea. PRC publications already identified this area as "an ideal graveyard for imperialist invaders," which was why the commander of the Chinese Fourth Field Army wondered if MacArthur would put his neck in this noose. If he did, he would be operating in territory uniquely suited to soldiers schooled in Maoist military tactics, vintage 1930: "Lure the enemy to penetrate deep, . . . concentrate before hand under cover along the route through which [he] is sure to pass, suddenly descend on him while he is moving, encircle and attack him before he knows what is happening, and conclude the fighting with all speed."

There was a way to fight this type of opponent on this type of terrain, as Chiang Kai-shek had discovered in the mid-1930s: advance cautiously, cover one's flanks, build blockhouses, then advance cautiously again. Airpower, MacArthur's strong suit, had distinct limitations. He was no longer fighting North Koreans at the Pusan perimeter, where communist supply lines were very long and each heavy armored division needed 200 tons a day. The Chinese were a light infantry army with far fewer requirements and far less exposure to surveillance. By late November at least 300,000 Chinese soldiers were hiding in the mountains of north-central Korea. For days, spotter planes for Eighth Army artillery had seen nothing of an enemy that stood undetected on the flanks of widely separated, thinly supplied columns racing as fast as they could down narrow trails through rugged terrain—to "hit the jackpot" and get "home by Christmas," in MacArthur's words. Very few of them would ever get to the Yalu or quickly back to the United States. The American army, which had scarcely fired a shot for several days, was about to be slammed all along its line, prior to conducting the longest retreat in its history. When it stopped after 275 miles, on 15 January 1951, it was 80 miles south of the thirty-eighth parallel.[8]

"WE FACE AN ENTIRELY NEW WAR."
(MacArthur, 28 November 1950)

The strength of the Chinese lay in deception, tactical mobility in rugged terrain, and "no reluctance to engage in close hand-to-hand combat," especially at night. These were the vulnerabilities of the Americans they ambushed, for whom on-the-job-military training had dire consequences. By the time an experienced cadre of combat soldiers was created, many would be killed, captured, or rotated. Between the Pusan perimeter and the Yalu, the American army rounded up reserves and garrison soldiers, gave some crash instruction, and sent them to the front, where they learned to call in airpower and artillery, expending shells at a rate three times higher than what America had used in World War II. The critical assessment the Chinese made of American infantry in November replicated observations Matt Ridgway and James Gavin had been sending to the Pentagon since the war began: poor small-unit leadership, enlisted men easily stampeded, and infantry "entirely dependent" on heavy weapons of marginal utility at night.

In the winter of 1950, U.S. soldiers ran a military gauntlet with one thing on their mind: "How soon can we get t'Hell outa this goddam country." Once the Eighth Army, west of the Taebaek Mountains, and the X Corps, to the east, suffered some 14,000 casualties and retreated south, the PRC achieved its initial and minimal objective of preserving a buffer between it and the anticommunist world. "China had no alternative," said General Peng Dehuai, the commander of the Fourth Field Army, "but to teach the imperialists a lesson." The ensuing communist success was reminiscent of Inchon—a tactical victory over an extended enemy hit at a weak spot. In September America finally resolved to exploit Inchon and escalate its war aims. In November the PRC followed suit, at the command of Mao Tse-tung, who micromanaged his military more than Truman ever did.

There was no MacArthur in Chinese civil-military relations, aside from Mao, reminiscent of his adversary insofar as he too believed he was a man of destiny forging "a new turning point in history." MacArthur had hoped to humiliate the communists so badly that the PRC would crumble. Mao, who had grave doubts about war as late as October, wanted to exploit the fact that MacArthur stuck his neck deep into North Korea that November. The United States would have been invulnerable behind its defense perimeter. Now the Chinese infantry could hold the enemy army up for ransom, meaning Mao would not sign an armistice until the United States (1) withdrew all UN forces from all of Korea, (2) terminated all assistance to Taiwan, (3) handed over Chang Kai-shek's UN seat, and (4) gave Mao participation in the peace treaty to be signed with Japan. This last demand would force neutrality on the old enemy "rearing up again [as] a fascist power" and deny American forces bases by which it would inherit "the mantle of Japanese militarism" in northeast Asia. In short, with the United States driven back to Hawaii, China under Mao would resume its historic mission as the leader on the mainland and the western Pacific region of the world.

"The Schoolmaster was getting drunk with success," according to General Peng, a down-to-earth peasant who sardonically told confidants "Mao is stronger on strategy than tactics." In October, Peng had written that a feasible goal for his force was "a reasonable solution of the Korean problem." He must have shook his head at the *People's Daily* (January 1951), which told him to "drive the U.S. invasion army down to the sea." Experienced combat soldiers close to the fight in the field already saw serious trouble for the CCF, whose logistics capacity had been designed to support a perimeter defense along the Pyongyang-Wonsan line. That December, when American infantry did not panic and held their positions, they shaped targets for heavy weapons to do enormous damage. The First Marine Division, with close air support, inflicted some 50,000 casualties as they withdrew toward South Korea and gave Chesty Puller the chance to add another epigram to Marine Corps lore: "The enemy is in front of us, behind us, to the left of us, and to the right of us. The bastards won't escape *this* time." Short of ordnance, food, medicine, clothing, and transportation, the Chinese army had reached its own culminating point before its politburo ever announced that the thirty-eighth parallel was "obliterated forever [as a] demarcation line of political geography." American forces could use their strategic mobility to withdraw from contact, catch their breath, and prepare to meet an exhausted enemy. However, before the initial panic was to subside, the army equivalent of a Chesty Puller would have to assume field command because MacArthur had become the greatest panic monger in Korea.

A man of mercurial moods, MacArthur exuded optimism as long as total victory was credible. By 28 November, when his dream of destroying Asian communism vanished, he swung toward despair: "This command has done everything humanly possible within its capabilities but is now faced with conditions beyond its control and its strength." The Chinese objective, he wired the JCS, was "the complete destruction of all United Nations forces"; it was time to escalate or get out of Korea. This message kicked off a new round of discussion in the NSC, which had held in September that America should not run "a substantial risk of general war with the Soviet Union or Communist China." The new debate, which lasted the whole month of December, pitted old contestants against each other. The Defense Department argued with the State Department, while the president played judge and referee. Congress and the public retained their right to criticize whatever policy ensued.

The Defense Department's position was clear, as the service secretaries wrote on 4 December: "When we went into Korea we did not guarantee military victories; we did though undertake to persist in our policy of seeking a peaceful world through the medium of the United Nations." In concrete terms this meant that America could not afford to risk its ground forces in an area "not worth a nickel," according to Joe Collins, "while the Russians hold Vladivostok and [Port

Arthur] on the other flank." It made far more military sense to return to the defensive perimeter policy "on the islands and off the mainland." If American forces were pinned down and destroyed or held hostage in Korea, little might be left to keep Russia or China from what they really wanted, Japan and Formosa.

The State Department's position was more complicated and equivocal. Its international constituents—NATO and the UN—had been nervous when the United States crossed the thirty-eighth parallel in October and quietly suggested, in early November, not to move beyond the narrow neck of North Korea. The subsequent debacle opened the diplomatic floodgates, as Dean Acheson told the NSC on 3 December: "The present tendency among other countries is to criticize us rather than the Chinese Communists. . . . Many of our Allies [particularly the Labour Party governing England] would quit us and deal with the Soviet Union" if we went to war with the PRC. America could lose the Japan of Europe—its geopolitical base in the North Atlantic, as Acheson reminded the JCS: "We can bring U.S. power into play only with the cooperation of the British."

State opposed bombing vital targets anywhere near the Yalu, let alone the PRC itself. At the same time, it believed (much like Mao) that U.S. global credibility was on the line. "There is a danger of our becoming," Acheson said that December, "the greatest appeasers of all time if we abandon the Koreans and they are slaughtered. [However,] if there is a Dunkirk and we are forced out, it is a disaster but not a disgrace." What is more, according to Dean Rusk, that contingency would "force the Chinese Communists to make a really major effort at great cost to themselves" and subsequent moves "into Southeast Asia," a theme to which he would return when discussing Vietnam in the 1960s. In 1950 a last "stand" in Korea would give America more prestige than "if we were simply to bow out at this point."

Omar Bradley, JCS chairman, agreed that "appeasement is gaining in Europe. The Germans are already saying we have proved that we are weak." He advocated a blockade "and a good many other things to bother [China] though we would probably not use the A-Bomb." However, believing that the United States had about thirty-six hours to decide to make an orderly withdrawal or hazard the loss of its ground force, he felt neither "Acheson [nor] Rusk fully appreciated the complexities and risks" of "a military evacuation under heavy enemy fire," a point related to another issue Bradley mentioned on 3 December: "It was [not only] a race to get into the beachhead. . . . It was also a question of how long the American public will stand without saying we are at war with China." If American troops fled Korea with heavy casualties, the public and the Congress would demand a drastic response already foretold in statements of assorted people with decided influence on Capitol Hill.

Most proponents of the position that "we are at war in every sense of the word" advocated atomic weapons. They included the commanders of all major veterans' organizations, members of the Senate and the House (from Owen Brewster, a conservative Republican, to Paul Douglas, a liberal Democrat), and

Bernard Baruch, an adviser to presidents back to Woodrow Wilson and a man with enormous influence in Congress. Actually, these so-called public opinion leaders were trailing public opinion. Polls taken the week before the Chinese offensive showed that in a hypothetical war, let alone another Dunkirk, a 45 to 38 percent plurality favored dropping atomic bombs on Chinese cities. Nearly everyone in the Truman administration believed that this would activate the Sino-Soviet defense alliance. Even if Russia restricted its response to aircraft and submarines in the Korean theater, the "only chance left to save" the U.S. Army, said its chief of staff, would be "the use or the threat of the use of the A-bomb" against the USSR. The State Department's option—withdrawing in the face of heavy fire— was very risky business. According to George Marshall, the issue was "whether there was any way in which we could 'withdraw from Korea with honor.'"

Because Washington could not decide exactly what to do, it sent equivocal instructions to MacArthur. He was not supposed to "fight a major war" in Korea but was to inflict "maximum damage" to the enemy *there*. He was to hold if he could but never forget that his primary responsibility was the safety of his troops and Japan. MacArthur, having previously exploited every ambiguity in Defense Department messages, now demanded clarity from a government that lacked it: "Is it the present objective of United States political policy to maintain a military position in Korea . . . or to minimize losses by evacuation as soon as it can be accomplished? As I have before pointed out, under the extraordinary limitations and conditions imposed upon the command in Korea, its position is untenable, but it can hold for any length of time up to its complete destruction if overriding political considerations so dictate." Acheson knew that this "prosperity paper" written for the historical record really said: "If the administration does not expand the war to China, the blood of an American army will be on your pampered hands. You'll be impeached, if you're not hung." He did not know that Moscow had already saved him and the American army from the noose.[9]

THE DURABILITY OF LIMITED WAR

American contingency plans had always assumed that, in a war against China, U.S. forces would have to destroy (not just damage) bases in Manchuria to ensure that the army operated under air supremacy. Without it, the U.S. Army could not operate at all, as was well known to the secretary of defense, former army chief of staff in World War II. Unfortunately, on 28 November, when CCF ground forces went on the strategic offensive, the Chinese had 100 high-performance fighters and 200 bombers in Manchuria. Fortunately, these assets remained on the defensive: guarding the Yalu River Valley, hereafter known as MIG Alley.

"For some reason, the Chinese Communists have allowed us to maintain sole control of the air," the chief of naval operations said on 1 December, a mystery Washington never fully solved. In October 1951 Rusk told the British that the

Chinese "were capable of using air power offensively but for some reason chose not to do so." There certainly was no shortage of targets: roads jammed with vehicles, airfields clogged with planes, and best of all Pusan—the exposed and well-lit choke point for the UN logistics command. The destruction of the only deepwater pier and port in South Korea would have disarmed the Eighth Army, trapped it on the mainland, and left Japan without defense on the ground. Hence Admiral Sherman told the president that at the first suggestion of air attack, "we must hit back [Manchuria] or we cannot stay." Truman agreed, although he believed that this would probably start World War III. Like most people faced with a terrible dilemma, he said he would meet that problem "when it comes." Because it never came, Truman could continue to wage a limited war—or a "police action," as he liked to call it.

Because Chinese and Soviet documents are still being disclosed, explanations for why they never used airpower in an offensive role must be tentative. However, some things seem clear. Most Chinese Communist party members, including the foreign minister and the commander of the army, had not wanted to fight America even for a buffer area. After 1 December 1950, when China took the offensive, Chou En-lai, Lin Piao, and others still worried about attacks on the PRC. Mao, a political majority of one, undertook the campaign without air support. If asked to do the same, American military planners would have called this lunacy. So would Mao, before November 1950. On 2 October, when Stalin offered him heavy bombers, Mao reciprocated by saying that "once we are equipped with Soviet weapons, we will cooperate with the Korean comrades in counterattacks to annihilate American aggressor troops." When Stalin withdrew his offer on 11 October, Mao constricted his campaign plan: "We can only fight the puppet [ROK] army. We can establish bases in the vast mountainous areas north" of the narrow neck. Our soldiers "will attack Pyongyang and Wonsan only when they have clear superiority over the enemy in both air and ground forces."

In late November MacArthur's mad dash for the Yalu gave Mao another chance to win a crushing victory. His new campaign plan was based on the premise, as General Peng told his staff, that "the imperialists will run like sheep. Our problem is not Seoul. It is Pusan. Not taking it—just walking there!" A major offense without air attack on ground targets, what Peng warned against, was part intoxication by tactical success. It was also based on the old fear that if the CCF used bombers against UN command targets, the "Wall Street war mongers" might turn Manchuria's wheat fields, forests, mines, and machinery into a radioactive parking lot. Truman was planning nothing this extreme, although he did tell the British prime minister that "every airfield in sight would be bombed in order to protect our troops." Mao never backed Truman into this corner. Even in late 1951, when he had his own air force independent of the Soviet Union, Mao would not involve it in the ground war then around the thirty-eighth parallel. Since 1946, when he began to fear American involvement in the Chinese civil war, Mao sought (and eventually got) a defense compact with Stalin. Nonetheless, he still would not risk his interdiction assets far beyond their border bases because he knew something Truman could not know. Even if America bombed Manchurian airfields (and Manchuria itself), the Russians would still not retaliate against Pusan or other UN bases that could, according to the Pentagon, be "blown right out of sight" for lack of air defense.

In October Stalin wanted to save North Korea because he confronted the same situation Truman had faced in June: a government he created was about to be destroyed. However, even more than a blow to his prestige, he feared a direct clash with the United States, as indicated by his plan to set up Kim Il Sung as a ruler in exile that fall. To avoid these distasteful alternatives, Stalin passed the rescue mission to China, a new phase of his old master plan to foment communist expansion in Asia but maintain plausible denial. In November he recommitted fighters (not bombers) to defend China, lest the PRC not defend North Korea. Some 5,000 Russians would fly air defense, if only because Chinese and North Koreans would not be ready to handle MIG-15s until 1952. However, Stalin always placed strict rules of engagement on his pilots, to the advantage of the UN. Unable to take the initiative, they had to fight at America's convenience. Nor could they pursue enemy planes over water or south of the narrow neck of North Korea. If they did so or bombed ground forces, a Soviet pilot could be captured and explode Stalin's claim of noninvolvement.

This secret was known in the White House and the Defense Department. Only the American public was kept in the dark. In the heat of battle, air-to-ground communications, recorded on armed forces intercepts, were in guttural Russian, not Chinese. The administration never changed its top secret policy: "It is not wise at this time to attempt to hold Russia directly responsible," even in April 1951, when the president justified relieving MacArthur on grounds that bombing China would jeopardize the attempt "to prevent a third world war." Conclusive proof of the danger would be that some 70,000 members of the Soviet armed forces were operating from bases in Manchuria that MacArthur wished to bomb. The government feared that evidence Soviets were killing American pilots would stir "tremendous pressure" to escalate the conflict to "a war with Russia," exactly what Truman's proxy conflict was supposed to deter.

The president never knew how blessed he was by loose talk of a preventive attack on the Kremlin with nuclear weapons he called "the most terrible thing ever discovered." The Soviets apparently felt that unauthorized individuals in Washington spoke for "Truman and his equally obstinate and aggressive Secretary of State, that political half-wit Mr. Acheson." Having dropped the A-bomb on Japan to intimidate the Kremlin in 1945, they were looking for a pretext to nuke Moscow, so Moscow believed. "Hostile and spiteful," Truman intimidated Stalin with political motives and military assets he did not really have.

In 1950 the Strategic Air Command lacked the information (high-altitude reconnaissance) and the power (hydrogen bombs) "to seriously impair the capability of Soviet armed forces to advance rapidly into selected areas of Western

Europe, the Middle East, and the Far East." This official assessment shocked Truman when he finally requested a briefing on nuclear capability in February. He would approve a major rearmament plan (NSC-68) in November to attain what he called "full military parity" with Russia. Meanwhile, the Russians, ignorant about this closely held secret, continued to believe that America had "nuclear supremacy" in Europe. Stalin did not dare give air support to communist ground forces in Korea lest it set off a chain of events leading to what a senior Russian general described "as a crushing defeat of the Soviet Union."

Largely because the Soviets feared U.S. strategic nuclear supremacy, the war in Korea became asymmetrical, in the language of so-called political science. Only UN forces had battlefield air interdiction and tactical fire support. This not only exacerbated tensions within the communist camp (described later) but also aggravated the growing fault line between MacArthur and the Pentagon. The theater commander maintained that "every ounce of [Red China's] military and economic force was thrown into the Korean struggle." The JCS and Marshall testified to Congress that "we are fighting under rather favorable rules for ourselves." Not attacking Manchuria "was more than equalled by the advantages derived from not exposing our [own] vulnerability to air attacks."

Because American forces were so susceptible to airpower and did not know how safe they really were, the Pentagon wished to decentralize authority to respond to a potential Chinese air offensive. It also wished to bring the atomic bomb into the theater, if only to deter the Soviets in the Far East. However, both the president and the JCS feared delegating authority to MacArthur, since he "might make a premature decision" and thereby bring Russian air and naval power into the war, the Defense Department's nightmare scenario. Rather than risk that event, the JCS kept tight control over strategic assets; the atomic bomb arrived in Guam the day Truman relieved MacArthur.

MacArthur, who saw the world from the Pacific, argued that Korea was the soft underbelly of the Soviet empire, "at the end of an endless one-track railroad to a peninsular battleground that led only to the sea." Foolishly, the "Truman–Acheson–Marshall–Bradley–general staff group concentrated its resources at the center to the neglect of the vital ends." Senior positions at State, Defense, and Central Intelligence were held by former military men who had worked in the Office for Strategic Planning or held major commands in the European theater during World War II. In either case—or both—their nemesis had been the peripheral strategy and MacArthur's call to fight in "the Pacific first." His new plan to take on China must have had an all-too-familiar ring. George Marshall, who had said in November 1940 that "a serious commitment in the Pacific is just what Germany would like to see us undertake," said in November 1950 that to fight a "general war with the Chinese Communists would be to fall into a carefully laid Russian trap." Now that it had apparently sprung, the CIA director, Walter Bedell Smith, once General Eisenhower's chief of staff, warned that the Soviets can "bleed us to death in Asia while defeating the armament effort in Europe."

Truman had stumbled into the penalty of waging a proxy war. Having hoped to make a point to Russia without engaging it directly, he was expending scarce resources on a secondary opponent. Worst of all, he could not pull out of Asia in favor of Europe, as he, Acheson, Marshall, and Averell Harriman informed the British at an emergency meeting on 4 December: "No Administration in the United States could possibly urge the American people to take vigorous action in its foreign policy on one ocean front while on the other they seemed to be rolled back and to accept a position of isolation." With domestic credibility, congressional support, and the NSC-68 rearmament plan held hostage in Korea, the administration needed a field commander whom they could trust not to lose or escalate the war. They got him three days before Christmas.[10]

THE RISE OF MATTHEW RIDGWAY AND
THE FALL OF DOUGLAS MACARTHUR

On 23 December 1950 Lieutenant General Walton "Johnnie" Walker, the commander of the Eighth Army, died in a traffic accident. Once George Patton's "toughest son of a bitch," he was sixty-one years old, overweight, and a roadbound tanker who sped around at seventy miles per hour, which is how he died. His replacement, Matthew Bunker Ridgway, was a fifty-five-year-old infantryman with the stamina to force the U.S. Army out of its vehicles, to prepare the ground, plant a defense, and prevent an ambush. He had something else in abundance, presence: a ramrod backbone, blazing eyes, and a rock-hard jaw. "The force that emanated from him was *awesome*," said an aide. "You had the impression he could knock over a building with a single blow or stare a hole through a wall."

MacArthur never got along with Walker, which is a reason he split the X Corps from the Eighth Army. He had had far more faith in Ridgway, whose assignment he requested despite a suspicious past: war plans staff, European corps commander, and the army's deputy chief of staff for operations. (MacArthur would not reproach him as he did Robert Eichelberger in World War II: "You are a good friend of George Catlett Marshall.") When Ridgway reported for duty on 25 December, MacArthur said: "The Eighth Army is yours, Matt. Do with it what you like." Ridgway subsequently wrote: "No field commander could ask for more. . . . The full responsibilities were mine." If MacArthur was pressuring Washington to escalate or suffer a shameful defeat, he pulled the rug out from under himself when he handed over the Eighth Army, with the X Corps reattached.

When Ridgway immediately asked for permission to attack, MacArthur grinned broadly, probably because it confirmed his hunch that the latest commander of the Eighth Army would support MacArthur's new grand strategy: another Inchon-type operation but on a grander scale. Because "the entire military resources of the Chinese nation" were supposedly committed to Korea, MacArthur believed that the PRC was open "to [a] counter-invasion against vulnerable areas of the Chinese mainland." An amphibious operation such as he envisioned—American navy, air force, airborne, and logistics, with Chiang Kai-shek's 500,000 men—would not be easy to sell with the enemy on its way to Pusan; nor was Inchon the previous August. When he made his new proposal to the JCS on 30 December, he had in theater the man who had been Inchon's strongest advocate inside the Pentagon. Maybe Ridgway, who had commanded the Eighty-second Airborne in World War II, could pry the division loose from his friends in Washington and drop it on enemy airfields before the beach assault, a MacArthur tactic used in World War II.

Ridgway, no "yes-man," would later write of his pride in "preventing hair-brained tactical schemes which would have cost the lives of thousands of men," such as rescuing the French at Dienbienphu in 1954. Nonetheless, this "airborne soldier" who believed in operating behind enemy lines concurred "at once" with MacArthur's plan, although for reasons of his own: to divert Chinese operations from Korea, not overthrow Mao Tse-tung. Small compensation, the attack would have frightened Mao as much as Dean Acheson. The former had long feared that "the boss of imperialism" would launch deep envelopments into Chinese provinces known for "dissatisfaction among the national bourgeoise." One reason he wanted America thrown out of Korea was so he could deploy his army south of Manchuria. In 1951, when Acheson described the internal Chinese opposition as mere "disruptive influences without any centralized direction," Mao launched a campaign against the "democratic individualists" whom MacArthur hoped to foment with a landing beneath the Yangtze River.

The feasibility of MacArthur's plan may never be known. When Ridgway recommended it to Joe Colllins, a West Point classmate, it sunk like a rock. After that, Ridgway proceeded to accomplish what his mentor George Marshall sent him to Korea to do: create the military conditions for a political settlement without depleting America's strength in a secondary theater. MacArthur said that "there is no substitute for victory." Ridgway would say that in the era of cold war and containment he was not sure what "victory" meant, aside from "accomplish[ing] what you set out to do—which we did in Korea."

Ridgway had arrived in the theater directly from the Pentagon, where the initial panic subsided weeks before it did on the front lines. As early as 5 and 8 December, Marshall told cabinet meetings that "there *seems* to be some improvement in the Korean situation"; "for a time we can hold a line . . . unless exposed to heavy Communist air attacks." In early January 1951 Ridgway told the staff of the Eighth Army: "There will be no more discussion of retreat." When an operations officer inadvertently gave him the contingency plan to withdraw, he was relieved on the spot. Other officers got the message. On 15 January the Eighth Army launched its first substantial counterattack, from a line seventy-five miles south of the thirty-eighth parallel. The (heretofore) daring airborne leader conducted a low-risk, step-by-step return toward the border. It could not knock the communists out of Korea, but it would not give them another opportunity to penetrate gaps and encircle a major enemy force. On 17 March the UN command recaptured Seoul —and would never lose it again.

On 20 March the JCS informed MacArthur that the government would seek a negotiated settlement before anyone on either side could cross the thirty-eighth parallel one more time. In short, the Truman administration now defined "containment" as the restoration of the status quo. First Ridgway, the so-called miracle man who turned around a beaten army, robbed MacArthur of his luster. Now Truman and Acheson would rob him of his destiny to roll back, if not crush, Asian communism. In March 1951 MacArthur looked much like he did before the war: "tired and depressed"; "a beaten man"—well not quite. He had one last card to play, and he played it in defiance of a presidential directive (issued 5 December) to clear all policy statements through the Department of Defense. The day MacArthur received the latest JCS message, he wrote the Republican leader in the House of Representatives: "We must win." Four days later he issued a communiqué stating that he would accept a CCF surrender or depart from his "tolerant effort to contain the war" inside Korea and "doom Red China to the risk of imminent military collapse." Under these stipulations and threats, the Chinese would not negotiate at all. Acheson called it "sabotage." Robert Lovett, deputy secretary of defense, called it "the most popular public statement anyone has ever made." He warned Acheson that "if the president challenged it, he would be in the position at once of being on the side of sin."

MacArthur was really talking to America, not the PRC. He apparently thought he would win no matter how Truman reacted. If the president acquiesced, as he had done before, the military commander would control military policy. If he did not submit, MacArthur must be fired, as Truman and leading journalists were convinced he wished to be. Then, as the general told Ridgway, he could "raise hell" at home and say what he would tell the Senate and the press: "The true object of a commander in war was to destroy the forces opposed to him." "When men become locked in battle there should be no artifice under the name of politics." If MacArthur's pronouncements were not sustained by Congress, there was always the public in the 1952 election. However, his candidacy lay in the future. The next move was up to the president. Would he come out in favor of "sin"?

Truman had taken extraordinary steps to conciliate MacArthur. In January he sent him a personal note (unprecedented action for a president) to explain his policy. However, he now felt that MacArthur's "open defiance of my orders as Commander in Chief . . . left me no choice," except that of impairing "the most powerful and the greatest office in the history of the world," the presidency. If he allowed that to happen, Truman not only would commit what he thought was a mortal sin but also would passively preside over a military escalation that would leave America without NATO allies and UN support. If so, a full-scale war against China would destroy the raison d'être for the intervention in Korea—collective security against aggression. Apart from all these weighty matters, there was another issue, as Truman told one of his staff: "Everybody seems to think I don't have courage enough to do it."

In April 1951 Harry Truman was back where he had been on 25 June 1950. The issue was no longer *if,* it was *how*—then, to intervene in Korea; now, to relieve MacArthur. Truman already had a two-to-one public disapproval rating as of February 1951. How could he pit his reputation against that of a five-star general, even after the latter's retreat from the Yalu River? (In "a clash of personalities," said one presidential assistant, "MacArthur seems to outrank Truman.") White House aides knew that the average American citizen hardly studied the civilian supremacy clause of the Constitution or military strategy per Clausewitz. The public believed that a president's job was to help generals win a war; a general's job need not be to help a president conduct his policy.

Truman believed MacArthur would lose his aura as a soldier when he became a de facto politician arguing policy with his superiors rather than doing his duty in the field. Acheson concurred and advised that to limit the political explosion, the administration would have to discredit MacArthur's contention that the essential issue was whether soldiers or civilians should conduct war. Hence, he warned, the White House could not move without the secretary of defense and the entire JCS: "The thing had to be accomplished with a completely united front, with no cracks in it whatsoever." On this issue Generals Marshall and Bradley had far more credibility than the president, a former lieutenant in Battery D, 129th Field Artillery, Missouri National Guard.

Marshall was reluctant, to say the least. He always made a special effort to accommodate MacArthur, partly because he would not indulge his feelings against him. In April 1951, although the CINCFE gave the Defense Department what it called the "idiot treatment," Marshall had a new reason to counsel caution. Since 1949 he had testified in favor of what he called a hopeless cause—American military preparedness in time of peace. In late November 1950, when the administration finally made a firm commitment to long-term rearmament, it won initial support because the Chinese offensive created the impression that America was on "the brink" of global war. Then Ridgway, Marshall's protégé, pulled the public rug out from under mobilization by victories that "dulled" what Marshall called "the interest and urge" for defense. Because MacArthur had so much support in Congress, Marshall feared his relief would close what was left of the opportunity for enhanced preparedness.

Marshall denied MacArthur's charge of substantial disagreements between the Pentagon and Truman but never made as strong a statement against his brother officer as the "politicos" wished. The JCS, at least in late March, did not even want to attend a White House meeting about what they called "considerations" best left to the president and the secretary of state. Acheson had no doubt that this continuation of the "separation of military and political questions" would have been disastrous for him. It would be convenient for Omar Bradley, who recently had written: "Thirty-two years in the peacetime army had taught me to do my job, hold my tongue, and keep my name out of the papers." It also taught him to be deferential to Congress, which traditionally made military policy through appropriations bills. World War II had enhanced presidential power, but Acheson and Marshall could attest that Capitol Hill was not supine. Bradley was grateful to have been spared "the savage mauling the right-wing primitives" had given them. He knew his "Washington 'honeymoon'" would end if MacArthur were sacked and the JCS involved. About to retire after four decades in the service, he "did not relish going out on that sour note."

What is more, Bradley simply did not like the idea of relieving MacArthur for insubordination. Having read all the message traffic, and probably drafting some himself, he knew "there is little evidence that General MacArthur ever . . . acted in opposition to an order of the Joint Chiefs." (The gag order of December was Truman political policy simply mailed through the JCS.) That incident aside, MacArthur was hardly sent an order, only diffident suggestions, scarcely grounds for charges of disobedience. As for the CINCFE's plans to attack the Chinese mainland with air and naval power, they had some JCS support for reasons of their own. The JCS had no interest in an armistice that would "drain our military resources [by] keep[ing] them in Korea."

The Joint Chiefs never doubted that MacArthur and Truman had a "basic policy" disagreement, nor did they forget who was commander in chief. If a president wanted to replace a theater commander, he certainly could. However, the JCS did not recommend MacArthur's dismissal, despite White House claims that they did. They only "concurred," a technical term with a narrow meaning in the U.S. military. Their boss, the president, discussed the issue with them and gave them an opportunity to object. They did not; they had no grounds and probably welcomed Truman's decision if only because MacArthur "treated us as if we were children." They also wanted to establish a policy consensus. Because the theater commander openly argued for his own preference, he created "doubt, confusion and uncertainty in the minds of the public about military leadership . . . when confidence in it was very essential," that is, in the aftermath of the longest retreat in the history of the army. Bradley, although still wary, would discredit MacArthur's claim that he spoke for all military men. He thereby gave the president the cover to survive, although in a crippled condition.[11]

THE POLITICAL DEMISE OF HARRY S. TRUMAN

Despite "the unanimous concurrence" of the JCS, Truman had to weather a public and congressional outcry. In April he told reporters that there would be a strong initial reaction against sacking MacArthur but that in about six weeks America would come to its senses. In fact, the public would not conclude that he was correct for another seven years, when (in December 1958) Truman was finally more admired than MacArthur, although both trailed the Reverend Billy

Graham in public opinion polls. In December 1951, eight months after MacArthur's relief, 60 percent of the public disapproved of Truman's action and MacArthur was America's most admired man. It would now be up to Republicans, the minority political party for the last twenty years, to harness this resentment to regain control of Washington.

The *New York Post* felt compelled to remind its readers that "the President of the United States is a member of the human race." MacArthur, however, was also politically tainted by the war in Korea, which was only slightly less unpopular than Truman himself (35 percent favored the war, 27 percent the president). Millions of people would line parade routes to scream their approval of the general. Would they support a political party that would escalate a war they considered a blunder? Senator Lyndon Baines Johnson thought not, even if MacArthur must have felt his brief acquaintance was an awful ingrate. In 1942 the general gave this legislator on temporary military duty a Silver Star for flying one mission against the Japanese. LBJ wore this combat ribbon on his suit jacket for the rest of his life, even when orchestrating Democratic political strategy to maintain that MacArthur and his congressional supporters wanted to wage World War III for control of Korea.

Republicans were quite willing to use MacArthur as a "baseball bat with which to beat the administration," said Johnson's Senate staff. Its national committeemen were far less willing to have him and his military policy tied around their neck, especially once the JCS told Congress that MacArthur's plan could enlarge the conflict "to a full-scale war." At a minimum, it would require three to five more U.S. divisions on the ground in Korea; the South Koreans and Chiang Kai-shek could not suffice. MacArthur may have been the most admired American, but that was strictly spontaneous emotion. Only 36 percent of the public thought he would make a good president; 38 percent wanted him to run.

More than twice as many Americans (57 to 21 percent) wanted the next president to be a man whom MacArthur had privately called "a mere clerk, nothing more." Dwight D. Eisenhower, MacArthur's executive officer in the 1930s, had taken no public position on how to conduct the Korean War. His reticence was well planned, as he wrote his oldest friend: "So far as all the MacArthur–Korean–administration–partisan politics affair is concerned, I have kept my mouth closed in every language of which I have ever heard." This tactic displeased political ideologues and military strategists on all sides, but it made Ike more attractive to professional politicians. Republican leaders feared that endorsing MacArthur would alienate Ike, who once said about a possible MacArthur administration: "My God, anything would be better than that!"[12]

PEACE TALKS, POWS, STALEMATE, AND POLITICS

Marshall and the JCS came to Truman's rescue in Senate hearings and public speeches by maintaining that because of heavy Chinese casualties "the war in

Korea can [soon] be concluded on honorable terms," provided the public retained a little patience. In June, when the communists proposed and the UN accepted armistice negotiations, Truman's approval rating rose ten points. His presidency and public acceptance of limited war would depend on early peace and mutual withdrawal from Korea of Chinese and American armed forces—propositions supported by 71 percent of the country in mid-1951.

Journalists, diplomats, and the JCS all predicted that peace talks would take a month. The front lines ran roughly along the thirty-eighth parallel, ideal for a status quo antebellum settlement, since political and military maps coincided. MacArthur pointed to this "military stalemate" inside Korea to argue for taking the war to the PRC. Ridgway spoke for most non-Koreans when he said that the purpose of military action was to create "advantages in support of diplomatic negotiations." His mentor, George Marshall, told the Senate that the administration had rejected the goal of unconditional surrender. Washington had learned its so-called lesson, to be remembered in Vietnam, not to deploy its ground force beyond the border of the political entity under communist attack.

The greatest disparity between the warring parties was in prisoners of war (POWs). The communists had 11,559 enemy soldiers; the UN held 150,000, 38,000 of whom were Chinese who had surrendered en masse for the first time in the war after a botched counterattack conducted in May. That was a tactical victory for the United States, but so was Inchon back in September 1950. Once again, America would have to decide whether to exploit a success or settle for a restoration of the status quo: in this case the repatriation of all prisoners to all sides. Because it chose to take advantage of its POWs, not its short-lived opportunity to push the weakened Chinese back to the Pyongyang-Wonsan line, the war lasted for two more years and claimed 50,000 more U.S. casualties, much to the surprise of the Truman administration.

The original idea for voluntary (not mandatory) repatriation of POWs came from the Bureau of Psychological Warfare, an army department created by civilians because most soldiers were solely concerned with conventional war fighting. Four days after activating the agency in July 1950, the secretary of the army wrote the secretary of defense that America must "take political, psychological and some military steps to put the Kremlin on the defensive." One year later, when the bureau was recruiting émigrés from Eastern Europe for intelligence, propaganda, and special operations, its commanding officer pointed out that involuntary repatriation to any communist country would "have a very unfavorable effect on the entire defector program." America returned Russian refugees to face imprisonment or execution after World War II—crude but effective means of Stalinist control. If repeated, this "would make it very difficult to wage effective psychological warfare against the [Soviet] Red Army in event of war." As for its impact on the Korean War, Brigadier General Robert McClure wrote Joe Collins that "inducements to surrender will be meaningless if they result in the prisoner's death or slavery."

In August 1951, with a rhetorical flourish, the JCS advocated voluntary repatriation: "In light of the ideological struggle throughout the world for the minds of men, it would be of great value to establish . . . the principle of United Nations asylum from terrorism." That October, upon reconsideration, it withdrew its endorsement. Most officers (as opposed to civilians) never placed much hope in guerrillas and so-called defectors, who might well be communist infiltrators themselves. More important, they wanted to get their own men out of captivity and the armed forces out of Korea as fast as they could, even when it meant encouraging defectors not to defect, telling subordinates to remind them of the fate likely to afflict their families once they failed to return. Collins, Ridgway, and company now felt that the enemy would not accept any settlement that would have an "extremely adverse affect on world-wide Commie prestige."

America's primary propaganda target was the Warsaw Pact, but Asian communists were even more opposed to voluntary repatriation. The Chinese and the North Koreans were still engaged in a civil war. Letting their nationals choose Chiang Kai-shek or Syngman Rhee belied communist claims that they were the only legitimate governments of their respective nations. Hence one Chinese officer told armistice negotiators in January 1952: "If anybody dares to hand over any of [our] personnel captured by the other side to the deadly enemy [Chiang], the Chinese People will never tolerate it and will fight to the end."

A State Department policy planner in secret contact with Beijing about peace terms advised Washington to return all—but only—CCF soldiers: the United States was not in Korea "to protect a Chinese regime." However, by the time the PRC began to make distinctions between their POWs and those of its ally, Truman had formed his own firm conviction not to allow the involuntary return of men dragooned into one Red army or the other: either South Koreans rounded up in the summer of 1950 (about 10 percent of the NKPA) or former soldiers for Chiang Kai-shek, almost 60 percent of the Fourth Field Army and 70 percent of its POWs. The more the communists objected to Truman's policy, the more unequivocal the president became. In May 1952 he declared: "To return these prisoners of war in our hands by force would result in misery and bloodshed to the eternal dishonor of the United States and of the United Nations."

Now that Truman was hooked on voluntary repatriation, the army was stuck in Korea, reminiscent of its inspired idea to dump it on the UN in 1948. In neither case did the military consider how deeply Truman might feel about these issues. Neither it, nor the president, nor Mao Tse-tung, also expecting an imminent armistice, should have been shocked that repatriation would prevent a peace settlement while Truman was president. The cold war was a fight about images, as Truman implied when he told MacArthur back in January that his mission was not to annihilate the enemy (per World War II) but "to deflate the dangerously exaggerated political and military prestige of Communist China."

For the Truman administration, voluntary repatriation had become a political substitute for military victory much as Korea had always been a substitute for a showdown with the Soviet Union. In early 1950 Washington felt that "Moscow's monopolistic control of the means of shaping internal public opinion and its world-wide apparatus of Communist Parties and front organizations places it in a unique position in psychological warfare." By mid-1952 the State Department held that the "refusal of some 80,000 Communist POWs to return except at rifle or bayonet point to Communist control hits them in a most sensitive and vulnerable spot." Furthermore, the acceptance of the American position on the issue would "leave no shadow of doubt in any one's mind that our will has been imposed upon the enemy."

Truman and Acheson avoided words like "war" and "unconditional surrender" but insisted on explicit recognition of "the principle of no forcible repatriation," lest an armistice agreement "seriously jeopardize the psychological warfare position of the United States in its opposition to Communist tyranny." When Canada and Britain tried to broker an arrangement that would concede the substance of the issue but save face for America, Acheson warned them that their position "on this essential matter would bring grave disillusionment regarding collective security." Thus the man who told the Senate hearings on MacArthur that the war was a victory for "the idea of collective security" told the Commonwealth "there would be no NATO, no Anglo-American friendship" if it did not support America's POW policy.

Because Stalin knew how divisive the prisoner issue was for the Western alliance, he had no great incentive to make peace, especially when North Korea and China were paying the lion's share of the cost of the war with their blood. Because the Truman administration would not forsake the principle of noncoercion, its last hope was to escalate the conflict per the president's maxim that communists were "influenced solely by force." However, by 1952, after the enemy took advantage of the armistice talks to fortify their lines, Korea resembled World War I, except that that was merely trench, whereas this was tunnel warfare. Interconnected communist bunkers and overlapping strongpoints virtually prohibited a major ground attack. "It could not, repeat not, inflict a decisive military defeat," Ridgway warned Washington in March 1952: It would only run "a serious risk of a successful enemy counter-offensive."

In theory, since the United States controlled the seas, it could mount amphibious invasions behind communist lines. Mao Tse-tung, who had worried America would do this since 1949, now wished it would try. He had never relinquished his ambition to bring "our enemies to their knees and force them to come to [our] terms." After suffering 85,000 casualties in May 1951, he had to conduct a protracted defense at great expense to economic development. Because UN forces were not likely to punch through minefields and strongpoints 20,000 yards in depth, a new Inchon could end up worse than Anzio. Light forces conducting the envelopment would be isolated and destroyed. Then, with Americans divided, Mao could turn and "annihilate a large number of enemy forces with our tactical offensive at the front."

Memories of failed World War II operations had chilled army audacity since 1950. Even without knowing Mao's hopes and plans, things seemed a lot less promising in 1952. Peace talks and a rotation policy (compliments of Congress) drained U.S. units of experienced veterans and the will to fight. Ridgway was conducting operations for "advantages in support of negotiations," hardly a goal to inspire GIs putting in their year and growing very cautious as their time got short. "Don't lose—but don't win, either," became doctrine at the foxhole level; "hold the line, while diplomats muddle through," despite Ridgway's best efforts to retain the fighting edge.

This military stalemate on the ground made strategic bombing the one resource left to force the communists to accept voluntary repatriation. On 30 July 1952 the UN command began mass air attacks on North Korean towns, communication centers, hydroelectric plants, and everything else worth destroying. However, by this stage of the war, the Chinese were fielding 1,000 jet fighters and four antiaircraft divisions to protect lines of communication whereby trains and trucks delivered over 300,000 artillery rounds a month, up from 16,000 shells, the communist expenditure in August 1951. At the front, the enemy was too hardened and entrenched to knock out with airpower. One could have bombed above the Yalu River to "substantially increase the military pressure on the Communists," but, as Lovett said in December, "that might be World War III." The Far East air force dropped more tonnage in Korea than was dropped in the entire Pacific theater during World War II, with one big difference in these different wars. Franklin Roosevelt hit Berlin and Tokyo, not just Rome. Truman bombed North Korea—not China or Russia, his major opponent in the field and its major source of military supply. Kim Il Sung was ready to make peace on American terms, but he no longer mattered very much.

Truman's strategy of coercion was fundamentally flawed, as he himself tacitly confessed when he said (in an incident discussed later) that Eisenhower should go to Russia, not Korea, because Moscow would determine war or peace. Nonetheless, he could not or would not extend the attack to the PRC, let alone the Soviet Union, although a clear plurality of the public wished that he would. In fact, he could not even threaten China, since that would validate MacArthur's position, as noted by the PRC. (His "dismissal stemmed precisely from his advocacy of expanding the aggressive war.") The under secretary of defense cursed the Senate hearings on MacArthur for "contributing to the knowledge of the enemy in a shocking manner," including testimony of Marshall and Bradley that they were not ready to wage a general war. These and other statements were printed every day in the *New York Times,* along with commentary that the conflict "will not be extended to Communist China." For political self-defense Truman made it crystal clear that "we must try to limit the war to Korea."

Harry Truman finished his presidency somewhat as he began it in the final months of World War II, with one significant difference. In both wars he refused to lower his political demands to negotiate a compromise—then about unconditional surrender; now about voluntary repatriation. Unlike 1945, he would not dramatically enhance his military means, as revealed in his farewell address: "Starting an atomic war is totally unthinkable." Hence Truman could only do what he dared not do when he first entered the White House: say that "with patience and courage" America would win "in the long run." *Collier's* magazine had already called this an "endless continuation of [a] slaughter-and-be-slaughtered policy," the recent subject of a Joe and Stewart Alsop (syndicated) newspaper column: "We cannot resume the offensive in Korea because our national strength is not sufficient. We cannot build national strength without going on a full-war basis. We cannot expect the enemy to sign a truce unless punishment makes it worth his while to do so. And we cannot sign a truce and surrender ourselves."

Without resolving the dispute over repatriation, Truman still could have obtained a temporary cease-fire. While such a ploy would be useful in the upcoming election, he felt that it would just increase public pressure for demobilization, reminiscent of the way "we tore up a great fighting machine" after World War II. Hence, he discounted political advice not to admit diplomatic failure and declared an "indefinite recess" of negotiations. He also stepped up military pressure on the ground, resulting in the heaviest UN casualties since the lines stabilized in 1951. On this inauspicious note, which lowered his approval rating a few more points, Truman could only turn the election into a vote of confidence from the public, 70 percent of whom already said they could foresee no end to the war. The Republican candidate, Dwight David Eisenhower, probably did not need much help from the leader of the Democratic party. However, in politics, as in war, one can always use reinforcements, wherever one can get them.[13]

THE 1952 PRESIDENTIAL ELECTION

Harry Truman finally gave up all hope of running for reelection in March 1952, when his public approval rating hit 25 percent, the all-time low for a sitting president. He sought a surrogate faithful to his policies who could keep the White House out of Republican hands. He would have liked to run Omar Bradley, a de facto Democratic general after leading the JCS to support MacArthur's relief, or Averell Harriman, his ambassador-at-large, "the ablest [man] of them all." However, Bradley needed more political grooming and Harriman was a Wall Street tycoon, just the sort of stereotype Truman stoned in the 1948 election. Hence the president, who still controlled his party's convention when primaries were just "eye-wash," settled on Adlai Stevenson, of whom he knew little except that he had won a landslide victory for governor of Illinois and strongly supported the UN, where he served in the U.S. delegation at its founding in 1945.

Stevenson, a graduate of Choate and Princeton, was a lace-curtain Democrat of the Harriman–Lovett–Acheson variety, with one big difference: he did not like or admire Harry Truman one bit. Although he supported the president's foreign and military policy, he "was frantic to distance himself" from the man in the White House, whom he thought crude and surrounded by cronies. This frustrated and embittered Truman, who saw the election as a referendum on his presidency and a repudiation of the Republican party, whose "vile vicious campaign of lies" supposedly encouraged China to prolong the war.

Truman, who had vented his political spleen by writing unmailed letters to and about his enemies, now had a chance to make more of the "give 'em hell" speeches on which he thrived. He thereby redeemed his pledge at the Democratic convention: "I am going to take my coat off and do everything I can to help [Stevenson] win"—everything but stay home. Stevenson knew that he could not and should not run as a clone of Harry Truman. In fact, he and Eisenhower had a lot more in common with each other than either one had with Truman or with Robert Taft. They were both conservative on economic issues and international-ists in foreign affairs, especially their mutual conviction that America had to maintain close political, economic, and military relations with Europe. Further-more, both men also believed, as Ike privately confessed, that a "decent armistice" was the only feasible solution to the Korean War.

Neither Eisenhower nor Stevenson had much of an idea how to get an acceptable truce, let alone a permanent peace that would bring the war to "a deci-sive end." Escalation, à la MacArthur, would "increase the risk of global war" and almost certainly cost America defections from NATO, which Ike called "the last remaining chance for the survival of Western civilization." However, Eisen-hower did put a wrinkle on the Truman approach to the Korean War, as he told his closest confidants: "The only program I could offer is to organize and arm the necessary number of South Koreans to defend their own front lines and withdraw our own troops into reserve positions. This is far from a satisfactory solution but it is the only one that looks to me to have any sense."

By October 1952, the month before the election, Eisenhower's unsatisfac-tory solution had become the major policy of the Eisenhower presidential cam-paign. "Let it be Asians against Asians," the candidate said; "our boys do not belong on the front lines." Stevenson attacked this proposal as "scuttle and run," the same phrase the State Department had used against the Pentagon when it wanted to abandon the peninsula in 1947. Korea "is not a war that concerns just Koreans. It is our war too." Stevenson's logic was sound; his instinct was awful; "Koreanization" had three-to-one approval in the public opinion polls.

According to Stevenson, Korea was "a major turning point in history"; "America has been called to greatness," like England against Hitler. These words hardly struck a responsive chord in a nation that believed, by almost two to one, that the commitment was mistaken. If Stevenson had personal credibility and prestige, the public still might have listened to his call to accept "a costly strug-gle likely to take a long time." No such response would be given to a former civil-ian assistant to the secretary of the navy running against the former supreme military commander, Allied forces Europe. When America elected Eisenhower with 55 percent of the popular vote, most citizens still favored Democratic positions on domestic policy (43 to 33 percent). This did not stop defections, even from those who agreed that the Republicans were the party of the Great Depression. One woman told a reporter: "The Democrats seemed to be saying prosperity was more important than the life of my boy." Fifty-two percent of the nation said the war was the most important issue; seven out of eight voters said Eisenhower "could handle the Korean situation best."

As early as January 1952, Stevenson said that Ike was "a cinch" to win. Of course, things are never that clear in the heat of a campaign, especially after Truman's miracle comeback in 1948. Hence when some polls in October showed Eisenhower losing his big lead, he made the most important speech of the entire election: I shall "forgo the diversions of politics and concentrate on the job of ending the war. . . . I shall go to Korea." Omar Bradley thought this "pure show biz"; it said nothing about policy. It did mean that Eisenhower assumed responsibility for solving a conflict he felt might be unsolvable.[14]

EISENHOWER, ESCALATION, AND PEACE IN KOREA

When Eisenhower was army chief of staff in 1948, he was the Pentagon's strongest voice for removing all soldiers from Korea. In 1953, after 155,000 U.S. casualties, the issue was more complicated. Ike had to balance the demands of Republicans in Congress, who doubted he was a true Republican, against the wishes of the European allies, with whom he had worked for the last ten years. The party had indicted Truman for being "afraid to win." The allies suspected that an "anti-Communist 'hysteria'" engulfed Washington and that Joe McCarthy was making foreign policy. If Eisenhower appeased Republicans, he might lose NATO. If he appeased NATO, he could lose control of his party. Between NATO and the GOP stood the American public, most of whom wanted "to knock the Communists out of Korea once and for all"—so America could get out of Korea once and for all.

The Eisenhower administration found itself "in a position of trying to reconcile the irreconcilable." It might have taken solace that there were also differences between Russia and China. Immediately after Eisenhower's election in November, the PRC grew more fearful of impending escalation. Mao's nightmare scenario had always been a deadlocked war of attrition that America would try to break with strategic bombing, one reason he tried for a quick knockout of America from Korea in December 1950. Instead, the CCF passed their culminating point, the war bogged down into stalemate, and Eisenhower was elected on a pledge to end the war in Korea. Consequently, in November 1952, China made its first compromise on mandatory repatriation by accepting a commission of neutral nations to assume custody of POWs.

Stalin continued to oppose voluntary repatriation, as well he should. Otherwise, he could not tell his own soldiers, as George Kennan imagined he would:

"You fellows might just as well die fighting for our side, because if you get caught as a prisoner you'll be given back to us and we'll kill you anyway." China had more trepidations. It thought Truman was a paper tiger but that Eisenhower would definitely "intensify the war." The Soviets thought Truman was an "imperialist warmonger," unlike the president-elect. Stalin, according to Nikita Khrushchev, "always stressed Eisenhower's decency, generosity and chivalry in his dealing with his allies" during World War II. Now, in the fall of 1952, the Russian dictator predicted a reduction in world tensions and more American concessions to end the Korean War.

The Kremlin knew Eisenhower as a military statesman trying to soothe a fractious coalition. He was far more conciliatory in that role than was his real disposition as a short-tempered man uncomfortable with the concept of limited war. Even though he thought Korea "an awkward place to fight," his initial advice to Bradley and Truman had been "that an appeal to force cannot, by its nature, be a partial one." "Do everything necessary to finish the Korean incident quickly" in 1950. Now, in 1953, America should begin full mobilization and prepare to make "use of the A-bomb." Hence Mao, who never met Eisenhower, understood him better than did Stalin or American voters who had heard Ike say: "No one I know has presented any possible plans for attacking China."

As president, Eisenhower began to prepare both conventional and nuclear action against the PRC—an old plan for a new purpose. MacArthur proposed it to destroy Asian communism; Truman considered it to save the American army from being pushed into the sea. Eisenhower, unlike either of them, would attack China just to settle the war, as would the Pentagon in 1953, after enhancing its nuclear arsenal from 298 to 1,161 bombs since the beginning of the war. In November 1951 Bradley was already conceding that the military commitment to "inconclusive operations in Korea over an indefinite period of time with the attendant attrition of manpower and material may become unacceptable." After eighteen more months of buildup, he and Eisenhower, his West Point classmate, agreed they had to take "more positive action"; "small attacks on small hills would not end the war." It was necessary "to use the atomic bomb" and "expand the war outside of Korea." There were "no good strategic targets [left] within the confines" of the peninsula. Joe Collins was nearly the sole proponent (easily outvoted) for the old proposition that the UN had the military advantage in a war with sanctuaries on both sides.

Exactly what steps America would have taken can never be known. On 5 March 1953, a month after Mao's latest public vow to fight as long as "U.S. imperialism persists in holding Chinese and Korean prisoners of war," Stalin died. The surviving members of the Politburo became preoccupied with political succession and immediately began talking about deciding all international conflicts with "peaceful means." They rejected new Chinese requests for economic assistance, let alone more heavy weapons, burdens the PRC could not bear when it was already spending 40 percent of total expenditures on defense. If any proof were needed, the Soviet cold shoulder must have showed the PRC it could not expect what it claimed in November 1950: that America's "atomic bomb is a paper tiger" thanks to Russian reprisal. A week after returning from Stalin's funeral, where they surely discussed the war at great length with the Russians, China's leaders surprised Washington, which expected no substantial concessions as late as 2 April. Within days, China's foreign minister issued a statement accepting the mutual repatriation of only "prisoners of war who insist upon repatriation."

Lest China forfeit its new status as a military power (the most important result of the Korean War), it described the repatriation of 14,000 POWs to Taiwan as one of several "minor issues." In June, Syngman Rhee released some 20,000 Korean (no Chinese) internees, rather than hand them to a commission for ultimate adjudication. This gave the PRC an opportunity to camouflage its political retreat with a military offensive. It inflicted 40,000 more casualties on the ROK army in battle that enabled China to boast that it had won "a glorious victory" and "compelled [the enemy] to agree to a truce." The PRC really felt America's failure to concede total repatriation meant it still did not respect the "New China." America felt that China's boast that it had shown Third World countries that "US imperialism" could not defeat a "people's war" meant the PRC had yet to learn to forgo aggression. Newspapermen observing the final armistice proceedings at Panmunjon in mid-1953 said both sides looked as if they "were signing a declaration of war instead of a truce."[15]

PEACE WITH SOUTH KOREA, BUT WITHOUT THE UN

By June 1953 the United States, the UN, the USSR, the PRC, and North Korea came to an essential settlement. South Korea was the last holdout. When Russia and America held their respective zones of occupation, the thirty-eighth parallel was relatively peaceful because the peninsula was relatively unimportant, at least for them. After they left in 1948, a civil war began, and civil wars—fought by Syngman Rhee and Kim Il Sung or Abraham Lincoln and Jefferson Davis—cannot be solved by compromise, unless it is imposed by foreign powers. Because MacArthur leveled the NKPA to twelve understrength divisions never operating above a corps, North Korea fell under Chinese military and political control. South Korea was far less deferential to whomever was the president of the United States.

Rhee, described by the U.S. ambassador as "a zealous, irrational and illogical fanatic," knew he had substantial support among conservatives in Congress and the mass media, especially *Time-Life,* which declared that "our strategy must be devised to bring about decisive victory." Fortified by such statements, he threatened to continue the war, thereby forcing the administration to contemplate a coup. It was not conducted for two reasons: Washington could not find a compliant replacement, and America did not have enough manpower to stop the communists on the battlefield, control POWs, and handle civil disturbances in rear areas. The United States had to bribe its ally, which held out for a military alliance in the face of JCS opposition to any settlement keeping the armed forces in Korea. No accident, Joe Collins was the last holdout for a coup.

Other people bridled at Rhee's demand for bilateral security because it slighted the United Nations. This symbolized the demise of Harry Truman's dream. In 1945 he rejected proposals for a regional pact in the Pacific lest it weaken the hope the UN would embody collective security. Rhee's requirement, which has kept the army in Korea for the last forty years, simply recognized a fact about the UN capabilities and U.S. disenchantment. In July 1950 the public affairs division advised the rest of the State Department to "minimize reference to 'US forces'" and emphasize the United Nations. By the following January, the political bloom wore off the rose as the UN proved to be what Dean Acheson always said it was: ineffective or "window dressing" for the United States. The average American, who wanted collective security, was bitter about the burden of defending the world. Other nations, contributing less than 5 percent of the total UN force, said America deserved to bear the cost since it did not share authority for military policy. This left Acheson bitter toward critics of U.S. policy: "Anytime anybody wants to replace our seven divisions with seven divisions of their own, then *their* generals are entitled to a very great weight in the discussion."

The administration, if not the president, was not beyond using the United Nations to protect its policy of limited war from congressional and public criticism. It counseled patience while the UN studied selective economic sanctions. Public anger with the General Assembly, increasingly controlled by an Indian- and Egyptian-led bloc of countries critical of the West, eventually fell on Harry Truman, who continued to defend the UN long after former supporters faulted it for failing to condemn (let alone fight) China. One result was the rejection of Adlai Stevenson, one of the last great proponents of the UN as a "great experiment in collective security." Other results were comments—or lack of them—after the armistice in July. Whereas French newspapers and British government ministers said that Truman had saved the UN from disappearing like the League of Nations, Americans were less favorable. Eisenhower barely mentioned the UN contribution. In the Senate, some prominent politicians denied that collective security had played a major role in the conflict at all. By 1975 two nonpartisan participants at a conference commemorating the anniversary of the Korean War summarized the American mood. Historian: "There certainly was a principle of collective security applied in Korea, but under unique circumstances which have never been repeated." General (Ret.) J. Lawton Collins: It "never will be again, in my judgment." In the 1980s, when the United States finally rolled back Soviet communism, the right-wing Wilsonians in the Reagan administration barely disguised their disgust with the United Nations. In the hands of radicals from the Third World, it was "a cesspool," a "place of jackals," and a "huge propaganda Jamboree."[16]

FROM KOREA TO VIETNAM

Korea cost America over 54,000 dead, 100,000 wounded, and $54 billion (twice as much as World War I). NATO, now a functioning military command, took faith from the fact that the United States had fought a limited war for limited objectives. American commentators, more aware of the "mass demands for quick victories," felt it "inconceivable for any future Administration to contemplate that kind of rigorously defensive military action." (Just wait.) Eisenhower's secretary of defense said, "We can't afford to fight limited wars. We can only afford to fight a big war, and if there is one that is the kind it will be."

The "big war" meant strategic and conventional forces against Russia in Central Europe or China on its own territory. This was not the type of conflict America would wage in the 1960s. The U.S. Army would not be much better prepared for guerrillas in the Mekong delta than Task Force Smith was for North Korean armor on the way to Pusan. Nonetheless, Korea planted political seeds that would bloom in the war against the Viet Cong, a so-called surrogate for North Vietnam, a so-called surrogate for Mao Tse-tung. By then, Mao's real influence in Vietnam had ebbed from its high-water mark in the 1950s. When Kim Il Sung made his first rush toward Pusan, Chinese advisers encouraged Ho Chi Minh to escalate his own armed action against the French as part of what the Chinese called "a two-pronged blow" against American positions on both flanks. In 1953 John Foster Dulles announced that "a single Chinese Communist aggressive front extends from Korea in the north to Indochina in the south."

By 1952 the Korean War had a new justification, that of diverting communist resources from the "conquest" of French Indochina, now receiving more American military assistance than any country in the world except South Korea. Both NSC and State Department position papers stated that Chinese communist control of Southeast Asia will have "critical psychological, political and economic consequences" that could cost the West everything it gained in Korea: military credibility, prosperity for Japan, and political stability from Singapore to Paris. Acheson added a particular wrinkle reminiscent of positions he took in late June and early December 1950, when he said it was better to be knocked out of Korea than not expend resources there. He acknowledged that our strategy was "a muddled hodgepodge," that the communists had captured the nationalist movement, and that the French would not win. Acheson still told Britain's foreign secretary in 1952 that "we are lost if we lose Southeast Asia without a fight."

As always, there were dissenting opinions, especially from those who would have to conduct the operation. In the 1950s Joe Collins and Matt Ridgway gave a grim prediction of "a long and indecisive war" in which the United States' "will to fight might be worn down." Paraphrasing Bradley, they told the NSC that sending American armed forces to Vietnam risks "embroiling the U.S. in [the] wrong war, in the wrong place, at the wrong time." United States Marines already predicted who would win this debate. Two months after Mao Tse-tung said in October 1950 that tying down America in northeast Asia would prevent it from sending forces to Vietnam, the corps added new lines to an old British army marching song: "We're saying good-by to them all. We're Harry's police force on the call. So put your pack on. The next step is Saigon. Cheer up, me lads, bless 'em all."[17]

9

Vietnam: Getting in While Staying Out, the Strategy of Gradualism

Arguably, Vietnam was the most divisive—but least important—war in American history. The failure was certainly traumatic, as were 58,000 fatalities, 300,000 casualties, and $190 billion spent in vain. Eighty-two percent of Vietnam veterans, as well as 85 percent of the general public, blamed the politicians for not "allowing" U.S. forces to win. The politicians, Lyndon Johnson and Richard Nixon, said they should have used more military power, especially bombing Hanoi and Haiphong. Nonetheless, one wonders how different the world would have been if America had won. Defeat did not prevent America from retaining a major military position on the mainland of Asia (Korea), enhancing its influence in the Middle East, and seeing the collapse of the Soviet Union. The long-term impact of Vietnam was the intangible loss of confidence, known as the "Vietnam syndrome." The same cannot be said of South Vietnam, which suffered 225,000 military fatalities and ceased to exist as a nation-state.

Failure of any kind is difficult to accept, especially for those held responsible. In the 1990s Robert McNamara wrote, "We were wrong, terribly wrong," but the former secretary of defense did not speak for most senior members of the Johnson administration. Walt Rostow, Dean Rusk, and William Westmoreland—the national security adviser, the secretary of state, and the senior officer in the military theater—all claimed ultimate victory. They point out that America went to war in Vietnam to prevent communism from spreading far beyond the Mekong River. America fought; Thailand, Malaya, and Indonesia did not fall, let alone the rest of Asia, Africa, and Latin America, as many feared in 1964. Thus, they reason, "we lost the battle in Vietnam but won the war in Southeast Asia," having "achieved our strategic objectives" despite the military restrictions Rostow and Westmoreland had opposed. Lyndon Johnson's "wisdom," according to the general, "has been sustained by history."

These men did not point out that when the United States went to war in 1965, the administration debated the commitment in ways germane to Rostow's

334

claim. Rusk, McNamara, and Johnson himself defined success as "stalemate"; that is, the Red tide will stop once "denied a victory." Others were less sanguine. George Ball, the under secretary of state, and Clark Clifford, the president's counsel, proposed a "tactical redeployment to more favorable terrain in the overall Cold War," such as those nations that did not fall to communism. "If we don't win, it is a catastrophe. If we lose 50,000+ [men in Vietnam] it will ruin us."

Between Rusk and Ball stood John McNaughton, the assistant secretary of defense for international security, and William and McGeorge Bundy, the assistant secretary of state for the Far East and Johnson's first national security adviser. Like Ball, they said South Vietnam had indefensible borders, a communist neighbor that already "took over [the] nationalist movement," and a Viet Cong insurgency with "far more talent" than the government in Saigon. Like Rusk, they rejected retreat. Reminiscent of Dean Acheson (Bill Bundy's father-in-law) in the darkest days of Korea, they said "we must have kept promises, been tough, taken risks, gotten bloodied, and hurt the enemy very badly" in order to retain "our standing as the principal helper against Communist expansion." America would be in a "stronger position to hold the next line of defense, namely Thailand," if we "go down with our guns firing."

In geostrategic terms, Vietnam's primary function was to "buffer" more viable and valuable countries, which may explain the tendency, noted by Daniel Ellsberg, to escalate to postpone defeat, not win the war. In 1965 LBJ said that "we must delay and deter the North Vietnamese and Viet Cong as much as we can" but "only [do] what is absolutely necessary," as if anyone could know what a war might require. McNamara, translating presidential intent into a concept of military operations, proposed "a measured and controlled sequence of actions to persuade [Hanoi] to stop its intervention in the south"—or, at the least, "buy time measured in years" before Saigon finally fell. This plan would prove ineffective against an opponent as tough as North Vietnam. Nor was it ever persuasive to the senior officers of the U.S. armed forces who wanted to employ "maximum conventional military power" and deliver "a level of destruction [the enemy can not] overcome." Their preference denied, they came to react, Mac Bundy would complain, "more like a powerful wing of the Senate than troops under a commander in chief."

Aside from the American military, public opinion also presented a problem for the president. From the onset of the war, LBJ knew Americans wanted a quick victory or a fast exit but without humiliation. They got military strategy on what Ball called the "Goldilocks principle," not too hard and not too soft. The result was a protracted war fought to no one's satisfaction.[1]

THE KENNEDY COMMITMENT: CREDIBILITY BY PROXY

In February 1950, four months before the Korean War, the Truman presidency began the American effort against communism in Vietnam, then a colony of the

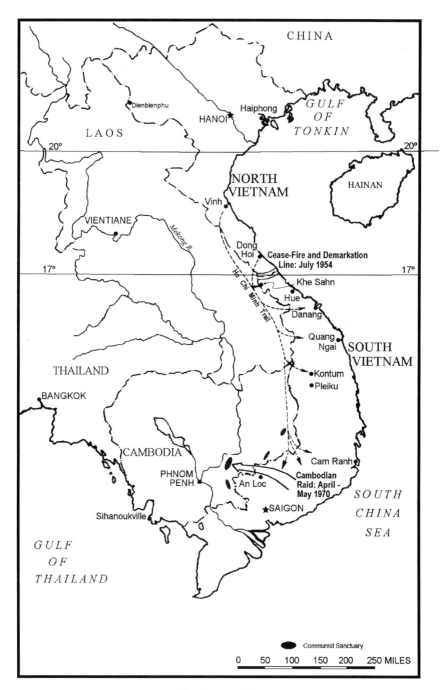

The Vietnam War

French Empire, to maintain France as a NATO ally and stop Indochina from becoming what was called a "Soviet satellite." When France withdrew from Southeast Asia in 1954 after defeat at Dienbienphu, the Eisenhower administration stepped into the vacuum with aid to Vietnamese anticommunists, who tended to be wealthy, urban Catholics who had worked with the French. Although occasionally tempted to take direct responsibility, Eisenhower held his troop commitment to 685 Saigon-stationed advisers and gave more attention to other crisis areas: Berlin, Cuba, and Laos, the so-called cork in the bottle whose loss would mean "the loss of most of the Far East."

John Kennedy, elected by a .001 percent plurality, became president in 1961. His pledge to reverse the pattern of "retreat, defeat, and weakness" prevalent since the Soviets launched *Sputnik* and Castro seized Cuba in the 1950s came back to haunt him after he withheld air support from an anti-Castro invasion and accepted a cease-fire ensuring communist control of eastern Laos. Republicans charged global "appeasement," painfully upsetting to the Kennedy retinue. First, as Bill Bundy admitted, the administration was "impregnated with the belief that Communism had gained a dangerous momentum." Second, the political career of the president's father had come to a crashing halt in 1940 when he was said to have appeased Hitler by opposing aid to England. In 1961 JFK told confidants, "There are just so many concessions that one can make to the communists and survive politically. We just can't have another defeat this year."

Laos was landlocked. Vietnam was accessible to America's strong suit—air and sea power—and was said to have had the best anticommunist army in Southeast Asia. "We have a problem," Kennedy said, "trying to make our power credible and Vietnam looks like the place." Partly in worry, partly in relief, he believed that guerrilla insurgencies in the Third World had become the main means of communist expansion. If he had to prove his capacity to contain the enemy, counterinsurgency in Vietnam was preferred to another confrontation over West Berlin, the main flash point of U.S.–Soviet rivalry from 1958 to 1962. Because Russia had, by most estimates, a seven-to-one advantage in conventional forces in Central Europe, Kennedy could do little more there than surrender the city or initiate a thermonuclear exchange that, according to official estimates, would kill 75 million Americans and 115 million NATO-nation Europeans.

Debatable for Europe, a resort to strategic weapons could seem ludicrous in Indochina, where America's immediate security was not at stake. Kennedy made much of this issue in the late 1950s when campaigning for the Democratic presidential nomination by attacking the Eisenhower defense policy for stockpiling nuclear warheads that could not "prevent the Communists from nibbling away at the fringe of the free world's territory or strength." For the superpowers, military conflict in a place like Southeast Asia had the same benefit the New World had for France and Britain in the eighteenth century. It was a place to struggle for advantage without risking a confrontation that could destroy either nation. At their summit conference in June 1961, Kennedy told Nikita Khrushchev, premier of the Soviet Union, that "the problem was how to avoid direct contact between [our] two countries as we support respective groups" outside Europe. The alternative, said Walt Rostow, Kennedy's resident expert on counterinsurgency, was "to seek out and engage the ultimate source of aggression"—Russia or China— "too damned dangerous and costly in a nuclear age."

Two weeks before Kennedy's inauguration, Khrushchev declared support for "wars of national liberation," specifically Vietnam, although Soviet policy was tentative in practice and subordinate to détente with the West. Kennedy thought that the speech, mostly about peaceful coexistence, was a "detailed blueprint" for "world domination." The relevant section, only four of the total fifty-four pages, was small enough to be dismissed if JFK were not obsessed but of convenient size to circulate through the new administration with presidential instructions to "read, mark, learn, and inwardly digest." Kennedy's own public statements were direct replies to Khrushchev: "We face a relentless struggle in every corner of the globe." How we shall fight guerrillas, such as those in Vietnam, "is one of the great problems now before the United States."

In Vietnam, what Kennedy called "anti-guerrilla activities which fall short of outright war" had not been tried and therefore had not failed. As in Korea, the U.S. military advisory mission, until mid-1961, had focused on a conventional invasion from the north. Now U.S. special forces would add social, economic, and political functions to the military training of the Army of South Vietnam (ARVN). The pupils, said Rostow, would "hold the line in Asia"; the teachers would "learn how to deal with indirect aggression," a subject of dispute in Washington. Everyone agreed that counterinsurgency was a blend of military and political measures. Nearly everyone disagreed about the relative amounts in the proper mixture.

"Counterinsurgency" and "antiguerrila" identified a target, not a technique. At West Point in 1962, Kennedy said these missions necessitated "a whole new kind of strategy, a wholly different kind of force, and therefore, a new and wholly different kind of military training." He did not specify what any of these elements were, aside from being "different." Rostow, a civilian expert in Third World economic development, emphasized external sponsors like China and new weaponry like helicopters, "uniquely effective in tracking down guerilla." Roger Hilsman—an assistant secretary of state, West Point graduate, and World War II guerrilla behind Japanese lines—emphasized internal discontent, political reform, and civil development. This was not as illogical as it might first appear. Whereas Rostow selected bombing targets in World War II, Hilsman knew firsthand that irregulars had limited military value and could not exist without indigenous support.

Robert Thompson, Britain's foremost expert on counterinsurgency, discussed it with Kennedy, whom he found a shallow dilettante. The CIA station chief in Vietnam complained the president was vague and could not "visualize the practical aspect of the problems on the ground." Each individual agency put forth its preference "devoid of any strategic concept" for a unified civil-military effort. For the army, "modern counterinsurgency warfare" meant multibattalion operations with armor and aircraft. One officer, falling into civic action to stop discontent at the village level, found "no doctrine, no established set of rules," not even a "clear statement of responsibilities."

Every institution has a vested interest in its special expertise. From the time George Washington argued with militia irregulars over who would make the main effort in the Revolutionary War, the U.S. Army's forte has been conventional warfare. Kennedy and McNamara said that America should enhance its nonnuclear capability for NATO. Their simultaneous call for special forces with a special doctrine for special missions in the Third World threatened further diversions of resources when special forces was already draining the best noncommissioned officers into low-tech, twelve-man teams. The army claimed that counterinsurgency was just a small form of conventional war and that "any good soldier can handle guerrillas." More to the point, one unidentified general later told a special forces captain: "I'll be damned if I permit the United States Army, its institutions, its doctrine, and its traditions to be destroyed just to win this lousy war."

In Vietnam, by October 1961, the insurgency was no longer content with political organization and small-unit ambushes. Communist forces began to consolidate into main-force battalion units, probably to slice South Vietnam in half, from Laos to the South China Sea. The JCS, believing Kennedy was "oversold" on counterinsurgency and America should be prepared to use all its power, advised sending 23,000 conventional soldiers from Southeast Asia Treaty Organization (SEATO) nations. If North Vietnam intervened, SEATO should counter with twelve divisions. If China intervened, send fifteen more divisions and conduct "an unremitting air and naval offensive to destroy the enemy's war-making capacity" (shades of Douglas MacArthur). Anything less "will make our ultimate task [defending Southeast Asia] proportionately more difficult."

Kennedy did not welcome this advice, although he probably was not surprised. Ever since serving in World War II, he thought the services were inept, if not narrow-minded. Now, upon hearing that the president must be ready to use nuclear weapons to "guarantee victory," the administration suspected that the JCS was seeking an excuse against intervention in an area they long considered "a serious diversion of limited U.S. capabilities." Partly for this reason, JFK brought out of retirement a special adviser whom he considered a "notable exception" to professional soldiers, General Maxwell Taylor: handsome as a movie star, a best-selling author, and an Eisenhower critic who coined the phrase that Kennedy made his own: "flexible response" in national defense. Taylor actually knew little about counterinsurgency: "It took me four months to understand what was on the President's mind." He still was ready to take Oval Office guidance and give it back to Congress, the public, and the press in the guise of expert opinion—important to people more impressed by the military than was JFK.

The Joint Chiefs naturally resented the president's emissary. Taylor himself liked to tell them that his "close personal relations with the President and his entourage" ensured military access to the White House through an honest broker reducing civil-military conflict. He took "political considerations" into account, felt MacArthur had been terribly wrong, and was thankful for the opportunity to help shape defense policy, something he was not able to do when he was army chief of staff under President Eisenhower. Taylor also told Kennedy and McNa-mara that he was distressed that the "amateur strategists of the New Frontier" had taken over military planning. In Vietnam he would fail to balance civilian supremacy and professional expertise. Older if not wiser in 1973, Taylor con-fessed he should have said in 1961: "Let's get several divisions and get them in there fast and clean this thing up and come home again."

In October 1961 Kennedy told Taylor he did not want to send large units to Vietnam, then dispatched him to report to the nation whether the president had to commit regular infantry divisions. Hardly a shock, Taylor said no. Aside from the president's agenda, he did not think the U.S. Army suited to jungle warfare in the highlands, where the Vietcong (VC) main-force units had planted their bases. He also had more faith than warranted in the potential of the ARVN and the leader of the government, Ngo Dinh Diem. "The South Vietnamese will really fight," he told his son, an army captain, "whereas these Laotians turn tail at the first threat." Best to upgrade and strengthen the American Military Assis-tance Command Vietnam (MACV), although that would make the United States "a limited partner in the war." Kennedy was not happy but liked the alternatives a lot less: either substantial escalation as the JCS proposed or pulling out and los-ing another country (like Cuba and Laos) to the communists. Soon thereafter, the president tripled the number of American military advisers in the theater, who now went beyond training to accompany the ARVN into combat against the VC.

Taylor's last act in this phase of the war was to replace the senior American officer in Vietnam with a new MACV commander. The incumbent, Lionel McGarr, was "a bull-dog for action," blunt with Diem, and ill suited for quasi-diplomatic missions. He had also become one of the few generals who under-stood how to conduct pacification. Whereas the JCS dismissed it as irrelevant and Taylor was still struggling to understand the topic, McGarr wrote Washington that driving enemy soldiers from a locale was insufficient. The government of South Vietnam (GSVN) had to uproot the hidden Viet Cong "infrastructure" pro-viding recruits, information, and supplies at the village level and replace it with political institutions responsible to and for the welfare of the peasantry. Because Saigon did not do this, the VC soon "regained control after clearance by military action," prophetic of American search and destroy after 1964.

Despite or because of McGarr's insight, he went into retirement. He could not overlook the chronic weakness of the GSVN, which mistrusted everything outside itself. This put McGarr on a collision course with Taylor, who always believed Diem could win the war "if he really tried" and selected for MACV Paul Harkins—described as "diplomatic to a fault" by Taylor and as "a born optimist" by Harkins himself. For the next two years, until replaced by another

Taylor protégé in mid-1964, Harkins wrote rosy reports and predictions that undercut critics from both ends of the military spectrum: the counterinsurgency proponents wanting less firepower and more attention paid to the VC infrastructure and the JCS hawks who continued to say that the only way to save Southeast Asia was to bomb Hanoi and cut off infiltration.

Why and how Harkins maintained the ARVN was winning was a mystery to his successor, William Westmoreland. Two things are clear. Harkins felt that his mission was "to help Diem fight," not to despair, as many others did, at the fundamental weakness of his government. The people to whom Harkins reported— Taylor, McNamara, and Kennedy—were all impatient and discouraged bad news. Taylor told him "to protect all the President's options," as opposed to the all-out war or defeat alternatives flexible response was supposed to supersede. McNamara applied pressure of his own. In late 1961 the secretary of defense told JFK that he would "look after" Vietnam. Soon he was planning field operations as the de facto desk officer in charge. This made perfect sense to someone like him who believed that insurgency was a "different form of war" and the military had not had "an original thought" since World War II. However, McNamara's special contribution toward achieving quick success was hardly helpful. He flooded carbines to self-defense militia units, which he called "the most important military people in Vietnam." Poorly paid and despised by the ARVN regulars, they surrendered, sold, or gave away their weapons to the Viet Cong, not armed systematically by North Vietnam until 1964.

In 1962 most of Washington grew complacent about Vietnam based on progress reports filed by Harkins in Saigon. Kennedy turned his short attention span and concern for crisis management to more imminent issues: nuclear weapons, civil rights, and Cuba. Meanwhile, VC platoons armed with U.S. weapons devised tactics against helicopters and formed more battalions to spring forth in 1963. However, there was an early warning system for danger in Vietnam. The military advisers whom Kennedy and Taylor placed in the field had not expected the conditions they saw, partly because Harkins withheld "sensitive" information from their training at Fort Bragg on the grounds it had "strong political intonations." Once in country, the men discovered the ARVN was not beating the insurgency in the military or the political arena. The most outspoken officer, John Paul Vann, would tell one general officer that "we couldn't win the war." Other advisers felt America should not try. They could not pass their message through MACV to the Pentagon. When Vann got an appointment to brief the JCS, Taylor knocked him off their calendar. Still, there were outside channels when the inside lines jammed with what one officer called the MACV "party line" that "we had found the secret to success and could expect an early end to the conflict." Advisers and CIA agents taking a drink at the Hotel Caravelle fraternized with American reporters, who became "the one gloomy spot" in the picture of progress, according to Washington officials.

McNamara dismissed this reportage for lacking the statistical data others concocted to meet his demands. Kennedy refused to consult these reporters, whom he thought a disadvantage of democracies, which had to conduct affairs out in the open. Hating them for lacking "any goddam patriotism," he would conclude that "the way to confound the press is to win the war." However, newspapermen got their message to the White House through an intermediary on an inspection tour of military assistance programs. Mike Mansfield—U.S. Senate majority leader, former intelligence officer, and professor of Asian history—had supported Diem since the 1950s, a far better investment than Laos. Now, after a long meeting in Saigon with journalists David Halberstam, Neil Sheehan, and Peter Arnett, he told the president in December 1962 that the GSVN was bound to lose, except if saved by "a truly massive commitment of American military personnel."

Kennedy, neither credulous nor pleased, responded that "this isn't what my people are telling me." Since 1956 he had said that Vietnam "represents a test of American responsibility and determination in Asia." However, according to an officer on Max Taylor's staff, he wanted "the fruits of victory" without paying "the price required to have them." Douglas MacArthur stunned him in 1961 with forceful arguments to stay off the Asian mainland. Now, in early 1963, he was ready to accept the Mansfield-MacArthur position. JFK got into Vietnam to establish his credibility and ward off criticism like that of *Time* magazine after the Bay of Pigs: President Kennedy "must seize" the opportunity to "throw back the challenges of Communism at whatever cost." ("Look at this shit," he complained to his staff.) After his triumph in the Cuban missile crisis of October 1962, he had far less need to prove a point in Vietnam.

There would be an international and domestic cost for liquidating the Vietnam commitment. According to Kennedy's personal pollster, 66 percent of the public then approved of American involvement, even "on a large scale if the Communist threat grew worse." The president hoped to limit the damage by claiming the anticommunist side had won the war. In the best case, he would then get what Henry Kissinger later called a "decent interval" before Saigon fell. In 1963, when Kennedy had 70 percent approval, he told a few of his close confidants, in utmost secrecy: "In 1965, I'll become one of the most unpopular Presidents in history. I'll be damned everywhere as a Communist appeaser. But I don't care. If I tried to pull out completely now from Vietnam [before reelection], we would have another Joe McCarthy scare on our hands."

One never can be sure what a president would do if he does not live to do it. In mid-1964 Robert Kennedy was asked what the administration would have done "if the [South] Vietnamese were about to lose." He gave an utterly frank answer: "We'd face that when we came to it." His brother, warming up for reelection, gave little indication of what he whispered to Roger Hilsman in the Oval Office: that he wanted to minimize his commitment in order to withdraw as soon as a good opportunity arose. He planned to tell a political audience in Texas about "our determined stand on behalf of freedom around the world, from West Berlin to Southeast Asia." Shot dead before he got to the podium, he left Vice

President Lyndon Johnson in a condition similar to that of Harry Truman in 1945: ignorant about a martyred president's hidden policy but stuck with his war-fighting rhetoric, in this case the prevention of "the impression that the wave of the future in Southeast Asia was China and the Communists."[2]

LBJ GOES TO WAR—OR NOT?

After Lyndon Baines Johnson became president in November 1963, high-ranking officials in foreign and defense affairs recognized a new tone at the White House. Whereas John Kennedy talked of withholding aid from South Vietnam, the new president expressed stronger views for stronger support: "I want 'em to get off their butts and get out in those jungles and whip hell out of some Communists. Then I want 'em to leave me alone, because I've got some bigger things to do right here at home." That meant his election in 1964, followed by legislation in health, education, and prosperity that would surpass that of his role model, benchmark, and rival for presidential immortality: Franklin Roosevelt. Vietnam was to be hidden from public view as long as possible, per LBJ's dictum that "if your mother-in-law has one eye and it's in the middle of her forehead, you don't keep her in your living room."

Unlike McNamara and Kennedy, Johnson had never been under an illusion that Vietnam was anything other than "a big juicy worm with a right sharp hook in the middle." In 1962, when others were receiving Pollyannaish reports from General Harkins at MACV, Johnson's military aide, relying on confidential sources in U.S. Army Pacific (based in Hawaii), told him that more assistance and advisers had "not reversed the level nor intensity of Viet Cong operations." If this bad news became public, as Kennedy acknowledged in 1963, it would damage the incumbent president, who would have to pull out and be labeled an appeaser or commit combat forces and be called another Democrat who got America into another war. "Whichever way Vietnam turns out," Johnson said repeatedly in 1964, "it is going to be my destruction."

In retrospect, what stands out is the broad-based opposition to withdrawal, approved by only 13 percent of the American people the month of Johnson's election. Even Senator William Fulbright and the greatest gadflys in the Saigon press, Halberstam and Sheehan, said Vietnam was "one of the five or six nations in the world that is truly vital to U.S. interests"; if America were "to dishonor" itself and pull out suddenly "under adverse conditions," political and psychological shock waves might "set off an unforseeable chain of events" that could "undermine our entire position in Southeast Asia," if not the world.

Subjected to this consensus, Johnson ran for president vowing while "we are not about to start another war, we're not about to run away from where we are." He was thereby in a perfect political position, appealing to the doves without being one himself. As policy (not politics), the moderate option (to maintain advisers but not send combat troops) was feasible only if "progress has been excellent," as McNamara proclaimed two months after confidentially telling the president, "I fear we are right at the point" at which America must decide whether to fight. That May, he was under tremendous White House pressure to find facts and figures supporting administration claims that the Vietnamese "are brave, effective fighters willing to sacrifice their lives in defense of their country," no matter that he heard from MACV commander William Westmoreland that Vietnam was a "bottomless pit."

Shortly before the election, Rostow warned LBJ to avoid the plight of Woodrow Wilson after 1916 and Roosevelt after 1940, subjected to charges of deceit for having promised not to enter combat. However, the position of his opponent, Barry Goldwater, that "we are at war in Vietnam" was too unpopular not to exploit. Whereas Kennedy had run on beating communism in 1960, Johnson ran on good times, received 61.1 percent of the vote but could not rest to enjoy it. On election day, he had to establish a committee to respond to Max Taylor's latest reports from Saigon: "We must soon adopt new and drastic methods to reduce and eventually end infiltration if we are ever to succeed in South Vietnam."

Despite enjoying the largest landslide in presidential history, LBJ still made Vietnam policy as imprecisely, incrementally, and belatedly as possible, not even giving MACV a simple mission statement. This oversight was not accidental, although it left 70 percent of the generals wondering what the national objective was. Johnson had at least three contradictory goals, each one dictating a different level of troop commitment:

1. Do not divert attention and resources from a fleeting opportunity for sweeping domestic legislation. "In politics," LBJ often said, "chicken salad can turn into chicken shit overnight."
2. Save Vietnam and his own stature lest the East Coast elite, conservatives in Congress, and the communists all "think we're yellow."
3. Avoid risking war with China or the Soviet Union, what John McNaughton called the "Korea syndrome." When military men predicted that they would not intervene, Johnson replied: "Are you more sure than MacArthur was?"

If LBJ were only interested in guarding his domestic agenda (as some historians maintain), he should have adopted the enclave strategy advised by Mike Mansfield and Bill Fulbright, old friends from Johnson's days as Senate majority leader. Whereas hawks said that would be like holding discussions with North Korea while pinned down at the Pusan perimeter in August 1950, they maintained that placing some 100,000 soldiers in defensive concentrations near the coast would be far less expensive than half a million men chasing enemy bands through the jungle. From these enclaves, America could negotiate a prolonged withdrawal along lines suggested by George Ball, letting the Viet Cong's political arm, the

National Liberation Front (NLF), run for election under UN auspices. Walter Lippmann, whom LBJ courted for his influence on the rest of the press, said that this would "let the place go Communist as gracefully as possible," Kennedy's apparent objective before he died. Johnson, a master of delay when it served his purpose, would have the Eighty-ninth Congress to pass and fund his Great Society. At best, the communist state of united Vietnam would emerge long after LBJ retired. Then he could still say, as he did in November 1963: "I am not going to lose Vietnam." His successor would do that.

Although spokesmen for Hanoi talked of delaying unification for fifteen to twenty years, Johnson rejected the enclave plan and other versions of "surrender on the installment plan." He simply could not stand "the thought of being responsible for America's losing a war to the Communists. Nothing would be worse than that." His conviction that "our national honor is at stake and we must keep our commitments" was typical of cold war presidents from Harry Truman to George Bush who felt the need to establish military credibility early in their administration. Kennedy hoped to do it in Vietnam but did it during the Cuban missile crisis, where the Vietnam monkey fell off his back to land on that of his successor. When still mulling over Southeast Asia after the 1964 election, LBJ read Joe Alsop, a premier columnist who wrote about him like *Time* wrote about his predecessor in 1961: "For Lyndon B. Johnson, Vietnam is what the second Cuban crisis was for John F. Kennedy. If [he] ducks the challenge, we shall learn what it would have been like if Kennedy had ducked."

Uncomfortable for anyone, these comparisons could be particularly painful for Johnson, whom Kennedy and McNamara described as a "very sensitive man with a huge ego" and "inferiority complex." His roots in a poor but ambitious family left him with awe, jealousy, and contempt for the American elite. He not only surrounded himself with JFK appointees; he was obsessed by thoughts that Robert Kennedy was waiting to rile up the Establishment and "reclaim the throne [with cries of] 'Coward! Traitor! Weakling!'" Then an underprivileged boy from south Texas would show less substance than a rich kid from Boston. "Hell," he told the NSC, invoking his region's monument, "Vietnam is just like the Alamo."

John Kennedy never told the public, the armed forces, or Johnson what to do if failing to defeat a communist insurrection. Too busy pretending he was winning in Vietnam, he did not say the alternative was retreat. In 1965, when failure could no longer be denied, virtually everyone in Washington, including the Kennedy coterie of McNamara and McGeorge Bundy, chose to elevate the conflict into a limited conventional war. Because insurgency was said to be touted as "the safe way to expand Communism," the administration, its congressional defenders, and its "wise men" advisers, like Dean Acheson, issued countless statements to the effect that America must show Hanoi and Beijing that this was not cheap. At best, U.S. efforts will "establish for the world that Communist externally inspired and supported wars of liberation will not work." At worst, said Bundy, the "reprisal policy will set a higher price for the future upon all adventures of guerrilla warfare." Unlike Douglas MacArthur in Korea, none of these men advocated the elimination of an established communist state, even North Vietnam. Bundy and McNamara only recommended using "our military power in the Far East to force a change [in] Communist policy."

Theoretically, there was an option other than escalation or defeat, available if the administration said wars of national liberation were internal wars by which native revolutionaries came to power through their own efforts. Once there, they were not likely to surrender their hard-won rule to anybody, ideology notwithstanding. This was Acheson's premise when he wooed Tito from Stalin in 1948. In 1965 it would have moved America to "play on Hanoi's fear of Peiping and the possible Liberation Front fear of being totally under Hanoi's domination," Bill Bundy wrote in June. However, to make this the basis of U.S. grand strategy would have meant "we are undercutting the whole international law and policy justification of our [past] action in South Vietnam." It seemed easier to bomb North Vietnam.

In September 1965, wars of national liberation showed signs of being paper tigers themselves. In Indonesia, in response to the assassination of five generals, Muslim soldiers and street gangs slaughtered some 500,000 members and supporters of the third-largest Communist party in the world. This removed a country of real strategic significance from what LBJ called the "Djakarta–Hanoi–Peking–Pyongyang axis." However, by the time a counterrevolution rescued "the greatest prize" in Southeast Asia, America was waging war in North and South Vietnam. Washington needed a rationale commensurate with its effort. "China fit this need," recalled the director of State Department intelligence. Seeing Indonesia slip into the anticommunist sphere, the PRC would send more support to North Vietnam to stop the dominoes from falling on the American side.

In 1950 Acheson and Truman initiated American assistance to keep Vietnam out of "the Soviet orbit." In 1965 another Democratic administration was eager to believe that in a series of confrontations from Korea to Cuba it convinced the USSR "of the futility of seeking political breakthroughs by military means." In retrospect, the Russians were not as benign nor the Chinese as aggressive as Washington believed. Khrushchev (not the Kremlin) learned the lesson Kennedy tried to tell him at Vienna—that he could not have bilateral détente with the West on nuclear weapons if he pursued expansion in the Third World. Two months after the Cuban missile crisis, the premier warned the Supreme Soviet (to Kennedy's immense satisfaction) that the so-called "paper tiger has atomic teeth." Soon thereafter, Khrushchev reassessed his policy of economic assistance to North Vietnam, even removed professors from its universities, and signed a nuclear test ban treaty with the United States. However, after his own ouster from power in late 1964, the Soviets reassessed once again and steadily increased their support to Hanoi.

This change in Soviet policy was not clear in 1965, when Beijing still attacked Moscow for "revisionism" and Hanoi criticized Russian condemnation of "adventurist policies." Rusk, McNamara, the CIA, Henry Kissinger, and Zbigniew Brzezinski (two part-time consultants seeking full-time employment) all said that the international task remaining for America was "to contain China in her expansionist phase." Then the so-called proponents of peaceful coexistence in Moscow would gain leverage in their struggle with "the most bellicose factions" of communism around the world. Under Kennedy, America had gone into Vietnam to prove his credibility to the USSR, that is, until he decided in late 1962 that "the threat in the years ahead is China." In 1965, under Johnson (with bipartisan support from Richard Nixon), the administration stayed to discredit Mao Tse-tung vis-à-vis Moscow. This policy helps explain LBJ's enduring illusion that "when the Chinese get a little weaker and the Russians stronger, we're going to have a peace." He asked McNamara in 1964: Why would the Kremlin "want to see the Chinese communists envelop Southeast Asia?"

If one could get beyond militant Red Chinese rhetoric (no easy task), one could see that since the Geneva Conference of 1954, China's main concern had been to keep foreign bases out of Indochina, meaning the United States and the USSR. Americans still believed that a victory for Ho Chi Minh, the leader of North Vietnam, was a victory for Maoist expansionism. Dean Rusk, a major player in the last proxy war (against North Korea to discourage Russia), said that unless discouraged now, "there will [soon] be a billion Chinese on the mainland, armed with nuclear weapons, with no certainty about what their attitudes toward the rest of Asia will be." Since other officials, including John Kennedy himself, had considered launching preemptive attacks on China's embryonic atomic facilities, Rusk could reason that a limited conventional war in Vietnam was a judicious option, especially when it also held out the hope of discrediting all communist wars of liberation. This kind of thinking, so prevalent in Washington, provided Walter Lippmann a last opportunity to get his final swipe at Woodrow Wilson through Rusk, his devotee. America's most prestigious political columnist wrote that the secretary of state was repeating the old "delusion," with a contemporary variation: America was "fighting a war to end wars"—but doing it without fighting China itself. "The Wilsonians at least believed that if they were to end wars they had to defeat the main aggressor," in their case Germany.

Lyndon Johnson stalked the White House, lamenting that war was more complicated than when FDR told Eisenhower: "Seek out the German army and destroy it." Eisenhower told LBJ to make sure China never "lacked appreciation of our determination to keep nations free by whatever means required." He nodded but was always more aware that General MacArthur's threats made the PRC, now with its own atomic bomb, the belligerent whom President Eisenhower had to threaten with nuclear weapons to end the Korean War. Beside him stood Dean Rusk, his closest adviser and the only member of the Truman administration to have dared try to stop MacArthur's charge toward the Chinese border in late 1950.

Rusk had been very reluctant to sink "American prestige on a losing horse," the government of South Vietnam. Once done in 1965, he would quote Truman in support of his contention that nothing but U.S. credibility prevented World War III. Rusk, unlike McNamara and McGeorge Bundy, never wavered from this rock-bottom belief once the casualties mounted. "Having lived through dark times" in Korea, he explained in retrospect, "I was not willing to yield to pessimism in Vietnam just because the outlook was bleak." Nor was Rusk willing to take "unacceptable risks" and "cross the flash point," as he did when he was the stongest voice inside the State Department for crossing the thirty-eighth parallel in September 1950. In 1965, despite statements from Mao, his foreign minister, and his army chief of staff not to fight unless attacked, Rusk began each day with the question: "Any sign of Chinese movement?" Since he believed the American people would never tolerate another war like Korea, the government would have to use nuclear weapons if the conflict brought in China.[3]

To exploit America's competitive advantage in air and sea power, Kennedy had moved containment in Southeast Asia from Laos to Vietnam. To maximize these capabilities in 1965 meant unrestricted action against Hanoi, the port city of Haiphong, and other high-value targets in the northern half of North Vietnam, not hit for various reasons. The USSR asked the United States to wage its war in South Vietnam; the United States hoped to enhance Soviet influence with Hanoi, highly unlikely if bombing gave China an "excuse for massive intervention." Moreover, the civilian strategists who staffed or advised the Pentagon felt mass destruction was not required. A "measured, controlled sequence of actions" was a relatively safe way of "signaling" firmness to China without direct threat. As for North Vietnam, unrestricted bombing would simply "shoot the hostage." The enemy might lose all fear if it had nothing more to lose.

Perfectly logical, this plan of operation would drop four times as much tonnage inside the South as the North, where 80 percent fell below the twentieth parallel, seventy-five miles south of Hanoi and Haiphong, much to the relief of Beijing, which sent a total of 320,000 soldiers to North Vietnam, largely to construct and defend transportation north of the twenty-first parallel. It produced the worst possible results, as the CIA expressly predicted and John McNaughton, its architect, eventually admitted: "a bridge here and there" did not inflict enough pain on Hanoi to desist but enough to increase its commitment to fight. The premise of bargaining by bombing lay in its false concept of the communist high command. In Max Taylor's words, they were "practical men [who] cannot wish to see the fruits of ten years of labor destroyed by slowly escalating air attacks."

Impatient for permission to destroy "all industrial and economic resources," most of the American military thought gradual escalation was absurd. The JCS begrudgingly accepted this plan because of civilian supremacy and the word of the secretary of defense that within a few months they would be permitted to place "very strong pressure" on Hanoi. When McNamara continued to conduct operations on the supposition that bombing should have "more deterrent than destructive impact," the military began to complain to the press of "being overruled on purely military matters by nonmilitary officials." Sympathetic senators agreed that "we are attacking the least important targets most, the more important targets less, and the most important targets not at all"—for example, power plants, railroad lines to China, and harbors handling shipments from the Soviet Union.

LBJ had a hunch about what military operations China would tolerate. He had hard experience with domestic politics, especially as a leading figure in the Senate hearings on Truman's dismissal of MacArthur. He knew enough to emulate FDR by appearing to eschew politics and defer to expert opinion on how to fight the war, as when he told the press he never made a military decision without JCS assent—perhaps the most egregious claim ever made by the man responsible for the phrase "credibility gap." The wide array of opinion and loose structure of the JCS enable any president to find at least one expert to agree with him. In 1965 this expert was Harold K. Johnson. "HK" or "Johnny," as he was known inside the army, became chief of staff in 1964, allegedly because he gave McNamara no grief. True or not, this infantryman never hid his belief that the war must be won on the ground. In March, before sending HK to report from Saigon, LBJ complained to the general: "Bomb, bomb, bomb. That's all you know. I want some solutions." To no one's suprise, HK reported back that infiltration should be stopped primarily by U.S. Army divisions that "can be defended as limiting the scope of the war by confining the physical presence to South Vietnam and southern Laos."

The president, having already stated that he was "ready to look with great favor on that kind of increased American effort," had no qualms at what McNaughton called the ground commitment, a "circuit-breaker" preventing geographic escalation. The White House was far less happy with supplementary messages from Generals Johnson, Westmoreland, Earle "Bus" Wheeler, chairman of the JCS, and Wallace Greene, commandant of the marines. Similar to military estimates made since 1953, they all said the deployment would necessitate 500,000 to 750,000 men, depending on the president's definition of success and provided "we do 'everything we can.' " There was "no likelihood," Westmoreland concluded, "of achieving a quick, favorable end to the war."

LBJ, afraid of a new MacArthur in his midst, was usually more polite to flag officers than to his civilian staff, especially when he ignored their military advice. However, when they announced these figures or leaked them to the press, they "got their ass chewed out" by the president himself. Other senior members of the administration simply discounted these estimates, believing the armed forces were shaking them down for more troops than they needed: 250,000 maximum, Bill Bundy thought at the time. In retrospect, some of the officers responsible for these estimates were shocked by their accuracy. Westmoreland and William DePuy, his MACV J-3 (plans and operations), would confess what they called their "basic error" in the war. "My biggest surprise," DePuy said in 1979, "and I have lots of company [was] I really thought the kind of punishment and pressure the North Vietamese and Viet Cong were under would have caused them to knock off." Eventually defeated by their "willingness to absorb losses" (800,000 fatalities, by

DePuy's count), he would admit he should have assessed the enemy more thoroughly than he had.

One can only assume that the U.S. military was using gloomy predictions (inadvertently correct) to send the president a message, as one favored reporter wrote in the *New York Times,* that "we must use what it takes to win." The same scare technique was employed by North Vietnam, whose premier would tell the Western press that "this is going to be a long, inconclusive war Americans do not like." He talked about protracted conflict to keep LBJ out of Indochina. American generals, like Harold Johnson, talked about protracted war to "get [the president] into this thing and win, or not go in at all." To escape political limitations on military operations, they repeatedly warned that without more force the war could last five to ten more years. No military man had to point out to a politician that this was a death sentence in American politics.

Whether dismal predictions were insincere or prudent, a disjunction existed between military means and civilian objectives. Government officals like McNamara and McNaughton usually maintained that America was fighting to show the enemy "that the odds are against their winning" and, by so doing, achieve "an acceptable outcome within a reasonable time." The president would use the same negative goals before the public ("deprive the communists of victory") but was far more heroic to a military audience: "My great-great-grandfather died at the Alamo" (not true); "nail the coonskin to the wall." Such pep talks were therapeutic for a cautious commander in chief who would not respond to memos asking whether the political objective was "a settlement short of total elimination of North Vietnam's intervention in the South." Eventually, the level of troop commitment would determine if the mission was the preservation of the territorial integrity of South Vietnam or merely helping the government survive a military emergency to "deal with what will remain a continuing and serious Communist problem." LBJ admitted in 1966: "I want to put off as long as I can, having to make these crucial decisions."

In theory, the president sets objectives, the Defense Department mobilizes the means, and the military finds the ways to fight America's wars. The armed services assumed the government would do what it had done in previous wars: declare a national emergency, call up reserves, and bring new tax bills to Capitol Hill. Otherwise, as McNamara warned Kennedy in 1961, the country would "get mired down in an inconclusive contest." However, by late 1963, McNamara defined flexible response as follows: "varying levels of pressure designed to make clear to the North Vietnamese . . . that we will escalate the conflict to whatever level is required to insure their defeat." Read closely, this meant sending signals. As for real escalation, he told Lyndon Johnson in mid-1965 that he differed from the JCS: "I have a very definite limitation of commitment . . . and I know they don't."

The president recognized that national mobilization would send a clear message to the communist world about determination not to be defeated. He also remembered that when Kennedy did this by mobilizing 120,000 reservists during the Berlin crisis of 1961, he irritated nearly everyone in Texas, a state very active in the National Guard and U.S. Army Reserves. In 1965 Johnson was nearly as anxious to conceal the conflict as he was to prove his credibility. If he mobilized America, he might have trouble convincing China and Russia that they were not at risk, especially since Khrushchev had referred to the Berlin call-up as a declaration of "preliminary war." He would also signal the American people that he was running up costs they would not accept over the long term. Reservists, let alone taxpayers, would demand that "their sacrifice produced some visible gain." Then, the administration feared, the "hard-line right wing" would promise a quick and decisive victory over the PRC, reminiscent of "the MacArthur crisis during the Korean War."

In mid-1964 Johnson asked his old mentor Senator Richard Russell (Dem.-Ga.) if Congress would impeach him for running out of Vietnam. It actually did what it has often done: let the president make the critical decision, then criticize whatever decision he made. LBJ hoped rather credulously that if he were nice and did not put Congress on the spot by calling up the reserves, they might be nice to him. Otherwise, he feared they would say: "You can't have guns and butter [his domestic legislation] and we're going to have guns."

In self-pity, Johnson asked McGeorge Bundy in 1964: "What the hell is Vietnam worth?" In mid-1965 he asked the JCS how they would "tell the American people what are the stakes." When a professional politician asks professional soldiers how to explain his policy, that policy stands on very shaky ground. The public did not want to let South Vietnam fall to communism, but its resolve was already slack. Private opinion polls commissioned by the White House found only a slight plurality for a major troop commitment and 69 percent already saying that Vietnam was "not very important." Whether LBJ's policy reflected public opinion or opinion reflected his reluctance to describe Vietnam as a major war, the president said he was trying to apply "the maximum amount of pressure with [the] minimum amount of danger," something that caused Eisenhower to describe Johnson as "a man at war with himself."

To avoid a direct war with China (that is, another Korea), Johnson risked a protracted war (that is, another Korea). George Ball identified another set of alternatives: pull out now and suffer a "short-term" loss in international prestige rather than stay and face a "major defeat." LBJ, foolish or not, was willing to risk a potential disaster rather than accept a sure loss in domestic support once Saigon fell. Moreover, limited war, despite its drawbacks, was not a foregone failure if the premise behind administration policy held up on the battlefield. Not a systematic strategy, it was the prevailing assumption behind statements like that of Walt Rostow, an economic historian specializing in industrial growth: Ho Chi Minh "has an industrial complex to protect: he is no longer a guerrilla fighter with nothing to lose." In the 1970s Harold Johnson recalled that "almost all of the individuals involved in the decision making process [believed] that a show of

force, a show of determination," would intimidate the enemy. This belief, he concluded, was difficult to refute because it was largely "unstated" and therefore not
debated.

Years later, Henry Kissinger would write that "the joys of peaceful construction held no temptation for . . . [the] fanatical ideologues in Hanoi." Like
most retrospective comments, this one understated how close to correct a failed
policy could be. North Vietnam always had a strong minority (sometimes a
majority) for postponing decisive action as late as 1973: "If we use our forces to
smash the Saigon army, it would open the possibility of a renewed war with the
United States." Back in 1964, before the prevailing assumption could be tested,
it was particularly suited for a president trying to scare Hanoi but not risk a major
war and still occupy the middle ground between hawks and doves. With the election over, LBJ asked General Johnson in mid-1965 for his opinion of Ho Chi
Minh's claim that they would fight for twenty years. The army chief of staff,
given a golden opportunity to use the threat of protraction to leverage a decision
for decisive escalation, immediately replied to the president: "I believe it. . . .
Best to get in and get the job done."

HK Johnson had already told reporters the war "could last 10 years," then,
off the record, said America would lose. Nonetheless, his boss, Robert McNamara, was anxious to "fight a limited war" that would "avoid building up public
pressure for drastic action." Within the government, many CIA, State Department, and Defense Department civilian experts were as apprehensive as the army
chief of staff. However, their opinion papers were rarely assembled for presentation to senior officials. Nor did they have much opportunity to assess the possibilities of failure. The president, fearing that critical studies would be leaked to
the media, kept his policies murky before implementation or abrupt enunciation
in the press.

Exactly what assumptions the president held is uncertain. Men he consulted
every day agree that "Lyndon Johnson really thought it terribly important people
should *not* know what he thought." While he often said "all I want to do is bloody
their noses a little bit" with 100,000 men, there are strong indications he was terribly disheartened, concluding as early as 1961 that "we had better be sure we are
prepared to become bogged down chasing irregulars and guerrillas over the rice
fields and jungles of Southeast Asia while our principal enemies China and the
Soviet Union stand outside the fray and husband their strength." In 1964 he said
he would soon have to make a "get in or get out" decision. When the time arrived
in 1965, he avoided the choice as best he could by adopting the prevailing
assumption he once described as nothing but "praying and grasping to hold on
. . . and hope [the communists] quit [which] I don't believe." In July the president privately predicted the war could require 600,000 men for an indefinite
duration. He asked Eisenhower: "Do you really think we can beat the Vietcong?"

Once the president bet on the middle-of-the road policy closest to the old
status quo, he spun a comforting delusion that it could actually work, no big

problem to a man who impressed one associate as having "a capacity for self-deception about the facts ten times greater than anybody I've ever met." In February 1967 Johnson yelled at Bobby Kennedy that he would win the war by July: Then "I'll destroy you and every one of your dove friends." Habitually, Lyndon Johnson was a tactician, predisposed to "frenetic activity" in domestic policy, his field of expertise, let alone in planning for Southeast Asia. In 1965 he mistook "crisis management" (fashionable after the Cuban missile crisis) for military strategy. If nothing else, his immersion in the details of the bombing of North Vietnam diverted his attention from the incompatibility of the war's various ends, ways, and means. It seemed easier to worry about airmen coming back from their missions than to sit still and confess, as he once did to startled reporters, "I don't know what the fuck to do about Vietnam. I wish someone would tell me."

Whatever the cause, the U.S. national commitment was understrength. LBJ deliberately understated his manpower needs and deployment plans once the administration determined that "the limited application of force for limited objectives has demanded that we avoid the emotion-rousing steps taken by governments in earlier wars." Dean Rusk believed that "a war psychology [was] too dangerous in a nuclear world." Lyndon Johnson replaced "unconditional surrender" with calls for "unconditional discussions." However judicious, neither one could answer a speechwriter's question: "How do you half-lead a country into war?"

Being prudent, the administration gave a distinct advantage to a totalitarian state proud to "mobilize the entire nation to defeat the U.S. imperialists." According to North Vietnam, "man and politics" would take priority over "bourgeois reliance on techniques," an ironic declaration from a political system full of techniques for motivating individuals to fight. Bill DePuy, widely thought to be the smartest general in the army, was well aware of the ideological strength of the communist side. He would make what he called "a coldly realistic" assessment of the situation: "We are going to stomp them to death. I don't know any other way." In the final analysis, U.S. firepower contained communist willpower for about ten years. It did not save Lyndon Johnson or win the war. Because Americans can neither abide military stalemate nor wage war without emotions, hawks and doves would unite to drive LBJ from the White House in 1968.

Before all this could explode in the president's political face, he would have to send ground forces off to meet the Army of North Vietnam (NVA). Because Johnson would not declare a national emergency, which would extend tours of duty in critical positions, the First Battalion of the Seventh Regiment, First Cavalry Division, lost four staff officers, two company commanders, eight of fifteen platoon leaders, and 160 men before deploying to Vietnam in 1965. That October in the Ia Drang Valley, it and the Second Battalion lost 200 killed and 242 wounded to the first NVA division operating inside South Vietnam. Back in July, upon hearing the president announce "it is not essential to order Reserve units into service," General Harold Johnson ordered his driver to take him to the White House, where he planned to resign over this "unconscionable" policy sure to erode "the quality of the Army." At the gate, he reconsidered and returned to the Pentagon. It was the beginning of three years of internal debate whether to resign over presidential refusal to use full military power.[4]

SEARCH AND DESTROY: FOR AND AGAINST

William "Westy" Westmoreland had grave reservations about deploying a large American ground force. The MACV commander had spent much of 1964 trying to prevent coups in Saigon, where "political chaos" led him to say that "a purely military solution" would not save the country from communism. In January 1965 he advised Washington that intervention "would at best buy time and would lead to ever increasing commitments until, like the French, we would be occupying an essentially hostile foreign country," where the ARVN would let the United States "carry the ball." Westy was also worried about the political foundation at home, that is, "whether or not our governmental structure, our body politic, was adaptable to the stresses and strains of a long commitment."

In March 1965, after General Johnson inspected South Vietnam for the president, Westmoreland became far less reluctant to request an army for his headquarters command. First of all, the Saigon government—unable "to foster national discipline, issue firm guidance, and give strong support"—would not survive without substantial intervention. Second, soldiers don't become generals by protesting they cannot accomplish their mission, as Westmoreland admitted when he later said "the armed services were not about to go to the Commander in Chief and say that we were not up to carrying out his instructions." Finally, the Pentagon, from McNamara to MACV, believed the enemy was moving out of guerrilla warfare into stage three of a Maoist insurgency: using large, conventional units far easier to locate and attack, as when intelligence identified NVA regulars in South Vietnam.

Heretofore, North Vietnam had been careful not to provoke an American reaction. Why its regiments appeared in 1965, when the Viet Cong were clearly winning the war, baffled U.S. officials, including Roger Hillsman, the resident expert on Asian guerrillas. The answer may lay in the fact that it would send many insurgents to thought-reform prisons and disparage their contribution after the war was won. The National Liberation Front recruited neutralists, Buddhists, peasants, and people from "bourgeois intellectual circles"—all against the Saigon ruling class. Aside from an inner core of communists, their ultimate loyalty was suspect to Hanoi, which did not want them to assume power through their own efforts, lest they remain independent from party control. To make sure no one challenged northern authority throughout all Vietnam, NVA regulars began to infiltrate the South in late 1964. This helped bring in regular American forces, which kept the NVA out of Saigon until 1975.

Without a mission statement from the White House, Westmoreland was free to deploy ground combat units where and how he wanted, as well as say they were "to maintain the initiative and go for victory, not a stalemate." This conventional soldier, who believed the conflict had entered its conventional stage, wanted to maximize America's strong suits—airmobility, helicopter gunships, and B-52s, "the most lethal weapon" in his arsenal. The means dictating the ways, Westy felt it best to "take the war" to main-force communist units in the highlands near the borders, where there would be fewer inhibitions against using massive firepower. American ground forces were to deplete the NVA in "an extended war of attrition." The ARVN, working behind this shield, was to pacify the densely populated coastal lowlands and wait for Westmoreland to turn the main battlefield over to it. This would give the Saigon government another chance to establish its legitimacy. It would also free most U.S. soldiers from civic missions in an alien culture, hardly their preferred responsibility. According to Private Bobby Muller, marine infantry: "Out in the bush the war was easy in a way because there was no ambiguity. Anybody you met was hard core NVA."

The search-and-destroy strategy would later be blamed for nearly every failure, from civilian massacres to the fall of Saigon. When Westmoreland and Bill DePuy described their concept in 1965 ("Go out, seek the enemy, and hit him whenever you can find him"), it was approved by McNamara, McGeorge Bundy, and Lyndon Johnson himself. No matter, the idea was barely proposed before it was criticized by the Marine Corps, the CIA, the U.S. embassy, and the army chief of staff. Each thought the concept of killing an elusive opponent faster than it could reconstitute was impractical in the jungle, where the enemy broke contact where and when it wished. They also thought that "the critical actions [of the war] are those that occur at the village, district, and provincial levels," where most people actually lived. They would have refocused America's effort from main-force units to guerrilla infrastructure and from heavy firepower toward "real—and not pretend—social revolution," all on the premise that "present US military actions are inconsistent with that fundamental of counterinsurgency doctrine which establishes winning popular allegiance as the ultimate goal."

One way or another, each critic of search and destroy stood outside the MACV mainstream. Long after the army ceased to be a constabulary force policing Indians, the Marine Corps retained similar missions in the Caribbean, where it had to defeat insurgencies without heavy weapons and large-unit sweeps. The CIA had been in the insurgency business itself when it recruited, supplied, and directed resistance units against the Axis (as the Office of Strategic Services) and against communist countries in the cold war. Ambassador Henry Cabot Lodge (grandson of Woodrow Wilson's nemesis) recruited a special team of embassy-based officers and civilians—Major General Edward Landsdale, Colonel Sam Wilson, Daniel Ellsberg, and John Paul Vann—who paid great attention to the peasants' struggle for existence, as did Harold Johnson, army chief of staff. Whereas Westmoreland and DePuy spent World War II in heavy combat with Germany, HK scrounged for food in the Philippines as a Japanese prisoner of war. Weighing only ninety pounds at liberation, he had a searing experience with

Third World living conditions few officers could imagine, except those advisers who found they had become part "politician, doctor, engineer, baby sitter, farmer, animal husbandry expert, and spy."

One month after Westmoreland proposed his search-and-destroy plan in July 1965, General Johnson gathered a group of former province and district advisers to assess its viability. Within nine months, they composed their own "Program for the Pacification and Long-Term Development of South Vietnam," commonly called the *PROVN Report*. Down at the hamlet level, they had confronted combat unit commanders who, like most soldiers in most American wars, cared little about anything but getting "the bad guys." In the *PROVN Report* they locked horns with MACV, which, according to the Defense Department, used seventy-five bombs and 150 shells per fatality: aiming at "places where the enemy might be, without reliable information he was there." Johnson came away with the impression that only 6 percent of artillery fire was aimed at observed targets, one reason for hundreds of thousands of civilian casualties.

Westmoreland had already pledged to "exercise restraint unnatural to war and the judgment of young men." He would maintain there were fewer civilian casualties in Vietnam than in any war in history, overstated but understandable in light of his previous experience in World War II and Korea, where whole countries were virtual free-fire zones. However, in those conflicts no one talked about the need to win the "hearts and minds" of the allied population or those of the *New York Times,* the *Wall Street Journal,* CBS, and NBC, each of whom would later ask how America could "save Vietnam if we destroy it in battle." Westmoreland and DePuy were well aware that "good-hearted but befuddled people" at home were "the real problem" in the Vietnam War. Nonetheless, aside from some province advisers who committed professional suicide by arguing with division commanders, few army officers would challenge the common infantry conviction that "when you are trying to survive, there is no such thing as too much firepower."

Most American soldiers, when not firing downrange, thought pacification meant charity: food, clothing, and military medical care. The counterinsurgency school thought differently but could not supplant search and destroy because of two intractable problems: the government of the South and the army of the North. Ed Landsdale and John Vann wanted to locate new "leaders who come from, think like, and are responsive to the majority" of the peasantry. Their recruits would isolate the hard-core communists and reconstitute the local militia infiltrated by the VC and despised by ARVN elites. Once rehabilitated, these units could defend their villages with shoulder-fired weapons and precise intelligence about the enemy, no need for heavy weapons that destroyed a hamlet "to save it" from the Reds. On occasion, MACV also talked about the need for a revolution in the countryside. However, the recommendation from Johnson's *PROVN* study that Americans become "more directly involved in internal affairs" drew a stiff reply from Westmoreland, always fearful of taking the place of colonial France: It "may defeat the objectives of U.S. policy, development of an independent, non-communist nation."

The U.S. embassy's elite counterinsurgency team thought itself far smarter than the army. Even so, it could not agree exactly what to do. Lodge hoped Lansdale would "be a sort of 'Lawrence of Arabia' to take charge under my supervision" of relations with South Vietnam. Landsdale, a former advertising executive, felt he could use his special gifts of persuasion; no need to resort to "colonial paternalism [which] will prove fatal to our cause." His boss and his disciple disagreed. Lodge and Vann believed the situation required "a strong, dynamic, ruthless, colonialist-type" proconsul who "really gives the orders," that is, men like them. Daniel Ellsberg, another member of the team, began to think the effort hopeless, at least by mid-1966. Unwilling to accept the alternative Bill DePuy gave to him—"more bombs, more shells, more napalm till the other side cracks"—Ellsberg saw the VC from close range: "boys in ragged black shoes and jerseys" but "too clean cut" to represent Saigon. He was moving toward his militant, antiwar position of 1968, when he said the United States was about to turn Vietnam into "a vast refugee camp." In the meantime, this former special assistant to the assistant secretary of defense helped convince McNamara to report to Johnson in late 1966 that "pacification has if anything gone backward; the VC political structure thrives," a significant event in McNamara's transition from hawk to dove.

Even if McNamara had told the president pacification was successful, it would not be easy for the White House to adopt it as the main effort. To be sure, the administration pushed and publicized health, welfare, and development programs, partly because LBJ was a devout New Dealer who wanted to bring "the healing miracles" of rural electrification to hamlets as he once brought them to Texas, partly because he was a cynic who said this would soothe the "sob sisters and peace societies" in the Democratic party. However, because Johnson was anxious "to get along [and] win the war" before the electorate tired of the effort, he did not want too "much effort placed on so-called social reforms." He, Dean Rusk, and Richard Russell (all southerners) were wary of what they seemed to feel was the latest brand of upper-crust New England imperialism. Lodge "thinks he's the emperor dealing with barbarian tribes," Russell told Johnson in mid-1964.

Whatever the legacy of the Civil War, any president would be wary of telling his field commander what Lodge told Johnson: that the "strategy of 'search and destroy' was wrong." First, LBJ never forgot Truman's politically fatal fight with MacArthur. Second, the counterinsurgency school presented no acceptable way to neutralize the NVA. If ground forces were to turn their backs to the border and break down to protect the pacification effort, how could they prevent main-force enemy units from building new staging bases a few miles from the populated coastal plains? The *PROVN Report* proposed that six divisions conduct a long-term occupation of the Laos section of the Ho Chi Minh Trail. (Westmoreland would have loved it, but he never had the gall to suggest something of this size.) The Marine Corps had a different proposal: unrestricted bombing that would inflict "damage of great magnitude" on all high-value targets from the railroads out of China to the harbor at Haiphong.

There had always been a symbiosis between high- and low-intensity warfare in Vietnam. Lodge and Max Taylor, early proponents, would have bombed the North rather than commit conventional American divisions in the South, where cultural friction between "grunts" and Vietnamese would feed the propaganda mills of the VC. The State Department ignored this issue, nor did it ask whether bombing could actually stop infiltration, disputed by McNamara and the CIA. It simply asked Victor Krulak, the marines' Pacific commander: "Do you want a war with the Soviet Union or the Chinese?" Lyndon Johnson had his own answer for the man who had tutored the Kennedys about winning counterinsurgency wars. He put his arm around Krulak, their favorite marine, and propelled him out the door. By tacit agreement between Washington, Beijing, and Moscow, a limited war could be waged as long as it was fought primarily within South Vietnam.

The proposal to wage unrestricted conventional war so one could prioritize pacification was only one of several ironies in a most paradoxical war. By 1965 it was already a commonplace that "we cannot defeat this armed enemy unless we win the people; yet unless we defeat the armed enemy, we cannot win the people." Harold Johnson gave contradictory recommendations that may have been the pinnacle of wisdom, since the war, the enemy, and public opinion were inconsistent at their roots. He told the president to mobilize the nation, "get in and get the job done"; his *PROVN Report* claimed America should be able to build a viable Vietnamese society "in less than 50 years." He condemned unobserved artillery fire as destructive and counterproductive to counterinsurgency; he also "deplored and opposed any intervention from the Washington level to impose limitations on further firepower application." The army must pursue the enemy "on a continued basis. The moment he can rest and restore himself, he comes bouncing back." In 1965 General Johnson said, "There has to be a solution to our problem but we have not yet found it." In 1973 he confessed, "I don't have the answer."

In mid-1966 Harold Johnson told Bill DePuy, now commanding the First Infantry Division, that if the army suffered more high casualties, like the thirty killed and 100 wounded in one of DePuy's companies, "the American people won't support this war." DePuy, architect of search and destroy, had recently sent out a small formation to search for an enemy battalion hiding from large units but likely to jump Americans exposed like bait. "The trick is to find them without being clobbered in the killing zone and then the reaction must be very rapid," with airmobility, gunships, and artillery. DePuy believed (and convinced even skeptical reporters) that he had the capability to "pile on" at the critical time and place, although he gave the opposition his professional respect: they "fight like tigers. We'd be proud of American troops of any kind who did as well against a large force that surprised them in the jungle."

DePuy's own combat initiation had come in World War II, where his Ninetieth Infantry Division took 18,000 casualties in six weeks when ambushed by German infantry—masters of fieldcraft, cover, and concealment like the enemy he faced in Vietnam. It was not good preparation for accepting General Johnson's prescient prediction about public opinion. "We went in[to Normandy]," DePuy would recall, "and said we would do it regardless of the cost. You went up the hill five, six times, and then you went up the seventh." In Vietnam, he knew the weak spot was "the home front," for which he had one response: the war "can only be won by the violence of combat," it was "being won in just that way," and "it will be a lot less unpopular once it is won"—so it seemed in 1966.[5]

PROGRESS OR DEADLOCK IN VIETNAM?

Pacification would remain, as Lyndon Johnson put it, "the other war," not the primary contest. Nonetheless, the counterinsurgency lobby had enough impact that Westmoreland dealt with it as any smart broker would, saying that their argument had merit, he already was performing the mission, he would devote more resources to it, and it would become the priority once the main-force war was won. In the meantime, search and destroy received over 95 percent of the money and 75 percent of the missions. One reason Westmoreland and DePuy were committed to "maintain the offensive on a seven-day-a-week, around-the-clock basis" was the question they frequently asked visitors: "How long have we got to win this war?" They—and their civilian superiors, such as Under Secretary of State Nicholas Katzenbach—recognized that "pacification is not the ultimate answer [because] we have neither the time nor the manpower." America had to mass (not disperse) its combat power to win the war before public patience ran out. As early as mid-1965, Washington officials were saying that "what we need more than anything else is some visible evidence of success for our efforts."

MACV's original concept of operations was to stop the Communist advance in 1965, take the offensive in 1966, and destroy the enemy by December 1967. Behind schedule from the outset, it believed it was ready to devastate most communist base areas and kill more soldiers than they could replace in January 1967, when DePuy led the largest search-and-destroy operation yet conducted, a multidivision sweep of enemy strongholds northwest of Saigon. After five months, four American-ARVN divisions killed 3,500 enemy soldiers, captured 5,000 tons of food, and destroyed 6,000 bunkers, tens of thousands of weapons, and countless rounds of ammunition. A week after the U.S. Army left, the VC returned. DePuy's assistant division commander wrote in the official after-action report: "The jungle is usually just too thick and too widespread to hope ever to keep [the enemy] from getting away." Main-force units moved their main bases across the border to Laos and Cambodia, which at least gave the coastal cities more breathing space. Otherwise, search and destroy in 1967 was not much different than in 1965, spoiling attacks on forward-positioned logistics that preempted a decisive communist offensive. The enemy was "hurt," Westmoreland wrote Washington in February, "but he was far from defeated."

Back in 1965, McNamara, the CIA, and State Department officials said that if the United States intervened in strength, the enemy would revert from stage three of an insurgency "back to their 1960–64 pattern" of irregular warfare, a prescient prediction insofar as they cut battalion-sized attacks 50 percent in 1966. McNamara took consolation that this would "stave off defeat in the short run." Others were more worried that this would create a permanent military stalemate in which the communists lacked the mass to defeat America but America was too heavy to trap elusive insurgents. MACV admitted that Vietnam "is a new kind of war," but rather than reexamine the basic premise that the conflict had entered a stage of conventional operations, DePuy and Westmoreland tried to "learn better ways of fighting" by distributing war-fighting lessons learned and recruiting "the smartest tactical US commanders."

By all accounts, from 1965 to 1968, the country deployed the best-trained and most well disciplined army it had ever had: the American "equivalent of a half-million-man Foreign Legion," said a reporter who had covered marines in World War II. The enemy still maintained a distinct advantage when Americans jumped off their helicopters humping ninety-pound packs in temperatures up to 110 degrees. The opposition hid mines, bunkers, and tunnels in elephant grass eight to fifteen feet high. When they decided to fight, said those who fought them, "they were absolute masters at choosing the right terrain at the right place at the right time to blow your crap away." When they chose avoidance (over 90 percent of the time), American infantry could not run down the opposition, which "can cover in 15 minutes what takes us four hours."

Westmoreland resented all accusations that he stuck to outmoded World War II tactics. The "Cloverleaf" sent small squads in all directions from a landing zone. The "Checkerboard" dropped separate units in every other grid square in what battalion commanders called "a bloody form of hide-and-seek." However inventive these formations, it still was doubtful whether any of them paid high dividends against an opponent who used "every bit of cover and concealment to perfection." Westy said "some of our ambush tactics are strikingly similar to those used in the Indian Wars." He failed to mention that germs and liquor conquered more warriors than the cavalry ever caught.

MACV's other response to stalemate, taking place at the strategic-operational level, gave Washington far more anxiety than new tactical techniques. By 1967, when search and destroy made substantial dents in enemy bases, the communists upgraded their cross-border sanctuaries. No longer just the terminus of supply trails for Russia's and China's best assault rifles, rockets, and mortars, these areas had become rest and training bases, storage depots, and sources of raw materials. Consequently, Westmoreland petitioned Washington that it was time "to deploy forces in Laos and cut off the enemy's access to the South." Since this was vital terrain that Hanoi could not relinquish, MACV could find, fix, and kill the enemy as search and destroy had failed to do within Vietnam. The alternative, Westmoreland warned an administration desperate for success, was "an unreasonably protracted war."

To execute this operation, an occupation (not a raid), the military requested 250,000 more soldiers, which would force the administration to mobilize the reserves, described inside Washington as breaking the "political sound barrier," where "the costs of Vietnam would become inordinate." LBJ was well aware that his middle-of-the-road strategy (fight the war inside South Vietnam) was disapproved two to one in opinion polls: "Every hawk, every dove, and every general seems to be against us." He was not surprised that public support for "total military victory" grew from 31 to 43 percent, nor did Robert McNamara, who predicted to the president that Westmoreland's requisition would raise "irresistible domestic pressures . . . 'to take the wraps off the men in the field.'" This would include chemical and nuclear weapons "if conventional efforts were not producing desired results," a particularly grim thought for a secretary of defense lacking the stomach to be a secretary of war.

For McNamara, whose worst curse during Vietnam was "Oh my God. We lost control," the means had become the goal. Whereas Washington once viewed Vietnam as a "laboratory, not only for this war, but for any insurgency," he now saw it as a training exercise for the American political system in "limited objectives being sought by limited [military] means." No small issue, he called this process "a necessity in our history because this is the kind of war we'll be facing in the next fifty years." If so, further escalation meant defeat—win, lose, or draw on the battlefield. This ambivalent hawk under JFK thereby became an ambivalent dove who still believed in the domino theory and the threat of communist expansion. "I didn't want to bomb Hanoi," he later told a biographer. "I didn't want to withdraw. I didn't have the answers. All I knew was we were in a hell of a mess."

The president also wanted to limit the war and keep the reserves at home, which McNamara considered his major accomplishment. In addition, he wanted undeniable military progress, which McNamara had not produced. At the least, LBJ wanted the army to convince the public that his claims of substantial improvement were true. That was the sine qua non for reelection one year away. To spike Westmoreland's troop request, a major step toward indefinite escalation, McNamara critiqued his strategy by saying the elimination of the main-force enemy (best accomplished outside South Vietnam) was not as important as pacification that "lessened destruction" and ran no risk of war with the PRC. Hence, to avoid a confrontation with China, he accepted one with MACV. He and his analysts in the Office of the Secretary of Defense (OSD) said that the army did not need to mobilize the reserves. It only needed to use its manpower efficiently, a slap at search and destroy. In private, MACV debated whether it was fighting the war correctly and concluded: "Nobody really knew the answer." What MACV knew, or fervently believed, was that a bunch of "uninformed" number crunchers working for McNamara knew a lot less. Westmoreland established his own systems analysis office to do briefing battles with OSD's "would-be strategists," who, according to DePuy, were making "a serious civilian intrusion into the business of the professional soldier."

This was not the only civil-military confrontation in mid- to late 1967, when the chairman of the JCS was warning the Pacific area commander that McNamara's views were "at considerable variance with our own thinking and proposals" about the war. Sixty-one percent of the public thought Vietnam was getting worse as different Senate committees held very different hearings on the war in Vietnam. Foreign Relations, a bastion for doves, investigated executive usurpation of congressional authority, a rather academic exercise. Its chairman, William Fulbright, knew Capitol Hill "was more warlike than the President," especially the Subcommittee on Military Preparedness, a stronghold for hawks ever since Lyndon Johnson used it as a forum to attack Harry Truman for conducting a "futile, indecisive, little war" in Korea.

In August 1967, when LBJ's political shoe was on the other foot, this committee summoned McNamara after first hearing from the JCS on the bombing of North Vietnam. Certainly no surprise to Chairman John Stennis, long a proponent of escalation, the military made headlines by complaining that restrictions on "lucrative" targets prevented decisive military success ("flat-out for all-out bombing"). McNamara's response was less anticipated, however contradictory. He said America was winning the war, lest he be tarred with stalemate. He also said in public what he said in private: that bombing, short of annihilating the enemy population, had "dubious prospects of successful results." The only thing it did, McNamara now believed, was run "a serious risk" of World War III: "Actions sufficient to topple the Hanoi regime will put us in a war with the Soviet Union and China."[6]

From the JCS perspective, born in World War II, any setback mandated an enhancement of military means, not a search for completely new methods to conduct an armed conflict. The JCS had begrudgingly accepted the doctrine of gradual escalation on grounds there would be no definitive limitations on military effort. Taken aback by McNamara's unequivocal defense of continual restrictions, they considered mass resignation, as advocated by Harold Johnson, a man with a bad conscience about Vietnam. "No one was really paying any attention" to their recommendations, he was said to have told his colleagues; "we had better be honest with the American people" by saying openly what was leaked anonymously: "Our senior military advisors are being overruled on purely military matters by nonmilitary officials." When asked about this by Stennis, McNamara replied that "the Constitution gives the responsibility of Commander in Chief to a civilian" who was not to "follow blindly the recommendations of his military advisors." His statement was irrefutable constitutional logic, to the acclaim of the *New York Times*. Made in a public forum, it plunged McNamara's stock even lower with the Congress, the electorate, and LBJ.

The next move was up to the JCS, whose chairman, "Bus" Wheeler, carefully selected by Lyndon Johnson, had always been anxious to avoid the impression that soldiers were "riding roughshod" over Washington. As a prop at presidential briefings or making speeches of his own, he supported LBJ's claim about a civil-military consensus. Now, in mid-1967, the day after HK Johnson's proposal for mass resignation, Wheeler responded, "We can't do it. This is mutiny." He once again implored his colleagues to "give it some time, maybe we can pull it out." While Wheeler waited for the right time to nudge LBJ toward decisive action, the president called a hasty news conference in the Oval Office to reiterate "no quarrels, no antagonisms, . . . [no] deep divisions" with the JCS. Hereafter, he carefully sought Wheeler's tacit approval. Without it, Johnson told McNamara, "I'm a man without a country."

No one knows exactly when or whether the president knew all the details of the secret meetings among the Joint Chiefs. By the time the story hit the news in late November, Johnson had sacrificed McNamara to a Congress-JCS coalition. Before the Stennis hearing commenced, he stopped calling McNamara on his private phone to OSD (the proverbial Johnson "deep freeze" for a persona non grata). Sensing their new opportunity the day the hearings started, the chiefs resubmitted recommendations to bomb in restricted areas of North Vietnam. The White House immediately approved fifty-seven of the seventy targets requested, although to be hit by small payload fighter-bombers, not the B-52s still used exclusively on tactical targets in South Vietnam. The next month, LBJ leaned back a little toward the dove side, offering Hanoi easier terms for bombing termination, while simultaneously telling Dean Acheson that the Senate "won't let us" do it.

McNamara had once been Johnson's lightning rod, attracting hostility away from the president's policy onto its loyal executive agent. Now he became too hot to hold. By late 1967 the president was searching for a new secretary of defense less susceptible to the Stennis subcommittee charge, supported by some 85 percent of the public, "that civilian authority consistently overruled the unanimous recommendations of [the] military commanders." Johnson needed unity; disagreement frightened the electorate. He also needed men with public standing to convey a message of military progress. In the war of public relations, the generals were still more optimistic, cooperative, and convincing than the national command authority. "How are we ever going to win?" LBJ asked Dean Rusk and McNamara, "It doesn't seem we can." McNamara had "no idea." Rusk suggested a strategy akin to the future communist Tet offensive: "All our forces should go on the offensive in an all-out effort to defeat the enemy in as many places as possible," that is, as long as they stayed inside South Vietnam. Westmoreland and the JCS objected. They wanted to mass combat power at specific locations outside the present geographic restrictions, something that tempted LBJ. "We have been too cautious for too long. If gradualism does not pay off early," he said long after it began, "the enemy must be fought with all resources . . . no sanctuary given."

After speaking tough to discharge his frustrations, the president reverted to business as usual, a far cry from carpet bombing, as was done in North Korea. Then, in a war of mutual sanctuaries, America had the advantage, particularly the port of Pusan, stacking ordnance and armaments twenty feet high. Now, as one aviator blurted out to White House aides in 1968: "I've flown through SAMs, flak, and automatic weapons fire . . . [to] hit the same wooden bridge three times. . . . I've seen the god-damned Russian freighters sitting there and the supplies stacked along the wharves. I can't hit them. 'It might start a wider war.' Well the war is too wide for me right now."

Lyndon Johnson had hoped to convince North Vietnam that "the game is not worth the candle," the war not worth the risk. When push ultimately came to shove, North Vietnam imposed this point on him. The president was long convinced that "our people won't stand firm" for a protracted war, but he worried even more about a confrontation with Russia or China. He asked the JCS what additional actions, "within present policy limitations," they could take before 12 March 1968—not coincidentally, the day of the New Hampshire presidential primary. They replied that "under current policy guidelines," there was nothing "in the near term which would result in a rapid or significantly more visible increase in the rate of progress." Hence, in December 1967, Johnson was back where he was in June 1965—still hoping for "a sequence [of events] in which we maintain pressure without widening the war; impose upon North Vietnamese increased losses; and then in time they would have to decide what to do in the face of the high losses and the continued frustration of their objective."

Unable to win within an acceptable duration without risking World War III, LBJ secretly explored diplomatic options available because he had never answered the question: "Is your aim in Vietnam to win the war or to seek a compromised negotiation?" America tried (1) to split the Viet Cong from the North Vietnamese, (2) to entice the NVA from the VC, and (3) to draw Soviet support from North Vietnam, all to no avail.

If the National Liberation Front were to break with Hanoi, it would have to have a substantial role in South Vietnam. Johnson desired "to broaden the government," if only to pacify the *New York Times,* but Saigon barely granted clemencies, let alone conduct talks, for fear of competition from the NLF. He would not pressure the regime (America's worst mistake "was getting rid of Diem") lest it collapse and discredit his claims to having built stability in Saigon. Tempting North Vietnam away from the VC would be more compatible with U.S. objectives. While the NLF talked of "the path of revolution laid down by our brothers in China," Hanoi was moving into the Soviet orbit, if only because Russian technology provided air defense. LBJ sensed an opening and explored what was called a "Laos-type solution," that is, a "standstill truce" acknowledging NVA zones in South Vietnam. Richard Nixon adopted this policy in 1972, along with something Johnson did not consider: wooing China from Hanoi. This compromise failed in 1967. The VC rejected all proposals that left the GSVN in Saigon; LBJ had revealed his readiness to make substantial concessions. The NVA prepared to negotiate but from a position of enhanced strength after a spectacular military victory planned for 1968.

The final diplomatic option involved the Soviet Union. Johnson had long expected assistance from the Kremlin on grounds that American intervention supported revisionist principles of peaceful coexistence versus Chinese militancy.

Wondering why Russia was not helping America back in 1964, he postulated that the Soviets were acting like Charles de Gaulle: resting under the U.S. nuclear umbrella while it waged the common fight against Red China. The administration never appreciated the fact that the Soviet Union was supporting Ho Chi Minh for much the same reason Washington opposed him—to contain the PRC. The Americans (so-called pragmatists) felt they were in a worldwide confrontation and Ho was a surrogate for Mao. The Russians (so-called ideologues) were far more specific and concrete. They wanted to contain Chinese territorial expansion and believed that a local strongman was exactly what they needed to rule a viable nation on China's southern flank. They were in no mood to do what they had done in 1962: deal with LBJ behind Ho's back like Khrushchev had dealt with Kennedy against Castro. In the Caribbean, the Soviets had been at a theater disadvantage, let alone fearful of thermonuclear war. Still, the Johnson administration was not ready to relive that ordeal and revive direct conflict with the Soviet Union to prevent it from sending equipment to the NVA. Now close to nuclear parity with the United States, Russia might respond to overt pressure with another blockade of Berlin, where it had an overwhelming conventional advantage, especially with America chest deep in Vietnam.

LBJ was unable to negotiate, nor was he willing to escalate like Roosevelt, Lincoln, and McKinley, all of whom won decisive battles before they faced reelection. Neither did he have the gall to accept Senator George Aiken's variant of John Kennedy's old solution, now privately endorsed by McGeorge Bundy—that is, declare victory and leave Vietnam. In late 1967, after Democratic congressmen complained that "nobody sees the light at the end of the tunnel. We are the victims of a poor public relations program," the president could only orchestrate a media blitz. In the throes of self-pity, LBJ felt "a climate of dissent and opposition" was created by East Coast metropolitan disdain for less-polished poor boys from the Southwest. However, he would not forfeit "the absolutely vital political base in the country," where the war would be won or lost. To "crank up" what he called his "propaganda effort," he toured the nation "in a fighting mood" that made Walt Rostow very nervous. Having warned LBJ in 1964 against unequivocal statements that America would not go to war, he now shuddered lest "hard evidence" and reporters come back to embarrass White House claims. No matter, Johnson was out "to change chicken shit to chicken salad," as he was wont to say, when he claimed a ten-to-one "kill ratio" in combat and "dramatic progress" in Vietnam.

Somewhat inadvertently, the media came to LBJ's support, however much he hated most reporters: "Don't they know I'm the only President they've got and a war is on?" Television did not show exactly what he wanted: "Ernie Pyles out there interviewing soliders who can tell how proud they are to do their duty." Nonetheless, it had so many pictures of so many soldiers jumping out of helicopters that the public, as well as many government officials, thought the operations must have had an irresistible momentum, no matter that camera crews entitled their output: "The Wily VC Got Away Again." Only 3 percent of the stories had combat footage with dead or wounded Americans. Eighty-three percent of the viewers felt more "hawkish" after watching the news.

For the vast majority of the American public, short-term success or failure had become the bottom line: if the war was being won, they approved the war. Whatever LBJ, Rusk, or Rostow may have believed about containing Communist China, the administration had not convinced the public that the national interest was at stake. Half said they did not know "what we are fighing for" in Vietnam; as many thought it would start World War III as thought it would prevent it. With the value of the effort not established, the cost of a prolonged war appeared too great by mid-1967, when fatalities reached 13,000, inflation reached its highest rate since the Korean War, and 81 percent of those polled expected several more years of war. The president was temporarily able to stop the political hemorrhage by re-creating an aura of optimism that made significant progress—in America, not Vietnam. In March 1967, 33 percent thought the country was winning, compared with 50 percent in November. In August, 39 percent approved Johnson's presidency, as did 48 percent in January 1968. On 28 January, LBJ sent reprints of the recent polling data to the leading figures in the Democratic party. Also celebrating, halfway around the world, his ARVN allies took leave for Tet.

Even the *New York Times* was impressed: Lyndon Johnson "remains one of the most formidable political showmen in American history." The president could not have carried the message alone, since the credibility gap between his claims and the facts had become a national cliché. To convince Americans that America was winning the war, he needed the military, ideally "some colorful general like MacArthur, . . . to go to Saigon and argue with the press," an ironic wish from a man who once said to Westmoreland: "I hope you don't pull a MacArthur on me." Unable to summon a dead man, Johnson got replacements, less imposing than his ideal choice but more credible than he. Omar Bradley (age seventy-four) went over, reported to Walt Rostow that "we were well on the way to winning the war," and published a *Look* magazine article ghostwritten by his second wife, a Hollywood screenwriter, claiming Vietnam was "a war at the right time, the right place, and with the right enemy," in contrast to his famous critique of MacArthur during Korea. Harold Johnson, back from his own inspection tour, where he received many of the same briefings as Bradley, was "unleashed on the White House Press Corps," at Rostow's suggestion, in mid-August. He told a skeptical audience, who brought up McNamara's criticism of search and destroy, that "by the first of the year . . . we will see very real evidence of progress" and that "we are very definitely winning in Vietnam."

The most important expert witness went from (not to) Vietnam. Johnson brought Westmoreland back home to address Congress, the public, and the press. He once declined these missions but took the opportunity to lobby for expanding the war. In private, the general was judicious: "We are making steady progress, although undramatic" and "not mathematically provable." He would not guarantee success, at least to the president, as long as military restrictions remained. However, before the National Press Club and on Capitol Hill, this hero with 68 percent approval uttered a line that nullified his message that the war had become "a question of putting maximum pressure on the enemy anywhere and everywhere we can." He was about to become a bumbler for saying: "I have never been more encouraged. The end begins to come into view."

Looking back long after the Tet offensive, one wonders why senior officers said "tremendous progress has been made" and "the military war in Vietnam is nearly won." To begin with, they were quite uneasy spending "an inordinate amount of time . . . in domestic politics"—something best left "up to the politicians"—and doing it to support a military strategy they all wanted to change. They were also very skeptical about their Saigon ally, whom they praised to the press, per White House requests, while privately complaining about "corruption everywhere." Hence generals, who were painting rosy public scenarios, were simultaneously warning each other (1) that the armed forces would "take the fall" if the president's policy failed—Harold Johnson to JCS; (2) that "we must [be] careful . . . to avoid charges that the military establishment is conducting an organized propaganda campaign"—Westmoreland to Johnson; and (3) that "we must not be over optimistic. . . . It is a common American characteristic to oversell"—MACV to unit commanders.

Westmoreland would confess in his memoirs that "it was difficult to differentiate between pursuit of a military task and such related matters as public and congressional support." It was particularly difficult, since he and other senior commanders had long been saying that "the only thing that can defeat us is for the American people to get tired of the war." These combat veterans of World War II and Korea could not grasp how they might be losing a war in the field without having lost a major battle. Westmoreland had fought at the Kasserine Pass, Johnson at Bataan and the Chorgchon River. Those were huge defeats; nothing happened on that scale in Vietnam. In 1965 HK Johnson said that America should fight all out or not fight at all. By 1967 the nation was committed, and this former POW of Japan did not acknowledge defeat. If he did, he would have died in captivity.

In the armed forces, unlike the press and Congress, negativism was disloyalty if there was any hope at all. LBJ kept hope alive by ignoring McNamara's recommendation for an unequivocal rejection of all military requests for more troops, new bombing targets, and ground maneuver operations outside Vietnam. He could hint and dangle future escalation before the high command, who never really knew their ultimate constraints. This had a military downside for the hawks and a political downside for the doves. The services stuck with tactics that could only win the war if the president removed restrictions, as they assumed he eventually would. European allies, White House staff, and OSD officials wanting de-escalation asked LBJ to "take command" of the high command—that is, run the armed forces like a Lincoln, Truman, or Churchill. They were sorely depressed when he refused. Anthony Eden visited Washington and said: "Winston and I would have never let the military interfere in policy the way President Johnson has."

These comparisons were not completely fair. The British Constitution kept generals away from parliamentary committees; Harry Truman had more protection because the Joint Chiefs were on his side. LBJ, in a weaker position, usually avoided direct discussions with senior officers. (When he had one in November 1965, the chief of naval operations called it "the worst experience I can imagine.") This lack of contact impaired the formation of effective policy. As DePuy confessed in 1988, no soldier said, "Look, Mr. President, you can't get there from here." Nonetheless, by avoiding civil-military confrontations, Johnson got Rostow to get "support for your president" while shaking down the armed services for data indicating there was "light at the end of the tunnel." This attempt to prove success was not done without risk. LBJ gambled in the face of growing evidence that the enemy would launch "kamikaze attacks" to achieve "some tactical victory," as he warned the Australian cabinet (not the American people) in late December 1967. "We face dark days ahead."[7]

TET: SNATCHING DEFEAT FROM THE JAWS OF VICTORY

In 1965 "stalemate" was not necessarily a dirty word. Rusk felt and McNamara said that if the enemy can "see that there is no hope for victory," we can force "negotiations that will preserve the independence of South Vietnam." By early 1967 a new consensus held that stalemate was the enemy's objective, best stated by Nicholas Katzenbach: "Hanoi uses time the way the Russians used terrain. [It] hopes for mounting dissension, impatience, and frustration caused by protracted war."

Government opinion was no more correct in 1967 than in 1965, when officials believed Hanoi would be intimidated by fear of destruction of its industry. The North would not give up territorial expansion, although the issue was hotly debated within its government. It did reject protracted conflict, at least as it described "a long, inconclusive war" to the Western press. The Communist party Central Committee, rejecting guerrilla-political war, chose to "take the initiative," accelerate the pace of the action, and "launch big battles." At the Ia Drang Valley in November 1965, the U.S. First Cavalry Division, inflicting some 3,500 fatalities, foiled the first NVA attempt to conclude the war. Not falling back to protraction, the party resolved in December "to win a decisive victory in the southern battlefield" by killing 60,000 U.S. soldiers in the next two years. They would try for a decisive victory three more times: Tet (1968), the Spring Offensive (1972), and Spring Victory (1975). The last one being successful, Hanoi conquered Saigon.

Party resolutions "to deal a decisive blow to the enemy" were one thing, the battlefield another. In constant motion to avoid U.S. firepower, most main-force units fought only two or three battles a year. Then win, lose, or draw, they broke contact before a skirmish became a slugfest. Communist forces regulated their losses to tolerable levels but, by December 1967, had killed only 16,000

Americans. Their officers claimed to have "annihilated dozens of U.S. battalions," but progress was clearly far behind schedule. Field commanders confessed that they had to do something to counteract "the fear of protracted war," the growing "lack of conviction in our mission," and "reluctance, hesitation, dejection, inactivity, and desertion." In Hanoi, where bombing (thanks to the Stennis hearings) caused substantial malnutrition and disease, 200 senior government officials were arrested for "conterrevolutionary crimes"—communist code for defeatism, now a capital offense.

MACV was about the only U.S. agency to doubt communist strategy was to wait out America's public will. To say this was to admit that search and destroy was doing no damage when it certainly was, although not enough to force surrender. After engagements in September 1967 with the largest enemy units since the Ia Drang, MACV maintained that the enemy had decided "to make a major effort to reverse the downward trend" and seek "at least one spectacular victory for propaganda purposes" prior to negotiations to stop protracted war. "I hope they try something," Westmoreland told a reporter at his National Press Club speech in November; "we are looking for a fight."

MACV expected the enemy to attack a key American outpost on a major route of entry near the border, where they could mass men, artillery, and ammunition from their Laos sanctuaries, much as they had done against France at Dienbienphu in 1954. If successful, they would occupy substantial hinterland during the ensuing diplomatic conference, bound to reflect the military facts. Then Saigon would not rule all of South Vietnam and Westmoreland would fail his own criteria for success: the enemy would be "free to move through large areas of the country without official detection" by the official government condemned to a permanent state of siege. However, if "a go-for-broke [military] campaign" were defeated, there would finally be a real possibility of forcing the communists to bargain from a position of weakness—at least that was what the White House hoped in late 1967, when it allowed MACV to make Khe Sahn, LBJ's special Alamo, bait for 40,000 NVA in a four-month siege.

The army felt the enemy's desperate search for a major victory would seal its coffin and prove to doubters in the CIA, OSD, and the press that it had reached the coveted "crossover point" where the communists lost more soldiers than they could replace. True, some prisoners, captured documents, and defectors suggested the enemy was planning something to "split the sky and shake the earth" in the urban areas, strange to conventional soldiers, for whom wars were fought between conventional armies. The so-called General Uprising must be a diversion to keep American attention from Khe Sahn, an opportunity to fight "on our terms, on our ground, and within supporting range of our [best] weapons," delivering 110,000 tons of bombs and 150,000 artillery rounds in this area of operation, over five times the kilotons dropped on Hiroshima. One senior intelligence officer later said about Tet, the most important event in the entire conflict, "If we'd gotten the whole [enemy] battle plan, it would not have been believed."

The Communist party, in accordance with its doctrine of military and political struggle, planned to combine soldiers in conventional attack with a civilian insurrection against the Saigon regime, the weakest link in the anticommunist effort because Americans were imperialists (not colonialists) who left their "puppets" incompetent and corrupt. The communist underground had assured Hanoi that, from 4 million sympathizers, it recruited hundreds of thousands ready to rebel. This report was perfectly credible to an organization that thought itself the vanguard of the masses. It was also believed by CIA analysts, who intercepted this figure and made it the basis of their charge that Westmoreland was undercounting the enemy so he could claim he was winning the war. In fact, the number proved to be what a senior communist commander subsequently called "an illusion based on our subjective desires." Some "city penetration elements" were fabricating success to continue to enjoy comfortable conditions they did not want to lose if sent to the highlands to face search and destroy. Other VC, more committed to the cause, wanted to play a dominant role in a decisive victory that would give them equal "right[s] to determine the political future of the south" before Hanoi established complete control. Motivation notwithstanding, when mass uprisings of the local population never occurred at Tet, the underground's "rosy reports to higher levels" were discredited in the Politburo. In Saigon, Westmoreland was vindicated, although no one seemed to notice at the time.

On 30 January 1968, throughout Vietnam, some 84,000 enemy (more VC than NVA) attacked government installations on the premise that "we only need to make a swift assault to gain total victory." The ARVN, on leave for the holiday, for once reacted rapidly, to the surprise of America and Hanoi. In their finest military hour, they threw back, killed, or captured most of the enemy in two or three days. Communists held Hue for three weeks and a battered wall at the U.S. embassy in Saigon for eight hours. Hue was "an unprecedented victory of scientific quality," about the highest praise Marxists can give. The embassy action was ignored, at least initially, by Hanoi. The political target was public opinion in South Vietnam, which did not care what happened at a foreign compound. Lyndon Johnson cared, even confessed to his advisers "we had the people believing we were doing very well in Vietnam when we actually were not."

Tet, more hype than substance, was made to order for American TV, desperately looking for what it called "shooting bloody." Despite expanding Saigon bureaus and expense accounts, it had not yet found much "irresistible sensationalism." Suddenly Saigon and Hue resembled a Hollywood gunfight, if not World War II. Said one cameraman, just outside the capital: "For the first time Vietnam really looked like the documentary war footage I grew up watching." Pictures are an excellent medium for portraying destruction, confusion, fear, and blood. According to TV news (20 February 1968): "Marines are so bogged down in Hue that nobody will predict when the battle will end." (Four days later the town was secured.) For Johnson, desperate to show progress, the media finally carried extensive combat at the time he was saying it was winding down. Unlike World

War II, where military success or failure could be traced on a map, there was little to refute a dramatic picture, no matter how misleading it was.

The Defense Department gathered numerous statistics, but its reports were ambiguous: some signs of progress, some of failure. Privately, analysts confessed they could not determine the "effectiveness of our military policy," bombing North Vietnam or hunting enemy forces on the ground. Others admitted they could not even agree on a definition of success, at least for pacification in the counterinsurgency war. The public might also say they could not define "progress," but they knew what they saw on TV, on magazine covers, and in front-page photos. The information was real but fragmented and devoid of explanatory context. Cameras depict casualties on the cameraman's side of the wire; the press was showing defeat during a military success. LBJ complained about the coverage, but things evened out in the end. He previously had profited from footage so overstating accomplishments that the public was not prepared for pictures of real combat—that is, chaos and "Americans getting the hell kicked out of them." CBS News anchor Walter Cronkite, the most trusted man in America, had been told that Vietnam was a counterinsurgency campaign where pacification and politics were the main effort. Seeing what looked like a World War II battle, he said: "What the hell is going on? I thought we were winning the war."

Desperate for support, Johnson turned again to Westmoreland: "Make a brief personal comment at least once a day . . . to reassure the public here that you have the situation under control." The next day, when the president looked at the front page for MACV's statement that the Tet offensive was "running out of steam," he saw a belated announcement of his own request for a 10 percent tax increase. He also saw the most memorable photograph of the 1960s: the summary execution of a Viet Cong prisoner on a street corner in Saigon. Blended at a glance, these features seemed to prove that the end was not in sight. Actually, the taxes Johnson avoided in 1965 were needed to stem inflation, not increase military spending. The average citizen was not the only confused party. One set of government officials dismissed what another set was saying when it conflicted with TV coverage, an espisodic method of communication ill suited for sustained analysis. Harry McPherson, a White House speechwriter very close to LBJ, confessed, "I put aside my own access to confidential information [from Walt Rostow] and was more persuaded by what I saw on the tube. . . . I was fed up with the optimism that seemed to flow without stopping from Saigon."[8]

THE HIGH COMMAND IN THE CORRIDORS OF POLITICAL POWER

Even Earle Wheeler and Bill DePuy, now stationed in the Pentagon, were engulfed in what Westmoreland called the media-based "impression that the Tet offensive was the worst calamity since Bull Run." After briefings in Saigon lifted their gloom, they felt Tet might force the country to "decide whether we are going to face up to this challenge or not." Not wanting the "not" option, they still hoped for LBJ's permission to enlarge and win the war. When limited ways and means proved inadequate, Lincoln gave more resources and authority to Grant; Roosevelt gave them to Marshall. While neither Wheeler nor Westy ever talked of unconditional surrender, they said, "We can win the war if we apply pressure upon the enemy relentlessly in the north and in the south"—and now the west, requesting 250,000 more soldiers to invade Laos and Cambodia.

Wheeler and Westmoreland agreed on what they wanted but not on how to get it. Long "against too gloomy an appraisal," MACV described Tet as a tactical victory to be made decisive by "a corps-size operation astride the most critical choke points" of the Ho Chi Minh Trail. The chairman of the Joint Chiefs, more familiar with Washington, knew better. Since 1965 he had been trying to nudge LBJ toward escalation, a "dirty word" in Washington, he wrote Westmoreland in 1966. The White House said it would reinforce "to avoid defeat" and stave off "disaster"— nothing about winning the war. Consequently, Wheeler told LBJ that Tet "was touch and go." He told MACV that the administration won't "accept a defeat," but don't predict victory. Say "there is tough fighting ahead, and that the enemy has residual capabilities not yet committed." Westmoreland, having said he was doing fine, now wrote that he needed at least 40,000 more soldiers, causing LBJ to wonder if different people were writing different cables from different headquarters in Saigon.

This so-called crisis was an opportunity for Wheeler to resubmit his long-standing plan for national mobilization, largely to acquire 300,000 more soldiers to constitute a worldwide reserve (total cost $12.5 billion). To get White House consent at a time of steep inflation and a plunging dollar on the international exchange, he said it was needed to prevent the collapse of Vietnam. This scenario, leaked to the press by OSD civilians, among them Daniel Ellsberg, reinforced the public's perception that Tet was a bad defeat. Meanwhile, Creighton "Abe" Abrams, the MACV deputy commander, no confidant of Westy, was kept in the dark about requisitions but summoned to Washington, where he said: "Mr. President, we've got plenty of troops. . . . It's beginning to turn our way." Another first-class military conspiracy bites the dust.

The tactical confusion on the military side of civil-military relations did not help resolve the chronic conflict inside the Johnson administration, which did not know, in Rostow's words, "whether we are being asked to send forces to prevent a radical deterioration in our side's position or to permit [Westmoreland] to conduct a vigorous offensive." In the president's most militant speech (described later), LBJ admitted that "we are not doing enough to win the war the way we are doing it now." Then he immediately said that "we are constantly trying to find additional things that it is reasonable, prudent, and safe to do." With China an unpredictable player, it was not prudent and safe to win the war, according to Clark Clifford, the new secretary of defense.

Clifford was "appalled [that] the military was utterly unable" to present him with a "plan for attaining victory." General officers tried to point out that it was impossible to attain victory under all the restraints OSD imposed. When MACV's chief of staff suggested "aggressive operations into southern North Vietnam and southern Laos," Clifford replied that they must think of reducing, not expanding, the effort. Right or wrong, it is hard for anyone to solve difficult problems by limiting the effort they expend.

Immediately after Tet, when LBJ told Wheeler to send Westmoreland "everything he wants," the president got some dissenting opinions beyond the doves in OSD. National mobilization required approval from the barons on the Senate Armed Services Committee, John Stennis and Richard Russell, long saying to "go in and win or get out." In 1968 their price for troop enhancement was strategic (not "piecemeal") escalation: invading Laos, bombing the rail lines with China, and mining Haiphong harbor. The first two could lead to war with the PRC, the last with the Soviet Union. An attack on American vessels in the Gulf of Tonkin had been LBJ's excuse to bomb North Vietnam in 1964. If Russia were looking for its own provocation, he feared it could cite a similar attack on shipping. "Don't you remember the Battleship *Maine*?"

Hawks and doves united against Johnson's centrist position. Friendly senators called Rostow to say that their strongest constituent supporters were "just sick" of the war. On 16 March Wheeler wrote Westmoreland that their scheme had failed (it actually made things worse): "The gloom and doom of Tet had affected public support. The latest polls show that 69 percent favor phased withdrawal of our forces from Southeast Asia." In this political environment, Clark Clifford convinced LBJ to convene another meeting of his prestigious senior advisers—Dean Acheson, Robert Lovett, John McCloy, and others—who had made him feel, said Bill Bundy, that "he should not fall short of the standards set by those men who had played leading parts in World War II and the American successes in the Cold War." In 1965 they told this less-than-proud graduate of a Texas teachers college that he had no "choice [in Vietnam] except press on." In 1967 Acheson repeated the message and reminded everyone how he had held his ground in Korea despite the "great outcry to get out" in 1951. In 1968 Clifford detected the group had changed its mind, as had Clifford during Tet.

Before LBJ listened to the "wise men," they listened to Bill DePuy, sent by the JCS to brief their meeting because Wheeler was recovering from a trip to the Philippines. The army chief of staff would have overstated Tet as a setback, if not a defeat. DePuy embellished in the opposite direction because, as he recently wrote his old First Infantry Division, "The mood in America is as bad as it can get." (When the army wins the war—"and I think you can"—it will "make liars out of a lot of people.") DePuy was too emotionally invested to convince skeptics already convinced, as Acheson told Johnson, that "the Joint Chiefs of Staff don't know what they are talking about." When DePuy made a flimsy claim about 80,000 enemy killed and three times that many wounded, one wise men asked: "Who the hell is there left for us to be fighting?"

The president met with the wise men immediately after this flaying of the last vestige of military credibility, caught between Wheeler's portrait of imminent danger and DePuy's claim of decisive victory. LBJ must have found ironic what he heard from Acheson, the group's senior member, no master of public opinion when he was Harry Truman's secretary of state: Mr. President, "the American people" will simply not give you the time "to force the enemy to sue for peace." Johnson mumbled, "The establishment bastards have bailed out" and blamed Ted and Bobby Kennedy for causing everyone to recommend "surrender." He thereby assuaged his Alamo guilt complex about running from a fight and sacrificing (as of then) about 20,000 soldiers who would die in vain if the war effort failed. Johnson later wrote that if these men "had been so deeply influenced by the reports of the Tet offensive, what must the average citizen in the country be thinking?" On 31 March he announced he would not run for reelection. Three days later Hanoi broadcast its official statement to the effect that Tet had worked just as planned: "The General Offensive and Uprising of the South Vietnam Armed Forces and people have inflicted on the U.S. aggressors and their lackeys a fatal blow. . . . The U.S. defeat is already evident."

Hanoi had hit Lyndon Johnson square in the forehead, largely by accident, although most Americans never saw Tet that way. Antiwar critics had their own vested interest in NVA military genius. They had been predicting U.S. failure, and, like LBJ, their credibility was at stake. Communist casualties and retreat were beyond reasonable debate, but the doves assumed that no one except MACV and the ARVN could have made such a terrible tactical mistake. They supposed Ho Chi Minh must have aimed at U.S. public opinion, as believed the president, OSD, and the American embassy in Saigon. Each had long felt the war would be decided inside America, where "morale, fatigue, and psychological factors" were obvious targets for the enemy. LBJ would conclude that Ho tried "to win in this country what he could not win from [fighting] men out" in Vietnam.[9]

A NEW MILITARY COMMANDER, AN OLD MILITARY POLICY

On 31 March 1968 President Johnson declared he soon would send 13,500 of the 206,000 men MACV requested: nothing more about the future. The next day, without LBJ's approval, Clark Clifford announced the adoption of "de-Americanization" and no further reinforcements. Continuing this method of operation in the Nixon administration under the name of "Vietnamization," Melvin Laird would do repeatedly what Clifford did on April Fools' Day, when the secretary of defense handed the president a public fait accompli for force reduction.

On the same day LBJ announced his limited reinforcement, he moved Creighton Abrams up to MACV commander from the deputy position neither he nor Westmoreland ever wanted him to have. When Harold Johnson could not convince Westy to adopt the *PROVN Report* in 1966, he sent Abe, the army vice chief of staff, to Saigon as MACV heir apparent. After Tet shattered Westmoreland's credibility, even with the president for whom he risked his reputation, he was moved out to be army chief of staff, LBJ's consolation for "playing on the team to help me." To make room for Westy, HK was retired. This former POW and Distinguished Service Cross recipient spent his final years berating himself to Vietnam veterans for failing to resign in protest over LBJ's strategy: "I am now going to my grave with that burden of lapse in moral courage on my back." Not unique, the entire JCS left the Pentagon wondering "Why did I go along with this kind of stuff?" General Johnson's replacement was equally bitter over his removal from "the mainstream of the war" and shipment to the Washington "merry-go-round," "particularly in view of the scarcity of brass rings this carnival season." Westmoreland told MACV colleagues he might not even be confirmed "because the Senate would hold him responsible for all our failures" in Vietnam.

By all accounts, including that of George S. Patton, Westmoreland's replacement had been the best U.S. tank commander in World War II. But despite his talent for shock action, Abrams based his long-range planning on *PROVN,* the counterinsurgency manifesto suddenly irrelevant in Vietnam. Both sides believed that the other was vulnerable to what communist headquarters called "continuous attacks aimed at securing final victory," what the United States called "smashing" the enemy "wherever he appears; peace talks be damned." From March to June, as America mounted its largest ground offensives in the entire war, another 5,300 of its soldiers died, a fatality rate greater than in Korea and the Pacific theater of World War II, as well as being the last nail in LBJ's political coffin. In November 1967, 50 percent of the public believed the country was making progress in Vietnam as did 33 percent in March 1968. The irony was that America never made greater progress than it did because of the communist plan for a "Great Uprising" in early 1968. The U.S. Army could always wear down the NVA, a conventional force "trying to win a battle like we do." It never had a solution for insurgency guerrillas who would "sneak around and ambush whatever they could." Nor could it neutralize the VC infrastructure, very hard to hit until Tet, where these masters of withdrawal hung on in fury. Some 25,000 VC died (versus 6,000 NVA); "we lost our best people," survivors would recall.

Those VC not killed were often disenchanted, like the U.S. public itself. In late 1967, communist central headquarters in South Vietnam (COSVN) drastically intensified taxation and conscription on the promise of a quick, conclusive victory. Then, at Tet, it sent its irregulars into ARVN strongholds with assurance of reinforcement from the main-force units Westmoreland had pinned down at Khe Sahn. Thereafter, although the National Liberation Front claimed to have "caused [Saigon's] eventual collapse," it fell into the same subordinate status the North Korean Army had in 1951. By June 1968, after Hanoi sent down another 150,000 men, over 70 percent of the communist soldiers in South Vietnam were NVA, as were 90 percent of the main-force battalions by 1972. Before Tet, the communists employed the type of guerrilla-conventional force combination that bedeviled the British in the American Revolution. In 1975, when the VC was a shadow of its former self, eighteen heavy NVA divisions conducted a conventional invasion. "They behave," one old insurgent complained, "as if they had conquered us." By then the NLF (may it rest in peace) had done its job for Hanoi by planting in the minds of many Americans an enduring image that the Vietnam War was a civil war conducted by an ill-supplied band of indigenous guerrillas.

The average American citizen was not the only person to fail to understand the ramifications of Tet. In late February, when the CIA's "best estimate" was "no better than a standoff" for the next ten months, Walt Rostow said our "only hope" was that the NVA would mount one more offensive. Then the armed forces might "clobber them between [late March] & 15 May. Just like Lincoln in 1864." Rostow, having long used references to the Civil War to attack his own era's peace Democrats, must have known the analogy was strained. In 1864, to the consternation of other politicians, Lincoln sought 500,000 new soldiers on the eve of a national election, far more men than Wheeler wanted in 1968. He did not have to pray for another enemy offensive, since Grant and Sherman were heading toward Richmond and Atlanta, the functional equivalents of Hanoi and Haiphong. Creighton Abrams, whose role model was Grant, could not even execute Rostow's relatively modest plan, the invasion of Laos and the demilitarized zone, which Rostow depicted as an opportunity to conquer "a peace in the next three months—without the loss of a single battle or skirmish—as General Winfield Scott did" in the Mexican War. In early 1969 the U.S. embassy would write Washington that the enemy "could have been knocked out of the war completely had he been pursued in the manner that U.S. forces pursued the German and Japanese armies."

LBJ dreamed of "knock[ing] the hell out of" North Vietnam. Rusk said on *Meet the Press* that "some of our mistakes, if you like, have been through an effort to bring a peaceful conclusion without an enlargement of the conflict." No matter, while messages drafted by Rostow told MACV to maintain "constant, relentless, persistent pressure," they contained the standard proviso to "avoid any sudden or dramatic increase in out-of-country operations." Americans had carte blanche to fire millions of rounds into unobservable areas as long as they did not land in some other country. Sanctuaries right across the border—to which the enemy withdrew, set up rockets, and shelled American bases with virtual impunity—remained a no-fire zone for U.S. artillery, never mind ground maneuver. Rusk reverted to his old position that Korea had proved the strategic defensive could win the war, especially after the "severe military setback" communist forces suffered at Tet. Meanwhile, Abrams lost what he called "a moment of supreme opportunity" to capitalize on this tactical success. Despite calls to "pour it on in South Vietnam," the war bogged down in stalemate on the eve of a presidential election, reminiscent of 1952. Because only 25 percent of the public could foresee an "honorable settlement," the party in power was not likely to retain the White House in 1969.[10]

THE 1968 ELECTION: MANDATE FOR SOME SORT OF CHANGE

Unlike politics in other wars where the opposition party attacked the president, Johnson's strongest supporter was the Senate Republican leader, Everett Dirksen. His strongest critics had been his strongest supporters in 1964, as Vice President Hubert Humphrey warned him in February 1965: "Our political problems are likely to come from Democratic liberals, independents, [and] labor if we pursue an enlarged military policy very long." Tet spread this discontent to the rank and file, as mentioned by an antiwar activist in the New Hampshire presidential primary: "For the first time a large proportion of the country was capable of being convinced that the government had lied to them." The Johnson forces tacitly agreed. "There they go," rued one machine Democrat, standing in front of a factory gate, "all our voters straight home to [watch the war on] television." Senator Gene McCarthy, the antiwar candidate, polled about 10 percent before Tet. After it, he stated, "We are in a much worse position [in Vietnam] than we were two years ago." His spokesman predicted Saigon would not last the month. Neither he nor Hanoi had to apologize for their fallacious predictions. McCarthy got 42 percent of the vote, exactly twice as high as public approval for LBJ's "handling" of the war.

Lyndon Johnson was outraged by the holiday sneak attack during a truce. For the first time, he could sound a lot like FDR: "Your President has come to ask you, and all the other people of this nation, to join us in a total national effort to win the war." Nonetheless, his most militant rhetoric of the entire conflict came three years too late. The public would not react to Tet as if it were Pearl Harbor, a "dastardly act [as] every schoolboy ought to know." James Rowe, chairman of Citizens for Johnson, wrote the president: "Everyone wants to get out and the only question is how." The Tet offensive "came as a shock to the American people, including me, because we all believed the United States was doing very well militarily." Hardly a shock, the president had already told Vietnam's ambassador: "I've tried my best, but I can't hold alone."

Rowe always maintained "there is always a trend" in each election; two trends were clear in 1968. In March, 33 percent of those polled thought America was making progress in Vietnam, compared with 18 percent in June; 37 percent thought intervention was a mistake in mid-1967, compared with 54 percent in October 1968. Aside from that, nearly everything was ambivalent. From late February to mid-March 1968, "doves" increased from 26 to 42 percent, outnumbering "hawks" for the first time. Meanwhile, those who wanted to "withdraw" entirely (not just "reduce" the commitment, as pollsters defined "doves") fell from 19 percent in 1966 to 9 percent on the eve of the election, when outpolled by those who favored escalation almost two to one. (The only members of Congress to have voted against the Gulf of Tonkin resolution, Senators Morse and Gruening, were both defeated.) The major party candidates for president, fully aware of these conflicting tendencies, had to distance themselves from Lyndon Johnson, condemned by stalemate, without leaning to either extreme. It was not an easy tightrope to walk for a natural dove like Hubert Humphrey or a hawk like Richard Nixon.

Political facts and ambition drew both men toward the center. Nixon could not hold out for "an all-out victory" in the face of advice from the Republican establishment, such as John McCone, and the fact that 77 percent of the voters expected "a compromise peace settlement." By 1967, after spending fifteen years criticizing Truman, Kennedy, and Johnson for not allowing "our Commanders in the field to end the war with a military victory," he was saying that the conflict "is a limited one with limited means and limited goals," something he began to call "peace with honor." This term, once used by LBJ, was never defined. Privately, Nixon wondered, "What the hell does it really mean?" As a challenger using sophisticated polls conducted every day, he knew he need only say he was a new man "with fresh ideas" running against "the tired old men around the president."

Humphrey had to create even greater distance from LBJ, having defended his policies despite private feelings that "America is throwing lives and money down a corrupt rat hole." In mid-September his campaign manager advised him, "Let's face it, as of now we're lost." Two weeks later he called for a total cessation of bombing the North, the reduction of American troops, and new elections in the South, with NLF participation. LBJ, then in hard negotiations with Hanoi, said, "Nixon is following my policies more closely than Humphrey."

Nixon was reiterating much of what he had said when he ran for vice president after Eisenhower promised peace in Korea: "The swift, overwhelming blow that would have been decisive two or three years ago is no longer possible now" (1968); "When we had superior power a year and a half ago, we should have used that power [but] we are no longer able to force a military decision" (1952). In both elections the bottom line was shame on the Democrats, not on me. To extricate America from Vietnam without a surrender that would rob it of its status as a world power, Nixon promised to "de-Americanize" the war, something Eisenhower had called "Koreanization." He also proposed "a dramatic escalation of our efforts on the economic, political, diplomatic, and psychological fronts," military escalation conspicuously absent. This meant convincing other communist nations to pressure Hanoi, presumably a renegade state dangerous to everyone's self-interest. Johnson himself tried this last tactic in discreet, diplomatic channels carefully sealed from leaks to the press. Its failure being secret, it was plausible to the public this election campaign.

Humphrey, by comparison, was caught in a bind. As he moved to the left, Johnson withheld money his financiers controlled. The Democrats also lost votes to George Wallace, the third-party candidate with a blue-collar base that despised the peace wing of the party, one reason the public (by a two-to-one margin) felt Nixon would handle the war better than any Democrat. It is remarkable that Humphrey came as close as he did, getting 42.7 percent of the popular vote versus

43.4 for Nixon. However, the game was not nearly as close as the score. Adding the Wallace element (which Nixon would get in 1972), Humphrey lost 56.9 percent of the vote, a repudiation of an administration exceeded only in the depth of the Great Depression and the election after World War I. Nixon, who received 40 percent of Johnson voters in 1964, would now see if he could do any better before coming up for reelection in 1972.[11]

FROM ELECTION 1968 TO 1972

In late December 1972, when North Vietnam was ready to sign a final settlement, a reporter asked Henry Kissinger to explain the enemy's motives. Nixon's national security adviser replied: "I have enough trouble analyzing our own motives." The Byzantine policies of the Nixon administration, where one agency barely knew what another one was doing, have mystified far better minds than mine. However, the bottom-line motivation of the president was consistent. While still a candidate, he concluded that there was no feasible way to win the Vietnam War. He would also proclaim, "I will not be the first President of the United States to lose a war." The difference between victory, which Nixon could not have, and defeat, which he would not accept, was his frequently repeated phrase: "peace with honor." His first term in office was a search for a definition of that phrase and for ways to force North Vietnam to accept stipulations respecting America's status as a world power. Through this frustrating process, Nixon would swing back and forth between extreme (but related) alternatives to prolonged war: a "strong impulse," said Colonel Al Haig, his military confidant, "to get out of Vietnam as fast as possible at almost any price" and "an equally strong impulse to 'bomb North Vietnam back to the Stone Age.'" In 1972 Nixon would be reelected in a political landslide because he had discovered effective terms and means. He would then resign in disgrace because some of the ways he hid what he was doing were "high crimes and misdemeanors," the Constitution's definition of an impeachable offense.

Nixon assumed office expecting to end the war inside six months and then turn to problems that really "could be devastating to America's security and survival": the Soviet Union, NATO, and the Middle East. He planned to leverage Russia to leverage North Vietnam, what Johnson had tried but failed to do. Kissinger knew all about that effort, having been an intermediary himself. New administrations are apt to believe old ones failed for poor execution, not flawed policy. Kissinger asked for Soviet help at least ten times in 1969, always getting an evasive reply confirming Nixon's suspicion that Russia was just stalling "to extract everything [it could get] out of America's quandary in Vietnam." Nixon threatened to "end the war one way or the other this year," then promised them "something more dramatic than could now be imagined." The Kremlin did not want to admit what Nixon could not imagine—that it had limited leverage on

North Vietnam, which took $5 billion over ten years' time and treated it with the contempt frontline fighters have for the quartermaster corps.

The "short-term problem" of Vietnam would come to absorb Nixon's presidency on the military and diplomatic fronts. He would trade concessions on strategic weapons of concern to "a few sophisticates" for Soviet help handling Hanoi "in a way that I can survive in office." Unsuccessful, Nixon had to reach out to China, which Russia blamed as a pernicious influence on North Vietnam. He hoped Mao could leverage Ho or at least threaten Russia with a Sino-American détente that could leverage Moscow to leverage Ho. Once a peripheral theater in the cold war against Russia and China, Vietnam thereby mitigated American hostility toward the communist superpowers.

Nixon also planned to exert a lot more military pressure to drive Hanoi to an acceptable settlement. This would not be easy. In 1969 its position was what it had been since 1965: any settlement must include a "coalition of transition" bearing a remarkable resemblance to the NLF. Nixon proved quite flexible in dealing with China, but even he could never claim that "peace with honor" meant deposing the government in Saigon.

In June 1969 the administration began to withdraw American ground forces from South Vietnam to buy time at home for diplomacy to deliver Hanoi. It was the first major breach in the Johnson policy of mutual withdrawal: once proposed by doves in the name of de-escalation and attacked by Nixon for leaving one's ally at the mercy of the Viet Cong. The new Nixon (old Fulbright) position was predicated on three conditions: enhanced ARVN performance, reduced enemy activity, and suitable progress in negotiations. Before they were ever stated, these conditions were ignored. Immediately after the new secretary of defense, Mel Laird, made his first trip to Vietnam in March, he told the president what Al Haig would later confirm: the ARVN had not improved much. He then forced the White House to withdraw 60,000 men. Because Congress was increasingly impatient with the war, Nixon felt OSD needed an experienced horse trader with close friends on Capitol Hill. When he selected this eight-term representative from Wisconsin, that is what he got—to his regret. Whenever the president hesitated to make the next withdrawal, "the cheesebelt Richelieu" (as Laird was known in Washington) would announce it at his early morning briefings, strategically scheduled before Kissinger met the press. If chastised for making a promise Nixon could not afford to retract, he would claim budget necessity. Unimpressed, the White House knew this "masterful manipulator of Congressional committees" shaped the budget with his buddies behind its back.

Kissinger acknowledged that "domestic support" had become the most important factor in the war, but he "wasn't a politician," according to Laird. "All he worried about was that Vietnamization would undercut his diplomacy." No nation could demand mutual withdrawal while withdrawing unilaterally. North Vietnam's representative to the peace talks held in Paris pointed this out whenever Kissinger forgot that "the struggle at the negotiating table . . . reflects the realities on the battlefield," disconcerting for the White House and for MACV. To give "the ARVN the best chance" possible, Creighton Abrams would have slowly removed half the Americans over four years' time and kept another 200,000 in country for another decade. Also part of Abe's discomfort, clearly visible to others, was his sense of what Laird's mission statement ("maximum assistance" and minimum combat) would do to the remnants of his own army. They pulled back into populated enclaves with little left to do outside vice, boredom, corruption, and criminal activity.

Whatever Vietnamization and "peace with honor" meant to Washington, most American soldiers simply hoped they were on their way home. Those who remained were a chip to be bargained for concessions whenever the peace talks got beyond the propaganda stage. Finding no good reason to fight when the country "didn't [seem to] give a damn about me or the sacrifice I and thousands of others were making in their name," soldiers conducted what they called "search and avoid" operations, reminiscent of the ARVN, whom Americans condemned as cowards. When "the lifers" from the regular army tried to disrupt this live-and-let-live arrangement with the enemy, there was passive, if not active, resistance: from simple refusals to go out on patrol to cash bounties for killing one's commander. From 1965 to 1967 the army America sent to Vietnam was the best force it had fielded to that date. By 1971, when substantially more soldiers were evacuated for drug abuse than for wounds received in battle, the army was the worst ever as measured by desertion, disobedience, and disunity: young grunts versus old veterans, blacks versus whites, combat soldiers versus "REMFS" (rear echelon blankety-blanks). By 1972, official policy had caught up with the de facto rules of engagement. Helicopter pilots had to radio for permission to return enemy fire. Likely to wait two to thirty minutes, they simply got out of the area as quickly as they could.

From 1969 to 1972 the senior noncommissioned officers (in the service since World War II) were leaving it after their second or third tours in Vietnam, cursing the army as if they were antiwar protesters. Staying behind to go down with the ship, the captain, Creighton Abrams, muddled through conflicting orders from Laird and the White House to prevent the NVA from winning while executing his withdrawal. It was "the most difficult position of any American combat commander in history," according to the chairman of the JCS. It was also a front-row seat for observing the demise of the army Abrams served so long. In the process, he became a devout Catholic, began heavy drinking (typical of lifers; the grunts were into dope), spent long nights listening to Wagner, and began to grow the cancer that killed him in 1974, the only army chief of staff to die in office.

The army's readiness for combat was on a decade-long decline that prolonged the war in Vietnam for two reasons. By not constantly attacking the enemy, ground forces failed to apply enough pressure to force suitable concessions. Neither would they suffer enough fatalities to force Congress to set a date for withdrawal. By process of elimination, Nixon chose a military strategy reminiscent of

America's lend-lease, airpower, sea-power plan in the early days of World War II. Since the ARVN was hardly the Soviet army, which bore the overwhelming brunt of land warfare before mid-1944, bombers would be even more important for Nixon than for FDR. If rebuffed by North Vietnam, he planned to renew the bombing Lyndon Johnson had stopped in late 1968—this time "a savage, decisive blow" on Hanoi, not Robert McNamara's idea of limited pressure for limited objectives. To keep the plan secret from Congress, it was kept secret from Mel Laird and handled by Al Haig—Kissinger's military assistant and a Bill DePuy battalion commander back in 1967. There was still no consensus that this would end the war in the South. But Nixon was hardly the man to discard any plan simply because it did not pass critical examination by Ivy League–educated analysts and "a bunch of pantywaist left-wing liberals" in the CIA and the NSC with ties to the East Coast Democratic Establishment. Nixon thought that they and their ilk had been out to get him since the late 1940s, when young Congressman Nixon led the partisan attack on Alger Hiss and Dean Acheson.

Nixon loved to describe himself as "a tough, bold, strong leader" able to transcend the mediocre cowards around him, à la his role models, Patton and MacArthur. However, when push came to shove in late 1969, he shoved the strategic bombing plan back into the files. Nixon has said that a large antiwar demonstration in Washington robbed his ultimatum to Hanoi of credibility. A real Patton or MacArthur would have said "bombs away." Nixon's perception of the antiwar movement dictated a different response. Although he gladly campaigned against it in 1972, he thought that even Daniel Ellsberg—now a radical denouncing Nixon's "immoral, illegal and unconstitutional war"—was just a stalking horse for pillars of the Establishment like Averell Harriman and the Bundy brothers, whom Nixon despised, envied, and feared because they (supposedly) would do anything to hurt him out of pure hatred. In these circumstances the administration did not have what Kissinger called "the stomach for the domestic outburst we knew renewed bombing would provoke."

Unwilling to attack the head of the dragon at Hanoi or Haiphong, Nixon began to bomb its tail in Cambodia. When news about this secret operation leaked to the press, he asked the FBI to wiretap reporters, Defense Department officials, and others he distrusted. J. Edgar Hoover refused lest he catch hell from Congress. The White House henceforth ran its own wiretap operation and broke into the office of Ellsberg's psychiatrist. This began the Watergate activities that drove Nixon from office; it was Ellsberg's greatest contribution to ending the war.

Because the bombing of Cambodia could not do substantial military damage, Nixon gave the JCS and MACV the mission they had wanted since 1967—more important in April 1970 if only because it gave the army a tangible objective that might reinvigorate its morale: "Take out all those sanctuaries. Make whatever plans are necessary." Creighton Abrams was told to "act as a Patton rather than [Bernard] Montgomery," rather presumptive to tell Patton's favorite battalion commander. The commander in chief, U.S. Armed Forces Pacific, got into the spirit by proposing that America bomb Hanoi, blockade Haiphong, and conduct amphibious raids to "create anxiety in the minds of the enemy as to our willingness to escalate and our broad capability to exploit his many weak spots." Admiral John McCain obviously took President Nixon too literally.

Publicly described as a temporary "incursion" to facilitate a permanent withdrawal, the operation captured some 40 percent of enemy supplies in the area, the most successful logistics raid of the entire war. Inside three months, the NVA reconstituted its cache. Tipped off early, they fled before U.S.–ARVN forces could make decisive contact. In the United States, militant protests arose at many universities: the more elite the college, the larger the uprising. The JCS, having planned to sweep fifty miles in an operation lasting up to four months, were "aghast" to hear Nixon promise Congress to stop the penetration at twenty-one miles, remove all forces inside eight weeks, and send none back there again. Nixon ordered all soldiers and civilians to say the incursion was an "enormous success." Military men in Vietnam told reporters the operation was oversold and undercut for "political considerations."

In Cambodia the NVA improved the Ho Chi Minh Trail to restock their sanctuaries. By 1972 they were better prepared to charge from these bases thirty-five miles to Saigon. In the U.S. Senate the doves became the dominant opinion, as shown in the congressional ban on funding new ground operations in Cambodia or Laos. As usual, the politicians were following public opinion, for which the incursion was another watershed. By May 1970, 58 (vs. 29) percent of the public wanted to continue to withdraw soldiers even if the GSVN collapsed. One year later, 76 percent wanted all troops home by 31 December. As Nixon later put it, the big issue was whether he could end the conflict on his terms before Congress "just voted us out of the war."

After the Cambodian incursion, the George McGovern bill slashing funds for all military operations in Southeast Asia was placed on the back burner because Nixon withdrew another 250,000 soldiers and American fatalities fell to ten per week. North Vietnam was not incapacitated. It was only avoiding an "unfavorable fight to the death" while making long-term preparations for its greatest offensive. In April 1972, one hundred fifty thousand soldiers armed with Russian heavy weapons were to attack across the demilitarized zone and the Laotian and Cambodian borders when some 60,000 American soldiers (primarily logistics) remained in Vietnam. To the NVA, they must have looked like more POWs to be held for ransom.

The NVA was right to suppose that Vietnamization was inexorable in an election year. They were wrong to think that they knew more about American politics than Richard Nixon. In March the president secretly ordered the removal of "all American [ground] combat forces . . . before the Democratic Convention." This gave him the domestic leeway to use unrestricted airpower, if not for the fear that strategic bombing could still mean war with Russia or China. In 1969 he and Kissinger had a golden opportunity to break this international constraint when the Sino-Soviet split moved beyond rhetoric to hostile fire on the Manchurian-Siberian border. By 1971 the Soviets had enlarged airfields, deployed nuclear missiles, and placed 1 million soldiers on China's northern flank.

This military situation was propitious for a Sino-American understanding provided Nixon removed American installations from Taiwan, holy ground for right-wing Republicans, his erstwhile colleagues. It was also important for the U.S. Navy, proponents of the offshore perimeter defense in the Pacific since 1945. By keeping the China initiative secret from the State and Defense Departments, Nixon and Kissinger kept it secret from their constituents on Capitol Hill, who faced a fait accompli when the president went to China in 1972. As for the navy, its opposition was sapped when Thomas Moorer, the new JCS chairman, was caught spying on the White House. Kissinger was outraged and wanted him fired. Nixon and his staff knew the chiefs only "wanted to know what was going on." They still took advantage of their opportunity and let Moorer "know that we had the goods. After this, the admiral was presunk."

Quid pro quo for Taiwan, the PRC drew farther from North Vietnam, a direction it had been going since Hanoi solidified relations with the Soviet Union in 1966. China had feared Moscow would force Hanoi to compromise with the United States in return for "superpower collusion" against them. In the early 1970s it reduced aid to Hanoi some 25 percent in hopes of collusion with America against the Soviet Union. It did not embargo its communist neighbor but made it very clear that an American attack would not cause war, a far cry from the geopolitical situation in 1965. Then Nixon had called Vietnam "a confrontation between the United States and Communist China"; Kissinger wrote that America "must strengthen" the "peaceful coexistence" brand of Soviet Marxism against its militant Maoist competition "around the world." In 1972, with different interests at stake, the NSC adviser would justify bombing Hanoi because it strengthened the "dove" (pro-Chinese) faction versus the "hawk" (pro-Soviet bloc) in the communist party of Vietnam.

Having made arrangements with China in February 1972, Nixon reached a similar understanding with the Soviet Union, implicit in the summit meeting held in Moscow that May. While Americans toasted their hosts, the United States bombed and mined Haiphong for the first time in the war. It hit Russian ships and killed Russian sailors, something Lyndon Johnson feared would cause World War III. The Soviets surrounded Hanoi and Haiphong with their best air defense equipment, but, similar to their aid to China during the Korean War, they would not give their clients aircraft to destroy the platforms for the American attack. They once were afraid Harry Truman might launch nuclear weapons. They now were afraid Richard Nixon would cut off U.S. grain and capital. By August, subjected to the most intensive and prolonged bombing to date, North Vietnam was openly chastising both the PRC and the Soviet Union for "serving their own immediate interests at the expense of the revolutionary movement."

Nixon was determined to bomb and mine North Vietnam despite Defense

Department and CIA doubts that it would be effective, positions dating back to McNamara. Their stance was supported by cables from MACV, which wanted to dedicate all airpower to the battle in South Vietnam. Nixon, who never had confidence in "the bureaucrats" at the Pentagon, now lost it in Creighton Abrams (Mel Laird's man), who diverted B-52s to support America's last soldiers in the field. The president would have sacked Abe and made Al Haig MACV commander if it were not for the secretary of defense, the press, Congress, and the army, which did not like recently promoted brigadier generals filling four-star commands. Still, within five days of the NVA invasion, Nixon dared override "professional advice" and thereby assumed responsibility if the campaign failed. As he directed missions north of the seventeenth parallel—and gesticulated with his pipe, as if he were MacArthur—he bellowed to subordinates: "I intend to bring the enemy to his knees"; "the bastards have never been bombed like they're going to be bombed this time."

From May through October, 155,548 tons of explosives fell on North Vietnam, not sufficient to keep the NVA out of Saigon, according to Haig, the Max Taylor of the Nixon administration. The president's personal military adviser believed—and Nixon recorded—that "all the air power in the world and strikes on Hanoi-Haiphong aren't going to save South Vietnam if the South Vietnamese aren't able to hold on the ground." When the president wrote these words (on 2 May), 35,500 enemy soldiers had flooded out of Cambodia and surprised 3,000 ARVN, with twenty-five American advisers, at An Loc, just sixty-five miles from Saigon. To the communist senior regional commander this critical road net was "the strategic battlefield which would determine the outcome of the war."

The battle of An Loc lasted sixty-six days, due to NVA strength and error. They surrounded their opponents to prevent them from bringing up artillery. They thereby prevented a retreat, which could become a stampede—a mistake rarely made by the VC, weaker in firepower but more adroit. With noplace to go, the ARVN held its positions while its American advisers called in massive airpower in what became a battle of terrible attrition. This made the bombing of the North effective. When McNamara and John McNaughton had argued that it could not stem the war in the South, they had been talking about a light infantry communist army that carried most of its supplies. In 1972 the enemy had become a heavy force expending 78,000 artillery rounds at An Loc. They needed a steady resupply of ammunition, weapons, and entire military units. "Linebacker"—code name for the bombing—hit railroads, bridges, and highways with precision-guided bombs (a recent innovation) that made reconstitution virtually impossible. By September the communist Spring Offensive had ground to a halt.

Nixon said An Loc vindicated Vietnamization, a very important issue this election year. Like search and destroy for Lyndon Johnson, it was Nixon's way of showing progress in the Vietnam War. If the country believed that the president's refusal to cut and run had bought time for the ARVN to defend itself, the electorate could have its cake and eat it, too: 73 percent wanted all Americans out, but 74 percent supported Nixon's contention "that it is important that South Vietnam not fall into the control of the Communists." As if to prove Nixon was right and his critics wrong when he said that the ARVN had "substantially exceeded our original expectations," the White House brought the senior American adviser at An Loc home to testify. Unfortunately, from the moment John Kennedy first sent Americans into the bush, they returned with sober stories. No exception, Colonel William Miller confidentially told Haig, Senator John Stennis, and William Westmoreland that although many ARVN soldiers were heroic, they held their position by "the skin of their teeth" with advisers making plans, calling in air strikes, and grabbing control when ARVN officers panicked. Without men like him down in the weeds, the NVA would have been in Saigon long before "Wild Bill" Miller got to Washington.

Nixon's military strategy was great reelection tactics: bombing North Vietnam (approved in polls by three to one) and claiming to have removed all ground forces, favored by 76 percent. Nixon would not admit that the conflict had returned to an advisory war because to keep any U.S. soldiers in the field would be unacceptable to the electorate and to Hanoi, now willing to compromise at the Paris peace talks. America had tacitly conceded mutual withdrawal by Vietnamization (1969) and calls for a cease-fire in place on the eve of the last congressional election, October 1970. In May 1972 Kissinger made the concession explicit, perhaps because the president (Walter Mitty's George Patton) did not want to do it himself; it was certainly not a victory, only peace with honor. Hanoi did not reciprocate until 8 October, when it finally agreed to a peace treaty that reflected the situation on the battlefield: the NVA would remain in the areas it conquered and the Saigon government (not a flimsy coalition of neutralists and communists) would control the other 75 percent of South Vietnam and receive continuous material aid that gave it a chance to survive without American soldiers on the ground.

Kissinger had always been anxious to negotiate an agreement that would give the negotiator enormous credit. If he failed and the war continued, he feared becoming the next Walt Rostow: a fellow Ivy League professor (Jewish, to boot) banished to a fate worse than death—a state university not frequented by the international elite. Bobbing between stardom and the gallows, Kissinger announced on 26 October, during his first televised press conference, that "peace is at hand." Not quite! Nguyen Van Thieu, leader of the Saigon government, refused any settlement that left any NVA on any plot of land inside South Vietnam. This hardly shocked Richard Nixon, who knew all about Thieu's record of sabotaging negotiations on the eve of an election, having encouraged him to do it to Lyndon Johnson in October 1968. When Saigon was the problem, why did Nixon want to keep the war a campaign issue, as he did when he claimed that "there were differences to work out" with Hanoi in order to avoid "peace with surrender"? Why wait until after the November election to send Haig to Saigon to talk of taking "brutal action," a code name for a coup against one's ally like Diem's deposal in 1963?

Partisan political strategy in the first Nixon administration revolved around tracking "what moves and concerns the average guy," especially the George Wallace–hard-hat Democrats. They did not trust Republicans on lunch-pail economic policy. However, Nixon was acutely aware that they supported him (or he supported them) on social and cultural issues such as welfare reform and opposition to school busing, which he made the fulcrum of his domestic policy in 1970. The war was another cultural concern, as Nixon knew full well from sophisticated polling that broke down the electorate by age, ethnicity, income, education, and so forth. It revealed that swing voters hated the antiwar movement even more than the war itself. They not only attributed protraction to aid and comfort to the enemy but also were disgusted by what they believed was an attack on morality: the so-called evil trinity of "acid, abortion, and amnesty." This may have been true of just a radical fringe of the antiwar movement that attracted publicity because it was sensational. Nonetheless, Franklin Roosevelt was loved for his enemies (the rich); George McGovern, the Democratic candidate, was hated for his friends. Blue-collar voters were not allowed to forget about people who felt Nixon's determination to uphold American power was an imperialist perversion. White House operatives worked overtime to make Democrats "guilty by association" through a "maximum number of pictures of rowdy people around McGovern."

When asked which candidate could do a better job of dealing with the Vietnam situation, Nixon beat McGovern by more than two to one in late September. He had done to the Democratic left what Lyndon Johnson had done to the Republican right in 1964: occupy the center by saying that after the election Americans would not be fighting but no ally would be lost to communism. However, the war and "left-wing liberals" would be hot-button issues only if America remained at war in some way. In October 1968, after Johnson stopped bombing North Vietnam, rumors of peace briefly catapulted Humphrey ahead of Nixon in the polls. Now in 1972, said the White House operative in charge of polling data, "our great fear" was that a preelection settlement "would let people say, 'Well, thank goodness the war is over. Now we will elect a Democrat because Democrats always do more in peacetime'" on economic issues.

No treaty being signed, Nixon resumed bombing North Vietnam (not yet Hanoi and Haiphong proper) on 2 November. Five days later, for the first time in history, a Republican presidential candidate won a majority of the blue-collar and/or Catholic households, as well as 60.7 percent of the total vote. But Nixon and his staff to the contrary, the election did not symbolize "the passing of the old establishment" from power and the rise of a "truly New Majority." Nixon garnered support from acknowledged elitists like Walter Lippmann, impressed that Nixon was not "trying to be the savior of the world," unlike Woodrow Wilson or George McGovern, both of whom believed "that man is by nature good and can be made perfect by making the environment perfect."

Other prominent men—Democrats themselves—also supported Nixon, once the most partisan and hated Republican. They were anxious to protect, if not resurrect, the principle of presidential authority and an assertive foreign policy. Dean Acheson, Nixon's political punching bag back in 1950, died in 1971, two years after he became an unofficial adviser to his old adversary based on their common discomfort at congressional control in the hands of Senator Fulbright, "a dilettante Fool." Acheson's place in Democrats for Nixon was taken by John Connally, a stand-in for Lyndon Johnson, who supported Nixon behind the scenes, and by Jimmy Roosevelt—FDR's oldest son and a highly decorated World War II marine. In 1968 he had planned to campaign for Johnson: aside from my "credit with the liberals . . . about 30 percent of the country remember mother and dad." In 1972 he campaigned against McGovern more than he did for Nixon, who once Red-baited him, along with Acheson: the president's opponent offers "an abject pull-out of all United States forces after which he would go to Hanoi to 'beg' for the release of our prisoners. . . . Not exactly a glorious chapter for American history."[12]

SOME BOMBS, SOME PEACE, SOME HONOR

After Nixon's reelection, Kissinger visited Saigon, where he received sixty-nine changes to the agreement with Hanoi. Thieu, never feeling the war would stop because America left, withheld consent to leverage a firm commitment for continued support. When Kissinger presented Thieu's stipulations at the next session of the peace talks, North Vietnam restated its old demands for a coalition government in South Vietnam. In theory, Nixon could have made a unilateral settlement in return for America's POWs. Since he could have made that deal his first day in office, he could not have justified the 20,000 fatalities sustained in pursuit of "peace with honor."

As late as November 1972, Nixon said the Korean armistice set a precedent—utter poppycock about negotiations that left 160,000 communist soldiers in South Vietnam. Just as significant was the political situation in the United States, where the doves picked up three more Senate seats despite Nixon's victory. Hence the president could not offer Thieu what Eisenhower gave Syngman Rhee in return for accepting much better conditions: a defense alliance guaranteed by U.S. soldiers on the ground. Nixon would have to prove the credibility of his personal pledge to "react very strongly and rapidly to any violation of the agreement" before Saigon would sign and Hanoi obey any treaty.

The bombing Nixon conducted in December 1972 may have occurred for another reason besides realpolitik. Nixon had vowed he would not be the first president to lose a war; he had not said he would win it. The last American raid of the war gave him one more chance to do what he had planned to do in 1969, before his nerve failed his martial self-image—strike "a savage, decisive blow against North Vietnam." He told the chairman of the JCS: "This is your chance to use military power effectively to win this war, and if you don't, I'll consider you responsible."

Linebacker II had a different array of targets than Linebacker I, a battlefield air interdiction campaign. After the Spring Offensive failed, there was no battlefield to interdict. Communist forces were exhausted, short of resources, and (admittedly) "no longer capable of fighting," at least for the time being. Airpower now had to be strategic bombing—the first time B-52s attacked Hanoi and Haiphong. The last important news heard by Congress, the press, and the public was Kissinger's pronouncement that "peace is at hand." News of the "Christmas bombing" shocked America nearly as hard as it hit North Vietnam.

Nixon's hopes to the contrary, his critics were not intimidated by his plurality in November. George McGovern, an old B-17 pilot, already called bombing North Vietnam "the most barbaric act committed by any modern state since the death of Adolf Hitler." The *Washington Post* described Linebacker II as "the most savage and senseless act of war ever visited, over a scant ten days, by one sovereign people upon another." In a war noted for hyperbole on all sides, this might win the prize. Forget comparisons to Hitler. It did not hold a candle to the U.S. Air Force in World War II, which never took the same precautions to reduce collateral damage. According to the North Vietnamese, 1,600 people died in two weeks; in contrast, 45,000 Germans were killed in three days at Dresden, and 84,000 Japanese in one night at Tokyo.

Whatever the damage, North Vietnam and the United States were both exhausted by late December. Hanoi and Haiphong suffered from bomb shock and the sheer terror of not knowing what to expect. In the American camp, resistance also collapsed. A state-of-the-art missile defense shot down fifteen B-52s, causing the American public to turn against bombing not on grounds it was "inhuman or immoral" but because "we lost [too] many American lives." "The outrage," said Haig, "grew to such proportions that every single adviser [excluding him, John Connally, and the JCS] was calling the President daily, hourly, and telling him to terminate the bombing." When LBJ did this to get negotiations in 1968, he allowed the NVA to replenish its antiaircraft artillery. Now that B-52s had destroyed this weaponry, more missions "would have been a milk run," said the deputy director of the CIA. No matter, Congress moved to pass its own restrictions on airpower, which Haig called "national suicide from the standpoint of ever negotiating a settlement." The American military "had reached the limit of domestic possibilities," Kissinger explained to Thieu.

Mutually exhausted, the United States and North Vietnam agreed to return to their diplomatic positions as of October, with a few cosmetic changes on minor issues to mollify Saigon, still embittered but more confident that it could count on America. In the tradition of U.S. politics, everybody got something; nobody got everything: 250,000 NVA remained in Laos, Cambodia, and the Central Highlands where Westmoreland once conducted search and destroy. The Saigon government remained the Saigon government, enabling Nixon to announce to America in January 1973 that "we today have concluded an agreement to end the war and bring peace with honor in Vietnam." America, not Vietnam, got peace;

there were 3,000 violations within three weeks of the cease-fire. Honor, like beauty, was in the eye of the beholder. The country had not "cut and run," thereby emboldening the forces that would doom all hope for international stability. Granted the settlement was far from perfect, but Nixon and Kissinger believed that "to get an iron-clad, crystal-clear agreement, we would have had to fight another year or two"—simply not an "option" for a "democracy." America also got what Kissinger called time to "heal its wounds."

In 1973 only a few Americans were disappointed with the settlement, although they were the people who knew the details best. The NSC's expert on Indochina said that "we bombed the North Vietnamese into accepting our concession," unilateral withdrawal; Dean Rusk would call it "tantamount to surrender." The JCS shared these sentiments but could do nothing about their disappointment over not bombing the North until all NVA left the South. The war had robbed the military, especially army chief of staff Westmoreland, of its power to appeal to the public and shape policy over the president's head. Even Senators Barry Goldwater and John Stennis were urging South Vietnam to sign the treaty Kissinger negotiated. The American right had no place else to go. The military had no place to speak. "For us," said Richard Nixon, speaking for the government consensus, "the important principle is that the Agreement does not hand over the political future to the Communists. Our friends [in Saigon] have every opportunity to demonstrate their inherent strength"—ominous words indeed. Time would tell if the mandate of the 1972 election (no U.S. troops but no Red victory) held up better than the same mandate did after 1964.[13]

FROM PEACE WITH HONOR TO THE FALL OF SAIGON

America would now see if its blood and treasure created what Nixon would call "a viable non-Communist enclave" or what Kissinger had called a "decent interval" before South Vietnam fell to a stronger state. If the latter, at least the United States would face "different consequences than that of simply packing up and pulling out." Of course, there was a third possibility they both wished to avoid: an indecently short interval and the humiliation heretofore evaded.

Both parties in the South were far more concerned with Hanoi than with America's worldwide credibility. The National Liberation Front suspected that Paris (1973) might be another Geneva (1954), when the insurgency was left to fend for itself as the North regrouped and recovered from war. President Thieu, their competition, was even less enthralled. He signed the accords only when the Nixon administration described them as "a legal foundation . . . for more aid to Vietnam" and because the president personally promised that "we will respond with full force [code name B-52s] should the settlement be violated." This pledge came with a promise of public disclosure that was never fulfilled. The JCS and the Defense Department, let alone Congress and the public at large, never knew of anything more than what Kissinger vaguely called "intentions" and "presumptions" until the NVA were in Saigon. Nixon's election mandate quickly became obsolete after disclosures of criminal behavior and a White House cover-up, collectively known as Watergate. To salvage his presidency, Nixon claimed indispensability in national security and foreign affairs. His case would not be helped by a revelation that the so-called peace treaty was just a cease-fire enforced by what Kissinger privately called a "hair-trigger U.S. readiness which may be challenged at any time." Nixon's political survival aside, if America were to salvage credibility for other commitments after Saigon fell, it would be best to deny having made any "legal commitment" at all.

Congress—"mean and testy" and Democratic—might not have honored a personal pledge of the president. Thanks to Nixon's penchant for secrecy, it need not face that issue. More important, thanks to Nixon's removal of military personnel, Congress no longer faced "the simple fact" that had made it compliant since 1965: "Our troops are in South Vietnam and we must supply them." On 1 July 1973 it passed a resolution, sponsored by George McGovern, that forbade "combat activities by United States military forces in or over or from off the shores of North Vietnam, South Vietnam, Laos or Cambodia": finis for Nixon's pledge to Thieu of "swift and severe retaliatory action" to enforce the treaty; the triumph of McGovern's policy a year after its resounding defeat.

Henry Kissinger once quantified a "decent interval" as five years, not five months. He was furious at what he called "one of the most vindictive, cheap actions that I've seen the Congress take." In fact, the battle over national security policy had already been lost during a fundamental shift in the distribution of institutional power. The White House lost the will to debate the Vietnam commitment in the midst of Watergate, let alone approve Kissinger's request for an air strike on the "bumper-to-bumper military traffic" rolling down the Ho Chi Minh Trail. By late April even Kissinger told Haig—the last holdout for military action—they could not renew bombing because it "will crystallize all the Congressional opposition."

Kissinger had only two other options to keep South Vietnam afloat: promise the "heroic fanatics" in Hanoi economic aid if it waited the decent interval or else convince the "cold-blooded practitioners of power politics" in the Kremlin to curtail shipments to North Vietnam. Having lost his reputation as a genius once his treaty broke down, he could do neither. Recent testimony about harsh treatment of American POWs and Soviet dissidents had left a bitter taste on Capitol Hill, where Senator Henry "Scoop" Jackson, the last of a dying breed of cold war Democrats, had more influence than anybody from the White House. Whereas Jackson prevented economic assistance to the Soviets, Nixon rejected Russian suggestions for mutual defense against China. The Soviet response was no surprise to Kissinger. Denied commensurate rewards, they could not "resist taking advantage of an opportunity to alter the power balance" in Southeast Asia. While American aid dramatically decreased, Russian assistance remained at $650 million a year.

As early as mid-1973, Hanoi said Nixon "will not dare to apply strong measures such as air strikes or bombing attacks in either North or South Vietnam." It used its freedom to perfect lines of communication and forward-position its supplies so that the next major operation would not literally run out of gas. By 1975 the Ho Chi Minh Trail had become a network of concrete bridges and metal-surfaced highways lined with radar-guided, quad-mounted, antiaircraft guns ready for another battlefield air interdiction campaign like the one conducted in 1972. To add final insurance against the reintroduction of American airpower, Hanoi planned its decisive attack for 1976, the next presidential election year. In the spring of 1975 it merely planned to grab some provincial capitals and move closer to Saigon. Before the NVA knew what was happening, according to one reporter, the ARVN began "losing the war faster than the Communists could win it."

Once again, there were numerous acts of great heroism by ARVN enlisted men. "If properly led into an engagement," Westmoreland's aide wrote in mid-1964, they "will not flinch." Eleven years later, the rank and file could not compensate for the inadequate officers, who were the first to panic. Nor could twenty-five years of American assistance (back to Truman in 1950) overcome the cancer in South Vietnam's body politic. If anything, massive amounts of American assistance created a bonanza of crime and corruption that shocked American soldiers, hardly monks themselves. This "venality" and an inflation rate four times that of other Southeast Asian nations created "the every-man-for-himself morality" by which the ARVN grabbed their possessions, collected their families, and fled the field in 1975. In the final analysis, said Westmoreland, it "just didn't have the stuff." In January 1965 Bill Bundy noted "the weakness we all recognize in the Saigon political situation." Twenty-nine years later, he said "we were only a little sanguine, but still too sanguine about the South Vietnamese."

After 1973, what Creighton Abrams called the "glue that [had] kept everything together" was absent from the ARVN, that is, American advisers on the ground who assumed command in emergencies and guaranteed the presence of U.S. airpower. Despite this absence, the leaders of South Vietnam never lost their complacency because they never thought America would allow the demise of its own credibility. Guess again. Kissinger, unable to secure even a "decent interval" for his ally, could only hope to get the humiliation out of the headlines. "Why don't those people die fast?" he asked the White House press secretary. "The worst thing that could happen would be for them to linger on."

If America had reintervened, it might have had assistance from China, now desperate to contact Kissinger, what was left of the Viet Cong, and even President Thieu: anybody to contain Hanoi and its friends in the Soviet Union. Kissinger, however, was primarily concerned with absolving himself, which made him no different than anybody else. Thieu blamed the White House, never grasping the role of Congress or public opinion. The White House blamed the Congress. Congress blamed the ARVN for giving up whatever weaponry it got. A few weeks before the NVA crashed into Saigon, America's last support mission to South

Vietnam returned to Washington and filed its last request for B-52 bombings and emergency shipments of heavy weapons. Reminiscent of John McNaughton in 1965 (and Dean Acheson in 1952), it concluded that "the style with which we do things is as important as the substance," especially when "continued U.S. credibility worldwide hinges on whether we make an effort, rather than on actual success or failure." Congress, afraid that any assistance would drag advisers and troops "back into the quagmire," asked if equipment would really save Vietnam. State and Defense officials answered that if the ARVN "go down," it should not be because "we didn't give it to them."

Gerald Ford, who replaced Nixon after his forced resignation in 1974, was not above posturing and finger-pointing, although not blameless himself. As House minority leader in 1965, he attacked Lyndon Johnson's strategy from a hawk position: "There is no substitute for victory." By 1973 he had changed his stance when he and Mel Laird delivered votes for the congressional ban on military action in Southeast Asia, lest House Republicans (in danger from Watergate) be smeared in next year's congressional election. In 1975 President Ford had to lie in the bed he helped make. Although old friends on Capitol Hill told him that "the American people and the elected Congress had decided to close the book" on Vietnam, he gave a Churchillian address to Congress on 10 April in which he requested emergency military aid. He received virtually no applause—an unprecedented event, as every TV viewer knows. After that (if not before), Ford was primarily concerned with not assuming ownership or responsibility for "Nixon's war." On 29 April the NVA raised its flag over Diem and Thieu's presidential palace, somewhat to the shock of old VC who clutched their own banner, retained ideas of independence, and soon underwent compulsory "reeducation" at the hands of their old allies from Hanoi. Six days earlier, Ford had addressed an audience of American college students wildly enthusiastic for his new applause line: "America can regain the sense of pride that existed before Vietnam. But it cannot be achieved by refighting a war that is finished as far as America is concerned."[14]

Postscript: Vietnam to the Balkans

> *[Americans] mistake tactics for strategy. . . . the absence of a solid, coherent, and consistent policy is their big flaw.*
>
> Andrei Gromyko, Soviet foreign minister, 1975

In the 1970s the Soviet Union defined "peaceful coexistence" the way Nikita Khrushchev had used the term in the early 1960s, to John Kennedy's alarm: "supporting the struggle for national liberation" without directly engaging the West in a military confrontation that would be a "calamity to civilization as a whole." After the NVA, armed to the teeth with Russian weapons, streamed into Saigon, the Soviet Union appeared to be on a five-year roll in the Third World: South Yemen, Nicaragua, Ethiopia, Somalia, Syria, Iraq, Mozambique, Angola, and Afghanistan. "It's now our turn," according to Kremlin officials who felt they were "riding the crest of a wave," as did the Somali who told an American reporter, "We have learned there is only one superpower."

Henry Kissinger had spent four years fighting for a "decent interval" to prevent these proverbial dominoes from tumbling around the world. The day after Saigon fell, he told the senior members of the Ford administration that America would "pay a price for what happened in Southeast Asia" and that those responsible, certainly not them, would be repudiated like Neville Chamberlain following Munich. In 1976 the country elected Jimmy Carter, hardly Winston Churchill. Kissinger sank into even deeper reveries about national "self-doubt, division, irresolution," and ultimately the decline of the West.

Neither Kissinger nor the Kremlin imagined that the Soviets were about to "blunder," as one Politburo member put it, "into a really serious mess." In 1975 they appeared to be the big winner among the big powers in Southeast Asia, as Kennedy once feared they would be. The Soviet Union got what Russia had wanted for some two centuries—major bases in the southeast Pacific at America's old bastions, Da Nang and Cam Ranh Bay. China ended up the big loser, as Lyndon Johnson once hoped it would be. By the late 1970s the PRC faced what it had opposed since the Geneva Accords of 1954: Russian military installations and an Indochinese superstate on its southern flank. With America's connivance, they subsequently supported Cambodians based in Thai sanctuaries. Hit, run, and return operations would cost Vietnam some 50,000 soldiers (nearly as many as America had lost in Southeast Asia) and their Soviet paymasters over $10 billion in a war of attrition neither Hanoi nor Moscow could afford.

Constructing military policy in a pluralistic democracy has never been a bed of roses, as this entire book maintains. Nonetheless, in the 1980s, America stumbled onto a successful strategy under Ronald Reagan, who did not spend "one nano-second" in analysis or planning, according to one of his NSC advisers. This hands-off president never tightly managed his factious administration manned at key positions by Republican critics of détente and cold war Democrats looking for a home after Scoop Jackson lost control of their party to the likes of George McGovern. Hawks, especially Al Haig, Reagan's first secretary of state, wanted to take direct military action against Cuba, which he called the Latin American source of communist expansion. The JCS reverted to military methods of operation as of 1960, before Kennedy's doctrine of flexible response doomed them to defeat in Vietnam. As formulated in the so-called Weinberger Doctrine, named for Reagan's secretary of defense, the armed forces would go all out (highly unlikely) or not go to war at all. Reagan's way of managing this dispute was to find an "acceptable compromise" among competing positions. Between doing nothing and high-intensity conflict fell aid to insurgents against Soviet clients, a far more cost-effective policy than counterinsurgency. In money, to say nothing of blood and demoralization, America spent approximately ten dollars for every dollar Moscow sent to rebels in the 1960s. In the 1980s, when the Soviet economy was already reeling from falling prices for its petroleum exports, the shoe was on the other foot. According to the Kremlin's own figures, it spent ten times more money propping up its allies than Washington spent on guerrillas knocking them down.

Even before Reagan took office in 1981, the Soviets realized that they were overcommitted in Afghanistan, their most damaging investment by far. Reminiscent of Washington in the 1960s, the Kremlin felt it could not lose face lest doing so would kick over its own set of dominoes, the last one being Russian control of the Soviet Union. Kissinger and Richard Nixon, proponents of stability and the balance of power, might have been sympathetic. They had only hoped to teach Moscow to exercise more restraint; not so Ronald Reagan and his anticommunist Wilsonians, such as Richard Perle, who had fought détente tooth and nail from Scoop Jackson's Senate office. They believed in rolling back "the evil Empire" with a fervor not seen in Washington since the Korean War. (Said the CIA director: "If America challenges the Soviets at every turn and ultimately defeats them in one place, that will shatter the mythology [of Marxist inevitability], and it will all start to unravel.") The Soviets lamented their condition, pleaded for help, even threatened the equivalent of Richard Nixon's Christmas bombing. This only caused the Reagan administration to increase its assistance to anticommunist zealots who fought with the tenacity of the old Viet Cong.

In Afghanistan, the Soviets spent more than just $100 billion to sustain a regime as inept as America's erstwhile ally in Saigon. It suffered 14,500 dead, 53,700 injured or wounded, and almost 500,000 hospitalized, mostly for viral hepatitis. Soviet military medicine was equipped to treat the wounded, not disease from poor sanitation. These men were sent home, where the financial cost of their recovery became an added burden to a political system already in economic decline. When the rest of the Soviet army finally left Afghanistan in 1989, it was racked with drug abuse, desertion, and demoralization reminiscent of American soldiers in the last three years of Vietnam. The Red Army was in no condition to hold back the dominoes when the Warsaw Pact crumbled after the demonstrative evidence that client governments need not stay in power. "The Mujahadin in the hills . . . were the real liberators of Eastern Europe," at least according to one Russian dissident.[1]

While the Soviets were falling into a counterinsurgency quagmire, the American army was flushing drugs, disobedience, and inexperience out of its own system. In 1972 an exhausted Creighton Abrams passed up retirement to become chief of staff and fulfill what he called his "destiny to rebuild the Army." (His dying words to his vice-chief were "Boy I want to be there when we get back on our feet.") The Reagan administration, not content with funding guerrillas at the low end of the spectrum of conflict, financed a system of high-intensity military training conceived by Bill DePuy, Abrams's personal choice to get the army's attention off Vietnam and onto modern, mechanized warfare, such as it would conduct in Desert Storm. But despite visible signs of recovery, the armed forces retained emotional scars, as noted by civilians who used the term "Vietnam syndrome" to refer to the Pentagon's reluctance to use force without first having "a strong consensus of support and agreement for our basic purposes"—now virtually impossibile in the United States.

The Ford, Reagan, and Bush administrations desperately sought a victory by direct action of the armed forces to excise the doubt that crippled American power "badly bitten by the Vietnam bug" since the Tet offensive. The month after Saigon fell in 1975, Gerald Ford and Kissinger suddenly thought they had an "opportunity" to "reassure our allies and bluntly warn our adversaries that the U.S. was not a helpless giant." Cambodia, "a fifth-rate state," had the temerity to seize the merchant vessel *Mayaguez* on the high seas. America suffered ninety-one casualties—forty-one dead—when navy jets and marines launched an attack to rescue hostages already being returned to American hands. Nonetheless, Ford said, "The gloomy national mood began to fade." "It's good," one congressman concurred, "to win one for a change."

The *Mayaguez* turned out to be a flash in the pan. Grenada (1983) may have been what one reporter called "a lovely little war," but 800 Cuban militiamen were hardly worthy opponents, nor were 3,500 Panamanians in 1989. The Persian Gulf, according to President George Bush, finally provided the victory that disproved the "perception, [in the] aftermath of Vietnam, that the U.S. wouldn't fight, wouldn't go all out." This self-described disciple of Lincoln, Eisenhower, and Theodore Roosevelt seized Iraq's conquest of Kuwait in 1990 to rehabilitate the U.S. military image. He therefore insisted that "there will be no concessions" and worried that Saddam Hussein might agree to American demands. The day before the massive ground offensive began against Iraq, the president told reporters: "When this is over we will have kicked, for once and for all, the so-called Vietnam syndrome." Three weeks later an unnamed officer at the Pentagon agreed: "The stigma of Vietnam has been erased. That's one of the reasons a complete and total victory was necessary."

After the armistice the president and congressmen gushed: "We know now that the American people are willing to go to war and to win." Nonetheless, the military triumph did not dissolve the chronic problem of conducting war in a democracy, where the electorate retains the final authority of ratification or rejection. In 1992 the public was so preoccupied with taxes, unemployment, the deficit, and crime that Desert Storm could not reelect the commander in chief. Surveys showed that about 10 percent of the electorate said that the war influenced their vote. Two percent said foreign policy was a major concern. Bush even lost the vote of Zbigniew Brzezinski, who coined the term "Vietnam syndrome" when he was national security adviser in the Carter administration.

Leadership in a war did not save the White House for the incumbent. Nor did parades and applause for military units erase senior officers' habitual worries about support from civilians, the Congress, and the press if the going got tough. Take the case of Colin Powell, chairman of the JCS. In 1968 his second tour in Vietnam began soon after a platoon in his brigade committed the notorious My Lai massacre. In 1991 he terminated combat operations before they fulfilled their objective of destroying Iraq's Republican Guard. The American media, reminiscent of Tet, had finally obtained vivid pictures of destruction at the so-called highway of death out of Kuwait: mostly abandoned vehicles, actually fewer than fifty dead Iraqi soldiers. "We did not need another situation," Powell later explained, "where a large number of civilians were killed with Peter Arnett [from CNN, who made his reputation in Vietnam, running] all over the place."

In 1992–93 most military officers (active duty or retired) opposed involvement in long-term, relatively low-intensity conflicts, where civilian casualties were inevitable. In fact, they worried that the four-day ground war in the Persian Gulf exacerbated the problem of sustained domestic support by spoiling the American public with unrealistic expectations. When asked on television if the U.S. military "is still suffering from the Vietnam syndrome," Lieutenant General (Ret.) Brent Scowcroft, national security adviser in the Bush administration, replied that "if ground forces enter Bosnia, the U.S. people will soon ask 'what are we doing there, since those people don't want peace.' " By implication, he was saying that America was willing to commit its fighting men to areas where there is no fighting, which was President Bill Clinton's stipulation in 1995, when U.S. troops went to Bosnia.

With the nation wary of running risks in the Balkans, attention soon turned to the latest threat, America's erstwhile ally against the Soviet empire. After militant Muslim fundamentalists drove the Russians from Afghanistan, their leaders took their talents to new places, bombing U.S. military facilities in Saudi Arabia and the World Trade Center in New York. As for Bosnia itself, as this book headed to its publisher, the House of Representatives had just gone on record to terminate the mission in mid-1998, the eve of the next congressional election. The secretary of defense, reflecting the opinion of the armed forces, favored the resolution. The secretary of state and the director of the NSC objected that Congress would tie the president's hands, as if his options were not already bound by the nation's reluctance to sustain casualties. The outcome of the debate in Washington (more political than military) may well depend on Clinton's standing after probes of campaign contributions, perjury, and sexual harassment.[2]

This factious policy over Bosnia has a familiar historical ring. Branches of the American government are divided. Military progress and stalemate are likely to be issues in the next election, already affecting partisan positions in regard to the Balkans. Congress, controlled by the political opposition, seems unlikely to stop the military mission it has publicly opposed, probably because it wants the commitment to come back and haunt the president. The White House, knowing bloodshed will resurrect memories of Clinton's draft dodging during the Vietnam War, seems determined to make the mission as safe as possible. British, no American, soldiers have arrested war criminals; those nabbed were merely minions bereft of bodyguards. All in all, the commander in chief has trouble commanding the armed forces, who slip their real opinions to Congress and the press. Justified or not, they have a moral aura that he lacks; they are thought to stand above politics. In conclusion, it is difficult to use military power for political purposes when political institutions are in conflict. It is even more difficult when the public supports the claim that the armed forces take no part in political affairs, especially when a president's political health is at stake.

Notes

Working under space limitations, I have discarded the traditional academic footnote form for three reasons: (1) I would rather use the allotted pages for text, (2) this book is primarily one of synthesis, rather than research in unpublished sources, and (3) the target audience is the well-informed generalist, as well as academics. The former may not care about standard footnotes; the latter will not see many sources unknown to experts. The books and articles, listed in sequential order by topics discussed in the text, constitute some 25 percent of the entire material consulted: the most important works for my particular interests and the places I found most quotes, all of which are from the historical participants, none from historians. Also selected to save space, the footnote form cites subtitles only if the subject matter is not clear from the main title. If anyone would like to know all the sources for any or all paragraphs or sections, I would be happy to send them.

INTRODUCTION

1. Basil H. Liddell-Hart, *Encyclopaedia Britannica* (1929), s.v. "strategy"; Arthur F. Lykke Jr., "Toward an Understanding of Military Strategy," in *Military Strategy: Theory and Application* (U.S. War College, 1989), pp. 3–8; Carl von Clausewitz, *On War* (Princeton University Press, 1976), pp. 86–89, 115–121, 605–607; Peter Kalm (ca. 1750), quoted in Douglas Edward Leach, *Arms for Empire: A Military History of the British Colonies in North America, 1607–1763* (Macmillan, 1973), pp. 279–280.

1. PERENNIAL ISSUES IN AMERICAN MILITARY STRATEGY

Many of the historical examples presented here are explained fully in subsequent chapters. For example, for Lincoln's lack of discussion with Grant, see chapter 4. For Wilson's rejection of unconditional surrender, see chapter 6.

1. Joel Achenbach, "War and the Cult of Clausewitz," *Washington Post,* 6 Dec. 1990,

p. D1; Davies in Maurice Matloff, *Strategic Planning for Coalition Warfare* (Chief of Military History, 1953, 1959), 2:287; Theodore White, ed., *The Stilwell Papers* (William Sloane, 1948), p. 256; Captain John S. McKean, "War and Policy," *Proceedings of the United States Naval Institute* 40 (Jan. 1914): 8–9; Jonathan Clarke, "The Conceptual Poverty of U.S. Foreign Policy," *Atlantic Monthly,* Sept. 1993, 55; Michael Pearlman, *To Make Democracy for America:* (University of Illinois Press, 1984), pp. 51, 89, 156; Ronald Reagan, with Richard G. Hubler, *Where's the Rest of Me?* (Duell, Sloan and Pearce, 1965), p. 139; Arthur Hadley, "Goodbye to the Blind Slash Dead Kid's Hooch," *Playboy Magazine,* Aug. 1971, p. 206; Samuel Flagg Bemis, *John Quincy Adams and the Foundations of American Foreign Policy* (Norton, 1973), chaps. 15, 16; David Eisenhower, *Eisenhower at War, 1943–1945* (Vintage Books, 1987), pp. 412–417, 421–423; Martin Blumenson, *The Patton Papers: 1940–1945* (Houghton Mifflin, 1974), p. 537.

2. Tuvia Ben-Moshe, *Churchill: Strategy and History* (Lynne Rienner, 1992), pp. 225, 240–241; Michael P. Riccards, "Waging the Last War: Winston Churchill and Presidential Imagination," *Presidential Quarterly Studies* 16 (spring 1986): 219–222; Louis J. Halle, *Dream and Reality: Aspects of American Foreign Policy* (Harper and Row, 1959), pp. 303–304; James T. Westwood, "Some Notes on Strategy," *Military Review* 65 (Oct. 1985): 65; George P. Shultz, "Shaping Foreign Policy: New Realities and New Ways of Thinking," *Foreign Affairs* 63 (spring 1985): 706; Warner R. Schilling, "Civil-Naval Politics in World War I," *World Politics* 7 (July 1955): 573; Thomas Riise-Kappen, "Public Opinion, Domestic Structure, and Foreign Policy in Liberal Democracies," *World Politics* 43 (July 1991):487, 511–512; Miroslav Nincic, *Democracy and Foreign Policy* (Columbia University Press, 1992), *passim;* J. William Fulbright, "American Foreign Policy in the 20th Century under an 18th-Century Constitution," *Cornell Law Quarterly* 47 (fall 1961): 2, 6–7, 12; Henry Kissinger, *Years of Upheaval* (Little, Brown, 1982), p. 806; Clark Clifford, *Counsel to the President* (Random House, 1991), pp. 128, 517; General John R. Galvin, "How We Can Nuture Military Strategists?" *Defense* 89 (Jan./Feb. 1989): 26, 28; Deborah Shapley, *Promise and Power: The Life and Times of Robert McNamara* (Little, Brown, 1993), 211–215, 451–453.

3. Bob Woodward, *The Commanders* (Pocket Books, 1991), pp. 111–115, 311–313, 362; Capt. John Vinton (13 Nov. 1840) in William B. Skelton, *An American Profession of Arms* (University Press of Kansas, 1992), p. 282; T. Harry Williams, "The Macs and the Ikes," *American Mercury* 75 (Oct. 1952): 32–39; John McCloy in Forrest Pogue, *George C. Marshall* (Viking, 1963–87), 3:460.

4. Larry Bland, ed., *George C. Marshall: Interviews and Reminiscences* (Marshall Research Library, 1991), p. 452; Marshall in Matloff, *Strategic Planning for Coalition Warfare,* 1:255, and Pogue, Marshall, 2:330, 346; Rachel Sherman Thorndike, *The Sherman Letters* (Da Capo Press, 1969), pp. 195, 301; Antoine H. Jomini, *The Principles of the Art of War* (1838); I. B. Holley, *General John M. Palmer* (Greenwood, 1982), p. 66; George McClellan, *Report of the Organization and Campaigns of the Army of the Potomac* (Sheldon, 1864), p. 441; Clayton James, *Years of MacArthur* (Houghton Mifflin, 1970–85), 3:361.

5. John F. Marszalek, *Sherman: A Soldier's Passion for Order* (Free Press, 1993), chap. 7; Stephen E. Ambrose, *Eisenhower* (Simon and Schuster, 1983–84); 1:96, 269; 2:592; Col. George A. Lincoln and Col. Richard G. Stilwell, "Scholars' Debouch into Strategy," *Military Review* 40 (July 1960): 60, 70; David Trask, *The War with Spain in 1898* (Macmillan, 1981), pp. 253, 281, 284, 292–293; Julian Corbett, *Some Principles of*

Maritime Strategy (1911), pp. 15–16; Alfred Thayer Mahan, *The Problem of Asia* (Little, Brown, 1900), p. 21, and *Lessons of the War with Spain* (Little, Brown, 1899), p. 21; Stimson (ca. March 1942) in Eric Larrabee, *Commander in Chief: Franklin Delano Roosevelt, His Lieutenants, and Their War* (New York: Touchstone, 1987), p. 173.

6. Robert L. Goldich, "The Evolution of Congressional Attitudes toward a General Staff in the 20th Century," in *Defense Organization: The Need for Change* (Senate Committee on Armed Services, 1985), pp. 260–263; C. Kenneth Allard, *Command, Control, and the Common Defense* (Yale University Press, 1990), pp. 123–131; Dudley W. Knox, "The Role of Doctrine in Naval Warfare," *United States Naval Institute Proceedings* 1 (Mar.–Apr. 1915): 328, 332–333, 353; Gen. Thomas T. Handy in Ray S. Cline, *Washington Command Post* (Chief of Military History, 1951), pp. 198–199; Paul H. Douglas, *In the Fullness of Time* (Harcourt, Brace, Jovanovich, 1971), pp. 113–124, 346–348; Calvin William Enders, "The Vinson Navy" (Ph.D. diss., Michigan State University, 1970), pp. 201–202; Robert Mahon, *History of the Militia and the National Guard* (Macmillan, 1983), pp. 201–202, 216, 222, 230, 257; Lewis Sorley, "Creighton Abrams and Active-Reserve Integration in Wartime," *Parameters* 21 (summer 1991): 45–46, 49.

7. Eisenhower in John Newhouse, *War and Peace in the Nuclear Age* (Knopf, 1989), pp. 104–105; Roger Brown, *Republic in Peril* (Norton, 1974), pp. 85–86; Roy P. Balser, ed., *Collected Works of Abraham Lincoln* (Rutgers University Press, 1953), 4:263, 5:49, 343; Arthur S. Link, ed., *The Papers of Woodrow Wilson* (Princeton University Press, 1966–), 40:536, 46:320; Sir William Wiseman (British intelligence) in David French, *Strategy of the Lloyd George Coalition* (Clarendon Press, 1995), p. 65.

8. Kurt William Nagel, "Empire and Interest: British Colonial Defense Policy (Ph.D. diss., Johns Hopkins University, 1992), pp. 359, 366; Kenneth Waltz, *Man, the State, and War* (Columbia University Press, 1959); Perry Miller, *Nature's Nation* (Harvard University Press, 1967), pp. 23–46; various speakers and newspapers in Steven Watts, *The Republic Reborn: War and the Making of Liberal America* (Johns Hopkins University Press, 1987), pp. 74–77, 84, and in Robert W. Johannsen, *To the Halls of Montezumas: The Mexican War in the American Imagination* (Oxford University Press, 1985), pp. 208, 241, 309; James McPherson, *For Cause and Comrades: Why Men Fought in the Civil War* (Oxford University Press, 1997), pp. 106, 178; Daniel R. Beaver, *Newton D. Baker and the American War Effort* (University of Nebraska Press, 1966), pp. 34, 90, 218; "Remarks at Pemiscot County Fair," 7 Oct. 1945, *Truman Presidential Papers* (Government Printing Office, 1961), p. 380; Dulles (1954) in Marc Trachtenberg, *History and Strategy* (Princeton University Press, 1991), p. 139; Nixon and Kissinger in Elmo R. Zumwalt Jr., *On Watch: A Memoir* (Quadrangle, 1976), pp. 319–320, 414; Pearlman, *To Make Democracy for America,* passim; Philip Caputo, *A Rumor of War* (Holt, Rinehart and Winston, 1976), pp. 322–323, 332; JFK in Lloyd Gardner, *Pay Any Price* (Ivan Dee, 1995), pp. 43–44.

2. THE COLONIAL AND REVOLUTIONARY WARS FOR NORTH AMERICA

1. Amherst on Indian auxiliaries and American militia in John Cuneo, *Robert Rogers of the Rangers* (Richardson and Steirman, 1987), p. 95; and Edward Leach, *Roots of Conflict: British Armed Forces and Colonial Americans* (University of North Carolina Press, 1986), p. 132; British soldier quoted in Lee McCardell, *Ill-Starred General: Braddock of the Coldstream Guards* (University of Pittsburgh Press, 1958), p. 180.

2. Jeremy Black, "British Foreign Policy in the Eighteenth Century: A Survey," *Journal of British Studies* 26 (Jan. 1987): 28; Daniel A. Baugh, "Great Britain's 'Blue-Water' Policy, 1689–1815," *International History Review* 10 (Feb. 1988): 42–46; Max Savelle, *The Origins of American Diplomacy* (Macmillan, 1967), pp. 230–231, 369–372, 400, 451, 459; William Pencak, *War, Politics, and Revolution in Provincial Massachusetts* (Northeastern University Press, 1981), pp. 126–127; Marie Peters, *Pitt and Popularity: The Patriot Minister and London Opinion during the Seven Years' War* (Clarendon Press, 1980), pp. 5, 28, 82–89, 149, 274.

3. Peters, *Pitt and Popularity,* pp. 25–27, 42, 111; James Corbett, *England in the Seven Years' War* (Longmans, Green, 1907), 1:28–29; Francis Parkman, *Montcalm and Wolfe* (Houghton Mifflin, 1884), pp. 87–90, 211, 267, 358, 400; Edward Hamilton, ed., *Adventure in the Wilderness: American Journals of Louis Antoine de Bouganville* (University of Oklahoma Press, 1964), pp. 251, 282; James Titus, *The Old Dominion at War* (University of South Carolina Press, 1991), pp. 59–60, 88, 89, 121–122; John C. Fitzpatrick, ed., *Writings of Washington* (Government Printing Office, 1931–44), 1:493, 502; W. J. Eccles, *Essays on New France* (Oxford University Press, 1987), pp. 112–116; Fred Anderson, *A People's War: Massachusetts Soldiers and Society* (Norton, 1984), pp. 35–39, 58–60, 178, 229; J. Clarence Webster, ed., *The Journal of Jeffrey Amherst* (University of Chicago Press, 1931), pp. 132, 154, 166–167, 210; George A. Rawlyk, *Nova Scotia's Massachusetts* (McGill-Queen's University Press, 1973), pp. 66, 159–163, 172–174, 205–206.

4. Reed Browning, *Duke of Newcastle* (Yale University Press, 1975), esp. pp. 182–183, 210, 241–243, 268, 283; Jeremy Black, *Pitt the Elder* (Cambridge University Press, 1992), passim; William Corey to Pitt (ca. March 1756) in Peter Paret, "Colonial Experience and European Military Reform at the End of the Eighteenth Century," *Bulletin of the Institute of Historical Records* 37 (1964): 47; Richard Middleton, *The Bells of Victory* (Cambridge University Press, 1985), esp. pp. 86, 96–97, 141, 196, 204; Gertrude Selwyn Kimball, ed., *Correspondence of William Pitt When Secretary of State* (Macmillan, 1906), 1:138–139, 2:302; Peter E. Russell, "Redcoats in the Wilderness," *William and Mary Quarterly* 35 (Oct. 1978): 650–651; Parkman, *Montcalm and Wolfe,* pp. 524, 536.

5. George III in Don Cook, *Long Fuse: How England Lost the American Colonies* (Atlantic Monthly Press, 1995), p. 12; John Ferling, *Wilderness of Miseries* (Greenwood Press, 1980), pp. 84, 164; Leach, *Roots of Conflict,* pp. 78, 130–131; Black, *Pitt the Elder,* pp. 195, 203, 215, 234, 241, 266–267, 291–299; John Brewer, *The Sinews of Power* (Knopf, 1989), pp. 22, 127–132; Jack P. Greene, "The Seven Years' War and the American Revolution," *Journal of Imperial and Commonwealth History* 8 (1979–80): 90–95, 100; J. C. D. Clark, *The Language of Liberty* (Cambridge University Press, 1994), pp. 238, 254, 264, 272.

6. James Pritchard, "French Strategy and the American Revolution," *Naval War College Review* 47 (autumn 1994): 84–105; Eccles, *Essays on New France,* pp. 124, 145–148, 150; Dave Palmer, *The Way of the Fox: American Strategy, 1775–1783* (Greenwood Press, 1975), pp. 97–106, 200–204; Richard K. Showman, ed., *Papers of General Nathanael Greene* (University of North Carolina Press, 1976–), 2:302, 6:220; Piers Mackesy, *The War for America, 1775–1783* (Harvard University Press, 1965), pp. 338, 343, 367, 401–406, 429, 512–513.

7. John Shy, *People Numerous and Armed* (Oxford University Press, 1976), pp. 151–154, 217–219; Fitzpatrick, *Writings of Washington,* 6:110–111, 7:46–47, 8:70–71, 10:267, 19:481, 20:49, 209; Paul David Nelson, "Citizen Soldiers or Regulars," *Military*

Affairs 43 (Oct. 1979):126–132; Don Higginbotham, "American Militia," in Higginbotham, *Reconsiderations on the Revolutionary War* (Greenwood Press, 1978), pp. 151–154, 217–219; Gordon S. Wood, *The Radicalism of the American Revolution* (Knopf, 1992), pp. 71, 120–121, 179–190, 221–223, 232–234, 295; Mark V. Kwasny, *Washington's Partisan War* (Kent State University Press, 1996), pp. 149, 217–218, 293–294; Orville Murphy, "French Contemporary Opinion of the American Revolutionary Army" (Ph.D. diss., University of Minnesota, 1957), esp. pp. 115–121, 159, 212; Burgoyne and sergeant quoted in Richard Ketchum, *Saratoga* (Henry Holt, 1997), pp. 142, 415; Showman, *Papers of Greene*, 1:362–363, 2:303.

8. Sidney Kaplan, "Rank and Status among Massachusetts Continental Officers," *American Historical Review* 56 (Jan. 1951): 318–321; James D. Scudieri, "The Continentals: A Comparative Analysis of a Late 18th C. Standing Army" (Ph.D. diss., City College of New York, 1993), pp. 123–124, 133–136, 384; Fitzpatrick, *Writings of Washington*, 3:371, 4:81, 6:386, 10:238.

9. Palmer, *Way of the Fox*, pp. 159, 162; Mackesy, *War for America,* esp. pp. 155, 171–173, 184, 308–309, 414, 465–467; Cook, *Long Fuse,* pp. 226, 290–296, 314–315, 322, 323, 333, 334, 340; Charles Royster, *A Revolutionary People at War* (Norton, 1981), pp. 146–150, 178–185.

10. Royster, *Revolutionary People at War,* pp. 152–162; Gordon Wood, *The Creation of the American Republic* (Norton, 1972), 124, 424, and passim; Clark, *Language of Liberty,* pp. 204, 215, 363; Nathan O. Hatch, *Sacred Cause of Liberty* (Yale University Press, 1977), pp. 17, 36, 59–60, 88; Paul Smith, *Loyalists and Redcoats* (Norton, 1972), esp. chap. 8; Daniel Timothy Miller, "Fire from the Hearth" (Ph.D. diss., University of Indiana, 1992), pp. 111, 184, 236–238, 274, 291–292; Mackesy, *War for America,* pp. 88, 401; Cook, *Long Fuse,* p. 326; French minister and King George in Eccles, *Essays on New France,* pp. 154–155; Burgoyne in Ketchum, *Saratoga,* p. 108.

3. 1812 AND MEXICO

1. Ronald Hatzenbuehler and Robert Ivie, *Congress Declares War: Rhetoric, Leadership, and Partisanship* (Kent State University Press, 1983), pp. 48–53, 117; Roger Brown, *Republic in Peril* (Norton, 1974), pp. 68, 74, 177, 241; J. C. A. Stagg, *Mr. Madison's War: Politics, Diplomacy, and Warfare in the Early American Republic, 1783–1830* (Princeton University Press, 1983), pp. 20, 60–61, 67, 74, 116–117; Richard Hofstadter, *The Idea of a Party System: The Rise of Legitimate Opposition in the United States, 1780–1840* (University of California Press, 1969), esp. chap. 6; Jackson, "Division Orders," 7 March 1812, in John Spencer Bassett, ed., *Correspondence of Andrew Jackson* (Carnegie Institute, 1926–33), 1:221–222.

2. Hofstadter, *Idea of a Party System,* pp. 105–106; Don Hickey, *War of 1812: Forgotten Conflict* (University of Illinois Press, 1989), pp. 45, 163, 255–257, 266–267; Henry Adams, *History of the United States during the Administrations of Jefferson and Madison* (Library of America, 1986), pp. 440–441; Merrill D. Peterson, *Thomas Jefferson and the New Nation* (Oxford University Press, 1970), pp. 170, 197, 211–231, 833–834; Lawrence Delbert Cress, " 'Cool and Serious Reflection': Federalist Attitudes toward War in 1812," *Journal of the Early Republic* 7 (summer 1987): 127–129, 135–138.

3. John K. Mahon, *War of 1812* (University of Florida Press, 1972), passim; J. Mackay Hitsman, *Incredible War of 1812* (University of Toronto Press, 1965), pp. 39–56; John R. Elting, *Amateurs, to Arms!* (Algonquin, 1991), pp. 27–29, 33, 39–41, 59–60, 133; George F. G. Stanley, "The Indians in the War of 1812," *Canadian Historical Review* 31 (June 1950): 150; C. P. Stacey, "Naval Power on the Lakes, 1812–1814," in *After Tippecanoe: Aspects of War of 1812,* ed. Philip P. Mason (Michigan State University Press, 1963), pp. 56–58.

4. British in Adams, *History of the United States,* pp. 567, 1190–1197, 1186–1187; and C. J. Bartlee, "Gentlemen versus Democrats: Cultural Prejudice and Military Strategy in Britain," *War in History* 1 (July 1994): 142, 145–146, 159; Republicans in Mahon, *War of 1812,* p. 116; and Stagg, *Mr. Madison's War,* pp. 383, 392, 410; Federalists in Samuel Eliot Morison, *Dissent in Three Wars* (Harvard University Press, 1970), p. 10; and Adams (above), p. 1065; Irving Brandt, *James Madison* (Bobbs-Merrill, 1941–61), 6:365, 384; Charles Winslow Elliott, *Winfield Scott* (Macmillan, 1937), pp. 62–66, 149; Robert Remini, *Andrew Jackson* (Harper and Row, 1977–84), 1:293, 319.

5. Brandt, *James Madison,* 6:369, 375, 392; Republicans in Hickey, *War of 1812,* p. 307; and Brown, *Republic in Peril,* p. 190; Remini, *Andrew Jackson,* 2:75–76; Justin Butterfield in Tyler Dennett, ed., *Lincoln and the Civil War: Diaries and Letters of John Hay* (Dodd, Mead, 1939), p. 80; William B. Skelton, *American Profession of Arms* (University Press of Kansas, 1992), p. 114; Scott to unknown, 23 May 1814, Scott Papers, Library of Congress.

6. Democrats quoted or described in Thomas R. Hietala, *Manifest Design: Anxious Aggrandizement in Late Jacksonian America* (Cornell University Press, 1985), pp. 87, 116, 119; Norman Graebner, ed., *Manifest Destiny* (Bobbs-Merrill, 1968), pp. iii, 145, 157; and Robert W. Johannsen, *To the Halls of Montezumas* (Oxford University Press, 1985), chap. 2; Daniel Walker Howe, *Political Culture of American Whigs* (University of Chicago Press, 1979), passim; Robert E. Shalhope, "Thomas Jefferson's Republicanism and Antebellum Southern Thought," *Journal of Southern History* 42 (Nov. 1976): 547–552; John Niven, *John C. Calhoun and the Price of Union* (Louisiana State University Press, 1988), pp. 210, 214, 337–341; Richard H. Brown, "The Missouri Crisis, Slavery, and the Politics of Jacksonianism," *South Atlantic Quarterly* 65 (winter 1966): 68–72.

7. Milo Milton Quaife, ed., *The Diary of James K. Polk* (A. C. McClurg, 1910), 1:400, 2:227, 239–242, 331, 432–433; David M. Pletcher, *Diplomacy of Annexation* (University of Missouri Press, 1973), pp. 274–275, 287, 290, 396; Charles A. Lofgren, "Force and Diplomacy," *Military Affairs* 31 (summer 1967): 61–63; Gene M. Brack, *Mexico Views Manifest Destiny, 1821–1846: An Essay on the Origins of the Mexican War* (University of New Mexico Press, 1975), pp. 162, 166; Thomas Hart Benton, *History of Working of American Government for Thirty Years* (Appleton, 1854), 2:680; Ernest McPherson Lander, *Reluctant Imperialists: Calhoun, the South Carolinians, and the Mexican War* (Louisiana State University Press, 1980), pp. 151–152.

8. Samuel J. Watson, "Manifest Destiny and Military Professionalism," *Southwestern Historical Quarterly* 99 (Apr. 1996): 469–472, 479, 484, 487; Quaife, *Diary of James K. Polk,* 1:94; K. Jack Bauer, *Mexican War* (Macmillan, 1974), pp. 71, 74, 86, 246, 364; Scott and Jackson quoted in Timothy Johnson, *Winfield Scott, The Quest for Military Glory* (University Press of Kansas, 1998), pp. 69, 88, 119, 146–147; Elliott, *Winfield Scott,* pp. 146–148, 217–230, 468; W. Nathaniel Hughes and Roy Stonesifer, *Life and Wars of Gideon J. Pillow* (University of North Carolina Press, 1993), pp. 45–58, 79–90, 199;

J. Knox Walker to Pillow, 26 May 1847, Polk Papers, Series 4, Roll 58, Library of Congress Microfilm; Edwin A. Miles, "The Whig Party and the Menace of Caesar," *Tennessee Historical Quarterly* 27 (winter 1968): 346–366; Mark E. Neely, "Lincoln and Mexican War," *Civil War History* 24 (Mar. 1978): 8–10; Winfield Scott, *Memoirs* (Sheldon and Company, 1864), 2:416; Lee in Charles Dufour, *The Mexican War: Compact History* (Hawthorn Books, 1968), p. 287; Kirby Smith, Hill, and McClellan quoted and Pillow cited in George Smith and Charles Judah, eds., *Chronicles of the Gringos* (University of Mexico Press, 1968), pp. 78, 240, 438, 440, 458–459.

9. Frederick Merk, *Manifest Destiny and Mission in American History* (Vintage, 1963), pp. 123, 186; Justin H. Smith, *The War with Mexico* (Macmillan, 1919), 1:98–99, 378, 2:89, 124–125, 131–138, 317; E. B. Long, ed., *Personal Memoirs of U. S. Grant* (Grosset and Dunlap, 1962), pp. 70, 85; Brack, *Mexico Views Manifest Destiny,* pp. 82, 107; James W. Pohl, "The Influence of Antoine Henri de Jomini on Winfield Scott's Campaign in the Mexican War," *Southwestern Historical Quarterly* 77 (July 1973): 88–89, 97; Smith and Judah, *Chronicles of Gringos,* pp. 228, 307, 404; Scott to Secretary of War Marcy, 28 April 1847, in House Exec. Doc. no. 56, 30th Cong., 1st sess.; Allan Peskin, *Volunteers: Mexican War* (Kent State University Press, 1991), pp. 250–255; Skelton, *American Profession of Arms,* pp. 72, 77, 297–299, 345; Douglas W. Richmond, "Andrew Trussell in Mexico: A Soldier's Wartime Impressions, 1847–1848," in *Essays on Mexican War,* ed. Douglas W. Richmond (Texas A&M University Press, 1986), pp. 91, 96; McClellan in Dufour, *Mexican War,* p. 99.

10. Norman A. Graebner, "Party Politics and Trist Mission," *Journal of Southern History* 19 (May 1953): 155–156; Quaife, *Diary* of James K. Polk, 2:466, 3:196, 283, 309–310, 347–348, 365; Marcy to Scott, 14 April 1847; Scott to Marcy, 14 May 1847; and Scott to the Mexican nation, 11 May 1847: all in House Exec. Doc. no. 56, 30th Cong., 1st sess.; quartermaster in Smith and Judah, *Chronicles of the Gringos,* p. 442; Hughes and Stonesifer, *Life and Wars of Gideon J. Pillow,* pp. 75–76; "Mexican War Letters of Col. William Bowen Campbell of Tennessee, Written to Governor David Campbell of Virginia, 1846–1847," *Tennessee Historical Magazine* 1 (June 1915): 136, 151; Pletcher, *Diplomacy of Annexation,* pp. 514, 518, 538–540, 542, 548; Col. Vincent Esposito, "War as a Continuation of Politics," *Military Review* 34 (Feb. 1955): 60.

11. Melba Porter Hay, ed., *The Papers of Henry Clay* (University of Kentucky Press, 1959–91), 10:323, 329; Charles M. Wiltse, ed., *The Papers of Daniel Webster* (University Press of New England, 1974–84), 6:228, 236, 288; William H. Sampson, ed., *Letters of Zachary Taylor from Battle-fields of Mexican War* (Genesse Press, 1908), pp. 51, 90; Roy Franklin Nichols, *Franklin Pierce* (University of Pennsylvania Press, 1958), pp. 161–162, 195, 204, 215; Whigs quoted in Johnson, *Scott,* pp. 214–215.

12. Hietala, *Manifest Design,* pp. 185–187; Lander, *Reluctant Imperialists: Calhoun,* pp. 15–17, 35, 154–156, 175; Lt. Thomas Williams (USMA, 1837) and Taylor in Smith and Judah, *Chronicles of Gringos,* pp. 74, 418; Long, *Memoirs of U. S. Grant,* pp. 22, 24, 151.

4. CIVIL WAR: POLICY OUT OF POLITICAL CONTROL

1. Paul Escott, *After Secession: Jefferson Davis and the Failure of Confederate Nationalism* (Louisiana State University Press, 1978), pp. 12, 233, 236, 248; William W.

Freeling, "Editorial Revolution, Virginia, and the Coming of Civil War," *Civil War History* 16 (Mar. 1969): 70, 71; *Official Records of Robert Dinwiddie: Lieutenant-Governor of Colony of Virginia* (Society of Virginia, 1884), 2:114; Rachel Sherman Thorndike, ed., *The Sherman Letters* (Da Capo Press, 1969), pp. 221–222; William C. Davis, *Jefferson Davis* (HarperCollins, 1991), pp. 78–80, 194–195, 274, 304, 390–391, 562, 592–595; James M. McPherson, *What They Fought For, 1861–1865* (Louisiana State University Press, 1994), pp. 15–16, 35–36, 47, 52–54, 60–63, and *For Cause and Comrades* (Oxford University Press, 1997), pp. 110, 114; Roy Basler, ed., *Complete Works of Abraham Lincoln* (Rutgers University Press, 1953), 4:235–236, 437; J. Mills Thornton, *Politics and Power in a Slave Society* (Louisiana State University Press, 1978), pp. 214–217; Larry E. Nelson, *Bullets, Ballots, and Rhetoric: Confederate Policy for the Presidential Contest of 1864* (University of Alabama Press, 1980), pp. 129, 133, 149–150; Stephen E. Woodworth, *Davis and Lee at War* (University Press of Kansas, 1995), pp. 65, 156–159; Robert F. Durden, *The Gray and the Black: The Confederate Debate on Emancipation* (Louisiana State University Press, 1972), pp. 45, 80, 93, 120, 124, 221, 246; Stephen V. Ash, *When the Yankees Came: Conflict and Chaos in the Occupied South* (University of North Carolina Press, 1995), pp. 8, 41, 59.

2. Basler, *Complete Works of Abraham Lincoln,* 4:30, 271, 439, 7:332–333; Earl Hess, *The Union Soldier in Battle* (University Press of Kansas, 1997), pp. 124–125; McPherson, *What They Fought For,* pp. 28–29, 32, 46, and James M. McPherson, *Battle Cry of Freedom* (Oxford University Press, 1988), p. 309; George Rable, *The Confederate Republic* (University of North Carolina Press, 1994), pp. 50, 123; H. Wayne Morgan, "Civil War Diary of William McKinley," *Ohio Historical Quarterly* 69 (1960): 283; Bertram Wyatt-Brown, *Southern Honor, Ethics and Behavior in the Old South* (Oxford University Press, 1982), pp. xi–xii, 109–110; Phillip Paludan, "American Civil War Considered as Crisis in Law and Order," *American Historical Review* 77 (Oct. 1972): 1013–1034; Mark Grimsley, *The Hard Hand of War* (Cambridge University Press, 1995), pp. 88, 91, 97, 154; Stephen Sears, *The Civil War Papers of George B. McClellan* (Ticknor and Fields, 1989), p. 5; Brooks Simpson, *Let Us Have Peace: Grant and the Politics of War and Reconstruction* (University of North Carolina Press, 1991), p. 11; Thorndike, *Sherman Letters,* pp. 78, 221; Mark A. DeWolfe Howe, ed., *Home Letters of General Sherman* (Scribner's, 1909), p. 189.

3. McClellan in Stephen Sears, *George B. McClellan: Young Napoleon* (Ticknor and Fields, 1988), pp. 20, 215–216, 226, 323, and *Civil War Papers of McClellan,* pp. 16, 46, 57, 60, 97, 103, 117, 134, 211, 246, 258–259, 288; and in George Smith and Charles Judah, eds., *Chronicles of the Gringos* (University of Mexico Press, 1968), pp. 25, 459; officers in Stephen Sears, *Landscape Turned Red: Antietam* (Warner, 1983), p. 364, and McPherson, *For Cause and Comrades,* p. 157; John Y. Simon, ed., *Papers of Ulysses S. Grant* (Southern Illinois University Press, 1967–), 10:97, 418; Grant in Tyler Dennett, ed., *Lincoln and the Civil War: Diaries and Letters of John Hay* (Dodd, Mead, 1939), p. 242; McPherson, *For Cause and Comrades,* p. 116; Hess, *Union Soldier in Battle,* p. 87.

4. Sam Watkins, *"Co. Aytch": A Side Show of the Big Show* (1882; reprint, Collier, 1973), pp. 24, 39, 202; Gerald F. Linderman, *Embattled Courage: Experience of Combat in American Civil War* (Free Press, 1987), passim; Patty Griffith, *Battle Tactics of the Civil War* (Yale University Press, 1987), p. 132; Hess, *Union Soldier in Battle,* pp. 137, 144; Robert Bruce, *Lincoln and Tools of War* (Bobbs-Merrill, 1956), chap. 7; Lorenzo M.

Crowell, "The Illusion of the Decisive Napoleonic Victory," *Defense Analysis* 4 (Dec. 1988): 329–346.

5. Alan Nevins, *The War for the Union* (Macmillan, 1959–71), 1:334, 2:88–91, 118, 140, 202, 298; McPherson, *Battle Cry of Freedom,* p. 500; Charles A. Jellison, *Fessenden of Maine* (Syracuse University Press, 1962), pp. 140–145; Cong. John J. Crittenden (Dem.-Ky.) and Sen. Sherman in *Congressional Globe,* 37th Cong., 2d sess., 23 Dec. 1861, 6 Jan. and 9 July 1862, pp. 163, 193, 3198; Simon, *Papers of Ulysses S. Grant,* 5:142–143, 145, 226, 9:155, 156; Basler, *Complete Works of Lincoln,* 5:49, 145–146, 494, 509.

6. Lincoln quoted and described in Mary A. Livermore, *My Story of the War* (Worthington, 1896), pp. 555–556; and Shelby Foote, *The Civil War* (Random House, 1958–74), 2:119; Clifford Dowdey, ed., *The Wartime Papers of R. E. Lee* (Little, Brown, 1961), p. 389; Grant in "The Military Leadership of North and South," in *Why the North Won the Civil War,* ed. David Donald (Collier Books, 1962), p. 51; John F. Marszalek, *Sherman: Soldier's Passion for Order* (Free Press, 1993), p. 308; William T. Sherman, *Memoirs* [Library of America, 1990 [orig. 1875]), pp. 365, 729.

7. Simon, *Papers of Ulysses S. Grant,* 10:16, 222, 292, 327, 340, 460; Walter D. Kamphoefner, "German-Americans and Civil War Politics," *Civil War History* 37 (Sept. 1991): 232–246; Richard West, *Lincoln's Scapegoat General: Benjamin Butler* (Houghton Mifflin, 1965), pp. 31, 75, 213, 239; Basler, *Complete Works of Lincoln,* 1:381, 4:532, 5:486, 494, 7:243–244, 324, 437, 444, 499; Dennett, *Lincoln and the Civil War,* pp. 33, 91, 115, 176; David Donald, *Lincoln* (Simon and Schuster, 1995), pp. 490–491, 525; E. B. Long, ed., *Personal Memoirs of U. S. Grant* (Grosset and Dunlap, 1962), pp. 47, 434; John Simon, "Grant, Lincoln, and Unconditional Surrender," in *Lincoln's Generals,* ed. Gabor Borritt (Oxford University Press, 1994), p. 170; Bruce Catton, *Grant Takes Command* (Little, Brown, 1968), pp. 135, 219, 301, 338, 340, 369, 410; William Glenn Robertson, *Back Door to Richmond: The Bermuda Hundred Campaign* (University of Delaware Press, 1987); esp. pp. 89, 108, 153–155, 225–235; Nevins, *War for the Union,* 4:23, 41, 50; Brooks Simpson, "Great Expectations," in *The Wilderness Campaign,* ed. Gary Gallagher (University of North Carolina Press, 1997), pp. 8, 24; *Official Record of the Rebellion* [hereafter *OR*], Series 1, 33:885–886, 1283, 36/1:20–21, 38/5:149, 46:19; McPherson, *For Cause and Comrades,* pp. 162, 165–166, 170, 177; David Long, *The Jewel of Liberty: Lincoln's Re-election and the End of Slavery* (Stackpole, 1994), chap. 11.

8. Charles Royster, *The Destructive War: William Tecumseh Sherman, Stonewall Jackson, and the Americans* (Knopf, 1991), pp. 90, 98, 101, 141, 361, 392; Thorndike, *Sherman Letters,* pp. 115, 159–163, 182, 185; Howe, *Home Letters of Sherman;* Simon, *Papers of Ulysses S. Grant,* 2:62, 4:264, 6:275, 293; Marszalek, *Sherman,* pp. 41, 55, 71, 91, 151, 195–196, 412; *OR,* Series 1, 13:743, 17/2:236, 280, 39/2:131–132, 248, and 3:162, 44:13; Lee Kennett, *Marching through Georgia* (HarperCollins, 1995), pp. 262, 274–282.

9. Richard Berlinger, Herman Hattaway, Archer Jones, and William Still, *Why the South Lost the Civil War* (University of Georgia Press, 1986), pp. 64–81, 126, 266, 439–440, 479–480; Walter Lord, ed., *The Fremantle Diary* [orig. 1864]; p. 114; Ella Lonn, *Desertion during the Civil War* (Century, 1928), p. 309; Watkins, *"Co. Aytch,"* pp. 218–219; Carl Degler, *At Odds: Women and the Family in America from the Revolution to the Present* (Oxford University Press, 1980), pp. 104–105; Bell Irvin Wiley, *Life of Johnny*

Reb (Louisiana State University Press, 1978), pp. 210, 240–241; 309; Lloyd Lewis, *Sherman: Fighting Prophet* (Macmillan, 1932), pp. 449, 451–452.

10. Basler, *Complete Works of Abraham Lincoln*, 5:59, 6:149, 374; Morris McGregor and Bernard Nalty, eds., *Blacks in United States Armed Forces: Documents* (Scholarly Resources, 1977), 2:107, 114, 118, 131, 212; Bell Irvin Wiley, *Life of Billy Yank* (Louisiana State University Press, 1978), p. 115; Thomas Wentworth Higginson, *Army Life in a Black Regiment* (Norton: 1984 [orig. 1869]), pp. 88, 124, 150; Leon Litwick, *Been in Storm So Long: Aftermath of Slavery* (Knopf, 1979), chap. 2; McPherson, *For Cause and Comrades*, pp. 27, 48, 57, 126–127, 152, 154; Long, *Jewel of Liberty*, pp. 189–190.

5. THE SPANISH-AMERICAN WAR

1. Republicans in Leonard D. White, *The Republican Era: 1869–1901* (Free Press, 1958), pp. 21, 24, and Lester Langley, *The Cuban Policy of the United States* (Wiley, 1968), pp. 59–72; Sherman (11 Feb. 1870) in *Congressional Globe,* 41st Cong., 2d sess., 1870, p. 1206; John A. S. Grenville and George Berkeley Young, *Politics, Strategy, and American Diplomacy: 1873–1917* (Yale University Press, 1966), pp. 55, 65, 70, 113, 123–124, 141; Gerald Eggert, "Our Man in Havana: Fitzhugh Lee," *Hispanic American Historical Review* 47 (Nov. 1967): 464, 470, 477; politicians in Ernest May, *Imperial Democracy* (Harper and Row, 1973), p. 33; and Richard Hofstadter, "Cuba, Philippines, and Manifest Destiny," in his *Paranoid Style in American Politics and Other Essays* (University of Chicago Press, 1979), pp. 153–154; *Spanish Diplomatic Correspondence and Documents*, 1896–1900 (Government Printing Office, 1905), pp. 28, 30–31; Sherman in *Congressional Record,* 54th Cong., 1st sess., 1898, p. 2727; Fitzgerald, Pasco, Morgan, and Wheeler in *Congressional Record,* 54th Cong., 2d sess., 1898, pp. 2106, 2606, 3968–3969, 3816–3819.

2. William Widenor, *Henry Cabot Lodge and the Search for an American Foreign Policy* (University of California Press, 1980), pp. 108, 114; politicians in May, *Imperial Democracy,* chaps. 10–12, and Charles S. Olcott, *William McKinley* (Houghton Mifflin, 1916) 2:25–30; Schofield in *Chicago Tribune,* 3 April 1898; Bingham and Bailey in *Congressional Record,* 54th Cong., 2d sess., 1898, pp. 2610–2611; Sandburg in Gerald Lindermann, *Mirror of War: American Society and Spanish-American War* (University of Michigan Press, 1974), p. 93; Cervera and officials in French Ensor Chadwick, *The Relations of the United States and Spain* (Scribner's, 1911), 1:108, 116–117, 2:171, 438; John L. Offner, *Unwanted War: Diplomacy of the United States and Spain over Cuba* (University of North Carolina Press, 1992), pp. 86–87, 121, 146.

3. Army-Navy Board, "Report for Sec. of War," 4 Apr. 1898, National Archives, RG 94; Lee to Wm. Day, 9 Mar. 1898, Day MSS, Library of Congress; Mark Russell Schulman, *Navalism and Emergence of American Sea Power, 1882–1893* (Naval Institute Press, 1995), chap. 1; Sec. of Navy John D. Long in David Traxel, *1898: Birth of the American Century* (Knopf, 1998), p. 95; Graham Cosmas, *Army for Empire: U.S. Army in the Spanish-American War* (University of Missouri Press, 1971), pp. 5, 38; Ronald Spector, *Professors of War: Naval War College* (Naval War College Press, 1977), pp. 47, 91–95; Elting Morison, ed., *Letters of Theodore Roosevelt* (Harvard University Press, 1951–54), 1:717,

759, 2:892, 811–812; Robert Wooster, *Nelson A. Miles* (University of Nebraska Press, 1993), pp. 14–15, 22–28, 215, 220; messages between Miles, War Dept., and Sec. of War Alger in *Correspondence Relating to War with Spain* (Government Printing Office, 1902), 1:8–9, 24, 46–47; Olcott, *William McKinley*, 2:55.

4. Newspapers and public commentary in John Joseph Leffler, "From the Shadows into the Sun: Americans in the Spanish-American War" (Ph.D. diss., University of Texas, 1991), pp. 41, 43, 165, 199; Butler in Allan Nevins, *Hamilton Fish* (Dodd, Mead, 1936), p. 886; Forrest and Sherman in *New York Times,* 9 and 23 Dec. 1873; Willard B. Gatwood, *"Smoked Yankees" and the Struggle for Empire: Letters from Negro Soldiers* (University of Illinois Press, 1971), pp. 30, 57; John Pettegrew, " 'The Soldier's Faith': Turn-of-the-Century Memory and Modern American Nationalism," *Journal of Contemporary History* 31 (Jan. 1996): 64–66; newspapers and brigadier general (Lawton) on Rough Riders in Michael Pearlman, *To Make Democracy Safe for America* (University of Illinois Press, 1984), pp. 18–19.

5. David Trask, *The War with Spain* (Macmillan, 1981), pp. 239–241, 290–293, 300; correspondence between Shafter, navy, and McKinley in *Annual Reports of Navy Department,* 1898, 55th Cong., 3d sess., House Doc. 3, pp. 608, 610, 625, 629–630; Joseph G. Dawson, "William T. Sampson and Santiago," and Graham Cosmas, "Joint Operation in the Spanish-American War," both in *Crucible of Empire: The Spanish-American War,* ed. James C. Bradford (Naval Institute Press, 1993), pp. 54–55, 62, 108–111.

6. Kennan in Traxel, *1898,* p. 202; Richard N. Ellis, "Copper-Skinned Soldiers: Apache Scouts," *Great Plains Journal* 5 (spring 1966): 56; American and Spanish soldiers in Stephen Crane, "How Americans Make War" (1898), in *The Works of Crane,* ed. Fredsom Bowers (University of Virginia Press, 1971), 9:231; and Chadwick, *Relations of the United States and Spain,* 2:263; messages between Washington and flag officers, *Correspondence Relating to War with Spain,* 1:118–154, 200; Dewey in Traxel, *1898,* p. 224; Spanish military in Chadwick (above), 1:377, 2:138, 263; Joseph Wheeler, *History of the Santiago Campaign* (Lamson, Wolfe, 1898), pp. 128–129; G. J. A. O'Toole, *Spanish-American War* (Norton, 1984), pp. 284–285, 329–330, 341; Pershing in Traxel, *1898,* p. 209.

6. WORLD WAR I

1. William Widenor, *Henry Cabot Lodge and the Search for an American Foreign Policy* (University of California Press, 1980), pp. 70, 120–121, 203, 263; Arthur S. Link, ed., *The Papers of Woodrow Wilson* (Princeton University Press, 1966–), 2:195, 3:287, 27:113, 30:394, 472–473, 33:349, 535, 38:365, 40:67–69, 534, 536, 539; Avner Offer, "The Working Classes, British Naval Plans and the Coming of the Great War," *Past and Present* 107 (1985): 205–207, 213–216; Paul Birdsall, "Neutrality and Economic Pressures," *Science and Society* 3 (spring 1938): 223–224; Charles Seymour, ed., *The Intimate Papers of Colonel House* (Houghton Mifflin, 1926–28), 1:114, 293; Ernest May, *The World War and American Isolationism* (Harvard University Press, 1959), pp. 157, 182–183, 242–243; John Mueller, *Retreat from Doomsday: Obsolesence of Major War* (Basic Books, 1989), pp. 27–28; David Stevenson, *The First World War and International Politics* (Oxford University Press, 1991), pp. 7, 93; Walter Lippmann, "Terms for Japan," *Washington Post,* 12 July 1945.

2. Fiorello La Guardia, *The Making of an Insurgent: Autobiography* (Lippincott,

1948), pp. 138–140; Seward Livermore, *Woodrow Wilson and the War Congress* (University of Washington Press, 1966), pp. 71, 76, 119, 251; John A. Thomas, *Reformers and War: The Role of Progressives* (Cambridge University Press, 1987), pp. 29, 181, 186; Stephen Vaughn, "Prologue to Public Opinion: Walter Lippmann's Work in Military Intelligence," *Prologue* 15 (fall 1983): 155.

3. Edward M. Coffman, *The War to End All Wars: American Military Experience in World War I* (University of Wisconsin Press, 1986), pp. 152, 174–175, 264; David French, *Strategy of the Lloyd George Coalition* (Clarendon Press, 1995), pp. 3–12; David Stevenson, "French War Aims and the American Challenge," *Historical Journal* 22 (1979): 881, 883; John W. Chambers, *To Raise an Army* (Free Press, 1987), pp. 130–133, 144–145.

4. John J. Pershing, *My Experiences in the World War* (Stokes, 1931) 1:15, 29, 38–40; Daniel Beaver, *Newton D. Baker and the American War Effort* (University of Nebraska Press, 1966), pp. 140–141; David Lloyd George, *War Memoirs* (Little, Brown, 1936), 5:439; Georges Clemenceau, *Grandeur and Misery of Victory* (Harcourt, Brace, 1930), pp. 65, 72; W. B. Flower, *British-American Relations, 1917–1918: The Role of William Wiseman* (Princeton University Press, 1969), pp. 259, 292.

5. Donald Smythe, *Life of John J. Pershing* (Scribner's and University of Indiana Press, 1973–86), 1:195–200, 2:17, 71, 294; Pershing, *My Experiences,* 1:151–153, 194, 2:189; David Trask, *The AEF and Coalition Warmaking* (University Press of Kansas, 1993), pp. 71, 72, 113; Robert L. Bullard, *Personalities and Reminiscences of the War* (Doubleday, 1925), pp. 38, 276; James Rainey, "The Training of the American Expeditionary Forces in World War I" (Master's thesis, Temple University, 1981), pp. 36–37, 43–46, 104, 107, 266; *United States Army in the World War, 1917–1919* (Army Historical Division, 1948), 1:77, 14:303–306, 312–314, 319, 347–348; George C. Marshall, *Memoirs of My Service in the World War* (Houghton Mifflin, 1976), p. 122; Larry Bland, ed., *George C. Marshall: Interviews and Reminiscences* (Marshall Research Library, 1991), p. 260.

6. Coffman, *War to End All Wars,* pp. 222, 245–253, 349–352; Smythe, *Life of John J. Pershing,* 1:254, 2:198–200, 210–213, 227–230, 233; Pershing, *My Experiences,* 2:157, 246, 250, 254, 367; Bland, ed., *George C. Marshall,* pp. 26, 228–229, 243; Paul Braim, "The Test of Battle: AEF in Meuse-Argonne" (Ph.D. diss., University of Delaware, 1983), pp. 172, 183–184, 215, 219; Gregory Martin, "German Strategy and Military Assessments of the American Expeditionary Forces," *War in History* 1 (July 1994): 164, 190–191; Stephen J. Lofren, "Unready for War: Army and World War I," *Army History* 22 (spring 1992): 15–16; Gen. Robert Bullard and various doughboys in James Seidule, "Morale in the American Expeditionary Forces During World War I" (Ph.D., Ohio State University, 1997), pp. 21, 174, 255; E. David Cronon, ed., *Cabinet Diaries of Josephius Daniels* (University of Nebraska Press, 1963), pp. 312, 339, 341, 346; Woodrow Wilson, *History of American People* (Harper and Brothers, 1902), 5:6, 49–50, 99; Link, *Papers of Woodrow Wilson,* 48:451, 51:117, 409, 410, 419, 473, 629, 645; Sec. of Treasury McAdoo in *New York Times,* 13 Oct. 1918; Joseph Tumulty, *Woodrow Wilson as I Knew Him* (Doubleday Page, 1921), pp. 158, 309–312; Bullitt Lowry, *Armistice 1918* (Kent State University Press, 1996), pp. 39, 45–48, 67–68, 146–148, 159.

7. Widenor, *Lodge and Search for American Foreign Policy,* pp. 20, 186, 203, 285, 315–316, 347; Henry Cabot Lodge, *Early Memoirs* (Scribner's, 1913), pp. 112, 115, 123–125; Livermore, *Woodrow Wilson and the War Congress,* pp. 169–173; Edwin Weinstein, *Wilson: Medical and Psychological Biography* (Princeton University Press, 1981),

p. 362; Wesley Bagby, *The Road to Normalcy: The Election of 1920* (Johns Hopkins University Press, 1962), pp. 46–47, 56, 94; Tumulty, *Woodrow Wilson as I Knew Him,* p. 502.

8. Robert Sherwood, *Roosevelt and Hopkins* (Harper and Brothers, 1948), pp. 204, 227, 263; Robert A. Divine, *Second Chance: Triumph of Internationalism in America during World War II* (Atheneum 1971), pp. 169, 171, 212–213; Walter Lippmann, *U.S. Foreign Policy* (Little, Brown, 1943), p. 106; Robert Ferrell, ed., *Off the Record: Truman's Private Papers* (Penguin, 1982), pp. 307, 403–404; Robert Donovan, *Tumultuous Years: The Truman Presidency* (Norton, 1982), p. 199.

7. WORLD WAR II

1. Joint Strategic Survey Committee, "Quadrant and European Strategy," 5 Aug. 1943, National Archives, RG 165; Marshall to Spencer Carter, 14 June 1948, Marshall Research Library.

2. Frank Freidel, *Franklin D. Roosevelt: Apprenticeship* (Little, Brown, 1952), pp. 237, 241, 348, 359; Samuel Rosenman, ed., *Public Papers and Addresses of Roosevelt* (Harper and Brothers, 1938–50), 6:407, 8:463–464, 9:640, 10:189; Robert Sherwood, *Roosevelt and Hopkins* (Harper and Brothers, 1948), 127, 302, 418, 438, 554; Theodore Wilson, *First Summit: Roosevelt and Churchill, 1941* (University Press of Kansas, 1991), pp. 2, 17, 151, 231, 232, 289; Stephen Westbrook, "The Rainey Report and Army Morale, 1941," *Military Review* 60 (June 1980): 11–24; Larry Bland, ed., *George C. Marshall: Interviews and Reminiscences* (Marshall Research Library, 1991), pp. 471, 476, 530, and *Papers of Marshall* (Johns Hopkins University Press, 1984–), 3:321.

3. Mark Lowenthal, *Leadership and Indecision: American War Planning, 1937–1942* (Garland, 1989), pp. 408–414, 424–426; Robert Dallek, *Franklin Roosevelt and American Foreign Policy* (Oxford University Press, 1979), pp. 310–311; Maurice Matloff, *Strategic Planning for Coalition Warfare* (Office of Chief of Military History, 1953–59), 1:13–14; "Conversation with Marshall," 23 July 1947, Robert Sherwood Papers, Harvard University; Forrest Pogue, *George C. Marshall* (Viking, 1963–87), 1:153, 170–171, 203–227, 2:238, 3:12–13.

4. Alfred Chandler, ed., *Papers of Dwight Eisenhower* (Johns Hopkins University Press, 1970–), 1:388–393; Pogue, *George C. Marshall,* 2:99, 287, 3:270–271; "General: Man of the Year," *Time,* 3 Jan. 1944, p. 15; Richard Leighton and Robert Coakley, *Global Logistics and Strategy* (Chief of Military History, 1955–67), 1:35, 65, 72–73, 94–95, 126–127, 132, 200, 203, 605, 633, 2:120–121, 203, 237–240, 353; Ray Cline, *Washington Command Post: Operations Division* (Chief of Military History, 1951), pp. 145, 152–154, 173–174.

5. Dwight D. Eisenhower, *Crusade in Europe* (Doubleday, 1948), p. 160; Winston Churchill, *The Second World War* (Houghton Mifflin, 1948–53), 3:673; [LTG] Frederick Morgan, *Overture to Overlord* (Doubleday, 1950), p. 294; Sherwood, *Roosevelt and Hopkins,* pp. 314–315, 557–560, 582, 592, 601–602, 878; Matloff, *Strategic Planning,* 1:192, 221–222, 237–240, 2:131; Tuvia Ben-Moshe, *Churchill: Strategy and History* (Lynne Rienner, 1992), pp. 61, 69, 250, 260; "Meeting of Combined Chiefs of Staff (CCS)," 16 Jan. 1943, in *Foreign Relations of the United States* [hereafter *FRUS*]: *Conferences at Washington and Casablanca,* p. 587; "Unity of Command," *New York Times,* 11 Mar.

1942; Bland, *George C. Marshall,* p. 590; Adm. William Leahy, *I Was There* (McGraw-Hill, 1950), pp. 96–97, 106; English diplomat quoted in Lowenthal, *Leadership and Indecision,* p. 1010; Henry Stimson and McGeorge Bundy, *On Active Service in Peace and War* (Harper and Brothers, 1948), p. 425.

6. Bland, *George C. Marshall,* pp. 590, 593, 598; Thomas Buell, *Master of Sea Power: Biography of Fleet Admiral Ernest King* (Little, Brown, 1980), pp. 208, 216–218, 265, 301, 336–337; King biographer Robert Love's phrase in Kenneth Hagen, ed., *In Peace and War: Interpretations of American Naval History* (Greenwood Press, 1978), p. 275; Field Marshall John Dill in Churchill, *Second World War,* 4:439; Matloff, *Strategic Planning,* 1:34–36, 159, 182, 211, 268–269, 2:111, 165–166, 220, 223; *FRUS: Conferences at Washington and Casablanca,* pp. 603–604; [Gen.] Albert C. Wedemeyer, *Wedemeyer Reports!* (Henry Holt, 1958), pp. 238–239.

7. Mark Stoler, *Politics of the Second Front* (Greenwood Press, 1977), pp. 77–78, 83, 101, 107–108; Robert Divine, *Foreign Policy and U.S. Presidential Elections, 1940–1948* (Franklin Watts, 1974), pp. 100, 127, 157–158, 162; Matloff, *Strategic Planning,* 1:272–273, 2:282, 338–345, 367, 398, 430–431, 491, 497; Buell, *Master of Sea Power,* pp. 389–390; "Roosevelt-Giraund Conversation," 15 Jan. 1943, and JCS Meeting, 7 Jan. 1943, *FRUS: Conferences at Washington and Casablanca,* pp. 506–508, 611–612; Allan Winkler, *The Politics of Propaganda: Office of War Information* (Yale University Press, 1978), pp. 133–135, 142; Bland, *George C. Marshall,* pp. 14–15, 289, 326, 342, 574, 616; Asst. Sec. of State Sumner Welles describing FDR's motivation in John L. Chase, "Unconditional Surrender Reconsidered," *Political Science Quarterly* 70 (June 1955): 272–275; Gerhard Weinberg, *A World at Arms: A Global History of World War II* (Cambridge University Press, 1994), pp. 461–469, 598; Harry Hopkins, "We Can Win in 1945," *American Magazine* 136 (Oct. 1943): 100; Marshall in Glen C. H. Perry, *"Dear Bart," Washington Views of World War II* (Greenwood Press, 1982), p. 207; FDR in Elliott Roosevelt, *As He Saw It* (Duell, Sloan and Pearce, 1946), pp. 108–109; Stimson and JCS planners in Diane Clemens, "Averell Harriman, John Deane, the Joint Chiefs of Staff, and the 'Reversal of Co-operation' with the Soviet Union in April 1945," *International History Review* 14 (May 1992): 280, 298–299, 300–303.

8. U.S. Joint Planners, "Strategic Plan for Defeat of Japan," 14 May 1943, in *FRUS: Conferences at Washington and Quebec,* p. 292; Minutes of Pacific Conferences, 3 Jan., 6 May, and 29 Sept.–1 Oct. 1944: all in King Papers, Box 10, Naval Historical Center; Carl Enders, "The Vinson Navy" (Ph.D. diss., Michigan State University, 1970), pp. 10–12, 132, 138; Vinson quoted in *New York Times,* 1 June 1942; Louis Morton, *Strategy and Command: First Two Years* (Chief of Military History, 1962); Buell, *Master of Sea Power,* pp. 245, 386, 394, 451; Joseph Alexander, *Utmost Savagery: Tawara* (Naval Institute Press, 1995), pp. 15, 77–78, 93; Holland Smith, *Coral and Brass* (Scribner's, 1949), pp. 139, 161; Nimitz and Bucker in George Feiffer, *Tennozan: Okinawa and the Atomic Bomb* (Ticknor and Fields, 1992), pp. 236, 243; Japanese in Leon Sigal, *Fighting to a Finish: Politics of War Termination, 1945* (Cornell University Press, 1988), pp. 34–35, 39, 228; Richard Wheeler, *Special Valor: U.S. Marines and the Pacific War* (Harper and Row, 1977), pp. 209–210; old marines in Eric Bergerud, *Touched with Fire: The Land War in the South Pacific* (Penguin, 1996), pp. 444, 450; William Styron, "Fortunate Son," *New York Times Book Review,* 16 June 1991; Philip Caputo, *A Rumor of War* (Holt, Reinhart and Winston, 1977), p. 8.

9. JCS and CCS planners, Dec. 1943, *FRUS: Conferences at Cario and Tehran,* pp. 766, 780; Stephen Taaffe, *MacArthur's Jungle War: 1944 New Guinea* (University Press of Kansas, 1997), passim; Stimson, FDR, and Marshall in Michael Schaller, *Douglas MacArthur* (Oxford University Press, 1989), pp. 63–65, 77–87; Marshall and Knox in Charles Brower, "The Joint Chiefs of Staff and National Policy: American Strategy and the War with Japan" (Ph.D. diss., University of Pennsylvania, 1987), pp. 28, 199; Meeting of CCS with Roosevelt and Churchill, 23 Jan. 1943, *FRUS: Conferences at Washington and Casablanca,* pp. 545, 550, 553, 718; MacArthur quoted in Taaffe (above), pp. 55, 233; JCS to Nimitz and MacArthur, 12 June 1944, and Memorandums on Future Operations in the Pacific, 1944 in WWII Strategic Plans Division Records, Box 163, Naval Historical Center; King, Spruance, Nimitz, and aviators quoted in E. B. Potter, *Nimitz* (Naval Institute Press, 1976), pp. 283, 300, 303; and Clark Reynolds, *The Fast Carrier: Forging of an Air Navy* (Krieger, 1978), pp. 66–67, 76, 161, 167, 173, 205, 321.

10. Pogue, *George C. Marshall,* 1:256; George C. Marshall, "Profiting by War Experiences," *Infantry Journal* 18 (Jan. 1921): 37; Bland, *George C. Marshall,* p. 286; Eisenhower quoted and the entire campaign discussed in Martin Blumenson, *The Battle of the Generals: Untold Story of the Falaise Pocket* (Morrow, 1993), pp. 20, 22, 211, and passim; Carlo D'Este, *Patton: Genius for War* (HaperCollins, 1995), pp. 298, 322; Omar Bradley, *A Soldier's Story* (Henry Holt, 1951), pp. 375–377; [Gen.] James Gavin, *On to Berlin* (Bantam, 1979), p. 298.

11. Alvin D. Coox, "Japanese Military Intelligence in the Pacific Theater," in *The Intelligence Revolution,* ed. Walter Hitchcock (Office of Air Force History, 1991), p. 200; Army War Plans, 18 Aug. 1943, and Marshall (Feb. and Mar, 1945), in Brower, "JCS and National Policy," pp. 143, 273; Cooke and Marine Corps (1937) in Edward Miller, *War Plan Orange: U.S. Strategy to Defeat Japan* (Naval Institute Press, 1991), pp. 202, 221–22, 365–366; Marshall in Stimson Diary, 14 June 1943, Yale University; Nimitz (1965) in Thomas Buell, "Adm. Spruance and Naval War College," *Naval War College Review* 23 (Mar. 1971): 33; E. B. Sledge, *With the Old Breed at Peleliu and Okinawa* (Bantam, 1991), pp. 149, 263, 321; and marine in Feiffer, *Tennozan,* p. 287.

12. Matloff, *Strategic Planning,* 2:136, 185, 231, 514; JCS memorandum, 29 June 1945, Japanese diplomatic messages, Stimson to Truman, 16 July 1945: all in *FRUS: Conference of Berlin,* 1945, 1:833, 911, 2:1255–1256, 1285, 1294, 1322; D. M. Giangreco, "Casualty Projections for the Invasion of Japan," *Journal of Military History* 61 (July 1997): 538–543; Stimson Diary, 2 July 1945; Leahy, *I Was There,* pp. 160–161, 259; U.S. intelligence and Japanese quoted in Robert Newman, *Truman and the Hiroshima Cult* (Michigan State University Press, 1995), pp. 24, 38, 50; Marshall (1946) in Thomas Schoenbaum, *Waging Peace and War: Dean Rusk* (Simon and Schuster, 1988), p. 127; newspapers and officials cited in John Chappell, *Before the Bomb: How American Approached the End of the Pacific War* (University of Kentucky Press, 1997), pp. 6–9, 41–46; Col. [David] Marcus, "Surrender Terms for Japan," 14 Mar. 1945, National Archives, RG 165, Box 505; "Comparison of Proclamation of July 26, 1945 with the Policy of the Department of State," attached to Minutes, Secretary's Staff Committee [hereafter SSC], 25 July 1945, National Archives; *FRUS: Cairo and Teheran,* pp. 323, 389, 532, 554, 864; Truman in Stimson Diary, 19 June 1945; Truman, "The Military Career of a Missourian," Senatorial Papers, Truman Presidential Library; John McCloy, "Memorandum for Chief of Staff," 20 May 1945, National Archives, RG 165, Box 504; Stimson,

Memorandum for President, 2 July 1945, Stimson Diary; Stimson and Bundy, *On Active Service*, p. 632; Marshall, Memorandums for Sec. of War, 15 May and 9 June 1945, Marshall Research Library; Pogue, *George C. Marshall*, 4:17–18, 400; Marshall to Asst. Sec. in Schoenbaum, *Waging Peace and War*, p. 119; JCS, MacArthur, and Nimitz in Grace Person Hayes, *The History of the JCS in World War II: War against Japan* (Naval Institute Press, 1982), p. 706.

13. SSC Minutes, Feb.–Aug. 1945, State Department Records, National Archives; R. H. Winnick, ed., *Letters of Archibald MacLeish* (Houghton Mifflin 1983), p. 326; Acheson, 7 July 1945, and Japanese diplomats in *FRUS: Conference of Berlin, 1945*, 1:901, 2:1291; *Gallup Poll: Public Opinion, 1935–1971* (Random House, 1972), 1:488–489; *Washington Post*, 9 May 1945; Truman quoted by Averell Harriman in *The Korean War: 25-Year Perspective*, ed. Francis H. Heller (Regents Press of Kansas, 1977), p. 230; Byrnes and Cordell Hull in Sigal, *Fighting to a Finish*, pp. 127–128; "Comparison of Proclamation of July 26, 1945, with the Policy of the Department of State," attached to Minutes, SSC, 25 July 1945, and Grew in SSC Meeting, 10 July 1945: both National Archives; Stimson Diary, 18 June 1945; Sweden to Sec. of State, 6 April 1945, *FRUS, Japan*, 6:477; Japanese diplomats and warriors in Robert Butow, *Japan's Decision to Surrender* (Stanford University Press, 1954), pp. 69, 183, 205; Republican senators in *New York Times*, 23 July 1945, p. 11; and *Congressional Record*, 79th Cong., 1st sess., 1945, pp. 7129, 7439; Gilbert Fite, *Richard B. Russell* (University of North Carolina Press, 1991), pp. 2, 132, 176; Russell in *Congressional Record*, 79th Cong., 1st sess., 1945, pp. 8671–8672; Marshall, "Remarks on Demobilization of Army to Members of Congress," 20 Sept. 1945, Marshall Research Library; Truman to Marshall, 18 Aug. 1945, Truman Presidential Library [hereafter TPL], Japanese Army Intelligence Estimate, 1 July 1945, in Donald Detwiler and Charles Burdick, eds., *War in Asia and the Pacific* (Garland Press, 1980), 12:7–8; Truman, interviewed by Noyse, 22 Jan. 1954, Truman Presidential Library; Truman in John Morton Blum, ed., *The Price of Vision: Diary of Henry Wallace* (Houghton Mifflin, 1974), p. 474.

14. Truman to MacArthur, 14 Aug. 1945, *FRUS: Japan*, 6:648; Harry S. Truman, *Memoirs* (Doubleday, 1956), 1:431–432; marine in D. Clayton James, *Years of MacArthur* (Houghton Mifflin, 1970–85), 2:785; Jerrold Schecter, ed., *Khrushchev Remembers* (Little, Brown, 1990), p. 82; Averell Harriman to Sec. of State, 25 Oct. 1945, *FRUS: British Commonwealth and Far East, 1945*, p. 786; Charlie Ross to Truman, 11 Aug. 1945, Ross Papers, TPL.

15. *FRUS: Conference of Berlin 1945*, 1:927, 2:410–411; Rusk in Schoenbaum, *Waging Peace and War*, p. 120.

8. KOREA

1. State-War-Navy Subcommittee, 30 Apr. 1945; Stalin to Truman and Truman to Stalin, 17 and 22 Aug. 1945; Joint Staff, JCS, 11 Oct. 1945: all in *FRUS, 1945*, 6:534, 670, 687–688, 744–745; Hodge and staff in James Schnabel, *Policy and Direction: First Year* (Center for Military History, 1972), pp. 14, 25; aide in Michael Schaller, *Douglas MacArthur* (Oxford University Press, 1989), pp. 162–163; Acheson to Oliver Franks, 24 Dec. 1949, *FRUS*, 7:927; Soviet offical (n.d.) in Thomas Schoenbaum, *Waging Peace and*

War: Dean Rusk in the Truman, Kennedy, and Johnson Years (Simon and Schuster, 1988), p. 208; Truman in David Lilienthal, *The Atomic Energy Years* (Harper and Row, 1964), p. 595; Dean Acheson, *Present at Creation: My Years in the State Department* (Signet, 1970), p. 528; Acheson on Formosa in *New York Times,* 4 Jan. 1950, p. 1; Acheson, 10 Oct. 1953, "Princeton Seminar," TPL, Independence, Mo.

2. MG John J. Chiles, "Oral Reminiscences," TPL; Clark Lee and Richard Henschel, *Douglas MacArthur* (Henry Holt, 1952), p. 193; MacArthur, "Formosa Must Be Defended," *U.S. News and World Report,* 1 Sept. 1950, p. 32; MacArthur on Marshall in Joseph Goulden, *Korea* (McGraw-Hill, 1982), p. 188; MacArthur in Mathew Ridgway, *Korean War* (Doubleday, 1967), p. 27; State Dept. Office of Public Affairs, Memo, 6 March; Rusk, Memo, 30 May; Acheson, Conversation with Cong. Christian Herter, 24 Mar.: all in *FRUS, 1950,* 1:185–187, 6:349–351; Dulles, Conversation with Truman, 28 Apr. 1950, in Stephen Pelz, "U.S. Decisions on Korean Policy," in *Child of Conflict: Korean-American Relationship,* ed. Bruce Cummings (University of Washington Press, 1983), p. 125; Omar Bradley and Clay Blair, *A General's Life* (Simon and Schuster, 1983), pp. 530, 532–534.

3. Truman in Francis Heller, ed., *Korean War: 25-Year Perspective* (Regents Press of Kansas, 1977), p. 114; *Time,* 3 July 1950, p. 7; aide, Rusk, and advisers in Glenn Paige, *The Korean Decision* (Free Press, 1968), pp. 114, 124–125, 174–175, 331, 393; Kathryn Weathersby, *Soviet Aims in Korea, 1945–1950: New Evidence from Russian Archives* (Woodrow Wilson International Center for Scholars, 1993), pp. 26–31; Bradley and Acheson in *FRUS, 1950,* 7:158, 182; J. Lawton Collins, *War in Peacetime* (Houghton Mifflin, 1969), p. 393; Truman in Beverly Smith, "Why We Went to War in Korea," *Saturday Evening Post,* 10 Nov. 1951, 80; comments of soldiers per "police action" rhetoric in T. R. Fehrenbach, *This Kind of War: Study in Unpreparedness* (Pocket Books, 1964), p. 172; Truman in Paige (above), pp. 188, 284, 337; comments about UN in Robert Divine, *Second Chance: Triumph of Internationalism . . .* (Atheneum, 1971), pp. 146–148, 279–281, 308–314; and Robert Donovan, *The Presidency of Harry S. Truman* (Norton, 1977–82), 2:203; JCS, 12 July 1950, in James Schnable and Robert Watson, *History of Joint Chiefs of Staff: Korean War* (Glasier, 1979), 3:137; State Dept. officals in *FRUS, 1950,* 1:332; and Paige (above), pp. 117–118.

4. Dulles, 29 June 1950, and State Dept. officals, 13 and 14 July, in *FRUS, 1950,* 7:237–238; Truman and MacArthur in Schaller, *Douglas MacArthur,* pp. 181, 190–191; *Life* reporter in Goulden, *Korea,* p. 90; MacArthur, JCS, and marine general Oliver Smith in Schnable and Watson, *History of JCS: Korea,* 3:72–73, 107; Vernon Walters, *Silent Missions* (Doubleday, 1978), p. 197; and D. Clayton James, *Years of MacArthur* (Houghton Mifflin, 1970–85), 3:430, 467–470, 475; Truman on Jenner in Donovan, *Presidency of Harry S. Truman,* 2:267; Secs. of army, air force, and navy to Sec. defense, 24 Aug. 1950, National Archives, RG 330, Box 179; unidentifed NKPA general in Russell Spurr, *Enter the Dragon, China's Undeclared War against the U.S. in Korea* (Henry Holt, 1988), p. 96; Ridgway in Clay Blair, *Forgotten War* (Times, 1987), p. 320.

5. Bradley to Sec. defense, *FRUS, 1950,* 7:540–541; Burke Davis, *Marine: Life of Chesty Puller* (Bantam Books, 1964), pp. 258–259; author's interview with Col. (Ret.), Joseph Pizzi [in charge of Eighth Army, enemy order of battle, 1950], 26 Feb. 1996; Robert Lovett, Mar. 1950, in *FRUS,* 1:178–179, 191, 198; Paul Hoffman, Charles Murphy, and Acheson at NSC Meetings, May and Sept. 1950, Reel 1, University Publications

of America; sec. army to sec. defense, 3 Aug. 1950, National Archives, RG 330, Box 179; Dept. of State and Dept. of Defense memorandum, July and Aug. 1950, *FRUS,* 7:503, 533; JCS and MacArthur, Sept. 1950, in Schnable and Watson, *History of JCS: Korea;* Nitze and Acheson in "Princeton Seminar," 1954, Reel 4; Cabinet Meeting, 29 Sept. 1950, Connelly MSS, Box 1, TPL.

6. Marshall and JCS to MacArthur and Bradley to British in Schnable and Watson, *History of JCS: Korea,* pp. 238, 242, 263; Charles Murphy in Donovan, *Presidency of Harry S. Truman,* 2:265, 284; Tydings and Chair Republican National Committee in *New York Times,* 11 Oct. 1950, p. 6; Rusk, *As I Saw It* (Norton, 1990), p. 169; FEC J–2 in Roy Appleman, *South to Naktong, North to Yalu* (Army Center of Military History, 1961), p. 759; CIA, memos on Chinese and Russian intervention, 12 Oct. 1950, *FRUS,* 7:933–938; Ridgway, *Korean War,* pp. 61, 81, 143; Bradley and Blair, *General's Life,* p. 577; Shu Guang Zhang, *Mao's Military Romanticism: China and the Korean War* (University Press of Kansas, 1995), pp. 86–88, 94–96, 102–106, 107; Peng in Spurr, *Enter the Dragon,* p. 169.

7. Unnamed Democratic and successful Republican candidates for U.S. senator, Everett Dirksen, in Heller, *Korean War,* pp. 127, 192; Truman, Cabinet Meeting, 7 Nov. 1960, Connaly MSS, Box 1, TPL.

8. Author's interview with Col. (Ret.) Joseph Pizzi, 26 Feb. 1996; MacArthur and JCS in Schnable and Watson, *History of JCS: Korea,* pp. 277–285; Collins, 21 Nov., *FRUS, 1950,* 7:1138–1139; columnists Arthur Krock and James Reston in *New York Times,* 9 and 21 Nov. 1950: both p. 32; "Conversation with Congressman McKinnon," 5 Dec. 1950, Elsey Papers, Box 92, and 71st Meeting of NSC, 10 Nov. 1950, President's Secretary's Files: both in TPL; Willoughby's estimates in Appleman, *South to Naktong,* p. 762; author's interview on 23 Aug. 1995 with LTG [then LTC] Philip Davidson, in J–2, Far East Command, 1950; *Time,* 16 Oct. 1950, p. 26; Ridgway Diary, 15 June 1951, Ridgway MSS, Army War College; CCF Gen. Peng in Jian Chen, "China's Changing Aims during the Korean War," *Journal of American–East Asian Relations* 1 (spring 1992): 25; American Mucciso, Memo of Conversation with MacArthur, 17 Nov., *FRUS, 1950,* 7:1175; Memo for Sec. Lovett, Brief of MacArthur's J-2, 13 Nov. 1950, National Archives, RG 330, Box 180; Marshall in Schnable and Watson (above), pp. 296–297; Chou En-lai, 24 Oct. 1950, in Sergei Goncharov, John Lewis, and Xue Litai, *Uncertain Partners: Stalin, Mao, and the Korean War* (Stanford University Press, 1993), pp. 193–194; MacArthur in Appleman (above), pp. 760, 763, 777; Mao on MacArthur in Zhang, *Mao's Military Romanticism,* p. 285.

9. Gavin et al., Memo for General Hull, 20 Dec. 1950, National Archives, RG 330, Box 180; Mao and Chou En-lai quoted in Jonathan Pollack, "Korean War and Sino-American Relations" and Chen Xiaolu, "China's Policy towards the United States, 1945–1955," both in *Sino- American Relations, 1945–1955,* ed. Harry Harding and Yuan Ming (Scholarly Resources, 1989), pp. 190, 219, 224; Peng in Spurr, *Enter the Dragon,* pp. 84, 253; MacArthur in Schnable and Watson, *History of JCS: Korea,* pp. 336–337; service secretaries to sec. defense, 4 Dec. 1950, National Archives, RG 330, Box 180; Collins, Acheson, CNO Forrest Sherman, Rusk, Bradley, Marshall, 28 Nov. and 1, 3, and 19 Dec. 1950: all in *FRUS,* 7:1119, 1324–1327, 1329, 1345; Bradley and Blair, *General's Life,* p. 614; JCS-MacArthur message traffic in Schnable and Watson (above), pp. 396–411; Acheson, *Present at Creation,* p. 664.

10. Adm. Forrest Sherman and Truman, 28 Nov. and 1 Dec., in *FRUS, 1950,* 7: 1243–1244, 1248, 1278; Rusk in Rosemary Foot, *The Wrong War* (Cornell University Press, 1985), p. 168; Stalin and Mao in Goncharov Lewis, and Litai, *Uncertain Partners,* pp. 167, 173–178, 180; Peng in Spurr, *Enter the Dragon,* p. 285; Truman, 7 Dec., *FRUS, 1950,* 7:1431; service secretaries to sec. defense, 28 Nov. 1950, National Archives, RG 330, Box 180; Paul Nitze in Jon Halliday, "Rewriting History: A Secret War," *Far East Economic Review* 156 (22 Apr. 1993): 33; Strobe Talbott, ed., *Khrushchev Remembers* (Little, Brown, 1970–74), 1:361, 2:356; General Harmon report in David Rosenberg, "American Atomic Strategy and Hydrogen Bomb Decision," *Journal of American History* 66 (June 1979): 72, 83–84; Gen. Dmitry Volkognov, 22 June 1993, quoted in Foreign Broadcast Information Service, *Russian International Affairs,* pp. 11–12; JCS and Marshall in John Wiltz, "MacArthur Hearings of 1951: Secret Testimony," *Military Affairs* 39 (Dec. 1975): 168; C. L. Sulzberger, "Footnote: MacArthur on the Eve of Korea," *New York Times,* 11 May 1951, p. 10; Marshall, 28 Nov., *FRUS, 1950,* 7:1243; Smith at NSC meeting, 9 Nov. 1950, President's Secretary's Files, TPL; *FRUS, 1950,* 3:1732–1734, 1770.

11. Walter Winton in Clay Blair, *Ridgway's Paratroopers: American Airborne in World War II* (William Morrow, 1985), pp. 3–4; MacArthur in Ridgway, *Korean War,* p. 83; Ridgway in Heller, ed., *Korean War,* p. 34; MacArthur to JCS, 30 Dec. 1950, in James, *Years of MacArthur,* 3:550–551; Ridgway, *Soldier* (Harper and Brothers, 1956), p. 201; Ridgway to Collins, ca. 30 Dec. 1950, in U.S. Senate, *Military Situation in the Far East* [hereafter *MacArthur Hearings*], 82d Cong., 1st sess., 1951, pp. 2956–2957; Mao, 2 Oct. and 5 Aug. 1950, in William Stueck, *Korean War: International History* (Princeton University Press, 1995), p. 100; and Goncharov, Lewis, and Litai, *Uncertain Partners,* p. 163; Fehrenbach, *This Kind of War,* 409–410; MacArthur described in Goulden, *Korea,* p. 453; Lovett, 24 Mar. 1951, in Schaller, *Douglas MacArthur,* p. 233; Truman in Schoenbaum, *Waging Peace and War,* p. 221; and Donovan, *Presidency of Harry S. Truman,* 2:355; Acheson, "Princeton Seminar," 2 Feb. and 14 Mar. 1954, Reels 3 and 7, TPL; messages between White House and Marshall per testimony at Senate hearing on MacArthur in "MacArthur, 1950–1952" folder, Marshall Research Library, Lexington, Va.; Omar Bradley, *A Soldier's Story* (Henry Holt, 1951), p. 147; Bradley and Blair, *General's Life,* pp. 633, 635, 638; Bradley, memo, 24 Apr. 1951, and interview in Schnable and Watson, *History of JCS: Korea,* pp. 345–346, 541.

12. Sen. Johnson's staff in Schaller, *Douglas MacArthur,* pp. 246–247, 249; Marshall and Bradley in *MacArthur Hearings,* pp. 610, 731 747–748; Eisenhower to "Swede" Hazlett, 21 June 1951, in Louis Galamobos, ed., *Papers of Dwight David Eisenhower* (Johns Hopkins University Press, 1970–), 12:370; MacArthur and Eisenhower in Steven Ambrose, *Eisenhower* (Simon and Schuster, 1983–84), 1:478, 511, 2:32.

13. Marshall, 12 May 1951, *MacArthur Hearings,* p. 667; Ridgway, 30 May 1951, in Schnabel, *Policy and Direction,* pp. 390–395; Frank Pace (sec. army) to sec. defense, 3 Aug. 1950, National Archives, RG 330, Box 179; McClure to Gen. Collins, 5 July 1951, in Barton Bernstein, "Struggle over Korean Armistice," in Cumings, *Child of Conflict,* p. 276; CNO Fechteler to sec. defense, 15 Oct. 1951, PSBF, Box 32, TPL; PRC and U.S. officials in Stueck, *Korean War,* pp. 252, 261, 266, 270, 279, 294; Truman, 7 May 1952, *Truman Presidential Papers,* p. 121; Truman to MacArthur, 13 Jan. 1951, in Harry S. Truman, *Memoirs* (Doubleday Doran, 1956), 2:435; State Dept., 20 May and 13 Nov. 1952, in Rosemary Foot, *A Substitute for Victory: Politics of Peacemaking at the Korean*

Armistice Talks (Cornell University Press, 1990), pp. 127, 158; Truman to sec. defense, 23 May 1952, Charles Murphy MSS, Box 14, TPL; Acheson to Truman, 15 Nov. 1952, Acheson MSS, Box 71, TPL; Acheson in Stueck (above), p. 299; Ridgway to JCS, 1 Mar. 1952, Ridgway MSS, Box 20, Army War College; Zhang, *Mao's Military Romanticism,* pp. 170–175; American soldiers in Fehrenbach, *This Kind of War,* p. 535; Lovett at Cabinet Meetings, 12 Sept. and 5 Dec. 1952 and 14 May 1951, Connelly MSS, Box 1, TPL; PRC newspaper, 18 Aug. 1953, in Pollack, "Korean War and Sino-American Relations," p. 229; *New York Times,* 18 Apr. 1951, p. 30; Truman, "Radio Report to American People," 11 Apr. 1951, and "Farewell Address," 15 Jan. 1953, *Truman Presidential Papers,* 1951:226, 1952–53:378; "Year of Decision," *Collier's,* 30 June 1951; Alsop column, *Washington Post,* 24 Aug. 1952, p. 58.

14. Bradley and Blair, *General's Life,* pp. 653–657; Truman and George Ball (Stevenson adviser) in David McCullough, *Truman* (Simon and Schuster, 1992), pp. 889, 891, 906; Truman, 28 Nov. 1952, in Schaller, *Douglas MacArthur,* p. 216; John Barlow Martin, *Adlai Stevenson* (Doubleday, 1975–77), 1:236, 523–524, 540, 550, 568; Robert Divine, *Foreign Policy and U.S. Presidential Elections, 1952–1960* (New Viewpoints, 1974), pp. 14, 39–40, 71; voter interviews in Samuel Lubell, *The Revolt of the Moderates* (Harper and Brothers, 1956), pp. 39–43.

15. Roper public opinion poll in *Time,* 22 Sept. 1952, p. 26; Undersec. of State Walter Bedell Smith, 19 May 1953, *FRUS, 1952–1954,* 15:1053; Kennan, "Princeton Seminar," 14 Mar. 1954, Reel 1, TPL; Bradley to sec. defense, "U.S. Courses of Action in Korea," 3 Nov. 1951, National Archives, RRG 330, Box 233; Dwight D. Eisenhower, *Mandate for Change* (Doubleday, 1963), p. 95; JCS to sec. defense, 19 May 1953, and NSC Meeting, 13 and 20 May 1953: all in *FRUS, 1952–1954,* 15:1012–1017, 1060–1065; Speech of 7 May 1953 in Michael Y. M. Kau, ed., *The Writings of Mao Zedong, 1949–1976* (M. E. Sharpe, 1986), 1:317; Mao and other PRC officals in Zhang, *Mao's Military Romanticism,* pp. 12, 245, 249; James Reston in Stueck, *Korean War,* p. 342.

16. Ambassador Walter Robertson, 2 July 1953, in Schnable and Watson, *History of JCS: Korea,* p. 1022; "Response," *Life,* 30 Apr. 1951, p. 34; asst. sec. public affairs, special guidance, no. 51, 27 July 1950, National Archives, RG 330, Box 233; Acheson, Princeton Seminar, 14 March 1954, Reel 2; historian (Norman Graebner) and Collins in Heller, ed., *Korean War,* p. 105; Reaganites in Jay Winik, *On the Brink: The Dramatic, Behind-the-Scene Saga of the Reagan Era and the Men and Women Who Won the Cold War* (Simon and Schuster, 1996), pp. 223–225, 248.

17. George Kennan, Irving Kristol, and Sec. Defense Charles Wilson in Kenneth Waltz, "Electoral Punishment and Foreign Policy Crisis," in *Domestic Sources of Foreign Polcy,* ed. James Rosenau (Free Press, 1967), pp. 276–277, 291–292; Dulles in Foster Rhea Dulles, *American Foreign Policy toward Communist China, 1949–1969* (Thomas Crowell, 1972), p. 139; Acheson at Cabinet Meeting, 20 Oct. 1950, Connelly MSS, Box 1, TPL; and in Robert McMahon, "Harry S. Truman and Roots of U.S. Involvement in Indochina," in David Anderson, *Shadow on the White House: Presidents and Vietnam War, 1945–1975* (University Press of Kansas, 1993), pp. 36–37; Collins and Ridgway in Robert Buzzanco, "Prologue to Tragedy: U.S. Military Opposition to Intervention in Vietnam, 1950–1954," *Diplomatic History* 17 (spring 1993): 207, 209, 211–212; marine song in Fehrenbach, *This Kind of War,* p. 394.

9. VIETNAM

1. Polls cited in John Ranelagh, *The Agency: CIA* (Simon and Schuster, 1986), p. 469; and Gaines Foster, "Coming to Terms with Defeat," *Virginia Quarterly Review* 66 (winter 1990): 32; Robert McNamara, *In Retrospect* (Times Books, 1995), p. xvi; Dean Rusk, *As I Saw It* (Norton 1990), p. 496; Rostow, Westmoreland, and Bundy in Ted Gittinger, ed., *Johnson Years: Vietnam Roundtable* (Johnson Library, 1993), pp. 78, 128, 191–192; Ball in William C. Gibbons, *U.S. Government and Vietnam War* (Government Printing Office, 1984–94), 3:322; Clark Clifford, *Counsel to the President* (Random House, 1991), pp. 412, 419; Clifford in Lloyd Gardner, *Pay Any Price: Johnson and the Wars for Vietnam* (Ivan Dee, 1995), p. 249; McNaughton and Bundys in *Pentagon Papers: Gravel Edition* (Beacon Press, 1971), 3:624–625, 684–686; and Gibbons (above), pp. 12–13.

2. Bundy in Gibbons, *U.S. Government and the Vietnam War,* 2:41; Stewart Alsop, "Kennedy's Grand Strategy," *Saturday Evening Post,* 31 Mar. 1962, pp. 12, 14; Rostow, JCS, and McGarr in *FRUS: Vietnam, 1961,* 1:61–62, 351, 450–451, 478; Rostow, 11 Apr. 1964, in Walt W. Rostow, *The Diffusion of Power* (Macmillan, 1972), p. 287; Roger Hilsman, *To Move a Nation* (Dell, 1967), pp. 415–416; Andrew Krepinevich, *The Army and Vietnam* (Johns Hopkins University Press, 1985), pp. 37, 191; Robert Thompson, *Make for the Hills* (Leo Cooper, 1989), pp. 135–137; William Colby, *Lost Victory* (Contemporary Books, 1989), pp. 108–109; unidentified general in Brian Jenkins, *The Unchangeable War* (Rand Corporation, 1972), p. 3; Richard Reeves, *President Kennedy* (Simon and Schuster, 1993), pp. 53, 66, 168, 183, 188, 222, 230, 305–306, 311, 350, 443, 637; Taylor in H. R. McMaster, *Dereliction of Duty: Lyndon Johnson, Robert McNamara, the Joint Chiefs of Staff, and the Lies that Led to Vietnam* (HarperCollins, 1997), p. 105; Oral Histories by Taylor, Harkins, and Gen. William Rosson, Military History Institute, Army War College [hereafter AWC]; Edwin Guthman, ed., *Robert Kennedy in His Own Words* (Bantam, 1988), p. 315; "Transcript of Huntley-Brinkley Report," 9 Sept. 1963, *President Kennedy Public Papers,* 3:659.

3. Bill Moyers, "Flashbacks," *Newsweek,* 10 Feb. 1975, p. 76; John Newman, *Kennedy and Vietnam* (Warner Books, 1992), pp. 226–228; Johnson quoted by colleagues in Gittinger, *Johnson Years,* p. 44; Fulbright in Gibbons, *U.S. Government and Vietnam War,* 3:305; David Halberstam, *The Making of a Quagmire* (Random House, 1965), pp. 315–319; and Neil Sheehan, "Not a Dove, but No Longer a Hawk," *New York Times Magazine,* 9 Oct. 1966, p. 140; McNamara to Johnson, 14 May 1964, Johnson Library Tapes; Gardner, *Pay Any Price,* p. 142; Taylor and M. Bundy in Gibbons (above), 2:359–365; Johnson (ca. 1970) in Doris Kearns, *Lyndon Johnson and the American Dream* (New American Library, 1977), pp. 264–265, 271; McNamara and M. Bundy in Gibbons (above), 3:436, and *Pentagon Papers: Gravel Edition,* 3:690; William Bundy in Gibbons (above), 3:441; Lyndon Johnson, *Vantage Point* (Popular Library, 1971), pp. 119, 125, 131, 136; Johnson to McNamara, 21 Mar. 1964, and to Bundy and Russell, 27 May 1964, Johnson Library Tapes; George Herring, *LBJ and Vietnam* (University of Texas Press, 1994), p. 19; Walter Lippmann, "The Secretary Misunderstood," *Newsweek,* 6 Nov. 1967, p. 23; Rusk, *As I Saw It,* p. 435; Rusk, Memorandum, 18 Apr. 1964, *FRUS, 1964–1968,* 1:244; Edgar Snow, "Interview with Mao," *New Republic,* 27 Feb. 1965, p. 17.

4. John McNaughton, 5 May 1967, and JCS, ca. June 1965, in Wallace Thies, *When Governments Collide: Coercion and Diplomacy in the Vietnam Conflict* (University of

California Press, 1980), pp. 104, 174; JCS and McNamara (1965) in McMaster, *Dereliction of Duty,* pp. 187–188, 254; unidentified generals and Sen. Stuart Symington in *U.S. News and World Report,* 14 Feb. 1966, p. 26; Vincent Demma, "Suggestions for the Use of Ground Forces, June 1964–March 1965," unpublished Center for Military History Paper; Gen. Johnson and other JCS estimates, and administration fears of right wing: all in Gibbons, *U.S. Government and the Vietnam War,* 3:157, 166, 354, 381, 421, 425, 445; Gen. DePuy, Oral History, AWC; reporter Hanson Baldwin in *New York Times Magazine,* 21 Feb. 1965, p. 9, and *Army* 25 (Sept. 1975): 2; McNamara to Kennedy, 5 Nov. 1961, and to Ambassador Lodge, 12 Dec. 1963, *FRUS, 1961,* 1:539–540 and *FRUS, 1961–1963,* 4:702; McNamara, *In Retrospect,* p. 189; Eisenhower quoted in Herring, *LBJ and Vietnam,* pp. 42, 54; Gen. Johnson, Oral History, AWC; LBJ in Gardner, *Pay Any Price,* pp. 55, 169, 221, 248 and McNamara, *In Retrospect,* pp. 190–191; LBJ described by Under Secretary of State Nicholas Katzenbach on *The American Experience: LBJ,* National Public Television, 24 Sept. 1992; DePuy in Keyes Beech, *Not without the Americans* (Doubleday, 1971), p. 307.

5. Westmoreland in Blair Clark, "Westmoreland Appraised," *Harper's,* Nov. 1970, pp. 96, 98; and Gibbons, *U.S. Government and the Vietnam War,* 3:159–160, 362–364, 385, 4:81; Cecil Currey, *Edward Landsdale* (Houghton Mifflin 1988), pp. 290–297; author's interview with Sam Wilson, 13 Feb. 1989; Neil Sheehan, *Bright Shining Lie: John Paul Vann* (Random House, 1988), pp. 336, 614–615, 681–682; [army adviser] Peter Dawkins, "The United States Army and the 'Other' War in Vietnam," (Ph.D. diss., Princeton University, 1979), pp. 30, 71, 76, 171, 259; Ellsberg in *Rolling Stone,* 5 Nov. 1987, pp. 221, 224; Lodge and LBJ in Anne Blair, *Lodge in Vietnam* (Yale University Press, 1995), pp. 88, 97; Lodge, Landsdale, and Ellsberg in Gibbons (above), 4:43–45, 58, 62–64, 474–476; Russell to LBJ, 27 May 1964, Johnson Library Tapes; DePuy, personal letters, 1966, DePuy MSS, AWC; Victor Krulak, *First to Fight* (Naval Institute Press, 1984), pp. 198–199, 200–202; Gen. Johnson, Oral History; DePuy in Ward Just, *Military Men* (Avon, 1970), p. 20.

6. LTG (Ret.) Philip Davidson [MACV, J-2], *Vietnam at War* (Presido Press, 1988), pp. 384, 410, 426, 430; Katzenbach in *Pentagon Papers,* 4:508; LTG Bernard Rodgers, *Cedar Falls–Junction City: A Turning Point* (Department of the Army, 1974), pp. 74, 157, 174–175; McNarmara and others in Gibbons, *U.S. Government and the Vietnam War,* 3:380–382, 402–403, 451; Westmoreland/COMUSMACV, MSS, 1966 Correspondence, AWC; [WWII correspondent] Robert Sherrod, "Notes on a Monstrous War," *Life,* 27 Jan. 1967, p. 22B; Robert Graham, "Vietnam: Infantryman's View," *Military Affairs* 48 (July 1984): 133–138; Charles F. Brower, "Strategic Reassessment in Vietnam: Westmoreland's 'Alternative Strategy' of 1967–1968," *Naval War College Review* 64 (spring 1991): 30, 40; Westmoreland's request, McNamara's response, reports on pacification and MACVs vs. OSD: all in Gibbons (above), 4:88, 98, 154–155, 395, 413, 556, 626–629, 712–715; 789, 900, 909, 930–931; Sen. LBJ in *Congressional Record,* 12 Dec. 1950, p. 987, and 14 Sept. 1952, 81st Cong. 2d sess., pp. 16458–16459; McNamara in Gibbons (above), pp. 645–646.

7. JCS revolt in Mark Perry, *Four Stars* (Houghton Mifflin 1989), pp. 161–164; LBJ, McNamara, and Rusk in Gibbons, *U.S. Government and the Vietnam War,* 4:786, 786–789, 876, 938; aviator, Cong. Lester Wolfe, and LBJ in Frank Vandiver, *Shadows of Vietnam: Lyndon Johnson's Wars* (Texas A&M University Press, 1997), pp. 229, 254, 298; LBJ in Gardner, *Pay Any Price,* p. 384; Ronnie Ford, *TET 1968* (Frank Cass, 1995), p. 94; Larry Berman, *Lyndon Johnson's War* (Norton, 1989), pp. 58, 60, 84–85, 121, 124–125; Kathleen

J. Turner, *Lyndon Johnson's Dual War: Vietnam and the Press* (University of Chicago Press, 1985), pp. 144, 151, 188–189; John Muller, *War, Presidents, and Public Opinion* (Wiley, 1973), p. 167; Samuel Zaffiri, *Westmoreland* (William Morrow, 1994), pp. 192–193, 199, 245–246; for military's private comments, see Jeffrey Clarke, *Advice and Support: The Final Years* (Center for Military History, 1988), p. 283; and William Hammond, *Public Affairs: Military and the Media* (Center for Military History, 1988–96), 1:291–297.

8. McNamara, Katzenbach, and other government officials in Gibbons, *U.S. Government and the Vietnam War*, 4:86, 92, 888; Michael Lanning and Dan Cragg, *Inside the VC and NVA* (Ivy, 1992), esp. pp. 196, 203, 222–223, 233–237; Westmoreland to Wheeler, 20 Dec. 1967, in *LBJ National Security File, Vietnam*, Reel 5; James Wirtz, *Tet Offensive: Intelligence Failure* (Cornell University Press, 1991), pp. 20, 49–53, 117–119, 125–127, 156, 270; Ford, *TET 1968*, pp. 29, 47, 48–49; [NVA Gen.] Tran Van Tra, *History of the Bulwark B2 Theater* (Foreign Broadcast Information Service, 1983), 5:35; John Brigham, "The NLF's Foreign Relations and the Vietnam War" (Ph.D. diss., University of Kentucky, 1994), p. 98; LBJ (6 Feb. 1968) in Robert Schulzinger, *A Time for War* (Oxford University Press, 1997), p. 263; Peter Braestrup, *Big Story: How the American Press and Television Reported the Crisis of Tet* (Westview Press, 1977), 1:38–40, 308–309; Cronkite in Don Oberdorfer, *TET!* (Doubleday, 1971), pp. 158, 248–251; McPherson in Herbert Schandler, *Lyndon Johnson and Vietnam* (Princeton University Press, 1977), pp. 81–82.

9. William Westmoreland, *A Soldier Reports* (Doubleday, 1976), p. 430; DePuy to mother, 1 Mar. 1968, DePuy Papers, AWC; Wheeler and Westmoreland per troop requests in Gibbons, *U.S. Government and the Vietnam War*, 4:558, 611, 667; Tet message traffic in Zaffiri, *Westmoreland*, pp. 309–315; Herring, *LBJ and Vietnam*, pp. 137, 154, 161, 182; Schandler, *Lyndon Johnson and Vietnam*, pp. 101–110; Stennis and Russell in Gibbons (above), pp. 549, 685–686; Abrams in Lewis Sorley, *Thunderbolt: General Creighton Abrams and the Army of His Times* (Simon and Schuster, 1991), p. 222; Clifford, *Counsel to the President*, pp. 497–498, 512–513; Gen. William Rosson, Oral History, AWC; DePuy to MG Keith Ware, 14 Mar. 1968, DePuy Papers; William Bundy, unpublished history of Vietnam War in Johnson Library; Acheson and Wheeler, in Vandiver, *Shadows of Vietnam*, pp. 303, 307; Acheson and Radio Hanoi in Oberdorfer, *TET*, pp. 312–314, 323; Johnson in Gardner, *Pay Any Price*, pp. 453–454 and Turner, *Johnson's Dual War*, p. 232.

10. Herring, *LBJ and Vietnam*, pp. 61, 168, 182; CNO in McMaster, *Dereliction of Duty*, p. 262; Harry Summers, "Survivor of Bataan: Harold Johnson's Undoing Was Vietnam," *Vietnam* 3 (Dec. 1990): 56; Westmoreland, Abrams, and LBJ in Ronald Spector, *After Tet* (Vintage, 1994), p. 10, 240, 296; Ford, *TET 1968*, pp. 111, 128; old VC veterans in Brigham, "NLF's Foreign Relations," pp. 191, 195; and Stanley Karnow, *Vietnam* (Viking, 1983), pp. 534, 545; Rostow, Rusk, and Johnson in Gardner, *Pay Any Price*, pp. 480, 452, 506, 523; Rusk, *As I Saw It*, pp. 472, 497; author's interviews with veterans, esp. W-2 Terry Washburn, 3 May 1995.

11. McCarthy and LBJ workers in Lewis Chester, Godfrey Hodgson, and Bruce Page, *American Melodrama: Presidential Campaign of 1968* (Viking, 1969), pp. 79, 93, Roger Morris, *Uncertain Greatness: Kissinger and Foreign Policy* (Harper and Row, 1977), p. 10; and Oberdorfer, *TET!* pp. 242, 330; LBJ and Rowe in Turner, *Johnson's Dual War*, pp. 222, 237–240; Carl Solberg, *Hubert Humphrey* (Norton, 1984), pp. 377, 392; Nixon quoted and Republican establishment described in Richard Whalen, *Catch the Falling Flag* (Houghton Mifflin, 1972), pp. 17, 26, 29, 35.

12. Kissinger, Laird, and Abrams in Walter Isaacson, *Kissinger* (Simon and Schuster, 1992), pp. 237, 416, 471; Haig in Elmo R. Zumwalt, *On Watch* (Quadrangle, 1976), p. 399; Richard Nixon, *Memoirs* (Grosset and Dunlap, 1978), pp. 341, 406–407, 600; Laird and Nixon described in Henry Kissinger, *White House Years* (Little, Brown, 1979), pp. 32, 239, 477–478; Nixon quoted, Laird and army described in Hammond, *Military and the Media*, 2:67–68, 108, 111, 150, 391; Col. Robert Heil, "The Collapse of the Armed Forces," *Armed Forces Journal* 108 (7 June 1971): 30–38; Sorley, *Thunderbolt*, pp. 296–298, 372–373; Nixon quoted in Alexander Haig, *Inner Circles* (Warner Books, 1992), p. 277; McCain to Abrams, 4 May 1970, Abrams MSS, AWC; Nixon to JCS, 1 May 1972, in Nixon, *Memoirs*, pp. 454, 607; Nixon in Isaacson (above), pp. 247–248; Kissinger and Nixon in Seymour Hersh, *Price of Power* (Summit, 1983), pp. 506, 522; author's interview with Col. Miller, 3 Jan. 1995; H. R. Haldeman, *Haldeman Diaries* (Putnam, 1994), pp. 436, 440, 450; Charles Colson in Hersh (above), p. 591; "Walter Lippmann at 83," *Washington Post*, 25 Mar. 1973, pp. C1, C4; Jimmy Roosevelt, *New York Times*, 4 Oct. 1972, p. 47.

13. Nixon, *Memoirs*, 734; critics in Marvin Kalb and Bernard Kalb, *Kissinger* (Dell, 1975), pp. 471–472; public reaction in Hammond, *Military and the Media*, 2:210; Haig and CIA asst. director in Gerald S. Strober, ed., *Nixon: Oral History* (HarperCollins, 1993), pp. 185, 189; Kissinger and Haig in Nguyen Tien Hung and Jerrold Schecter, *Palace File* (Harper and Row, 1986), pp. 143, 156, 353; and Isaacson, *Kissinger*, pp. 137, 279–280; Nixon in Zumwalt, *On Watch*, p. 414; John Negroponte in Hung and Schecter (above), p. 146; Rusk, *As I Saw It*, p. 491; Message to Congress, 1 May 1973, *Nixon Presidential Papers*, p. 390.

14. Nixon in *Time*, 2 Apr. 1990, p. 48; Isaacson, *Kissinger*, p. 313; Brigham, "NLF's Foreign Relations," pp. 186–188; Nixon, Kissinger, and Ford in Hung and Schecter, *Palace File*, pp. 1–2, 111, 114, 308, 338; Henry Kissinger, *Years of Upheaval* (Little, Brown, 1982), pp. 302–333, 319, 325–326, 359; Arnold Isaacs, *Without Honor: Defeat in Vietnam and Cambodia* (Random House, 1984), pp. 86, 145, 334, 383, 401; Capt. Dave Palmer, 1964, Westmoreland MSS, AWC; Westmoreland, Bundy, and others in Gittinger, *Johnson Years*, pp. 91, 97–99; David Anderson, "Gerald R. Ford and President's War in Vietnam," in *Shadow on the White House: Presidents and the Vietnam War*, ed. David Anderson (University Press of Kansas, 1993), p. 186; Trong Nhu Tang, *Viet Cong Memoir* (Vintage, 1986), pp. 263–268.

POSTSCRIPT

1. Georgi Arbatov, Nicholas Shishlini, and other former Soviet officials in *Messengers from Moscow*, "Episode 4, The Center Collapses," PBS Television, Feb. 1995; Kissinger (1975) in Robert Schulzinger, *A Time for War: United States and Vietnam* (Oxford University Press, 1997), p. 327; Gromyko, Kissinger (after 1975), and NSC adviser Robert McFarland in Peter Rodman, *More Precious than Peace: The Cold War and the Struggle for the Third World* (Scribner's, 1995), pp. 177–179, 191–195, 259, 452–453, 541; CIA director William Casey in Jay Winik, *On the Brink: The Dramatic Saga of the Men and Women Who Won the Cold War* (Simon and Schuster, 1996), p. 447; dissident quoted and effects discussed in Douglas Borere, "The Afghan War: Communism's First Domino," *War and Society* 12 (Oct. 1994): 132, 135, 137–139.

2. Abrams quoted and discussed in Bruce Palmer, 29 May 1975, Abrams Oral History Project, Military History Institute; [Sec. Defense] Caspar Weinberger, "The Uses of Military Power," *Defense,* Jan. 1985, p. 5; Gerald Ford, *A Time to Heal* (Berkeley, 1980), pp. 267–276; Bush in Richard Brookhiser, "A Visit with George Bush," *Atlantic,* Aug. 1992, p. 22 and Bush, Exchanges with Reporters in Kennebunkport and the Soviet Peace Proposal, 17 and 19 Feb. 1991, *Weekly Compilation of Presidential Documents,* 27:183–184; unnamed officer quoted in "The Military's New Image," *Newsweek,* 11 Mar. 1991, p. 50; Powell quoted and issue discussed in Michael Gordon and Bernard Trainor, *The Generals' War: Inside Story of the Conflict in the Gulf* (Little, Brown, 1995), pp. 327, 416, 423, 463; Scowcroft on *This Week with David Brinkley,* 9 May 1993.

Bibliographical Essay

Rather than list all the books, articles, and documents previously mentioned in the notes, this section emphasizes the works I found essential to understanding how America has conducted its wars. The notes primarily identify the source of quotes; this essay identifies the source of ideas.

1. PERENNIAL ISSUES IN AMERICAN MILITARY STRATEGY

Louis Halle, *Dream and Reality: Aspects of American Policy* (1959), and Miroslav Nincic, *Democracy and Foreign Policy* (1992), describe the strengths and weaknesses of political pluralism. While excellent for the military ethic, Samuel Huntington's *The Soldier and the State* (1957) is less useful on actual behavior. Martin Van Creveld, *The Transformation of War* (1991), emphasizes that human beings are reluctant to risk their lives for political self-interest. For the often understated influence of Congress, see James M. Lindsay, "Congress and Defense Policy: 1961–1986," *Armed Forces and Society* 13 (spring 1987): 371–401; and Robert L. Goldich, "The Evolution of Congressional Attitudes Toward a General Staff in the 20th Century," in *Defense Organization: The Need for Change* (1985). Robert Mahon, *History of the Militia and the National Guard* (1983), is indispensable for the political power of the reserves. For thoughts about the passivity of democracy, see Kenneth Walz, *Man, the State, and War* (1982).

2. THE COLONIAL AND REVOLUTIONARY WARS FOR NORTH AMERICA

Daniel Baugh, "Great Britain's 'Blue-Water' Policy, 1689–1815," *International History Review* 10 (1988): 33–58, is the best short discussion of British strategy. Richard Middleton, *The Bells of Victory* (1985), makes the case that there was no English strategy at all. Francis Parkman, *Montcalm and Wolfe* (1884), is excellent on the cultural conflicts between Europeans, Indians, Canadians, and Americans. For conflicting views of war between different American colonies, compare James Titus, *The Old Dominion at War* (1991), with Fred Anderson, *A People's War: Massachusetts Soldiers and Society* (1984). George A. Rawlyk, *Nova Scotia's Massachusetts* (1973), shows the great diversity within the most militant American colony.

Dave Palmer, *The Way of the Fox* (1975), emphasizes Washington's military flexibility. John Shy, *People Numerous and Armed* (1976), shows the complexity of the Revolutionary War. J. C. D. Clark, *The Language of Liberty* (1994), stresses religious motivation, while Charles Royster, *A Revolutionary People at War* (1981), shows specifically how religion affected the war effort. Don Higginbotham, "American Militia," in his *Reconsiderations on the Revolutionary War* (1978), is excellent on force structure. Because militiamen, unlike Washington, have not had their papers collected, we may never know exactly what they were thinking. Jackson Turner Main, *Political Parties before the Constitution* (1974), emphasizes their activity in postwar democratic politics. Although not focusing on the militia per se, Gordon Wood, *The Radicalism of the American Revolution* (1992), helps explain its ideology during the war.

3. 1812 AND MEXICO

Roger Brown, *Republic in Peril* (1974), J. C. A. Stagg, *Mr. Madison's War* (1983), and Lawrence Delbert Cress, " 'Cool and Serious Reflection': Federalist Attitudes toward War in 1812," *Journal of the Early Republic* 7 (summer 1987): 123–145, explain the partisan motivation of the War of 1812. Richard Hofstadter, *The Idea of a Party System* (1969), explains the nature of partisanship at the time. Don Hickey, *War of 1812* (1989), and John Mahon, *War of 1812* (1972), are excellent on military operations. Henry Adams, *History of the United States during Administrations of Jefferson and Madison* (1986 edition), remains a treasure of information on domestic politics, war fighting, diplomacy, and much else.

Thomas Hietala, *Manifest Design* (1985), Robert Johannsen, *To the Halls of Montezumas* (1985), and Richard H. Brown, "The Missouri Crisis, Slavery, and the Politics of Jacksonianism," *South Atlantic Quarterly* 65 (winter 1966): 68–72, give the partisan Democratic background to the Mexican War. William B. Skelton, *American Profession of Arms* (1992), and Samuel J. Watson, "Manifest Destiny and Military Professionalism," *Southwestern Historical Quarterly* 99 (April 1996): 467–498, explain the feelings of the regular army. Nathaniel Hughes and Roy Stonesifer, *Life and Wars of Gideon J. Pillow* (1993), and Timothy D. Johnson, *Winfield Scott* (1998) tells the story of the premier antagonists inside the American Army. For the peace settlement, see David M. Pletcher, *Diplomacy of Annexation* (1973), and Norman Graebner, "Party Politics and Trist Mission," *Journal of Southern History* 19 (May 1953): 137–156. Justin H. Smith, *The War with Mexico* (1919), remains one of the best general histories ever written of any war.

4. THE CIVIL WAR

James McPherson, *For Cause and Comrades* (1997), is the best single work on political motivation. Robert F. Durden, *The Gray and the Black* (1972), and Larry Nelson, *Bullets,*

Ballots, and Rhetoric (1980), delineate the Confederate debate over political priorities—independence or the preservation of slavery. Stephen Sears, *George B. McClellan* (1988), is excellent, although Mark Grimsley, *Hard Hand of War* (1995), shows that many other Union officers also feared crime and anarchy in their ranks. The best discussion of the North's demand to escalate the intensity of the war is Alan Nevins, *The War for the Union* (1959–71), vols. 1 and 2. For Lincoln's military leadership, see Tyler Dennett, ed., *Lincoln and the Civil War: Diaries and Letters of John Hay* (1939). For Grant, politics, and the operational level of war, see John Simon, "Grant, Lincoln, and Unconditional Surrender," in *Lincoln's Generals,* ed. Gabor Boritt (1994), and James Schneider, *The Structure of Strategic Revolution* (1994). The best discussion of the 1864 election is David Long, *The Jewel of Liberty* (1994). John Marszalek, *Sherman* (1993), explains a very complex soldier. Bertram Wyatt-Brown, *Southern Honor* (1982), and Richard Berlinger, Herman Hattaway, Archer Jones, and William Still, *Why the South Lost the Civil War* (1986), discuss the military strengths and weaknesses of Southern culture. Leon Litwick, *Been in Storm So Long* (1979), is excellent on black soldiers.

5. THE SPANISH-AMERICAN WAR

Ernest May, *Imperial Democracy* (1973), and John Offner, *Unwanted War* (1992), are the best discussions of the domestic political background. Gerald Lindermann, *Mirror of War* (1974), John Pettegrew, " 'The Soldier's Faith': Turn-of-the-Century Memory and Modern Nationalism," *Journal of Contemporary History* 3 (1996): 49–73; and Richard Hofstadter, "Cuba, Philippines, and Manifest Destiny," in Hofstadter, *Paranoid Style in American Politics and Other Essays* (1979), explain the public interest in war and Cuba. For mobilization, see Graham Cosmas, *Army for Empire* (1971). For military strategy, see John A. S. Grenville and George Berkeley Young, *Politics, Strategy, and American Diplomacy* (1966), and David Trask, *The War with Spain* (1981). French Ensor Chadwick, *The Relations of the United States and Spain* (1911), explains how and why naval engagements in the Caribbean were militarily decisive.

6. WORLD WAR I

Ernest May, *The World War and American Isolationism* (1959), William Widenor, *Henry Cabot Lodge and the Search for an American Foreign Policy* (1980), Seward Livermore, *Woodrow Wilson and the War Congress* (1966), and John Thomas, *Reformers and War* (1987), explain domestic political factors. For international affairs and coalition politics, see David Stevenson, *The First World War and International Politics* (1991), W. B. Flower, *British-American Relations, 1917–1918: Role of William Wiseman* (1969), and David Trask, *The AEF and Coalition Warmaking* (1993). The best works on military mobilization are John Chambers, *To Raise an Army* (1987), Daniel Beaver, *Newton D. Baker and the American War Effort* (1966), and David Kennedy, *Over Here* (1980). For American military operations, Edward M. Coffman, *War to End All Wars* (1986), and Donald Smythe, *Life of John J. Pershing* (1973–86), are indispensable. The foreign and domestic factors of the armistice are explained in E. David Cronon, ed., *Cabinet Diaries of Josephius Daniels* (1963), Joseph Tumulty, *Woodrow Wilson as I Knew Him* (1921), and Bullitt Lowry, *Armistice 1918* (1996). For the short- and long-term aftermath of Wilson and the war, see Wesley Bagby, *Road to Normalcy* (1962), and Robert Ferrell, ed., *Off the Record: The Private Papers of Harry S. Truman* (1982).

7. WORLD WAR II

For the political mood in American, see John Morton Blum, *V Was for Victory* (1976), and Theodore Wilson, *First Summit: Roosevelt and Churchill* (1991). For Roosevelt's state-craft, see Robert Sherwood, *Roosevelt and Hopkins* (1948), and Robert Dallek, *Franklin Roosevelt and American Foreign Policy* (1979). Mark Lowenthal, *Leadership and Indecision* (1989), and Maurice Matloff, *Strategic Planning for Coalition Warfare* (1953–59), are excellent on grand (or high) strategy. For campaign planning, see Forrest Pogue, *George C. Marshall* (Viking, 1963–87), vols. 2 and 3, Ray Cline, *Washington Command Post* (1951), and Louis Morton, *Strategy and Command* (1962). For the conflict between risk taking and caution within the armed forces, see Martin Blumenson, *The Battle of the Generals* (1993), Edward Miller, *War Plan Orange* (1991), and Clark Reynolds, *The Fast Carrier* (1978). For the international and bureaucratic politics of unconditional surrender, see Gerhard Weinberg, *A World at Arms* (1994), and Leon Sigal, *Fighting to a Finish* (1988). The best study yet written on the military implications of domestic war-weariness is Charles Brower, "The Joint Chiefs of Staff and National Policy: American Strategy and the War with Japan" (Ph.D. diss., 1987).

8. KOREA

For the domestic and international political background, see Robert Donovan, *Presidency of Harry Truman* (1982), Dean Acheson, *Present at Creation* (1970), William Stueck, *Korean War: International History* (1995), and James Schnabel, *Policy and Direction* (1972). Glenn Paige, *The Korean Decision* (1968), is a classic study of U.S. government decision making. James Schnable and Robert Watson, *History of Joint Chiefs of Staff: Korean War* (1979), explains the war at the highest military level. To understand it at the operational and tactical levels, see Clay Blair, *Forgotten War* (1987), and T. R. Fehren-bach, *This Kind of War* (1964). D. Clayton James, *Years of MacArthur* (1985), vol. 3, is remarkably thorough and fair. Michael Schaller, *Douglas MacArthur* (1989), is biased but very insightful. Sergei Goncharov, John Lewis, and Xue Litai, *Uncertain Partners* (1993), and Shu Guang Zhang, *Mao's Military Romanticism* (1995), explain Soviet and Chinese policy at the strategic and tactical levels. We have no thorough study of the Chinese con-cession on the POW issue, largely because the PRC, while releasing many documents on the war, has kept this topic secret. Rosemary Foot's books *The Wrong War* (1985) and *Sub-stitute for Victory* (1990) are essential for understanding American policy after MacArthur's dismissal. Robert Divine, *Foreign Policy and U.S. Presidential Elections, 1952–1960* (1974), and Samuel Lubell, *The Revolt of the Moderates* (1956), explain Eisenhower's election in the context of Korea.

9. VIETNAM

David Halberstam, *The Best and the Brightest* (1972), remains very useful on domestic political issues, as is Richard Reeves, *President Kennedy* (1993). For Johnson, see Ted Gittinger, ed., *Johnson Years: Vietnam Roundtable* (1993), and Lloyd Gardner, *Pay Any Price* (1995). For civil-military relations, see George Herring, *LBJ and Vietnam* (1994), H. R. McMaster, *Dereliction of Duty* (1997), and Mark Perry, *Four Stars* (1989). For search and destroy versus counterinsurgency, see William Westmoreland, *A Soldier Reports* (1976), Andrew Krepinevich, *The Army and Vietnam* (1985), Victor Krulak, *First to Fight* (1984), William Colby, *Lost Victory* (1989), and Neal Sheehan, *Bright Shining Lie* (1988). For gradual escalation and the air war, see Wallace Thies, *When Governments Collide* (1980), and Mark Clodfelter, *The Limits of Air Power* (1989). Communist policy, strategy, and tactics are explained in Douglas Pike, *PAVN: People's Army of Vietnam* (1986), Michael Lanning and Dan Cragg, *Inside the VC and NVA* (1992), and John Brigham, "The NLF's Foreign Relations and the Vietnam War" (Ph.D. diss., 1994). The best military studies of Tet are Ronnie Ford, *TET 1968* (1995), Don Oberdorfer, *TET!* (1971), and James Wirtz, *Tet Offensive* (1991). Its political implications are covered in Peter Braestrup, *Big Story* (1977), and Herbert Schandler, *Lyndon Johnson and Vietnam* (1977). The best book yet published on the war during the Nixon administration is William Hammond, *Public Affairs: Military and the Media, 1969–1973* (1996); it is much more than its title indicates. Walter Isaacson, *Kissinger* (1992) and Jeffrey Kimball's *Nixon's Vietnam War* are also indispensable. The best studies on the so-called peace settlement of 1973 and its aftermath are Nguyen Tien Hung and Jerrold Schecter, *Palace File* (1986), and Arnold Isaacs, *Without Honor* (1984).

POSTSCRIPT

For Soviet expansion and the American reaction to it, see Peter Rodman, *More Precious Than Peace* (1995), and Jay Winik, *On the Brink* (1996). For the resurrection of America's armed forces, see James Kitfield, *Prodigal Soldiers* (1995).

Index